Financial Inclusion, Sustainability, and the Influence of Religion and Technology

Awais Ur Rehman
Faculty of Management Sciences, University of Central Punjab, Pakistan

Arsalan Haneef Malik
College of Business Management, Department of Accounting and Finance, Institute of Business Management (IoBM), Karachi, Pakistan

IGI Global
PUBLISHER of TIMELY KNOWLEDGE

A volume in the Advances in Finance, Accounting, and Economics (AFAE) Book Series

Published in the United States of America by
IGI Global
Business Science Reference (an imprint of IGI Global)
701 E. Chocolate Avenue
Hershey PA, USA 17033
Tel: 717-533-8845
Fax: 717-533-8661
E-mail: cust@igi-global.com
Web site: http://www.igi-global.com

Library of Congress Cataloging-in-Publication Data

Names: Rehman, Awais, 1984- editor. | Malik, Arsalan, 1988- editor.
Title: Financial inclusion, sustainability, and the influence of religion and technology / edited by Awais Rehman, Arsalan Malik.
Description: Hershey, PA : Business Science Reference, [2024] | Includes bibliographical references and index. | Summary: "This book explores the complex relationship between financial inclusion and sustainability, and identifies ways they can mutually reinforce each other"-- Provided by publisher.
Identifiers: LCCN 2023058623 (print) | LCCN 2023058624 (ebook) | ISBN 9798369314753 (hardcover) | ISBN 9798369314760 (ebook)
Subjects: LCSH: Financial exclusion. | Sustainable development. | Finance--Religious aspects.
Classification: LCC HG176.55 .F56 2024 (print) | LCC HG176.55 (ebook) | DDC 332--dc23/eng/20240130
LC record available at https://lccn.loc.gov/2023058623
LC ebook record available at https://lccn.loc.gov/2023058624

This book is published in the IGI Global book series Advances in Finance, Accounting, and Economics (AFAE) (ISSN: 2327-5677; eISSN: 2327-5685)

British Cataloguing in Publication Data
A Cataloguing in Publication record for this book is available from the British Library.

For electronic access to this publication, please contact: eresources@igi-global.com.

Advances in Finance, Accounting, and Economics (AFAE) Book Series

Ahmed Driouchi
Al Akhawayn University, Morocco

ISSN:2327-5677
EISSN:2327-5685

Mission

In our changing economic and business environment, it is important to consider the financial changes occurring internationally as well as within individual organizations and business environments. Understanding these changes as well as the factors that influence them is crucial in preparing for our financial future and ensuring economic sustainability and growth.

The **Advances in Finance, Accounting, and Economics (AFAE)** book series aims to publish comprehensive and informative titles in all areas of economics and economic theory, finance, and accounting to assist in advancing the available knowledge and providing for further research development in these dynamic fields.

Coverage

- Health Economics
- Applied economics
- Economics of Risks, Uncertainty, Ambiguity, and Insurance
- Auditing
- Economics of Migration and Spatial Mobility
- Economics Geography
- Taxes
- Statistical Analysis
- Internet Banking
- Comparative Accounting Systems

IGI Global is currently accepting manuscripts for publication within this series. To submit a proposal for a volume in this series, please contact our Acquisition Editors at Acquisitions@igi-global.com or visit: http://www.igi-global.com/publish/.

The Advances in Finance, Accounting, and Economics (AFAE) Book Series (ISSN 2327-5677) is published by IGI Global, 701 E. Chocolate Avenue, Hershey, PA 17033-1240, USA, www.igi-global.com. This series is composed of titles available for purchase individually; each title is edited to be contextually exclusive from any other title within the series. For pricing and ordering information please visit http://www.igi-global.com/book-series/advances-finance-accounting-economics/73685. Postmaster: Send all address changes to above address.

Titles in this Series

For a list of additional titles in this series, please visit: www.igi-global.com/book-series/advances-finance-accounting-economics/73685

Exploring Central Bank Digital Currencies Concepts, Frameworks, Models, and Challenges
Guneet Kaur (University of Stirling, UK) Pooja Lekhi (University Canada West, Canada) and Simriti Popli (Kaplan International College, UK)
Business Science Reference • copyright 2024 • 359pp • H/C (ISBN: 9798369318829) • US $325.00 (our price)

Harnessing Blockchain-Digital Twin Fusion for Sustainable Investments
Syed Hasan Jafar (Woxsen University, India) Raul Villamarin Rodriguez (Woxsen University, India) Hemachandran Kannan (Woxsen University, India) Shakeb Akhtar (Woxsen University, India) and Philipp Plugmann (SRH Hochschule für Gesundheit Gera, Germany)
Business Science Reference • copyright 2024 • 441pp • H/C (ISBN: 9798369318782) • US $290.00 (our price)

Harnessing Technology for Knowledge Transfer in Accountancy, Auditing, and Finance
Samuel Kwok (Xi'an Jiaotong-Liverpool University, China) Mohamed Omran (Xi'an Jiaotong-Liverpool University, China) and Poshan Yu (Xi'an Jiaotong-Liverpool University, China & European Business University of Luxembourg, Luxembourg)
Business Science Reference • copyright 2024 • 279pp • H/C (ISBN: 9798369313312) • US $275.00 (our price)

Cases on Economic Crisis Impact on Multinational Corporations
Kyla Latrice Tennin (College of Doctoral Studies, University of Phoenix, USA) and Samrat Ray (International Institute of Management Studies (IIMS), India)
Business Science Reference • copyright 2024 • 225pp • H/C (ISBN: 9798369315446) • US $275.00 (our price)

The Role of Financial Inclusion for Reaching Sustainable Development Goals
João Jungo (University of Aveiro, Portugal) Mara Madaleno (GOVCOPP, University of Aveiro, Portugal) Anabela Botelho (GOVCOPP, University of Aveiro, Portugal) and Eyup Dogan (Abdullah Gul University, Turkey)
Business Science Reference • copyright 2024 • 326pp • H/C (ISBN: 9798369305225) • US $275.00 (our price)

Artificial Intelligence and Machine Learning-Powered Smart Finance
Sanjay Taneja (Graphic Era University (Deemed), India) Amandeep Singh (Chitkara Business School, Chitkara University, India) and Pawan Kumar (Chandigarh University, India)
Business Science Reference • copyright 2024 • 347pp • H/C (ISBN: 9798369332641) • US $295.00 (our price)

IGI Global
PUBLISHER of TIMELY KNOWLEDGE

701 East Chocolate Avenue, Hershey, PA 17033, USA
Tel: 717-533-8845 x100 • Fax: 717-533-8661
E-Mail: cust@igi-global.com • www.igi-global.com

Editorial Advisory Board

Table of Contents

Section 3
Challenges and Opportunities

Detailed Table of Contents

For a very long time, in France, the Christian and state solution to protecting the poor was to ban interest-bearing bank loans, thus excluding them from protection and placing them de facto in the hands of uncontrolled greedy usurers. A first solution was to introduce Catholic charitable pawnshops in France charging low interest rates, then the mission of social utility of Monts-de-Piété was recognized by the government in France by their transformation into municipal credit institutions in the early 20th century. Furthermore, with regards to deposits, the Caisses d'Epargne were created by philanthropic bankers in the 19th century to educate the population in the virtues of saving. In the last 20 years, using new opportunities provided by European Union directives, some fintechs such as notably Nickel were active in banking inclusion to combat poverty.

This study aims to conduct a bibliometric analysis on the intersection of financial inclusion, religion, and technological advancements, with a particular focus on the role of Islamic banking and Fintech in promoting financial access. Employing an in-depth bibliometric approach, the study analyzes citation patterns, co-authorship networks, and keyword co-occurrence using VOSviewer, based on a systematic literature review. A meticulously selected set of keywords related to financial inclusion, exclusion, and religion facilitated a comprehensive search across major academic databases, yielding 110 relevant articles. The analysis reveals a significant thematic cluster around the convergence of financial inclusion,

Islamic banking, and Fintech, particularly within the Indonesian context. This highlights the emerging scholarly interest in exploring how technological innovations and Islamic financial principles can together foster inclusive financial systems. The regional focus underscores the socio-economic dynamics unique to Indonesia, suggesting a broader relevance for similar contexts globally. Despite its comprehensive scope, the study acknowledges limitations such as potential publication bias and the exclusion of non-indexed literature. It underscores the need for qualitative research to complement bibliometric findings and address the complex dynamics between religion and financial inclusion. From a policy perspective, it advocates for regulatory frameworks that support Fintech growth within Islamic banking, aiming to promote inclusive, culturally responsive financial systems. This research contributes to the literature by offering a systematic bibliometric analysis of the nexus between religion, financial inclusion, and technology. It highlights the importance of integrating Islamic finance and Fintech to enhance financial access, urging a global dialogue on culturally responsive financial solutions for economic empowerment and poverty reduction.

This chapter offers a comprehensive examination of the intersection of Islamic finance and financial inclusion, shedding light on how Islamic financial principles can contribute to expanding financial access and promoting economic inclusivity. Examining the fundamental principles of Islamic finance reveals the inclusive foundations upon which this financial system is constructed. It has also examined the case studies and real-world examples to illustrate the tangible effects of Islamic finance on marginalised populations and economies. This chapter investigates the impact of financial technology (Fintech) and Islamic microfinance institutions on the availability of Islamic financial products. The chapter discussed the limitations of Islamic finance, which include a prohibition on interest, restrictions on loans and investments, and sector limits. Innovative products provide financing alternatives. In addition, the chapter discuss how the challenges of standardisation, regulatory compliance, and consumer awareness impede the widespread adoption of Islamic finance in practise. For Islamic financial services to contribute more effectively to financial inclusion, addressing these issues requires industry cooperation, regulatory support, and consumer education.

The study presents a review of existing research on bank profitability determinants in Africa. Using the literature review methodology, it was found that bank profitability determinants differ across countries in all regions of Africa. Some suggested areas for future research are to explore the impact of circular economy, fintech activities, pandemic, and uncertainty on the profitability of African banks. The implication of the review findings is that bank profitability determinants will remain a contested research agenda in the banking literature.

Section 2
Financial Inclusion and Its Outcomes

The objective of this study is to analyse the financial inclusion impacts on the financial stability of Islamic banks in Pakistan. This study used balance panel data of 15 full-fledged Islamic banks and Islamic windows from 2011 to 2021 by employing the feasible generalized least squares (FGLS) estimation technique to count the heteroskedasticity and potential endogeneity issue. The results of the present study lend support to the notion that financial inclusion as assessed by bank branches, financing, and availability of ATMs plays a substantial role in stimulating the financial stability of Islamic banks.

This chapter employs bibliometric analysis to deeply explore the interplay between financial inclusion and sustainability, addressing key research questions. The trend of publications shows a notable rise, particularly following the 2015 introduction of the United Nations Sustainable Development Goals (UNSDGs). Performance analysis indicates China's leading role in terms of document production and citations. Collaboration patterns highlight important authors and groups to underscore worldwide cooperation. Co-occurrence networks reveal diverse study clusters, while word clouds visually represent major themes from authors' keywords and paper titles. Conclusively, this chapter presents future research directions, such as cross-disciplinary studies; technological developments; longitudinal impact assessments; environmental, social, and governance (ESG) integration; and regional studies in the present field of study. Practically, it offers guidelines for aligning financial practices with sustainability goals, promoting international collaboration, informed policymaking, and strategic insights.

This study employs bibliometrics and a systematic literature review to comprehensively analyze Sukuk and Green Sukuk research trends from 2011 to 2023. Key terms such as "Islamic finance," "Sukuk," and "green bonds" are identified through bibliometric analysis, revealing their central role. The systematic literature review uncovers dominant themes, notable authors, and publication trends. Findings indicate a transformative potential in fostering financial inclusion and sustainability. The study underscores the importance of international collaboration, highlights key contributors like Malaysia and Indonesia, and provides insights for practitioners and policymakers. Despite positive trends, research gaps necessitate further exploration for a nuanced understanding of Sukuk's impact on sustainability goals.

The significance of access to formal bank accounts becomes evident as it enables individuals to safely transfer and receive funds, make everyday transactions, and make investments to hedge against financial shocks, among others. The present study aims to investigate the extent to which financial inclusion has been adopted by individuals from poor and non-poor backgrounds and males and females across OIC and non-OIC economies. The outcome of the extent of access to financial accounts and financial services—digital payment, savings, borrowing, and financial well-being in terms of financial resilience and financial worrying—is also conducted among the vulnerable group. The study utilises the global findex database, which consists of data from 128,000 individuals across 123 economies, to provide an empirical description of financial inclusion. The outcome of the examination of the disparity of marginalised groups yields valuable insights into the recognition of associated challenges and opportunities for bridging the existing gap.

Financial inclusion (FI) is perceived as an imperative tool for reducing poverty and stimulating economic growth. In particular, FI provides access to capital and financial services to small and medium-sized enterprises (SMEs) and enables them to manage their finances, mitigate risks, expand operations, facilitate innovation, and drive job creation. SMEs are considered the backbone of an economy regardless of the level of development of that economy. However, their potential is not fully tapped yet and is hindered

Foreword

In the contemporary era, we find ourselves amidst a landscape characterized by both opportunities and challenges. On the one hand, technological advancements present boundless opportunities for human advancement. Conversely, the fragility of the financial ecosystem and the ongoing degradation of the environment present formidable risks to human well-being and survival. It appears that a quest is underway to ascertain an optimal equilibrium, wherein the integration of cutting-edge technological frontiers is leveraged to effectively address the core concerns essential to humanity's welfare.

Financial Inclusion, Sustainability, and the Influence of Religion and Technology is a timely exploration of this dynamic ecosystem, delving into the intricate interplay between these profound themes. This edited volume, meticulously curated by Dr. Awais Rehman and Dr. Arsalan Haneef Malik, explores beyond the traditional boundaries of financial inclusion and sheds light on the multifaceted dimensions that shape a financially inclusive and sustainable future. Each chapter, meticulously crafted by a team of esteemed contributors, offers a distinct perspective on the intricate relationships between the book's central themes.

The exploration starts with a historical lens, examining religion's evolving dynamics and its impact on financial inclusion practices. It discusses in-depth the role of religion, specifically Islamic finance, in fostering financial inclusion. Through case studies and real-world examples, the book delves into the practicalities of Islamic microfinance and its impact on marginalized communities. Subsequent chapters delve into the transformative potential of technology, particularly Industry 4.0, in bridging the financial access gap. Moreover, the book demonstrates the intricate connection between financial inclusion and sustainability, offering valuable insights for policymakers and practitioners seeking to align financial practices with long-term environmental and social goals. The book concludes by highlighting the need for further research, dialogue, and concrete steps towards a future where financial inclusion and sustainability are not competing priorities, but rather, two sides of the same coin.

Financial Inclusion, Sustainability, and the Influence of Religion and Technology is not just an informative resource; it serves as a call to action. More importantly, the book moves beyond academic discourse by offering a practical resource for a broad audience. Whether you are a seasoned researcher, a policymaker navigating the complexities of financial inclusion, or an individual simply curious about the future of finance, this book offers valuable insights. I invite you to embark on this intellectual journey, explore the diverse perspectives presented, and contribute your voice to the ongoing discourse. It's an invitation to engage in a crucial conversation about shaping a more inclusive and sustainable future for all.

Mohamed Eskandar Shah
College of Islamic Studies, Hamad Bin Khalifa University, Qatar

Preface

We are delighted to present *Financial Inclusion, Sustainability, and the Influence of Religion and Technology*, the first book to comprehensively explore the intricate interplay between these critical factors. This groundbreaking work delves into the nuanced connections between financial inclusion, sustainability, and the crucial role of religion in shaping this landscape. We examine the influence of technology in this dynamic ecosystem, offering a comprehensive analysis that pushes the boundaries of traditional academic discourse.

While *Financial Inclusion, Sustainability, and the Influence of Religion and Technology* serves as a valuable resource for academics and researchers, we recognize its potential as a powerful tool for education as well. Each chapter is meticulously crafted to be suitable for classroom use, fostering active learning and engaging discussions.

To enhance the learning experience and spark intellectual curiosity, we have included thought-provoking assessment activities at the end of each chapter. The authors have skillfully crafted the assessment materials to maximize their utility for both teachers and students. Recognizing this potential, the questions and assignments are designed to serve as valuable building blocks for classroom discussions. This allows teachers to plan their lectures, accordingly, ensuring a well-structured and engaging learning experience. For students, these assessments offer a unique opportunity to not only solidify their understanding of the fundamental concepts but also to explore the practical implications of the various topics. By actively engaging with the thought-provoking questions and assignments, students can begin to envision their future career paths and even formulate potential research topics for further exploration, fostering a spirit of intellectual curiosity and paving the way for groundbreaking future endeavors.

This book is not merely an academic endeavor; it serves as a practical resource for a broad spectrum of readers. Whether you are an academic researcher, a policymaker, a financial sector practitioner, or an individual intrigued by the evolving financial landscape, the insights presented here will offer valuable perspectives and inspire meaningful action.

The content is meticulously organized to cater to a diverse audience, from university teachers and students to researchers, practitioners, and financial sector stakeholders. We explore potential business opportunities in financial inclusion products and services, aligned with Sustainable Development Goals (SDGs), providing practical insights that can inform policy guidelines and shape a more inclusive and sustainable future.

The book delves into a wide range of topics, from the challenges and prospects of branchless banking to the critical role of information technology in financial inclusion. Each chapter provides a nuanced exploration of its subject matter, enriching the overall understanding of the intricate relationships between financial inclusion, sustainability, religion, and technology.

We invite readers to embark on a journey of discovery within the rich tapestry of this compilation. Explore the diverse perspectives presented, engage in the ongoing discourse about the future of finance, and be part of the transformative force driving towards a financially inclusive and sustainable world. It is our sincere hope that this book serves as a catalyst for further research, dialogue, and action, paving the way for a brighter future for all.

SECTION 1: THE FOUNDATIONS

Chapter 1: Christianity and State Behavior in France: A Brief History of Banking Inclusion Initiatives in France Since Renaissance (1637 - 2023)

Jean Michel Rocchi from Sciences Po Aix takes us on a historical journey through the evolution of banking inclusion in France, highlighting the intricate relationship between Christian and State solutions to protect the poor. Beginning with the prohibition of interest-bearing loans, the chapter unfolds various initiatives, including Catholic charitable pawnshops, Monts-de-Piété's transformation, and recent fintech endeavors. By exploring these historical perspectives, the chapter offers insights into the evolving landscape of banking inclusion in France.

Chapter 2: Bibliometric Insights into Religion's Impact on Financial Inclusion and Exclusion

Authored by Misbah Khan, Farah Naz, Saima Khan, and Misal Ijaz from Kinnaird College for Women, this chapter employs bibliometric analysis to dissect the evolving dynamics at the intersection of financial inclusion, Fintech, and religion. Through VOS viewer analysis, the authors reveal thematic clusters, emphasizing the contemporary significance of probing the interplay between technology, Islamic financial principles, and inclusive financial systems. The chapter provides practical implications for policymakers, practitioners, and scholars, offering avenues for addressing challenges through technological integration and religious considerations.

Chapter 3: Empowering Communities: The Nexus of Islamic Finance and Financial Inclusion

Written by Shama Mushtaq, Muhammad Idrees, Laraib Manzoor, Noreen Akhtar, Basharat Ali, Muhammad Roman, and Sara Akram, this chapter delves into the inclusive underpinnings of Islamic finance and its impact on marginalized communities. Utilizing case studies and real-world examples, the authors explore the role of Fintech and Islamic microfinance organizations in enhancing financial access. The chapter identifies challenges and advocates for industry cooperation, regulatory assistance, and consumer education to improve the adoption of Islamic financial services.

Chapter 4: Bank Profitability Determinants in Africa: A Review of Literature

Presented by Peterson Ozili of the Central Bank of Nigeria, this chapter reviews existing research on bank profitability determinants in Africa. The author highlights the diversity of determinants across African countries, suggesting potential future research areas, including the impact of circular economy, fintech activities, pandemics, and uncertainty on bank profitability. The review underscores the contested nature of bank profitability determinants in the African banking literature.

SECTION 2: FINANCIAL INCLUSION AND ITS OUTCOMES

Chapter 5: Catalyzing Financial Stability and Unveiling the Influence of Financial Inclusion in Pakistan's Islamic Banking Sector: Financial inclusion and Financial stability

Ejaz Aslam, Anam Iqbal, and Muhammad Ishfaq from Minhaj University explore the impact of financial inclusion on the financial stability of Islamic banks in Pakistan. Using panel data, the chapter reveals that financial inclusion, measured by bank branches, financing, and ATMs, plays a substantial role in stimulating the financial stability of Islamic banks.

Chapter 6: Financial Inclusion and Sustainability: A Contemporary and Future Perspective from Bibliometric Analysis

Authored by Fiaz Ahmad, Calvin W. H. Cheong, Rana Hussain, Ahmad Salman, Khalil Hussain, Muhammad Khalid Shahid, and Muhammad Akram Naseem, this chapter conducts a comprehensive bibliometric analysis of financial inclusion and sustainability studies. The authors highlight trends, collaboration patterns, and research directions, providing practical implications for practitioners to align financial practices with sustainability goals.

Chapter 7: Financial Inclusion in Sukuk and Green Sukuk: A Case Study Through Bibliometric and SLR

Sumiya Tahir and Farah Naz from Kinnaird College for Women delve into Sukuk and Green Sukuk research trends from 2011 to 2023. Employing bibliometrics and systematic literature review, the chapter identifies key terms, highlights international collaboration, and underscores transformative potential in fostering financial inclusion and sustainability. Despite positive trends, the study acknowledges research gaps, emphasizing the need for further exploration for a nuanced understanding of Sukuk's impact on sustainability goals.

Chapter 8: Financial Inclusion, Sustainability, and Financial Wellbeing in OIC and Non-OIC Countries

Waqas Shair, Saem Hussain, Muhammad Asif, and Azra Niamat examine the significance of access to formal bank accounts across OIC and non-OIC economies. Utilizing the Global Findex Database, the chapter empirically describes financial inclusion's impact on digital payment, savings, borrowing, and financial well-being. The study uncovers disparities among marginalized groups, offering valuable insights into challenges and opportunities for bridging existing gaps.

Chapter 9: Impact of Financial Inclusion on SME Growth: A Bibliometric Analysis of OIC and Non-OIC Countries

Humera Mahmood, Deniz Yoruk, and Mark Gilman from Birmingham City University conduct a bibliometric analysis to review the literature on the impact of financial inclusion on SME growth in OIC and non-OIC countries. The chapter aims to provide deep insights into the overlooked influences in the existing literature, contributing to the understanding of the complex nexus between financial inclusion and SME growth.

SECTION 3: CHALLENGES AND OPPORTUNITIES

Chapter 10: Inflation-Targeting Monetary Policy Framework in Nigeria: The Success Factors

Peterson Ozili returns to explore the transition of Nigeria to an explicit inflation-targeting regime in 2023. The chapter identifies critical success factors, including economic agent monitoring, central bank credibility, independence, reduced budget deficits, limited dollarization, effective communication, financial development, and addressing security challenges. The study anticipates that these factors will play a pivotal role in taming high inflation in Nigeria.

Chapter 11: The Interplay Among Financial Inclusion, Corruption, and Phishing

Bilal Chishty, Rafia Ayub, and Syed Hasan from the Institute of Business Management scrutinize the complex relationship among financial inclusion, corruption, and phishing. Focusing on technology and sustainability, the chapter emphasizes the need for holistic approaches to balance inclusivity and protection against corruption and cyber threats. The authors advocate for collaborative efforts among scholars, policymakers, and practitioners to effectively handle challenges and capitalize on opportunities in our interconnected society.

Chapter 12: Unleashing the Potential of Industry 4.0 for Financial Inclusion

Saeed Mousa from Rennes School of Business explores the transformative potential of Industry 4.0 technologies in reshaping financial inclusion. The chapter investigates how technologies like mobile devices, the internet, blockchain, and AI can bridge gaps in financial access, fostering a more inclusive and equitable global economy. Through case studies, the chapter provides an in-depth examination of benefits, challenges, and ethical considerations associated with Industry 4.0's role in promoting financial inclusion.

Financial Inclusion, Sustainability, and the Influence of Religion and Technology stands as a comprehensive exploration into the intricate dynamics shaping the global financial landscape. This edited reference book, curated by Awais Rehman and Arsalan Malik, brings together a wealth of knowledge from scholars and practitioners, addressing the multifaceted dimensions of financial inclusion, sustainability, and the profound impacts of religion and technology.

The concept of financial inclusion has transcended its traditional boundaries, evolving into a subject of paramount interest for policymakers and academics. This collection not only illuminates the complex relationships between financial inclusion, sustainability, religion, and technology but also provides invaluable insights that extend beyond disciplinary confines. The esteemed contributors have skillfully crafted a narrative that examines the far-reaching effects of financial inclusion on various societal elements.

Each chapter in this edited reference book contributes a unique perspective, enriching our understanding of the intricate relationships between financial inclusion, sustainability, religion, and technology. As editors, we commend the diverse range of topics covered by our esteemed contributors and hope this compilation sparks further research, dialogue, and actionable insights for a more inclusive and sustainable financial future.

The book navigates through the challenges posed by the intersection of religion and technology, offering solutions that leverage technology while acknowledging the unique risks associated with the rise of digitalization in finance. In the wake of the COVID-19 crisis, the importance of digital financial inclusion has become more pronounced, underlining the need for cost-effective service delivery.

The ambitious yet focused objectives of the book aim to unravel the nexus between financial inclusion and sustainability, dissecting the roles played by religion and technology in this intricate relationship. Each chapter, authored by experts in their respective fields, contributes to this overarching theme by identifying best practices, challenges, and opportunities for leveraging religion and technology to foster financial inclusion and sustainability.

This book is not confined to academic circles alone; it serves as a practical resource for a broad spectrum of readers. Whether you are an academic researcher, policymaker, practitioner, or an individual intrigued by the evolving financial landscape, the insights presented here offer valuable perspectives. The content is organized to cater to a diverse audience, from university teachers and students to researchers, practitioners, and financial sector stakeholders.

The exploration of potential business opportunities in financial inclusion products and services, aligned with Sustainable Development Goals (SDGs), provides practical insights that can inform policy guidelines. The book is structured to cover a wide array of topics, ranging from challenges and prospects of branchless banking to the critical role of information technology in financial inclusion. Each chapter provides a nuanced exploration of its subject matter, contributing to the overarching theme of understanding and enhancing the complex relationships between financial inclusion, sustainability, religion, and technology.

We express our gratitude to the contributors who have embraced the challenge of examining diverse dimensions, from the role of information technology in financial inclusion to the nuanced intersections of religion and finance. Their work encompasses critical discussions on Islamic finance, behavioral aspects, and the role of technology, offering a comprehensive understanding of these intricate relationships.

We encourage readers to immerse themselves in the wealth of insights provided in this compilation, explore the varied perspectives presented, and actively participate in the ongoing conversation surrounding the future of finance. Our genuine aspiration is that this book serves as a catalyst, inspiring additional research, meaningful dialogue, and tangible actions toward the realization of a world that is both financially inclusive and sustainable.

Awais Ur Rehman
Faculty of Management Sciences, University of Central Punjab, Pakistan

Arsalan Haneef Malik
College of Business Management, Department of Accounting and Finance, Institute of Business Management (IoBM), Karachi, Pakistan

Section 1

The Foundations

Chapter 1
Christianity and State Behavior in France:
A Brief History of Banking Inclusion Initiatives in France Since the Renaissance (1637–2023)

Jean Michel Rocchi
Sciences Po Aix, France

ABSTRACT

For a very long time, in France, the Christian and state solution to protecting the poor was to ban interest-bearing bank loans, thus excluding them from protection and placing them de facto in the hands of uncontrolled greedy usurers. A first solution was to introduce Catholic charitable pawnshops in France charging low interest rates, then the mission of social utility of Monts-de-Piété was recognized by the government in France by their transformation into municipal credit institutions in the early 20th century. Furthermore, with regards to deposits, the Caisses d'Epargne were created by philanthropic bankers in the 19th century to educate the population in the virtues of saving. In the last 20 years, using new opportunities provided by European Union directives, some fintechs such as notably Nickel were active in banking inclusion to combat poverty.

INTRODUCTION

"Financial inclusion is a key enabler to reducing poverty and boosting prosperity" [1]

World Bank

According to the World Bank definition "*Financial inclusion means that individuals and businesses have access to useful and affordable financial products and services that meet their needs*"[2]. Moreover, Financial inclusion has been identified as an enabler for 7 of the 17 Sustainable Development Goals

DOI: 10.4018/979-8-3693-1475-3.ch001

(SDG) of United Nations Organization. While the G20 affirmed its commitment to implement the "*G20 High-Level Principles for Digital Financial Inclusion*".

Historically however, in the Christian world, this growing consensus in favor of banking inclusion has been anything but self-evident as it took a great deal of time and effort to emerge. The aim of this chapter, in presenting the French case, is to show that for centuries, Christian thought, heir to Aristotle's philosophy, prohibited interest-bearing loans to private individuals in order to avoid increasing the precariousness of the poor and notably serfdom in the event of inability to repay. Paradoxically, this prohibition of most of the population had the disadvantage of exposing the poor, obliged to borrow to the unlimited greed of usurers. Such exclusion in order to protect them soon proved to be counter-productive and damaging. The response of the local Catholic Church was therefore to develop in France the *Monts-de-Piété* (Christian charitable pawnshop) since 1637, in order to bank the poor, before the French authorities launched the *Crédit Municipal* network to replace the *Monts-de Piété* in 1918.

Governments continued over time to increase banking inclusion, for example in providing savings accounts by newly launched *Caisses d'Epargne* (savings institutions) in 1818. More recently, in the late 2000s and 2010s, European Union directives on means of payment and electronic money challenged the oligopoly formed by the major European banks, aiming at lowering the banking products and services costs and promoting the inclusion of individuals by fintechs.

The argument of this chapter proceeds in five parts. First, examination of banking world history which considers banking exclusion as the way to protect the poor. Second, the *Mont-de-Piété* (1637-1918) a catholic pawnshop solution in France to struggle against usury will be presented. Third, the transformation of *Monts-de-Piété* into *Crédit Municipal* and its practical consequences will be analyzed. Fourth, the creation of *Caisse d'épagne* (1818), a savings institution with a seminal role to educate the poor to the virtue of saving. Fifth will emphasizes on recent change in European environment since the 2010s through new European directives, the presentation of the *Compte-Nickel'* case, and a quick overview of banking inclusion's policy influence on banking stability.

1. IN ANTIQUITY AND THE MIDDLE AGES, THE POOR WERE PROTECTED BY BEING EXCLUDED FROM USURY LOANS AND, LESS FREQUENTLY, BY HAVING THEIR DEBTS CANCELLED

In this first section, we'll take a quick look at the role played by interest-bearing loans in some of the world's major civilizations.

The first interest-bearing loans in history appeared in the Middle East

The first traces of banking activity and interest rates appear on the Enmetena cone and lead us to Mesopotamia around 2,400 BC. (Goetzmann & Rouwenhorst, 2005). According to Homer & Sylla (2005) in Mesopotamia according to famous Code of Hammourabi (Circa 1,700 B.C.): "*The maximum rate of interest was set at 33,3% per annum for loans of grain, repayable in kind, and at 20% per annum for loans of silver by weight. [...] If a higher than legal interest rate was collected by subterfuge, the principal of the debt was canceled. Land and movables could be pledged for debt, as could the person of the creditor, his wife, concubine, children, or slaves. Personal slavery for debt, however, was limited to three years.*"(p.3) Van de Mieroop (1997) notes that despite the code there were exceptions, as debt with no interest rate or, on the contrary, a rate of up to 50% or more in the event of late repayment. Van de Mieroop (1997) also emphasizes that often the kings were obliged to intervene to declare all consumer debt null and void in order to avoid social unrest as in the edict *issued by Ammisaduqa of Babylonia (ruled 1646-1626): 'The arrears of the tenant-farmers, shepherds, flayers, herders, and crown tributaries are remitted in order to strengthen them and to treat them justly. The collector may not act against the household of the crown tributary'* ". (p.206).

In Greece and Rome, the risks to social order persist and are attracting the attention of those in power.

Homer & Sylla (2005) emphasizes the very different choices made in Greece imposed by economic crisis and widespread personal slaver for debt: " *around 600 B.C., the legal history of classical Greece began with the laws of Solon.[...]. In contrast to the Code of Hammurabi, the laws of Solon did away with all limits on the rate of interest. They reduced or canceled many debts. They permitted hypothecation, but they forbade personal slavery for debt. These laws endured for centuries.*" (p.3) According to Aristotle (1996) in Greece in the fourth century B.C.: "*The most hated sort [of wealth], and with the greatest reason, is usury, which makes a gain out of money itself, and not from the natural object of it. For money was intended to be used in exchange, but not to increase at interest. And this term interest, which means the birth of money from money, is applied to the breeding of money because the offspring resembles the parent. That is why of all modes of getting wealth this is the most unnatural.*" (p.25) As emphasizes Homer & Sylla (2005) Rome's choices were not so different than the Babylonian one while: " *The famous semi traditional Twelve Tables, dating from around 450 B.C., insofar as they deal with credit, resembled the Code of Hammurabi more than they did the laws of Solon. Interest on loans was limited to no more than 81,3% per annum. Higher than legal interest was penalized by fourfold damages. Personal slavery for debt was permitted, but the physical well-being of the slave was protected.*"(p.3-4)

The original Christian vision reverts to the pragmatism of ancient societies and prohibits all forms of interest-bearing loans.

By breaking with the pragmatism of ancient societies (Babylon, Greece and Rome), which aimed to limit the excesses of usury to protect itself from the major political and social risks involved, the Christian doctrine's total prohibition of lending at interest paradoxically freed usurers *de facto* from any legal constraints, whether they operated in plain sight or clandestinely. The Church Fathers, then theologians, based on both the *Old* and the *New Testament* of the *Holy Bible* as notes Le Goff (2019) in his seminal book: "*Mutuum date, nihil inde sperantes*" ("lend freely, hoping nothing thereby.") (Luke, 6, 35); but also, *"you shall not lend at interest to your brother, whether it be a loan of money, or of living, or anything from which interest is demanded*" (Levitical, XXV, 36) and finally "*Thou shalt not lend upon usury to thy brother; usury of money; usury of victuals; usury of anything. Unto a stranger thou mayest lend upon usury; but unto thy brother thou shalt not lend upon usury...*" (Deuteronomy 23:19-20) The Jews, who recognize only the *Old Testament* and rely in particular on Deuteronomy, could lend at interest to non-Jews, i.e. in practice in France and Europe to Christians who, according to their beliefs, were not part of God's chosen people, and were therefore not their "brothers" in the sense of their sacred books. Homer & Sylla (2005) emphasizes the importance of another sacred text in the corpus to forbid: *"He that hath not given forth upon usury, neither hath taken any increase . . . he is just, he shall surely live, saith the Lord God." '(Ezekiel 18:8).* As Le Goff (2019) also reminds us, as early as the 5th century A.D., Pope Leo I, known as the Great, who reigned from 440 to 461, exclaimed sternly: *"Fenus pecuniae, funus est animae"* (usurious profit from money is death to the soul).

In the Carolingian Empire, Emperor Charlemagne support Christianism expansion and prohibits the lending of money at interest in the capitulary *Admonitio generalis* (General admonition) of 789: "*Lending money for interest (usury) was forbidden to all.*" (Fried, 2016). Charlemagne then reaffirmed this position in a capitulary of 808, which defined usury as the practice of asking for more in return than was originally received. Fichtenau (1966) emphasizes nevertheless a voluntary paradox the absence of sanction against usurers in the capitularies because they were powerful persons: *"although they denounced such practices, never laid down any sanctions against the taking of interest and usury. [...] Only in the stormy year 829 was the enforcement of the prohibition included among the demands of those who set out to protect the poor against 'the innumerable varieties of usury practiced by the great'* ". (p.151) Conversely, McKitterick (2008) is much more positive on this prohibition: "*Not only was this Admonitio rapidly and widely disseminated, but there is every indication [...] of the rapid impact and implementation of this decree*" (p.240).

The Usurers of the Middle Ages: Demonic Individuals Not Belonging to Christianity

Lapidus (1991) emphasizes medieval definition of usury by "moralists" as Robert of Courçon: "*usury is a sin resulting from the fact of receiving or aiming at receiving something above the principal" (De Usura)*"(p.3) Lapidus (1991) also notes the argument of Gregory of Nazianze *(fourth century A.D.), against usurers " taking his affluence not from the cultivation of the earth but from the destitution of the poor*" (p.4) As Le Goff notes (2019), the cornerstone of twelfth-century canon law is Gratian's decree, which postulates *"Quicquid ultra sortem exigitur usura est"* (anything demanded beyond capital is usury). What's more, he goes on to explain that the activity of usury itself constitutes a triple sin: first, the mortal sin of greed ("*avaricia*"); second, theft because it is the theft of time which belongs only to God, and third, it is a sin against justice.

Le Goff (2019) speaks of the "*accursed usurer*" whose activity is in essence diabolical, since it is in fact against nature (itself a divine creation), as Thomas Aquinas emphasizes in his famous formula "*nummus no parit nummos*" (money doesn't produce money), a reasoning that is directly in line with Aristotelian thought. Originally published in 1304, "*Inferno*" is the volume 1 of Dante Alighieri's The *Divine Comedy*, and Canto 17 is dedicated to fraudsters and usurers - hell is promised to them without the slightest doubt (Alighieri, 1996).

The Council of Trier in 1227, held in Germany, forbade all paid deposits with bankers (hence, in the Middle Ages, bankers were paid to protect the sums entrusted to them), and at the Council of Lyon in 1274, France, it was decided to deprive usurers of Christian burial if they failed to repent and make reparation for their wrongs. (Bonin, 1992). While in ancient times non-repayment of a loan often led to slavery in many societies, in the Middle Ages in France it still led to "serfdom" (Mollat, 2006).

Goetzmann and Rouwenhorst (2005) brilliantly summarize the theological problematic selling time is against the "divine plan": "*According to William of Auxerre (ca. 1120) 'The usurer acts contrary to natural law, for he 'sells time, which is common to all creatures'*" (p.5). Throughout the Middle Ages and Modern Times, the reference to the episode in the *Holy Bible* (New Testament) in which Jesus chases the money-changers out of the Temple remains omnipresent, bringing opprobrium on both the money-changers and usurers as represented on Figure 1 hereafter.

The First Developments Which Announces a Future Abandonment of the Original Doctrine

A first evolution in the usury thought was the acceptance of the principle of the *lucrum cessans* (shortfall or earnings foregone) which is very close to the contemporary concept of opportunity cost. As lapidus

Figure 1. Christ expelling money-changers from the temple
Source: Classic painting from the French Master Nicolas Colombel, 1682.

(1991) explains Thomas Aquinas accepted the l*ucrum cessans* principle: *"In his contract with the borrower, the lender may, without any sin, stipulate an indemnity to be paid for the prejudice he suffers while being deprived of what was his possession; this is not to sell the use of money, but to receive a compensation. Besides, the loan may spare the borrower a greater loss than the one to which the lender is exposed. It is thus with his benefit that the first makes up the loss of the second" (Summa Theologica, II-II, q.78, a.2, ad. 1)*" (p. 6).

Lutzel (2008) also mentioned the *damnus emergens* (loss incurred) and the *periculum sortis* (risk of not being repaid on time). Nevertheless, before the creation of the *Monts-de-Piété*, the Catholic Church's disapproval of interest rates was in practice very similar to that of the Muslim religion. What separated the two visions was the fact that the Catholic religion gradually separated the reasonable interest rate, which became licit, from usury, which remained rejected because of its excessive nature. It wasn't until

1515 that a Lateran Council fully legitimized the interest rate for Catholic pawnbroking (Bonin, 1992), which brings us to the case of the *Monts-de-Piété*.

2. THE NEW RELIGIOUS ANSWER TO BANKING THE POOR: THE DEVELOPMENT OF THE *MONT-DE-PIÉTÉ* SYSTEM IN MODERN FRANCE (1637-1918)

The first Mont-de-Piété were born abroad, before spreading to France. The *Monts-de-piété* (*mons pietatis*) were at the origin of "*social microcredit*" (Pastureau, 2013), which, contrary to popular belief, is by no means a new idea.

First Appearances in London and Then Italy

Indeed, the first "pilot" (Praszkier, 2023) *mons pietatis* was founded in England, and more precisely in London, by Bishop Michael Nothburg in 1361, who entrusted 1,000 marks to be used to set up a charitable pawnbroking establishment that would grant interest-free loans to the poor. (Bader-Saye, 2013). As emphasizes Praszkier (2023) "*However, because the bank did not receive any interest at all, it was not a viable enterprise*". (p.368).

Commonly the launch of the *Monte di Pietà* is attributed to Franciscan priest Bernardino da Feltre in Perugia in the year 1462. Toaff (2004) remarks: "*As of 1462, the year in which the Monte di Pietà in Perugia was founded and generally deemed by scholars to be chronologically the first Monte di Pietà*" (p.239). Soon after an impressive expansion began in Umbria and Marche regions of central Italy, as well as in the areas of Tuscany, Lazio, Veneto, and Abruzzi. Praszkier (2023) notes complementarily: "*The idea was based on the one hand, on the desire to combat poverty and, on the other hand, to make the system sustainable, generating modest income from the newly sparked businesses that became successful*". (p.368) Success was almost immediate, and similar institutions soon sprang up all over Italy. (Rzegocki, 2021) Before founding a Monte di Pietà there was an immutable pattern of events described by Toaff (2004) in the following words which begin by a preach of a Franciscan very hostile to Jewish usurers, but also to local notables considered to be their accomplices, who had to make amends. Monte dei Paschi di Siena, founded in 1472, is considered the oldest bank still active in the world. (Rocchi, 2020) But things didn't stop there, as this model gradually spread to many European countries: Belgium, France, Germany, Austria, Spain, and back in England (Puglisi & Barcham, 2008).

The Franciscans Win a Theological Debate in Italy With Far-Reaching Consequences Against the Dominicans

Hence, in the 16th century, things took a turn for the better in the Catholic Church, as Pope Leo X (reigned 1513-1521) authorized pawnshops (the first form of Catholic banking in Europe) to compete with the high rates charged by usurers. (Rocchi, 2020). Praszkier (2023) categorize retrospectively Bernardino da Feltre as one of the "*Changers-for-Good*". Nevertheless, the *Monte di Pièta* acceptance was difficult as explains Bader-Saye (2013): "*The theoretical challenge came especially from the Dominicans (following Aquinas) who charged the Franciscans with back-door usury. Although initially no interest was returned to depositors (and thus no profit was made from the loans), the very act of charging an administrative fee, usually about 5 percent of the loan, smacked of usury by another name. The Franciscans countered that the fee was canonically acceptable since it staved off the disastrous consequences of borrowing from the exploitative moneylenders*". (p.126) The fact that the Franciscan practicality of offering the poor an alternative to usurers prevailed, despite a weakness in the theological debate with the Dominicans, will have fundamental consequences.

Bader-Saye (2013) highlights the fundamental changes brought about by the acceptance of *Mons pietatis*: "*Islam is the only Abrahamic tradition that has preserved its prohibition on usury. As such, it provides an interesting contrast to Western banking practices that have become accepted by Jews and Christians. Further, it provides a vision of what might have arisen in Christian countries if the Dominicans had won the medieval debate*" (p.130).

The Birth of Monts-de-Piété in France: First Successes and Opposition From Loan Sharks

The first French *Mont-de-Piété* (Haley, 1995; Pastureau, 2011) in Paris was founded in 1637 by Théophraste Renaudot (also known as the first modern journalist as founder of *La Gazette* in 1631), before expanding to many other major cities. The project of *Mont-de-Piété de Paris* is supported by King Louis XIII and his prime minister the Cardinal de Richelieu, a friend of Renaudot.

Soon after the death of the King and the Cardinal, under pressure from usurers who charge 120% interest per year, the parliament decides that *Mont-de-Piété* activity will terminate in 1644.

The Second Birth of Monts-de-Piété

More than a century later, the Lieutenant General of the Paris Police convinces the King Louis XVI, aware of the abuses, to re-establish the *Mont-de-Piété de Paris* with letters patent of 1777. The social character is clearly indicated, as Halay (1992), points out: "*it provides inexpensive cash relief to borrowers without other resources, and the resulting profit will be fully applied to the relief of the poor and the improvement of charitable homes*". (p.51) Framboisier de Beaunay the drafter of the patent becomes the first director of the re-established institution. As emphasizes Deschodt (1993): "*A year after its creation, the institution had received 128,508 items in pledge, worth 8,509,384 pounds, lent at 5% a year. The average rate of usury was 10% per month - you can see what immense losses the profession was making.*" (p.32)

It should be noted that as early as 1610, a *Mont-de-Piété* had been created in Avignon, which was then part of the Papal state before its attachment to France only in 1791. Similarly, in 1628, a Mont-de-Piété was created in Lille, then part of the United Provinces dependent on the Spanish Empire before attachment to France in 1667.

The success of the *Monts-de-Piété* attracted the attention of the French public authorities in a context of growing de-Christianization following the French Revolution of 1789. The Mont-de-Piété de Piété de Paris was briefly closed in 1795, under the Terror regime, during which several bankers were guillotined.

The Third Birth of Monts-de-Piété

The Mont-de-Piété reopened definitively in 1797 under the Directoire regime, although it changed its name to *Crédit Municipal de Paris* in 1918, as will be explained later. Between 1806 and 1872, in keeping with its social orientation, the Mont-de-piété paid out more than 25 million francs to support hospital funds (Haley, 1992). In the Napoleonic empire since September 3, 1807, penalties have been imposed for usury, i.e. any loan with an interest rate higher than 6% for commercial transactions and 5% for civil transactions. (Chaibi, 2010) Even today, the Banque de France regularly publishes usury rates for various loans to individuals, which banks may not exceed under pain of severe penalties This is far remote from the thinking of the English utilitarian philosopher Jeremy Bentham (2014), whose *A Defense of Usury* first appeared in 1787 in response to Smith's (1999, 2003) *Wealth of Nations* fist published in 1776, which advocated limiting interest rates.

Religion and Banking in Modern France

The first theologian to accept interest-bearing loans was the French Protestant theologian Jean Calvin; in his *letter to Claude de Sachin*, dated 1545, proposes a distinction must be made between the licit nature of an interest-bearing loan made to a rich person who will be able to make the money work for them and get richer, from loans granted to the poor, which remain forbidden because it would only increase their precariousness (Rocchi, 2020). Hence, from the 16th to the 18th century bankers in France were either Jews or Protestants (Rocchi, 2020). In 1830, the Papacy changed its mind and canon law recognized the legality of interest-bearing loans, allowing Catholics to enter the profession. The first major Catholic bank in France *Union Générale*, went bankrupt in 1882 against a backdrop of stock market crisis and embezzlement. (Bonin, 1992) In his seminal Weber (2002) firstly published in 1905 attributes the emergence of capitalism mainly to Calvinist beliefs.

The Rapid and Continuing Success of Mont-de-Piété

In the 19th century, the success of the Paris pawnshop was such that it was no longer just seen as an antechamber for the destitute, in fact, many classes of society, and even some eminent figures, sought him out. Surprisingly enough, King Louis-Philippe's third son, the Prince de Joinville François-Ferdinand d'Orléans, deposited his watch to pay off a gambling debt. Somewhat ashamed, he claimed to his mother queen Marie-Amélie to have left it at his aunt's house. Hence the expression "*ma tante*" (my aunt) to describe the *Mont-de-Piété.* (Halay, 1992) Another popular nickname attached to the institution is "*le clou* " (the nail), where small pawned items were supposed to be hung. (Deschodt, 1993) During the 19th century, illustrious Frenchmen with money problems would turn to this service, including impressionist painter Claude Monet, poet Paul Verlaine and novelist Emile Zola in his youth, as well as illustrious borrowers such as Joséphine de Beauharnais (future Empress) and the Comtesse de Castiglione, mistress of Italian Prime Minister Cavour and later Emperor Napoleon III (Deschodt, 1993). In the 20th century, the famous playwright Sacha Guitry pawned *La Rouge*, a famous work by the painter Henri de Toulouse Lautrec (Halay, 1992). Nevertheless, the most important clientele, numerically speaking, remained the common people. As an example of this success, in 1847, the *Monts-de-Piété* granted 4,300,000 loans (Hoffman et al., 2001), compared with a French population of around 36 million. In the 19th century, people came to pawn mattresses, umbrellas, bicycles, watches and art objects, then in the 20th century radio sets, televisions and electrophones (Halay, 1992). Popular novelist Eugène Sue's plan for an interest-free pawnshop is mocked by Karl Marx (Jeanblanc, 2002). On the other hand, utopian socialist and anarchist theorist Proudhon's (with the support of worker's organizations) competing project for a *Banque du peuple* (meaning People's Bank) with initial capital provided by popular subscription (Chaibi, 2010), aroused enthusiasm for a time in working-class and progressive circles, soon proved to be an illusory project that ended in liquidation before the bank had even begun operations. (Chaibi, 2014) This alternative project was largely born out of a criticism of the very restrictive policy of the *Monts-de-Piété* and its costs (Chaibi, 2010): "*Before being pledged, the item was submitted to an auctioneer for appraisal, who naturally depreciated it. If the pledgor was unable to recover his property, the pledge was sold at auction, and the sum returned to the debtors was less than the value of the lost item. [...] Interest rates in Paris were as high as 9%, to which 0.5% had to be added as a pricetag fee*" (pp. 36-37).

During the Second Republic, the laws of March 8, April 12 and June 24, 1851 gave priority to the role of local authorities: the *Mont-de-piété* became a *public utility establishment*, created by decree of the President of the Republic, with a board of directors chaired by the local mayor.

The Black Legend of Mont-de-Piété: First Scams and Dramatic Events

In 1815, Mister Baron became director of the *Mont-de-Piété de Paris*, and soon began to draw down funds in his favor. The embezzlement of funds lasted around 15 years, and was discovered in 1830 (Deschodt, 1993).

Then, in the course of the French Second Empire (1852-1870), an attempt to defraud the *Mont-de-Piété de Paris* was thwarted. Numerous "*reconnaissances* " (acknowledgements) issued by the *Mont-de-Piété de Paris* were presented and appearing as authentic, but mysteriously, the corresponding pledged items could not be found. These had been sold to merchants, and the swindler had stolen official documents from the Mont-de-Piété in Paris, which he simply had to fill in. He was identified thanks to the information provided by the purchasers of his forgeries, arrested and taken to the police station, where he pierced his heart with a compass taken from his pocket (Dulac, 1993). This scam was made possible by the fact that the resale of acknowledgements was only prohibited in 1919, whereas in Belgium it had been since 1848 (Deschodt, 1993).

Deschodt (1993) tells the story of a tragic event: *"Among the thieves, the unfortunate Marie Launay, a kitchen maid, hanged in the Place de Grève for having tried to pawn a gold watch and silver cutlery stolen from her masters in 1780*" (p.13).

Another drama, in December 1868, a woman of around 35 years presented herself in the establishment to try and pawn some worthless clothes, but was refused. Deschodt (1993) recounts the unfortunate end: "*She collapsed on the way down the stairs. The doorman came to her aid, while a thief snatched her parcel. She was taken to a pharmacy, where she was unable to regain consciousness. The local police commissioner had her admitted to the Charité hospital, where she died two hours later, without opening her eyes or uttering a word, dead of hunger...*" (p.20).

Public Decision-Making and Acts of Philanthropy to Liberate Pledged Objects

In the midst of the revolutionary turmoil, on October 9, 1789, King Louis XVI, in an attempt to ease tensions and relieve the population, withdrew the hefty sum of 300,000 livres from his personal coffers in order to free up the wages of the most destitute (Haley, 1992).

In 1870, as also indicates Haley (1992) the government of National Defense during the Franco-Prussian war, in view of the restrictions it had imposed, decided that: *"lingerie, sheets and shirts deposited for loans of up to fifteen francs would be returned to their owners*" (p.52).

Complementarily in some cases, philanthropists made also substantial donations to free up pledged objects, as in the case of the Maréchale de Mac-Mahon, wife of the first President of the French Third

Figure 2. Le Mont-de-Piété of Paris painting from Ferdinand Heilbuth (1826-1889)
Source: "Musée des beaux arts" of Dijon (France).

Republic, or in 1901 the famous Brazilian aviator Santos Dumont, who shared a prize with the institution. (Deschodt, 1993). As explain Albert (2016b), surprisingly the disengagement operation is a semi-failure: "*From November 19 to 30, only 2,534 items were claimed for 17,370 frs, barely a third of the 50,000 frs donated by the aviator*" (p. 78).

Hereafter on Figure 2 a representation of the *Mont-de-Piété de Paris* at the mid of the XIXth century.

N.B: To the right: "*engagements*", the commitment counter were pawnbroking items are registred. We can see on the painting that: "*Pawnbroking is a woman's job*" (Albert, 2016a)

3. THE FRENCH GOVERNMENT ANSWER TO BANKING THE POOR: THE CRÉDIT MUNICIPAL NETWORK

On October 24, 1918, a decree from French President Raymond Poincaré transformed the *Monts-de-piété* into *Crédit Municipal* (municipal credit unions) after approval of the transformation by the municipal councils concerned. (Dulac, 1993) The Paris pawnshop thus became the *Crédit municipal de Paris*, as did the pawnshops in Lyon, Avignon and Bordeaux, as did all the others. The change of name reflected the development of banking activities alongside pawnbroking. The *Mont-de-Piété* thus became a credit institution, subject to banking legislation regulating pawnbroking and making it a public service, the monopoly of which was granted to specialized municipal banking institutions. According to Elgey (2003) the evolution proved a success until a huge scandal in the 1930s initiated by the famous swindler

Alexandre Stavisky*: " From the outset, it was clear that pawnbrokers, considered to be charitable organizations, had access to the financial market, where they could borrow money at 6% and then pawn at 8%. The margin is low, unless the volume of deposits is high"*[3]

The Attempt to Defraud the Orléans Municipal Credit Bank Was a Resounding Failure

Elgey (2003) recounts the organization of the attempted swindle of the Credit Municipal d'Orléans. Desbrosses, the director of the Mont de Piété, is no stranger to René Hayotte, Stavisky's right-hand man of many years. Desbrosses joins forces with the swindling duo. The Alex Company (founded by Stavisky), whose corporate purpose is jewelry trading, borrows from Bayonne's Crédit Municipal, pledging authentic jewelry as collateral for appraisal. After credit approval, the originals are replaced by imitations, so the institution's safe only holds fakes, but thanks to this system, the money flows in.

Elgey (2003) explains that nevertheless the first attempt turned out to be a disaster*:"But in 1931, faced with the threat of an audit by the Ministry of Finance, it became urgent to redeem the bonds, since it was impossible to present the pledges: a counter-expertise would prove their lack of value. [...] In four years, Alexandre Stavisky raised 65,327,216.70 francs. However, after repaying loans in advance, buying back counterfeit bonds, paying discounting fees and paying intermediaries, he disbursed 69,035,685.55 francs. For Stavisky, the Crédit municipal d'Orléans affair ended with a loss of 4 million francs..."*[4].

The Bayonne Municipal Credit Affair: A Major Fraud With Huge Political Consequences

He then decided to turn to *Crédit Municipal de Bayonne*, in particular to have the cash needed to finish recovering the counterfeit jewels from the Credit Municipal d'Orléans before the audit. Jankowski (2002) which describes *"the heart of fraud"* shows that the initial project as presented by deputy Garat was fully in line with financial orthodoxy of the Credit Municipal network practices: "*In September 1930, after the summer recess and his seminal encounter with Stavisky, Garat proposed to the city council of Bayonne that it creates a crédit municipal. It would operate under the same nineteenth-century statutes as all the others, issue bonds at 5 percent interest to raise cash for the loans it would make at 7 percent, and use the difference to cover its operating expenses and contribute to the general good of the town. This appealed to the assembled councilors, who twice voiced their enthusiasm with their votes*" (p.102).

The *Crédit Municipal de Bayonne* opened in 1931 and began operations with a manager named Tissier, chosen by Stavisky and instructed by Garat to obey Stavisky and not the Board of Directors. (Jankovski, 2002). In his history of the city of Bayonne Pontet (1991) explains the complex scam and its collapse with its huge political consequences: "*In this creation, he receives the encouragement of the Minister of Commerce [...] Stavisky gained control of the establishment by getting it managed by a person he trusted, a certain Tissier. With the help of accomplices, Stavisky then placed 200 million worth of counterfeit savings bonds in Paris banks and insurance companies. On December 24, 1933, the fraudulent operations were discovered; the director of Crédit Municipal was arrested, followed by the deputy mayor, Joseph Garat. The next day, Stavisky was found dead, and the day after that, the press reported a recommendation from the Minister of Colonies to buy Crédit Municipal de Bayonne bonds*" (p.271).

Figure 3. Illustration from the Petit Journal showing the arrest of Gustave Tissier, director of Bayonne's Crédit municipal in 1933, a front man for Alexandre Stavisky
Source: https://www.lefigaro.fr/histoire/archives/2019/01/07/26010-20190107ARTFIG00261-affaire-stavisky-la-mort-de-l-escroc-fit-vaciller-la-republique-en-1934.php

A Scandal With Serious Political Consequences That Does Not Call Into Question the Existence of the Municipal Credit Network

As explains Fortescue (2000): "*The Stavisky Affair provoked one of the most important domestic political crises in France during the 1930s. [...] Allegedly a number of people with government connections were also involved in this scandal, but before the truth could be established Stavisky was found dead by the police (8 January 1934)*" (p.186).

The investigation led to the suicide, but the press almost unanimously concluded that Stavisky had been murdered to avoid explosive revelations (*Le Canard Enchainé, Le Temps, L'Action Française...*).

Figure 4. Current logo of the Crédit Municipal de Paris
Source: https://www.creditmunicipal.fr/

Fortescue (2000) notes: "*It was widely assumed that the police, acting on government orders, had murdered Stavisky*" (p.186).

Moreover, the magistrate investigating the case, Councilor Albert Prince, was found on February 20, 1934, torn to pieces on the track of the Paris-Dijon train, on which he had been tied up (Jankowski, 2002; Cornut-Gentille, 2010).

Jankowski (2002) emphasizes the court sentence for the former director of the Crédit Municipal de Bayonne: "*Tissier reaped seven years' hard labor for his pains at Bayonne*"(p.259). Most of the swindler's numerous accomplices received lighter sentences, including the deputy mayor Garat, whose court found that there had been no personal enrichment, Arlette Stavisky (wife of the swindler) was exonerated (Jankowski, 2002).

As noted Laroche-Signorile (2019): *"the swindler's death cause to flicker the Republic in 1934"* by encouraging the riot of February 6, 1934. (p.294) Passmore (2013) notes: *"the alleged cover-up of the affair symbolized professional politicians' manipulation of the system for gain, especially through interference in the judiciary"* (p.294).

Nevertheless, the *Crédit Municipaux* network did not suffer too much from the scandal, but the public authorities, both national and municipal, realized that it was essential to exercise much more effective and strict control over their activities. In 2024, the *Municipal Credit* network is still present in all the most important cities of France offering microcredit and more diversified banking services (Since the French banking law of 1984).

Hereafter on Figure 4 the current logo of Crédit Municipal de Paris which explicitly refers to the first *mons pietatis* in Perugia.

N.B.: The Griffin on the logo is a reference to the coat of arms of the city of Perugia, the Griffin was also known according to myth as the dedicated and inflexible guardian of the treasure and gold mines of the Greek god Apollo, having per motto "*Win or Die*".

4. LEARNING THE BENEFITS OF POPULAR SAVINGS ACCOUNTS: THE CREATION OF THE *CAISSE D'EPARGNE* AND *LIVRET D'ÉPARGNE*

The second pillar has been to provide the general public with savings tools and educate them to build up precautionary savings and overcoming poverty (Gueslin, 1987, 2007).

The Beginnings of Savings Banks in Europe

The world's first savings banks were founded in continental Europe, and more specifically in Germany. In 1778, the "*Erparnisklasse der Allgemeine Versorgungsanstalt*", literally the savings section of the General Provident Institution, was founded in the City of Hamburg (Gaudez and Schacchi, 1989), soon after in 1786, they were established in Detmold, Oldenburg and Kiel, followed by Altona and Göttingen in 1801, before gradually becoming more widespread.

Switzerland was the second country to be convinced, with the opening of a "*Dienstenzinskasse*" literally the servant's fund in Berne in 1787, followed by a "*Caisse d'Epargne et de Dépôts*" in the Canton of Geneva in 1789, and further savings banks in Zurich in 1805, before gradually becoming more widespread. (Gaudez and Schacchi, 1989).

In the Anglo-Saxon countries, the forerunners were Mrs Priscilla Wakefield in Great Britain, who founded the Tottenham Benefit Bank in 1804, the country's first savings bank, and the Reverend Dr Henry Duncan in Scotland, who founded the Ruthwell Savings Bank in 1810 (Gaudez and Schacchi, 1989). As Thieveaud and Kang (1991) note, the legislature is very active in the control and development of new financial institutions: *"From 1817 to 1853, eight Saving Banks Acts were passed in England, successively improving the regulatory provisions and extending the system to Ireland (1828)*" (p.73).

Earlier French Projects Had Failed in the Face of Opposition From the Church and Then the Constituent Assembly

The idea of savings banks is also an old French one, as Gueslin (1989) explains, since two previous projects had failed: firstly, in 1611, Hugues Delestre's project met with the hostility of the Church to the idea of remunerating savings by paying an interest rate.

In the aftermath of the 1789 French Revolution, the economist Joachim Lafarge proposed a "*Tontine viagère et d'amortissement*" (life and amortization tontine) project to the Constituent Assembly, which was rejected. Anglo-Saxon-inspired projects will therefore see the light of day.

Philanthropic and Cosmopolitan French Bankers at the Helm

Benjamin Delessert, whose banker father had sent him to study in the United Kingdom, had attended Adam Smith's lectures and had been impressed by the first savings banks. (Duet, 1991) The Catholic aristocrat Duke of de la Rochefoucault-Liancourt, future first president of the *Caisse d'Epargne de Paris* had lived not only in the U.K. but also in the U.S. (Daumy, 2023).

The creation of the *Caisse d'Epargne de Paris* was authorized by royal decree on June 29, 1818 (Gueslin, 1989). As Thieveaud and Kang (1991) underlines "*The Banque de France gave its blessing to the savings banks, generously lending in 1820 to the Caisse de Paris. But neither the savings nor the Bank ever intended to join forces.*" (p.74) As Gueslin (1989) points out: "*Almost all the founders of the Caisse d'Epargne de Paris belonged to the business world (at least 21 out of 25). They include some of the biggest names in finance: Delessert, James de Rothschild, Jacques Laffitte, Pillet-Will, Hottinguer, Jean-Charles Davillier, Scipion Périer... The Duc de La Rochefoucauld-Liancourt, from a noble court family, must be set aside, as Baron de Staël is present as a grandson of Necker.* "(p.393-394) As Esquiros (1844) emphasizes, the first step was to copy the admired English experience: *"We must stop for a moment to consider the savings banks of England, which served as a model for our own"* (p.753).

In 1818, under the reign of King Louis XVIII, the *Caisse d'Epargne de Paris* and the *Livret d'Epargne*, with an interest rate at inception of 5%, were born. Benjamin Delessert, a protestant philanthropic banker from Swiss origin and founder of the *Caisse d'Epargne de Paris*, set himself the mission of combating social instability and promoting the notions of providence and social protection in order to fight poverty and try to eradicate it. A Foundation to promotes its ideas and goals is still active in France[5] . The founders describe themselves, in La Rochefoulcaud-Liancourst's beautiful phrase, as "*friends of humanity*". (Duet, 1991). Daumy (2023) describes the important role of the Duke of La Rochefoucauld-Liancourt "*liberal aristocat and reformer*" and first President of the *Caisse d'Epargne de Paris*, while the vice-president was Benjamin Delessert: "*In 1818, he helped found the Caisse d'Épargne et de Prévoyance de Paris, alongside Baron Benjamin Delessert and other Protestant bankers bankers such as Jacques Lafitte.*"(p.174) According to Thieveaud and Kang (1991) the primary objective was preparing retirement: "*However modest are a worker's wages,*" said La Rochefoucauld-Liancourt in 1825, " *We had to teach him [...] and finally to accumulate enough to protect him in old age from the rigors of indigence.* " (Speech by the Duke of La Rochefoucauld to the General Meeting of Directors and Administrators of *Caisse d'Epargne de Paris*, August 28, 1825), p.71. In 1835, the famous poet and politician Lamartine referred to the institution as an "*élan vers le bien*" (impetus for goodness)" (Duet, 1991).

A Great Success Despite Karl Marx's Isolated Opposition to the Project

By 1843, 644,000 accounts had already been opened in the Caisses d'Epargne in France. (Hoffman et al., 2001). Gilormi (2013) summarizes the objectives of these philanthropic bankers in the following terms:" *For their founders, the Caisses d'Epargne had a moral, social and educational purpose. They help to combat gambling, intemperance and dissipation, and accustom workers to foresight. [...] In this way, savings provide relief for piety mounts, hospices and charitable institutions*" (p.6). Gueslin (1991) explains: "*In their minds, the Caisses d'épargne had nothing to do with the traditional banking sector, but were simply social welfare institutions, not so very far removed from charitable societies*" (p.250).

There was, however, one very dissonant voice, that of the economist and communist theorist Karl Marx, who was living in Paris at the time, and poured out a torrent of hatred for the reformist institution likely to distract the worker from his natural goal of making revolution. According to Duet (1991), Marx "*saw in the savings bank system 'a machine of oppression', 'the golden chain by which the state binds a large part of the working class*'" (p.13-14).

When their founder Benjamin Delessert died on March first 1847, there were already more than 350 *Caisses d'Epargne* in France, and Delessert, justifiably proud of his work, had the following engraved on his tombstone: "*Ci-gît l'un des cofondateurs des Caisses d'Epargne*" (Here lies one of the co-founders of the Caisses d'Epargne).

The Long-Standing and Growing Influence of Caisse des Dépôts et Consignations

As Thiebeault and Kang (1991) point out, the 1837 Act was a milestone in the history of both the State and society. As the State took on the role of "*moral guarantor*", the role of *Caisse des Dépôts et Consignations* in the management of *Caisses d'Epargne* is reaffirmed and clarified. As Christen-Lécuyer (2004) shows, the French state's more or less explicit guarantee of its involvement was reflected in the fact that, during the economic and social crisis of 1848, funds were placed with the *Caisse des Dépôts et Consignations*, turning a de facto philanthropic project into a relay for state policy.

The Rapidly Aborted Plan to Merge Monts-de-Piété and Savings Banks

As Haley (1992) points out, a man named Courtet de l'Isle presented in 1840 a project to merge *Caisses d'épargne* and *Mont-de-Piété*, inspired by an experiment conducted in Metz since 1820, justified in the following terms: "*Thus is realized an idea of high morality, since, by this simple combination, one inspires the fear of misery in the worker momentarily in ease and the hope of ease in the miserable worker who sees beside him the result of pension and work*" (p.53).

The reform, which was the subject of a serious study, was not adopted in the end. The reasons were as follows the practical implementation of such a merger was deemed complex and risky, and was abandoned.

Despite Temporary Crises: A Constant Success Right Up to the Present Day

In 1870, the state once again intervened to limit customer withdrawals and avoid the risk of panic. This gradual shift from a purely private project to public supervision reinforced the image of risk-free savings attached to the "*Livret A*". Precisely, de Coninck (2012) has carried out a longitudinal study (1818-2008) of the *Livret de Caisse d'Epargne* (savings account booklet), highlighting its immense success and contribution to banking inclusion. The passbook was liquid, and the money available very quickly, which underpinned its great success: around 1913, 38% of the population held one, and around 1988, 53 livrets were held for every 100 inhabitants. These figures are probably underestimated, since Duet (1991) gives an even more impressive statistic: "*We must not forget, either, that more than 45 million French people hold a Caisse d'Epargne passbook, i.e. 8 out of 10 French people (of all ages). What company can announce such a high rate of distribution of its product*" (p.3).

This "livret" (booklet) allows savers to be identified only by their first and last names, but other individual characteristics: year of birth, profession, place of residence, signature, etc… As emphasizes de Coninck (2012) the passbook soon became an instrument of police control: "*numerous letters from the Prefecture of Police were addressed to the General Agent of the Paris Savings Bank to find out whether such and such a person (...) might possibly have a passbook there*" (p.133). The Caisse d'Epargne has conveyed an entire popular imagination, embodied in its logo, which has evolved considerably over time, as shown in Figure 5.

The Squirrel, the current emblem, is a reference to an animal reputed to be friendly, astute and far-sighted. It was preceded in the 1930s by the ant (a direct reference to a famous fable by Jean de La Fontaine, which pitted the working forward-looking ant against the spendthrift cicada. While, in the 1920s by the beehive, a reference to the hard-working nature of the bee.

Caisse d'Epargne played a great role in women financial inclusion. Between 1875 and 1881, French women could open a savings account on their own, but could only withdraw funds with their spouse. Moreover, with the laws of April 9th, 1881 and July 20th, 1895, women could now open and use their savings books alone, without the intervention of their husbands, both at the *Caisse d'Epargne* and at the *Caisse Nationale d'Epargne Postale* (equivalent products available at the French post office network). Only quite recently a new law was allowing women to open a bank account in their own name and to work without their husband's consent (law of July 13, 1965). The *Caisse d'épargne* network, which had become a mutual bank, merged in 2009 with another major mutual network, the "*Banques populaires*", to

Figure 5. Evolution of the logo of Caisse d'Epargne from 1920 to the present day
Source: https://www.moneyvox.fr/banque/actualites/59812/comment-ecureuil-est-devenu-embleme-de-la-caisse-epargne

form BPCE, the 2nd largest banking network in France, with 100,000 employees, 6 million "sociétaires" (members) who own the group and 35 million customers in 40 countries worldwide.

5. NEW EUROPEAN FINTECH OPPORTUNITIES (PSD 1 & 2 AND EMD 1 & 2 DIRECTIVES): THE "COMPTE-NICKEL" CASE AND THE INFLUENCE OF THE BANKING INCLUSION POLICY ON BANKING STABILITY

In this final section, we'll look at three points in turn: the new European environment created by the emergence of fintechs; the role of the French fintech Nickel in banking inclusion; and finally, the stabilizing effect (or otherwise) of inclusion policy on banking stability.

The New European Framework

As banking regulation is a competence of the European Union, banking inclusion is de facto directly dependent on the policy advocated by European directives.

PSD1 (Payment Services Directive 1) in force in December 2009 was designed by the European Union to regulate payment services to all EU member states (including France) and the European Economic

Area (EEA). It came into force in December 2009, in order to offer better services, and thus protect consumers. PSD2 prohibits overcharging, i.e. the application of surcharges on credit card payments.

Morevover, a second directive, the E-Money Directive or the electronic money (EMD1) introduced in 2009 was reinforced by EMD2 in 2015 to increase cashless transaction with a high security level. The objective of the European Commission is to increase competition in lowering prices for consumers, in order to improve inclusion. New players such as fintechs born from the decline of the banking monopoly consequently to these two directives have taking initiatives to bank the unbanked.

The Role of Fintechs in Promoting Inclusive Banking

A practical definition of Nickel is provided by Machkour & Abriane (2020) " *Fintech BtoC (business-to-consumer) which are aimed at the general public, for example the 100% digital "neobanks", without an agency, which offer a low-cost account and payment card*"(p.499)

Even if France is one of the most banked countries in the world, Nickel attracted more than 3 million customers (Rocchi, 2022) in *"creating a new demand"* (Kim et al., 2020) while targeting people on low incomes or in precarious situations (people who suffer from banking ban, employees on fixed-term contracts, the unemployed, students who are not in higher education, etc).

Nickel's model is based on a double duality: on the one hand, inclusion associated with technology, and on the other, phigital access through authorized tobacconists (physical) but also via the internet (digital), as Rocchi (2021) points out.

Le Bret (2017a) co-founder of Nickel describes its business model in the following terms: " *The Nickel Account, a "bankless account" that can be opened at your local tobacconist's, is not only socially responsible, it is also easy to use. It takes just a few minutes to open an account by scanning identity documents and setting up an electronic customer file.*"(p.58) Pinos (2015) points out that compte-nickel is positioned primarily as a reaction to the existing banking offer, which is controversial: " *Under the slogan "100% useful 0% toxic", the Nickel account is precisely positioned as the solution to the most common shortcomings in the attitude of banks towards opaque pricing, and the final cost of services sold.*"(p.286). Croutsch & Roux (2015) classify compte-nickel as a" *low-cost*" player nevertheless having a success exceeding expectations: "*This account, which imposes no income, deposit or assets, has also found fans beyond its initial target group and vulnerable populations.*" (p.92)

In addition, Benavent (2017) describes a "disruptive player": "*Nickel's success is not simply due to the targeting of the unbanked, giving them access to a payment card and an account in just a few minutes in the network of tobacconists. Very quickly, the value of the Nickel account has not only been for populations neglected and excluded from traditional banking, but has also extended to regular customers who expect greater simplicity. A disruptive potential is created*". (p.13) for all the reasons mentioned above, it is clear that Nickel contributes to the Sustainable Development Goals (SDGs) of the United Nations Organization.

Chesneau (2019) describes the relationship between fintechs and traditional banks in terms of "coopetition", meaning that head-on competition in some areas does not exclude cooperation in others, as embodied in open APIs2 in particular.

In 2017, Compte-Nickel was acquired by the universal bank BNP Paribas to address Bottom of the Pyramid (BOP) customers. Then, BNP Paribas since 2020 launch internationalization by creating subsidiaries in Spain, Portugal, Belgium and recently in Germany

The measures that have contributed to the rise in bank deposits and savings accounts are more in line with the increased stability of commercial banks, hence an increased access to placements will enhance resilience of the real economy and consequently the financial system stability (GPFI, 2012; Cull et al., 2012; Khan, 2011). For instance, in 1983 the *Livret d'Epargne Populaire* (LEP) was created, a specific savings account which is subject to maximum income requirements for its holder, only granted to French tax residents because LEP provides attractive tax-free interests. On the other hand, policies to support the economy in the wake of Covid 19, such as state-guaranteed loans (*Prêts Garantis par l'Etat* or PGEs), have exposed the banking system - and above all the state, which provides a guarantee up to 90% of the granted loan by commercial banks to businesses including sole traders and craftsmen. At the moment, these risks are still difficult to measure especially in the long term (Bach et al. 2021), but seem not negligible.

DISCUSSION AND AREAS FOR FUTURE RESEARCH

Our study demonstrates the direct influence of Catholic thought, even if it has evolved significantly over the centuries. France (now a secular country) remains fairly representative of the Latin countries of Southern Europe, whereas Northern Europe has been marked by the spirit of Protestant capitalism (Weber, 2002), and such a study in these countries would certainly differ significantly from our own. Indeed, until the French Revolution, banking in France was dominated by religious minorities (Protestants and Jews).

Academic research on the influence (positive or negative) of inclusion on system stability remains extremely limited to date, which is a pity. Indeed, a positive influence of inclusion on the solidity of the banking system would be a powerful incentive for this policy. Conversely, it goes without saying that a negative link would not be conducive to the legitimacy of SGPs. Almost everything remains to be demonstrated on these points, and so the research agenda remains considerable.

CONCLUSION

"Experience has taught us that, in the affairs of life, a timely help has all the importance of a treasure."

Théophraste Renaudot, founder of the *Mont-de-Piété of Paris.*[6]

The protection of populations at risk was historically conceived as requiring their exclusion from banking activity, solution which quickly proved to be a remedy worse than the disease by handing them over to loan sharks. As Bader-Saye emphasizes (2013): "Y*unus sounds .almost like a fifteenth-century Franciscan when he writes, "In the past, financial institutions always asked themselves, 'Are the poor credit-worthy?' and always answered no. As a result, the poor were simply ignored and left out of the financial system, as if they didn't exist. I reversed the question: 'Are the banks people-worthy?' When I discovered they were not, I realized it was time to create a new kind of bank*" (p.129).

In France, since the Renaissance, these populations have been gradually reintegrated and today the fintechs born of the new legal framework imposed by the European Union since 2010s have almost fully completed the banking of the unbanked. We have tried to demonstrate, using the French case as a starting point, that banking inclusion is not a new idea, dating back to 1637, when the *Mont- de-Piété de Paris* was created, and that over the years, a wide variety of solutions have been developed to strengthen

Table 1. Chronology of banking exclusion and inclusion

Name	Date	Country	Event
Banque de France	2024	France	The law on usury rate or maximum legal interest rate is still in place. https://www.banque-france.fr/statistiques/taux-et-cours/taux -dusure
BPCE	2023	France	Caisses d'épargne which are mutually held bank are a part of BPCE, France's second-largest banking group, with 100,000 employees, 9 million "sociétaires" (members) who own the bank and 35 million customers, thanks to a presence in 40 countries worldwide.
Crédit Municipaux	2023	France	Branches in all main cities of France.
Crédit Municipal de Paris	2018	France	Launch of "Livret Paris Partage" savings booklet.
BPCE	2009	France	On July 31, 2019, the merger between the Banques Populaires and the Caisses d'Epargne became effective, and the new BPCE group was equally owned by the two mutual banking networks.
Crédit Municipaux	1984	France	According to the new banking law they became banking institutions.
Crédit Municipaux	1954	France	Authorization to grant consumer credit notably to civil servants.
Alexandre Stavisky	1934	France	In January, Alexandre Stavisky was discovered dead in a chalet in Chamonix by the police who had come to arrest him. The investigation concluded that he had committed suicide, but this official version failed to convince a large part of public opinion, which was convinced that he had been murdered to avoid revelations of complicity in high places.
Alexandre Stavisky	1930-1933	France	Huge organized swindle at Bayonne's Crédit Municipal uncovered in December, suggesting political protection based on corruption. The director of Crédit Municipal de Bayonne, an accomplice of Stavisky, was the most heavily convicted.
Alexandre Stavisky	1929	France	Failure in the scam of Crédit Municipal d'Orléans. The swindler is obliged to redeem all the bonds issued, which will result in heavy losses for him and his accomplices.
Raymond Poincaré	1918 Oct.24th	France	The President of the Republic decides by decree that, with the agreement of the municipal councils, each Mont-de-Piété will become a public utility institution called "Crédit Municipal". From now on, beyond credits, they can also receive deposits.
Mont de Piété de Paris	1892	France	Real estate loans are authorized.
Banque populaire	1878	France	Creation of the first banque populaire, a mutually held bank.
Monts-de-Piété de Paris	Second-Empire	France	Large scam attempt in using forged " reconnaissances" or acknowledgements (unfilled genuine documents stolen).
Monts-de-Piété	1851	France	By law a "public utility establishment" under supervision of municipalities.
Pierre-Joseph Proudhon	1849	France	Failure of the project "Banque du Peuple".
Mr Baron	1830	France	Discovery of the fraudulent activities of the director of Mont-de-Piété de Paris that began in 1815.
Benjamin Delessert	1818	France	Foundation of the Caisse d'Epargne de Paris.
Dr Henry Duncan	1810	Scotland	The reverend Duncan launches the Ruthwell Savings Bank, the first Savings Bank in Scotland.
Napoléon Bonaparte	1807	France	Law on usury rate (limitation of interest rates in the French Empire at that time western Europe).
Napoléon Bonaparte	1804	France	The Mont-de-Piété de Paris was granted a monopoly on pawnbroking by decree.
Mrs Priscilla Wakefield	1804	England	Foundation of the Tottenham Benefit Bank, the first savings bank in the UK.
Mont-de-Piété de Paris	1797	France	Re-opening of the MPP.
Mont-de-Piété de Paris	1795	France	*De facto* the doors of MPP are closed.
Terror period	1793-1794	France	Banks are closed and some bankers are beheaded.
Jeremy Bentham	1787	England	Publication of the book *Defense of Usury,* collected letters against state limitation of interest rate.

Table 1. Continued

Name	Date	Country	Event
Marie Launay	1780	France	A kitchen maid is hanged in the "Place de Grève" for having tried to pawn a gold watch and silver cutlery stolen from her masters.
Framboisier de Beaunay	1778 Feb. 9th	France	The King's advisor and drafter of the letters patent became the first director of the establishment, which now stands at its heir's (the "Credit Municipal de Paris") current address. Interest rate is at 10% per annum.
Jean-Charles-Pierre Lenoir	1777 Dec. 9th	France	The Lieutenant General of the Paris Police convinces the King Louis XVI to re-establish the Mont-de-Piété of Paris with letters patent.
Usurers	XVIIIth	France	Annual interest rate up to 120% per annum.
Parliament	1644 March first.	France	Decision to end of Mont-de-Piété under the pressure of usurers.
King Louis XIII	1643	France	Dies on May 14th in Saint-Germain en Laye.
King Louis XIII	1643	France	Authorizes 58 towns to create "Monts-de-Piété" (charitable pawnshops).
Cardinal de Richelieu	1642	France	The prime minister dies on December 4th in Paris.
Théophraste Renaudot	1637	France	The king authorizes him to create the Paris Mont-de-Piété. (The first in France).
Théophraste Renaudot	1631	France	King Louis XIII's physician and philanthropist, he was appointed " Commisaire général des pauvres" (General Commissioner for the Poor) by his friend, the Prime Minister Cardinal de Richelieu.
Wenceslas Coeberger	1628	Lille	Creation of the Mont-de-Piété of Lille, which grants loans to the poor at 12%. At this time, the city belongs to the United Provinces, part of the Spanish Empire. The town didn't become part of France until 1667, when it surrendered to the French King Louis XIV.
Bartholomé Masurel	1610	Lille	"Fondation Masurel" interest-free loans to the poor.
Congrégation de Notre-Dame de Lorette	1610	Avignon	Creation of a Mont-de-Piété in Avignon then part of the "enclave des papes" (papal territory), which was not attached to France until 1791.
Jean Calvin	1545 Nov.7th	France & Switzerland	Letter to Claude de Sachin the industrial and commercial loan is licit (but consumer credit is not).
Lateran Council	1515	Italy	Interest rate is legitimate for Catholic pawnbroking (Monte di Pièta).
Bernardino da Feltre	1463	Italy	Foundation of the first *mons pietatis* in Perugia which charged low interest rate. Franciscans support prevails from Dominicans opposition.
Michael Nothburg	1361	England	Foundation of the first *mons pietatis* in London no interest rate charged.
Dante Alighieri	Circa 1307	Italy	In the *Divine Comedy* the place of "usurers" is in "Inferno".
Council of Lyon	1274	France	Decision to deprive usurers of Christian burial if they failed to make reparation for their wrongs
St. Thomas Aquinas.	1225-1274	Italy	*"Nummus non parit nummos"*
Council of Trier	1227	Germany	Prohibition is made to paid for deposits with bankers.
Charlemagne	789	Europe	In the Carolingian Empire, which roughly encompassed France, Germany and northern Italy, usury was strictly forbidden under the proclamation of the capitulary *Admonitio Generalis* (General admonition) constantly confirmed.
Pope Leo I ("The Great")	5th century A.D.	Rome	Usury destroys the soul.
Aristotle	384-322 B.C.	Greece	Commercial chrematistics, which includes usury, is unnatural and therefore unacceptable. (*Nicomachean Ethics*)
"Twelve Tables" (Laws)	Circa 450 B.C.	Rome	*Interest on loans was limited to 8% per annum. Beyond was penalized by fourfold damages. Personal slavery for debt was permitted, but the physical well-being of the slave was protected.*
Laws of Solon	Circa 600 B.C.	Greece	Reduction and cancelation of many debts, personal slavery for debt is forbidden. But no limit to interest rate.
Code of Hammourabi	Circa 1,700, B.C.	Babylonia	*Limitation of interest rates: 331/3% per annum for loans of grain, repayable in kind, and at 20% per annum for loans of silver by weight. Personal slavery for debt is limited to three years.*
Cone of Enmetena	Circa 2,400 B.C.	Mesopotamia	*First evidence of banking operations and interest rate.*

Source: The author.

banking inclusion. Today, this policy based on proactive banking legislation needs to be analyzed also at the level of the single European market. In the banking sector, it is the law that protects and makes rights effective, which validates the famous formula of the Dominican and "*progressive Catholic*" thinker Lacordaire in the mid of the XIXth Century.

"*Between the strong and the weak, between the rich and the poor, between master and servant, it is freedom that oppresses and the law that sets free*".[7] Henri Lacordaire

ACKNOWLEDGMENT

The author extend sincere gratitude to

- The Editor and the International Editorial Advisory Board (IEAB) of this book.
- All anonymous reviewers who provided very constructive feedback for thorough revision, improvement, extension, and fine-tuning of the chapter.
- Dr Ivan Topalovic who assisted to complete this task.

REFERENCES

Albert, A. (2016a). Le genre du prêt sur gage: rapports de pouvoir au Mont-de-Piété de Paris (années 1850 – années 1920). *Genre & Histoire*. Printemps. doi:10.4000/genrehistoire.2462

Albert, A. (2016b). Une incomprehension de la pauvreté? La crise du Mont-de-Piété de Paris à la Belle Époque. *Les Études Sociales, 2*(164), 63-86. https://www.cairn.info/revue-les-etudes-sociales-2016-2-page-63.htm doi:10.3917/etsoc.164.0063

Alighieri, D. (1996). The Divine Comedy. Volume 1, Inferno. Oxford University Press.

Aristotle. (1996). Politics, Book. In *Aristotle. The politics and The Constitution of Athens*. Cambridge University Press.

Ashta A., Assadi D., & Durand N. (2021). Capture d'innovation: étude de cas d'une néo-banque à mission sociale et défis pour les pays en développement. *ISTE OpenScience*, 1–21 doi:.OP.2021.0673 doi:10.21494/ISTE

Bach, L., Ghio, N., Guillouzouic, A., & Malgouyres, C. (2021). *Rapport d'évaluation de la contrainte pour les entreprises du remboursement des prêts garantis par l'État (PGE)* [Rapport de recherche]. Rapport IPP n°32, Institut des politiques publiques (IPP). https://shs.hal.science/halshs-03693262

Bader-Saye, S. (2013). Disinterested Money. Islamic Banking Monti di Pietà, and the Possibility of Moral Finance. *Journal of the Society of Christian Ethics, 33*(1), 119-138. doi:10.1353/sce.2013.0015

Benavent C. (2017). Disruption à l'âge des plateformes. *Économie & Management, 165*, 11-17.

Bentham, J. (2014). *A Defense of Usury. Shewing the Impolicy of the Present Legal restraints on the Terms of Pecuniary Bargains, in a Series of Letters to a Friend.* Cambridge University Press.

Bonin, H. (1992). *La banque et les banquiers en France, du Moyen-Âge à nos jours*. Larousse.

Chaibi, O. (2010). *Proudhon et la banque du peuple (1648-1849)*. Éditions Connaissances et Savoirs.

Chaibi, O. (2014). Le crédit des travailleurs »: un aperçu du crédit populaire en France de 1848 à 1914. *Vie sociale*, *3*(7), 13-29.

Chesneau, D. I. (2019). Fintechs et banques coopération et coopétition, *Réalités industrielles. Annales des Mines*, 45–50.

Christen-Lécuyer. (2004). *Histoire sociale et culturelle des Caisses d'Epargne en France: 1818–1881*. Economica.

Coninck, S. de. (2012). *Le livret de Caisse d'épargne (1818-2008): une "passion" française*. Economica.

Cornut-Gentille, P. (2010). *Un scandale d'État: l'affaire Prince*. Perrin.

Croutsche, J.-C., & Roux, M. (2015). La fixation du prix des produits et services bancaires. *La Revue des Sciences de Gestion*, *271*, 89-95. doi:10.3917/rsg.271.0089

Cull, R., Demirgüç-Kunt, A., & Lyman, T. (2012). *Financial inclusion and stability: what does research show?* openknowledge.worldbank.org

Daumy, J.-C. (2023). Des salons à l'Assemblée constituante: le du de Liancourt ou la formation d'un aristocate libéral et réformateur (1768-1827). *Parlements(s), Revue d'histoire politique*, *2*(38), 159-175.

de Lutzel, E. (2008). Prêter aux pauvres avec intérêt? Une révolution du XVème Siècle. *Finance & Bien Commun*, *1*(30), 115-119. https://www.cairn.info/revue-finance-et-bien-commun-2008-1-page-115.htm doi:10.3917/fbc.030.0115

Deschodt, E. (1993). *Histoire du Mont-de-Piété, Collection « Documents*. Le Cherche Midi Editeur.

Duet, D. (1991). *Les Caisses d'Epargne*. PUF.

Dulac, S. (1993). *Histoire du Mont-de-Piété en France*. Rondeau. https://www.historia.fr/les-mauvaises-affaires-dalexandre-stavisky

Esquiros, A. (1844, September). Les Caisses d'Epargne. *Revue des Deux Mondes (Paris, France)*, *7*(5), 751–782. https://www.jstor.org/stable/44690223

Fichtenau, H. (1966). *Carolingian Empire. The Age of Charlemagne*. Harper Torchbooks.

Fortescue, W. (2000). *The Third Republic in France: 1870 - 1940*. Routledge.

Fried, J. (2016). Charlemagne (P. Lewis, Trans.). Harvard University Press.

Gaudez, P., & Schacchi, P.-H. (1989). *Les Caisses d'Epargne en Europe*. ESKA.

Gilormini, P. (2013). *Aux origines du groupe Banque Populaire Caisse d'Epargne: Philantropie libérale et solidarisme républicain*. Electronic Working Paper Series, ESDES Recherche.

Goetzmann, W. N., & Rouwenhorst, K. G. (2005). *The Origins of Value. The Financials Innovations that Created Modern Capital Markets*. Oxford University Press. doi:10.1093/oso/9780195175714.001.0001

GPFI. (2012). The G20 Basic Set of Financial Inclusion Indicators. Global Partnership for Financial Inclusion.

Gueslin, A. (1987). *L'invention de l'économie sociale. Le XIXème siècle français.* Economica.

Gueslin, A. (1989). *L'invention des Caisses d'épargne en France: une grande utopie libérale. Revue Historique, 282.* https://www.jstor.org/stable/40955304

Gueslin, A. (1991). *Aux origines de l'État-providence: la mise en place du modèle français des Caisses d'épargne. Revue d'histoire moderne et contemporaine, 38*ᵉ. https://www.jstor.org/stable/20529732

Gueslin, A. (2007). *Mythologies de l'argent: essai sur l'histoire des representations de la richesse et de la pauvreté dans la France contemporaine (XXe-XXe siècles).* Economica.

Halay, T. (1994). *Le Mont-de-Piété des origines à nos jours.* L'Harmattan.

Hoffman, P., Postel-Vinay, G., & Rosenthal, J.-L. (2001). *Des marchés sans prix, une économie politique du crédit à Paris.* EHESS.

Homer, S., & Sylla, R. (2005). *A History of Interest Rates* (4th ed.). Wiley.

Jankowki, P. (2002). *A Confidence Man in the Republic of Virtue.* Cornell University Press.

Jeanblanc, H. (2002). Karl Marx à la découverte des mystères de Paris. *Cahiers d'Études Germaniques, 42*, 135-153. https://www.persee.fr/doc/cetge_0751-4239_2002_num_42_1_1590 doi:10.3406/cetge.2002.1590

Khan, H. R. (2011). Financial Inclusion and Financial Stability; Are They Two sides of the Same Coin? In *Address at BANCON 2011.* Reserve Bank of India.

Kim, W.C., Mauborgne, R., & Pipino, M. (2020). *Fintech: Compte-Nickel Creating New Demand in the Retail Banking Sector.* INSEAD.

Lapidus, A. (1991). Information and Risk in the Medieval Doctrine of Usury during the Thirteenth Century. In *Perspectives on the History of Economic Thought.* Edward Elgar. https://paris1.hal.science/hal-00721678

Laroche-Signorile. (2019), Affaire Stavisky: la mort de l'escroc a fait vaciller la République en 1934. *Le Figaro Histoire.* https://www.lefigaro.fr/histoire/archives/2019/01/07/26010-20190107ARTFIG00261-affaire-stavisky-la-mort-de-l-escroc-fit-vaciller-la-republique-en-1934.php

Le Bret, H. (2013). *No Bank. L'incroyable histoire d'un entrepreneur de banlieue qui veut révolutionner la banque.* Les Arènes.

Le Bret, H. (2016). Le Compte-Nickel: un compte pour tous, sans banque. *Le Journal de l'école de Paris du Management, 6*, 24–30.

Le Bret, H. (2017). Vers un monde sans banques? [Towards a world without banks?]. In Annales des Mine- Réalités industrielles (nº 4, pp. 56–59). FFE.

Le Goff, J. (2019). *Le Moyen Âge et l'argent. Essai d'anthropologie historique.* Perrin.

Llorca, M. (2017). Les banques aux prises avec les fintech. *L'économie politique, 3*(75).

Machkour, B., & Abriane, A. (2020). Industry 4.0. and its Implications for the Financial Sector. *Procedia Computer Science, 177*, 495–502. doi:10.1016/j.procs.2020.10.068

McKitterick, R. (2008). Charlemagne. The Formation of a European Identity. Cambridge University Press.

Passmore, K. (2013). The Right in France from the Third Republic to Vichy. Oxford University Press.

Pastureau, G. (2011). Le Mont-de-piété en France: une réponse économique aux problèmes sociaux de son époque (1462-1919). *Revue d'histoire de la protection sociale, 1*(4), 25-40. doi:10.3917/rhps.004.0025

Pastureau, G. (2013). Le microcrédit social: un "argent secours" en perspective historique - Le cas du prêt sur gages au Crédit municipal de Bordeaux. In *Economies et finances*. Université Montesquieu - Bordeaux IV.

Pinos, F. (2015). *Inclusion financière et populations précarisées: effets des business models des services financiers en France. Economies et finances* [Thèse]. Université de Bordeaux.

Pontet, J. (1991). *Histoire de Bayonne, ebook*. Privat.

Praszkier, R. (2023). Three-dimensional delineation of Changers-for-Good: From practice to conceptualization. *Possibility Studies & Society, 1*(3), 361–379. doi:10.1177/27538699231177149

Puglisi, C. R., & Barcham, W. L. (2008). Bernardino da Feltre, the Monte di Pieta and the man of sorrows: Activist, microcredit and logo. *Artibus et Historiae, 29*(58), 35–63. https://www.jstor.org/stable/40343649

Rocchi, J. M. (2020). *Des banques en ligne aux néobanques*. Franel Editions. doi:10.14375/NP.9782384910243

Rocchi, J. M. (2021). Competition Between Neobanks and Online Banks in the French Retail Banking Market and Reactions from Universal Banks. In A. Sghari & K. Mezghani (Eds.), *Influence of FinTech on Management Transformation* (pp. 191–216). IGI Global. doi:10.4018/978-1-7998-7110-1.ch009

Rocchi, J. M. (2022). How to Build a Leading So-Called Neobank and Pursue its Growth? The Case of the FinTech Nickel in Europe. In J. D. Santos (Ed.), *Cases on Digital and Management Issues in Modern Organizations* (pp. 177–199). IGI Global.

Rzegocki, M. (2021). *The mounts of piety: A case study in Christian innovation*. Acton Institute. https://www.acton.org/publications/transatlantic/2021/06/23/mounts-piety-case-study-christian-innovation

Smith, A. (1999). *The Wealth of Nations, Books IV-V*. ePenguin.

Smith, A. (2003). *The Wealth of Nations*. Books I-III. Penguin Classics.

Thivaud, J.-M., & Kang, Z. (1991). Épargne, retraite, prévoyance idéale: Les caisses d'épargne, la Caisse des retraites et la Caisse des dépôts et consignations (1816-1850). *Revue d'Economie Financiere, 1*(1), 65–92. doi:10.3406/ecofi.1991.1779

Toaff, A. (2004). Jews, Franciscans, and the First monti di Pieta in Italy (1462–1500). In *Friars and Jews in the Middle Ages and Renaissance*. Leiden: Koninklijke Brill.

Van de Mieroop, M. (1997). *The Ancient Mesopotamian City*. Oxford University Press. doi:10.1093/oso/9780198150626.001.0001

Weber, M. (2002). *The protestant ethic and the "spirit" of capitalism and other writings*. Penguin.

ENDNOTES

1 https://www.worldbank.org/en/topic/financialinclusion/overview
2 https://www.worldbank.org/en/topic/financialinclusion/overview
3 https://www.historia.fr/les-mauvaises-affaires-dalexandre-stavisky
4 https://www.historia.fr/les-mauvaises-affaires-dalexandre-stavisky
5 https://www.institut-benjamin-delessert.net
6 Quoted in Haley (1992). p.54.
7 https://www.nytimes.com/2012/09/27/opinion/UN-general-assembly-on-the-rule-of-law.html

APPENDIX

QUESTIONS AND ANSWERS

1) Was the Legalization of Interest-Bearing Loans in France Inevitable?

Lending at interest was practiced in France in the Middle Ages by a religious minority, the Jews, who were poorly integrated and hated by part of the population because this activity remained illegitimate. From the Renaissance onwards, the Protestants, another religious minority, began to lend interest to merchants. When the Catholic Church authorized the Monts-de-Piété at the end of the 15th century, it settled a violent theological dispute between the Franciscans and the Dominicans. It wasn't until the mid-nineteenth century that the Pope changed canon law and simply legalized interest-bearing loans in Christendom.

2) When It Comes to Bank Credit, Has the Protection of Borrowers Through Exclusion That Prevailed in the Middle Ages Disappeared in Contemporary France?

The answer is no. There are important reminders of this vision. First of all, in 1807, Emperor Napoleon 1st imposed a usury rate (i.e. a maximum interest rate). This principle remains in force, and today the Banque de France protects private individuals by checking that commercial banks respect the maximum rates in force for different types of credit. Even though France is officially a secular country, there can be little doubt of the Catholic religious influence, since, for example, the commercial banks of our Anglican neighbors in the UK can charge much higher interest rates than in France.

If the borrower falls into over-indebtedness due to the bank's failure to comply with the legislation (lenders are prohibited from lending to individuals above a maximum debt ratio stipulated by law), the loan will be considered illegal and null and void, and the borrower will be exempt from repaying it.

3) In Terms of Savings Products, Has the Protection of Savers Through Exclusion Disappeared?

Savings products considered complex and risky are prohibited from sale to ordinary retail investors, and are reserved for sophisticated investors or professional investors.

European MIFID 1 and 2 legislation, applicable in France, has strengthened the ban on commercial banks and asset management companies selling financial products that are unsuited to the customer's financial profile.

4) Is Pawnbroking, as Practiced by the Monts-de-Piété, the Ancestor of Microcredit as Practiced in India or Bangladesh, for Example?

The similarity lies in the fact that lending to the poor means targeting a segment of the market that conventional banks are not traditionally interested in, because it is deemed risky and unprofitable. There's a famous French saying that says, "on ne prête qu'aux riches" (You only lend to the rich).

The main difference is that Mont-de-Piété grants consumer credit to individuals. The Grameen Bank, set up in 1983 by Muhammad Yunus in Bangladesh, not only grants loans to individuals, but also to micro-businesses and self-entrepreneurs, particularly in villages, through a large number of rural branches.

In addition, the Mont-de-Piété and today the Crédit Municipaux are only present in large cities. From a capital point of view, the Crédit Municipaux are entirely municipalities-owned, whereas the Grameen Bank is 97% owned by its customers and only 3% by the Bangladeshi government. From a capital point of view, it is much closer to the French cooperative banks, which are owned by their member-customers.

5. How Would You Describe Today's Regulations in Favor of Inclusive Banking in a Country Like France?

The legislation is complex and resembles a Russian doll system. In fact, there are three levels of objectives and regulations: on a global level, the UN's recommendations; on a regional level, due to our membership of the European Union, there is a second level of regulations and objectives; and finally, although banking regulations are a European responsibility, they need to be transposed into our country's legislation to take account of local specificities.

MCQ

1. The Pope authorized interest-bearing loans in:
    a. 1230
    b. 1430
    c. 1630
    d. 1830
2. The first modern pawnshop was set up in Italy in:
    a. Perugia
    b. Rome
    c. Milan
    d. Florence
3. The creator of the Monts-de-Piété in France was:
    a. Voltaire
    b. Victor Hugo
    c. Charles Baudelaire
    d. Théophraste Renaudot
4. The creator of the Caisses d'Epargne was:
    a. Karl Marx
    b. Benjamin Delessert

   c. Proudhon
   d. None of the above
5. Legislation on the usury rate (interest rate ceiling) dates back to:
   a. 1207
   b. 1407
   c. 1607
   d. 1807
6. The Mont-de-Piété de Paris, first establishment in France dates from:
   a. 1237
   b. 1437
   c. 1637
   d. 1837
7. The "Twelve Tables" Laws were a regulation in force in:
   a. Rome
   b. Athens
   c. Babylon
   d. Aachen
8. The prohibition of interest-bearing loans in the Carolingian Empire dates back to:
   a. 589
   b. 789
   c. 989
   d. None of the above
9. Mons pietatis was founded in London, by Bishop Michael Nothburg in:
   a. 1161
   b. 1261
   c. 1361
   d. 1461
10. The famous French swindler Alexandre Stavisky was found dead in:
   a. 1914
   b. 1924
   c. 1934
   d. None of the above

ASSIGNMENT: FURTHER READINGS

About the History of Risk Management:

Bernstein, P. L. (2012). *Against the Gods: the Remarkable Story of Risk*, Wiley.

About the History of Money:

Weatherford, J. (1997). *The History of Money*, Crown Pub.

About the History of Capitalism:

Braudel, F. (1992). *Civilisation and Capitalism, 15th-18th, Volume I: The Structure of Everyday Life: The Limits of the Possible*, University of California Press.

Braudel, F. (1992). *Civilisation and Capitalism, 15th-18th, Volume II: The Wheels of Commerce*, University of California Press.

Braudel, F. (1992). *Civilisation and Capitalism, 15th-18th, Volume III: The Perspective of the World*, University of California Press.

About Banking History:

Goetzmann, W. N., Rouwenhorst, K. G., (2005). *The Origins of Value: The Financial Innovations that Created Modern Capital Markets*, Oxford University Press.

Goetzmann, W. N., (2016). *Money Changes Everything: How Finance Made Civilization Possible.* Princeton University Press.

LESSONS LEARNED

Lessons Learned 1: Both Inclusion and Exclusion Can Protect the Retail Customers of Commercial Banks, Depending on the Circumstances and the Times

Based on your one knowledge cand you provide an example of this counter-intuitive phenomenon?

Lesson Learned 2: Morality and Law Regarding an Economic Sector Can Evolve Significantly Over the Centuries

Can you think of an example of this phenomenon in your own country?

MCQ ANSWERS

1. d, 2 a., 3. d., 4. b., 5. d., 6. b., 7.a., 8. b., 9. c, 10. c.

Chapter 2
Bibliometric Insights Into Religion's Impact on Financial Inclusion and Exclusion

Misbah Khan
Kinnaird College for Women, Lahore, Pakistan

Farah Naz
https://orcid.org/0000-0002-4707-5443
Kinnaird College for Women, Lahore, Pakistan

Saima Khan
Kinnaird College for Women, Lahore, Pakistan

Misal Ijaz
Kinnaird College for Women, Lahore, Pakistan

ABSTRACT

This study aims to conduct a bibliometric analysis on the intersection of financial inclusion, religion, and technological advancements, with a particular focus on the role of Islamic banking and Fintech in promoting financial access. Employing an in-depth bibliometric approach, the study analyzes citation patterns, co-authorship networks, and keyword co-occurrence using VOSviewer, based on a systematic literature review. A meticulously selected set of keywords related to financial inclusion, exclusion, and religion facilitated a comprehensive search across major academic databases, yielding 110 relevant articles. The analysis reveals a significant thematic cluster around the convergence of financial inclusion, Islamic banking, and Fintech, particularly within the Indonesian context. This highlights the emerging scholarly interest in exploring how technological innovations and Islamic financial principles can together foster inclusive financial systems. The regional focus underscores the socio-economic dynamics unique to Indonesia, suggesting a broader relevance for similar contexts globally. Despite its comprehensive scope, the study acknowledges limitations such as potential publication bias and the exclusion of non-indexed literature. It underscores the need for qualitative research to complement bibliometric findings and address the complex dynamics between religion and financial inclusion. From a policy perspective,

DOI: 10.4018/979-8-3693-1475-3.ch002

it advocates for regulatory frameworks that support Fintech growth within Islamic banking, aiming to promote inclusive, culturally responsive financial systems. This research contributes to the literature by offering a systematic bibliometric analysis of the nexus between religion, financial inclusion, and technology. It highlights the importance of integrating Islamic finance and Fintech to enhance financial access, urging a global dialogue on culturally responsive financial solutions for economic empowerment and poverty reduction.

1. INTRODUCTION

Given the dynamic and evolving landscape of global finance, the exploration of religion's impact on financial inclusion and exclusion offers a timely and critical lens through which to understand the complexities of accessing financial services (Kania, 2022). In recent years, the intersection of religious beliefs and financial behaviours has emerged as a pivotal area of study, reflecting broader societal shifts towards understanding the nuanced ways in which cultural and religious factors shape economic practices (Ahmad, Lensink, & Mueller, 2023; Ali, Devi, Furqani, & Hamzah, 2020; Aziz & Naima, 2021; Kim, Yu, & Hassan, 2020; Umar, Ado, & Ayuba, 2019). Amidst the backdrop of increasing global interconnectedness, financial inclusion has ascended as a paramount goal for international development agendas, aiming to bridge the gap between those who can access financial services and those who are systematically excluded (Gu, Gao, Zhu, & Ye, 2023).

The World Bank and other institutions champion financial inclusion as a key driver of economic empowerment, poverty alleviation, and equitable growth (Salman & Nowacka, 2020). However, despite concerted efforts, significant portions of the global population, particularly in developing regions, remain marginalized from the formal financial system. This exclusion is not solely a consequence of economic barriers but is also intricately linked to socio-cultural factors, among which religion plays a consequential role. Religion, with its profound influence on individual and community values, ethics, and behaviors, intersects with financial practices in complex ways (Fathallah, Sidani, & Khalil, 2020). It can dictate the ethical frameworks within which financial transactions are conducted, influence attitudes towards saving, investing, and borrowing, and even shape the financial products and services deemed acceptable (Sarofim et al., 2020). Consequently, understanding the impact of religion on financial inclusion and exclusion requires a nuanced analysis that goes beyond traditional economic metrics.

Having said that, the role of religion in our soceity, is critical in imparting ideals in civilizations having a profound impact on individuals' attitudes and actions in their daily financial practises (S. Kumar, Sahoo, Lim, & Dana, 2022). At the macro level, religion, for example is considered a contextual, cultural, or environmental element while on the other hand, it may be regarded a component that builds networks at the micro level (Henley, 2017). Religion's impact on financial inclusion is a multifaceted phenomenon that intertwines deeply with cultural, social, and economic aspects of society (Kim et al., 2020). At its core, religion shapes individuals' values, ethics, and behaviors, which in turn influence their financial decisions and practices (Fathallah et al., 2020). This relationship is critical to understanding the broader concept of financial inclusion, which encompasses the availability and equality of opportunities for individuals and businesses to access financial services. Firstly, religious doctrines and ethical teachings can directly affect how people engage with financial systems (Sarofim et al., 2020). For instance, Islamic finance, guided by Sharia law, prohibits interest (riba) and speculative investments (gharar), leading to the development of unique financial products and services that comply with these principles

(Svoboda, 2024). Such religious guidelines ensure that financial practices align with the faith's ethical standards, offering inclusive financial solutions for followers who might otherwise be excluded from conventional financial systems.

Moreover, religion often plays a role in forming community networks and social capital, which are essential for financial inclusion, especially in regions with limited access to formal financial services (Abdu & Adem, 2021). Religious communities can facilitate trust and cooperation among members, providing a foundation for informal financial support systems such as rotating savings and credit associations (ROSCAs) or mutual aid (Amaroh & Masykuroh, 2023). These systems can serve as vital access points to financial resources for individuals who are marginalized or underserved by traditional banking institutions. Additionally, the impact of religion on financial inclusion extends to influencing policy and regulatory frameworks within financial markets (Khmous & Besim, 2020). In countries where religion is a significant aspect of the social fabric, financial policies and products may be tailored to accommodate religious practices and beliefs (Ammerman, 2020). This can lead to the creation of regulatory environments that foster inclusive financial systems, accommodating a diversity of religious practices and ensuring that financial services are accessible to all segments of the population.

In addition to this, the impact of religion on financial exclusion intertwines socio-cultural, economic, and religious beliefs, affecting how individuals and communities engage with the financial sector (Sharma & Díaz Andrade, 2023). Financial exclusion refers to the inability of individuals or communities to access necessary financial services in an appropriate form (Ozili, 2021). This exclusion can manifest in various ways, including lack of access to banking, loans, insurance, and investment opportunities, often leading to a reliance on informal or predatory lending practices. One of the primary ways religion impacts financial exclusion is through the ethical and moral guidelines it provides, which can influence attitudes towards money, savings, lending, and interest rates (Fernández-Olit, Martín Martín, & Porras González, 2020). For example, Islamic finance operates under Sharia law, which prohibits usury (Riba) - the charging of interest on loans (Kuyateh, 2022). This religious principle has led to the development of a comprehensive Islamic banking system that offers interest-free loans and other financial products.

In regions where Islamic banking is not readily available or integrated into the broader financial system, Muslims may find themselves financially excluded from conventional banking services that do not align with their religious beliefs (Riaz, Burton, & Fearfull, 2023). Additionally, religious institutions themselves often play a direct role in financial inclusion or exclusion. In some communities, religious organizations provide financial services, such as microfinance loans to their members, promoting inclusion among populations that might otherwise be excluded from the formal financial sector (Gyapong, Gyimah, & Ahmed, 2021). These faith-based financial initiatives can offer vital support, fostering economic empowerment and development within religious communities.

However, the influence of religion on financial exclusion is not always positive (Ali, Devi, & Bustomi, 2020). In some cases, religious beliefs can lead to self-exclusion from financial services. Certain individuals or groups may avoid engaging with the financial system due to a perceived incompatibility between their religious values and the practices of conventional banking, such as the aforementioned issue of interest on loans (Grais & Pellegrini, 2006). This self-exclusion can hinder economic opportunities and perpetuate cycles of poverty within communities. Moreover, the social and cultural norms shaped by religion can also indirectly contribute to financial exclusion. For instance, in some religious contexts, women may face restrictions on their ability to work or own property, limiting their access to financial services and credit. Such gender-based exclusion has significant implications for the economic well-being of women and their families, affecting their ability to participate in and benefit from financial systems (Cabeza-García, Del Brio, & Oscanoa-Victorio, 2019).

In light to this, the purpose of this article is to synthesize current academic insights on the interplay between religion and financial inclusion and exclusion, aiming to unify diverse perspectives within the field. To achieve this, we will conduct a systematic review of the literature, complemented by a comprehensive bibliometric analysis. This dual approach aims to illuminate key themes, trends, and significant contributions that have shaped our understanding of how religious beliefs intersect with financial practices. By identifying gaps in the existing research, this study not only seeks to chart a course for future inquiries but also to foster a deeper comprehension of the complex dynamics at play.

Our primary objective is to deliver a bibliometric analysis of the literature surrounding the relationship between financial inclusion and religion. Through examining citation patterns, co-authorship networks, and keyword co-occurrence, we intend to offer a detailed overview of the research landscape, highlighting the evolution of discourse and pinpointing areas ripe for further exploration. This is motivated by the recognition that, despite the critical importance of the topic—especially in multicultural and multireligious contexts—there has yet to be a systematic literature review and bibliometric analysis addressing the nexus of religion, financial inclusion, and exclusion.

The significance of this research lies in its potential to advance our understanding of how religious beliefs influence financial behaviors and access to financial services, integrating insights from various academic disciplines. By mapping the intellectual terrain of this field, we aim to elucidate the ways in which religious principles and financial practices intersect, identifying both commonalities and divergences across different cultures and religious traditions. Ultimately, this study aspires to enrich the dialogue on creating financial systems that are inclusive and respectful of diverse religious and cultural values. By highlighting significant findings and emerging perspectives within the literature, we hope to inform policymakers, financial service providers, and community leaders, guiding efforts to promote financial practices that accommodate a wide array of religious beliefs and practices. This comprehensive analysis seeks not only to enhance academic understanding but also to contribute practical insights for enhancing financial inclusion in a way that acknowledges and embraces the diversity of religious experiences and values.

2. METHODOLOGY

This research employs an in-depth methodological framework for conducting a systematic review and bibliometric analysis of the literature on the nexus between religion and financial inclusion. This methodology is tailored to provide a comprehensive exploration of the primary themes, research trends, and emerging viewpoints in the literature, thus shedding light on the intricate relationship between religious beliefs and financial behaviors. The study aims to chart the chronological progression of research on this topic, examining the expansion of scholarly work, variances in research emphasis across regions, and the introduction of new insights. The objective is to unearth key themes and discussions in the literature that explore the impact of religion on financial inclusion and exclusion, through a thorough review of academic writings. Essential research questions for this study include: identifying the journals that focus on this topic, tracking the development of research on the intersection of religion and financial inclusion/exclusion, pinpointing specific religions and regions that have received more attention, determining the most seminal works and key scholars in this field, assessing whether themes can be grouped into clusters, and recognizing under-researched topics, religions, and regions that may warrant further study.

2.1. Literature Search Strategy

To find relevant articles, a range of keywords related to financial inclusion (including financial inclusion, financial participation, financial services, ownership, savings, bank credit usage, and digital financial inclusion) and financial exclusion (such as financial isolation, financial exclusion, and lack of financial access), along with keywords linked to religion (like religiosity, religion, spirituality, religious, spiritual, faith, Islam, Hinduism, Christianity, Buddhism, and Judaism), were utilized. These keywords led to 110 searches, from which relevant papers will be selected for detailed analysis. The search strategy encompasses a wide array of leading academic databases, such as EBSCOhost, Sciencedirect, JSTOR, Emerald, Springer, Wiley Online Library, Web of Science, Elsevier, and Taylor and Francis, among others. These databases were chosen for their extensive coverage of scholarly literature across a range of disciplines, ensuring a diverse and comprehensive corpus for analysis. Moreover, the strategy includes manual examination of pertinent journals and publications in the fields of economics, sociology, religious studies, and finance to ensure a thorough literature review. The gathered data will be subjected to bibliometric analysis using tools like VOSviewer, focusing on citation patterns, co-authorship networks, and keyword co-occurrence to highlight influential publications, prominent authors, and emerging topics. The review will synthesize these findings, summarizing the main themes, trends, and gaps in the literature, and highlighting significant contributions and scholars in the field, thus providing readers with an extensive overview of the current state of research.

2.2. Inclusion and Exclusion Criteria

The inclusion criteria for the selection of relevant literature encompass scholarly articles, research papers, and academic publications that provide substantial insights into the relationship between religious beliefs and financial inclusion. The selected literature is expected to offer empirical evidence, theoretical frameworks, and critical analyses that contribute to a comprehensive understanding of the evident dynamics that shape financial behaviors and access within religious communities. Conversely, the exclusion criteria involve the exclusion of non-peer-reviewed publications, opinion pieces, and non-academic sources that lack empirical evidence or theoretical rigor. Publications that do not directly contribute to the scholarly discourse on the intersection of religion and financial inclusion are excluded from the analysis to ensure the integrity and academic rigor of the study.

2.3. Data Extraction and Analysis

The data extraction process involves the systematic collection of relevant information, including publication titles, authors, publication dates, abstracts, keywords, and key findings. The extracted data is organized and synthesized using a structured framework that facilitates the categorization of key themes, research trends, and emerging perspectives within the literature. The data extraction process aims to identify the key contributions and seminal works have influenced the discussion on religion and financial inclusion, thereby providing valuable insights into the evolving research landscape in this field.

3. RESULTS

3.1. Document Type

The analysis of bibliometric data pertaining to financial inclusion and religion reveals a diverse landscape of scholarly contributions. With a predominant focus on articles, it is evident in figure 1 that there is a strong and ongoing exploration of the relationship between financial inclusion and religion within academic circles. The presence of reviews suggests a concerted effort to synthesize existing literature, providing comprehensive overviews that aid researchers and practitioners. The inclusion of book chapters' points to a contextualization of the subject within broader academic frameworks, possibly as part of collaborative projects. Editorials contribute to an active discourse, allowing scholars to express opinions on current issues and trends. Additionally, the existence of books indicates a commitment to in-depth exploration, potentially authored by subject matter experts. Conference papers highlight an engaged academic community, participating in dialogues and knowledge exchange. Together, these document types suggest an interdisciplinary exploration and collaboration within the scholarly community. Analysing trends over time and collaboration patterns among authors and institutions could offer deeper insights into emerging areas and potential collaborative opportunities.

Figure 1. Document type

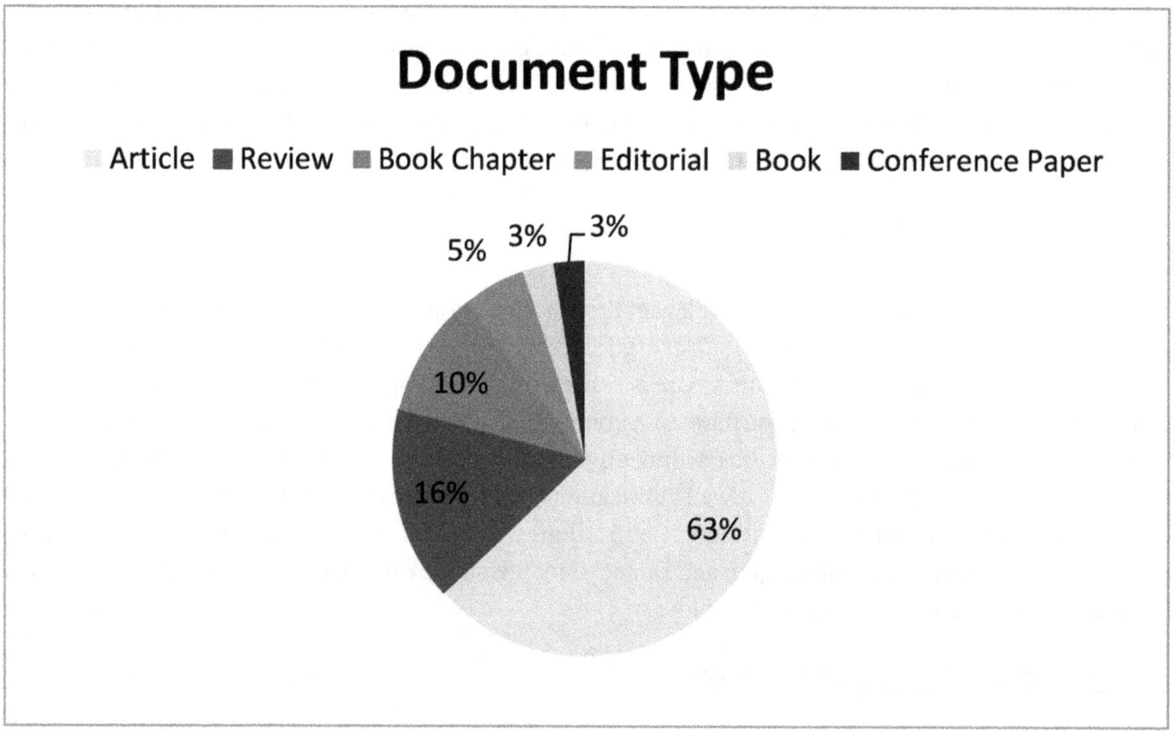

3.2. Journals

Table 1 shows a peek into the journals that has shown highest number of publication in the relevant area, with all the others journal not mentioned with maximum count of 1. There has not been much focus in this area and hence it can be seen that most prominent research were done by journals at the count of two articles per journal. This could anticipate that there is either lack of focus or some gap in this area of academia.

Table 1. Journals count

International Journal Of Islamic And Middle Eastern Finance And Management	22
Journal Of Financial Regulation And Compliance	22

The most repeated authors (Table 2) with prominent publication in relevant topic is Hassan, M.K who is Professor of Finance and Hibernia Professor of Economics and Finance, University of New Orleans. The rest of the author had one publication to their name with reference to topics that revolved around financial inclusion and religion.

Table 2. Author names

Hassan, M.K.	22
All the rest	11

3.3. Main Themes

3.3.1. Religion, Culture, and Financial Inclusion

The first research cluster (Figure 2) within the domain of religion and financial inclusion centers on a comprehensive exploration of three interlinked aspects: culture, religion, and financial inclusion. Within this framework, cultural dynamics are acknowledged as being occasionally influenced by religious tenets, thereby contributing to instances of social exclusion or isolation. This interplay between culture and religion becomes particularly significant within the context of financial inclusion initiatives, as both elements play pivotal roles in shaping societal norms and structures. Notably, a substantial emphasis is placed on the initial discussions within these studies, where the focus is directed toward the examination of social dynamics related to gender, ethnicity, and the associated stigmas.

While religion can foster financial inclusion, it can also be a significant determinant of financial exclusion, particularly in contexts where religious beliefs and cultural norms discourage or prohibit certain financial practices. Studies have shown that in some religious communities, the avoidance of

Figure 2. Network visualization

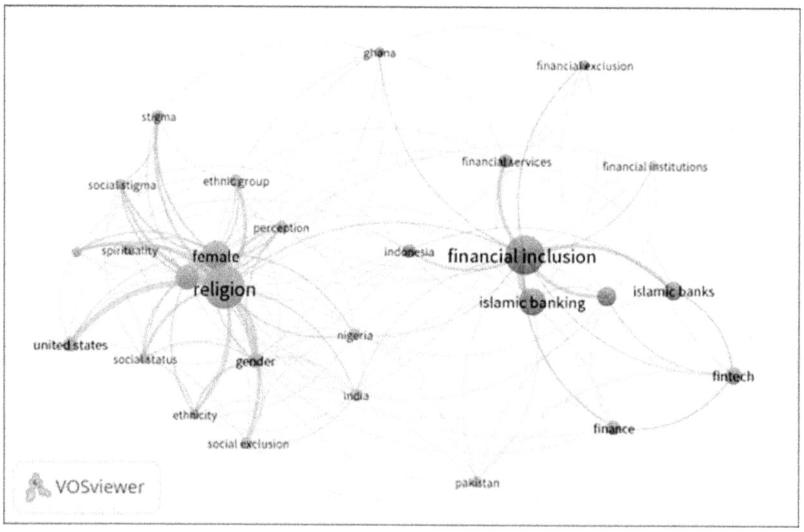

interest-based financial transactions is rooted in religious doctrines, leading to the voluntary exclusion of individuals from mainstream financial services. Tinta, Ouédraogo, and Al-Hassan (2022) emphasize the impact of religious beliefs on the financial practices of certain communities, illustrating how religious norms may lead individuals to opt for informal financial arrangements or alternative financial systems that align with their religious values.

Religious beliefs and practices play a fundamental role in shaping individuals' worldviews, ethical frameworks, and moral values. These religious underpinnings often extend to financial decision-making, guiding individuals' attitudes towards savings, investments, and borrowing. Research conducted by Ahmad et al. (2023) highlights the pervasive impact of Islamic finance principles on the financial practices of Muslim communities, emphasizing the significance of religious norms in shaping ethical and Sharia-compliant financial behaviors. Similarly, studies by Kim et al. (2020) and Umar et al. (2019) underscore the influence of Christian ethical principles on financial decision-making, illustrating how religious teachings inform individuals' approaches to wealth accumulation, expenditure, and charitable giving.

Moreover, the intersection of religion and financial practices is not limited to individual behaviors but also extends to communal and institutional levels. Religious organizations often play a pivotal role in facilitating financial inclusion through the provision of ethical financial services and microfinance initiatives tailored to meet the specific needs of their respective communities. The study by Aziz and Naima (2021) elucidates the role of Islamic financial institutions in promoting financial inclusion among marginalized Muslim communities, underscoring the importance of religiously compliant financial products and services in fostering economic empowerment and social development.

Furthermore, the cultural and religious dimensions of financial exclusion extend beyond the realm of individual behaviors and practices. McIntyre, Quaye, Anning-Dorson, Lanivich, and Adomako (2023) sheds light on the ways in which religious institutions and cultural norms influence the accessibility and availability of formal financial services within specific geographic regions. Religious values and practices often shape the regulatory frameworks and institutional practices of financial institutions, thereby impacting the accessibility of financial services for individuals belonging to certain religious communities.

3.3.2. Financial Inclusion and Islamic Banking

Among all religion unbiasedly attempted to be analysed, Islamic finance stands out as a distinctive domain that has not only influenced but has also formalized specific rules governing financial service access. Islamic finance operates on principles derived from Islamic law (Sharia), emphasizing ethical and equitable financial practices. The formal shaping of rules within Islamic finance has propelled it to the forefront of academic investigations into financial inclusion.

The literature on Islamic finance and financial inclusion illuminates a nuanced understanding of how religious principles can be integrated into formal financial systems. Islamic finance, by design, emphasizes ethical considerations, risk-sharing, and avoidance of exploitative practices, thereby contributing to a financial system that aligns with principles of justice and fairness. A significant focus in the literature is on how Islamic finance addresses the financial needs of marginalized groups, thereby contributing to inclusive economic development. Studies explore the impact of Islamic microfinance on empowering women and economically disadvantaged communities, highlighting the potential of Islamic finance to mitigate financial exclusion. Furthermore, researchers examine the regulatory frameworks and policy initiatives that promote Islamic finance as a means to enhance financial inclusion, emphasizing the need for a supportive environment. Islamic microfinance products and operations differ from typical interest-based microfinance due to Shari'ah principles which prohibit charging interest. Smolo and Ismail (2011) adds up to this viewpoint, where he finds out that Shari'ah aims to protect property rights, stress moral principles, encourage risk-taking, and advance social justice in addition to restricting interest.As a consequence, Islamic microfinance may assist significantly by providing distinctive products that adhere to Shari'ah laws (M. K. Hassan, Alshater, Hasan, & Bhuiyan, 2021). Alam, Hassan, and Said (2015) analyse the efficacy of Islamic microcredit operations in the context of Maqasid Al-Shariah and conclude that IMFIs are enhancing the welfare of their clients. They claim that, except intelligence, IMFIs in Bangladesh help achieve all of the essential components of Al-daruriyyat. The challenges that prevent Islamic MFIs from operating at the same level as conventional MFIs are the subject of a substream of research. Rahman and Dean (2013) discuss few issues, such as increasing transaction costs, sustainability, and market penetration. Market penetration is impacted by IMFIs' weak branch networks.

3.3.3. Fintech and Financial Inclusion (in Terms of Islamic Bank and Fintech Access to Conservative Religion)

The banking industry's contribution to the execution of Islamic microfinance and the role of the Islamic microfinance banking model in Bangladesh in reducing poverty and empowering women (Bhuiyan, Siwar, Ismail, & Omar, 2017). The involvement of Islamic banks in the creation of microfinance products has drawn attention from researchers (Farooqi, Qamar, & Chachi, 2017; A. Hassan & Saleem, 2017). Aliyu, Yusof, and Naiimi (2017) concentrate on the viability of Islamic banks and put forth a theoretical Islamic microfinance institution that enhances the welfare of society. In accordance with the findings from research of Ayaz, Shah, Shaheen, and Yusuf (2019), it identifies several barriers preventing Islamic banking from offering microloans. These challenges are comparable to those that IMFIs are currently facing (refer to research stream one), and they highlight the necessity of a legal framework, backing from the government, a diverse range of products, and effective operations. The significance of Islamic banks as a cutting-edge strategy for enhancing the impact of microfinance programmes on sustainable development is also examined in Wajdi Dusuki (2008). It suggests assisting underprivileged entrepre-

Figure 3. Publication by year

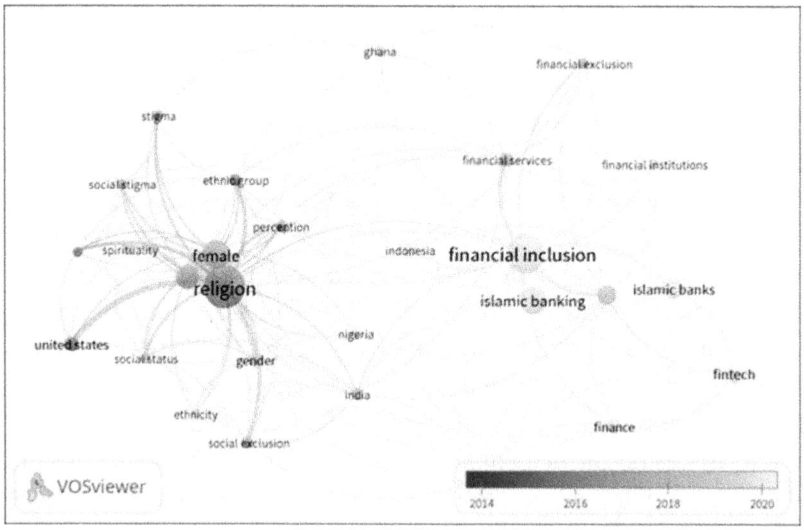

neurs with microloans through special purpose entities (SPVs). validate claims made by Bhuiyan et al. (2017) using case-based evidence.

3.4. Publication by Year

For the analysis of year focus on keywords (Figure 3), there was a restriction on the selection to a maximum of five papers per designated period. Consequently, any research falling below this stipulated threshold was relegated to the status of supplementary or peripheral applications. Examining the literature within this confined framework, a discernible trend emerges, highlighting a noteworthy concentration of scholarly attention on the confluence of financial inclusion, Fintech, and Islamic banking. This thematic cluster has surged in prominence, captivating researchers and academics in the field. Notably, a substantial volume of these investigations centers on the Indonesian context, indicating a regional specificity and perhaps reflecting the distinctive financial landscape of the country. The conjoining of financial inclusion with Fintech and Islamic banking in scholarly discourse signifies a contemporary and dynamic intersection within the broader spectrum of financial studies. Researchers are drawn to explore the synergies, challenges, and opportunities posed by the integration of technological innovations, Islamic financial principles, and the imperative of fostering financial inclusion. The choice of Indonesia as a focal point for many of these studies suggests a recognition of the unique socio-economic context and the particular relevance of this intersection within the Indonesian financial landscape. In essence, the prevalence of studies in this thematic cluster underscores the evolving nature of financial research, with an increasing emphasis on the integration of emerging technologies and Islamic financial practices to address the imperative of inclusive financial systems. The specific limitation on the number of papers per period has, in turn, facilitated a more concentrated and in-depth exploration of this dynamic and multifaceted research domain.

Figure 4. Average citation

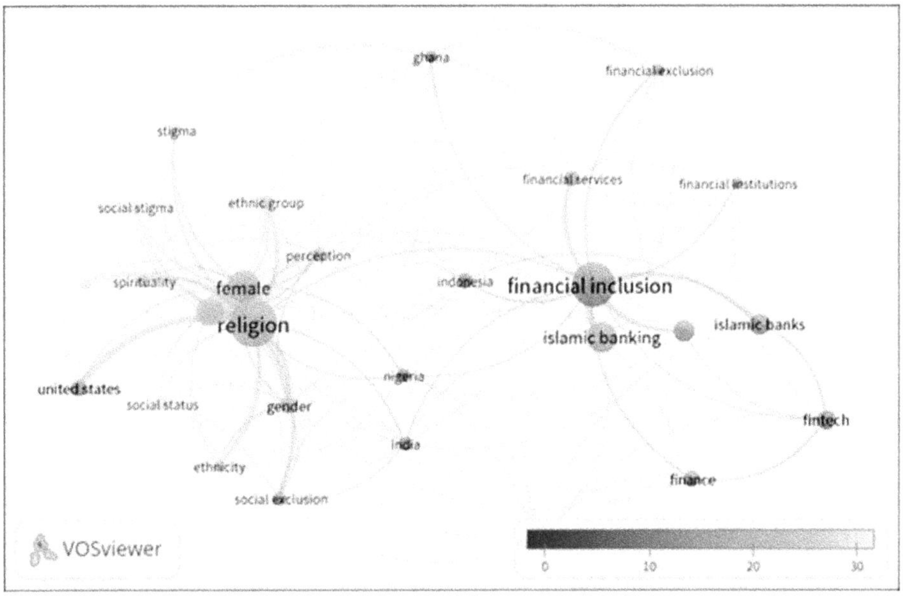

3.5. Average Citation

Citation analysis of keyword is a method of bibliographical reference analysis (Seglen, 1989) which allows to analyse most frequently cited keywords in the main work and their nexus. According to certain scholars, it portrays the paper's quality unfairly. By pointing out fundamental works, it aids in our understanding of an area or subject. From the above data (Figure 4) it can be seen that the most cited work is social status ethnic group, spirituality and stigma when it comes to discussing financial inclusion

Figure 5. Country visualisation

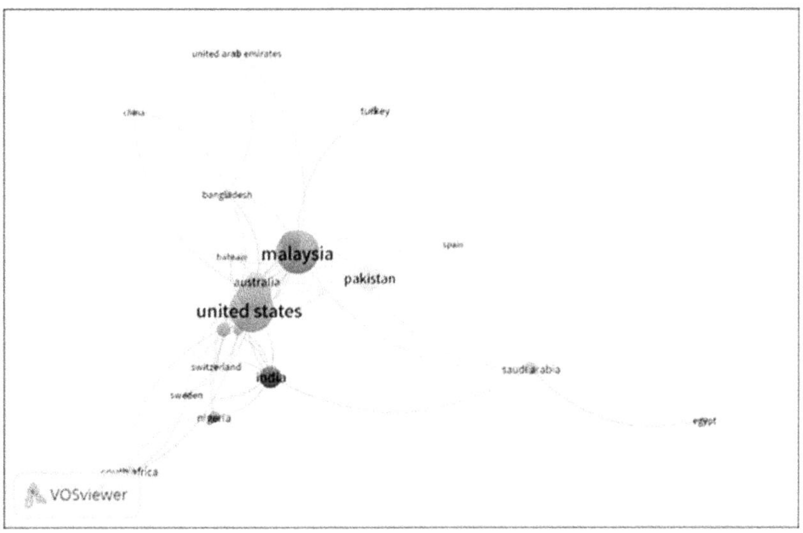

and religion. Although this topic has not been biased towards Islamic banking and included all possible religion studies on financial inclusion, but since Islamic banking is only active religion based banking and financial inclusion from interest system is obligatory in Islam hence, naturally it can be seen that there is a cluster of Islamic Banking as well in this study.

3.6. Country Visualisation

Indonesia, India, and Pakistan are among the most frequently mentioned countries with more in-need people (Figure 5 & Figure 6); this could be related to their need for microfinance. Malaysia is well-known since it is a centre for Islamic financial education. The United States, Japan, and New Zealand—all nations that fund scientific research—as well as Saudi Arabia, a significant Muslim nation, have authors writing on Islamic microfinance. The International Journal of Islamic and Middle Eastern Finance and Management, the International Journal of Social Economics, and the Journal of Humanomics—later renamed the International Journal of Systems and Ethics—rank first, second, and third, correspondingly. The influence of religion on financial inclusion varies across different cultural and geographical contexts, reflecting the diverse ways in which religious beliefs and practices intersect with local economic and social structures. R. Kumar and Pathak (2022) highlight the cultural nuances that shape the relationship between religion and financial inclusion, emphasizing the need for context-specific approaches to understanding the role of religion in shaping financial behaviors and access to financial services. This contextual understanding is essential for designing inclusive financial systems that cater to the diverse religious and cultural preferences of individuals from various communities.

Moreover, the role of religious institutions and leaders in promoting financial inclusion has been a subject of growing interest among researchers and policymakers. Studies have underscored the pivotal role of religious leaders in advocating for financial literacy and promoting the accessibility of ethical financial products and services within their communities. Ezzahid and Elouaourti (2022) emphasize the significance of partnerships between religious institutions and financial organizations in promoting financial inclusion and promoting responsible financial practices, highlighting the potential of collaborative efforts in addressing the challenges of financial exclusion.

Figure 6. Country visualization

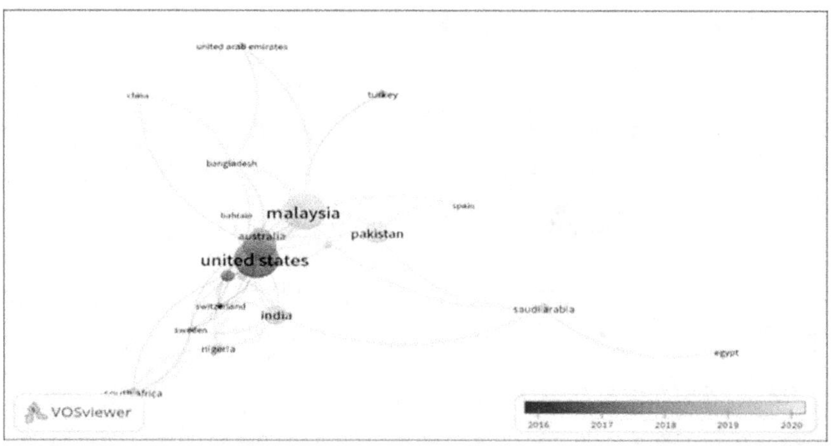

Figure 7. Financial inclusion

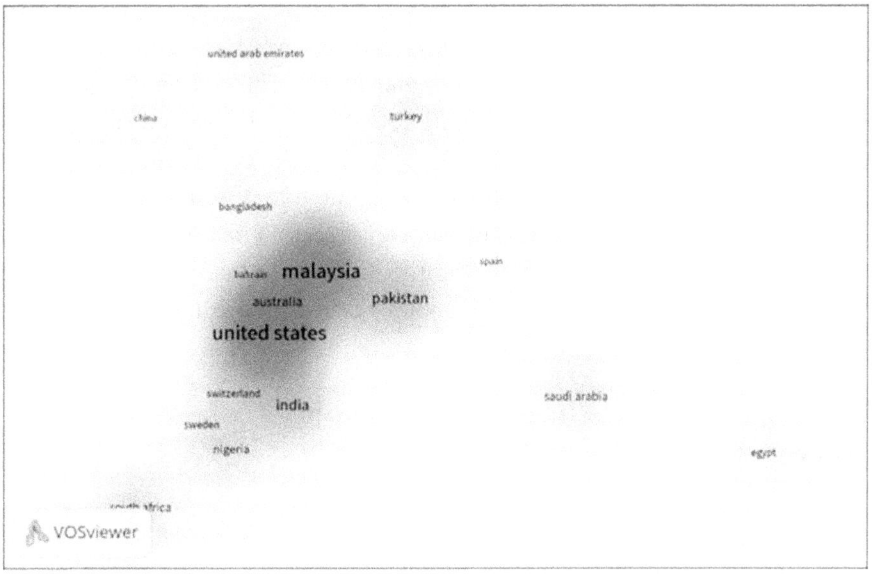

The more frequently studied domain in the research relevant to region and financial inclusion has been India, Pakistan, Malaysia, Bangladesh and Nigeria (Figure 7). Followed by other countries, these countries may have been active in religion and financial inclusion studies academically since these countries have a significant influence of religion on financial service usage.

4. DISCUSSION

While the integration of religious values into financial practices presents opportunities for fostering inclusive financial systems, it also poses certain challenges that need to be addressed. The tension between religious principles and financial innovations often necessitates the development of financial services and goods that respect Islamic morality and conform to sharia. Scholars have pointed out the need guaranteeing the importance of ensuring the transparency and ethical integrity of Islamic financial practices, calling for robust regulatory frameworks and governance mechanisms to uphold the principles of fairness and social justice within Islamic financial systems (Ali, Devi, Furqani, et al., 2020). Furthermore, the integration of religious values into mainstream financial systems requires a nuanced understanding of the diverse religious and cultural preferences of individuals from various communities. The study by Xiao and O'Neill (2016) emphasises the need of taking cultural sensitivity into account when creating financial services and products that are customised according to the distinctive needs and tastes of religious communities, emphasizing the need for inclusive and culturally responsive financial practices that respect the religious beliefs and values of individuals. The evolving discourse on religion and financial inclusion has witnessed the emergence of new research trends and perspectives that reflect the changing dynamics of global financial settings. Researchers have begun to explore the part of technology and digital innovations in promoting financial inclusion among religious communities, emphasizing the potential of digital financial services in overcoming the barriers of physical distance and accessibility.

Studies have highlighted the transformative influence of mobile banking and digital payment systems in expanding financial access for individuals in distant and underserved areas, underscoring the role of technology in fostering inclusive financial ecosystems (Ezzahid & Elouaourti, 2021).

Moreover, the growing emphasis on sustainable and ethical finance has prompted researchers to examine the potential of religious values in promoting socially responsible and environmentally sustainable financial practices. The study by Henley (2017) emphasizes the significance of integrating religious principles into sustainable finance initiatives, highlighting the role of religious institutions and leaders in promoting ethical investment and responsible financial practices that align with the values of social justice and environmental stewardship. This growing focus on sustainable finance reflects the broader shift towards inclusive and socially conscious financial systems that prioritize the well-being of both individuals and communities.

5. CONCLUSION

The research within the defined domain, guided by the constraint of a maximum of five papers per period, has provided valuable insights into the evolving landscape of financial inclusion, Fintech, and Islamic banking. The deliberate limitation on the number of selected papers served as a methodological tool to enhance precision and focus, encouraging a meticulous examination of research outputs. This discerning approach facilitated a clear understanding of the thematic cluster that emerged prominently, particularly the intersection of financial inclusion, Fintech, and Islamic banking, with a notable concentration of studies in Indonesia. The research findings underscore the contemporary relevance of exploring the interplay between technological advancements, Islamic financial principles, and the imperative of developing inclusive financial systems. The regional specificity observed, particularly in the context of Indonesia, suggests an acknowledgment of the unique socio-economic dynamics shaping the financial landscape in the country. The prominence of this thematic cluster within the limited scope of selected papers points to the increasing scholarly interest and recognition of the significance of addressing financial inclusion challenges through the lens of emerging technologies and Islamic finance. The application of a constraint on paper selection has not only provided a focused exploration but has also prompted a deeper examination of the specific nuances within the chosen thematic cluster. It will be anticipated that more studies in this area will improve our understanding of the complicated relationships among financial inclusion, Fintech and Islamic banking, offering insights that can inform policy, practice, and academic discourse in the dynamic field of finance.

The study acknowledges certain limitations inherent in the methodology, including the potential for publication bias and the inherent subjectivity in the selection of keywords and search terms. The reliance on academic databases may result in the exclusion of relevant literature that is not indexed in the selected databases. Furthermore, the study acknowledges the limitations of bibliometric analysis in capturing the full complexity of the relationship between religion and financial inclusion, emphasizing the need for qualitative research approaches to complement the findings of the bibliometric analysis.

Despite these limitations, the study aimed to provide a complete and rigorous analysis of the existing literature, offering valuable insights into the complex dynamics that underpin the relationship between religious beliefs and financial practices. By addressing these limitations through a meticulous and systematic approach to data collection and analysis, the study aimed to contribute to the advancement of knowledge and the promotion of inclusive and culturally responsive financial systems worldwide.

Given the evolving landscape of financial inclusion, Fintech, and Islamic banking, several avenues for future research emerge from our study. First, there is a compelling need to explore the integration of Fintech solutions within Islamic banking frameworks across different regions beyond Indonesia. Comparative studies could offer deeper insights into how various socio-economic and cultural contexts influence the adoption and effectiveness of such integrations. Secondly, the growing interest in the intersection of financial inclusion and religious principles suggests an opportunity for research into other religious frameworks and their influence on financial practices. Examining similarities and differences across religions could uncover universal principles that promote inclusive financial systems. Thirdly, the study's findings point to the potential for Fintech to democratize access to financial services.

Future research could delve into the development of specific Fintech tools or platforms tailored for Islamic banking customers, assessing their impact on financial inclusion metrics. Moreover, the limitations highlighted in our methodology underscore the importance of qualitative research to complement bibliometric analyses. Ethnographic studies, in-depth interviews, and case studies could provide nuanced understandings of the relationship between religion, financial inclusion, and technology, capturing the lived experiences of individuals and communities. Lastly, policy-focused research is crucial. As our findings indicate a need for regulatory frameworks that support Fintech growth within the Islamic banking sector, future studies should investigate effective policy models and regulatory practices that balance technological innovation with Shariah compliance, ensuring that financial services are inclusive, equitable, and culturally responsive. By addressing these areas, future research can build upon our findings, contributing to the development of financial systems that not only respect cultural and religious values but also leverage technology to expand financial access and reduce global poverty.

By identifying key areas for further research and emphasizing the importance of inclusive, technology-driven financial services, the study aims to inspire a concerted effort among academics, policymakers, and practitioners to address the challenges and harness the opportunities presented by this dynamic field. From a policy perspective, the research underscores the necessity of creating regulatory frameworks that accommodate the growth of Fintech within the Islamic banking sector. Policymakers are tasked with the challenge of ensuring that these financial innovations do not only comply with Shariah laws but also actively promote financial inclusion. There is a clear implication for the development of policies that support the expansion of digital financial services that are accessible, affordable, and appropriate for underserved and unbanked populations, particularly in regions where Islamic banking is prevalent.

For practitioners within the finance industry, the study offers insights into the potential for Fintech solutions to enhance the accessibility and appeal of Islamic banking services. Financial institutions, including banks and Fintech startups, can leverage these findings to innovate and tailor their offerings, ensuring they meet the financial needs and preferences of their target markets. There is an opportunity to design and implement financial products that not only adhere to Islamic principles but also take advantage of technological advancements to reach wider audiences. On a global scale, the study's implications extend to the promotion of inclusive finance as a means to achieve economic empowerment and reduce poverty. The integration of Fintech and Islamic banking principles can serve as a model for developing financial systems that respect cultural and religious values while leveraging technology to increase financial access. This research, however, encourages a global dialogue on the importance of culturally responsive financial solutions in achieving broader financial inclusion objectives.

REFERENCES

Abdu, E., & Adem, M. (2021). Determinants of financial inclusion in Afar Region: Evidence from selected woredas. *Cogent Economics & Finance*, *9*(1), 1920149. doi:10.1080/23322039.2021.1920149

Ahmad, S., Lensink, R., & Mueller, A. (2023). Religion, social desirability bias and financial inclusion: Evidence from a list experiment on Islamic (micro-) finance. *Journal of Behavioral and Experimental Finance*, *38*, 100795. doi:10.1016/j.jbef.2023.100795

Alam, M. M., Hassan, S., & Said, J. (2015). Performance of Islamic microcredit in perspective of Maqasid Al-Shariah: A case study on Amanah Ikhtiar Malaysia. *Humanomics*, *31*(4), 374–384. doi:10.1108/H-12-2014-0072

Ali, M. M., Devi, A., & Bustomi, H. (2020). Determinants of Islamic financial exclusion in Indonesia. *Journal of Islamic Monetary Economics and Finance*, *6*(2), 373–402. doi:10.21098/jimf.v6i2.1093

Ali, M. M., Devi, A., Furqani, H., & Hamzah, H. (2020). Islamic financial inclusion determinants in Indonesia: An ANP approach. *International Journal of Islamic and Middle Eastern Finance and Management*, *13*(4), 727–747. doi:10.1108/IMEFM-01-2019-0007

Aliyu, S., Yusof, R. M., & Naiimi, N. (2017). The role of moral transaction mode for sustainability of banking business: A proposed conceptual model for Islamic microfinance banks in Nigeria. *International Journal of Social Economics*, *44*(12), 2238–2256. doi:10.1108/IJSE-07-2016-0205

Amaroh, S., & Masykuroh, E. (2023). Financial Attitude, Trust, and ROSCAs' Member Commitment: Social Relations as Mediating Factor. *Global Business & Finance Review*, *28*(3), 35–49. doi:10.17549/gbfr.2023.28.3.35

Ammerman, N. T. (2020). Rethinking religion: Toward a practice approach. *American Journal of Sociology*, *126*(1), 6–51. doi:10.1086/709779

Ayaz, M., Shah, H. S., Shaheen, S., & Yusuf, J. B. (2019). *Islamic microfinancing by the banking sector of Pakistan: Problems and solutions*. Academic Press.

Aziz, A., & Naima, U. (2021). Rethinking digital financial inclusion: Evidence from Bangladesh. *Technology in Society*, *64*, 101509. doi:10.1016/j.techsoc.2020.101509

Bhuiyan, A. B., Siwar, C., Ismail, A. G., & Omar, N. (2017). The Islamic microfinancing contributions on sustainable livelihood of the borrowers in Bangladesh. *International Journal of Business and Society*, *18*(S1), 79–96.

Cabeza-García, L., Del Brio, E. B., & Oscanoa-Victorio, M. L. (2019). *Female financial inclusion and its impacts on inclusive economic development.* Paper presented at the Women's Studies International Forum. 10.1016/j.wsif.2019.102300

Ezzahid, E., & Elouaourti, Z. (2021). Financial inclusion, mobile banking, informal finance and financial exclusion: Micro-level evidence from Morocco. *International Journal of Social Economics*, *48*(7), 1060–1086. doi:10.1108/IJSE-11-2020-0747

Ezzahid, E., & Elouaourti, Z. (2022). Financial inclusion, financial frictions, and economic growth: Evidence from Africa. *Journal of African Business*, *23*(3), 731–756. doi:10.1080/15228916.2021.1926856

Farooqi, A. H., Qamar, M. U. R., & Chachi, A. (2017). Role of Islamic microfinance scheme in poverty alleviation and well-being of women implemented by Islami Bank Bangladesh Limited. *İslam Ekonomisi ve Finansı Dergisi, 3*(1), 1-32.

Fathallah, R., Sidani, Y., & Khalil, S. (2020). How religion shapes family business ethical behaviors: An institutional logics perspective. *Journal of Business Ethics, 163*(4), 647–659. doi:10.1007/s10551-019-04383-6

Fernández-Olit, B., Martín Martín, J. M., & Porras González, E. (2020). Systematized literature review on financial inclusion and exclusion in developed countries. *International Journal of Bank Marketing, 38*(3), 600–626. doi:10.1108/IJBM-06-2019-0203

Grais, W., & Pellegrini, M. (2006). *Corporate governance and Shariah compliance in institutions offering Islamic financial services* (Vol. 4054). World Bank Publications. doi:10.1596/1813-9450-4054

Gu, F., Gao, J., Zhu, X., & Ye, J. (2023). The impact of digital inclusive finance on SMEs' technological innovation activities—Empirical analysis based on the data of new third board enterprises. *PLoS One, 18*(11), e0293500. doi:10.1371/journal.pone.0293500 PMID:37917741

Gyapong, E., Gyimah, D., & Ahmed, A. (2021). Religiosity, borrower gender and loan losses in microfinance institutions: A global evidence. *Review of Quantitative Finance and Accounting, 57*(2), 657–692. doi:10.1007/s11156-021-00958-5

Hassan, A., & Saleem, S. (2017). An Islamic microfinance business model in Bangladesh: Its role in alleviation of poverty and socio-economic well-being of women. *Humanomics, 33*(1), 15–37. doi:10.1108/H-08-2016-0066

Hassan, M. K., Alshater, M. M., Hasan, R., & Bhuiyan, A. B. (2021). Islamic microfinance: A bibliometric review. *Global Finance Journal, 49*, 100651. doi:10.1016/j.gfj.2021.100651

Henley, A. (2017). Does religion influence entrepreneurial behaviour? *International Small Business Journal, 35*(5), 597–617. doi:10.1177/0266242616656748

Kania, R. (2022). *Why and how financial inclusion policy develop? A case study from Indonesia.* University of Birmingham.

Khmous, D. F., & Besim, M. (2020). Impact of Islamic banking share on financial inclusion: Evidence from MENA. *International Journal of Islamic and Middle Eastern Finance and Management, 13*(4), 655–673. doi:10.1108/IMEFM-07-2019-0279

Kim, D.-W., Yu, J.-S., & Hassan, M. K. (2020). The influence of religion and social inequality on financial inclusion. *The Singapore Economic Review, 65*(01), 193–216. doi:10.1142/S0217590817460031

Kumar, R., & Pathak, D. (2022). Financial awareness: A bridge to financial inclusion. *Development in Practice, 32*(7), 968–980. doi:10.1080/09614524.2022.2028731

Kumar, S., Sahoo, S., Lim, W. M., & Dana, L.-P. (2022). Religion as a social shaping force in entrepreneurship and business: Insights from a technology-empowered systematic literature review. *Technological Forecasting and Social Change, 175*, 121393. doi:10.1016/j.techfore.2021.121393

Kuyateh, M. A. (2022). Shariah Compliance Prohibitions in Islamic Banking and Finance: The Case of Riba, Gharar and Maysir. *Journal of Islamic Banking & Finance, 39*(1).

McIntyre, N., Quaye, E. S., Anning-Dorson, T., Lanivich, S., & Adomako, S. (2023). Investigating the impact of religiosity on entrepreneurial intentions. *Journal of Business Research, 156*, 113528. doi:10.1016/j.jbusres.2022.113528

Ozili, P. K. (2021). *Financial inclusion research around the world: A review.* Paper presented at the Forum for social economics. 10.1080/07360932.2020.1715238

Rahman, R. A., & Dean, F. (2013). Challenges and solutions in Islamic microfinance. *Humanomics, 29*(4), 293–306. doi:10.1108/H-06-2012-0013

Riaz, U., Burton, B., & Fearfull, A. (2023). Emotional propensities and the contemporary Islamic banking industry. *Critical Perspectives on Accounting, 94*, 102449. doi:10.1016/j.cpa.2022.102449

Salman, A., & Nowacka, K. (2020). *Innovative financial products and services for women in Asia and the pacific*. Academic Press.

Sarofim, S., Minton, E., Hunting, A., Bartholomew, D. E., Zehra, S., Montford, W., Cabano, F., & Paul, P. (2020). Religion's influence on the financial well-being of consumers: A conceptual framework and research agenda. *The Journal of Consumer Affairs, 54*(3), 1028–1061. doi:10.1111/joca.12315

Seglen, P. (1989). Use of citation analysis and other bibliometric methods in evaluation of the quality of research. *Tidsskrift for den Norske Laegeforening: Tidsskrift for Praktisk Medicin, ny Raekke, 109*(31), 3229-3224.

Sharma, H., & Díaz Andrade, A. (2023). Digital financial services and human development: Current landscape and research prospects. *Information Technology for Development, 29*(4), 1–25. doi:10.1080/02681102.2023.2199189

Smolo, E., & Ismail, A. G. (2011). A theory and contractual framework of Islamic micro-financial institutions' operations. *Journal of Financial Services Marketing, 15*(4), 287–295. doi:10.1057/fsm.2010.24

Svoboda, A. (2024). Investing in the Islamic world: Opportunities, challenges, and implications. *Economics and Finance, 12*(1), 13–21. doi:10.51586/2754-6209.2024.12.1.13.21

Tinta, A. A., Ouédraogo, I. M., & Al-Hassan, R. M. (2022). The micro determinants of financial inclusion and financial resilience in Africa. *African Development Review, 34*(2), 293–306. doi:10.1111/1467-8268.12636

Umar, U. H., Ado, M. B., & Ayuba, H. (2019). Is religion (interest) an impediment to Nigeria's financial inclusion targets by the year 2020? A qualitative inquiry. *Qualitative Research in Financial Markets, 12*(3), 283-300.

Wajdi Dusuki, A. (2008). Banking for the poor: The role of Islamic banking in microfinance initiatives. *Humanomics, 24*(1), 49–66. doi:10.1108/08288660810851469

Xiao, J. J., & O'Neill, B. (2016). Consumer financial education and financial capability. *International Journal of Consumer Studies, 40*(6), 712–721. doi:10.1111/ijcs.12285

APPENDIX

Multiple Choice Questions

1. What are the main challenges of integrating religious values into financial practices?
    a) Difficulty in finding investment opportunities that comply with religious principles. b) Tension between religious beliefs and financial innovations. c) Lack of qualified professionals with expertise in both finance and religion. d) Resistance from traditional financial institutions.
2. How can financial services and products be designed to be Sharia-compliant?
    a) Offering fixed-income products with guaranteed returns. b) Avoiding interest-based transactions and promoting profit-sharing models. c) Investing only in ethical and socially responsible companies. d) Providing financial education programs on Islamic finance principles.
3. What is the primary benefit of using technology like mobile banking in promoting financial inclusion among religious communities?
    a) Increased access to financial services regardless of geographic location. b) Ability to conduct transactions anonymously, respecting religious privacy concerns. c) Reduced risk of fraud and financial scams compared to traditional methods. d) Lower transaction costs compared to conventional banking services.
4. How can religious values be best integrated into sustainable finance initiatives?
    a) Encouraging investments that support environmental protection and social justice. b) Promoting financial literacy and responsible financial behavior among religious communities. c) Partnering with religious institutions to develop and implement sustainable finance programs. d) Lobbying governments to adopt policies that incentivize sustainable investments.
5. What is a potential limitation of relying solely on academic databases for research on religion and financial inclusion?
    a) Difficulty in capturing the lived experiences of individuals and communities. b) Overrepresentation of studies from developed countries compared to developing nations. c) Bias towards certain religious perspectives and exclusion of others. d) Lack of access to unpublished research and industry reports.
6. Which of the following is NOT a key area for future research identified in the study?
    a) The impact of artificial intelligence and blockchain technology on Islamic finance. b) Comparative studies on the integration of religious values and financial inclusion across different regions. c) The role of financial inclusion in promoting religious tolerance and understanding. d) Development of culturally sensitive financial products tailored to specific religious communities.
7. What is the main implication of the study for policymakers regarding Fintech and Islamic banking?
    a) Need for regulatory frameworks that balance innovation with Sharia compliance. b) Importance of promoting financial literacy and consumer protection measures. c) Encouragement of competition between Islamic and conventional financial institutions. d) Investment in infrastructure development to improve access to financial services.
8. What is a critical ethical consideration when integrating religious values into financial systems?
    a) Ensuring transparency and accountability in all financial transactions. b) Avoiding discrimination against individuals based on their religious beliefs. c) Balancing the interests of religious

institutions with those of financial institutions. d) Protecting the privacy of individuals' financial information.

9. How can financial institutions best achieve financial inclusion while respecting diverse religious and cultural preferences?
    a) Offering a wide range of financial products and services to cater to different needs. b) Partnering with religious and community organizations to build trust and understanding. c) Designing marketing campaigns that are sensitive to religious and cultural values. d) Implementing flexible and adaptable financial regulations that accommodate diverse practices.
10. What is the primary role of regulatory frameworks in ensuring the fairness and social justice of financial systems?
    a) Protecting consumers from predatory financial practices and scams. b) Promoting competition and ensuring a level playing field for all financial institutions. c) Encouraging financial inclusion and access to financial services for underserved populations. d) Balancing the interests of different stakeholders, including investors, borrowers, and the government.

Answers to MCQs

1. b) Tension between religious beliefs and financial innovations.
2. b) Avoiding interest-based transactions and promoting profit-sharing models.
3. a) Increased access to financial services regardless of geographic location.
4. a) Encouraging investments that support environmental protection and social justice.
5. a) Difficulty in capturing the lived experiences of individuals and communities.
6. c) The role of financial inclusion in promoting religious tolerance and understanding.
7. a) Need for regulatory frameworks that balance innovation with Sharia compliance.
8. b) Avoiding discrimination against individuals based on their religious beliefs.
9. b) Partnering with religious and community organizations to build trust and understanding.
10. a) Protecting consumers from predatory financial practices and scams.

Assignment Topics on Religion and Financial Inclusion/Exclusion

1. **Case Study: A Specific Religious Community and Financial Inclusion Challenges:** Choose a specific religious community (e.g., Muslims, Hindus, Christians) and analyze their unique challenges in accessing financial services. Investigate the specific reasons for exclusion, explore existing initiatives addressing these challenges, and propose potential solutions based on religious values and technological advancements.
2. **Ethical Considerations in Integrating Religious Values and Financial Innovations:** Analyze the ethical complexities of integrating religious values into financial products and services. Consider issues like transparency, fairness, potential discrimination, and the role of religious institutions. Discuss how technology can be used ethically to promote financial inclusion while respecting religious principles.
3. **The Future of Fintech and Sharia-Compliant Finance:** Explore the potential of emerging technologies like blockchain and artificial intelligence to revolutionize the Islamic finance industry.

Discuss the challenges and opportunities these technologies present for ensuring Sharia compliance, promoting financial inclusion, and fostering economic growth.

4. **Comparative Analysis: Religion and Financial Inclusion Across Regions:** Conduct a comparative study of how different religious communities in various regions (e.g., Middle East vs. Southeast Asia) approach and experience financial inclusion. Analyze the influence of cultural and legal frameworks, religious interpretations, and financial infrastructure on access to financial services.
5. **Policy Recommendations for Inclusive and Culturally Sensitive Financial Systems:** Develop a set of policy recommendations for policymakers, financial institutions, and religious organizations to promote financial inclusion that considers diverse religious and cultural preferences. Consider issues like regulatory frameworks, financial literacy, product development, and partnerships with community organizations.

Short Questions

1. Briefly describe the main challenge of integrating religious values into financial practices.
2. What is one way financial services can be designed to be Sharia-compliant?
3. What is the main benefit of mobile banking for financial inclusion among religious communities?
4. What is one ethical consideration when integrating religious values into financial systems?
5. What is one way financial institutions can promote financial inclusion while respecting religious preferences?

Long Questions

1. Discuss the pros and cons of integrating religious values into financial systems, considering both opportunities and potential challenges.
2. Analyze the role of technology in promoting financial inclusion among religious communities, drawing on specific examples of successful initiatives.
3. Describe the current state of research on the relationship between religion and financial inclusion, identifying key findings and potential areas for future study.
4. Develop a plan for designing a financial product or service that is both Sharia-compliant and caters to the specific needs of a particular religious community.
5. Compare and contrast the approaches to financial inclusion taken by different religious communities around the world, considering the influence of cultural and legal contexts.

Chapter 3
Empowering Communities:
The Nexus of Islamic Finance and Financial Inclusion

Shama Mushtaq
https://orcid.org/0009-0005-8604-5174
University of Agriculture, Faisalabad, Pakistan

Muhammad Idrees
University of Agriculture, Faisalabad, Pakistan

Laraib Manzoor
https://orcid.org/0009-0000-4041-9437
International Islamic University, Islamabad, Pakistan

Noreen Akhtar
University of Agriculture, Faisalabad, Pakistan

Basharat Ali
Government College, Faisalabad, Pakistan

Muhammad Roman
University of Jhang, Pakistan

Sara Akram
https://orcid.org/0000-0001-7281-0086
School of Sociology and Anthropology, Guangzhou, China

ABSTRACT

This chapter offers a comprehensive examination of the intersection of Islamic finance and financial inclusion, shedding light on how Islamic financial principles can contribute to expanding financial access and promoting economic inclusivity. Examining the fundamental principles of Islamic finance reveals the inclusive foundations upon which this financial system is constructed. It has also examined the case studies and real-world examples to illustrate the tangible effects of Islamic finance on marginalised populations and economies. This chapter investigates the impact of financial technology (Fintech) and Islamic microfinance institutions on the availability of Islamic financial products. The chapter discussed the limitations of Islamic finance, which include a prohibition on interest, restrictions on loans and investments, and sector limits. Innovative products provide financing alternatives. In addition, the chapter discuss how the challenges of standardisation, regulatory compliance, and consumer awareness impede the widespread adoption of Islamic finance in practise. For Islamic financial services to contribute more effectively to financial inclusion, addressing these issues requires industry cooperation, regulatory support, and consumer education.

DOI: 10.4018/979-8-3693-1475-3.ch003

INTRODUCTION

The Islamic finance industry has grown substantially in Asia over the last 2 decades. The Muslim populations in different Asian countries, especially in Southeast Asia, are increasing. Rapid Muslim population growth and improving living standards may enhance the popularity of Islamic finance as a keen alternative to conventional financing mechanisms. In addition, investors from the Middle East and Asia are increasingly seeking to invest in products that are in line with their religious beliefs.

Understanding the Significance of Financial Inclusion

Financial inclusion, defined as universal access to affordable and effective financial services, has emerged as a pivotal driver of economic growth and poverty reduction. According to Asli (2017) Financial inclusion means that adults have access to and can effectively use a range of appropriate financial services. In an increasingly interconnected world, the ability to participate in the formal financial system is fundamental to an individual's or a community's socioeconomic progress. This section will delve into the multifaceted importance of financial inclusion, elucidating its impact on economic stability, wealth distribution, and individual prosperity. Financial inclusion affects, and is influenced by, the level of financial innovation, poverty levels, the stability of the financial sector, the state of the economy, financial literacy, and regulatory frameworks which differ across countries (Ozili, P. 2020).

In particular, we will emphasize the role of financial inclusion as a linchpin for achieving the United Nations' Sustainable Development Goals (SDGs), with a particular focus on SDG 1 (No Poverty), SDG 5 (Gender Equality), and SDG 8 (Decent Work and Economic Growth). Ozili (2022) explained that financial inclusion improves the economic aspect and social aspect of sustainable development as it allows providers of financial services to put social considerations first before profit. Financial inclusion acts as an enabler for these goals, facilitating poverty alleviation, empowering women, and fostering economic growth, ultimately contributing to a more equitable society.

Islamic Finance as a Catalyst for Financial Inclusion

Islamic finance, rooted in ethical and Sharia-compliant principles, has gained global recognition not only for its ethical foundations but also for its potential to enhance financial inclusion. Mohieldin et al (2015) defines financial inclusion as the concept initially referred to the delivery of financial services to low-income segments of society at affordable cost. During the past decade, the concept of financial inclusion has evolved into four dimensions: easy access to finance for all households and enterprises, sound institutions guided by prudential regulation and supervision, financial and institutional sustainability of financial institutions, and competition between service providers to bring alternatives to customers. This section will elucidate the core tenets of Islamic finance, emphasizing its prohibition of usury (Riba), endorsement of risk-sharing, and asset-backed financing. By doing so, we will highlight the inherent inclusivity embedded within Islamic finance.

Furthermore, we will explore how Islamic microfinance institutions, by offering benevolent loans (Qard al-Hasan) and microinsurance (Micro Takaful), have become powerful tools for promoting financial inclusion, especially among marginalized and underserved populations. These institutions prioritize the provision of financial services to those who have traditionally been excluded from the formal financial system.

OBJECTIVES OF THE CHAPTER

1. **Analyzing the Principles and ethical consideration of Islamic Finance:** This section aims to provide a comprehensive understanding of the principles that underpin Islamic finance. We will delve into concepts such as the prohibition of Riba, the significance of risk-sharing, and the ethical considerations that guide Islamic financial transaction. As explained by Elasrag (2011) Money must be put to practical use in creating real value for the participants of the transaction.
2. **Exploring Islamic Microfinance:** Here, we will explore the practical applications of Islamic microfinance and financial technology (Fintech) in expanding financial access. Case studies and real-world examples will illustrate the impact of these innovative approaches in reaching underserved communities. Additionally, we will discuss the role of blockchain and smart contracts in ensuring Sharia compliance in Fintech solutions.
3. **Exploring Islamic Fintech:** In the era of rapid technological advancement, Fintech has emerged as a transformative force in Islamic finance, reshaping financial services while adhering to Sharia principles. This intersection of technology and Islamic finance is driven by the need for efficiency and accessibility, as well as compliance with ethical and religious standards. This part of chapter will discuss its details.
4. **Evaluating the Impact of Islamic Finance on Financial Inclusion:** This objective involves a rigorous assessment of the tangible outcomes resulting from the implementation of Islamic finance principles. It includes an examination of the economic empowerment of marginalized populations, increased access to financial services, and the role of Islamic finance in fostering entrepreneurship and small business development. the coming years, Islamic finance could account for a substantial share of financial services in several countries, meeting the preferences of significant numbers of people, enhancing financial inclusion and intermediation, and contributing more broadly to financial stability and development (Mohieldin, M. 2012).
5. **Addressing limitations, Challenges and Opportunities:** The final objective will delve into the challenges and opportunities inherent in the realm of Islamic finance and financial inclusion. Regulatory barriers, lack of awareness, and scalability issues will be discussed as challenges. In contrast, we will explore opportunities arising from the adoption of financial technology, international collaboration, and knowledge sharing among stakeholders in the financial inclusion landscape.

1. ISLAMIC FINANCE: PRINCIPLES AND ETHICAL FOUNDATIONS

1.1. Sharia Compliance in Islamic Finance

In the world of Islamic finance, adherence to Sharia law is paramount. This section will delve into the key principles that make Islamic finance Sharia-compliant.

1.1.1. Prohibition of Riba (Usury or Interest)

At the core of Islamic finance lies a resolute prohibition of Riba, commonly understood as usury or the charging of interest on financial transactions. According to Franzoni (2018), In particular riba occurs when there is an interest rate, whether positive or negative, that is fixed. Islamic financial institutions operate on a principle of equitable risk-sharing, ensuring that profits and losses are shared among all parties involved. We will explore how this prohibition fundamentally reshapes the financial landscape, fostering ethical transactions and equitable wealth distribution. Komijani and Taghizadeh (2018) also discussed this phenomenon in their study that Islamic banking returns on investments are based on underlying economic activities and/or assets that structure the contractual relationship between transacting parties, it is possible to use the asset-based nature and risk-sharing aspects of Islamic finance for greater integration with the real economy and to improve the overall economic balance between the real and the finance sector. The research of Abdullah (2016) explained the Islamic banking product design and development, is that it enhances the ability to block the legal means to an unlawful outcome (Sadd al-dhara'i), thereby avoiding harm (al-darar) attributed to usury (Riba), and upholding what is in the public interest (maslahah), in order to fulfil one of the objectives of the Shari'ah (maqasid al-Shari'ah), which is to protect wealth (hafiz al-mal).

1.1.2. The Concept of Risk-Sharing (Mudarabah)

Islamic finance champions the concept of Mudarabah, which represents a unique form of profit and loss sharing between investors and entrepreneurs. According to Mumtaz et.al (2015), the principle of participation lies at the heart of Islamic finance, ensuring that increases in wealth accrue from productive activities. This section will elucidate how Mudarabah encourages risk-taking, entrepreneurship, and innovation within the financial ecosystem. Readers will gain insight into how this risk-sharing mechanism differs from conventional finance and its implications for financial inclusion. Islamic finance approves profit-and-loss sharing, with risk sharing being a consequence of that, according to a critique of the argument that the Islamic financial system is superior to the conventional one due to its emphasis on risk sharing (Hasan, 2015)

1.1.3. Asset-Backed Financing (Murabaha)

Asset-backed financing, known as Murabaha, is a hallmark of Islamic finance. It involves the sale of goods at a transparent markup rather than the charging of interest. Mumtaz et al (2015) defines murâbaḥah, is a deferred payment sale transaction where the intention is to facilitate the acquisition of goods and not to exchange money for more money (or monetary equivalents) over a period of time. The mechanics of Murabaha promotes ethical financial transactions. It facilitates access to credit for individuals and businesses while ensuring financial inclusivity.

1.2. Ethical Considerations

Beyond Sharia compliance, Islamic finance is deeply rooted in ethical considerations that prioritize social justice, equitable wealth distribution, and risk mitigation.

1.2.1. Social Justice and Wealth Distribution (Zakat and Sadaqah)

Central to Islamic finance is the principle of Zakat, which obligates Muslims to contribute a portion of their wealth for the betterment of society. This section will delve into how Zakat, and its voluntary counterpart Sadaqah, serve as mechanisms for wealth redistribution, poverty alleviation, and social justice. Mohieldin et.al (2011) describes that Independent social spending, according to Islam, is the best possible way for members of the Islamic social order to promote a more equitable distribution of wealth and resources. We will also explore how these principles enhance financial inclusion, particularly for disadvantaged communities.

1.2.2. Risk Mitigation through Takaful (Islamic Insurance)

Takaful, the Islamic alternative to conventional insurance, embodies the principles of mutual cooperation and shared responsibility. Ullah (2023) explained in a study that Takaful operates on the principles of mutual cooperation, risk sharing, and social solidarity, which are in line with the principles of Islamic law. Takaful operates and plays its role in risk mitigation for individuals and businesses. By sharing risks collectively, Takaful contributes to economic stability and financial resilience, factors critical for fostering financial inclusion.

2. ISLAMIC MICROFINANCE: EMPOWERING COMMUNITIES

2.1. Concept and Framework of Islamic Microfinance

This section delves into the intricate world of Islamic microfinance, a powerful tool for uplifting underprivileged communities while adhering to Sharia principles. Islamic development bank defines that Microfinance plays a significant role in providing sustainable livelihoods to disadvantaged groups all over the world.

2.1.1. Qard al-Hasan (Benevolent Loan)

Qard al-Hasan, also known as a Benevolent Loan, is a term used in Islamic finance and Islamic banking to describe an interest-free or zero-interest loan made with the primary objective of supporting someone in need. In Arabic, "Qard" implies loan, while "Hasan" denotes kind or friendly. This type of loan is based on ethical and humanitarian goals, as well as Islamic financial principles that prohibit the charging or payment of interest, known as "riba" in Islamic finance. The research of Widiyanto et al., 2011 shows that Qard al-Hasan financing, a free-interest financing model supported by prominent figures in society and Muslim religious leaders, is effective in empowering the economic activities of the needy and has the potential to be developed further as a poverty alleviation model.

The following are Qard al-Hasan's primary qualities and philosophies:

1. **No interest**: Qard al-Hasan is unique in that it is an interest-free loan. In contrast to regular loans, which charge interest on the principal amount, an Islamic charity loan does not charge interest or usury.
2. **Purely Charitable:** The primary reason for giving a Qard al-Hasan is to help someone in need, provide financial assistance, or solve a humanitarian concern. It is a type of charitable giving in the form of a loan.
3. **Repayment:** While Qard al-Hasan does not require interest, the borrower must repay the principal amount borrowed. The borrower must repay the entire amount received, with no additional fees.

4. **There is no advantage. Motive:** The lender is not interested in profiting from the loan. The lender's intention is entirely altruistic, and there is no chance of profit on the borrowed cash.
5. **Social and Ethical Considerations:** Qard al-Hasan embodies the social and ethical values of Islamic finance. It promotes cooperation, solidarity, and assistance to those in need, particularly during times of financial trouble.
6. **Documentation:** Even if the borrower is a family member or close friend, the benevolent loan should be documented to maintain transparency and to clarify the terms of repayment.

Qard al-Hasan is widely used to assist persons in financial need, fund humanitarian projects, assist with education costs, and provide assistance during calamities. It is a method of advancing the Islamic finance and ethics values of social justice and communal welfare.

2.1.2. Microtakaful: Microinsurance in Islamic Microfinance

In the context of Islamic microfinance, microtakaful, also referred to as microinsurance, is a financial service that provides insurance coverage to low-income individuals and micro-entrepreneurs in accordance with Islamic principles. It blends microfinance ideas, which focus on providing financial services to the economically underprivileged, with Takaful concepts, which are the Islamic equivalent of insurance. According to Nikunjkumar (2013), Microtakaful is a concept established for poor people in Muslim countries. It covers high risk, as opposed to takaful. Microtakaful is characterized as "a mechanism for providing Shariah-based protection to underprivileged Muslims at a reasonable cost."

The following are the main components and features of Microtakaful:

1. **Microfinance and Microinsurance Integration:** Microtakaful combines microfinance and microinsurance services to provide financial security to people who might not have access to traditional insurance. This integration is consistent with the larger goals of Islamic finance and microfinance, which are to promote financial inclusion and economic empowerment.
2. **Risk-Sharing (Tabarru) Principle**: Microtakaful is based on the risk-sharing (Tabarru) principle in Islamic banking. Participants contribute to a common fund, which is used to compensate individuals who have suffered a covered loss in the case of a covered loss. This is consistent with the Islamic financial prohibitions on "gharar" (uncertainty) and "riba" (usury).
3. **Community-Based approach:** Microtakaful is frequently based on a community-based approach, in which individuals from a similar economic background or geographic area pool their resources and share risks.
4. **Affordability of Premiums:** Microtakaful items are designed to be inexpensive for low-income persons and micro-entrepreneurs. To ensure accessibility, premiums are reduced to a bare minimum.
5. **Risk Coverage**: Microtakaful provides coverage for a variety of risks that low-income individuals may experience, including health, accidents, property damage, and natural disasters. It provides a safety net for these vulnerable groups.
6. **Sharia Compliance:** Microtakaful products and activities are built on Islamic principles. This involves avoiding investing in non-Sharia-compliant activities (such as drinking and gambling) and sticking to ethical and moral standards.

7. **Financial Inclusion**: Microtakaful helps to achieve the greater objective of financial inclusion by giving excluded people a way to secure their assets and livelihoods. This has the potential to increase economic stability and reduce poverty.
8. **Education and Awareness:** Microtakaful providers frequently engage in financial literacy and education activities to ensure that participants understand the insurance products' terms, benefits, and circumstances.

Microtakaful has grown in popularity in areas of the world where Islamic finance and microfinance meet. It is a tool for social and financial empowerment, helping people with limited financial means to avoid risks and protect their economic well-being. Incorporating Islamic values into microinsurance demonstrates a commitment to providing ethical and equitable financial services to all. Microtakaful strengthens low-income people's resilience and secures their financial security.

Micro takaful, a Sharia-compliant micro-insurance system, has developed as an effective method for safeguarding poor communities against unforeseen catastrophes. Here are some recent and impactful examples that demonstrate its successful application in various regions:

1. **Bima Salaam, Indonesia (2013):** Provided death and disability Micro takaful to low-income rural residents.

Impact: Over ten million participants are covered, providing financial stability and comfort of mind.

Quantitative data: According to World Bank research conducted in 2022, Bima Salaam beneficiaries had a rise in household 12% increase income and a 15% decrease in financial vulnerability as compared to non-participants (Konyak et al., 2022).

2. **Takaful Al-Aman, Bangladesh (2010):** focuses on crop loss Micro takaful to protect farmers against natural calamities.

Impact: Over 1 million farmers have been insured, increasing resilience and minimizing financial shocks.

Quantitative data: According to an Islamic Development Bank report from 2021, Takaful Al-Aman reduced poverty among participating farmers when compared to non-participants (Islam, 2020).

4. **Baraka Takaful, Pakistan (2005):** It focuses on Sharia-compliant Micro takaful solutions that address women's vulnerabilities.

Impact: Women's access to healthcare, financial independence, and social mobility have improved.

Quantitative data: A study by Wei et al., 2021 found that by the use of Baraka Takaful raise the female business ownership and a reduction in household poverty among participants.

These examples demonstrate how Micro takaful can be effectively used to meet the specific requirements of vulnerable groups in a variety of places. Micro takaful, which emphasizes risk-sharing, community engagement, and Sharia-compliant principles, has the potential to become a major tool for advancing financial inclusion and social development worldwide.

2.2. Case Study

To provide a tangible perspective on the impact of Islamic microfinance, this section presents compelling case studies that highlight its transformative potential.

2.2.1. Grameen-Jameel: A Pioneering Islamic Microfinance Institution

Grameen-Jameel: Bridging Financial Inclusion and Islamic Principles

Grameen-Jameel is a remarkable institution that exemplifies the seamless integration of Islamic finance and microfinance principles. Founded as a collaborative initiative between Grameen Foundation and Abdul Latif Jameel Community Initiatives (ALJCI), this institution has been instrumental in addressing the financial needs of marginalized communities, particularly in the context of Islamic ethics.

Historical Perspective

The roots of Grameen-Jameel trace back to the groundbreaking work of Nobel laureate Muhammad Yunus and the Grameen Bank in Bangladesh. Inspired by the Grameen Bank's success in providing microloans to impoverished individuals, Grameen-Jameel set out on a mission to replicate and adapt these principles within the framework of Islamic finance.

Key Features and Methodologies

- **Interest-Free Financing**: At the core of Grameen-Jameel's approach is the provision of interest-free microloans, aligning with Islamic prohibitions against usury. These loans are extended to entrepreneurs and small business owners, enabling them to expand their enterprises or launch new ventures. The concept of interest-free microloans is deeply rooted in Islamic finance, which strictly prohibits usury, or the charging of interest on loans (Aslan, 2017). In a study Rahyan (2023) studied and concluded that Interest-free finance is often based on risk-sharing, this can encourage greater collaboration and trust between lenders and borrowers and can lead to more successful business ventures.
- **Profit-and-Loss Sharing**: Grameen-Jameel incorporates the Islamic concept of Mudarabah, a profit-and-loss sharing arrangement. This means that the institution shares in the risks and rewards of the businesses it supports. If a business succeeds, the entrepreneur and Grameen-Jameel both benefits. Also, Mirakhor and Krichene (2010) defines the most important dimension of Islamic finance: its ability to facilitate high growth of employment and income with relatively low risk to individual investors and market participants.

In the context of Indonesian Islamic banking, the stability of Islamic banking has been associated with profit-loss sharing financing, particularly in Mudarabah financing (Widarjono & Mardhiyah, 2022).

- **Community-Centered Approach**: The institution prioritizes community development, working closely with local partners and community leaders to identify the specific needs and opportunities within each target area (Daly and Frikha, 2016). This approach ensures that financial solutions are tailored to the unique circumstances of each community. For instance, Abdul-Rahman et.al (2016) stated that Musharaka will certainly open up opportunities for entrepreneurs to also invest and provide their own start-up capital. This will also indirectly reduce incompetence and mismanagement of businesses as they had initially contributed their own capital. When profits are shared, so are the risks which are shared accordingly.

- **Women's Empowerment**: Grameen-Jameel places a strong emphasis on empowering women entrepreneurs. It acknowledges the pivotal role that women play in community development and economic growth. By providing women with access to finance and resources, the institution contributes to gender equality and social progress. The emphasis on empowering women entrepreneurs by Grameen-Jameel aligns with the broader discourse on the role of Islamic finance in promoting women's economic empowerment. Research in this area has explored the impact of Islamic microfinance on women's empowerment, the intersection of and women's entrepreneurship, and the role of Islamic finance in fostering entrepreneurship and economic growth (Islam, 2020; Muhammad et al., 2021; Althalathini et al., 2020)

Impact and Success Stories

Through a rigorous commitment to its principles and methodologies, Grameen-Jameel has achieved notable success. It has witnessed countless stories of entrepreneurs who have transformed their lives and communities through access to interest-free microfinance.

- Economic Upliftment: The institution has played a pivotal role in lifting communities out of poverty. By providing financial resources and business support, it has contributed to increased incomes and improved living standards for many.
- Job Creation: Grameen-Jameel's support for small businesses has not only generated income for entrepreneurs but also created job opportunities within communities. This multiplier effect has a far-reaching impact on local economies.
- Women's Empowerment: A significant portion of Grameen-Jameel's clients are women. Through access to microloans and support, these women have become financially independent, gaining decision-making power within their households and communities.

Challenges and Future Prospects of Grameen-Jameel

While Grameen-Jameel has achieved remarkable success, it has not been without challenges. The institution faces issues related to scalability, regulatory compliance, and access to capital for expansion. However, its commitment to its mission and principles remains unwavering.

Looking ahead, Grameen-Jameel continues to explore innovative ways to leverage technology and partnerships to extend its reach and impact. The institution recognizes that financial inclusion, coupled with adherence to Islamic principles, can be a powerful force for positive change, and it remains dedicated to this noble endeavor. Dhaoui (2015) defines that the Grameen model has all the potential for eradication of poverty from Muslim societies in a manner that is compatible with Islamic Shariah – both in letter and spirit.

3. FINANCIAL TECHNOLOGY (FINTECH) IN ISLAMIC FINANCE

In an era of rapid technological advancements, Fintech has emerged as a transformative force within the realm of Islamic finance. As Hassan (2020) stated that in this modern era, Islamic finance cannot operate without technology. Rabbani et al., 2021 confirms that the development of the Islamic Fintech Ecosystem and companies confirms the potential for further growth and use of Fintech tools in Islamic banking and finance while preserving Sharia norms. According to Islamic Finance Development report 2018, Fintech is also playing a part to push towards improving Islamic social finance such as zakat and charity using blockchain technology, which will boost transparency in their collection, management and distribution. This section delves into the innovative intersections of Fintech and Islamic finance, highlighting how technology is reshaping financial services while ensuring adherence to Sharia principles.

3.1. Fintech Innovations in Islamic Finance

3.1.1 Peer-to-Peer (P2P) Islamic Lending

The rise of P2P lending platforms has revolutionized the accessibility of Islamic finance. These platforms facilitate direct lending between individuals or businesses, eliminating intermediaries. Within an Islamic context, these platforms adhere to the principles of Mudarabah and Musharakah, ensuring profit-and-loss sharing between investors and entrepreneurs. Muneer et.al (2022) in their research confirms that the integration and collaboration between Islamic P2P lending and Islamic banks would promote the positive development trend of the business cycle, especially for the small business sector. Thus P2P not only democratizes access to finance but also aligns with Islamic risk-sharing principles.

The Islamic finance sector is experiencing a substantial overhaul, propelled by the swift integration of financial technology (Fintech) solutions. These technologies are not only simplifying existing processes, but also revealing new possibilities for expansion and inclusivity. Below are few prominent illustrations and current progressions that demonstrate the ever-changing environment of incorporating Fintech in Islamic finance:

1. **Robo-advisors for Sharia-compliant investments:** Platforms such as Wahed Invest and InvestMee employ algorithms to offer tailored investment guidance and wealth management services that align with Islamic norms. This enhances the accessibility and convenience of Sharia-compliant investing, particularly for younger cohorts.
2. **Blockchain-powered Sukuk issuance:** Utilizing blockchain technology in Sukuk issuance provides enhanced transparency, security, and efficiency. Emirex and Wahed Invest are utilizing blockchain technology to streamline the process of issuing and trading, resulting in cost reduction and the attraction of new investors.
3. **AI-driven risk assessment and fraud detection:** Islamic finance institutions are progressively using AI-driven techniques to scrutinize extensive datasets and discover potential dangers in transactions. This measure ensures adherence to Sharia norms and mitigates the risk of fraudulent activities, thereby safeguarding the interests of both financial institutions and investors.
4. **Mobile banking and digital wallets:** The increasing popularity of mobile banking and digital wallets such as Barq and TawakkalPay is enhancing the accessibility of Islamic financial services, particularly in locations with limited access to traditional banking services. These platforms pro-

vide an easy and safe means for users to oversee their financial matters, utilize Sharia-compliant products, and conduct transactions.

5. **Crowdfunding platforms for ethical investments**: crowdsourcing sites catering to ethical investments, such as Islamic Markets and EthisCrowd, are facilitating the opportunity for individuals to engage in projects that adhere to ethical standards and comply with Sharia principles through crowdsourcing. This promotes the practice of social impact investing and facilitates the connection between investors and firms that share their beliefs.

3.2. Ensuring Sharia Compliance in Fintech

Blockchain and Smart Contracts

Blockchain technology, with its inherent transparency and security features, has found a natural home in Islamic finance. The immutable nature of blockchain ensures the integrity of transactions, a crucial element in Sharia compliance. Smart contracts, built on blockchain, automate complex Islamic financial agreements, reducing the potential for disputes and ensuring adherence to Islamic contractual principles. Truby et al., (2022) argue that blockchain has the ability to mediate and harmonise differing sharia compliance regimes thus opening up a single digital market for Islamic financial products and services.

3.2.1 Regulatory Frameworks

As Fintech continues to reshape Islamic finance, regulatory bodies are adapting to ensure Sharia compliance. These frameworks guide the development and operation of Fintech solutions within the Islamic finance industry. They serve to protect consumers, maintain financial stability, and uphold ethical and religious standards.

The integration of Fintech into Islamic finance represents a harmonious fusion of tradition and innovation. It enables financial institutions to reach underserved Muslim populations, fosters financial inclusion, and empowers individuals to make ethical financial choices. Hassan (2023) defines that Fintech can help the Islamic financial industry to become more competitive in the global market. Moreover, it showcases how technology can amplify the principles of fairness, transparency, and risk-sharing inherent in Islamic finance, ultimately contributing to the broader goals of financial inclusion and social justice.

4. IMPACT OF ISLAMIC FINANCE ON FINANCIAL INCLUSION

Islamic finance, with its ethical underpinnings and inclusive principles, holds the potential to significantly impact financial inclusion. Enhancing financial inclusion or access to finance can make critical contributions to the economic development. Conventional mechanisms such as micro-finance, small-medium-enterprises (SME), and micro-insurance to enhance financial inclusion have been partially successful in enhancing the access to finances (Mirakhor and Iqbal, 2012). This section explores the multifaceted ways in which Islamic finance can address the challenges of financial exclusion, particularly among marginalized populations.

Islamic finance has been having a significant impact on poverty reduction, job creation, and women's empowerment. The following sources give quantifiable evidence as well as specific success stories to demonstrate the impact of Islamic financing in these areas:

Umar et al., 2021 investigated the effectiveness of the Centre for Zakat Management (CZM) in Bangladesh in using zakat funds to promote entrepreneurship and the empowerment of disadvantaged women in rural areas in the pursuit of poverty eradication. Anis and Kassim (2016) conducted a study to demonstrate the effectiveness of zakat-based efforts in alleviating poverty and empowering underprivileged women in Bangladesh. The study focused on the important factors that determined the success of female entrepreneurs. Amsami et al. (2021) discovered a substantial relationship between microcredit funding, poverty reduction, and women's empowerment. The study emphasizes the favourable impact of microfinance on poverty reduction and women's economic empowerment.

Nugroho et al. (2020) stressed the relevance of Islamic banking in poverty reduction in their study. They discovered that diverting more Islamic bank money towards the community improves welfare and lowers poverty rates. According to Dao and Liu (2017), removing financial constraints has a greater influence on job creation for smaller firms and production structures that rely more on labor. This shows that Islamic financing has the potential to help with employment creation. Berger (2021) emphasized the importance of local finance and the growth of service jobs in the post-industrial economy. The author speculated that Islamic financing could have a significant impact on service industry employment.

These factual evidence and specific case studies demonstrating the impact of Islamic financing on poverty reduction, job creation, and women's empowerment, hence confirming Islamic finance's critical role in promoting economic development and social inclusion.

4.1. Islamic Finance and the Unbanked Population

4.1.1 Reaching the Rural and Remote Areas

One of the defining features of Islamic finance is its emphasis on reaching underserved communities, including those residing in rural and remote areas. Dhaouni (2015) studied that Islamic microfinance providers offer services at a micro level directly to poor and low-income clients constitute the backbone of the system. Conventional banks often find it economically unviable to establish branches in these regions. Islamic financial institutions, however, have devised innovative strategies to bridge this gap. Through mobile banking, agent banking, and microfinance initiatives, they bring financial services directly to the doorstep of the unbanked, enabling them to access savings, credit, and investment opportunities.

4.1.2 Facilitating Financial Literacy

Financial illiteracy is a formidable barrier to financial inclusion. Islamic financial institutions go beyond providing financial services; they also prioritize financial education. These institutions conduct financial literacy programs that empower individuals with the knowledge and skills needed to make informed financial decisions. By combining services with education, Islamic finance promotes sustainable financial inclusion.

4.2. Economic Empowerment through Islamic Finance

4.2.1 Entrepreneurship and Small Business Development

Islamic finance places a strong emphasis on entrepreneurship and small business development. Through mechanisms like Mudarabah and Musharakah, entrepreneurs can access funding while sharing profits and losses with investors. Sadr (2008) defines, Greater access to financial services, which Islamic Finance (IF) promotes, would help in reducing income inequality, unemployment, and poverty besides accelerating economic growth. This encourages entrepreneurship and fosters the growth of small and medium-sized enterprises (SMEs). SMEs play a pivotal role in job creation and economic development, contributing to financial inclusion on both individual and community levels.

4.2.2 Supporting Sustainable Livelihoods

Beyond economic empowerment, Islamic finance aligns with principles of sustainability. Financial instruments such as Sadaqah and Zakat channel resources toward poverty alleviation and social welfare. These mechanisms help disadvantaged individuals and communities improve their livelihoods, breaking the cycle of poverty and fostering financial inclusion.

Islamic finance's commitment to ethical and inclusive finance positions it as a formidable tool for addressing the global challenge of financial exclusion. According to Obaidullah (2008), the provision of financial services to the poor helps to stem up aggregate household income and economic security, as well as create demand for other goods and services such as nutrition, education, and health care; and thus stimulating the local economies. By extending its reach to the unbanked, prioritizing financial literacy, and promoting entrepreneurship and sustainable livelihoods, Islamic finance exemplifies its potential to create a more inclusive and just financial landscape, ultimately contributing to the achievement of broader sustainable development goals.

5. LIMITATIONS, CHALLENGES, AND OPPORTUNITIES IN THE PRACTICAL IMPLEMENTATION OF ISLAMIC FINANCE

5.1 Limitations

Prohibition of interest: The prohibition of interest in Islamic finance means that banks cannot charge interest on loans. This can make it difficult for individuals and businesses to access financing, especially for large projects or long-term investments. A study by Rayhan (2023) explains that interest-free finance structures may be less profitable than interest-based finance structures, particularly for lenders.For example, a business that needs to borrow money to expand its operations may have difficulty finding an Islamic bank that is willing to lend to them without charging interest.

Prohibition of uncertainty: The prohibition of uncertainty in Islamic finance means that banks cannot invest in businesses or projects that involve a high degree of risk. Mumtaz et al., (2015) eleborate that transacting parties have a moral duty to disclose information before engaging in a contract and prohibiting excessive uncertainty (gharar) as manifested by contract ambiguity. This can limit the range of investment opportunities available to Islamic investors. For example, an Islamic investor may not be able to invest in a new technology company that is still in its early stages of development, as this would be considered a risky investment.

Prohibition of certain sectoral investments: Islamic finance prohibits investment in certain sectors, such as alcohol, tobacco, gambling, and pornography. This can limit the investment options available to Islamic investors and make it difficult for them to diversify their portfolios. For example, an Islamic investor may not be able to invest in a company that manufactures alcoholic beverages or tobacco products.

How these limitations can impact individuals and businesses:

The limitations of Islamic finance principles can impact individuals and businesses in a number of ways. For example:

Individuals: Individuals may have difficulty obtaining financing for large purchases, such as a home or a car. They may also have difficulty finding investment opportunities that align with their Islamic values.

Businesses: Businesses may have difficulty accessing financing for expansion or new projects. They may also have difficulty finding investors who are willing to invest in their business.

Despite the limitations, Islamic finance is a growing industry and is becoming increasingly popular around the world. There are now a number of Islamic banks and financial institutions that offer a wide range of products and services. Additionally, there are a number of Islamic investment funds that invest in a variety of sectors.

Here are some examples of how Islamic finance products and services can be used to overcome the limitations of Islamic finance principles:

Murabaha: Murabaha is an Islamic financing contract in which the bank purchases an asset on behalf of the customer and then resells it to the customer at a profit margin. Numan et al., (2022) stated that in Murabaha the asset is delivered to the customer and he can use it but the ownership will be held by bank until all payment is done. This can be used to finance large purchases, such as a home or a car.

Ijarah: Ijarah is an Islamic leasing contract in which the bank leases an asset to the customer for a fixed period of time. Numan et al (2022) documented that bank will also monitor the use of product to see if that it is used for a halal or permissible work according to Islam bank will retain its ownership This can be used to finance business equipment or real estate.

Sukuk: Sukuk is an Islamic bond that represents ownership in an asset, such as a real estate project or a business. Mumtaz et al., (2015) studied that sukuk are certificates of equal value representing undivided shares in ownership of tangible assets, property right, and services This can be used by businesses to raise capital and by investors to invest in a variety of sectors.

It is important to note that Islamic finance is a complex and evolving field. There is no one-size-fits-all solution to the limitations of Islamic finance principles. However, by understanding the principles and products available, individuals and businesses can find ways to overcome these limitations and meet their financial needs.

5.2 Challenges in the Practical Implementation of Islamic Finance

There are following challenges that can impact the widespread adoption of Islamic financial services and limit their impact on financial inclusion:

The challenges of standardization, regulatory compliance, and consumer awareness can hinder the widespread adoption of Islamic financial services and limit their impact on financial inclusion in the following ways:

- **Standardization:** The lack of standardization can make it difficult for banks and other financial institutions to develop and offer Islamic products and services that meet the needs of their customers. Hakimah and Apnizan (2012) Lacking in terms of standardization may cause serious leakage to its growth. This can lead to a limited range of Islamic products and services being available to consumers.
- **Regulatory compliance:** The complexity and cost of regulatory compliance can make it difficult for banks and other financial institutions to offer Islamic products and services. This can lead to higher costs for consumers and a limited supply of Islamic products and services in the market.
- **Consumer awareness:** The lack of consumer awareness about Islamic finance products and services can make it difficult for consumers to access and use these products and services. This can lead to consumers being underserved by the financial system and being excluded from the benefits of financial inclusion.

Steps that can be taken to overcome the challenges in the practical implementation of Islamic finance:

- **Standardization:** Industry bodies and regulators can work together to develop and implement standards for Islamic finance products and services.Alvi (2009) standardization will allow more time for stakeholders, especially, scholars, to innovate. This also can help to reduce the costs and complexity of developing and offering Islamic products and services, and it can also make it easier for consumers to compare products and services from different providers.
- **Regulatory compliance:** Regulators can work with banks and other financial institutions to develop regulatory frameworks that are supportive of Islamic finance. Ernawati et al (2022)The regulation can improve market discipline, and through the supervision from the higher authority, they will increase cost and profit effeciently. This can help to reduce the costs and complexity of regulatory compliance, and it can also help to encourage innovation in the Islamic finance sector.
- **Consumer awareness:** Industry bodies, regulators, and financial institutions can work together to raise awareness of Islamic finance products and services among consumers. Ernawati et al (2022) presented that the position of public awareness is essential as a mediator of knowledge and regulation in promoting the development of the Islamic financial industry. This can be done through educational campaigns, public awareness campaigns, and other initiatives.

By taking steps to overcome the challenges in the practical implementation of Islamic finance, the industry can help to promote the widespread adoption of Islamic financial services and expand their impact on financial inclusion.

Bridging the Gap: Practical Solutions for Islamic Finance Implementation

The ethical and inclusive ideas of Islamic finance could considerably improve financial equality. The practical application of this notion faces hurdles that can slow its progress. Here are some practical ways to close the gap and maximize its potential:

Collaboration and Standardization

Standardize Sharia interpretations: Promote international organisations like AAOIFI and IFSB to give standard Sharia guidelines to ease cross-border transactions and boost investor trust.

Facilitate regulatory collaboration: Help national regulators and central banks coordinate Islamic finance regulations across jurisdictions to improve operational efficiency.

Implement knowledge sharing mechanisms to help regulators and financial institutions share best practices and increase transparency.

Innovation and Expertise

Use technology and encourage financial specialists and Sharia scholars to study and build cutting-edge Sharia-compliant products.

Sharia boards vary: Promote different expertise on Sharia boards and knowledge sharing among scholars from other locations to broaden perspectives.

Clear instructions: Establish clear Sharia-compliant product development frameworks for financial institutions to maintain consistency.

Awareness and Accessibility

Publicly educate customers and financial institutions about Islamic finance's benefits.

Specialized training programs: Develop Islamic finance training programmes with universities and financial organizations to help professionals learn key skills.

Digital platforms: Create user-friendly platforms and mobile apps to make Islamic financial goods and services more accessible.

Human Capital and Labor Force

Academic programs: Establish Islamic finance academic programs and certifications in universities and financial institutions.

Training and development: Offer internal Islamic finance training for financial professionals.

Promote mentorship and internships to develop new talent in the sector.

Liquidity and Infrastructure

Create secondary markets for Sharia-compliant assets like Sukuk to increase liquidity and attract investors. Promote Sharia-compliant infrastructure investment to boost Islamic finance.

Promote collaboration and consolidation: Encourage Islamic financial institutions and sovereign wealth funds to pool their resources for large infrastructure projects.

Technology and Ethics

Sharia-compliant Fintech creates Islamic finance-specific financial technology solutions. Blockchain-based Sukuk issuance and Sharia risk assessment using AI are examples.

Fintech companies and Islamic financial institutions should collaborate to innovate and increase efficiency. Implement strict data privacy laws and improve cybersecurity to ensure Islamic banking technology is used ethically.

5.3 Opportunities for Future Growth/Unleash the Potential: Islamic Finance Growth and Inclusion Strategies

Islamic banking can improve financial inclusion and economic development in addition to tackling current issues. These tactics, policies, and joint ventures can boost its growth:

Technological Leverage

Sharia-compliant Fintech solutions like robo-advisors for microinvestments, blockchain-based crowdfunding platforms for ethical ventures, and AI-powered financial risk assessment tools must be developed and implemented. Expanding digital infrastructure and internet connectivity in poor areas will enable fair Islamic financial services.

Mobile banking and financial literacy: Encourage financial inclusion and responsible financial behavior by creating user-friendly mobile banking apps and financial literacy **programs for specific demographics and needs.**

Product Diversity and Innovation: Focus on underserved segments: Develop microfinance, insurance, and asset management tools for women, youth, and rural communities. Expand Sharia-compliant investing choices, such as Sukuk for infrastructure projects, equity funds for ethical enterprises, and REITs. Encourage R&D will foster collaboration between financial institutions, colleges, and Sharia experts to develop Sharia-compliant financial products.

Policy and Regulation Support

Harmonization and standardization: Promote worldwide collaboration to harmonize Sharia interpretations and regulatory frameworks, reducing ambiguity and facilitating cross-border commerce. To grow the business and encourage participation, provide specific tax exemptions and subsidies for Islamic financial institutions and investors.

Regulator capacity building: Invest in regulator training and capacity building to ensure they can monitor and support Islamic finance growth.

Additional Considerations

Promote financial literacy: Continue funding Islamic financial literacy initiatives that emphasize responsible resource management.

Encourage ethics: Maintain high ethical standards in Islamic finance to build confidence and attract investors and clients.

Decision-making using data: Data and analytics can help you understand market trends and customer needs for product development and outreach.

Islamic finance may promote financial inclusion, economic growth, and social good by using these methods, fostering collaboration, and emphasizing ethics. Islamic finance has a bright future, but it needs innovation, collaboration, and ethical and inclusive practises.

6. CONCLUSION

6.1. Key Takeaways

Throughout this exploration of the nexus between Islamic finance and financial inclusion, several key takeaways have emerged, shedding light on the potential and significance of this relationship.

6.1.1 The Inclusive Foundations of Islamic Finance

Islamic finance, rooted in ethical and Sharia-compliant principles, inherently promotes financial inclusion. It operates on the premise of social justice, wealth distribution, and risk-sharing, which align with the goals of financial inclusion. The prohibition of Riba (usury or interest) and the emphasis on risk-sharing create a financial ecosystem that is inclusive by design.

6.1.2 Realizing the SDGs through Financial Inclusion

Financial inclusion is not merely an economic pursuit but a powerful tool for achieving the United Nations' Sustainable Development Goals (SDGs). Islamic finance intersects with seven of the 17 SDGs, particularly those related to gender equality (SDG 5) and decent work and economic growth (SDG 8). Lanzara (2021) states the role of Islamic public- private partnership (PPPs) projects in bridging the huge infrastructure investment gap related to sustainable development goals (SDGs), as SDGs are seen as an opportunity for the growing of Islamic finance industry. It plays a pivotal role in addressing poverty, promoting economic empowerment, and supporting sustainable livelihoods.

6.2. Future Prospects

As we contemplate the future, the role of Islamic finance in advancing financial inclusion appears poised for significant expansion.

6.2.1 The Expanding Role of Islamic Finance

Islamic finance is poised to extend its influence as a catalyst for financial inclusion on a global scale. With continued innovation, strategic partnerships, and targeted investments in Fintech solutions, it can reach previously underserved populations, including those in remote areas and marginalized communities.

6.2.2 A Vision for Inclusive Global Economies

Looking ahead, there is a compelling vision of inclusive global economies where Islamic finance serves as a bridge to connect individuals and communities to mainstream financial services. This vision entails not only economic empowerment but also social justice, poverty alleviation, and sustainable development.

In closing, the integration of Islamic finance and financial inclusion holds the promise of creating more equitable and prosperous societies. By embracing the principles of Islamic finance, leveraging Fintech innovations, and nurturing international collaboration, we can work towards a future where financial inclusion becomes a reality for all, fulfilling the aspirations of the Sustainable Development Goals and fostering a world that leaves no one behind.

REFERENCES

Abdul-Rahman, A., & Mohd nor, S. (2016). Challenges of profit-and-loss sharing financing in Malaysian Islamic banking. *Geografia : Malaysian Journal of Society and Space*, *12*, 39–46.

Abdullah, A. (2016). Examining U.S. approvals of Islamic financing products and the Islamic theory of lawful profit. *International Journal of Islamic and Middle Eastern Finance and Management*, *9*(4), 532–550. doi:10.1108/IMEFM-09-2015-0107

Althalathini, D., Al-Dajani, H., & Apostolopou, N. (2020). Muslim women's entrepreneurship in conflict zones: Religiosity, culture, and gender egalitarianism. *Proceedings - Academy of Management*, *2020*(1), 13878. doi:10.5465/AMBPP.2020.13878abstract

Alvi, I. (2009, May). *Standardization of Documentation in Islamic Finance & Role of the International, Islamic Financial Market (IIFM).* Paper presented at Islamic Financial Sector Development (IFSD), Forum 2009, Ashgabat, Turkmenistan.

Aslan, I. (2017). Interest- free banking: reasons for choosing Islamic banking in bingol city. *Press academia, 3*(1), 257-268. doi:10.17261/Pressacademia.2017.411

Daly, S., & Frikha, M. (2016). Banks and economic growth in developing countries: What about Islamic banks? *Cogent Economics & Finance*, *4*(1), 1168728. doi:10.1080/23322039.2016.1168728

Demirguc-Kunt, A., Klapper, L., Singer, D., Inclusion, F., & Inclusive, G. A. (2017). *Review of Recent Empirical Evidence.* World Bank Group, Policy Research working paper 8040.

Dhaoui, E. (2015). *The role of Islamic Microfinance in Poverty Alleviation: Lessons from Bangladesh Experience.* Tunisian Institute for Competitiveness and Quantitative Studies, Munich Personal RePEc Archive, Paper No. 63665.

Elasrag, H. (2011). *Principals of the Islamic finance: A focus on project finance.* Munich Personal RePEc Archive, MPRA Paper No. 30197.

Ernawati, E., Rosnawintang, R., & Nusantara, A. (2022). The Effect of Public Awareness on the Islamic Financial Industry's Development. *Significant: Journal Ilma Ekonomi.*, *11*(2), 399–414. doi:10.15408/sjie.v11i2.25816

Franzoni, S., & Allali, A. (2018). Principles of Islamic Finance and Principles of Corporate Social Responsibility: What Convergence. *Sustainability (Basel), 10*(3), 637. Advance online publication. doi:10.3390/su10030637

HasanM. (2023)The Impact of Financial Technology (Fintech) on the Financial and Banking Services Sector and Its Applications in the Islamic Financial Industry. doi:10.2139/ssrn.4369683

Hasan, Z. (2015). *Risk sharing versus risk transfer in Islamic Finance: A critical appraisal.* . doi:10.12816/0021394

Hassan, M. K. (2020). Introduction: Islamic Finance and Contemporary Challenges. *Arab Law Quarterly, 35*(1-2), 1-5. https://www.isdb.org/sites/default/files/media/documents/2021-02/ISLAMIC%20MICROFINANCE%20FOR%20WOMEN%20FINAL.pdf doi:10.1163/15730255-BJA10067

Hussain, M., Nawaz, M. A., Aqdas, R., & Riaz, M. (2020). The Influence of Islamic Finance. *Financial Inclusion and Governance on the Economic Growth of Islamic Countries., 25*, 216–226.

Hussain, M., Shahmoradi, A., & Turk, R. (2015). *An Overview of Islamic Finance.* IMF Working Paper, International Monetary Fund, WP/15/120.

Islam, M. (2020). Role of Islamic microfinance in women's empowerment: Evidence from rural development scheme of Islami bank Bangladesh limited. *Isra International Journal of Islamic Finance, 13*(1), 26–45. doi:10.1108/IJIF-11-2019-0174

Islamic Development Bank. (2018). An overview of Islamic banking and finance in Asia. Routledge Handbook of Banking and Finance in Asia. doi:10.4324/9781315543222-28

Kazim, S. (2008). Islamic Finance for Micro and Medium Enterprises. Islamic Research Training Institute and University Brunei Darussalam.

Konyak, O., Das, S., & Patra, N. (2022). Impact of Nagaland state rural livelihood mission (nsrlm) on livelihood status of women in Nagaland. *Agricultural Reviews.* , doi:10.18805/ag.R-2358

Lanzara, F. (2021). Islamic finance and Sustainable Development Goals. A bibliometric analysis from 2000 to 2021. *European Journal of Islamic Finance.* https://ssrn.com/abstract=3857617

Mirakhor, A., & Iqbal, Z. (2012). *Financial Inclusion: Islamic Finance Perspective.* . doi:10.12816/0004974

Mohieldin, M. (2012). Realizing the potential of Islamic finance. World Bank Publications.

MohieldinM.IqbalZ.RostomA.FuX. (2015)The Role of Islamic Finance in Enhancing Financial Inclusion in Organization of Islamic Cooperation (OIC) Countries. *Islamic Economic Studies, 20*(2). https://ssrn.com/abstract=3158639

Muhammad, S., Ximei, K., Saqib, S. E., & Beutell, N. J. (2021). Entrepreneurial income and wellbeing: Women's informal entrepreneurship in a developing context. *Sustainability (Basel), 13*(18), 10262. doi:10.3390/su131810262

Muneer, M. (2022, September). Fintech in Islamic finance literature: A review. *Heliyon, 8*(9), e10385. doi:10.1016/j.heliyon.2022.e10385 PMID:36060472

Nikunj Kumar Gor. (2013). Microtakaful-islamic insurance for deprived: innovation, sustainability and inclusive growth. *International Journal of Business, Economics and Law, 3*(2).

Obaidullah, M., & Khan, T. U. (2008). *Islamic Microfinance Development: Challenges and Initiatives.* Islamic Research & Training institute Policy Dialogue Paper No. 2. doi:10.2139/ssrn.1506073

OziliP. (2020). Financial Inclusion Research Around the World: A Review. Socially Responsible Investment journal. doi:10.2139/ssrn.3515515

Ozili, P. K., & Inclusion, F. (2022)Sustainability and Sustainable Development. Advance online publication. doi:10.2139/ssrn.4185735

Rabbani, M. R., Bashar, A., Nawaz, N., Karim, S., Ali, M., Rahiman, H. U., & Alam, M. S. (2021). Exploring the role of Islamic fintech in combating the aftershocks of covid-19: The open social innovation of the Islamic financial system. *Journal of Open Innovation, 7*(2), 136. doi:10.3390/joitmc7020136

Rayhan, A. (2023). *Interest-Free Finance for A More Equitable Future*. doi:10.13140/RG.2.2.33212.21129/1

Thomson Reuters. (2018). *Islamic Finance Development Report 2018.* Thomson Reuters. Retrieved from: https://ceif.iba.edu.pk/pdf/Reuters-Islamic-finance-development-report2018.pdf

Truby, J., Dahdal, A., & Ismailov, O. (2022). The Role and Potential of Blockchain Technology in Islamic Finance. *European Business Law Review, 33*(2), 175–192. Advance online publication. doi:10.54648/EULR2022005

Ullah, Dey, Shahriar, & Shahriar. (2023). *A Review of Literature on Takaful and Conventional Insurance. Evidence from Bangladesh.* Munich Personal RePEc Archive, MPRA Paper No. 117463.

Wani, Tali, Ashraf, & Sikandar. (2022). An Over view of Islamic micro finance. *Journal of Emerging Technologies and Innovative Research, 9*(9), 422-429.

Wei, W., Sarker, T., Żukiewicz-Sobczak, W., Roy, R., Alam, G., Rabbany, G., Hossain, M. S., & Aziz, N. (2021). The influence of women's empowerment on poverty reduction in the rural areas of bangladesh: Focus on health, education and living standard. *International Journal of Environmental Research and Public Health, 18*(13), 6909. doi:10.3390/ijerph18136909 PMID:34199117

Widarjono, A., & Mardhiyah, Z. (2022). Profit-loss sharing financing and stability of Indonesian Islamic banking. *International Journal of Islamic Business and Economics (Ijibec), 6*(1), 1–16. doi:10.28918/ijibec.v6i1.4196

Widiyanto, W., Mutamimah, S., & Hendar, H. (2011). *Effectiveness of Qard Al-Hasan financing as a poverty alleviation model. Economic Journal of Emerging Markets, 3, 27-42.* doi:10.20885/EJEM.V3I1.2318

Yaacob, H., & Abdullah, A. (2012). Standards Issuance for Islamic Finance in International Trade: Current Issues and Challenges Ahead. *International Congress on Interdisciplinary Business and Social Science 2012, Social and Behavioral Sciences, 65*, 492 – 497.

APPENDIX

Discussion Questions

1. How does asset-backed financing, as described in the case study, address the ethical concerns raised by some people regarding traditional interest-based financing?
2. What are the potential challenges of implementing asset-backed financing in different economic and cultural contexts?
3. How can asset-backed financing be adapted to meet the needs of different types of businesses and individuals?
4. How does asset-backed financing compare to other forms of financing, such as debt financing and equity financing, in terms of risk and return?
5. What role can asset-backed financing play in promoting financial inclusion and economic development?

Multiple Choice Questions (MCQs)

1. What is the underlying principle of asset-backed financing?
   a) Borrowing money based on creditworthiness
   b) Selling an asset with a deferred payment agreement
   c) Investing in a pool of real estate assets
   d) Providing financial aid to individuals in need
2. Which type of asset is NOT typically used in asset-backed financing?
   a) Accounts receivable
   b) Inventory
   c) Intellectual property
   d) Personal loans
3. What is the term used for the markup in a Murabaha transaction?
   a) Interest rate
   b) Profit margin
   c) Loan fee
   d) Service charge
4. Which statement is TRUE about the ownership of the asset in a Murabaha transaction?
   a) The seller retains ownership until full payment
   b) The buyer becomes the owner upon signing the agreement.
   c) Ownership is shared proportionally between the seller and buyer.
   d) Ownership remains unclear until the final payment is made.
5. Which regulatory body is responsible for overseeing and promoting Islamic finance globally?
   a) International Monetary Fund (IMF)
   b) World Bank Group
   c) Accounting and Auditing Organization for Islamic Financial Institutions (AAOIFI)
   d) Organisation for Economic Co-operation and Development (OECD)
6. What is the primary benefit of asset-backed financing for borrowers, as described in the case study?

a) Lower interest rates compared to traditional loans
b) Flexibility in choosing the repayment schedule
c) Access to credit without strict credit score requirements
d) Ability to retain ownership of the financed asset

7. Which statement is FALSE about Sukuk?
   a) They are considered Sharia-compliant financial instruments.
   b) They represent ownership interests in underlying assets.
   c) They generate returns through profit sharing instead of interest payments.
   d) They function similarly to bonds in traditional finance.
8. Which type of financial institution typically acts as the intermediary in asset-backed financing transactions?
   a) Insurance company
   b) Investment bank
   c) Credit union
   d) Microfinance organization
9. What is the main risk associated with asset-backed financing for lenders?
   a) Market fluctuations affecting the value of the underlying asset
   b) Difficulty in repossessing the asset in case of default
   c) Uncertainty about the borrower's financial stability
   d) All of the above
10. What is NOT a potential application of asset-backed financing, as described in the case study?
    a) Financing the purchase of a car
    b) Funding infrastructure development projects
    c) Providing working capital for businesses
    d) Issuing student loans for higher education

Short Answer Questions

1. Explain the mechanics of Murabaha transactions, as described in the case study.
2. Discuss the potential limitations of asset-backed financing in terms of its ability to meet the needs of all individuals and businesses.
3. Describe how asset-backed financing can be used to promote financial inclusion.
4. Compare and contrast the risks and benefits of asset-backed financing with another form of financing, such as debt financing.
5. Evaluate the potential impact of asset-backed financing on the development of the Islamic economy.

Assignment Topics

1. Research and report on the history and development of Islamic finance.
2. Compare and contrast the regulatory frameworks for Islamic finance and traditional finance in different countries.
3. Analyze the use of asset-backed financing in a specific industry or sector.

4. Develop a case study of a business that has successfully used asset-backed financing to achieve its financial goals.
5. Write a persuasive essay arguing for or against the wider adoption of asset-backed financing as a tool for economic development.

Answers to Multiple Choice Questions

Q1: (b), Q2: (d), Q3: (b), Q4: (a), Q5: (c), Q6: (c), Q7: (d), Q8: (b), Q9: (d), Q10: (b)

Chapter 4
Bank Profitability Determinants in Africa:
A Review of Literature

Peterson K. Ozili
https://orcid.org/0000-0001-6292-1161
Central Bank of Nigeria, Nigeria

ABSTRACT

The study presents a review of existing research on bank profitability determinants in Africa. Using the literature review methodology, it was found that bank profitability determinants differ across countries in all regions of Africa. Some suggested areas for future research are to explore the impact of circular economy, fintech activities, pandemic, and uncertainty on the profitability of African banks. The implication of the review findings is that bank profitability determinants will remain a contested research agenda in the banking literature.

1. BACKGROUND

The objective of this paper is to provide a concise overview of the advances in the African bank profitability determinants literature, to understand the state of research in the field and offer directions for future research. During the review, the study focused mostly on the post-2010 literature, and illuminate the issues that are particularly significant in the literature.

Bank profitability is crucial for the continuity of banking business. Bank profitability is of interest to external parties such as regulators, shareholders, tax authorities, accounting standard setters, financial economists, banking academics, the public and investor analysts. There is so much attention on bank profitability for many reasons. The most important reason is because, when banks declare a profit, some of the profit is allocated as (i) provisions for loan loss (ii) regulatory reserves, (iii) dividend to shareholders, (iv) tax payments, (v) bonuses to employees, (vi) corporate social responsibility expenses, and (vii) some profit is reinvested into the banking business. These allocation expectations, which are either statutory or discretionary, both justify the attention given to the profitability of banks from internal and

DOI: 10.4018/979-8-3693-1475-3.ch004

external parties. Take the case of a bank regulator, for example. Bank regulators want banks to be profitable at all times. Regulators would be worried if all or most regulated banks report significant losses in the same year because it can tarnish the reputation of the regulator. Bank regulators can grant regulatory forbearance to banks that have financial difficulties in the short term, to avoid transmitting distress in the inter-bank market. Of course, there may be concern that bank managers could take advantage of their important status in the financial system to report false profit or inflated profit in order to meet their profit projections and to entice investors, and this is a highly debated issue in the earnings management literature (see, for example, Cao (2022), Ozili (2022), and Ertan (2022)).

Bank profitability is also very important for the proper functioning of firms in the real sector of the economy. Profitable banks can perform their financial intermediation function effectively by allocating credit to economic agents who undertake production and investment activities that contribute to higher economic output. Given the importance of bank profitability for economic growth, economists and researchers are interested in bank profitability determinants. Many studies provide extensive insight into the determinants of bank profitability in developed countries, but such insights are limited for developing countries particularly African countries. Knowledge about bank profitability determinants in African countries is limited in the literature.

Majority of the profitability studies have focused on bank profitability determinants while only few studies focus on the antecedents and consequence of bank profitability. Some studies explore bank profitability during booms and recessions (Dietrich and Wanzenried, 2011; Albertazzi and Gambacorta, 2009); how profit persistence contribute to bank stability (Ali and Puah, 2019; Le, 2020; Ozili 2021a); the role of earning management in profit persistence (Ozili, 2018; Ozili and Outa, 2017); how regulation affects bank profitability (Ozili, 2015; Latridis and Persakis, 2012); impact of competition on bank profit (Yuanita, 2019); how corporate governance affects bank profit (Peni and Vähämaa, 2012; Aebi, Sabato and Schmid, 2012); as well as bank profitability impacts across other regions (Pasiouras and Kosmidou, 2007; Ozili and Uadiale, 2017, etc.). Despite the extensive research on bank profitability determinants, there are few studies from emerging countries, particularly African countries. This review study summarizes the mainstream bank profitability literature, and thereafter, focus the discussion on African bank profitability determinants. In Africa, banks are important because most African countries have a bank-based financial system. Yet, there is little research on African bank profitability determinants, compared to the similar research conducted in other regions.

The review adds to existing research that investigate the determinants of bank performance. It also adds to the research that explore the nexus between bank profit and financial regulation designed to make the banking system safer (Lee and Chih, 2013; Xu, Hu and Das, 2019). The review study also adds to the earnings management literature by considering the potential for managers to understate or overstate bank profit in order to meet their opportunistic financial reporting objectives, and whether such behavior reduces the transparency of reported profits in banks (see, Cohen et al 2014; Ozili and Thankom, 2018; Ozili, 2019).

The remaining sections of the study are organized in the following way. The methodology used to conduct the review is reported in section 2. The review of studies that investigate the determinants of bank profitability in African countries is reported in section 3. Some suggestions for further research are presented in section 4. The concluding remarks are presented in section 5.

2. REVIEW METHOD

The review was conducted using published articles. The search for content was limited to abstract search and a search on the body of articles and using Google as the primary search engine. The search result yielded 34 articles. Therefore, the study used the 34 studies to conduct the review. The inclusion criteria are that the articles included in the review are post-2010 articles, and the articles are published in a journal. Regarding the exclusion criteria, studies that are published prior to 2010 were excluded. Also, thesis and dissertation papers were excluded from this review.

3. BANK PROFITABILITY DETERMINANTS IN AFRICAN REGION

3.1. The African Banking Sector: Challenges and Opportunities

In the last decade, many African countries witnessed sustained economic growth which is partly due to sustained financial sector development. Despite this, the banking system in many African countries remain either developing or under-developed. African banking systems are still highly concentrated as five banks own over 60 percent of the entire banking assets in the industry in many African countries. Bank intermediation is also inefficient in the region as shown by the high interest rate, small bank size, low intermediation and significant entry and exit barriers. Access to credit is also a significant issue in the region as African countries are among the countries with the lowest access to credit indicators in the world and it constrains banks' ability to generate enough profit. Notwithstanding these challenges, African banks are also benefiting immensely from a stable macroeconomic environment which assists in the development of the banking sector and in the persistence of bank profitability in the region. Some African countries are undergoing reforms and structural changes that would position the banking sector for higher profitability and growth.

3.2. Sub-Saharan African Countries

Focusing on Sub-Saharan African countries, Francis (2013) investigates the determinants of bank profit in Sub-Saharan Africa during the 1999 to 2006 period. They focus on 216 commercial banks from 42 African countries, and measured profitability using net interest margin, return on assets and return on equity. The explanatory variables were total asset growth, equity capital ratio, deposit size, efficiency ratio, change in GDP and the rate of inflation. They found that internal and external factors are significant factors affecting bank profitability. Ozili (2017) investigates bank profitability determinants in Africa. The author used several measures of profitability and found that the volume of total assets, minimum risk capital and provision for loan loss are factors affecting bank profit, with risk capital having a stronger effect than the other determinants for listed banks.

Another research by Sarpong-Kumankoma et al (2018) focused on banks from four countries in Sub-Saharan Africa from 2006 - 2012. They showed that cost efficiency is a crucial factor influencing the persistence of bank profit, while bank concentration did not have any impact on bank profit. Tarus and Manyala (2018) also investigate some factors affecting the interest rate spread of banks in Sub-Saharan African countries during the 2003 to 2012 period. They focus on 20 sub-Saharan African countries and found that high inflation and strong governance institutions decrease the interest rate spread of banks. They also found that bank concentration leads to increase in the interest rate spread of SSA banks.

Overall, the dominant profitability determinants for African banks in the Sub-Saharan region are capital regulation, inflation, operating cost and bank concentration.

3.3. West Africa

Studies from West Africa have interesting findings. In Ghana, Boadi et al (2017) investigate whether bank profitability is affected by SMEs funding in Ghana. The authors use the panel regression method estimation technique, and they found that SMEs funding and GDP growth are significant factors affecting bank profit in Ghana. They also found that the real value of SMEs loan is depleted by high inflation, thereby eroding the interest income on the loans to SMEs. In a related study, Alhassan et al (2016) analyse twenty-six banks in Ghana during 2003 to 2011 and found that technical efficiency positively affects the profit of banks. They further observe that there is low persistence of profit which might be caused by having a competitive banking industry.

Mireku et al (2018) investigate whether commercial bank presence improves profitability in Ghana during the 2007 to 2013 period. They showed that increase in bank branches leads to higher bank profit, while credit risk and management quality did not improve profitability. However, they observe that bank profit is also enhanced by internal and external factors. Adelopo et al (2018) investigate banks in the ECOWAS regional group, to identify the factors affecting bank profit before, during and after the great recession. They use fixed effect estimations. The variables used are internal and external variables affecting bank profit, and they found that the internal factors had a significant influence on bank profit in the three periods, and the significance vary across the periods.

Ozili (2015) focused on the factors that determine bank profit after the adoption of Basel capital regulation in Nigeria. The study used three profitability metrics: ROE, NIM and ROA. The analysis was estimated using fixed effect regression. The findings show that regulation had an insignificant impact on the profit of Nigerian banks. It was also found that nonperforming loans impacted the interest margin of banks, and the size of a bank and cost-to-income ratio had a considerable influence on ROA. Ozili (2015) conclude that the significance of bank profitability determinants depends on the profitability metric employed. Chidozie and Ayadi (2017) in their study focused on external factors influencing bank profit in Nigeria. They found that crude oil price negatively affects the profit of banks in Nigeria. Zaccheaus and Ajuwon (2019) investigate whether bank profit is affected by volatile oil price. They investigate twelve large commercial banks between 2006 to 2015. They found a significant effect of volatile oil price shocks on the profit of banks in Nigeria, indicating that the transmission mechanism through which oil price impacts the profit of banks is a direct mechanism. In another related study, Ozili and Uadiale (2017) examined whether ownership concentration influences the profit of banks in Nigeria. In the study, ownership was measured as the proportion of direct equity share held by a majority shareholder. They conducted some empirical analysis and found that ownership concentration increases the interest margin of banks.

Overall, the dominant bank profitability determinants in West Africa are market power, inflation, monetary policy, real interest rates, exchange rates, capital regulation, cost efficiency, and rising nonperforming loans.

Table 1. Reviewed articles

S/N	Region	Number of Articles
1	Sub-Saharan African countries	4
2	West Africa	8
3	Middle East and North Africa (MENA)	6
4	Southern Africa	5
5	East Africa	5

These are 28 articles in total. The remaining 6 articles that were reviewed can be found in sections 1 and 5

3.4. Middle East and North Africa (MENA) Studies

For instance, in the case of Tunisia, Ben Naceur and Goaied (2008) investigate the factors that affect bank profit for the 1980 to 2000 period. Two performance indicators were used: ROA and NIM. They found that bank capital, overheads, and better stock market development positively affect the profit of banks. Abdullah and Tan (2017) investigate the factors affecting the profit of commercial banks in eleven Middle East and North African (MENA) countries during the 2004 to 2014 period. It was found that credit risk reduced the profit of banks in non-oil exporting countries. Elkhayat and ElBannan (2018) assessed whether privatizing public banks affect their profit and focused on the MENA region. Thirty-six countries were analysed, and they found that privatization had an insignificant impact on bank profit, but the region witness a reduction in credit risk due to the privatization. They conclude that the privatization certainly improved cost efficiency and reduced credit risk for privatized banks.

Ammar and Boughrara (2019) were interested in whether revenue diversification improve the profit of banks. They examined two hundred and seventy-five banks in 14 fourteen MENA countries from 1990 to 2011. They use GMM regression estimation and found a strong positive association between revenue diversification and bank profit. They also observe that non-interest activities did not improve the profit of banks, rather it leads banks to insolvency.

One notable observation from the MENA profitability literature is the impact of political transition on the profit of banks. War and conflict in the region make banks unstable for many reasons, and empirical evidence supports this hypothesis. Ghosh (2016) investigates bank profitability during the Arab spring period covering 2000-2012 to determine its impact on the profit of banks in MENA region. The author found that the Arab spring lowered the profit of banks and increased the risk of banks. Bitar (2016) took into account the Arab spring transition period when investigating the impact of Basel capital regulation on the risk and profit of banks in MENA region. The author found that compliance with the Basel capital requirements helped to protect MENA banks against certain risks and improved their profit.

Overall, the dominant factors affecting bank in the region are bank size, bank ownership type, cost efficiency and bank risk.

3.5. Southern Africa

In the southern Africa region, some studies such as Du Toit and Cuba (2018) investigate the relationship between the cost efficiency and profit of South African banks before, during and after the great recession. They focused on banks that were listed on the Johannesburg Stock Exchange from 2004 to 2012.

They observe a significant link between bank profit and changing business cycles. Seemule et al (2017) investigate the determinants influencing the profit of banks in Botswana and found that bank liquidity and GDP are significant factors influencing the profit of banks. Garcia and Trindade (2019) examined the determinants of the profit of seventeen banks in Angola and found that ownership has a strong positive impact on the profit of Angola banks. Kumbirai and Webb (2010) analyse the case of South Africa during 2005 to 2009. They found that banks performed better before the crisis but witnessed significant poor performance during 2008 and 2009 at the peak of the crisis. Abel and Le Roux (2016) examine bank profitability determinants in Zimbabwe from 2009 to 2014 during the period when Zimbabwe adopted a multi-currency system. They employ a fixed effect model and show that profitability is significantly driven by bank risk.

Overall, the dominant factors affecting bank profit in Southern African region are bank ownership type, financial crisis, and bank risk and bank liquidity.

3.6. East Africa

Bank profitability studies in East Africa is limited. Only few studies exist on the factors influencing bank profit in this region. Mdoe et al (2018) found that Kenyan banks have high profit persistence. Amin, Sanusi, Kusairi and Abdallah (2019) analysed the association between the risk and profit of banks in Tanzania. They found a negative association between risk and profit, implying that supervisors in Tanzania would need to consider the trade-off between risk and return. Kodongo et al (2015) investigate the effect of leverage on the profit of listed firms in Kenya, and they found that leverage significantly and negatively affect firm profitability but does not affect firm value.

Kapur and Gualu (2012) examine the effect of ownership structure on the profit of eight Ethiopian commercial banks from 2001 to 2008. They found that private banks performed better than public banks. Private banks had higher profit, fewer loan default, and stronger capital ratio than public banks. Lelissa (2014) examine the factors influencing the profit of banks in Ethiopia and found that internal factors largely determine changes in the profit of banks. Bank capital, liquidity status, bank size and real GDP growth rates did not significantly influence profitability.

Overall, these studies show that the dominant bank profitability determinants in East African region are leverage, and bank risk.

4. DIRECTIONS FOR FURTHER RESEARCH

4.1. Fintech Revolution and Bank Profitability

There is few research on the impact of fintech activities on the determinants of bank profitability. 'Fintech' combines financial services with digital innovation. Fintech activity may negatively impact banks' profit because fintech lenders are less regulated or are regulated within a sandbox, which puts them in an advantageous competitive position over banks (Ozili, 2021b). Future studies can explore how fintech activities affect the profit margins of banks.

4.2. Uncertainty and Bank Profitability

There is few research on the effect of uncertainty on the profit of banks. Banking activity is sensitive to uncertainty particularly economic policy uncertainty that is caused by unexpected changes in monetary policy, fiscal policy, and regulatory policy. Such uncertainty affects bank profitability through reduced bank lending and loan repricing (Danisman et al, 2020). Future studies can explore the how economic policy uncertainty affects bank's return on asset, return on equity, and net interest margin.

4.3. Effect of Pandemic on Bank Profitability

There is few research on the impact of pandemic on the profit of banks. A pandemic, such as the Covid-19 pandemic, disrupts banks' revenue streams for an indeterminate period, increase the fixed costs of banks, lead to poor credit quality in banks, and lead to deteriorating balance sheets. These combined effects will impact the profit of banks. Generally, the impact of pandemics on bank profit may differ due to different risk management practices across banks, and differences in regulatory and supervisory quality. Further research can explore the impact of pandemics on the profit of banks.

4.4. Bank Profitability in the Circular Economy

No studies have examined how the circular economy would affect bank profit. The circular economy emphasize efficiency in waste reduction (Ozili and Opene, 2021). In the circular economy, banks will have opportunities to diversify their revenue stream by lending to the recycling sector, and this may increase the profit of banks. But no research has investigated the prospects of higher bank profit in the circular economy. Future studies can explore the profitability prospects of banks in a circular economy.

4.5. Other Areas

Future researchers in this topic can undertake a more comprehensive analysis of the specific economic, political, and regulatory conditions in each of the African regions, and provide an overview of the regional characteristics and their potential impact on bank profitability. Case studies could also be used to provide real-world examples for the impact on bank profit in the regions. Future research can also examine how significant economic and political events in these regions, such as financial crises, changes in leadership, and political instability, may impact bank profitability. In addition, future studies can explore the impact of macroeconomic factors, such as GDP growth, inflation, exchange rates, interest rates, and monetary policies, on bank profitability. Furthermore, it would be interesting to investigate the impact of risk management and the regulatory environment on profit of banks in each region.

5. CONCLUSION

I reviewed the literature on the factors influencing the profit of banks across several regions of the world. The findings from the review revealed that the factors influencing the profit of banks differ across countries and several regions including the African region. The study offered some suggestions for future research such as the need to explore the impact of circular economy, fintech activities and pandemic on bank profitability. A profitable banking environment will undoubtedly promote greater financial development and expand lending to the real sector to increase the level of economic activities. Nevertheless, there are policy debates on what constitutes the uniform determinants of bank profitability. The academic literature also shows that bank profitability determinants differ according to bank specific, external, and time-varying factors. In the future, there will be a continuous search for factors influencing bank profit. Therefore, the study concludes that the factors influencing bank profit will remain a contested research agenda in the banking literature

REFERENCES

Abdullah, N., & Tan, Y. (2017). Profitability of commercial banks revisited: New evidence from oil and non-oil exporting countries in the MENA region. *Investment Management and Financial Innovations*, *14*(3), 62–73. doi:10.21511/imfi.14(3).2017.06

Abel, S., & Le Roux, P. (2016). Determinants of banking sector profitability in Zimbabwe. *International Journal of Economics and Financial Issues*, *6*(3).

Adelopo, I., Lloydking, R., & Tauringana, V. (2018). Determinants of bank profitability before, during, and after the financial crisis. *International Journal of Managerial Finance*, *14*(4), 378–398. doi:10.1108/IJMF-07-2017-0148

Aebi, V., Sabato, G., & Schmid, M. (2012). Risk management, corporate governance, and bank performance in the financial crisis. *Journal of Banking & Finance*, *36*(12), 3213–3226. doi:10.1016/j.jbankfin.2011.10.020

Albertazzi, U., & Gambacorta, L. (2009). Bank profitability and the business cycle. *Journal of Financial Stability*, *5*(4), 393–409. doi:10.1016/j.jfs.2008.10.002

Alhassan, A. L., Tetteh, M. L., & Brobbey, F. O. (2016). Market power, efficiency and bank profitability: Evidence from Ghana. *Economic Change and Restructuring*, *49*(1), 71–93. doi:10.1007/s10644-015-9174-6

Ali, M., & Puah, C. H. (2019). The internal determinants of bank profitability and stability. *Management Research Review*, *42*(1), 49–67. doi:10.1108/MRR-04-2017-0103

Amin, M. A. M., Sanusi, N. A., Kusairi, S., & Abdallah, Z. M. (2019). Inverse relationship of financial risk and performance in commercial banks in Tanzania. *Innovations*, *11*, 4–1.

Ammar, N., & Boughrara, A. (2019). The impact of revenue diversification on bank profitability and risk: Evidence from MENA banking industry. *Macroeconomics and Finance in Emerging Market Economies*, *12*(1), 36–70. doi:10.1080/17520843.2018.1535513

Bitar, M., Saad, W., & Benlemlih, M. (2016). Bank risk and performance in the MENA region: The importance of capital requirements. *Economic Systems*, *40*(3), 398–421. doi:10.1016/j.ecosys.2015.12.001

Boadi, I., Dana, L. P., Mertens, G., & Mensah, L. (2017). SMEs' financing and banks' profitability: A "good date" for banks in Ghana? *Journal of African Business*, *18*(2), 257–277. doi:10.1080/15228916.2017.1285847

Cao, Y. (2022). Bank earnings management and performance reporting of comprehensive income. *Journal of Accounting and Public Policy*, *41*(5), 106996. doi:10.1016/j.jaccpubpol.2022.106996

Chidozie, U. E., & Ayadi, F. S. (2017). Macroeconomy and banks' profitability in Nigeria. *African Research Review*, *11*(2), 121–137. doi:10.4314/afrrev.v11i2.10

Cohen, L. J., Cornett, M. M., Marcus, A. J., & Tehranian, H. (2014). Bank earnings management and tail risk during the financial crisis. *Journal of Money, Credit and Banking*, *46*(1), 171–197. doi:10.1111/jmcb.12101

Danisman, G. O., Demir, E., & Ozili, P. (2021). Loan loss provisioning of US banks: Economic policy uncertainty and discretionary behavior. *International Review of Economics & Finance*, *71*, 923–935. doi:10.1016/j.iref.2020.10.016

Dietrich, A., & Wanzenried, G. (2011). Determinants of bank profitability before and during the crisis: Evidence from Switzerland. *Journal of International Financial Markets, Institutions and Money*, *21*(3), 307–327. doi:10.1016/j.intfin.2010.11.002

Du Toit, E., & Cuba, Y. Z. (2018). Cost and profit efficiency of listed South African banks pre and post the financial crisis. *Research in International Business and Finance*, *45*, 435–445. doi:10.1016/j.ribaf.2017.07.175

Elkhayat, N., & ElBannan, M. A. (2018). State Divestitures and Bank Performance: Empirical Evidence from the Middle East and North Africa Region. *Asian Economic and Financial Review*, *8*(2), 145–171. doi:10.18488/journal.aefr.2018.82.145.171

Ertan, A. (2022). Real earnings management through syndicated lending. *Review of Accounting Studies*, *27*(4), 1157–1198. doi:10.1007/s11142-021-09607-7

Francis, M. E. (2013). Determinants of commercial bank profitability in Sub-Saharan Africa. *International Journal of Economics and Finance*, *5*(9), 134–147.

Garcia, M. T. M., & Trindade, M. J. (2019). Determinants of banks' profitability in Angola. *African Journal of Economic and Management Studies*, *10*(1), 116–128. doi:10.1108/AJEMS-06-2018-0161

Ghosh, S. (2016). Political transition and bank performance: How important was the Arab Spring? *Journal of Comparative Economics*, *44*(2), 372–382. doi:10.1016/j.jce.2015.02.001

Kapur, D., & Gualu, A. K. (2012). Financial performance and ownership structure of Ethiopian commercial banks. *Journal of Economics and International Finance*, *4*(1), 1–8.

Kodongo, O., Mokoaleli-Mokoteli, T., & Maina, L. N. (2015). Capital structure, profitability and firm value: Panel evidence of listed firms in Kenya. *African Finance Journal*, *17*(1), 1–20.

Kumbirai, M., & Webb, R. (2010). A financial ratio analysis of commercial bank performance in South Africa. *African Review of Economics and Finance*, *2*(1), 30–53.

Latridis, G. E., & Persakis, A. D. (2012). Bank profitability determinants under IFRSs. *International Journal of Economics and Accounting*, *3*(1), 77–99. doi:10.1504/IJEA.2012.045523

Le, T. D. (2020). The interrelationship among bank profitability, bank stability, and loan growth: Evidence from Vietnam. *Cogent Business & Management, 7*(1), 1840488. doi:10.1080/23311975.2020.1840488

Lee, T. H., & Chih, S. H. (2013). Does financial regulation affect the profit efficiency and risk of banks? Evidence from China's commercial banks. *The North American Journal of Economics and Finance, 26*, 705–724. doi:10.1016/j.najef.2013.05.005

Lelissa, T. B. (2014). The determinants of Ethiopian commercial banks performance. *European Journal of Business and Management, 6*(14), 52–62.

Mdoe, I. J., Omolo, J. O., & Wawire, N. H. (2018). Bank Competition in Kenya. *Journal of Industry, Competition and Trade*, 1–20.

Mireku, K., Sakyi, E. A., & Agana, J. A. (2018). Does Commercial Banks Presence Enhance Profitability in Ghana? *Global Business Review, 19*(6), 1449–1461. doi:10.1177/0972150918794969

Naceur, B. S., Goaied, M. (2010). The determinants of commercial bank interest margin and profitability: evidence from Tunisia. *Frontiers in Finance and Economics, 5*(1), 106-130.

Ozili, P. K. (2017). Bank profitability and capital regulation: Evidence from listed and non-listed banks in Africa. *Journal of African Business, 18*(2), 143–168. doi:10.1080/15228916.2017.1247329

Ozili, P. K. (2019). Bank income smoothing, institutions and corruption. *Research in International Business and Finance, 49*, 82–99. doi:10.1016/j.ribaf.2019.02.009

Ozili, P. K. (2021a). Banking sector earnings management using loan loss provisions in the Fintech era. *International Journal of Managerial Finance.*

Ozili, P. K. (2021b). Bank profitability determinants: Comparing the United States, Nigeria and South Africa. *International Journal of Banking and Finance, 16*(1), 55–78.

Ozili, P. K. (2022). Big 4 auditors, bank earnings management and financial crisis in Africa. *Journal of Financial Reporting and Accounting, 20*(2), 215–232. doi:10.1108/JFRA-10-2020-0306

Ozili, P. K., & Outa, E. (2017). Bank loan loss provisions research: A review. *Borsa Istanbul Review, 17*(3), 144–163. doi:10.1016/j.bir.2017.05.001

Ozili, P. K., & Uadiale, O. (2017). Ownership concentration and bank profitability. *Future Business Journal, 3*(2), 159–171. doi:10.1016/j.fbj.2017.07.001

Ozili & Opene. (2021). The role of banks in the circular economy. *World Journal of Science, Technology and Sustainable Development.*

Pasiouras, F., & Kosmidou, K. (2007). Factors influencing the profitability of domestic and foreign commercial banks in the European Union. *Research in International Business and Finance, 21*(2), 222–237. doi:10.1016/j.ribaf.2006.03.007

Peni, E., & Vähämaa, S. (2012). Did good corporate governance improve bank performance during the financial crisis? *Journal of Financial Services Research, 41*(1-2), 19–35. doi:10.1007/s10693-011-0108-9

Sarpong-Kumankoma, E., Abor, J., Aboagye, A. Q., & Amidu, M. (2018). Differences in bank profit persistence in Sub-Saharan Africa. *African Journal of Economic and Management Studies*, *9*(4), 512–522. doi:10.1108/AJEMS-03-2017-0037

Seemule, M., Sinha, N., & Ndlovu, T. (2017). Determinants of Commercial Banks' Profitability in Botswana: An Empirical Analysis. *IUP Journal of Bank Management*, *16*(2).

Sufian, F. (2009). Determinants of bank profitability in a developing economy: Empirical evidence from the China banking sector. *Journal of Asia-Pacific Business*, *10*(4), 281–307. doi:10.1080/10599230903340205

Sufian, F. (2011). Profitability of the Korean banking sector: Panel evidence on bank- specific and macroeconomic determinants. *Journal of Economics and Management*, *7*(1), 43–72.

Tarus, D. K., & Manyala, P. O. (2018). What determines bank interest rate spread? Evidence from Sub-Saharan Africa. *African Journal of Economic and Management Studies*, *9*(3), 335–348. doi:10.1108/AJEMS-05-2017-0094

Xu, M. T., Hu, K., & Das, M. U. S. (2019). *Bank profitability and financial stability*. International Monetary Fund. doi:10.5089/9781484390078.001

Yuanita, N. (2019). Competition and bank profitability. *Journal of Economic Structures*, *8*(1), 31. doi:10.1186/s40008-019-0164-0

Zaccheaus, O. D., & Ajuwon, O. S. (2019). Oil Price Dynamics and The Nigerian Banks Profitability. *Journal of Developing Areas*, *53*(2), 91–107. doi:10.1353/jda.2019.0023

APPENDIX

Discussion Questions

1. Identify three determinants of bank profitability.
2. Identify the determinant of bank profitability that is common in West African countries and in sub-Saharan African countries.
3. Identify the determinant of bank profitability that is common in East African countries and in Southern African countries.

Assessment questions

1. Which of the following is NOT a determinant of bank profitability in the chapter.
   (a) Bank risk
   (b) Cost efficiency
   (c) Cryptocurrency
   (d) Monetary policy
2. Which of the following is NOT a determinant of profitability in sub-Saharan Africa.
   (a) Inflation
   (b) Operating cost
   (c) Migration policy
   (d) Bank concentration
3. Which of the following is NOT a determinant of profitability in West African countries.
   (a) Inflation
   (b) Operating cost
   (c) Loan loss provision
   (d) Bank concentration
4. Which of the following is a suggested area for future research
   (a) Bitcoin
   (b) Fintech revolution
   (c) Uncertainty
   (d) Pandemic

Answers to Discussion Questions:

1. leverage, bank risk, bank ownership type, financial crisis, bank liquidity, bank size, cost efficiency, market power, inflation, monetary policy, real interest rates, exchange rates, capital regulation, cost efficiency, nonperforming loans, capital regulation, operating cost and bank concentration.
2. Inflation
3. Bank risk

Assessment Questions:

1. C.
2. C.
3. C.
4. B.

Section 2

Financial Inclusion and Its Outcomes

Chapter 5
Catalyzing Financial Stability and Unveiling the Influence of Financial Inclusion in Pakistan's Islamic Banking Sector

Ejaz Aslam
Minhaj University, Pakistan

Anam Iqbal
Minhaj University, Lahore, Pakistan

Muhammad Ishfaq
Minhaj University, Lahore, Pakistan

ABSTRACT

The objective of this study is to analyse the financial inclusion impacts on the financial stability of Islamic banks in Pakistan. This study used balance panel data of 15 full-fledged Islamic banks and Islamic windows from 2011 to 2021 by employing the feasible generalized least squares (FGLS) estimation technique to count the heteroskedasticity and potential endogeneity issue. The results of the present study lend support to the notion that financial inclusion as assessed by bank branches, financing, and availability of ATMs plays a substantial role in stimulating the financial stability of Islamic banks.

INTRODUCTION

Financial inclusion, often regarded as a cornerstone of economic development, has garnered significant attention in the realm of banking and finance (Bhardwaj, Hedrick-Wong, & Howard, 2018). This idea captures the notion of providing businesses and individuals in all societal strata with access to basic financial services and opportunities, with a special emphasis on those who have historically been left out of the formal financial system (Neaime & Gaysset, 2018). Its effects go well beyond simple ac-

DOI: 10.4018/979-8-3693-1475-3.ch005

cessibility, as financial inclusion has become a potent force that has the ability to drastically alter the environment surrounding the financial stability of Islamic banks and the financial industry as a whole (Banna et al., 2022).

One of the primary tenets of the contemporary financial landscape, financial inclusion has a significant impact on the dynamics of economic development, social equity, and general well-being (Banna & Alam, 2020). The stability of banking systems is inextricably linked to the importance of financial inclusion, which is commonly understood as the availability and accessibility of basic financial services to all facets of society (Aslam, Ur-Rehman, & Iqbal, 2021). This mutually beneficial relationship is a crucial aspect of current financial research and policy discussions.

The development of finance is contingent upon financial inclusion. On the other hand, reduced disparities and destitution are a result of increased accessibility to financial amenities and products (Okonkwo & Nwanna, 2021). Researchers and policymakers including both developed and developing countries have emphasized the importance of financial inclusion (Eid, Al Houl, Alqudah, & Almomani, 2023). Thus, easier availability of formal financial services for households and corporations helps to advance financial conditions and reduce hardship in emerging as well as developed nations (Pham & Doan, 2020).

Financial stability can be attained when a nation's financial system operates smoothly and effectively. This is because crises in the system are less likely to occur when financial risks are properly evaluated and controlled. Second, economies everywhere strive to improve economic inclusion as a component of their plans to expand the economic and financial industries by granting access to financial services (Khan & Aslam, 2018; Vo, Nguyen, & Thi-Hong Van, 2021). Therefore, for all adults in the community to have access to reasonably priced goods and services that meet their needs, they must all be financially included, eventually stimulating financial stability. (Malik et al., 2022).

Pakistan is a developing country, there is a significant need for financial inclusion. According to State Bank of Pakistan[1] around186 cellular mobile connection in Pakistan, only 11.3 million, 16.44 percent of Pakistanis use mobile money, either from their own or other people's accounts. As a result, financial inclusion can have a significant impact on the evolution of the formal financial system since it will include a wide range of the public in having a large amount of money in the banking system, making money available for productive use, and eventually leading to positive changes in the development of the economy (Ahmad et al., 2021). Thus, stronger financial institutions are in a better position to offer products and services related to finance that greatly broaden financial inclusion. Although banks are essential for tying the financial system to the actual economy, financial inclusion makes monetary policy more effective at containing inflation by affecting a larger segment of the economy (Jungo, Madaleno, & Botelho, 2022). There is evidence that financial stability contributes to a nation's ability to develop sustainably (Musau, Salome & Munthe, 2018). On the other perspective, financial instability might significantly hinder the growth of developing countries. The country's growth process is significantly linked to its financial stability (Siddik & Kabiraj, 2018).

There are limited studies that are focused on the relationship between financial inclusion and financial stability of banks. According to certain research, financial inclusion is positively and significantly related with financial stability (Ahamed & Mallick 2019; Dienillah & Anggraeni, 2016) some found negative (Neaime & Gaysset 2018) and some found mixed results (Ratnawati, 2020). These authors argued that initiatives to increase financial inclusion ensure resource efficiency and strengthen the financial stability of the nation that has already put the improvement in financial infrastructure and professional regulation in place. Therefore, the present study establishes the link between financial inclusion and its impact on the financial stability of Islamic banks in Pakistan.

2. LITERATURE REVIEW

2.1 Financial Inclusion

Financial inclusion is the planned and implemented actions to ensure that financial services are readily available to everyone in the nation, particularly the needy and the poor (Ratnawati, 2020). According to Mehry et al. (2021), financial inclusion makes the formal financial system's operations available, usable, and accessible for everybody. Allam (2020) stated that the practice of granting individuals and businesses access to a broad range of reasonably priced, top-notch financial products and services is known as financial inclusion. Those services should be provided responsibly, sustainably, and with strong supervision. From a macroeconomic viewpoint, increased financial inclusion boosts savings, which results in better allocation of resources and more effective investment. Secondly, It fosters the development of small and medium-sized businesses (SMEs), which is beneficial for both income and employment status. The prior study consensus that bank branches, deposits, financing, ATMs and digital accounts are the main components of the financial inclusion (Bhatti et al., 2023; Jain et al., 2023; Ratnawati, 2020).

2.1.1 Banks Branches

Shihadehs et al. (2018) stated that large branch networks increase client engagement, outreach, and accessibility. According to empirical research, there is a positive relationship between Islamic banking financial stability metrics and bank branch expansion (Vo et al., 2020). An established bank branch network helps to mobilize deposits and makes the bank more accessible to customers, which draws in a wide variety of depositors and creates a more stable and dependable funding base. As a buffer against liquidity risks, this expanded deposit base in turn strengthens Islamic banks' financial stability.

Yangdol & Sarma (2019) and Malik et al. (2022) highlighted that increasing financial access through branches plays an important role in increasing the earnings of the people and assures the availability of services of financial institutions that assist people in carrying out economic activity. Several studies show the positive and significant relationship of bank branches with financial stability (Le et al., 2019a&b; Khan (2011). However, some researchers have different opinions about the impact of bank branches on financial stability. For instance, Ahamed & Mallick, (2019) stated that more branch networks may result in a lowering of lending standards which shows the negative consequence of the subprime mortgage crisis in the United States. In the light of the above discussion, the following hypothesis is formulated.

H_1: Bank branches enhance the financial stability of Islamic banks.

2.1.2 Bank Deposits

A major factor in promoting the financial stability of banks is bank deposits. For banks, deposits are a vital source of funding since they offer a reliable and affordable funding source (Ratnawati, 2020). A bank's ability to fulfil its short-term obligations is improved by this stability, which adds to its overall financial resilience. Deposit levels and measures of financial stability, like capital adequacy ratios and liquidity positions, have been shown to positively correlate empirically (Aslam, Ashraf, & Iqbal, 2022; Aslam, Azam, & Iqbal, 2020). The study of Han and Melecky (2013) finds that greater access to and use of bank deposits could dramatically cut down on emergency withdrawals boost the amount of steady funding available to banks and lessen the volatility of all bank deposits during recessions with the data set of 95 countries. In order to improve financial stability, scholarly literature highlights the significance of diversifying deposit sources (Kamal et al., 2021). Banks that draw in a diverse range of depositors are better equipped to weather shocks in particular market segments, which helps them maintain a stronger financial position. In the light of the above discussion, the following hypothesis is formulated.

H_2: Bank deposits enhance the financial stability of Pakistan.

2.1.3 Bank Investments

Investments are essential elements for promoting a bank's financial stability. A large portion of banking operations involve investments, and prudent management of these assets is essential to overall financial stability. Numerous empirical studies confirm that prudent investments—especially those that follow Sharia principles—are essential for promoting financial stability (Ahmad, Amjad, Aslam, 2018; Ratnawati, 2020). The stability of banks is ensured by a strong financial position, which is a result of diverse sources of revenue, sound investment practices, efficient risk management, and supportive regulatory frameworks. The study by Ratnawati (2020) stated that by enhancing the process of acting as a middleman between savings and investments, financial inclusion can help Asian nations achieve financial stability. Moreover, Jungo et al. (2022) discovered that financial inclusion enhanced financial stability in Latin American and Caribbean (LAC) and Sub-Saharan African (SSA) nations and found that equal opportunities for the country to obtain financing and increased financial inclusion is an appropriate factor in achieving financial stability for banks. In light of the above discussion following hypothesis is formulated.

H_3: Bank financing enhances the financial stability of Pakistan.

2.1.4. Automated Teller Machines (ATMs)

Automated Teller Machines (ATMs) indirectly contribute to the financial stability of banks by improving the availability and effectiveness of banking services. ATMs make banking services more accessible and facilitate a range of convenient transactions for users (Ratnawati, 2020). This accessibility helps banks maintain a steady and devoted client base by improving client loyalty and retention. ATMs give users a convenient way to manage their money by enabling both deposits and withdrawals. Routine transactions at ATMs can have a positive effect on banks' liquidity, which is a vital aspect of financial stability (Banna, Hassan, & Alam, 2020). Several studies find high levels of ATMs in banks stimulate the financial stability of banks (Eid, Al Houl, Alqudah, & Almomani, 2023: Ratnawati, 2020). In light of the above discussion, the following hypothesis is formulated.

H_4: Bank's ATMs enhance the financial stability of banks.

3 EMPIRICAL METHODOLOGY

3.1 Data and Sample

The study sample consisted of five full-fledged Islamic banks and ten Islamic banking branches of conventional banks. The data is collected from annual statements and banks' official websites that are openly available on bank websites and the State Bank of Pakistan (SBP) from 2011 to 2021. The total sample size consisted of 165 observations. The study sample will be selected only those banks that are alive and provide bank branches, bank financing, bank deposit, and ATM information on the provider. Similar data have been used for this kind of research in a number of earlier studies (Ahmad et al., 2019; Banna, et al., 2022; Ratnawati, 2020; Tahir et al., 2020).

3.2 Data Variables

Table 1 presents the details of the variables that are used in this study. There are several proxies used in the literature to assess the financial sustainability of banks. We employ two different metrics for banking stability that are consistent with financial inclusion to get around the issue of proxy-specific bias. ZEQTA and ZCAR are our proxies for Islamic banks' financial stability (Bhatti et al., 2023; Ratnawati, 2020). Financial inclusion consists of four variables bank branches, bank financing, bank deposits, and ATMs. Besides this, capital structure is used as a moderating variable and government expenditures, trade openness, and GDP per capita are control variables. Similar types of variables have been used for this kind of research in a number of earlier studies (Banna & Alam, 2020; Eid, Al Houl, Alqudah, & Almomani, 2023).

Table 1. Measurement of the variables

Sr.	Variables	Code	Measurement
Dependent variables			
I.	Financial Stability	ZEQTA	Proportion of ROA plus the equity asset ratio which is divided by the standard ROA
II.	Financial Stability	ZCAR	Proportion of ROA plus the capital asset ratio which is divided by the standard ROA
Independent variables			
I.	Bank Branches	BB	Total number of bank branches
II.	Bank Deposits	BD	Total bank deposits
III.	Bank Financing	BF	Total bank financing
IV.	Bank ATMs	ATM	Total number of bank ATMs
Control Variables			
I.	GDP Per Capita	GDPPC	The GDP of a country divided into a number of populations
II.	Government Expenditures	GEXP	Total government expenditure in fiscal year
III.	Trade Openness	TO	Imports, exports and GDP

Note: Author self-created

3.3 Statistical Model

To analyse the objective of this study Feasible Generalized Least Squares (FGLS) method employed because it is a potent statistical technique that enhances the precision of regression analysis in cases where data deviate from the assumptions of classical linear regression, such as heteroscedasticity or correlated errors (Greene, 2003; Weeks, 2002). FGLS is especially helpful as it offers more accurate and reliable parameter estimates than Ordinary Least Squares (OLS). FGLS increases the accuracy of confidence intervals and hypothesis testing by assigning optimal weights based on variances and covariances. It is a strong tool that provides a more precise examination of data with these features and increases the reliability of results when classical assumptions are broken. The following is the equation for the panel data model that assesses how financial inclusion affects financial performance and sustainability:

$$ZEQTA_{it} = \alpha_0 + \beta_1 \sum_3^k (FIN)_{it} + \beta_2 \sum_3^p (CONT)_{it} + \varepsilon_{it} \tag{1}$$

$$ZCAR_{it} = \alpha_0 + \beta_1 \sum_3^k (FIN)_{it} + \beta_2 \sum_3^p (CONT)_{it} + \varepsilon_{it} \tag{2}$$

In the above equations, i is for the bank and t for the time respectively. ZEATA and ZCAR present the financial stability of banks. FIN presents financial inclusion, and it is measured with branches of banks (BB), the deposits of the banks (DB), bank financings (BF), and bank ATMs. CONT presents a control variable that is measured with government expenditure (GEXP), trade openness (TO), and GDP Per capita (GDPPC). β_0 is the alpha / Intercept Parameter, and ε is the error term/disturbance term.

4. RESULTS AND DISCUSSION

4.1 Summary Statistics

Table 2 presents the descriptive statistics for the full sample, which includes 15 observations each year and 161 observations for the pooled sample, which are summarized during the years 2011 to 2021. The value of the bank Z-score is 6.195973, which is lower than the findings of Haneef et al. (2020) and Malik et al., (2022) for Asian nations as well as Siddik and Kabiraj (2018) for cross-country study. Moreover, the mean value of ZCAR is 0.7213 and the minimum and maximum values are -29 and 25, respectively.

The mean value of bank branches is 159.7785, higher than the finding for Asian countries. The maximum value is 815 and the minimum value is 3.33890 with a standard deviation of 187.05. The mean of the bank deposits is 71.56667, which is higher than the finding of Jungo et al. (2022) for developing countries and the standard deviation is 43.3333 while the minimum is 1.38629 and the maximum is 146. The mean value of bank financing is 70.6 with a standard deviation of bank financing is 43.2796 and a maximum value is 145. Moreover, the mean value of ATMs is 39 and the maximum and minimum values are 125 and 5, respectively. As a moderator variable, the mean value of capital structure is 0.875 with a max/min value is 0.997162 and -1.98271 with a standard deviation is 0.205.

As per the control variable, the mean value of government expenditure is 26.36016 which is greater than the finding of Ahmad et al. (2021) for China, the maximum value is 26.579, the minimum value is 26.136 with standard deviation is 0.1361. The mean value of Gross domestic product per capita (GDPPC) is 8.392787 which is less than the finding of Siddik & Kabiraj (2018) for cross countries based on 217 countries analysis, while, the maximum value is 8.49 minimum value is 8.292 and the standard deviation is 0.073. The mean value of trade openness is 71.566 which is less than the finding of Manu et al. (2011) for Africa, the maxim value is 146 and the minimum value is 1 while the standard deviation is 43.33395.

Table 2. Descriptive statistics

Variable	Obs	Mean	Std. Dev.	Min	Max
ZEQTA	165	6.195973	8.404366	1.22055	47.9672
ZCAR	165	0.72321	2.123	-29	25
Bank Branches	165	159.7785	187.05	3.38908	815
Bank Deposits	165	71.56667	43.33395	1.38629	146
165	165	70.6	43.27964	1	145
ATMs	165	39	42	5	125
Financial Leverage	165	0.8752537	0.2052094	-1.9827	0.99072
Govt. Exp.	165	26.36016	0.1361308	26.1362	26.5797
GDPPC	165	8.392787	0.0739591	8.29244	8.49625
Trade Openness	165	71.56667	43.33395	1	146

Note: Author self-created

4.3 Correlation and Multicollinearity

Table 3 shows the correlation matrix which presents the pattern of association between a variable that are bank branches (BB), Bank deposits (BD), bank financing (BF), financial leverage (FL), government expenditures (Gexp), GDP per capita (GDPPC) and Trade openness (TOP). The highest correlation is found between bank branches and bank deposits which is 0.6776 and the lowest association between bank branches and financial leverage is 0.2245. There is no Multicollinearity issue in explanatory variables because all coefficients are lower than 0.80 as suggested by (Gujarati & Porter, 2009). The association between bank deposits and trade openness is high which is 0.7776 lowest association between bank deposits and financial leverage is 0.421.

Table 3. Correlation matrix and multicollinearity

Variables	BB	BD	BF	ATMs	GEXP	GDPP	TOP
Bank Branches	1						
Bank Deposits	0.6776	1					
Bank Financing	0.6755	0.9238	1				
ATMs	0.2697	0.274	0.3468	1			
Govt. Exp.	0.2534	0.4326	0.4325	0.2534	1		
GDPPC	0.3131	0.5294	0.5292	0.4326	0.8482	1	
Trade Openness	0.6716	0.7776	0.7433	0.4325	0.4122	0.5144	1

Note: Author self-created

4.5 Results and Discussion

In Table 4, FGLS estimation shows that bank branches have a negative and significant relationship with the financial stability of the bank is negative and in terms of ZEQTA, but it has a positive and significant relationship with ZCAR. Thus, H1 is accepted. These results are in line with the findings of Ratnawati (2020) who stated that bank branches play a significant role in the performance of the banking sector. Thus, our findings suggested that branch networks are essential to Islamic banks because they improve customer engagement, outreach, and accessibility—all of which ultimately support the banks' financial stability.

The bank deposits have a negative and significant association with both financial stability indicator of Islamic bank. Therefore H2 hypothesis is rejected. These results support the findings of Ratnawati (2020), who stated that enhancing the role of intermediaries between savings and investments, and financial inclusion can promote the financial stability of Islamic banks. This negative relationship indicates that Islamic banks do not fully utilize their deposits to generate profit that's the reason it harms the financial stability of Islamic banks. The present findings are also in line with the findings of (Cull et al. (2012; Han and Melecky, 2013; Pham and Doan, 2020).

Bank financing has a positive and significant relationship with the financial stability of Islamic banks. Therefore, H3 accepts that which indicates that bank financing enhances financial stability. These results support the findings of Adzimatinur & Manalu (2021) who state that the amount of financing is closely related to the real sector, so it directly affects financial stability. When a bank makes financing in multiple sectors of the economy it makes a profit, if one sector faces a loss then the other side covers the bank's loss. If a bank invests fully in only one sector, in case of loss all investments face loss. Therefore, financial institutions, especially banks invest in multiple sectors so that in case of loss recovery may be possible. Lastly, the bank ATMs have a positive but insignificant relationship with the financial stability of Islamic banks. Thus, H4 is rejected. The present results are in accordance with the findings of (Ratnawati, 2020) in Asian countries. The present results imply that Automated Teller Machines (ATMs) indirectly contribute to the financial stability of Islamic banks by improving the accessibility and efficiency of banking services.

Table 4. FGLS estimation financial inclusion impact on financial stability

Variables	ZEQTA	ZCAR
Bank Branches	-0.0101707	0.00568**
Bank Deposits	-0.579025***	-0.58443***
Bank Financing	0.123588**	0.076079**
Bank ATMs	1.34381**	5.838121**
Govt. Expenditures	1.06573	3.114411*
GDPPC	38.44336*	3.332374
Trade Openness	0.5761327***	0.6283226***
cons	-326.2192**	-93.64078**
No. of observation	165	165
F test (P- value)	0	0
R-square	0.4729	0.57129

Note: *, **, ***denote statistical significance at the 0.1, 0.05, and 0.001.

As per control variables, Government spending has a negative and significant link with financial stability. Our results are supported by the results of Vo, Nguyen, & Van (2021) state that an increase in government expenditures decreases financial stability. This might be due to the rising government expenses, the government imposes new taxes and duties to meet its expenses, and as a result, investment and financing activities start to move down. In a particular scenario, financial institutions face financial instability.

GDPPC positive and significant relationship with bank financial stability. When GDP per capita increases financial stability increase. The research backs up the argument made by (Ur Rehman, Aslam, & Iqbal, 2021) that a nation's economic strength is determined by its gross domestic product per capita (GDPPC). This result presents that a higher ratio of GDPPC increase the purchasing quality of individual and it may lead to improved credit quality among borrowers. Trade openness has a negative and significant relation with the financial stability of Islamic banks. The result is also consistent with the finding of Vo, Nguyen, & Van, (2021) who stated that trade openness has detrimental effects on financial stability.

5. CONCLUSION

Despite the dearth of empirical on financial inclusion, financial stability, and their causality, this research empirically investigated whether financial inclusion enhances the financial stability of Islamic banks. This research used panel data from 15 Islamic banks and Islamic windows from 2011 to 2021 in Pakistan. The Feasible Generalized Least Squares (FGLS) estimation technique was used to address the heteroscedasticity or correlated errors that arise in the classical linear regression.

Our study's findings confirm to the notion that financial inclusion as assessed by bank branches, financing, and ATMs plays a major role in stimulating financial stability in Islamic banks measured as ZEQTA and ZCAR. Besides this, the total number of deposits has a lesser effect on the financial stability of Islamic banks. Moreover, government expenditure and trade openness both have negative effects, as well. On the other side, GDPPC has a favourable effect on the financial stability of Islamic banks.

The study's findings will be beneficial for policymakers, regulators and top management of banks to give top priority to programs that expand banking services' accessibility, stimulate deposit mobilization, and make financing options easier for the Islamic banking industry. This could entail creating innovative deposit products, encouraging the opening of bank branches in underdeveloped regions, and making sure that the regulatory atmosphere is favourable for Islamic financing. To further enable people and businesses to make wise financial decisions, efforts should be focused on improving financial literacy. Regulatory bodies can enhance the resilience as well as the stability of Islamic banks and promote a more beneficial and resilient financial system for the Islamic banking industry.

This study is limited to addressing financial stability only in Islamic banks. The second limitation is related to the period of research which is from 2011 to 2021. The third limitation is about variables as this study uses quantitative variables and ignores behavioral variables like attitude and subjective norms etc. Thus, future studies could explore this study in the cross country and can compare it with the conventional banks with the help of the latest and vast data set. Moreover, future studies could take into account the household sector's incorporation into the financial system to raise living standards and poverty eradication. Similarly, use the information on other financial stability indicators, such as stock market volatility, increases or declines in bank deposits, financial crises, etc., when it becomes available to observe the overall impact of financial inclusion on financial stability.

REFERENCES

Adzimatinur, F., & Manalu, V. G. (2021). The Effect of Islamic Financial Inclusion on Economic Growth: A Case Study of Islamic Banking in Indonesia. Budapest International Research and Critics Institute (BIRCI-Journal): Humanities and Social Sciences, 4(1), 976–985. doi:10.33258/birci.v4i1.1699

Ahamed, M. M., & Mallick, S. K. (2019). *Is financial inclusion good for bank stability? International Evidence, 157*, 403–427.

Ahmad, M., Majeed, A., Khan, M. A., Sohaib, M., & Shehzad, K. (2021). Digital financial inclusion and economic growth: Provincial data analysis of China. *China Economic Journal*, *14*(3), 291–310. doi:10.1080/17538963.2021.1882064

Ahmad, S. (2019). The Role of Musharakah in the Economic Development of Tehsil Dargai, District Malakand, Khyber Pakhtunkhwa, Pakistan. *Islamic Banking and Finance Review*, *6*(1), 80–97. doi:10.32350/ibfr.2019.06.05

Allam, A. (2020). *Doctor of philosophy Three Essays on Financial Inclusion Allam*. Academic Press.

Aslam, E., Ashraf, M. S., & Iqbal, A. (2022). Impact of corporate image on customer loyalty of Islamic banks: The role of religiosity, collectivism, sight cues and CSR. *Journal of Islamic Marketing*, *14*(5), 1310–1324. doi:10.1108/JIMA-09-2021-0314

Aslam, E., Ur-Rehman, A., & Iqbal, A. (2021). Does Corporate Governance Matter for Asset Quality of Islamic Banks? *Bulletin of Monetary Economics and Banking*, *24*(2), 221–236. doi:10.21098/bemp.v24i2.1344

Babajide, A. A., Adegboye, F. B., & Omankhanlen, A. E. (2015). Financial inclusion and economic growth in Nigeria. *International Journal of Economics and Financial Issues*, *5*(3), 629–637. doi:10.38157/business-perspective-review.v2i2.149

Banna, H., & Alam, M. R. (2020). Islamic banking efficiency and inclusive sustainable growth: The role of financial inclusion. *Journal of Islamic Monetary Economics and Finance*, *6*(1), 213–242. doi:10.21098/jimf.v6i1.1089

Banna, H., Alam, M. R., Ahmad, R., & Sari, N. M. (2022). Does financial inclusion drive the Islamic banking efficiency? A post-financial crisis analysis. *The Singapore Economic Review*, *67*(01), 135–160. doi:10.1142/S0217590819420050

Banna, H., Hassan, M. K., & Alam, M. R. (2020). Digital financial inclusion, Islamic banking stability and sustainable economic growth. *Islamic Perspective for Sustainable Financial System*, *20*(1), 131–152.

Bhardwaj, M., Hedrick-Wong, Y., & Howard, T. (2018). *Financial inclusion for Asia's unbanked*. World Bank Blogs.

Bhatti, F. A., & Aslam, E., ur Rehman, A., Ashraf, S., Aslam, M., & Shabbir, M. S. (2023). Does intellectual capital efficiency spur the financial performance of banks? A comparative analysis of Islamic and conventional banks in Pakistan. *Al-Qantara*, *9*(3), 55–67.

Dienillah, A. A., & Anggraeni, L. (2016). Impact of Financial Inclusion on Financial System Stability in Asia. *Inclusion on Financial System Stability in Asia. Bulletin of Monetary Economics and Banking.*

Eid, Q. M. A., Al Houl, M. A. A., Alqudah, M. T. S., & Almomani, M. A.-A. (2023). The Role of Financial Inclusion in the Stability of Islamic Banks. *International Journal of Professional Business Review: Int. J. Prof. Bus. Rev.*, *8*(4), 7–19.

Greene, W. H. (2003). *Econometric analysis*. Pearson Education India.

Haneef, M., Manu, L. P., Adjasi, C. K. D., Abor, J., Harvey, S. K., Dienillah, A. A., ... Doan, T. P. L. (2020). The impact of financial inclusion on financial stability in Asian countries. *Journal of Asian Finance. Economics and Business*, *7*(6), 47–59. doi:10.13106/jafeb.2020.vol7.no6.047

Jain, V., Ramos-Meza, C. S., Aslam, E., Chawla, C., Nawab, T., Shabbir, M. S., & Bansal, A. (2023). Do energy resources matter for growth level? The dynamic effects of different strategies of renewable energy, carbon emissions on sustainable economic growth. *Clean Technologies and Environmental Policy*, *25*(3), 771–777. doi:10.1007/s10098-022-02432-9

Jungo, J., Madaleno, M., & Botelho, A. (2022). The Effect of Financial Inclusion and Competitiveness on Financial Stability: Why Financial Regulation Matters in Developing Countries? *Journal of Risk and Financial Management*, *15*(3), 122. Advance online publication. doi:10.3390/jrfm15030122

Kamal, A., Khan, M. M. S., Kazmi, U. E. R., Anis, W., Hussain, T., & Sualeh, M. (2021). Impact of Financial Inclusion and Corporate Social Responsibility on Islamic Banks Financial stability with the Moderating Role of Corporate Governance. *Indian Journal of Economics and Business*, *20*(1), 1–13.

Khan, S. A., & Aslam, E. (2018). Partnership Based Microfinance in Islamic Banks: Need, Application and Commandments in Modern Age. *Journal of Islamic Thought and Civilization*, *8*(1), 192–208. doi:10.32350/jitc.81.13

Malik, A. H., Md Isa, A. H., Jais, M., Ur Rehman, A., & Ali Khan, M. (2022). Financial stability of Asian Nations: Governance quality and financial inclusion. *Borsa Istanbul Review*, *22*(2), 377–387. doi:10.1016/j.bir.2021.05.005

Manu, L. P., Adjasi, C. K. D., Abor, J., & Harvey, S. K. (2011). Financial stability and economic growth: A cross-country study. *International Journal of Financial Services Management*, *5*(2), 121. doi:10.1504/IJFSM.2011.041920

Mehry, E.-B., Ashraf, S., & Marwa, E. (2021). The Impact of Financial Inclusion on Unemployment Rate in Developing Countries. *International Journal of Economics and Financial Issues*, *11*(1), 79–93. doi:10.32479/ijefi.10871

Musau, S., Muathe, S., & Mwangi, L. (2018). Financial inclusion, bank competitiveness and credit risk of commercial banks in Kenya. *International Journal of Financial Research*, *9*(1), 203–218. doi:10.5430/ijfr.v9n1p203

Neaime, S., & Gaysset, I. (2018). Financial inclusion and stability in MENA: Evidence from poverty and inequality. *Finance Research Letters*, *24*, 199–220. doi:10.1016/j.frl.2017.09.007

Okonkwo, J., & Nwanna, I. (2021). Financial Inclusion and Economic Growth in Nigeria: An Empirical Study. *International Journal of Research and Innovation in Social Science*, *05*(01), 323–330. doi:10.47772/IJRISS.2021.5113

Pham, M. H., & Doan, T. P. L. (2020). The impact of financial inclusion on financial stability in Asian countries. *Journal of Asian Finance. Economics and Business*, *7*(6), 47–59. doi:10.13106/jafeb.2020.vol7.no6.047

Ratnawati, K. (2020). The Impact of Financial Inclusion on Economic Growth, Poverty, Income Inequality, and Financial Stability in Asia. *The Journal of Asian Finance. Economics and Business*, *7*(10), 73–85. doi:10.13106/jafeb.2020.vol7.no10.073

Rehman, A., Aslam, E., & Iqbal, A. (2022). Intellectual capital efficiency and bank performance: Evidence from islamic banks. *Borsa Istanbul Review*, *22*(1), 113–121. doi:10.1016/j.bir.2021.02.004

Shihadeh, F. H., Hannon, A. M. T., Guan, J., Ul Haq, I., Wang, X., & Haq, I. ul, & Wang, X. (2018). Does Financial Inclusion Improve the Banks' Performance? Evidence from Jordan. In J. W. Kensinger (Ed.), Global Tensions in Financial Markets (pp. 117–138). Emerald Publishing Limited. doi:10.1108/S0196-382120170000034005

Siddik, M. N. A., & Kabiraj, S. (2018). Does financial inclusion induce financial stability? Evidence from cross-country analysis. *Australasian Accounting. Business and Finance Journal*, *12*(1), 33–46. doi:10.14453/aabfj.v12i1.3

Tahir, H., Hussain, S., Iqbal, A., Aslam, E., & Masri, R. (2020). Determinants of Return on Assets of Non-Financial Firm of Malaysia. *International Transaction Journal of Engineering, Management, &. Applied Sciences & Technologly*, *11*(11), 1–11.

Ur Rehman, A., Aslam, E., & Iqbal, A. (2021). Factors influencing the intention to give Zakat on employment income: Evidence from the Kingdom of Saudi Arabia. *Islamic Economic Studies*, *29*(1), 33–49. doi:10.1108/IES-05-2020-0017

Van, L. T.-H. H., Vo, A. T., Nguyen, N. T., & Vo, D. H. (2021). Financial Inclusion and Economic Growth: An International Evidence. *Emerging Markets Finance & Trade*, *57*(1), 239–263. doi:10.1080/1540496X.2019.1697672

Vo, D. H., Nguyen, N. T., & Thi-Hong Van, L. (2021). Financial inclusion and stability in the Asian region using bank-level data. *Borsa Istanbul Review*, *21*(1), 36–43. doi:10.1016/j.bir.2020.06.003

Weeks, M. (2002). *Introductory econometrics: a modern approach*. JSTOR.

Yangdol, R., & Sarma, M. (2019). Demand-side factors for financial inclusion: A cross-country empirical analysis. *International Studies*, *56*(2–3), 163–185. doi:10.1177/0020881719849246

Zhao, M., Yang, R., & Li, Y. (2020). Financial leverage, economic growth and environmental degradation: Evidence from 30 provinces in China. *International Journal of Environmental Research and Public Health*, *17*(3), 831. Advance online publication. doi:10.3390/ijerph17030831 PMID:32013117

ENDNOTE

1 https://www.sbp.org.pk/ecodata/index2.asp

APPENDIX

MCQ Questions (Multiple Choice Questions)

1. According to the study, which of the following aspects of financial inclusion has the most significant positive impact on the financial stability of Islamic banks in Pakistan? a) Total number of bank deposits b) Total number of bank branches c) Availability of ATMs d) All of the above

2. What statistical technique was used in this study to address potential issues in classical linear regression? a) Ordinary Least Squares (OLS) b) Feasible Generalized Least Squares (FGLS) c) Chi-Square Test d) Correlation Analysis

3. The study found a negative and significant relationship between _______ and the financial stability of Islamic banks. a) Government expenditure b) Trade openness c) GDP per capita d) Bank financing

4. Which of the following is NOT a limitation of the study as identified by the authors? a) Focus on Islamic banks only in Pakistan b) Limited data timeframe (2011-2021) c) Use of only quantitative variables d) Large sample size

5. Based on the study's findings, which action would likely be most beneficial for improving the financial stability of Islamic banks? a) Increasing the number of bank branches in developed areas b) Encouraging the creation of innovative deposit products c) Reducing government spending d) Limiting trade openness

6. The study mentions ________ as a possible reason why deposit levels have a negative impact on financial stability. a) Ineffective deposit mobilization strategies b) High number of non-performing loans c) Low-interest rates offered on deposits d) All of the above

7.3 What is the dependent variable in the regression model used in this study? a) Financial inclusion b) Bank profitability c) Financial stability of Islamic banks d) Government expenditure

8. Which of the following best describes the relationship between GDP per capita and financial stability according to the study? a) Positive and significant b) Negative and significant c) Positive and insignificant d) Negative and insignificant

9. The concept of "proxy" is mentioned in the study. What does it refer to in this context? a) A direct measure of a variable b) An indirect measure used to represent another variable c) A statistical test for significance d) A control variable used to account for external factors

10. The authors suggest that future research could explore including data on ________ to observe the overall impact of financial inclusion. a) Customer satisfaction with banking services b) Stock market performance c) Changes in bank regulations d) All of the above

Short Answer Questions

Briefly explain the concept of financial inclusion and its importance in the context of Islamic banking.

What are the main findings of the study regarding the relationship between financial inclusion and financial stability of Islamic banks?

Describe two limitations of the study as identified by the authors.

How does the study suggest that policymakers and regulators can promote financial stability in the Islamic banking sector?

What are some potential future research directions based on the insights from this study?

Discussion Questions

Discuss the potential challenges and opportunities associated with expanding access to banking services in developing countries.

How can Islamic banking principles be leveraged to promote financial inclusion and economic development?

Compare and contrast the potential effects of financial inclusion on conventional banks versus Islamic banks.

The study focuses on financial stability as a key outcome. Discuss other potential benefits or drawbacks of promoting financial inclusion in Pakistan.

How might technological advancements, such as mobile banking, influence the landscape of financial inclusion in the future?

Correct answers for Multiple Choice Questions.

1. b)
2. b)
3. a)
4. d)
5. b)
6. a)
7. c)
8. a)
9. b) **An indirect measure used to represent another variable** (Financial inclusion is likely measured through proxies like number of branches or ATMs)
10. d)

Chapter 6
Financial Inclusion and Sustainability:
A Contemporary and Future Perspective From Bibliometric Analysis

Fiaz Ahmad
https://orcid.org/0000-0002-6368-1881
Department of Economics and Finance, Sunway Business School, Sunway University, Malaysia

Calvin W. H. Cheong
Department of Economics and Finance, Sunway Business School, Sunway University, Malaysia

Rana Tanveer Hussain
School of Business and Management Science, Minhaj University Lahore, Pakistan

Ahmad Salman
Faculty of Hospitality and Tourism, Prince of Songkla University, Phuket Campus, Thailand

Khalil Hussain
https://orcid.org/0000-0003-0646-0190
School of Hospitality and Service Management, Sunway University, Malaysia

Muhammad Khalid Shahid
https://orcid.org/0000-0001-8593-9620
Department of Economics, Faculty of Accountancy and Management, Universiti Tunku Abdul Rahman, Malaysia & Institute of Business Administration, University of the Punjab, Lahore Pakistan

Muhammad Akram Naseem
Lahore Business School, The University of Lahore, Pakistan

ABSTRACT

This chapter employs bibliometric analysis to deeply explore the interplay between financial inclusion and sustainability, addressing key research questions. The trend of publications shows a notable rise, particularly following the 2015 introduction of the United Nations Sustainable Development Goals (UNSDGs). Performance analysis indicates China's leading role in terms of document production and citations. Collaboration patterns highlight important authors and groups to underscore worldwide co-operation. Co-occurrence networks reveal diverse study clusters, while word clouds visually represent major themes from authors' keywords and paper titles. Conclusively, this chapter presents future research directions, such as cross-disciplinary studies; technological developments; longitudinal impact assess-ments; environmental, social, and governance (ESG) integration; and regional studies in the present

DOI: 10.4018/979-8-3693-1475-3.ch006

field of study. Practically, it offers guidelines for aligning financial practices with sustainability goals, promoting international collaboration, informed policymaking, and strategic insights.

1. BACKGROUND OF FINANCIAL INCLUSION AND SUSTAINABILITY

Financial inclusion is a fundamental aspect of the current economic discourse, as it ensures that all sectors of society, particularly those discriminated and marginalised individuals can avail themselves of essential financial services. Financial inclusion and sustainability address the interest of marginalised areas, the neglected areas facing discrimination and exclusion from basic rights. In recent decades, there has been a significant transformation in the conceptualisation of financial inclusion, evolving from a narrow concentration on microfinance to a broader scope that incorporates a diverse range of financial services and products (Demirgüç-Kunt et al., 2017a). It is recognised that establishing a bank account is just one aspect of financial inclusion. The other crucial component entails the integration of individuals into the financial system, enabling them to handle their financial affairs proficiently and securely (Sarma & Pais, 2011; Ahmad et al., 2020; Hussain & Ahmad, 2021).

The concept of financial inclusion has evolved significantly over time. Initially centred on providing access to financial services, it now focuses on optimizing the utilisation of these services. This evolution is crucial for sustainable economic growth and poverty alleviation, which hinge on the careful allocation and management of financial resources (Demirgüç-Kunt, Klapper, & Singer, 2017; Elouaourti & Ezzahid, 2022a). As per the World Bank's definition, financial inclusion transcends mere possession of a bank account. It encompasses the active use of these accounts and related services to improve the quality of life (World Bank, 2018). An integral aspect of enhancing financial inclusion is a strong foundation in financial literacy. Huston (2010) emphasizes that financial literacy bolsters individuals' capacity to make informed financial decisions, thereby better managing financial resources. This literacy is pivotal in effective financial inclusion programs, enabling individuals to adeptly navigate the complexities of the financial world. Technological advancements have played a significant role in the expansion of financial inclusion. Innovations such as mobile banking and digital payment methods have been instrumental in this growth (GSMA, 2019; Elouaourti & Ezzahid, 2022b). These technologies have diminished barriers to financial access and facilitated more efficient use of financial services. This is particularly beneficial for individuals in rural and underserved areas, where traditional financial services are often limited (Ozili, 2018; Ezzahid & Elouaourti, 2019; Ezzahid & Elouaourti, 2021a)

The concept of sustainability, as initially outlined by the World Commission on Environment and Development (WCED) in 1987, strongly emphasised environmental considerations, which experienced a substantial expansion to incorporate social and economic dimensions (Brundtland, 1987). The European Commission (2007) further delineated sustainability as a triangular framework with People, Planet, and Prosperity serving as its vertices. Researchers endeavored to integrate this concept into academic discourse, describing it into three principal themes: social, economic, and technical dimensions (Hasna, 2007). Although certain researchers extended this concept into five dimensions (Seghezzo, 2009), due to sustained well-being relevance, sustainability have led to the acknowledgement of environmental, economic, and social dimensions as the fundamental dimensions of sustainability (Dempsey et al., 2011; Guillen-Royo, 2018). To effectively integrate sustainability into the realm of financial inclusion, it is imperative that financial decision-making processes duly consider the long-term implications on social and environmental aspects. The approach described in this process aims to safeguard the capacity of future generations to fulfil their needs by promoting sustainable development via the lens of financial activities (WCED, 1987; Elouardighi & Kenza Oubejja, 2023). The discourse of the literature posits that sustainability addresses the interest of the environment, society and governance where governance bring a system of financial inclusion to the marginalised communities and environment. The incorporation of ESG factors and the impact of technology on enhancing financial inclusion can offer significant insights to professionals in the financial industry (Elouardighi & Oubejja, 2023).

Bibliometric analysis is a powerful tool for examining the evolution and prevailing trends in scholarly and policy discussions pertaining to financial inclusion and sustainability. Through a systematic analysis of publishing patterns, citation networks, and subject concentrations, scholars can comprehensively comprehend the developmental trajectory of a particular area and the emergence of new themes (Ellegaard & Wallin, 2015). An imperative aspect of examining financial inclusion and sustainability is the adoption of a contemporary and progressive standpoint. The contemporary landscape has been reshaped by swift technological advancements, evolving regulatory structures, and an increasing recognition of the importance of inclusive and sustainable financial practices. Effective policy formulation and strategic decision-making necessitate the ability to anticipate forthcoming trends and challenges (Sachs et al., 2019).

The synergistic relationship between financial inclusion and sustainability highlights a persuasive relationship that necessitates collaborative efforts from governmental bodies, industries, and individuals in the same way, to collectively contribute towards the recognition of a sustainable future (Guillen-Royo, 2018; Ezzahid & Elouaourti, 2021b). The result of rigorous efforts in advancing financial inclusion is ultimately directed towards the betterment of humanity at the individual level because it is fundamentally related to the vision of ensuring a sustainable future for coming generations. To enhance the generalizability of the concept, this chapter explores the intricate relationship between financial inclusion and sustainability through the application of analysis. The aim is to comprehensively study and understand this topic's historical development, current state, and potential future trajectories. This approach will effectively identify potential areas for additional investigation and areas where further research is needed while offering valuable insights into the topic's status. The study addresses the following questions:

RQ1. What is the publication trend in financial inclusion and sustainability research?

RQ2. Which are the most influential articles and top contributing journals for financial inclusion and sustainability research?

RQ3. Which are the top contributing authors, institutions, and countries for financial inclusion and sustainability research?

This chapter contributes valuable insights to the financial inclusion and sustainability literature, offering theoretical and practical perspectives that enhance current understanding and guide future research in these fields. Researchers in financial inclusion and sustainability, regardless of their level of experience, can assess the level of interest in the topic throughout the scientific community over time by obtaining a summary and current understanding of its publication trend (RQ1). Furthermore, aspiring scholars can discover significant literature, such as the most influential articles and top contributing journals in the field (RQ2), as well as potential collaborators, such as authors, organisations, and nations (RQ3). The anticipated answers to the research questions are key to achieving our objective: delineating the relationship between financial inclusion and sustainability in a manner that supports sustainable development. The identified trends, patterns, and gaps provide strategic insights for policymakers, enabling stakeholders to align their efforts in financial inclusion with sustainable development goals.

2. FINANCIAL INCLUSION: DEFINITIONS AND SCOPE

At first, financial inclusion was included in sustainable development goals (SDGs) highlighting the importance and need of financial inclusion for SDGs. Later, this concept was defined by Demirgüç-Kunt et al. (2017b) and pertains to providing affordable financial services and products to individuals and enterprises, irrespective of their income levels. According to a study conducted by the World Bank in 2018, it has been demonstrated that the augmentation of financial inclusion has a crucial role in reducing poverty rates and expediting economic progress. According to Sachs et al. (2019), incorporating ESG factors is crucial for ensuring the sustainability of financial decision-making and investment. Recent literature has emphasised the importance of sustainable finance in achieving the SDGs (UNDP, 2020).

2.1 Financial Inclusion and Sustainability

Recent literature increasingly acknowledges the importance of integrating sustainable development with financial inclusion, highlighting this as a pivotal focus for current research and policy initiatives. According to Bateman et al. (2019), financial services possess not just accessibility but also ethicality and durability. Zhang et al. (2021) have found, through an empirical study, that a favourable correlation exists between financial inclusion in the attainment of SDG's. Bibliometric analysis is increasingly employed to delineate the research terrain within this field as it enables the identification of significant themes, authors, and publications in a meaningful way (Donthu et al., 2021b). This approach facilitates understanding the evolution of research trends over time and the impact of various studies in the domains of sustainability and financial inclusion (Aria & Cuccurullo, 2017).

The intersection of financial inclusion and sustainability has garnered significant attention in academic research. However, studies that effectively integrate these two concepts are scarce (Sachs et al., 2019). The existing body of literature on the correlation between financial inclusion and the Sustainable Development Goals (SDGs) remains limited, evidenced by the scarcity of comprehensive studies in this area (UNDP, 2020). There is a disparity in the level of attention given to integrating financial inclusion and sustainability between affluent and poor countries, with a greater emphasis on the latter (World Bank, 2018). It is vital to conduct studies that establish comparisons among diverse economic settings. However, insufficient data exists about the long-term impact of financial inclusion programs on sustainability targets, as highlighted by Demirgüç-Kunt et al. (2017), which makes this comparison difficult. Considering the need for an empirical investigation, this chapter intends to ascertain the extent to which technological interventions can effectively facilitate the adoption of sustainable financial practices. Further, limited bibliometric evaluations have been conducted to analyse the progression of research at the intersection of sustainability and financial inclusion (Aria & Cuccurullo, 2017). Therefore, this research employs bibliometric analyses to meticulously identify the most notable contributions and authors in this field, and to highlight emerging patterns and trends.

3. METHODOLOGY

The present work undertakes the collection of bibliometric data about research in financial inclusion and sustainability to conduct a comprehensive review. The Scientific Procedures and Rationales for Systematic Literature Reviews (SPAR-4-SLR) methodology is utilised and executed in this investigation. The technique encompasses three primary stages: assembling, arranging, and assessing articles (Paul et al., 2021). Figure 1 depicts the overview of the review process.

3.1 Assembling

Following an initial examination of relevant scholarly works in the preceding section, this research endeavour has discovered specific search terms associated with financial inclusion and sustainability. This identification aims to gather a comprehensive collection of papers about the topic. Subsequently, consultant's expertise was enlisted to assess the suitability of the keywords in accurately representing the concepts of sustainable financial inclusion and sustainability. This led to the amalgamation of two keywords, which are organised in the following manner within the search string:

"Financial inclusion" AND "Sustainability"

Following identifying pertinent search phrases, the investigation procured articles from Scopus, a widely recognised and reputable scientific database renowned for its extensive collection of scholarly papers (Comerio & Strozzi, 2019). According to Paul et al. (2021), Scopus was prioritised above the Web of Science (WoS) due to more significant number of articles available for review. This decision was based on the search query used in the "article title, abstract, and keywords" area of Scopus. The analysis of the search yielded a cumulative count of 283 documents.

3.2 Arranging

The present study employed the category (code) function inside the Scopus database to comprehensively analyse the search results, focusing on many parameters like the year of publication, subject area, document type, publication stage, source type, and language. The search results underwent filtration and restriction, focusing on the subsequent categories: "2023", "business, management, and accounting, Economics, Econometrics and Finance, Social Sciences", "article", "final", "journal", and "English" within those respective categories. The resulting corpus of 151 articles obtained from the compilation step was able to be organised. As proposed by Paul et al. (2021), the filters were applied, taking into consideration that 2023 was the most recent complete year of operation. The domains of business, management, accounting, economics, econometrics, finance, and social sciences encompass the study of financial inclusion and sustainability. The decision was made to exclude in-press articles due to their incomplete status. Additionally, non-journal sources such as books, book chapters, and conference proceedings were not considered as they may not have undergone thorough peer review. Furthermore, articles written in languages other than English were excluded due to our limited proficiency in those languages. Editorials and notes typically do not undergo the peer-review process, and including reviews may lead to the inclusion of overlapping perspectives. To mitigate the inadvertent omission of relevant research in the discipline, a total of 151 articles were selected following a rigorous screening process. The validity of this reduced corpus was further verified through a random cross-validation procedure, utilising additional databases such as Google Scholar, as well as reputable publisher platforms including Elsevier, Emerald, Sage, Springer, and Taylor and Francis (Goyal et al., 2021; Lim et al., 2021).

3.3 Assessing

This study employs bibliometric analytic methodology to examine a comprehensive corpus of 151 papers on the topic of "Financial Inclusion". The size of the corpus is considered relatively substantial. Bibliometric analysis is a quantitative approach to assessing scientific data from academic publications (Donthu et al., 2021a). Notably, bibliometric systematic reviews are increasingly used as the standard practice (Ellegaard & Wallin, 2015)

The literature evaluations encompass a diverse array of subjects, encompassing the broad field of business (Baker et al., 2020; Zupic & Cater, 2015) as well as the specific finance domain. Using quantitative tools, bibliometric analysis is employed to mitigate the inherent biases associated with manual and qualitative reviews. This approach, as supported by Broadus (1987) and Burton et al. (2020), is efficient when dealing with a substantial review corpus consisting of many articles, such as the present study, which encompasses 151 articles (Donthu et al., 2021a). This study employs a bibliometric analysis, utilising a performance analysis to examine the publication trend, top articles and contributing journals, authors, institutions, and countries, in line with previous reviews (Donthu et al., 2020, 2021d; Khan et al., 2021; Shahid et al., 2024). Furthermore, the study employs a scientific mapping technique through a temporal analysis utilising word clouds (van Eck & Waltman, 2017) and network analysis using keyword co-occurrence (Castriotta et al., 2019; Donthu et al., 2021a) in VOSviewer (van Eck & Waltman, 2017) to elucidate the primary themes and topics that underpin the intellectual framework of research on Financial Inclusion and Sustainability. This study presents a future research plan to enhance comprehension of the subject based on analysing relevant publications and identifying remaining gaps within each primary theme. The review findings are systematically given in the subsequent sections, whereby empirical evidence and tabular representations are utilised to substantiate the arguments.

Figure 1. Flowchart of systematic review procedure (Paul et al., 2021)

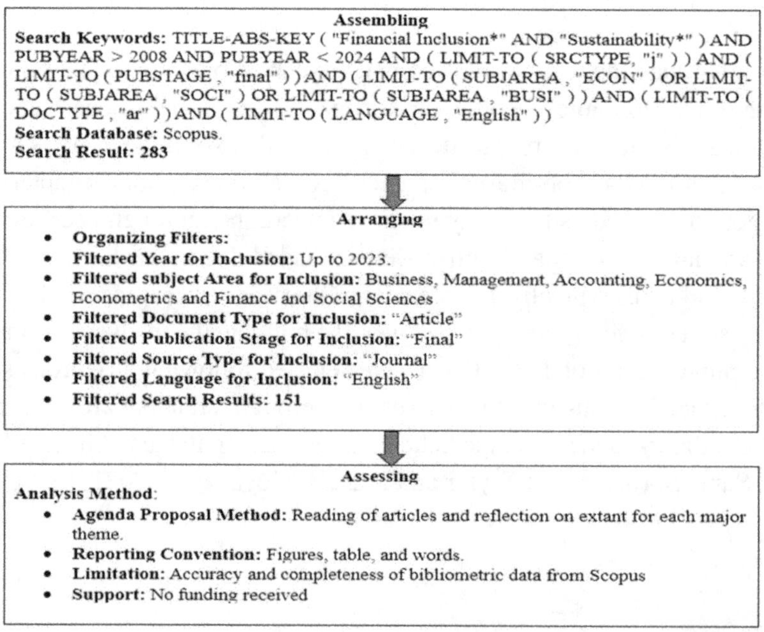

4. FINDINGS

4.1 Performance Analysis

Donthu et al. (2021a) define performance analysis as a bibliometric analytic approach used to evaluate the success of a research area, specifically in the context of financial inclusion and sustainability research. This approach employs bibliometric metrics to enhance rigour, like participant profiling in empirical investigations (Donthu et al., 2021a). This study conducts a performance analysis to ascertain the publication trend and identify the most essential articles, top contributing journals, prominent authors, institutions, and countries.

4.1.1 Article Production Overtime

Publications Trend for Financial Inclusion and Sustainability

The bar graph displays the annual count of articles published on financial inclusion and sustainability from 2009 to 2023. The adoption of the United Nations Sustainable Development Goals (UNSDGs) in 2015 marked a significant shift in the observable pattern of rising publication volume. The period from 2009 to the present, known as the "Post Global Financial Period," is marked by a shortage of activity. This could be attributed to the repercussions of the global financial crisis, as research on crisis management may have been prioritised over sustainability at that period. Research funding and objectives may be altered during crises to prioritise issues directly associated with immediate recovery.

Nevertheless, in 2015, when the UNSDGs were officially launched, there was an increase in the number of articles. The UNSDGs have provided a framework to address global financial inclusion and sustainability concerns. Pursuing these goals appears to have spurred study in this domain, perhaps due to increased consciousness, attention from decision-makers, and funding for sustainability-related projects. Since 2015, there has been a steady and significant increase in articles. The increasing trend results

Figure 2. Year-wise publication trends in financial inclusion and sustainability research

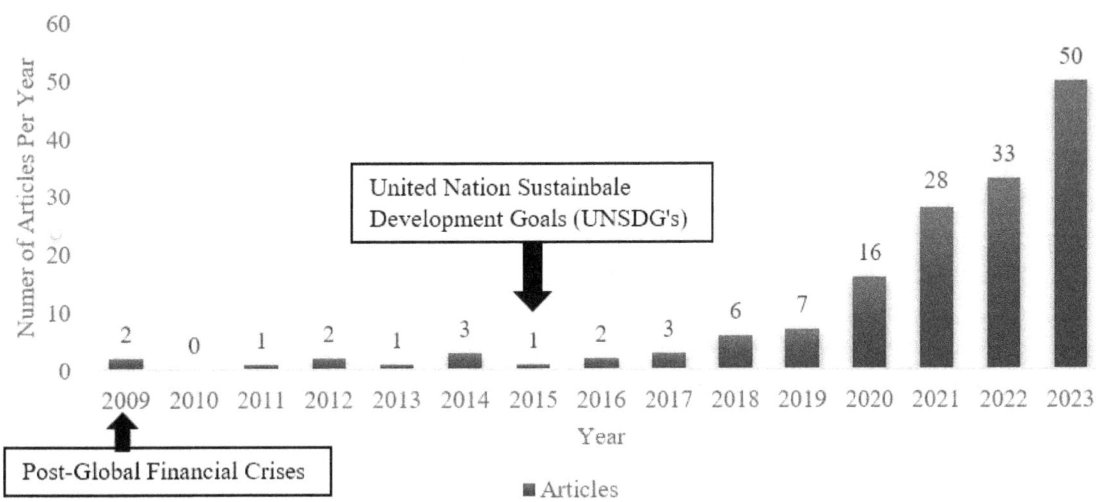

from the financial sector's growing focus on sustainability and the broader push for economic measures that foster sustainable development. In 2023, there is a significant increase to 50 papers, suggesting a convergence of factors such as heightened worldwide awareness, policy modifications, advancements in technology, and the maturation of the discipline as an area of research.

4.1.2 Most Influential Articles

Table 1 offers a comprehensive overview of the critical works in sustainability research and financial inclusion. The academic community has bestowed significant attention upon these works, evidenced by their substantial total citation counts (TC). The citations demonstrate their importance, relevance, and substantial impact on the ongoing discussion on financial inclusion and sustainability. Academics and researchers frequently refer to these publications to enhance comprehension, establish the foundation for novel information, and address significant matters in this interdisciplinary field. These articles encompass various topics related to financial inclusion and sustainability. They explore the correlation between the efficacy of microfinance institutions and economic freedom, the dynamics of sustainable economic development in specific regions, and the impact of digital financial inclusion on economic growth and environmental sustainability. Each publication provides a unique perspective, empirical evidence, and theoretical frameworks, enriching the existing knowledge of sustainability and financial inclusion research.

Including various publishing years underscores the papers' enduring significance and long-lasting impact. These articles, covering the period from 2017 to 2023, have maintained their relevance and are now essential resources for scholars, policymakers, and professionals seeking to understand and capitalise on the numerous opportunities and challenges at the intersection of finance, sustainability, and economic development. Ultimately, the papers listed in this table provides the fundamental basis for researching the topics of sustainability and financial inclusion. Their considerable number of citations underscores their importance as seminal sources that have shaped and continue to shape the trajectory of research in this crucial and constantly expanding field.

4.1.3 Top Contributing Journals

Table 2 portrays the list of the top contributors' sources; leading from the top is the journal "Sustainability (Switzerland)", which has the most significant number of publications (32), which suggests a significant interest and emphasis on sustainability and financial inclusion. TC suggests that the study has gained significant recognition and is actively utilised. With 421 citations, the journal "Sustainability (Switzerland)" again stands out, showcasing its significant influence. The *h*-index of Sustainability (Switzerland) is 11.

The performance of 'Sustainability (Switzerland)' is commendable, as it demonstrates a harmonious equilibrium between the quantity of articles and their influence. 'Sustainability (Switzerland)' undeniably surpasses the comparison in all three criteria, showcasing a significant contribution to the progress of sustainability and financial inclusion research. The H-indices of other journals indicate that they possess comparable utility to 'Sustainability (Switzerland)', although they have fewer articles and citations. Nevertheless, their general impact in the field appears to be diminished. Although lesser TP and TC in specific journals do not necessarily indicate inferior quality, they may indicate a more specific or specialised viewpoint. For instance, "Borsa Istanbul Review" and "European Business Organization

Table 1. Most influential articles for financial inclusion and sustainability research

Authors	Title	Source Title	Year	TC
Arner D.W.; Buckley R.P.; Zetzsche D.A.; Veidt R.	Sustainability, FinTech, and Financial Inclusion	European Business Organization Law Review	2020	144
Le T.-H.; Chuc A.T.; Taghizadeh-Hesary F.	Financial inclusion and its impact on financial efficiency and sustainability: Empirical evidence from Asia	Borsa Istanbul Review	2019	132
Ozturk I.; Ullah S.	Does digital financial inclusion matter for economic growth and environmental sustainability in OBRI economies? An empirical analysis	Resources, Conservation and Recycling	2022	114
Pradhan R.P.; Arvin M.B.; Nair M.S.; Hall J.H.; Bennett S.E.	Sustainable economic development in India: The dynamics between financial inclusion, ICT development, and economic growth	Technological Forecasting and Social Change	2021	74
Kamarudin F.; Anwar N.A.M.; Chien F.; Hussain H.I.; Sadiq M.	Efficiency of microfinance institutions and economic freedom nexus: Empirical evidence from four selected Asian countries	Transformations in Business and Economics	2021	74
Chen H.; Shi Y.; Zhao X.	Investment in renewable energy resources, sustainable financial inclusion and energy efficiency: A case of US economy	Resources Policy	2022	70
Gbongli K.; Xu Y.; Amedjonekou K.M.	Extended technology acceptance model to predict mobile-based money acceptance and sustainability: A multi-analytical structural equation modeling and neural network approach	Sustainability (Switzerland)	2019	68
Schinckus C.	The good, the bad and the ugly: An overview of the sustainability of blockchain technology	Energy Research and Social Science	2020	60
Kumar K.; Prakash A.	Developing a framework for assessing sustainable banking performance of the Indian banking sector	Social Responsibility Journal	2019	48
Yang L.; Zhang Y.	Digital financial inclusion and sustainable growth of small and micro enterprises-evidence based on China's new third board market listed companies	Sustainability (Switzerland)	2020	47
Mia M.A.; Lee H.-A.	Mission drift and ethical crisis in microfinance institutions: What matters?	Journal of Cleaner Production	2017	46
Moro-Visconti R.; Rambaud S.C.; Pascual J.L.	Sustainability in FinTechs: An explanation through business model scalability and market valuation	Sustainability (Switzerland)	2020	43
Lutfi A.; Al-Okaily M.; Alshirah M.H.; Alshira'h A.F.; Abutaber T.A.; Almarashdah M.A.	Digital financial inclusion sustainability in Jordanian context	Sustainability (Switzerland)	2021	39
Lopez T.; Winkler A.	The challenge of rural financial inclusion–evidence from microfinance	Applied Economics	2018	37
Anu; Singh A.K.; Raza S.A.; Nakonieczny J.; Shahzad U.	Role of financial inclusion, green innovation, and energy efficiency for environmental performance? Evidence from developed and emerging economies in the lens of sustainable development	Structural Change and Economic Dynamics	2023	35
Al-Okaily M.; Alsharairi M.; Natour A.R.A.; Shishan F.; Al-Dmour A.; Alghazzawi R.	Sustainable fintech innovation orientation: A moderated model	Sustainability (Switzerland)	2021	32
Gálvez-Sánchez F.J.; Lara-Rubio J.; Verdú-Jóver A.J.; Meseguer-Sánchez V.	Research advances on financial inclusion: A bibliometric analysis	Sustainability (Switzerland)	2021	29
Menyelim C.M.; Babajide A.A.; Omankhanlen A.E.; Ehikioya B.I.	Financial inclusion, income inequality and sustainable economic growth in Sub-Saharan African countries	Sustainability (Switzerland)	2021	28
Somanje A.N.; Mohan G.; Lopes J.; Mensah A.; Gordon C.; Zhou X.; Moinuddin M.; Saito O.; Takeuchi K.	Challenges and potential solutions for sustainable urban-rural linkages in a ghanaian context	Sustainability (Switzerland)	2020	27
Odugbesan J.A.; Ike G.; Olowu G.; Adeleye B.N.	Investigating the causality between financial inclusion, financial development and sustainable development in Sub-Saharan Africa economies: The mediating role of foreign direct investment	Journal of Public Affairs	2022	26

Note: TC= Total Citations (citations count)

Law Review" have a single piece on this subject. However, despite their limited publications, they have garnered several citations, indicating a significant impact. Altogether, these journals offer researchers and academics important platforms to publish their work, exchange ideas, and add to the continuing conversation around sustainability and financial inclusion. Researchers can evaluate the influence of

Table 2. Top contributing journals for financial inclusion and sustainability research

Journal	TP	TC	H-Index
Sustainability (Switzerland)	32	421	11
Economic Research-Ekonomska Istrazivanja	7	49	6
Resources Policy	7	110	3
Social Responsibility Journal	4	59	3
Enterprise Development and Microfinance	4	23	2
Technological Forecasting and Social Change	4	81	2
Economic Change and Restructuring	3	26	1
Indian Journal of Finance	2	5	2
Qualitative Research in Financial Markets	2	14	2
Sustainable Development	2	35	2
Australasian Accounting, Business and Finance Journal	2	10	1
Cogent Economics and Finance	2	1	1
Abac Journal	1	3	1
Applied Econometrics and International Development	1	4	1
Applied Economics	1	37	1
Borsa Istanbul Review	1	132	1
Economic Horizons	1	2	1
Economics And Sociology	1	13	1
Energy Research and Social Science	1	60	1
Equality, Diversity and Inclusion	1	1	1
European Business Organization Law Review	1	144	1

Note: TP= Total Publications, and TC= Total Citations

their work in this critical and multidisciplinary field by using this table to determine which journals are best for their research articles.

4.1.4 Top Contributing Countries

Table 3 highlights the production of documents and their impact measured by the number of citations by countries. As per the Scopus database, twenty-one countries are producing documents in the domain of financial inclusion and sustainability which includes eight developed and thirteen developing economies. This distribution offers insights into the global research landscape and the diverse perspectives on financial inclusion and sustainability. China is the global leader in the number of documents (16) and citations (167), as evidenced by the above table. This indicates that China has a significant influence and productivity in the selected field of research. India possesses double the number of documents compared to the country with the second highest count (101), although it has fewer citations (101). These findings indicate that while India generates a substantial volume of research, its impact in terms of citations is smaller than that of China. Malaysia, Spain, and Nigeria possess fewer documents than China and India; nevertheless, they still exhibit noteworthy citations. This indicates that their research

Table 3. Top contributing countries

Country Name	Documents	Citations	Nature of Economy
China	16	167	Developing
India	22	101	Developing
Malaysia	6	91	Developing
Spain	8	79	Developed
Nigeria	6	76	Developing
Germany	3	38	Developed
Jordan	1	32	Developing
Pakistan	3	27	Developing
Netherlands	1	18	Developed
United Kingdom	3	17	Developed
Indonesia	3	12	Developing
South Africa	2	9	Developing
Canada	1	5	Developed
Italy	1	4	Developed
United States	3	4	Developed
Palestine	1	3	Developed
South Korea	1	3	Developing
United Arab Emirates	1	3	Developing
Mexico	1	2	Developing
Ghana	1	1	Developing
Nepal	1	1	Developing

output is substantial and often cited compared to the number of articles they have produced. During this examination, the United States has been found to possess only three documents and four citations, which is relatively low considering its typical significance in research and academia. Given its historical supremacy in numerous scientific fields, this may be unexpected. It is imperative to bear in mind that these findings may not be representative of other academic disciplines. There exists a solitary document with a finite quantity of citations encompassing the countries of Ghana, Nepal, and Mexico collectively. This indicates that these nations' research output and influence on the selected topic are limited. The relatively small numbers of documents and citations in Jordan, the Netherlands, the United Kingdom, and Italy suggest a lower level of involvement in this specific area of research.

4.2 Science Mapping

Donthu et al. (2021a) define science mapping as an analytical method visually representing the available material and its connections within a specific field, such as sustainable finance research. The science mapping of sustainable finance research is conducted by utilising two bibliometric analysis techniques in VOSviewer. Firstly, a network analysis is employed to examine the co-occurrence of keywords, thereby uncovering the fundamental themes that form the intellectual framework of sustainable finance research over time. Secondly, a temporal analysis uses word clouds to dissect the primary topics that define sustainable finance research within each period.

4.2.1 Temporal Analysis Using Word Clouds for Sustainable Finance Research

The word cloud visualises the 100 most prominent terms associated with the author's sustainability and financial inclusion keywords. The size of each word in the phrase cloud corresponds to its frequency of occurrence in the literature. The often-employed terms in this field of study include "financial services," "economic growth," "financial inclusions," "sustainability," and "finance." "Sustainability" commonly focuses on maintaining long-term ecological equilibrium and the robustness of systems and processes. This concept holds significant importance in discussions concerning the current state of the economy. "Finance" and "financial services" imply a high appreciation for the financial tools and strategies that promote sustainable development. Financial inclusion refers to prioritising offering financial services to marginalised communities, a vital method for diminishing poverty and fostering sustainable economic growth.

The use of terms such as "microfinance," "economic growth," and "empirical analysis" highlights the emphasis on research that relies on data to establish connections between financial activity and economic growth. The mention of geographical locations such as "China" and "India" implies a focus on a specific region, maybe due to these countries' significant populations and thriving economies. This makes them valuable examples to study when examining financial inclusion. The terms "green economy," "energy efficiency," "alternative energy," and "carbon emission" imply a strong correlation between environmental concerns and the economic dimensions of sustainability. This exemplifies the multidisciplinary nature of sustainability studies, encompassing several fields, such as social policy, environmental science, and finance.

The word cloud also includes methodological terminology such as "regression analysis" and "econometrics," which refer to using quantitative tools for analysing and interpreting data in this field. The comprehensive analysis of the word cloud reveals that the study on financial inclusion and sustainability

Figure 3. World Cloud by author keywords top 100

Figure 4. World Cloud by most reported words in title top 50

is diverse, focusing on the areas where finance, economic development, and environmental stewardship intersect. Complex interconnections are examined through a variety of empirical methodologies.

The critical ideas encompassed in this context are "financial," "inclusion," "sustainability," "development," and "economic." The expressions mentioned suggest a scholarly emphasis on combining financial practices with sustainable development goals, which is crucial to the discussion on financial inclusion and sustainability. The terms "financial" and "inclusion" refer to a study focus that aims to enable all sections of society, particularly those who are disadvantaged, to access and utilise financial services. This is a crucial element of sustainable development as it fosters increased economic engagement and contributes to the battle against poverty.

The phrases "sustainability" and "sustainable" suggest simultaneously focusing on long-term economic growth feasibility and resilient environmental measures. This indicates that scientists incorporate social and ecological variables into their analysis rather than solely focusing on financial growth. The terms "microfinance," "green," "energy," and "efficiency" imply a need for a thorough examination of how microfinance services might contribute to the development of environmentally sustainable economies and energy consumption. The term "microfinance" emphasises the role of small-scale financial services in promoting inclusive economic growth.

The use of geographical phrases such as "countries," "India," and "rural" suggests that a significant percentage of the research focuses on examining financial inclusion and sustainability within specific national or local contexts. Understanding the opportunities and challenges present in different places is essential. The terms "digital," "fintech," "model," and "performance" indicate a fascination with the technological aspects of finance, the assessment of the effectiveness of these interventions, and the utilisation of innovative financial technology to foster inclusivity. The terms "empirical," "social," "institutions," "study," "research," "approach," and "evidence" imply different research techniques, primarily focusing on empirical studies to validate social theories and models related to sustainability and financial inclusion.

4.3 Network Analysis

The network analysis employs keyword co-occurrence throughout the entire corpus to reveal the fundamental themes that characterise the intellectual framework of sustainable finance research, spanning from its inception in 2009 to 2023. In contrast, temporal analysis employs word clouds and divides the collection of articles on financial inclusion and sustainability into periods to examine the chronological development of subjects in the field. Thematic similarity consolidates a wide range of topics in sustainable finance. This is achieved using keyword co-occurrence network analysis, which reveals this discipline's primary themes or knowledge departments.

4.3.1 Collaboration Between the Countries

Table 4 and Figure 5 provide a detailed representation of the frequency of international collaborations in producing academic papers and research publications between countries. To ascertain the countries that hold the utmost significance in this setting, we can evaluate the quantity and the intensity of cooperation between them. The data reveals that China and Pakistan have collaborated on research projects four times, indicating a significant level of cooperation between these two countries in the field of financial inclusion and sustainability.

China and Saudi Arabia have a robust relationship, which is seen in four specific cases. China and Indonesia have engaged in three collaborative endeavours, demonstrating a significant relationship in the field of research. The research collaboration between Malaysia and Pakistan is also noteworthy, as evidenced by their joint efforts in three distinct cases. China and Bangladesh have engaged in two collaborative efforts, demonstrating moderate research collaboration.

China and Poland have engaged in two instances of collaboration, demonstrating a notable scientific relationship. Poland, China, and Turkey have engaged in two instances of collaboration, indicating a mutual interest in research. China and the United Kingdom have engaged in two collaborative efforts, demonstrating their commitment to international research cooperation. India and Malaysia have engaged in two collaborations, signifying a degree of research cooperation or collaborative endeavours. Malaysia and Indonesia have engaged in two collaborative endeavours, potentially focused on regional research initiatives or academic interchange. Nigeria and the United Kingdom have engaged in two collaborations, suggesting the possibility of cooperative research or academic interaction. Pakistan and Saudi Arabia have collaborated, indicating mutual scientific interests or partnership endeavours.

Saudi Arabia and Tunisia have engaged in two collaborations, suggesting potential joint efforts in research or academic exchanges. Spain and Uruguay have engaged in two instances of collaboration, indicating a significant degree of research or academic cooperation. The United Kingdom and Oman have engaged in two collaborative endeavours, demonstrating mutual scientific interests or academic alliances. Australia and Luxembourg have engaged in a single collaboration, suggesting a somewhat infrequent yet noteworthy level of cooperation. China and France have previously engaged in a collaborative effort, indicating a partnership in research or academic interchange. China and Hong Kong have previously collaborated, maybe indicating a partnership in research or academic endeavours. China and Hungary have engaged in a singular research collaboration or partnership. China and India have previously engaged in collaboration, suggesting the occurrence of a distinct research endeavour or intellectual interchange between the two nations.

Table 4. Collaboration between the countries (top 20)

From	To	Frequency	Nature of Economy
China	Pakistan	4	Developing
China	Saudi Arabia	4	Developing
China	Indonesia	3	Developing
Malaysia	Pakistan	3	Developing
China	Bangladesh	2	Developing
China	Poland	2	Developing
China	Turkey	2	Developing
China	United Kingdom	2	Developing
India	Malaysia	2	Developing
Malaysia	Indonesia	2	Developing
Nigeria	United Kingdom	2	Developing
Pakistan	Saudi Arabia	2	Developing
Saudi Arabia	Tunisia	2	Developing
Spain	Uruguay	2	Developed
United Kingdom	Oman	2	Developed
Australia	Luxembourg	1	Developed
China	France	1	Developing
China	Hong Kong	1	Developing
China	Hungary	1	Developing
China	India	1	Developing

Figure 5. Collaboration between the countries

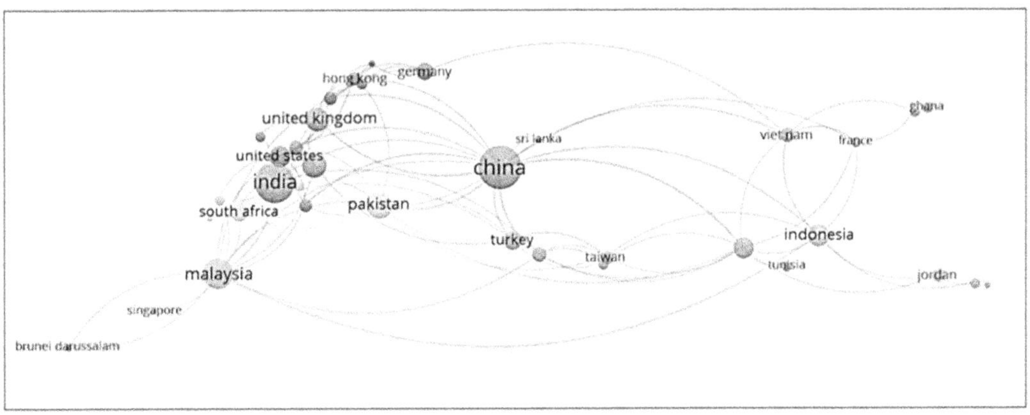

Within this framework, the significance of a nation in research collaboration can be evaluated by considering both the frequency and variety of its collaborative efforts. China is the most significant country in this context since it frequently collaborates with multiple countries, including Pakistan, Saudi Arabia, Indonesia, the United Kingdom, and others. The substantial involvement of China in research partnerships indicates its importance in the worldwide research arena. Additional significant nations encompass Pakistan, Saudi Arabia, Malaysia, and the United Kingdom, which collaborate with diverse countries.

4.3.2 Co-Authorship Analysis

Figure 6 presents a bibliometric analysis of authors' collaboration patterns in financial inclusion and sustainability domains. The importance of collaborative networks is a notable finding, as evidenced by the research conducted by authors such as Ofosu-Mensah Ababio J., Yiadom E.B., Mawutor J.K.M., Tuffour J.K., and Attah-Botchwey E. in 2023 and Shabir M. in 2022. The authors' significant biographical link indicates a substantial likelihood of active collaboration. Moreover, multiple clusters have formed due to grouping authors based on their participation patterns. In 2022, researchers Zhao F., Zhang Y., Alharthi M., and Zafar M.W. combined to form a coherent cluster with a high coupling score, suggesting a network of closely connected researchers. The same remains valid for Rehman A.U., Malik A.H., Md Isa A.H., and Jais M. in 2023. In addition, the table highlights the temporal aspect of collaboration by illustrating the distribution of research activity throughout many years. Notably, multiple authors contribute to various clusters across different periods, emphasising the dynamic nature of these collaboration networks in this field. The coupling scores and citation metrics provide insight into the significance of joint endeavour about the influence. Ozturk I. and Ullah S. collaborated in 2022, resulting in a remarkable number of citations and a notably strong coupling score, demonstrating the impact of their combined contributions. The authors' independent research paths are demonstrated by negative coupling scores, as seen in Gambetta N., Azcárate-Llanes F., Sierra-García L., and García-Benau M.A. in 2021.

Figure 6. Co-authorship analysis

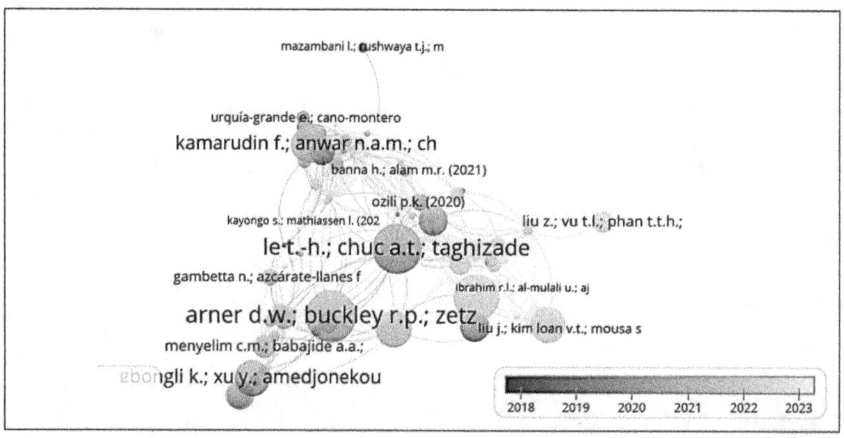

Figure 7. Co-occurrence network of author keywords

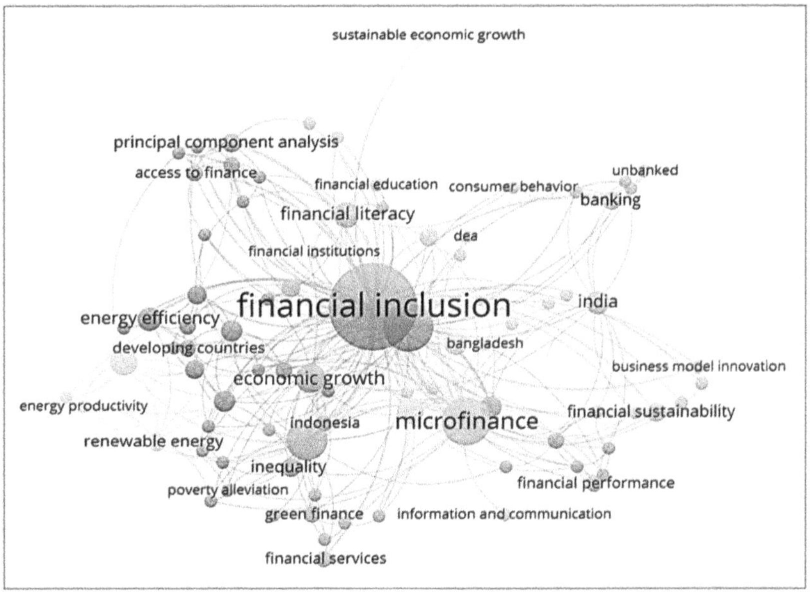

4.3.3 Co-Occurrence Network of Authors' Keywords

Figure 7 depicts the details of the co-occurrence of authors' keywords in clusters, which have been appended in detail as follows.

Cluster 1: Developing countries, digital financial inclusion, energy efficiency, financial development, financial innovation, globalisation, governance, human capital, natural resources, sustainable economic development. This cluster seems to focus primarily on financial and economic development topics. The text has keywords related to sustainable economic development, energy efficiency, financial inclusion, and rising nations. Due to its strong co-occurrence associations with other keywords, the term "developing countries" is prominent in this cluster. The terms "financial development" and "financial innovation" focus on progress's monetary aspects. The terms "natural resources" and "energy efficiency" indicate a connection between environmental issues and sustainable development.

Cluster 2: Artificial intelligence, blockchain, economic growth, emerging economies, financial services, green finance, innovation, poverty eradication, sustainable development. The cluster appears to prioritise innovation, technology, and economic expansion. The text comprises keywords related to blockchain technology, economic expansion, innovation, and artificial intelligence. The terms "blockchain" and "artificial intelligence" in this cluster suggest a focus on technological advancements. "Economic growth" and "emerging economies" highlight the significance of fostering economic advancement. The terms "green finance" and "sustainable development" both refer to the consideration of sustainability within the framework of technological progress.

Cluster 3: Access to finance, digitalisation, financial inclusion, financial stability, social inclusion, social sustainability, sustainable development goals (SDGs), and technology. This cluster focuses on three key areas: technology, financial inclusion, and achieving sustainable development goals. The emphasis on "financial inclusion" suggests that the primary objective is to ensure access to financial services. The term "technology" is frequently employed to imply that technology is necessary for attaining both financial and social inclusion. The Sustainable Development Goals (SDGs) demonstrate a dedication to tackling worldwide issues.

Cluster 4: Digitization, empowerment, fintech, microfinance institutions, social enterprise, social performance. This cluster notably focuses on the impact on society, the promotion of individual agencies, and converting analogue information into digital format. The text comprises terminology related to social enterprises, fintech (financial technology), and digitisation. The terms "microfinance institutions" and "fintech" refer to the intention of utilising technology to advance financial inclusivity. The terms "social enterprise" and "empowerment" focus on financial services that have a social impact and promote empowerment.

Cluster 5: Financial performance, Islamic microfinance, microcredit, poverty, social entrepreneurship. This cluster appears to be related to financial performance, poverty alleviation, and microfinance. The phrases "microcredit" and "Islamic microfinance" specifically focus on providing financial services in Islamic contexts. "poverty" and "social entrepreneurship" highlight the intention to utilise financial resources in addressing societal issues.

Cluster 6: Digital financial services, financial sustainability, Microfinance institutions, microfinance, operational efficiency. This cluster emphasises digital financial services, financial sustainability, and operational efficiency within microfinance and financial institutions. The words "microfinance" and "digital financial services" imply a growing integration of financial services with digital technology. The term "financial sustainability" refers to concerns over the enduring viability of financial institutions.

Cluster 7: Consumer behaviour, inclusion. This cluster is related to banking, consumer behaviour, and financial inclusion. The phrases "banking" and "consumer behaviour" refer to the study of how customers utilise financial services. The term "inclusion" underscores ensuring that financial services are readily available.

Cluster 8: Economic development, financial exclusion, inclusive growth, inequality, poverty alleviation, sustainability, women empowerment. This cluster focuses on economic development, poverty reduction, sustainability, and gender empowerment—the terms "sustainability" and "economic development" focus on achieving balanced growth. The terms "women empowerment" and "poverty alleviation" highlight concerns related to gender and societal matters. Financial exclusion refers to the mechanisms that hinder certain social groups and people from obtaining entry to the official financial system. This exclusion is evident in the groups' inability to access essential financial services (Leyshon and Thrift, 1995; Sinclair, 2001; Ozli, 2021).

Cluster 9: Financial education, financial institutions, financial literacy, sustainable development goals. The cluster seems interconnected with the Sustainable Development Goals (SDGs), financial literacy, financial institutions, and financial education. "Financial literacy" and "financial education" focus on enhancing individuals' understanding and knowledge of financial matters. The "sustainable development goals" underscores a commitment to addressing global challenges.

Cluster 10: Digital finance, financial efficiency, and social efficiency. The core focus of this cluster appears to be on financial efficiency, social efficiency, and digital finance. The primary emphasis of "digital finance" should be on digital financial services. The terms "social efficiency" and "financial efficiency" highlight the significance of impact and effectiveness.

Cluster 11: Energy productivity, Environmental Sustainability, Renewable Energy, Technological Innovation. This cluster is characterised by energy productivity, environmental sustainability, renewable energy, and technical innovation. The terms "environmental sustainability" and "renewable energy" focus on energy sources and sustainable practices. The term "technological innovation" suggests a correlation between sustainability and technology.

Cluster 12: Sustainable economic growth: This cluster primarily fosters sustainable economic growth. "Sustainable economic growth" underscores the significance of achieving a well-proportioned and stable expansion of the economy. These clusters demonstrate the connections between the keywords inside each cluster and the main topics and subjects addressed in the study domain. Researchers can utilise this data to identify patterns, explore conceptual relationships, and understand the structure of the field's study.

5. CONCLUSION

The bibliometric study of financial inclusion and sustainability research provides a comprehensive overview of the field's progress, prominent publications, and trends in international collaboration. The bar graph depicts the publishing trend, revealing a significant increase in scholarly output from 2009 to 2023. 2015 witnessed the highest point of this upward trend, coinciding with the introduction of the United Nations Sustainable Development Goals (UNSDGs). This indicates a growing commitment to aligning scientific efforts with global environmental objectives.

The performance analysis reveals a notable upward path in scholarly endeavours, as illustrated in Figure 2. Among the impactful studies, 'Sustainability' emerges as the journal with the highest number of publications. However, as detailed in Table 1, the European Business Organization Law Review's 142 citations underscores the significance of financial inclusion, sustainability, and fintech. Examining the top contributing nations reveals China's unequivocal supremacy, as it excels in the number of documents produced and the effect of citations. In contrast, India has many documents but a shallow impact in terms of citations. An essential factor to highlight is international collaboration, particularly with China, as demonstrated by forming alliances with Pakistan, Saudi Arabia, and Indonesia. The results of network analysis presented in Table 4 shows the need for scholarly contributions from developed economies in East Asia, Australia, and Europe. This approach fosters an exemplary understanding that can be generalised globally, promoting financial inclusion universally. The co-occurrence network of author keywords reveals thematic clusters that showcase the multidisciplinary nature of research, encompassing economic development, technology, social inclusion, and environmental sustainability. The word clouds visually represent significant topics such as sustainability, finance, economic growth, and financial inclusion.

The review concludes by providing recommendations for future research, which encompass multidisciplinary investigations, longitudinal assessments of impact, research on the integration of environmental, social, and governance (ESG) factors, studies that consider regional contexts, and exploration of the role of technological improvements in promoting financial inclusion and sustainability. Ultimately, the explanation of clusters in this chapter underscores the need for 'sustainable development' in developing countries instead of focusing sustainable economic development.' This paradigm shift aims to achieve sustainability and financial inclusion precisely where it is most needed i.e., in the developing parts of the world.

5.1 Practical Implications

Comprehensive financial inclusion and sustainability bibliometric analysis offers valuable implications for scholars, decision-makers, and practitioners. The noticeable increase in published works, particularly after 2015, demonstrates a renewed dedication to using research to tackle sustainability issues worldwide. Policymakers may leverage this momentum to underscore the necessity of regulations that promote ethical financial conduct aligned with sustainability goals and to shape policy choices based on empirical facts. The prominent role of China in document production and citations underscores its leadership in this academic domain and indicates potential opportunities for collaboration and knowledge exchange. Thematic clusters focusing on areas such as the incorporation of ESG factors and the impact of technology on enhancing financial inclusion can offer significant insights to professionals in the financial industry (Elouardighi & Oubejja, 2023). Moreover, the emphasis on multidisciplinary research highlights the importance of cross-sector collaboration in tackling the intricate nature of sustainability problems. Policymakers can tailor financial inclusion policies to specific socio-economic contexts by utilising regional studies, ensuring that initiatives are targeted and effective. Overall, the practical implications encompass opportunities for global cooperation, informed development of policies, and strategic guidance for professionals seeking to align financial strategies with sustainability objectives.

5.2 Future Research Direction

The outcomes of the bibliometric analysis offer valuable insights that can impact future research directions and have practical implications for practitioners, academics, and policymakers in the domains of sustainability and financial inclusion. Future research should prioritise multidisciplinary investigations, exploring how integrating finance, environmental science, social policy, and technology can comprehensively solve global challenges. Comprehending the lasting consequences of financial inclusion initiatives on ecological, social, and economic sustainability relies on conducting longitudinal impact evaluations. Areas that warrant more investigation include analysing how environmental, social, and governance (ESG) factors are incorporated into financial practices and assessing emerging technology's impact on digital financial services. Analysing the local environment can provide an intricate understanding of the specific challenges and benefits different communities face, informing the creation of targeted policy remedies. To establish financial systems that are both inclusive and sustainable, it is crucial to evaluate the effectiveness of existing legislation, encourage community participation, and enhance capabilities through financial education programs. Promoting worldwide efforts like the United Nations Sustainable Development Goals (UNSDGs) and establishing robust effect measurement frameworks will facilitate the progress of responsible financial practices globally and provide valuable data for evidence-based policymaking. Overall, these research directions have the potential to provide practical strategies that promote sustainability and enhance financial inclusion, aligning with broader objectives for global development.

REFERENCES

Ahmad, F., Hussain, R. T., & Shahzad, S. M. (2020). Measuring Financial Permanency of Firms in Emergent Economy: A Comparative Study on Financial Institutions of Pakistan. *Int. J. of Multidisciplinary and Current Research, 8*(2), 534-544.

Aria, M., & Cuccurullo, C. (2017). Bibliometrix: An R-tool for comprehensive science mapping analysis. *Journal of Informetrics, 11*(4), 959–975. doi:10.1016/j.joi.2017.08.007

Baker, H. K., Pandey, N., Kumar, S., & Haldar, A. (2020). A bibliometric analysis of board diversity: Current status, development, and future research directions. *Journal of Business Research, 108*, 232–246. doi:10.1016/j.jbusres.2019.11.025

Bateman, M., Blankenburg, S., & Kozul-Wright, R. (2019). The rise and fall of microfinance. *The Journal of Development Studies, 55*(7), 1205–1221.

Broadus, R. N. (1987). Toward a definition of "bibliometrics.". *Scientometrics, 12*(5–6), 373–379. doi:10.1007/BF02016680

Brundtland, G. H. (1987). *Our Common Future: The World Commission on Environment and Development*. Oxford University Press. Available at https://shorturl.at/hnOT6

Burton, B., Kumar, S., & Pandey, N. (2020). Twenty-five years of The European Journal of Finance (EJF): A retrospective analysis. *European Journal of Finance, 26*(18), 1817–1841. doi:10.1080/1351847X.2020.1754873

Castriotta, M., Loi, M., Marku, E., & Naitana, L. (2019). What's in a Name? An exploration of the emerging organisations conceptual structure. *Scientometrics, 118*(2), 407–437. doi:10.1007/s11192-018-2977-2

Comerio, N., & Strozzi, F. (2019). Tourism and its economic impact: A literature review using bibliometric tools. *Tourism Economics, 25*(1), 109–131. doi:10.1177/1354816618793762

Demirgüç-Kunt, A., Klapper, L., & Singer, D. (2017a). *Financial Inclusion and Inclusive Growth: A Review of Recent Empirical Evidence.* World Bank Policy Research Working Paper, (8040). Available at: https://shorturl.at/JORS4

Demirgüç-Kunt, A., Klapper, L., & Singer, D. (2017b). Financial inclusion and legal discrimination against women: Evidence from developing countries. *The World Bank Economic Review, 31*(3), 1–22.

Dempsey, N., Bramley, G., Power, S., & Brown, C. (2011). The social dimension of sustainable development: Defining urban social sustainability. *Sustainable Development (Bradford), 19*(5), 289–300. doi:10.1002/sd.417

Donthu, N., Kumar, S., Mukherjee, D., Pandey, N., & Lim, W. M. (2021). How to conduct a bibliometric analysis: An overview and guidelines. *Journal of Business Research, 133*, 285–296. doi:10.1016/j.jbusres.2021.04.070

Donthu, N., Kumar, S., Pandey, N., & Lim, W. M. (2021c). Research constituents, intellectual structure, and collaboration patterns in Journal of International Marketing: An analytical retrospective. *Journal of International Marketing, 29*(2), 1–25. doi:10.1177/1069031X211004234

Donthu, N., Kumar, S., Pattnaik, D., & Lim, W. M. (2021d). Abibliometric retrospection ofmarketing from the lens of psychology: Insights from Psychology & Marketing. *Psychology and Marketing, 38*(5), 834–865. doi:10.1002/mar.21472

Durisin, B., & Puzone, F. (2009). Maturation of corporate governance research, 1993–2007: An assessment. *Corporate Governance, 17*(3), 266–291. doi:10.1111/j.1467-8683.2009.00739.x

Ellegaard, O., & Wallin, J. A. (2015). The bibliometric analysis of scholarly production: How great is the impact? *Scientometrics*, *105*(3), 1809–1831. doi:10.1007/s11192-015-1645-z PMID:26594073

Elouaourti, Z., & Ezzahid, E. (2022a). Factors of regional financial inclusion in Morocco. *Regional Science Policy & Practice*, rsp3.12516. Advance online publication. doi:10.1111/rsp3.12516

Elouaourti, Z., & Ezzahid, E. (2022b). Financial services and firm performance, are there any differences by size? Worldwide evidence using firm-level data. *Journal of Economic Studies (Glasgow, Scotland)*, *50*(4), 858–880. Advance online publication. doi:10.1108/JES-10-2021-0526

Elouardighi, I., & Oubejja, K. (2023). Can Digital Financial Inclusion Promote Women's Labor Force Participation? Microlevel Evidence from Africa. *International Journal of Financial Studies*, *11*(3), 87–87. doi:10.3390/ijfs11030087

Elouardighi, I., & Oubejja, K. (2023). COVID-19 and the fate of Moroccan female-led firms: Regional level evidence. *Regional Science Policy & Practice*, *15*(8), 1740–1767. doi:10.1111/rsp3.12703

Ezzahid, E., & Elouaourti, Z. (2019). Financial development and total factors productivity channel: Evidence from Africa. *Indonesian Capital Market Review*, *10*(2). Advance online publication. doi:10.21002/icmr.v10i2.10827

Ezzahid, E., & Elouaourti, Z. (2021a). Financial Inclusion, Financial Frictions, and Economic Growth: Evidence from Africa. *Journal of African Business*, *23*(3), 1–26. doi:10.1080/15228916.2021.1926856

Ezzahid, E., & Elouaourti, Z. (2021b). Financial inclusion, mobile banking, informal finance and financial exclusion: micro-level evidence from Morocco. *International Journal of Social Economics*. doi:10.1108/IJSE-11-2020-0747

Goyal, K., Kumar, S., & Xiao, J. J. (2021). Antecedents and consequences of personal financial management behavior: A systematic literature review and future research agenda. *International Journal of Bank Marketing*, *39*(7), 1166–1207. Advance online publication. doi:10.1108/IJBM-12-2020-0612

GSMA. (2019). *State of the industry report on mobile money*. GSMA. https://www.gsma.com/sotir/#download

Guillen-Royo, M. (2018). *Sustainability and wellbeing: Human-scale development in practice*. Routledge. doi:10.4324/9781315762135

Hussain, R. T., & Ahmad, F. (2021). Measuring Financial Longevity of Firm in Emerging Economy: A Study on Islamic Financial Institutions of Pakistan. *Minhaj Journal of Economics and Organization Science, 1*(2), 9-27.

Huston, S. J. (2010). Measuring financial literacy. *The Journal of Consumer Affairs*, *44*(2), 296–316. doi:10.1111/j.1745-6606.2010.01170.x

Khan, M. A., Pattnaik, D., Ashraf, R., Ali, I., Kumar, S., & Donthu, N. (2021). Value of special issues in the Journal of Business Research: A bibliometric analysis. *Journal of Business Research*, *125*, 295–313. doi:10.1016/j.jbusres.2020.12.015

Leyshon, A., & Thrift, N. (1995). Geographies of financial exclusion: Financial abandonment in Britain and the United States. *Transactions of the Institute of British Geographers*, *20*(3), 312–341. doi:10.2307/622654

Lim, W. M., Yap, S. F., & Makkar, M. (2021). Home sharing in marketing and tourism at a tipping point: What do we know, how do we know, and where should we be heading? *Journal of Business Research*, *122*, 534–566. doi:10.1016/j.jbusres.2020.08.051 PMID:33012896

Lusardi, A., & Mitchell, O. S. (2014). The economic importance of financial literacy: Theory and evidence. *Journal of Economic Literature*, *52*(1), 5–44. doi:10.1257/jel.52.1.5 PMID:28579637

Ozili, P. K. (2018). Impact of digital finance on financial inclusion and stability. *Borsa Istanbul Review*, *18*(4), 329–340. doi:10.1016/j.bir.2017.12.003

Ozili, P. K. (2021). Measuring financial inclusion and financial exclusion. In *New Challenges for Future Sustainability and Wellbeing* (pp. 411–427). Emerald Publishing Limited. doi:10.1108/978-1-80043-968-920211022

Paul, J., Lim, W. M., O'Cass, A., Hao, A. W., & Bresciani, S. (2021). Scientific procedures and rationales for systematic literature reviews (SPAR-4-SLR). *International Journal of Consumer Studies*, *45*(4), O1–O16. doi:10.1111/ijcs.12695

Sachs, J., Thye, W. W., & Yoshino, N. (2019). *Handbook of Green Finance: Energy Security and Sustainable Development*. Springer. doi:10.1007/978-981-13-0227-5

Sarma, M., & Pais, J. (2011). Financial inclusion and development. *Journal of International Development*, *23*(5), 613–628. doi:10.1002/jid.1698

Seghezzo, L. (2009). The five dimensions of sustainability. *Environmental Politics*, *18*(4), 539–556. doi:10.1080/09644010903063669

Shahid, M. R., Khin, A. A., Seong, L. C., Shahbaz, M., & Ahmad, F. (2024). Mapping the Relationship of Research and Development Expenditures and Economic Growth through Bibliometric Analysis: A Theoretical Perspective. *Journal of the Knowledge Economy*. Advance online publication. doi:10.1007/s13132-024-01781-8

Sinclair, S. P. (2001). Financial exclusion: An introductory survey. CRSIS, Edinburgh College of Art/Heriot Watt University.

UNDP. (2020). *Sustainable Development Goals*. Retrieved from United Nations Development Programme website. Available at: https://www.undp.org/sustainable-development-goals

Van Eck, N. J., & Waltman, L. (2017). Citation-based clustering of publications using CitNetExplorer and VOSviewer. *Scientometrics*, *111*(2), 1053–1070. doi:10.1007/s11192-017-2300-7 PMID:28490825

World Bank. (2018). *The Global Findex Database 2017: Measuring Financial Inclusion and the Fintech Revolution*. World Bank Group. https://documents.worldbank.org/curated/en/332881525873182837/The-Global-Findex-Database-2017-Measuring-Financial-Inclusion-and-the-Fintech-Revolution

World Bank. (2018). *Global Financial Development Report 2017/2018: Bankers without Borders*. Available at: https://shorturl.at/pr028

World Bank. (2022). *Financial Inclusion*. Available at: https://shorturl.at/bgqsv

Zhang, Y., Posso, A., & Swanepoel, J. (2021). Financial inclusion and poverty reduction in Sub-Saharan Africa. *Economic Modelling*, *94*, 387–396.

Zupic, I., & Čater, T. (2015). Bibliometric methods in management and organisation. *Organizational Research Methods*, *18*(3), 429–472. doi:10.1177/1094428114562629

KEY TERMS AND DEFINITIONS

Bibliometric Analysis: The analysis of books, papers, and other publications using statistical techniques, particularly in the field of science, is known as bibliometrics. Large amounts of scientific data can be explored and analysed using this well-liked and rigorous method, which makes the data easy to understand through visualisation.

Clusters: It is a group of similar things of objects positioned closely together. In bibliometric analysis, it is used to understand the nature of various objects (i.e., keywords, countries etc.) to understand the association of objects.

Financial Inclusion: This term devised by the United Nations describes the efforts to make accessible financial products and services for all individuals and institutions. Specifically, it relates to making these services available for affordable transactions, payments, savings, credit and insurance under sustainable development.

Performance Analysis: It is an analysis technique being used in bibliometric analysis. It examines the contributions of research constituents (i.e., authors, sources, institutes etc.) to a given field of study.

Science Mapping: It is also a technique of bibliometric analysis which pertains to the intellectual interactions and structural connections among research constituents.

Sustainability: Sustainability is a goal to satisfy current needs without compromising the resources' capacity for future generations. It is an intention of long-term human existence by conserving scarce resources.

APPENDIX

Assignment Topics for Financial Inclusion and Sustainability

Class Assignment 1

Title: Analysing Global Collaboration in Financial Inclusion and Sustainability Research

Instructions: Based on the collaborative patterns mentioned in the provided information, conduct further research, and answer the following questions:

- Identify three pairs of countries that exhibit a substantial level of collaboration in financial inclusion and sustainability research. Explain why you think these collaborations are significant.
- Discuss the potential benefits of international collaboration in research, especially in financial inclusion and sustainability. Provide examples from the information provided.
- Select one author from the collaborative networks mentioned in the text and explore their research contributions. Discuss how their joint efforts contribute to the broader understanding of financial inclusion and sustainability.

Class Assignment 2

Title: Journal Impact Analysis: Sustainability (Switzerland) vs. Borsa Istanbul Review

Instructions: Based on the information about top contributing journals, compare the impact of two journals, "Sustainability (Switzerland)" and "Borsa Istanbul Review," in the field of financial inclusion and sustainability research.

- Analyse the key metrics (total publications, total citations, and H-index) for both "Sustainability (Switzerland)" and "Borsa Istanbul Review." Explain how these metrics reflect the influence of each journal in the field.
- Discuss the potential reasons behind the higher impact of "Sustainability (Switzerland)" compared to "Borsa Istanbul Review." Consider factors such as the number of publications, citations, and the H-index.
- Evaluate the statement, "Although lesser TP (total publications) and TC (total citations) in specific journals do not necessarily indicate inferior quality, they may indicate a more specific or specialised viewpoint." Apply this statement to the comparison between the two journals.

Take-home Assignments

1. **Cross-disciplinary studies:** Analyze how integrating finance, environmental science, social policy, and technology can address global challenges related to financial inclusion and sustainability.
2. **Longitudinal impact assessments:** Conduct long-term studies to understand the lasting impacts of financial inclusion initiatives on ecological, social, and economic sustainability.
3. **Incorporating ESG factors:** Investigate how environmental, social, and governance factors are currently integrated into financial practices and identify areas for improvement.

4. **Emerging technologies and digital financial services:** Assess the impact of new technologies like blockchain and AI on digital financial services and their potential contribution to sustainable financial inclusion.
5. **Regional studies:** Analyze the specific challenges and opportunities for financial inclusion and sustainability in different regions of the world.

Practical Implications:

6. **Evaluating existing policies:** Examine the effectiveness of current policies and regulations in promoting both financial inclusion and sustainability.
7. **Community participation:** Explore ways to encourage community participation in financial policy development and implementation.
8. **Financial education programs:** Develop and evaluate financial education programs to enhance individual and community capacity for responsible financial management.
9. **Global collaboration and SDGs:** Analyze the existing frameworks for global collaboration, such as the UN SDGs, and propose further improvements for promoting sustainable and inclusive financial practices worldwide.
10. **Impact measurement frameworks:** Design and implement robust impact measurement frameworks to track progress towards achieving financial inclusion and sustainability goals.

Additional Considerations:

- You can further refine these topics by focusing on specific aspects of the research questions, such as a particular region, technology, or policy area.

Quiz 1:

Question 1: What does the H-index of a journal, such as "Sustainability (Switzerland)," indicate? How does it reflect the journal's influence on financial inclusion and sustainability research?

Question 2: According to the information provided, why is 2015 highlighted in the bar graph depicting the publication trend in financial inclusion and sustainability research?

Question 3: Choose one cluster from the co-occurrence network of author keywords and explain the thematic focus of that cluster. How does it contribute to the multidisciplinary nature of research in financial inclusion and sustainability?

Quiz 2:

Question 1: Briefly explain the significance of the word cloud generated from the titles of research papers in financial inclusion and sustainability. What insights does it provide about prevalent themes in the research?

Question 2: Identify two countries mentioned in the analysis that demonstrate a high level of collaboration in financial inclusion and sustainability research. Discuss the potential reasons behind their collaborative efforts.

Question 3: Considering the bar graph illustrating the article production over time, why do you think there was minimal activity in the initial years (2009-2014), and what changed in 2015?

MCQs

1. **Which global event led to a significant increase in research on financial inclusion and sustainability?** (a) The financial crisis of 2008 (b) The adoption of the Paris Agreement (c) The introduction of the United Nations Sustainable Development Goals (UNSDGs) (d) The launch of the World Bank's Global Findex database
2. **Which research approach does NOT align with the future directions presented in the chapter?** (a) Cross-sectional surveys on the financial literacy of specific communities (b) Historical analysis of financial inclusion policies in developed countries (c) Case studies examining the impact of fintech on microfinance initiatives (d) Long-term studies tracking the environmental and social outcomes of financial inclusion projects
3. **Which area of research requires further investigation, according to the chapter?** (a) The optimal design of government subsidies for financial inclusion programs (b) The impact of traditional banking models on social inequality (c) The effectiveness of financial education programs in reducing poverty (d) The integration of environmental, social, and governance (ESG) factors into financial institutions' decision-making

Practical Implications

4. **What is the primary goal of evaluating existing policies on financial inclusion and sustainability?** (a) To identify and celebrate successful policies (b) To justify the need for increased government spending (c) To inform future policy revisions and improvements (d) To track compliance with international regulations **Answer:** (c) Policy evaluation aims to identify both strengths and weaknesses, informing revisions and improvements for better outcomes.
5. **How can community participation be enhanced in financial policy development and implementation?** (a) By increasing government funding for public awareness campaigns (b) By holding public consultations in major cities only (c) By involving local community leaders and organizations in the decision-making process (d) By relying solely on online surveys to gather feedback **Answer:** (c) Engaging local communities directly through leaders and organizations ensures their unique needs and perspectives are considered.
6. **What is the main purpose of promoting global collaboration and the UN SDGs related to financial inclusion and sustainability?** (a) To impose uniform financial regulations on all countries (b) To facilitate knowledge sharing and coordinated efforts (c) To provide financial aid to developing countries only (d) To establish a global ranking system for financial inclusion **Answer:** (b) Global collaboration and shared goals like the SDGs encourage knowledge sharing and joint efforts for faster progress towards financial inclusion and sustainability.

Additional Short Questions

7. Which country was identified as the leading publisher of research on financial inclusion and sustainability in the chapter?
8. What is a co-occurrence network used to illustrate in bibliometric analysis?

9. What are the major themes identified in the word cloud analysis based on author keywords and paper titles?
10. What practical recommendations does the chapter offer for financial institutions to align their practices with sustainability goals?

Answer Key

1. (c) The introduction of the United Nations Sustainable Development Goals (UNSDGs)
2. (b) Historical analysis of financial inclusion policies in developed countries
3. (d) The integration of environmental, social, and governance (ESG) factors into financial institutions' decision-making

Practical Implications

4. (c) To inform future policy revisions and improvements
5. (c) By involving local community leaders and organizations in the decision-making process
6. (b) To facilitate knowledge sharing and coordinated efforts

Additional MCQs

7. China
8. A visual representation of how frequently certain research terms appear together in the analyzed publications.
9. Themes will vary depending on the specific chapter content but could include digital finance, microfinance, poverty reduction, green finance, etc.
10. Examples include integrating ESG factors into investment decisions, offering sustainable financial products, and supporting green businesses.

Chapter 7
Financial Inclusion in Sukuk and Green Sukuk:
A Case Study Through Bibliometric and SLR

Sumiya Tahir
Kinnaird College for Women, Pakistan

Farah Naz
https://orcid.org/0000-0002-4707-5443
Kinnaird College for Women, Pakistan

ABSTRACT

This study employs bibliometrics and a systematic literature review to comprehensively analyze Sukuk and Green Sukuk research trends from 2011 to 2023. Key terms such as "Islamic finance," "Sukuk," and "green bonds" are identified through bibliometric analysis, revealing their central role. The systematic literature review uncovers dominant themes, notable authors, and publication trends. Findings indicate a transformative potential in fostering financial inclusion and sustainability. The study underscores the importance of international collaboration, highlights key contributors like Malaysia and Indonesia, and provides insights for practitioners and policymakers. Despite positive trends, research gaps necessitate further exploration for a nuanced understanding of Sukuk's impact on sustainability goals.

INTRODUCTION

It is essential to understand that the use of Sukuk as a substitute funding vehicle has shown to be a practical success in several Muslim nations rather than just a theoretical idea. Several studies show that a large proportion of Muslim countries struggle with external debt to obtain funds for infrastructure development. Even though these countries urgently require large-scale development programs their limited resources make it difficult for them to find local funding. As a result, many governments turn

DOI: 10.4018/979-8-3693-1475-3.ch007

to other nations or international financial organizations for financial support. This traditional method poses several difficulties for the country borrowing the money, such as the vulnerability to changes in the value of the home currency when the loan is in foreign currency. An increase in economic leverage and volatility is a result of external borrowing (Trabelsi, Umar, Dogah, & Vo, 2024). The vulnerability to changes in the price of commodities because of the country's heavy reliance on commodity exports. The advent of Islamic bonds sometimes referred to as Sukuk, is a novel development that has the potential to mitigate the drawbacks of borrowing from outside sources, lower economic leverage, and improve resilience to risk factors (A. Hasan, Gupta, Irfan, & Dias, 2024).

Sukuk can serve as a conduit for foreign investment, fostering the expansion and improvement of the regional economy. These investments can support a range of initiatives and projects that advance economic stability, infrastructure development, and general advancement (Surachman, Hermawan, Handayani, & Astuti, 2023). Sukuk's appeal to investors worldwide makes them a desirable option, encouraging cooperation and support for the development of the issuing nation. It's similar to welcome friends from other countries that support and believe in the constructive advancement of the country. To finance its development infrastructure, the Malaysian government issued the first sovereign sukuk (Uluyol, 2023).

The Islamic finance sector's primary goal is to achieve long-term gains and consistently engage in initiatives that advance the interests of the public. The Islamic finance, which prioritizes sustainability and the environment is expected to be one of the societal solutions to the pollution and harm to the environment (Musari & Hidayat, 2023). Regarding poor nations, the SDGs aim to lower poverty rates while enhancing the standard of living in terms of health, education, sanitation, availability of drinking water and preservation of marine and forest ecosystems. Countries all across the world had already concluded that financing was essential for the successful implementation of sustainable development before the SDGs were created the global development, encompassing both wealthy and developing nations (Brahmana & You, 2022).

Therefore, the Green finance like green sukuk is getting a lot of attention in the recent literature as a result of the increased global action on climate change. Investment products made with green sukuk still have a lot of room for improvement and require assessment (A. Rahman, Ahmad, Bin-Nashwan, Muneeza, Abdul Halim, & Markom, 2023). This study addresses the question of how much can be learned about green sukuk in terms of development patterns in the number of publications, development opportunities, and evaluation given the significance and enormous potential of the concept. This study's main goal is to shed light on the historical development, contemporary trends, and potential future applications of Sukuk and Green Sukuk in the context of Islamic finance and sustainable investing (Faisal, Gunawan, Cupian, Hayati, Apriliadi, & Fajri, 2023).

The concepts of sustainability and inclusion have come to light as potent threads running through the complex web of economic development in the colorful tapestry of global finance. Nestled at the intersection of these fundamental ideas is an engrossing investigation of "Financial Inclusion in Sukuk and Green Sukuk". Financial inclusion in Sukuk and Green Sukuk promotes equity, justice, and sustainable development, which is in line with the fundamental tenets of Islamic finance (Khan, 2023). These financial instruments serve to empower underprivileged groups, boost small and medium-sized enterprises (SMEs), and promote inclusive economic growth by increasing access to financial services. Green Sukuk adds to social effect and is in line with the Sustainable Development Goals by concentrating on ecologically sustainable projects. Through Sukuk funds, financial literacy programs and vocational training are included addressing economic difficulties and generating employment prospects (Asnaini, Isnaini, & Fryanti, 2023).

This strategy promotes a robust and inclusive financial system by drawing impact investors in addition to adhering to moral and responsible finance practices. The promotion of these programs by governments and regulatory assistance can be crucial in fostering an atmosphere that is conducive to the success of financial inclusion projects based on Sukuk. All things considered the incorporation of financial inclusion into Sukuk constitutes a holistic approach that blends social development, environmental sustainability, and economic empowerment (Khan, 2023). This innovative project explores the core of Islamic finance where Green Sukuk and its ecologically aware counterpart the Sukuk take center stage as financial instruments. It follows tell a story of scholarship, invention, and transformational potential as this study sets out on a path led by the dual guiding principles of ecological responsibility and financial inclusiveness. Get ready to explore the conceptual spaces where economic systems meet social welfare, and environmental awareness meets Islamic teachings to produce a story that transcends traditional limits (Qosim, Ratnasari, Wardhana, Fauziana, & Barkah, 2023).

The significant number of Muslim clients who are beginning to understand the benefits of financing money to Islamic banks is another factor contributing to this rise. Furthermore, the capital market industry made a 27% contribution to the growth of Islamic finance in 2018 compared to a 23% contribution in 2017 (Brahmana & You, 2022). The drive for Sukuk stems from the necessity of harmonizing financial practices with Islamic precepts, particularly the Quran's proscription against interest (riba). Designed to give investors a share in real assets or projects, sukuk is a noteworthy innovation that complies with Shariah and ethical financial standards. Investors seeking financial instruments that are both financially stable and ethically decent have found attraction in this approach, which emphasizes risk-sharing and asset-backing, and it has gained ground in both Islamic and conventional financial markets (Liu & Lai, 2021).

Sukuk issuance globally decreased somewhat in 2022, but ESG Sukuk increased by 35% annually. ESG Sukuk issued in 2022 totaled US$8.1 billion, up from US$6 billion in 2021.The amount of outstanding sukuk globally in 2022 was USD 765.3 billion, 7.6% more than the previous year. Multilaterals and sovereigns continue to be the primary issuers. Sukuk in default made up a small percentage of total issues 0.21%. Outstanding ESG sukuk volumes reached USD 24.5 billion (3% of global sukuk volumes) in 2022, growing 62.9% mostly as a result of the low-base impact. Frameworks and tactics for ESG sukuk and bond issuance were introduced by numerous authorities (fitch rating) (Ulfah, Sukmana, Laila, & Sulaeman, 2023).

Moreover, non-Muslim issuers from Europe, Asia, and Africa have also been drawn to this relatively young market. Following the worldwide financial crises, the sukuk market evolved into a novel phenomenon in the global financial system. It is a different approach to raising money to support sustainable economic development and satisfy the financial demands of businesses. Globally, academic and policymakers alike were interested in this market. In tandem with this curiosity and the ongoing sukuk issuance, a substantial body of literature has emerged on the subject (Trianto & Masrizal, 2021).

Research Question

1. How frequently do specific keywords related to financial inclusion occur in the identified trends and themes within discussions about Sukuk and Green Sukuk?
2. What connections do countries have in terms of financial inclusion through Sukuk and Green Sukuk?

3. Which journals have the most citations in the area of financial inclusion within Sukuk and Green Sukuk?
4. Who are the most influential authors contributing to the understanding of financial inclusion in Sukuk and Green Sukuk?
5. What trends and themes can be identified in discussions about financial inclusion within Sukuk and Green Sukuk?
6. How has previous literature evolved, and what opportunities and developments are revealed through a systematic literature review in the context of financial inclusion within Sukuk and Green Sukuk?

Objective

The primary objective of this study is to perform a thorough examination of Sukuk and Green Sukuk, covering their historical evolution, present-day patterns, and potential future developments. A quantitative evaluation of the Sukuk and Green Sukuk-related literature is part of the project. This methodology is being used in the study with the goal of quantifying the field's growth, trends, and key players. This study helped to learn a great deal about the background of Sukuk and Green Sukuk research by looking at publication trends, recognizing influential writers and organizations, and following the development of important themes and ideas. Simultaneously, a qualitative analysis is carried out on professional and academic research papers in order to discover gaps in the literature, classify study themes, and unearth important findings. Through a thorough content analysis of previous studies, the bibliometric review deepens our comprehension of Sukuk and Green Sukuk by exposing us to the subtleties and developing issues in the area (Faisal et al., 2023).

Significance of the Study

There are several stakeholders in the financial, investment, and policy areas who should find this research significant. It helps to clarify the historical development of Sukuk and Green Sukuk by providing insights into their progress. Additionally, by exploring current research trends, the study offers insightful advice to practitioners, policymakers, and academics who are attempting to negotiate these complex and dynamic financial markets. In conclusion, by providing a thorough examination of Sukuk and Green Sukuk's historical evolution, present trends, and potential futures, this research hopes to further knowledge of these financial instruments. This study aims to shed light on the journey that Sukuk and Green Sukuk have taken, highlighting their importance within the framework of morally and environmentally responsible finance, using the combined lens of bibliometric analysis (Musari & Hidayat, 2023).

RESEARCH METHODS

Methodology

This study takes a broad approach to examine the financial inclusion of sukuk and green sukuk by combining bibliometric analysis with a systematic literature review.In order to compile a wide selection of peer-reviewed publications published during the previous ten years, the research process starts with a thorough search on the Scopus database. Based on their applicability to the research topic, papers are chosen using predetermined inclusion and exclusion criteria. After that, the gathered data is put through bibliometric analysis with the aid of VOSviewer, an effective program for calculating and displaying author partnerships, co-citation patterns, and topic clusters (M. Rahman, Isa, Tu, Sarker, & Masud, 2020). In parallel, a comprehensive assessment of the literature is carried out in order to provide a qualitative summary of the most important discoveries, methodology, and new trends. The goal of integrating quantitative and qualitative insights is to offer a comprehensive perspective and produce insightful results. In parallel, a comprehensive assessment of the literature is carried out in order to provide a qualitative summary of the most important discoveries, methodology, and new trends (Rezkyarta & Irfany, 2023).

Bibliometrics

An analysis known as "bibliometrics" is done using bibliographies that are taken from books, articles, and journals (Koseoglu, Rahimi, Okumus, & Liu, 2016).The bibliometric method was first introduced and applied statistically to bibliographic data (Pritchard, 1969).According to research by (Pritchard, 1969) it may be applied in all academic domains that seek to quantify the relationship between every piece of documentation, including books, journal articles, and media, and it integrates mathematical and statistical methodologies (Wallin, 2005).

Data Collection

Take advantage of Scopus, a reputable academic database, to gather a wide range of academic papers. Relevance and currency are guaranteed by the inclusion criteria, which cover publications published in peer-reviewed journals within a given time span. In journal terminology, "ABCD" categorization typically refers to a ranking system that takes into account the journal's perceived impact or quality. Usually, there are four categories: A, B, C, and D. A signifies the greatest influence or quality, while D is the lowest. Researchers and academics can assess the importance of publications in their subject with the use of this system. Remember that different disciplines and institutions may have different particular criteria for classification (Ngoc & Tien, 2023).

VOS Viewer Analysis

Using the potent bibliometric tool VOS viewer for network analysis and visualization. To find important writers, journals, and subject groups in the literature, do co-citation analysis. This method provides a quantitative viewpoint on the field's intellectual structure. Use the bibliometric analysis tool VOS viewer to see how the literature is organized intellectually. To find important writers, journals, and groups of closely connected studies, use a co-citation analysis. Thematic clusters and possible research gaps will become apparent when these relationships are mapped (Liaqat, Altaf, Barutçular, Zayed, & Hussain, 2023).

Thematic Coding

Sort and evaluate the articles' content by using theme coding. It emphasized on the words co-occurrence, country wise analysis and conceptual elements associated with emerging developments in Islamic finance will be part of this process (Maulayati & Iswati).

2. Systematic Literature Review (SLR)

A study's assessment of prior research is crucial because, as all research begins with prior research, it will establish the study's direction, objectives, and driving force. In several research meant to analyze a topic; the literature review process is crucial. The literature review method, according to (Kitchenham, Brereton, Budgen, Turner, Bailey, & Linkman, 2009) has a number of goals, including finding gaps in prior research, determining what research has not been discussed, identifying significant variables pertinent to the discussion topic, examining prior research findings and gaining fresh perspectives, identifying the primary methodologies, and situating the research within the framework of the evolution of research topics (Dziopa & Ahern, 2011).

Search Strategy

Create a methodical search approach with pertinent keywords like "green sukuk," "sukuk," and "Financial inclusion."

Data Extraction and Synthesis

Extrapolate relevant information, such as study goals, methods, important conclusions, and consequences, from the chosen articles. Arrange and integrate this data to pinpoint recurring themes, differences, and

Table 1. Inclusion and exclusion criteria

Years	Articles Between 2011-2013
Type	Included in the article's criteria
Steps	Article in the final stage
Language	English articles only
Indexation	Articles with Scopus index and ABDC Journal Quality List

voids in the current body of work (Maulayati & Iswati).

Table 1. Criteria for Inclusion and Exclusion Requirements Acceptable for Pilot Years articles published from 2011 until 2023 Type Listed in the Article Requirements Actions Article nearing completion Articles in English only Indexing articles listed on the ABDC Journal Quality List and the Scopus index. Based on the predetermined inclusion and exclusion standards, drawn from a population of 280 articles. The 156 articles were filtered based on the predetermined inclusion and exclusion criteria, making them suitable for use as samples in this investigation (Paltrinieri, Hassan, Bahoo, & Khan, 2019). The following research procedures were followed:

Figure 1. Research steps (Paltrinieri, Hassan, Bahoo, & Khan, 2019)

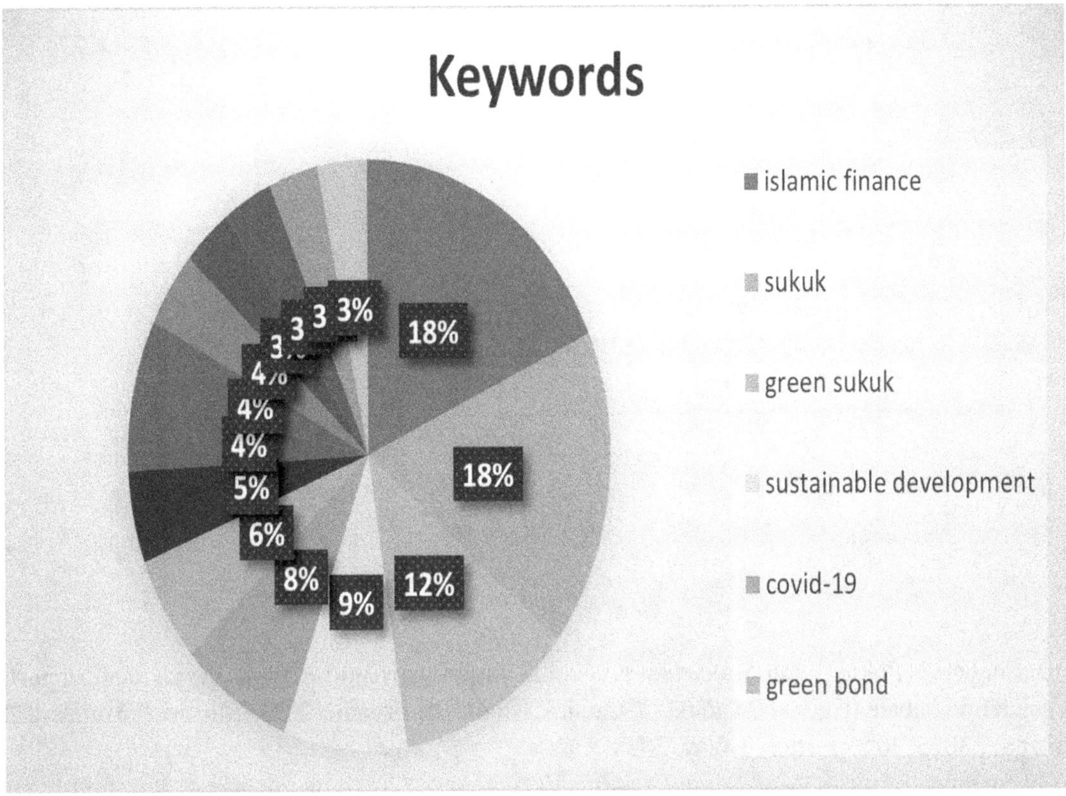

RESULTS AND ANALYSIS

Bibliometric Clustered Analysis

The steps involved in performing a bibliometric clustered analysis on financial inclusion in Sukuk and Green Sukuk literature are gathering and cleaning bibliometric data, choosing clustering parameters, and using an appropriate algorithm to find clusters. The detected clusters are then shown and interpreted using visualization tools like network graphs (M. Rahman et al., 2020).

- **Co-occurrence of keywords**
- **Country wise Analysis**
- **Author Analysis**

1. Co-Occurrence of Keywords

The research domain's interrelated links and theme concentrations are revealed through the analysis of keyword co-occurrence in the bibliometric assessment of financial inclusion in Sukuk and Green Sukuk literature. When keywords are systematically evaluated for how often they occur together, patterns become apparent that clarify dominant themes and relationships between ideas. Notable keywords such as

Figure 2. Chart of keywords

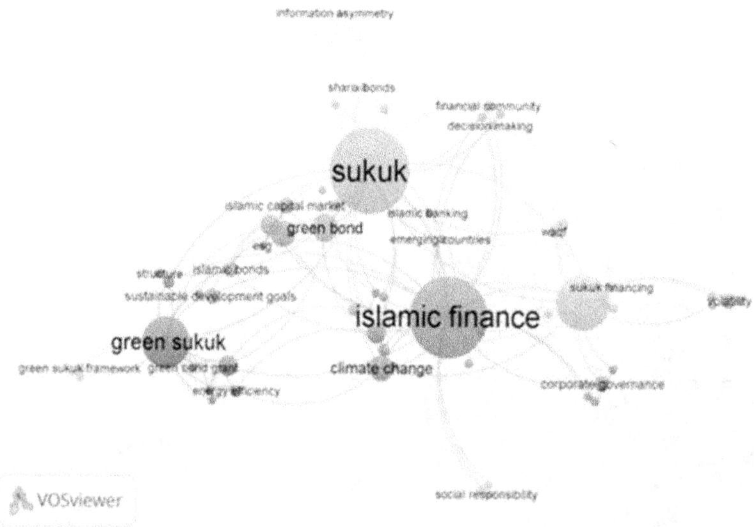

"Islamic finance," "Sukuk," and "green bonds" exhibit strong correlations, highlighting their importance in the academic debate (figure 02 and 03). (Asnaini, Isnaini, & Fryanti, 2023; Musari & Hidayat, 2023; Qosim et al., 2023; Rezkyarta & Irfany, 2023).

Co-occurrence of terms was examined using VOS viewer.228 keywords were identified from this process's data. The size of the node indicates the frequency of a keywording the abstracts and titles of 154 Sukuk, Green Sukuk, and financial inclusion-related articles. The findings presented in Figure 4 indicate that the term "Islamic finance" was most frequently used in connection with the terms "Sukuk" and "green bond" (Musari & Hidayat, 2023). Following these terms, the financial inclusion in Sukuk and Green Sukuk literature also commonly cited "green bonds," "energy efficiency," and "Green Sukuk framework" (Billah, Elsayed, & Hadhri, 2023).

Figure 3 presents a graphic representation of the frequency and relationship between particular terms in the financial inclusion bibliometric analysis of Sukuk and Green Sukuk literature.

Purple Cluster: Islamic Finance (Highest Cluster)

Focusing on the wide field of Islamic finance, the color purple represents the largest and most noticeable cluster in the research. This cluster probably covers a wide range of Islamic finance issues, such as market activities, financial products, and core principles. It has showed the most Interestingly, "Sukuk" is the most often referenced term, and it is closely associated with both "Islamic finance" and "green bond."

Peach Cluster: Sukuk Cluster

Sukuk is at the center of the second-largest cluster, which is peach-colored and indicates that Sukuk is a major player in the network. Various elements pertaining to Sukuk issuance, structures, and market dynamics may be included in this cluster.

Figure 3. Mapping of keywords

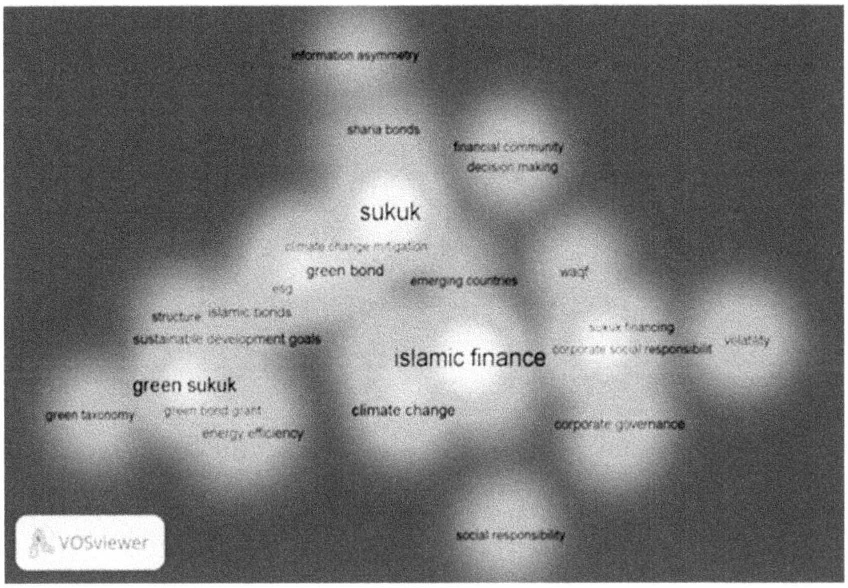

Red Cluster: Green Sukuk

The red-colored, third-highest cluster highlights Green Sukuk and its significance in sustainable finance. Topics like energy efficiency, green bond grants, and other sustainable financing initiatives are probably included in this cluster since they are associated with financial instruments that consider the environment. The following terms, which show notable repetition in the literature, are "green bonds," "energy efficiency," and "Green Sukuk framework," suggesting a theme focus on sustainability in the context of Sukuk. The graphic successfully conveys how Sukuk research is intertwined with important subjects pertaining to Islamic finance and environmental sustainability (Keshminder, SİNGH, WAHİD, & Abdullah, 2019).

The highly densely populated yellow cluster includes Green Sukuk, Sukuk, and Islamic finance. This points to a focused and interconnected conceptual network inside these domains. The co-occurrence map is a useful tool that indicates that "Sukuk" is a widely used and prominent phrase that is often used synonymously with terms such as Islamic finance, green Sukuk, Sukuk finance, and Sukuk financing The color yellow denotes the close relationship and dense network of studies, practices, and topics among Islamic finance, Sukuk, and Green Sukuk. Furthermore, the visualized mapping highlights that much of the Sukuk research is concentrated on investigating the performance of Sukuk instruments within the realm of Islamic financial investment (Dziopa & Ahern, 2011).

Blue and Green Keywords (Before 2021)

Keywords that appear before 2021 are highlighted in green, indicating a certain collection of ideas or themes that dominated the scene at the time. These green keywords most likely describe the field's well-established or basic subjects.

Figure 4. Density mapping of keywords

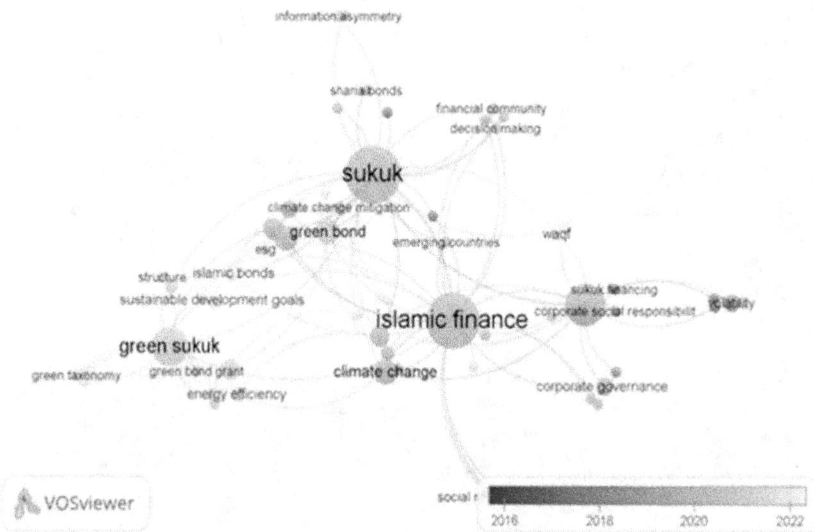

Figure 5. New trends in the keywords

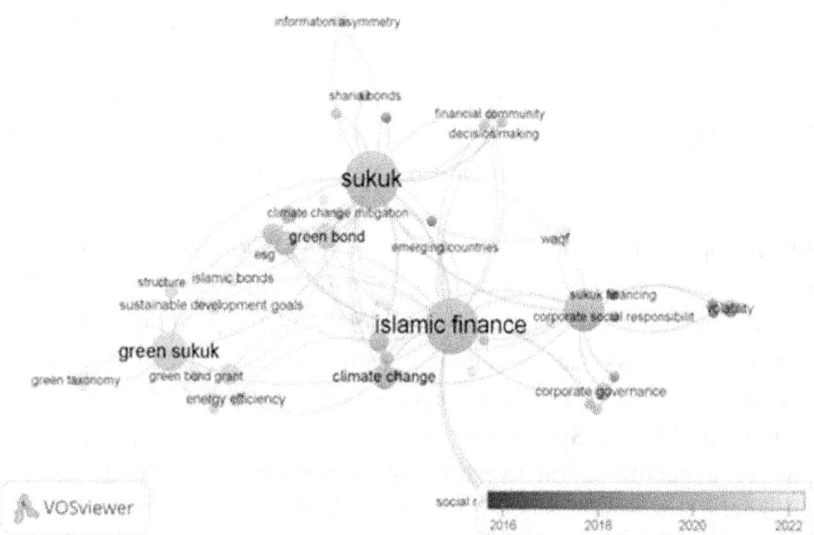

Figure 6. Countrywide analysis

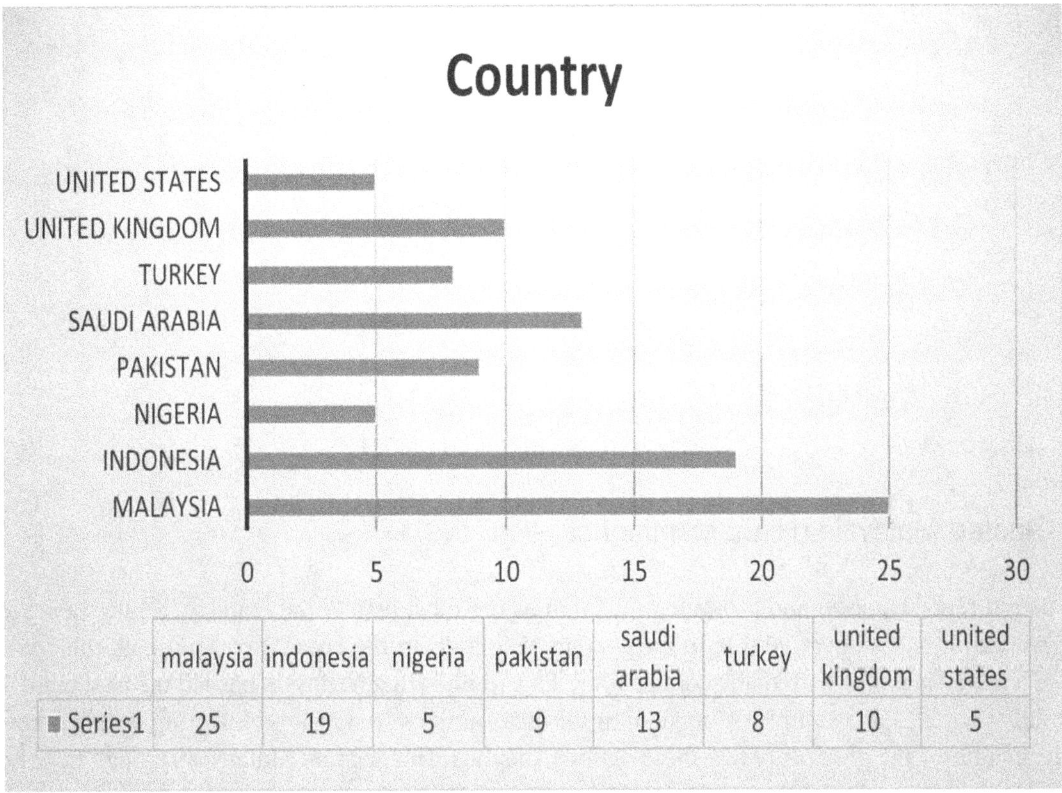

Green to Yellow Transition for Green Sukuk (2021 to 2022)

Green Sukuk becomes yellow in 2022 after turning green in 2021. This change in hue could be interpreted as a growing awareness of or attention to Green Sukuk during this time. A higher concentration or intensity in the connections within the Green Sukuk cluster is indicated by the shift to yellow. Now, it has moved towards the green sukuk. As interest in sustainable and ecologically conscious financial products has grown, there has been a discernible shift in study concentration towards Green Sukuk in recent years. Green Sukuk is a financial instrument that combines green finance and Islamic finance concepts to address environmental sustainability and ethical investment (Musari & Hidayat, 2023).

2. Country Analysis

Malaysia is the world's most emerging nation, as Figure 6 demonstrated. To further elaborate on the collaborative landscape around Sukuk research, it is interesting that Malaysia stands out as a pioneer in terms of both international collaborations and the sheer volume of research output produced. With its 13 Multi-Country Publications (MCP) and 10 Single-Country Publications (SCP), the data shows that Malaysia actively collaborates on research projects with scholars from other countries, demonstrating its dedication to promoting an international conversation on Sukuk and related financial instruments. This cooperative strategy underscores Malaysia's commitment to promoting knowledge-sharing globally and its position as a center of expertise for Islamic finance(Ramadhan, 2020).

Figure 7. Mapping view of countries

Red Cluster: Malaysia (Highest Influence)

With its red representation and prominent position as the most influential country, Malaysia is clearly playing a major and innovative role in the issuing of Sukuk. In the context of Malaysia, the color red denotes a robust network with many connections. This implies that Malaysia has led the way in the area, potentially acting as an example or inspiration for other nations.Malaysia's clustering with Turkey and Bangladesh raises the possibility that these nations, maybe influenced by Malaysia's model, have begun aggressively pursuing Sukuk issuance, drawing on knowledge and expertise from the country's market.

Green Cluster: Indonesia (Second Highest Influence)

As the country with the second-highest influence and the green representation, Indonesia also becomes a major player in Sukuk research, in addition to Malaysia's contributions, highlighting the collaborative and international nature of scholarly endeavors. The red color signifies its substantial influence in the field. Research on a range of Sukuk-related topics, including market development and sustainability integration, has been sparked by Indonesia's expanding Islamic financial industry. Writing Sukuk-related publications together demonstrates Indonesia's dedication to interacting with the global academic community and adding a range of viewpoints to the conversation as it develops. Cross

Blue Cluster: Saudi Arabia, UAE, UK (Issuing New Sukuk)

The UAE, the UK, and Saudi Arabia—represented in blue—form a distinct cluster that shows their combined influence and participation in the issuance of fresh Sukuk. Within this cluster, the blue tint denotes a cooperative or linked network. This could indicate a coordinated attempt on the part of these nations to encourage and increase the issuance of Sukuk, perhaps in order to meet the demands of their Muslim populations or to capitalize on the increasing interest in Islamic banking around the world. International discussion on Islamic finance instruments is enhanced by the sharing of knowledge and perspectives on issues like sustainability concerns, regulatory frameworks, and market dynamic (Kitchenham et al., 2009).

Figure 8. Mapping view of new trend among countries

Figure 8 showed that the clustered moved from green to yellow in the Bangladesh and Pakistan. Consider reading scholarly publications, going to conferences, and reviewing reports from financial institutions and regulatory agencies in Bangladesh and Pakistan to remain current on Sukuk and Green Sukuk trends. With their expanding Islamic finance industries, Bangladesh and

Pakistan are probably going to provide something special to the continuing conversations about Sukuk (Mukit, Muneeza, & Paltrinieri, 2021).

3. Author Analysis

I): The author has the highest publication
ii): The author has the highest cited number.

The co-authorship analysis illustrates how collaborative Sukuk research is, which emphasizes the value of teamwork. A more complete comprehension of the individual contributions might be possible with an in-depth examination of the most prolific writers and their associations. Examining the h-index, citation counts, and particular study issues linked to influential writers would clarify their influence on the area even more (Zupic & Čater, 2015).

I) The Author Has the Highest Publication

Kesh minder, J.S.

Number of Publications: The researcher with the greatest number of publications in Sukuk and Green Sukuk research is Kesh minder, J.S. Kesh minder's large corpus of work demonstrates a steady and committed interest in the topic and makes a substantial contribution to the academic conversation (Keshminder et al., 2019).

Research Focus: Kesh minder's writings would reveal certain study themes, techniques, and the development of their contributions over time with a thorough examination. Gaining knowledge of the

Figure 9. Comparative review of publication and citation in the context of author

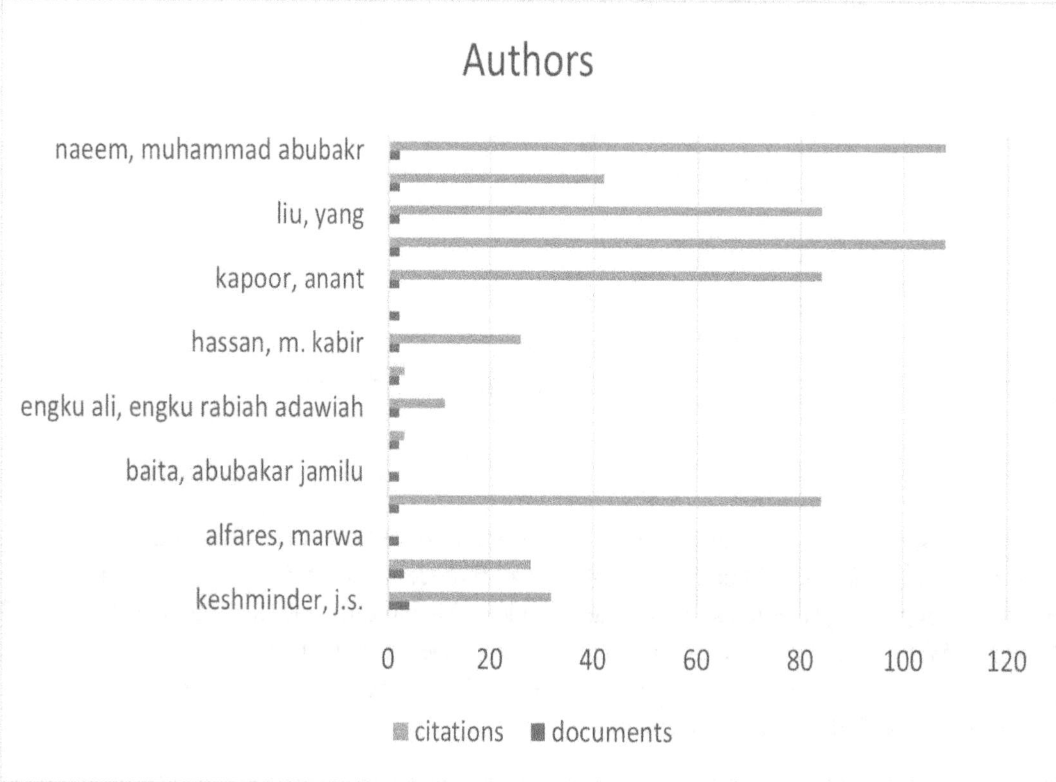

intricate aspects of Sukuk and Green Sukuk that Kesh minder has studied can help one appreciate the breadth of their influence and level of skill in the field (Keshminder et al., 2019).

ii): The Author Has the Highest Cited Number

Azhgaliyeva D., Kapoor A., Liu Y.

Citation Impact: Kesh minder's writings would reveal certain study themes, techniques, and the development of their contributions over time with a thorough examination. Gaining knowledge of the intricate aspects of Sukuk and Green Sukuk that Kesh minder has studied can help one appreciate the breadth of their influence and level of skill in the field (Azhgaliyeva, Kapoor, & Liu, 2020).

Influence on Research Landscape: The highest number of citations indicates that the research on Sukuk and Green Sukuk by Azhgaliyeva D., Kapoor A., and Liu Y. has reached a pivotal level. Their impact goes beyond the simple quantity of articles they have produced; rather, their contributions have had a substantial impact on the field's intellectual climate and following research directions (Azhgaliyeva, Kapoor, & Liu, 2020).

Figure 10. Number of publications in context of author

Collaborative Networks

Interdisciplinary and International Collaboration

Mapping Figure 11 indicates that examining collaborative networks involving Keshminder, J.S., Azhgaliyeva D., Kapoor A., and Liu Y. will demonstrate how multidisciplinary and global Sukuk research is. Gaining insight into the collaborative relationships amongst prolific writers illuminates the interchange of knowledge, variety of viewpoints, and teamwork that propels progress in the subject.To sum up, a detailed grasp of the dynamics of authorship in Sukuk and Green Sukuk research can be gained from the examination of Keshminder, J.S., and the most often cited authors, Azhgaliyeva D., Kapoor A., and Liu Y. A thorough understanding of the intellectual terrain of Sukuk studies is facilitated by examining their distinct contributions, areas of interest, and cooperative networks.

SYSTEMATIC LITERATURE REVIEW ANALYSIS

Financial inclusion in the Context of Sukuk and Green Sukuk

A systematic literature review is a thorough and rigorous research methodology that identifies, assesses, and synthesizes the body of scholarly literature that has already been written on a particular subject in an organized and objective manner, offering an overview of the state of knowledge in that field as it is today. It entails transparent methodology, predetermined criteria for study selection, and a thorough analysis to pinpoint research gaps and offer conclusions based on evidence(Dziopa & Ahern, 2011; Maulayati & Iswati).

Figure 11. Mapping view of collaborative networks of authors

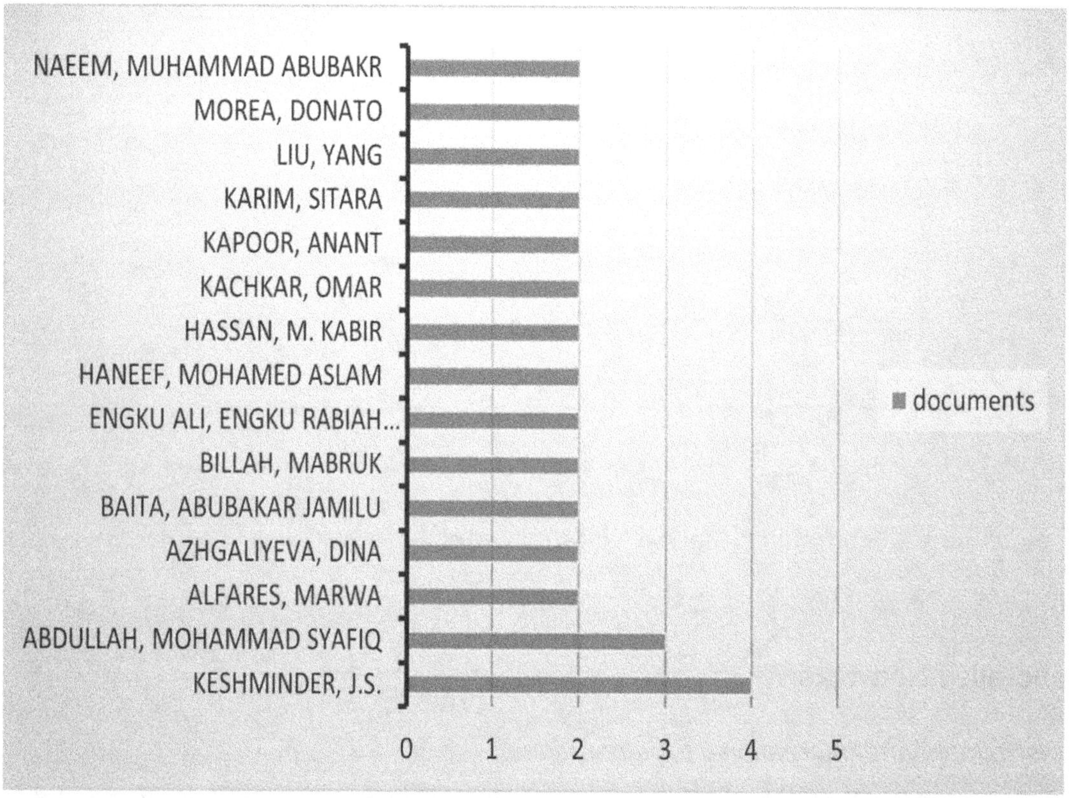

Table 2. Development and opportunity

Authors	Title	Model Development	Development and Opportunity
(Azhgaliyeva, Kapoor, & Liu, 2020)	Green bonds for financing renewable energy and energy efficiency in South-East Asia: a review of policies	Qualitative and interpretive methodologies	• The issuing of green bonds is beneficial, the proceeds from these bonds are sometimes used to finance projects overseas or to refinance previous loans, which may not necessarily encourage investments in energy-efficient and renewable energy projects inside ASEAN.
(Karim & Naeem, 2022)	Do global factors drive the interconnectedness among green, Islamic and conventional financial markets?	Vector Autoregressive (VAR) wavelet analysis	• The entire system connection demonstrates the time-varying characteristics of conventional, Islamic, and green financial markets. • This research provides additional proof that the interconnectedness of financial markets is influenced by global variables, especially in times of stress.
(A. Oseni, 2014)	Dispute management in Islamic financial institutions: a case study of near sukuk defaults	Examining the effects of debt restructuring in situations where a sukuk default is imminent or complete.	• The right dispute resolution system supports the underlying contracts; the law's importance in the more robust, stable, and sustainable Islamic financial sector cannot be discounted.
(Boujlil, Hassan, & Grassa, 2020)	Sovereign debt issuance choice: Sukuk vs conventional bonds	A selection of 602 traditional sovereign bonds and 143 Sukuk that were issued in 16 OIC nations between 2000 and 2015.	• In order to promote new debt products and expand and diversify their financial markets, countries with strong financial markets, positive economic indicators, high credit quality, and stable financial positions are more likely to issue sovereign Sukuk than bonds. • The government bases its decision to issue sovereign debt primarily on these factors as well as on particular events.
(Hafssa & Oumaima, 2020)	Blockchain and smart sukuk: new determinant of development of the sukuk market	The study evaluates smart sukuk's application strategies and structure.	• The use of blockchain technology and smart contracts, smart sukuk provide a forward-thinking solution to major problems facing the sukuk market, such as non-standard practices, excessive issuance costs, and a lack of investor diversity. • Their distinctive characteristics position them as catalysts for the future growth of the sukuk market by improving transparency, lowering fraud, and doing away with the need for middlemen.

Table 2. Continued

Authors	Title	Model Development	Development and Opportunity
(Surachman et al., 2023)	Evaluation of Sovereign Sukuk as a government financing instrument with stakeholder theory: a moving forward policy from Indonesia's experience	Stakeholder theory was used in this study's qualitative interpretative method to content analysis.	• The policy recommendations for every stakeholder include creating an SBSN Project Master Plan, making it less likely for working units in technical ministries to use project extension facilities, and putting in place a thorough system to support them with project planning, development, and service delivery.
(Naeem, Raza Rabbani, Karim, & Billah, 2023)	Religion vs ethics: hedge and safe haven properties of Sukuk and green bonds for stock markets pre- and during COVID-19	Hedge ratios and hedge effectiveness in portfolio	• In times of economic uncertainty, green bonds which are renowned for being safe haven investments offer risk-averse investors useful diversification choices and efficient hedging against a range of foreign equities.
(Hussain, Shahmoradi, & Turk, 2016)	An Overview of Islamic Finance	Qualitative and interpretive methodologies	• The empirical research on the stability of Islamic banks is inconclusive, but they highlight the need for customized risk management strategies because Islamic banks face distinct and shared risks in comparison to conventional banks. • These findings have important policy implications for macroeconomic policy, as Islamic finance is rapidly growing.
(Rizvi, Naqvi, Mirza, & Umar, 2022)	Safe haven properties of green, Islamic, and crypto assets and investor's proclivity towards treasury and gold	Vector Autoregressive (VAR)	• Green and Islamic bonds provide refuge only in times of normal market conditions. • In times of extreme or bearish volatility, however, assets such as gold, cryptocurrencies, and the US Treasury proved to be reliable sources of safety.
(Morea & Poggi, 2017)	An innovative model for the sustainability of investments in the wind energy sector: The use of green sukuk in an Italian case study	Net present value (NPV),the internal rate of return (IRR), the WACC,the annual debt service cover ratio (ADSCR) and the annual loan life cover ratio (ALLCR)	• In light of climate change concerns, the research establishes cost criteria and emphasizes the significance of incentives and Shari'ah-compliant Sukuk in promoting realistic and sustainable investments in the wind energy sector.
(Chong, 2021)	Enhancing trust through digital Islamic finance and blockchain technology	Interpretive methodologies	• The benefits of incorporating blockchain technology into Islamic finance are discussed, with a focus on smart Sukuk as an example. • This illustrates the potential advantages of Islamic financial technology
(Morea & Poggi, 2016)	Islamic finance and renewable energy: An innovative model for the sustainability of investments	Net present value (NPV) analysis method	• Continued investment in the wind energy sector.
(Ramady, 2012)	The GCC economies: Stepping up to future challenges	Qualitative and interpretive methodologies	• The GCC is a prominent regional bloc that plays a crucial role in worldwide politics and economics due to its advantageous geopolitical location, ample global energy supplies, and substantial financial reserves.
(N. Alam, Duygun, & Ariss, 2016)	Green Sukuk: An innovation in Islamic capital markets	Issuance mechanism of sukuk	• Green sukuk are Shariah-compliant investment instruments that finance renewable energy projects like wind farms, solar parks, and biogas facilities. • The primary goal of the creation of green sukuk is to solve environmental protection-related Shariah difficulties.
(Zain & Muhamad Sori, 2020)	An exploratory study on Musharakah SRI Sukuk for the development of Waqf properties/ assets in Malaysia	The critical review and analysis of past literature	• A sukuk model based on musharakah is being developed for waqf assets in Malaysia. • The model takes into account many factors, including the goal, functionality, Sariah contract, obligor, and return method.
(Liu & Lai, 2021)	Ecologies of green finance: Green sukuk and development of green Islamic finance in Malaysia	Documents analysis and interviews	• Mention how green sukuk is increasingly being adopted internationally.
(Zain & Muhamad Sori, 2020)	An exploratory study on Musharakah SRI Sukuk for the development of Waqf properties/ assets in Malaysia	Analysis the Case studies related to Sukuk. Conduct semi-structured interview	• Malaysian waqf properties are developed using a sukuk model based on Musharakah, which takes interviewee replies into account and describes elements such as the purpose, functionality, Sariah contract, obligor, and return method.

Number of Publications and Citation Trends in the Last Twelve Years

Based on Scopus data, an examination of publication and citation trends over the last 12 years indicates a steady but slow rise in scholarly production related to Sukuk and Green Sukuk. Notably, with 19 articles added to the growing body of research, 2020 saw the greatest number of publications. Simultaneously,

Figure 12. Number of publications and citation trends in the last twelve years

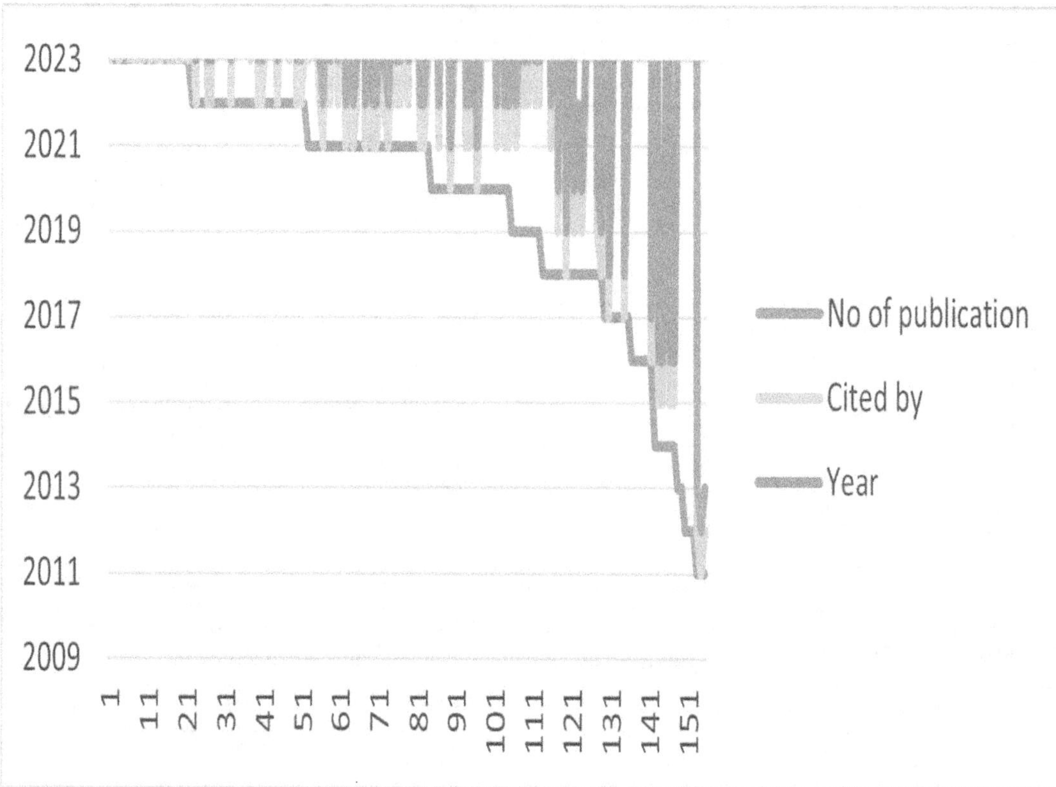

Figure 13. Number of citations

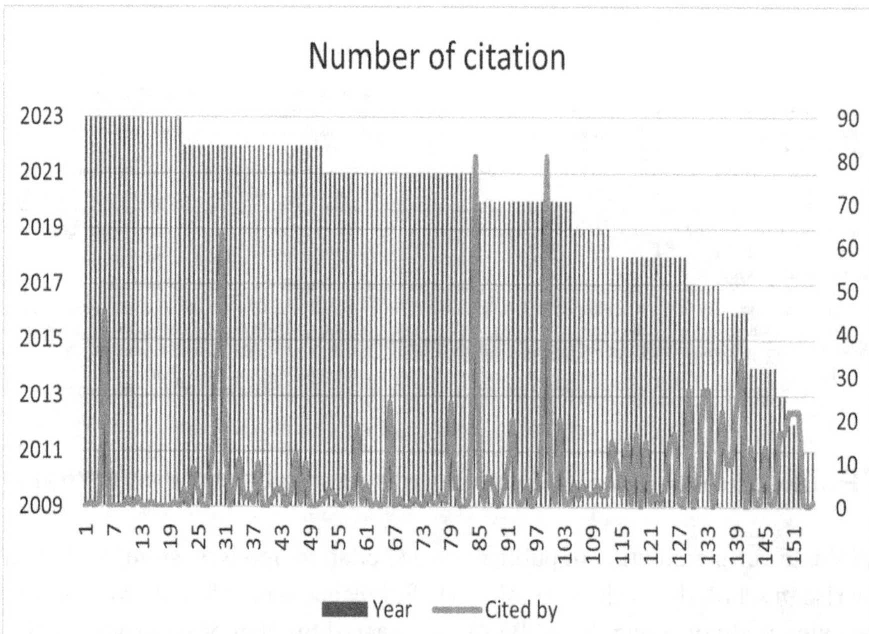

these articles attracted a great deal of attention, receiving 237 citations in one year, indicating the importance and pertinence of the study conducted during this time(Keshminder et al., 2019).

The year 2023 saw a significant increase with 83 publications released, demonstrating a considerable advancement compared to the initial years beginning in 2011. This further highlights the growing interest in Sukuk research. Essentially, the increasing trend in the quantity of publications and citations indicates a strong and developing body of research in the field of green sukuk. Researchers' and academics' growing interest in Sukuk is a sign of a sector that is dynamic and changing, with scholars actively adding to the body of information about the product, especially when it comes to sustainability and green financing. This encouraging trend points to further progress and in-depth study in the fascinating and significant fields of Sukuk and Green Sukuk(Kitchenham et al., 2009).

Table 3. Highest cited top journals

Authors	Title	Year	Source Title	Cited by
(Azhgaliyeva, Kapoor, & Liu, 2020)	Green bonds for financing renewable energy and energy efficiency in South-East Asia: a review of policies	2020	Journal of Sustainable Finance and Investment	81
(Karim & Naeem, 2022)	Do global factors drive the interconnectedness among green, Islamic and conventional financial markets?	2022	International Journal of Managerial Finance	63
(Naeem et al., 2023)	Religion vs ethics: hedge and safe haven properties of Sukuk and green bonds for stock markets pre- and during COVID-19	2023	International Journal of Islamic and Middle Eastern Finance and Management	45
(Hussain, Shahmoradi, & Turk, 2016)	An Overview of Islamic Finance	2016	Journal of International Commerce, Economics and Policy	34
(Rizvi et al., 2022)	Safe haven properties of green, Islamic, and crypto assets and investor's proclivity towards treasury and gold	2022	Energy Economics	32
(Morea & Poggi, 2017)	An innovative model for the sustainability of investments in the wind energy sector: The use of green sukuk in an Italian case study	2017	International Journal of Energy Economics and Policy	27
(Chong, 2021)	Enhancing trust through digital Islamic finance and blockchain technology	2021	Qualitative Research in Financial Markets	24
(Morea & Poggi, 2016)	Islamic finance and renewable energy: An innovative model for the sustainability of investments	2016	AEIT 2016 - International Annual Conference: Sustainable Development in the Mediterranean Area, Energy and ICT Networks of the Future	23
(Ramady, 2012)	The GCC economies: Stepping up to future challenges	2012	The GCC Economies: Stepping up to Future Challenges	22
(N. Alam, Duygun, & Ariss, 2016)	Green Sukuk: An innovation in Islamic capital markets	2016	Energy and Finance: Sustainability in the Energy Industry	22
(Zain & Muhamad Sori, 2020)	An exploratory study on Musharakah SRI Sukuk for the development of Waqf properties/assets in Malaysia	2020	Qualitative Research in Financial Markets	20
(Liu & Lai, 2021)	Ecologies of green finance: Green sukuk and development of green Islamic finance in Malaysia	2021	Environment and Planning A	19

Figure 14. Trends

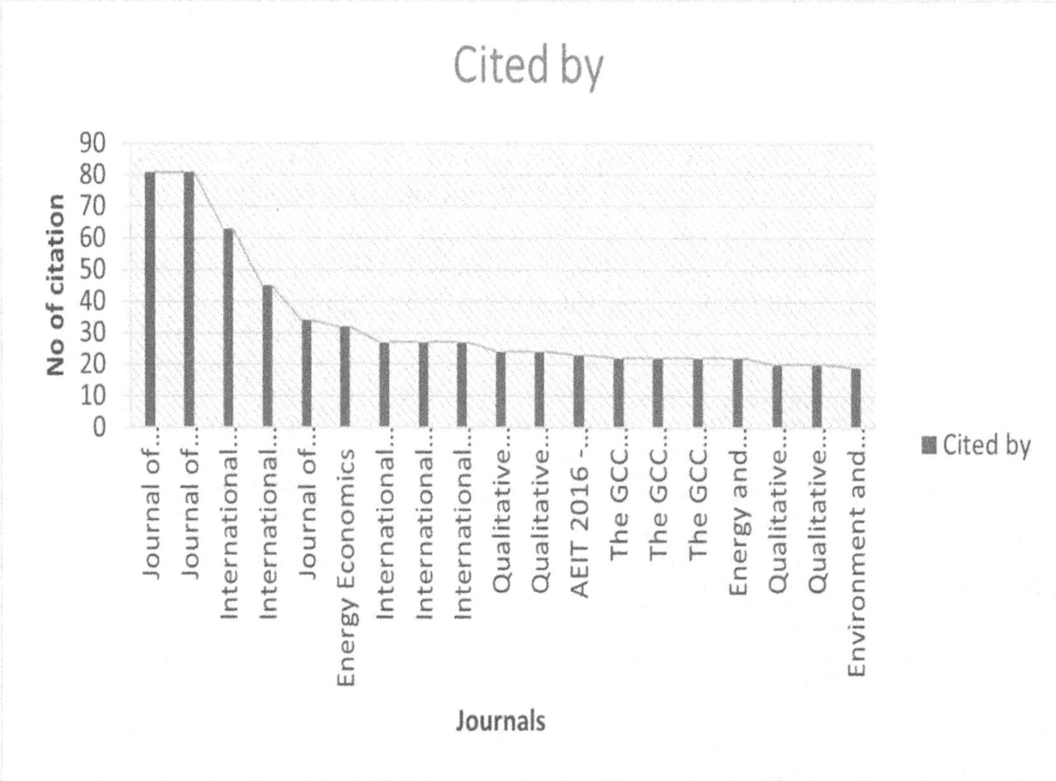

The Journal of Sustainable Finance is the most referenced journal in the field of Sukuk and Green Sukuk research, highlighting its significant influence on the direction of academic discussions about these financial instruments. The Journal of Sustainable Finance has a high citation count, indicating that it is a main source for cutting-edge advancements in Sukuk and Green Sukuk as well as for insights that have stood the test of time(Liu & Lai, 2021).

FINDINGS AND NEW TRENDS IN SUKUK AND GREEN SUKUK

Key Themes Identified

Dominance of Sukuk in Financial Inclusion Discourse

The term "Sukuk" is consistently and prominently present in the chosen literature, indicating its pivotal importance in conversations on financial inclusion, according to the systematic analysis (Yıldırım, Yıldırım, & Diboglu, 2020).

Interconnectedness With Islamic Finance Principles

Significant associations between the terms "Sukuk" and "Islamic finance" are revealed by keyword co-occurrence analysis, suggesting that Sukuk instruments and the more general ideas of Islamic finance are inextricably linked (Ahmed, Islam, Alabdullah, & Amran, 2019).

Growing Emphasis on Sustainability

Some aspects that stand out are the increasing focus on sustainability, which is demonstrated by the frequent occurrence of terms like "green bonds," "energy efficiency," and "Green Sukuk framework," which indicate a move toward ecologically conscious financial practices (Nehal, 2023).

Sukuk Risk Analysis and Management

The risk elements connected to Sukuk, such as credit risk, market risk, and liquidity risk, may be examined through research. Making informed decisions requires policymakers and investors to have a thorough understanding of these factors (Al-Sayed, 2013; R. Hasan, Ahmad, & Parveen, 2019; Homsi, Muhamad Sori, & Mohamad, 2023).

Digitization and Blockchain

The implementation of blockchain technology has the potential to improve sukuk issuance and trading efficiency and transparency. Blockchain technology has the potential to expedite the issuance process, shorten settlement times, and give investors access to a transparent and safe platform (Sa'ad & Ali, 2023).

Sukuk Trends in Hedging

Following the rules of Islamic banking, sukuk are expanding their function beyond capital raising to encompass hedging techniques. For risk management, Sukuk Al-Wakala, profit and loss sharing schemes, and asset-backed Sukuk are being investigated (Naeem et al., 2023). For the most recent information on the revolutionary potential of Sukuk in risk mitigation, keep up with market developments (Naeem et al., 2023; Rabbani, Billah, Shaik, Rahman, & Boujlil, 2023).

Innovation in Sukuk Structure

Governments and financial organizations can keep looking into new sukuk arrangements to satisfy the needs of a wide range of investors. This could involve arrangements like everlasting sukuk, hybrid sukuk, or other variants that address certain budgetary requirements (Abdul Kareem, Mahmud, & Elbishr Ali Hassan, 2023; Elhaj, Muhamed, & Ramli, 2015).

Market Behavior and Trends in Financial Market

The performance of Sukuk in comparison to traditional bonds, investor behavior, and market dynamics are all explored in empirical research on Sukuk (Baita, Malami, & Al-Faryan, 2023). It facilitates comprehension of Sukuk's risk-return profile and its effects on the larger financial market (Yilmaz, 2023).

Standardization and Regulatory Developments

The augmentation of regulatory frameworks and the standardization of sukuk structures have the potential to foster investor confidence and enable the issuing of sukuk across borders. A more liquid secondary market could be produced with the use of standardization (Abubakar, Nafees, Dorloh, & Aji, 2023).

Diversification of Sukuk Assets

The issuance of sukuk backed by non-traditional assets is one example of how the underlying assets of sukuk may be diversified. Perhaps a wider spectrum of investors will be drawn in by this diversification (Najeeb, Bacha, & Masih, 2017; Pirgaip, Arslan-Ayaydin, & Karan, 2021).

Green Sukuk Expansion

Green Sukuk, which is intended to finance eco-friendly initiatives, might rise even more. Green sukuk satisfy the growing demand from investors for sustainable and ethical investment solutions (A. Alam, Ratnasari, Jannah, & Ashfahany, 2023).

Growing Emphasis on Environmental, Social, and Governance (ESG) Criteria

An increased emphasis on ESG criteria in Sukuk and Green Sukuk structures is revealed by the systematic examination. In order to draw in socially conscious investors, issuers are progressively implementing ESG principles, which advances the broader sustainability goal (Azhgaliyeva, Kapoor, & Liu, 2020).

Role of Islamic Finance in United Nations Sustainable Development Goals (SDGs)

The alignment of Sukuk and Green Sukuk with the Sustainable Development Goals (SDGs) has been a recurrent issue in contemporary research. Academics underscore the capacity of these tools to support SDGs, particularly those pertaining to reducing poverty, renewable energy, and climate action. A study gap has been identified by the systematic analysis in the comprehensive evaluation of Sukuk and Green Sukuk's influence on sustainability objectives. Subsequent investigations have to concentrate on formulating resilient approaches to quantify the concrete impacts of these tools on social and environmental consequences (Liu & Lai, 2021).

FINDINGS OF THIS STUDY

The study's findings provide a thorough picture of the financial inclusion environment surrounding Sukuk and Green Sukuk, with a focus on the new sustainability trend. Intriguing insights into the changing dynamics of Islamic finance and it's fit with global sustainability goals can be gained from the examination of major themes and trends.

1. **Growing Interest in Green Sukuk:** The study brings attention to a significant change in the way Sukuk frameworks are incorporating sustainability elements. The industry's response to the increasing demand for socially responsible investments is highlighted by the introduction of Green Sukuk,

which is devoted to financing environmentally sustainable initiatives. It is clear that stakeholders are making a deliberate effort to include sustainability into the foundation of Sukuk structures because phrases like "renewable energy," "climate resilience," and "sustainable development" are frequently used in the examined literature. The results indicate that Islamic finance is actively assisting in the accomplishment of more general environmental goals in addition to adjusting to global sustainability trends (Ramadhan, 2020).

2. **Malaysia's Sustainable Leadership:** Malaysia is a leader in environmentally friendly Sukuk activities, particularly with regard to promoting Green Sukuk as a means of funding green projects. The nation's strong regulatory framework and aggressive participation show its dedication to coordinating Sukuk with international environmental objectives. Financial institutions can benefit from this leadership by strengthening their relationships with green initiatives and improving reporting transparency (Nurhanifah & Khomsatun, 2023).
3. **Visualizing the Sukuk Landscape:** The geographic distribution of Sukuk and Green Sukuk initiatives is depicted in Figure 14, which highlights the implementation of sustainable practices in the regions under investigation. Concentric circles draw attention to how intensely sustainable measures are implemented, with Malaysia serving as the main focus. Sukuk environment is changing, and new developments in Indonesia, the GCC, and Pakistan and Bangladesh offer a visual story of its evolution (Nurhanifah & Khomsatun, 2023).
4. **Indonesia's Inclusive Focus:** In an innovative approach, Indonesia uses Sukuk to promote financial inclusion by allocating money to address social and economic issues. Sukuk is in line with Indonesia's inclusive development plan due to its emphasis on "microfinance projects" and "community development". The results indicate that improving Sukuk structures—including microfinance Sukuk may make Islamic financing more widely available to a wider range of people (Nurhanifah & Khomsatun, 2023).
5. **Global Convergence towards Sustainability:** A global trend is demonstrating how sustainable finance ideas are being applied to Sukuk and Green Sukuk.. The worldwide movement towards sustainability suggests a concerted attempt to incorporate Islamic finance with moral and socially conscious values. Subsequent investigations ought to delve into the contextual elements that impact nation-specific patterns and carry out comparative evaluations to pinpoint optimal methodologies and prospects for international education (A. Rahman et al., 2023).
6. **Insights for Practitioners:** The research offers significant perspectives for professionals operating in the Islamic finance domain. Practitioners can contribute to the creation of novel financial products and make well-informed decisions by having a thorough awareness of the prevailing themes and changing trends. By pointing up areas that need further investigation and filling in research gaps, the study advances academics. Scholars can expand upon these results to investigate particular facets in greater detail, therefore contributing to the advancement of scholarly knowledge regarding Sukuk and its effects on sustainability and financial inclusion.

CONCLUSION

In conclusion, the paper that is supplied offers a comprehensive examination of bibliometrics, systematic literature reviews (SLRs), and research techniques with an emphasis on how Sukuk and Green Sukuk are changing between 2011 and 2023. These techniques are employed by the study in order to pinpoint publication patterns, important phrases, and cooperative endeavors within the academic discourse. Remarkable discoveries highlight the importance of concepts like "Islamic finance," "Sukuk," and "green bonds," demonstrating their centrality in scholarly discourse. Within Sukuk study, visualization technologies such as VOS viewer help to provide a more detailed understanding of theme concentrations and interrelated linkages. Acknowledged for its methodical and reusable methodology, the SLR technique highlights the rising connection between sustainability and Islamic finance by identifying recurring themes in the discourse on financial inclusion. Important writers and publications stand out as significant additions to the body of knowledge.

Scholarly production is steadily increasing, as seen by publication and citation patterns, with the Journal of Sustainable Finance being one of the most referenced sources. The analysis emphasizes the journal's long-lasting influence on research on Sukuk and Green Sukuk. Positive developments include the incorporation of sustainability elements, the focus on ESG standards, and alignment with the Sustainable Development Goals of the United Nations. Nevertheless, research gaps are noted, necessitating a more thorough evaluation of Sukuk's influence on social inclusion indicators and sustainability goals.

The conversation focuses on how Sukuk and Green Sukuk can promote financial inclusion in a sustainable framework by transforming the market. The Sukuk environment is changing as a result of Indonesia's inclusive approach, Pakistan and Bangladesh's early involvement, and Malaysia's sustainable leadership. The ramifications encompass practitioners and policymakers within the Islamic finance industry, proposing avenues for harmonizing products with sustainability objectives and developing regulatory structures that promote ethical financial conduct. In order to contribute to a more complex knowledge of the efficacy of sustainability-focused Sukuk in accomplishing sustainable development goals, the study recommends future research to look deeper into the long-term impact of these instruments. Overall, the analysis shows how the market is dynamic and changing and how Sukuk and Green Sukuk will play a key role in determining the direction of inclusive and responsible finance in the future.

Implications and Future Directions

The results' revealed trends have important ramifications for the Islamic banking industry's practitioners and policymakers. By utilizing these information, financial institutions can customize their Sukuk and Green Sukuk offers to better meet sustainability objectives and draw in a wider pool of investors. Future studies ought to focus more on the long-term effects of Sukuk with a sustainability focus on social and environmental results. Sturdy impact assessments and long-term research will help us acquire a more sophisticated understanding of how well these tools work to achieve sustainable development objectives (Musari, 2022). The policymakers have the potential to significantly impact the issuance of Green Sukuk for sustainable projects, improve investor education, and advance standardization. Subsequent investigations ought to concentrate on delving deeper into the causal connections between Sukuk, Green Sukuk, and financial inclusion. Additionally, they should examine the ways in which these financial instruments can help marginalized communities close the financial access gap (Hania, Endri, & Indra, 2022).

REFERENCES

AbdulKareem, I. A., Mahmud, M. S., & Elbishr Ali Hassan, E. M. (2023). The Application of Legal and Beneficial Ownership in Sukuk Structure in Malaysia and Nigeria. *Turkish Journal of Islamic Economics*, *10*(1).

Abubakar, Y. S., Nafees, S. M., Dorloh, S., & Aji, R. H. (2023). *The Concept of Sukuk and Its Applications in Contemporary Islamic Financial System*. Academic Press.

Ahmed, E. R., Islam, M. A., Alabdullah, T. T. Y., & Amran, A. B. (2019). A qualitative analysis on the determinants of legitimacy of sukuk. *Journal of Islamic Accounting and Business Research*, *10*(3), 342–368. doi:10.1108/JIABR-01-2016-0005

Al-Sayed, O. (2013). Sukuk risk: Analysis and management. *European Journal of Applied Social Sciences Research*, *1*(3), 67–76.

Alam, A., Ratnasari, R. T., Jannah, I. L., & Ashfahany, A. E. (2023). Development and evaluation of Islamic green financing: A systematic review of green sukuk. *Environment and Ecology*, *14*(1), 61–72.

Alam, N., Duygun, M., & Ariss, R. T. (2016). Green sukuk: An innovation in Islamic capital markets. In *Energy and finance: Sustainability in the energy industry* (pp. 167–185). Springer. doi:10.1007/978-3-319-32268-1_10

Asnaini, F., Isnaini, D., & Fryanti, Y. E. (2023). Exploring the potential of Islamic financial instruments in addressing economic challenges: the role of financial inclusion and institutional quality. *International Journal of Economics and Finance Studies*, *15*(1), 204–224.

Azhgaliyeva, D., Kapoor, A., & Liu, Y. (2020). Green bonds for financing renewable energy and energy efficiency in South-East Asia: A review of policies. *Journal of Sustainable Finance & Investment*, *10*(2), 113–140. doi:10.1080/20430795.2019.1704160

Baita, A. J., Malami, H. U., & Al-Faryan, M. A. S. (2023). Fiscal policy and sukuk market development in OIC countries. *Journal of Islamic Accounting and Business Research*, *14*(8), 1216–1231. doi:10.1108/JIABR-06-2022-0159

Billah, M., Elsayed, A. H., & Hadhri, S. (2023). Asymmetric relationship between green bonds and Sukuk markets: The role of global risk factors. *Journal of International Financial Markets, Institutions and Money*, *83*, 101728. doi:10.1016/j.intfin.2022.101728

Boujlil, R., Hassan, M. K., & Grassa, R. (2020). Sovereign debt issuance choice: Sukuk vs conventional bonds. *Journal of Islamic Monetary Economics and Finance*, *6*(2), 275–294. doi:10.21098/jimf.v6i2.1104

Brahmana, R. K., & You, H. W. (2022). Do Muslim CEOs and Muslim stakeholders prefer Islamic debt financing? *Global Finance Journal*, *54*, 100625. doi:10.1016/j.gfj.2021.100625

Chong, F. H. L. (2021). Enhancing trust through digital Islamic finance and blockchain technology. *Qualitative Research in Financial Markets*, *13*(3), 328–341. doi:10.1108/QRFM-05-2020-0076

Dziopa, F., & Ahern, K. (2011). A systematic literature review of the applications of Q-technique and its methodology. *Methodology: European Journal of Research Methods for the Behavioral and Social Sciences*, *7*(2), 39–55. doi:10.1027/1614-2241/a000021

Elhaj, M. A. A., Muhamed, N. A., & Ramli, N. M. (2015). The influence of corporate governance, financial ratios, and Sukuk structure on Sukuk rating. *Procedia Economics and Finance*, *31*, 62–74. doi:10.1016/S2212-5671(15)01132-6

Faisal, Y. A., Gunawan, I., Cupian, Hayati, A., Apriliadi, A., & Fajri, M. (2023). Examining the Purchase Intentions of Indonesian Investors for Green Sukuk. *Sustainability (Basel)*, *15*(9), 7430. doi:10.3390/su15097430

Hafssa, Y., & Oumaima, B. (2020). *Blockchain and smart sukuk: new determinant of development of the sukuk market.* Paper presented at the 2020 IEEE International Conference on Technology Management, Operations and Decisions (ICTMOD). 10.1109/ICTMOD49425.2020.9380613

Hania, B. T., Endri, E., & Indra, I. (2022). Identify the Issuance Problem of Corporate Green Sukuk in Indonesia. *Islamic Economics Journal*, *8*(2), 187–204. doi:10.21111/iej.v8i2.8404

Hasan, A., Gupta, S., Irfan, M., & Dias, R. M. (2024). Assessing Public Awareness of Islamic Finance and Interest-Free Banking in India. In Fintech Applications in Islamic Finance: AI, Machine Learning, and Blockchain Techniques (pp. 80-92): IGI Global.

Hasan, R., Ahmad, A. U. F., & Parveen, T. (2019). Sukuk risks–a structured review of theoretical research. *Journal of Islamic Accounting and Business Research*, *10*(1), 35–49. doi:10.1108/JIABR-06-2015-0026

Homsi, M. A., Muhamad Sori, Z., & Mohamad, S. (2023). Determinants of Sukuk credit rating: Evidence from issuing firms in Malaysia. *Journal of Islamic Accounting and Business Research*, *14*(8), 1324–1343. doi:10.1108/JIABR-05-2022-0127

Hussain, M., Shahmoradi, A., & Turk, R. (2016). An overview of Islamic finance. *Journal of International Commerce. Economic Policy*, *7*(01), 1650003.

IFSB, I. F. S. B. (2020). Retrieved from Karim, S., & Naeem, M. A. (2022). Do global factors drive the interconnectedness among green, Islamic and conventional financial markets? *International Journal of Managerial Finance*, *18*(4), 639–660.

Keshminder, J., Singh, G., Wahid, Z., & Abdullah, M. (2019). Green sukuk: Malaysia taking the lead. *Malaysian Journal of Consumer and Family Economics*, *22*(2), 1–22.

Khan, S. (2023). The impacts of Sukuk on financial inclusion in selected Sukuk markets: An empirical investigation based on generalized method of moments (GMM) analysis. *International Journal of Social Economics*, *50*(8), 1153–1168. doi:10.1108/IJSE-06-2022-0424

Kitchenham, B., Brereton, O. P., Budgen, D., Turner, M., Bailey, J., & Linkman, S. (2009). Systematic literature reviews in software engineering–a systematic literature review. *Information and Software Technology*, *51*(1), 7–15. doi:10.1016/j.infsof.2008.09.009

Koseoglu, M. A., Rahimi, R., Okumus, F., & Liu, J. (2016). Bibliometric studies in tourism. *Annals of Tourism Research*, *61*, 180–198. doi:10.1016/j.annals.2016.10.006

Liaqat, W., Altaf, M. T., Barutçular, C., Zayed, E. M., & Hussain, T. (2023). Drought and sorghum: A bibliometric analysis using VOS viewer. *Journal of Biomolecular Structure & Dynamics*, •••, 1–13. doi:10.1080/07391102.2023.2269279 PMID:37837436

Liu, F. H., & Lai, K. P. (2021). Ecologies of green finance: Green sukuk and development of green Islamic finance in Malaysia. *Environment and Planning A. Economy and Space*, *53*(8), 1896–1914.

Maulayati, R. R., & Iswati, S. (n.d.). *Sukuk Trend Analysis: Bibliometric and Systematic Literature Review from 2011-2021*. Academic Press.

Morea, D., & Poggi, L. A. (2016). *Islamic finance and renewable energy: An innovative model for the sustainability of investments*. Paper presented at the 2016 AEIT International Annual Conference (AEIT). 10.23919/AEIT.2016.7892766

Morea, D., & Poggi, L. A. (2017). An innovative model for the sustainability of investments in the wind energy sector: The use of green sukuk in an Italian case study. *International Journal of Energy Economics and Policy*, *7*(2), 53–60.

Mukit, M. M. H., Muneeza, A., & Paltrinieri, A. (2021). Contributions of Professor M. Kabir Hassan to the Islamic finance literature: A bibliometric study. *Jurnal Ekonomi Malaysia*, *55*(3), 49–76. doi:10.17576/JEM-2021-5503-04

Musari, K. (2022). Integrating green sukuk and cash waqf linked sukuk, the blended Islamic finance of fiscal instrument in Indonesia: A proposed model for fighting climate change. *International Journal of Islamic Khazanah*, *12*(2), 133–144. doi:10.15575/ijik.v12i2.17750

Musari, K., & Hidayat, S. E. (2023). The role of green sukuk in maqasid al-shariah and SDGs: Evidence from Indonesia. In *Islamic finance, fintech, and the road to sustainability: Reframing the approach in the post-pandemic era* (pp. 181–203). Springer. doi:10.1007/978-3-031-13302-2_9

Naeem, M. A., Raza Rabbani, M., Karim, S., & Billah, S. M. (2023). Religion vs ethics: Hedge and safe haven properties of Sukuk and green bonds for stock markets pre-and during COVID-19. *International Journal of Islamic and Middle Eastern Finance and Management*, *16*(2), 234–252. doi:10.1108/IMEFM-06-2021-0252

Najeeb, S. F., Bacha, O., & Masih, M. (2017). Does a held-to-maturity strategy impede effective portfolio diversification for Islamic bond (sukuk) portfolios? A multi-scale continuous wavelet correlation analysis. *Emerging Markets Finance & Trade*, *53*(10), 2377–2393. doi:10.1080/1540496X.2016.1205977

Nehal, S. (2023). Green Sukuk–A Viable Global Financing option for Climatic and Environmental Revolution (A Practical Instrument for the Development of Sustainable Energy Projects in Pakistan). *Karachi Islamicus, 3*(1).

Ngoc, N. M., & Tien, N. H. (2023). Quality of Scientific Research and World Ranking of Public and Private Universities in Vietnam. *International Journal of Public Sector Performance Management.*

Nurhanifah, A., & Khomsatun, S. (2023). Literature analysis of sukuk ratings in Indonesia bibliometric approach. *Journal of Science*, *12*(03), 4191–4201.

Oseni, A., U. (. (2014). Dispute management in Islamic financial institutions: A case study of near sukuk defaults. *Journal of International Trade Law & Policy*, *13*(3), 198–214. doi:10.1108/JITLP-12-2013-0034

Paltrinieri, A., Hassan, M. K., Bahoo, S., & Khan, A. (2019). A bibliometric review of sukuk literature. *International Review of Economics & Finance*.

Pirgaip, B., Arslan-Ayaydin, Ö., & Karan, M. B. (2021). Do Sukuk provide diversification benefits to conventional bond investors? Evidence from Turkey. *Global Finance Journal*, *50*, 100533. doi:10.1016/j.gfj.2020.100533

Pritchard, A. (1969). Statistical bibliography or bibliometrics. *The Journal of Documentation*, *25*, 348.

Qosim, N., Ratnasari, R. T., Wardhana, A. K., Fauziana, H., & Barkah, T. T. (2023). Eight Years of Research Related to the Green Sukuk in the Global Stock Exchange Market to Support the Implementation of SDG: A Bibliometric Review. *Journal of Islamic Economic and Business Research*, *3*(2), 161–180. doi:10.18196/jiebr.v3i2.204

Rabbani, M. R., Billah, S. M., Shaik, M., Rahman, M., & Boujlil, R. (2023). Dynamic connectedness, spillover, and optimal hedging strategy among FinTech, Sukuk, and Islamic equity markets. *Global Finance Journal*, *58*, 100901. doi:10.1016/j.gfj.2023.100901

Rahman, A., Ahmad, A. U. F., Bin-Nashwan, S. A., Muneeza, A., Abdul Halim, A. H., & Markom, R. (2023). Policy approach adopted for issuance of Green Sukuk: Is priority given to priority needed areas? *Journal of Islamic Accounting and Business Research*. Advance online publication. doi:10.1108/JIABR-10-2022-0279

Rahman, M., Isa, C. R., Tu, T.-T., Sarker, M., & Masud, M. A. K. (2020). A bibliometric analysis of socially responsible investment sukuk literature. *Asian Journal of Sustainability and Social Responsibility*, *5*(1), 1–19. doi:10.1186/s41180-020-00035-2

Ramadhan, I. A. (2020). *Green Sukuk issuance as an investment instrument for sustainable development.* Paper presented at the International Conference on Law, Governance and Islamic Society (ICOLGIS 2019). 10.2991/assehr.k.200306.189

Ramady, M. A. (2012). *The GCC economies: Stepping up to future challenges*. Springer Science & Business Media. doi:10.1007/978-1-4614-1611-1

Rezkyarta, A., & Irfany, M. I. (2023). Bibliometric Analysis of Sukuk Literatures. *Journal of Islamic Economics Literatures*, *4*(2). Advance online publication. doi:10.58968/jiel.v4i2.314

Rizvi, S. K. A., Naqvi, B., Mirza, N., & Umar, M. (2022). Safe haven properties of green, Islamic, and crypto assets and investor's proclivity towards treasury and gold. *Energy Economics*, *115*, 106396. doi:10.1016/j.eneco.2022.106396

Sa'ad, A. A., & Ali, E. R. A. E. (2023). Developing Smart Green Sukuk Structure Using Blockchain Technology. *Journal of Islamic entrepreneurship (Majallatu Riyadati Al-aamali Al-islamiati), 8.*

Surachman, E. N., Hermawan, R. P., Handayani, D., & Astuti, E. (2023). Evaluation of Sovereign Sukuk as a government financing instrument with stakeholder theory: A moving forward policy from Indonesia's experience. *Journal of Islamic Accounting and Business Research, 14*(2), 315–338. doi:10.1108/JIABR-03-2022-0066

Trabelsi, N., Umar, Z., Dogah, K. E., & Vo, X. V. (2024). Are investment grade Sukuks decoupled from the conventional yield curve? *International Review of Financial Analysis, 91*, 102981. doi:10.1016/j.irfa.2023.102981

Trianto, B., & Masrizal, M. (2021). Sukuk and Islamic banking financing: Their impacts on the real sector. *Journal of Islamic Monetary Economics and Finance*, *7*(4), 671–686. doi:10.21098/jimf.v7i4.1407

Ulfah, I. F., Sukmana, R., Laila, N., & Sulaeman, S. (2023). A structured literature review on green sukuk (Islamic bonds): Implications for government policy and future studies. *Journal of Islamic Accounting and Business Research*. Advance online publication. doi:10.1108/JIABR-10-2022-0255

Uluyol, B. (2023). A comprehensive empirical and theoretical literature survey of Islamic bonds (sukuk). *Journal of Sustainable Finance & Investment, 13*(3), 1277–1299. doi:10.1080/20430795.2021.1917224

Wallin, J. A. (2005). Bibliometric methods: Pitfalls and possibilities. *Basic & Clinical Pharmacology & Toxicology, 97*(5), 261–275. doi:10.1111/j.1742-7843.2005.pto_139.x PMID:16236137

Yıldırım, S., Yıldırım, D. C., & Diboglu, P. (2020). Does Sukuk market development promote economic growth? *PSU Research Review, 4*(3), 209–218. doi:10.1108/PRR-03-2020-0011

Yilmaz, E. (2023). Analyzing investor types and marketing strategies for sukuk: Insights from preference similarity theory and protection motivation theory. *Journal of Islamic Accounting and Business Research*. Advance online publication. doi:10.1108/JIABR-03-2023-0097

Zain, N. S., & Muhamad Sori, Z. (2020). An exploratory study on Musharakah SRI Sukuk for the development of Waqf properties/assets in Malaysia. *Qualitative Research in Financial Markets, 12*(3), 301–314. doi:10.1108/QRFM-09-2018-0099

Zupic, I., & Čater, T. (2015). Bibliometric methods in management and organization. *Organizational Research Methods, 18*(3), 429–472. doi:10.1177/1094428114562629

APPENDIX

1): Multiple Choice Questions (MCQs)
2): Short Answer Questions
3): Diverse Assignment Topics

Multiple Choice Questions (MCQs)

1. Which of the following best describes sukuk?
   a) Interest-based loans
   b) Equity financing
   c) Debt instruments compliant with Islamic law
   d) Asset-backed securities
2. Green sukuk are specifically designed to finance:
   a) Social projects
   b) Environmentally friendly projects
   c) Infrastructure development
   d) Technological innovations
3. What is the primary difference between conventional bonds and sukuk?
   a) Conventional bonds pay interest, while sukuk pay dividends.
   b) Sukuk are asset-backed, while conventional bonds are not.
   c) Sukuk can only be issued by governments, while conventional bonds can be issued by corporations.
   d) Sukuk have shorter maturity periods compared to conventional bonds.
4. Which Islamic finance principle prohibits the payment or receipt of interest?
   a) Murabaha
   b) Mudarabah
   c) Riba
   d) Wakalah
5. The process of securitizing and selling future receivables in Islamic finance is known as:
   a) Ijarah
   b) Musharakah
   c) Istisna
   d) Sukuk
6. What is Sukuk?
   a) Conventional mortgage b) Islamic bond c) Stock option d) Mutual fund
7. Which of the following is a key characteristic of Sukuk?
   a) Paying interest b) Being backed by physical assets c) Issued by non-Islamic financial institutions d) Speculative trading
8. Sukuk represents:
   a) Ownership in a debt obligation b) Ownership in a tangible asset c) Ownership in a company d) Ownership in a stock market index

9. The issuance of Sukuk is based on the principles of:
   a) Interest-based lending b) Risk-sharing and asset backing c) Speculative trading d) Fixed return on investment
10. Which Islamic finance principle does Sukuk comply with?
    a) Riba (interest) b) Gharar (uncertainty) c) Zakat (charitable giving) d) Shariah-compliant investment structures

Answers to MCQs

1. c) Debt instruments compliant with Islamic law
2. b) Environmentally friendly projects
3. b) Sukuk are asset-backed, while conventional bonds are not.
4. c) Riba
5. d) Sukuk
6. b) Islamic bond
7. b) Being backed by physical assets
8. b) Ownership in a tangible asset
9. b) Risk-sharing and asset backing
10. d) Shariah-compliant investment structures

Assessment Questions

1. Explain the concept of asset-backed securities in the context of sukuk.
2. Compare and contrast the features of green sukuk and conventional sukuk.
3. How do Islamic finance principles influence the structuring of sukuk?
4. Discuss the potential benefits and challenges of issuing sukuk for both issuers and investors.
5. Analyze the impact of regulatory frameworks on the growth of the sukuk market globally.

Diverse Assignment Topics

a) Conduct a case study on a recent green sukuk issuance, analyzing the project funded, the structure of the sukuk, and its impact on sustainable development.
b) Design a hypothetical sukuk issuance for a government or corporation, considering various asset classes and structuring options.
c) Explore the role of fintech and blockchain technology in enhancing transparency and efficiency in sukuk issuance and trading.
d) Investigate the market potential of sukuk in non-Muslim majority countries, assessing challenges and opportunities for expansion.
e) Develop a research paper discussing the evolution of sukuk as an alternative financing instrument and its potential to address infrastructure financing needs in emerging markets.

Chapter 8
Financial Inclusion, Sustainability, and Financial Wellbeing in OIC and Non-OIC Countries

Waqas Shair
https://orcid.org/0000-0001-6495-2922
Minhaj University, Lahore, Pakistan

Saem Hussain
https://orcid.org/0009-0007-8410-5561
Technological University Dublin, Ireland

Muhammad Asif
Independent Researcher, Pakistan

Azra Niamat
Independent Researcher, Pakistan

ABSTRACT

The significance of access to formal bank accounts becomes evident as it enables individuals to safely transfer and receive funds, make everyday transactions, and make investments to hedge against financial shocks, among others. The present study aims to investigate the extent to which financial inclusion has been adopted by individuals from poor and non-poor backgrounds and males and females across OIC and non-OIC economies. The outcome of the extent of access to financial accounts and financial services—digital payment, savings, borrowing, and financial well-being in terms of financial resilience and financial worrying—is also conducted among the vulnerable group. The study utilises the global findex database, which consists of data from 128,000 individuals across 123 economies, to provide an empirical description of financial inclusion. The outcome of the examination of the disparity of marginalised groups yields valuable insights into the recognition of associated challenges and opportunities for bridging the existing gap.

DOI: 10.4018/979-8-3693-1475-3.ch008

1. INTRODUCTION

Financial inclusion promotes equal access to financial services, seeking to remove obstacles that hinder individuals from engaging in the financial sector. Financial inclusion encompasses various financial products, such as banking services, loans, equity options, and insurance solutions. Measuring financial inclusion involves evaluating three key dimensions: the extent of access, the level of usage, and the overall quality. Access encompasses the accessibility and affordability of financial services, while usage gauges the frequency and variety of these services. Quality refers to financial products and services' suitability, convenience, reliability, and safety. The importance of financial literacy as a crucial aspect cannot be overlooked in the process of financial inclusion, as it is explicitly linked to the diffusion of financial inclusion (Agner & Desello, 2023). Recognising the importance of financial inclusion, it becomes evident that it is vital in attaining various social and economic objectives. These include reducing poverty, promoting income equality, fostering job opportunities, empowering women, and ensuring sustainable development (Park & Mercado, 2021). Numerous countries have implemented national financial inclusion strategies and policies to encourage and oversee financial inclusion within specific circumstances.

The fourth industrial revolution is commonly described as the broad diffusion and adoption of digital technologies. The emergence of digital technologies is potentially revolutionising the financial sector. The continuous digital revolution has significantly increased global account ownership over a decade, from 2011 to 2021. During this period, the percentage of adults with account ownership surged by 50 per cent, increasing from 51 per cent to 76 per cent (Demirgüç-Kunt et al., 2022.). The significance of a formal bank account becomes evident as it enables individuals to safely transfer and receive funds, make everyday transactions, and make investments to hedge against financial shocks, among others. Significant progress has been made in global financial inclusion, particularly in increasing the number of individuals with access to banking services. However, investigating a sustainable aspect of financial inclusion needs to be explored. Specifically, financial inclusion, with a particular focus on its distribution by income groups and gender categories. The present study aims to investigate the extent to which financial inclusion has been adopted by individuals from poor and non-poor backgrounds and males and females across OIC and non-OIC economies.

Account ownership has increased to 75 per cent globally, but there is a noticeable 4 per cent gender gap in account access. Men have a higher ownership rate at 78 per cent, while women have a slightly lower rate at 74 per cent (Demirgüç-Kunt et al., 2022). Similarly, there is an evident 8 per cent disparity in account ownership between the rich and the poor. Religion is a significant factor contributing to the lack of account ownership. Based on a recent Global Findex report, only 10 percent of unbanked adults worldwide view religion as an obstacle (Demirgüç-Kunt et al., 2021). Considering the worldwide account ownership statistics, it is crucial to analyse and compare the account ownership of individuals from both OIC and non-OIC countries, taking into account factors such as gender and income-group category. In addition, it is important to investigate the gap in the extent of financial service utilisation and financial wellbeing among women and individuals in lower income brackets of OIC and non-OIC. The contribution of this study in the existing literature is related to an attempt to figure out the gap in financial account access, financial services utilisation, and financial wellbeing across the gender and different income group in OIC and non-OIC. The existing literature is scant in relation to financial wellbeing as a measure of financial resilience and financial worrying.

The objective of the study is to figure out the gender gap and income-gap across the three dimensions of financial inclusion in OIC and non-OIC. The access by investigating the account ownership, and use by examining the extent of usage to financial services – digital payment, savings, and borrowing. On the other hand, exploring financial well-being, specifically in terms of financial resilience and worrying, covers the quality aspect of financial inclusion. The study contributes to the scholarly literature by providing insights into Sustainable Development Goal (SDG) 1, 'No poverty', specifically target 1.4, which pertains to enhancing access to financial services for poor individuals. Furthermore, the research endeavour contributes to the realisation of SDG 5, specifically focusing on 'Gender Equality', with a specific emphasis on target 5.a, which pertains to the attainment of gender parity concerning financial services. The outcome of the examination of the disparity of marginalised groups yields valuable insights into the recognition of associated challenges and opportunities for bridging the existing gap.

2. REVIEW OF LITERATURE AND THEORETICAL UNDERPINNING

2.1 Review of the Literature

Financial inclusion refers to the provision of accessible and affordable financial services to individuals who are economically disadvantaged to facilitate their active involvement in the formal economic system (UN, 2016). The significance of financial inclusion becomes apparent as it plays a direct role in enhancing economic growth, reducing poverty and income inequality, managing financial risk, and promoting financial stability (Kim et al., 2018; Neaime & Gaysset, 2018). The study of Duvendack et al. (2011) found that financial inclusion in terms of borrowing from formal financial institution is associated with better health, education, expenditure, and subjective well-being outcomes. The observed variations in the degree of financial inclusion across different countries can be attributed to several factors, such as the varying levels of digital finance, financial literacy, financial regulation, and economic policy uncertainty (Grohmann et al., 2018; Anarfo & Abor, 2020). The utilisation of financial instruments has been found to have a positive impact on various economic factors, such as savings, consumption, and productive investment (Ashraf et al., 2010). According to Bhandari (2009), the development of financially and socially sustainable inclusive financial systems must place a strong emphasis on prioritising poverty reduction.

In the literature, various studies have indicated a positive association between various socioeconomic factors and the likelihood of individuals possessing an account at a formal financial institution, engaging in formal savings, and accessing formal borrowing mechanisms (Zins & Weill, 2016). Specifically, individuals who exhibit characteristics such as higher wealth, greater educational attainment, younger age-cohort, residence in urban areas, employed, and married have been found to have higher probabilities of holding a formal financial account (Gupte et al.,. 2012; Nandru et al. 2016). The presence of specific country characteristics, such as well-established institutions, adequate legal frameworks, robust contract enforcement mechanisms, and political stability, have been identified as significant factors that contribute to the promotion of financial inclusion (Allen et al., 2016).

The influence of gender on financial inclusion is a noteworthy aspect to consider, as evidenced by the existence of a substantial gender disparity in terms of account ownership, formal saving, and formal credit (Fungácová & Weill, 2015). The lower representation of women in financial inclusion can be attributed to several factors, including inadequate documentation, limited financial literacy, geographical barriers, and religious considerations. It has been observed that women residing in developing nations frequently engage in occupations that are informal in nature, requiring minimal skill sets and offering wages that are relatively low (Ghosh & Vinod, 2017). Furthermore, it has been noted that women in these contexts face challenges in terms of their access to assets and resources, which are comparatively lower or constrained when compared to their male counterparts. According to a study conducted by Demirgüc¸-Kunt et al. (2013), it has been observed that religion can potentially have an impact on financial inclusion. Specifically, the study found that individuals who identify as Muslims tend to exhibit a lower tendency towards engaging in financial account ownership and saving as compared to those who do not identify as Muslims.

Financial well-being encompasses the ability to manage one's finances effectively, navigate unexpected financial challenges, achieve desired financial objectives, and enjoy a sense of financial independence (CFPB, 2015). Understanding the effects of money management stress and the importance of future financial security is crucial for one's overall well-being. According to research, there is a clear association between financial capability, financial literacy, planning, and overall financial well-being (Xiao & O'Neill, 2018). Additionally, having easily accessible liquid savings has been identified as a significant contributing factor (Gutter & Copur, 2011). Various factors such as age, education, income, marital status, and family structure play essential roles in shaping individuals' perceptions of financial well-being (Shim et al., 2009; Malone et al., 2010).

Although numerous studies have been conducted on the different aspects of financial inclusion. More studies are needed on the comprehensive examination of the dimensions of financial inclusion and its sustainability aspect across the OIC and non-OIC regions. There is a limited number of research available on the topic of financial wellbeing as a measure of financial resilience and financial worrying. This study contributes to the existing literature by examining financial inclusion in terms of access and usage, as well as the aspects of financial well-being, explicitly focusing on the marginalised segments of society such as women and the poor.

2.2 Theoretical Core

Sustainable development encompasses three primary dimensions: environmental, social, and economic perspectives (Alaimo et al., 2021). The interaction between the social and economic dimensions is a crucial focus of sustainable development (see Figure 1). It is of utmost importance related to the inclusion of gender parity as a social factor and the fair accessibility of financial services across different income groups. By including the marginalised segments of society, such as women and the poor, in the banking community and offering them a range of financial services, one can help improve their economic conditions. Ensuring the participation of all members of society undoubtedly enhances overall well-being by boosting the effectiveness of financial inclusion, fostering job opportunities, and driving economic growth.

The theory of social exclusion and inclusion is a multifaceted concept that stems from economic considerations of poverty and inequality (Sen, 2000). Social exclusion is the condition where individuals are deprived of essential resources, rights, goods, and services. On the contrary, social inclusion aims to provide opportunities and resources to those who are vulnerable to poverty and social exclusion, allowing them to actively engage in economic, social, and cultural activities. Given the backdrop of exclusion, Ozili's (2020) study listed twelve theories on financial inclusion/exclusion and its potential sources. Amongst these theories, public good theory states that everyone should take benefits associated with financial inclusion, and steps need to be undertaken to make it a public good. Vulnerable group theory points to the marginalised segment of society as unable to take the ongoing benefits associated with financial inclusion.

Figure 1. Theoretical framework on sustainability, financial inclusion, and its dimensions

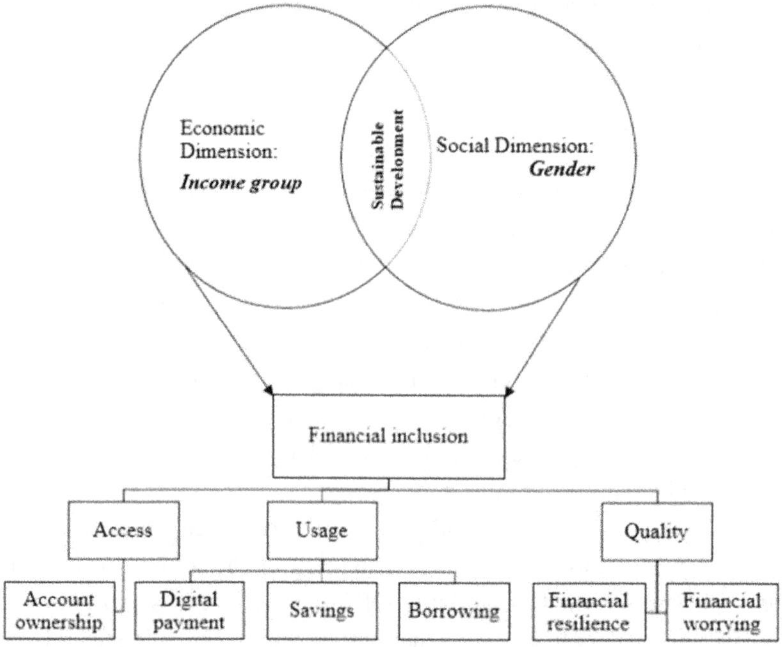

The three major dimensions of financial inclusion are access, usage and quality of infrastructure (Sarkar et al., 2023). An in-depth examination of financial inclusion and its associated dimensions is required because it is intricately linked to the wellbeing of individuals. Financial inclusion in terms of access to financial accounts not only empowers women economically but also facilitates the transition to social autonomy. The use of digital payments, formal savings, and borrowing plays an essential role in enhancing entrepreneurial activities, channelling the flow of liquidity, and bolstering the digital economy. The quality of financial inclusion is related to the available infrastructure to serve as an outcome base of financial wellbeing in terms of financial resilience and financial worrying to navigate short-term shock and stress management.

Put simply, the gender disparity and economically disadvantaged groups are likely to be excluded from the benefits of financial inclusion. These deprivations may appear as limited access to account ownership, utilisation of financial services, and overall financial wellbeing.

3. DATA AND EMPIRICAL METHODOLOGY

The present study seeks to examine the level of financial inclusion among individuals from different socioeconomic backgrounds and genders in both OIC and non-OIC economies. This study utilises the Global Findex Database, which includes data from 128,000 individuals across 123 economies, to empirically describe the financial inclusion status of the marginalised segment of society. Based on the provided sample, 35 countries are classified as OIC, while 88 countries are classified as non-OIC.

The focus of the study is not on establishing cause and effect relationships but instead on understanding the extent of gender and income gap in the access, use and quality of financial services across the

OIC and non-OIC zonation. For this purpose, this study relies on simple descriptive analysis and implies a weighted average to obtain country- and zonation-level estimates of financial inclusion across gender and different income groups.

4. FINANCIAL INCLUSION: DIMENSION OF ACCESS

The access to formal financial account is a major dimension of the financial inclusion because it is directly related to the wellbeing of the individuals. This section explores the developmental impact of the financial inclusion and penetration of the banked and unbanked individuals across the OIC and non-OIC zonation.

4.1. Developmental Impact of Financial Inclusion

Financial inclusion contributes to short-run economic growth and transmits its effects to the development of economies. It has positive developmental impacts on various dimensions, such as poverty reduction, inequality reduction, human development, and social cohesion. It increases savings, capital allocation, trade, and innovation, reducing capital costs and promoting investment (Abdelghaffar et al., 2023). It also reduces poverty by providing access to credit, savings, insurance, and payments, enabling poor households to invest in human and physical capital. Financial inclusion empowers disadvantaged groups, ensuring equitable distribution of economic benefits. It also improves health, education, and gender equality outcomes, strengthening social cohesion and trust (Ozili, 2023).

Bank account ownership is a crucial indicator of financial inclusion and access to formal financial services. It can significantly impact individuals' and households' credit, consumption, and wealth accumulation. Owning a bank account can facilitate access to affordable and formal sources of credit, such as credit cards and bank loans, and reduce reliance on informal alternatives. This can improve economic well-being by enabling households to smooth income shocks, invest in human and physical capital, and build credit history and reputation (Fitzpatrick, 2015). Bank account ownership can also affect consumption patterns and preferences, particularly for durable goods that require large upfront payments or credit financing. Owning a bank account can help households save and accumulate financial assets, such as deposits, stocks, bonds, and pensions. It also supports the accumulation and allocation of non-financial assets like housing, land, and vehicles by facilitating access to credit and reducing transaction costs (Prina, 2015).

Financial inclusion in the context of account ownership is a crucial aspect of economic growth. Access to bank accounts promotes economic growth by reducing the risk of theft or loss, encouraging savings and wealth accumulation, and enabling access to essential services like loans, insurance, and investment products. Access to bank accounts also allows individuals to participate in the formal financial system, receive and make payments, receive social safety nets transparently, and engage in economic activities. It also contributes to economic activities by providing secure money storage, payment access, credit access, enhancing financial literacy, better financial decision-making, and reducing counterfeit money circulation (Bruhn & Love, 2017). Research indicates that a unit increase in financial inclusion in the long run leads to a 0.50 per cent increase in economic growth (Sethi & Acharya, 2018).

4.2. Account Ownership Across the Countries

Considering the significant developmental impact of financial inclusion at both micro and macro levels, there is still a persistent effort within the global community to increase the number of individuals with bank account ownership. Based on the latest report from the Global Findex Database (2021), it has been found that approximately 76 per cent of individuals across the globe possess an account with a bank or a regulated financial institution that accepts deposits, which also includes mobile money service providers. However, the count of account ownership differs when examined at the country level, mainly focusing on the OIC and non-OIC economies. According to the data in Figure 2, it can be observed that 7 out of the 35 (or 20 per cent) reference OIC economies have an account ownership rate of 50 per cent or higher. Interestingly, 77 out of 88 (or 87.5 per cent) non-OIC economies have an account ownership

Figure 2. Account ownership across the OIC and non-OIC economies
Source: Authors' own calculation based on Findex database 2021

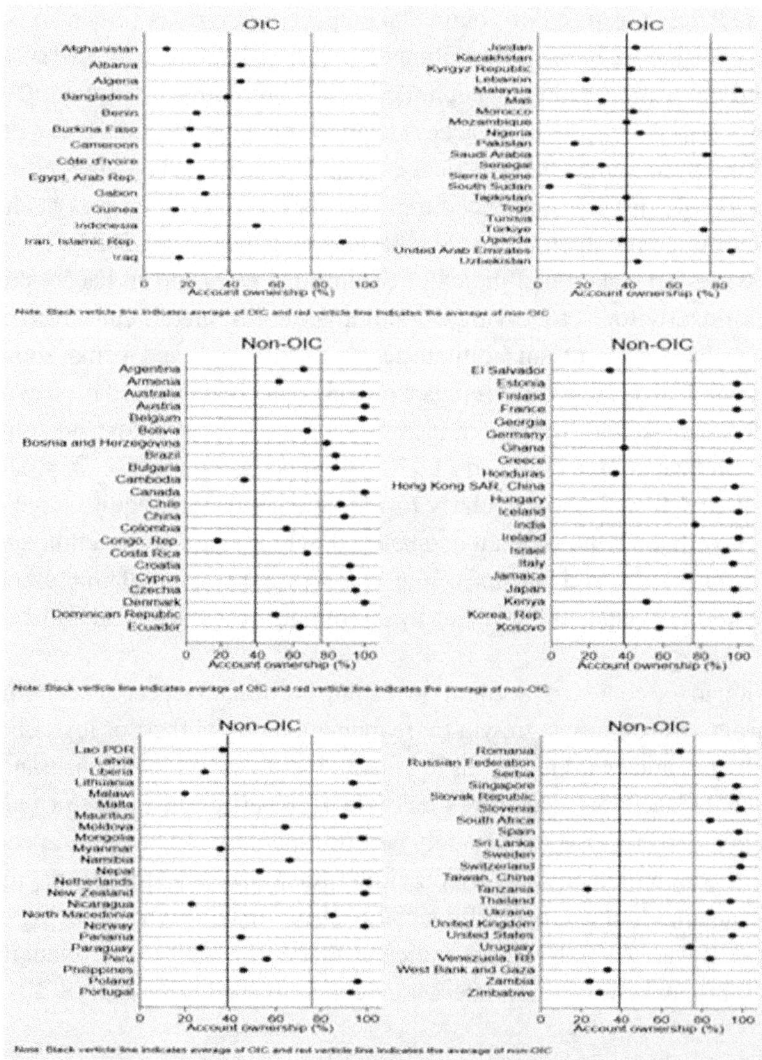

rate of 50 per cent or above. In non-OIC economies, the distribution of account ownership is skewed towards the upper limit, in contrast to the distribution in OIC economies. The lower level of account ownership in the OIC economies can be described by various socio-economic, demographic, cultural, and religious metrics.

4.3. Account Ownership Across the OIC and Non-OIC Groups

As mentioned in the previous section, there is a difference in account ownership between countries in the OIC and non-OIC groups. Examining the penetration of account ownership – in banks, mobile money accounts, and both – in different groups allows for a better understanding of the overall picture. We can obtain a single and comparable estimate by considering the OIC and non-OIC groups as separate units. Additionally, this analysis helps us assess the sustainability of account ownership. The results of this study have been conducted and are presented in Figure 3.

In the OIC unit, 39 per cent of individuals reported having a financial institution account, compared to 76 per cent in the non-OIC group (see Figure 3). Similarly, ownership of mobile money accounts is higher in the non-OIC, with a 5 per cent difference. Interestingly, individuals from the OIC group have a slightly higher rate of having both a bank account and a mobile money account, with a difference of only 0.5 per cent. The estimates of account ownership align with the findings in Figure 2, indicating that countries outside of the OIC group have a higher rate of account ownership. Religious values, among other factors, contribute to lower financial inclusion in OIC economies. People's preferences and behaviours regarding financial services can be influenced by religious norms, leading some to favour cash or kind savings over formal options. A significant number of unbanked individuals can be attributed to religious objections to interest-based services, particularly those prohibited in Islam. According to a recent Global Findex report, religion is identified as a hindrance by a mere 10 per cent of unbanked adults worldwide (Demirgüç-Kunt et al., 2021). The percentages rise to 24 per cent and 19 per cent in specific OIC countries like Iraq and Morocco, respectively.

Figure 3. Account ownership across the OIC and non-OIC

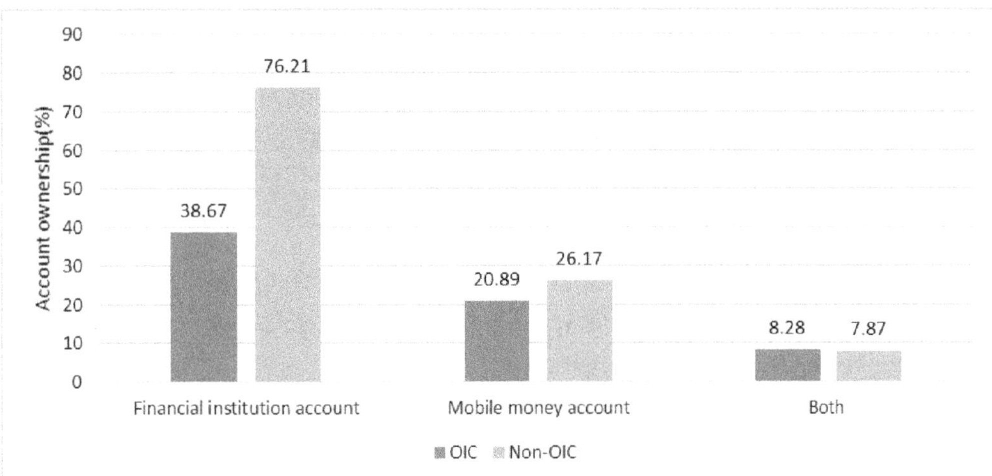

5. FINANCIAL INCLUSION AND SUSTAINABILITY

Financial inclusion is also subject to the provision of affordable financial services that meet the needs of individuals and enterprises responsibly and sustainably. It can contribute to achieving the Sustainable Development Goals (SDGs), which aim to end poverty, protect the planet, and ensure peace and prosperity by 2030. SDGs related to financial inclusion include achieving no poverty, zero hunger, good health and well-being, gender equality, decent work and economic growth, industry, innovation and infrastructure, and reduced inequalities. Financial inclusion can help people escape poverty by enabling them to save, invest, manage risks, and access opportunities. It can also enhance food security, promote sustainable agriculture, and reduce health outcomes by facilitating access to healthcare and promoting preventive behaviours.

Given the globally recognised importance of financial inclusion, the scope of this study is on SDG 1, 'No poverty', specifically target 1.4, which pertains to enhancing access to financial services for poor individuals. Furthermore, the aspect related to the realisation of SDG 5, specifically focusing on 'Gender Equality', with a specific emphasis on target 5.a, which pertains to the attainment of gender parity concerning financial services.

According to the Global Findex report, there has been a significant increase in global account ownership from 2011 to 2021, with a rise of 50 per cent (Demirgüç-Kunt et al., 2021). Nevertheless, it is crucial to compare the sustainable effects on vulnerable and marginalised populations within those economies. Figure 4 presents a comparison of the gender gap in account ownership. The 45-degree angle represents the equal distribution of account ownership across genders. In both non-OIC and OIC economies, there is a noticeable trend of higher account ownership among males compared to females. This is evident from the scatter plot, where most data points lie to the right of the 45-degree line. Likewise, Figure 5 illustrates a disparity in account ownership between those who are non-poor and those who are poor. The analysis reveals a noticeable gap in account access when considering gender and income. Given the pressing need for sustainability within marginalised communities, it is crucial to determine the extent of access to bank accounts within both OIC and non-OIC countries and among vulnerable populations.

There is a lack of equality in the distribution of bank account ownership among different gender and income groups in both OIC and non-OIC countries. Figure 6 presents the account ownership across various groups within OIC and non-OIC. This exercise evaluates the sustainability of account ownership. Financial account ownership mobile money account ownership, and both have income gaps in OIC and non-OIC nations. For instance, 42 per cent of non-poor OIC members have a financial account, compared to 32 per cent of poor. The non-OIC category also has a gender gap. Non-poor people from OIC and non-OIC nations have two levels of account ownership. Multiple opportunity differential contributes to the lower participation of the poor in accessing financial accounts. For example, limited income, high transaction costs, and participation in the informal economy often serve as economic obstacles to achieving financial inclusion. In addition, the challenges are compounded by factors such as limited access to technology, low levels of financial literacy, institutional barriers, absence of customised products, discriminatory practices, and a lack of awareness.

The gender gap in account ownership, with a difference of 11 per cent, is visible in Figure 6. On the contrary, there is no gender gap in account ownership in non-OIC nations. The account ownership across the males of OIC and non-OIC depicts a gap of 30 per cent. The lower participation of females in access to financial accounts in OIC can be attributed to factors such as lower incomes, limited education and work prospects, safety concerns, traditional gender roles, legal and regulatory constraints, and

Figure 4. Plot of account ownership by gender across OIC and non-OIC

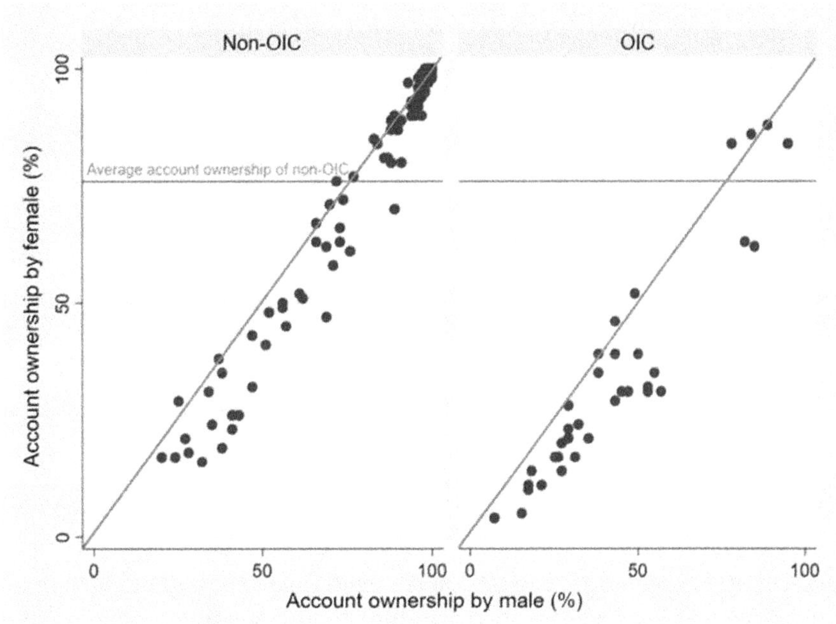

Figure 5. Plot of account ownership by income group across OIC and non-OIC

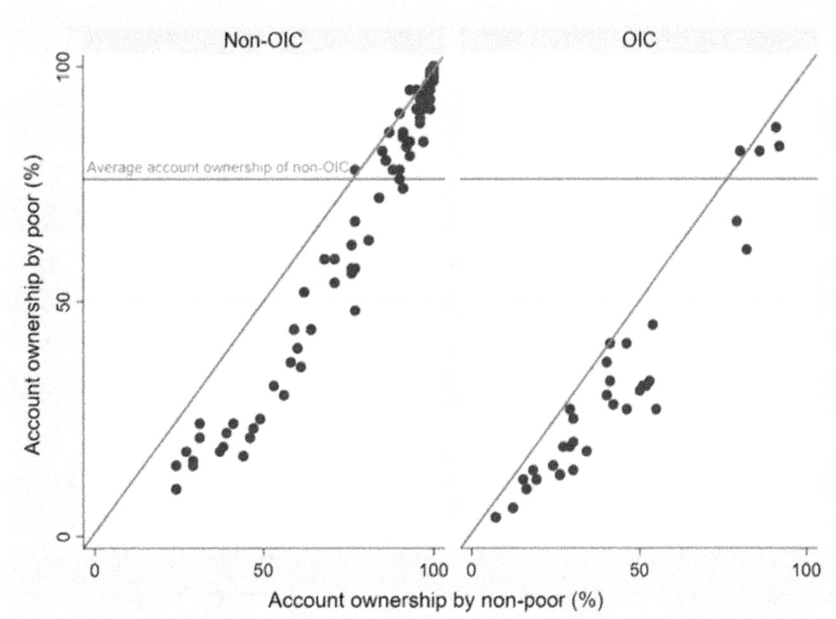

Figure 6. Sustainability aspect in account ownership across the OIC and non-OIC

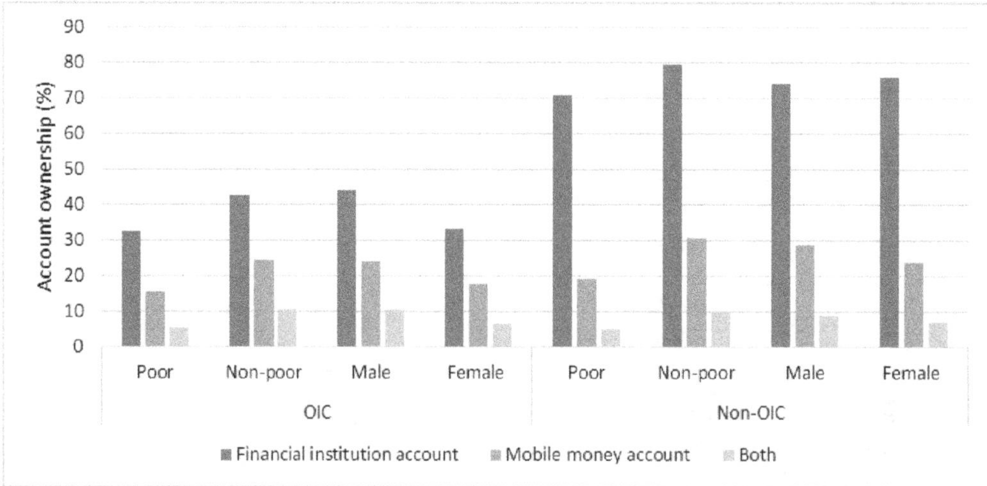

societal norms and cultural expectations can all contribute to financial limitations within households. In addition, a lack of financial literacy also restricts the ability to operate financial activities and associated benefits banks offer.

6. USE OF FINANCIAL SERVICES

The use of the financial services is related to the digital payment, formal savings and formal borrowing. The gender and income gap in the utilisation of the financial services across the OIC and non-OIC has been discuss in the current section.

6.1. Digital Payment

Financial services such as digital payment are an essential feature of financial inclusion. Digital payments include mobile money, debit or credit cards, and internet usage for sending or receiving money. The Global Findex 2021 reveals that 64 per cent of adults globally make or receive a digital payment, with 95 per cent in high-income nations and 57 per cent in developing economies (Demirgüç-Kunt et al., 2021). There are numerous benefits of digital payments for both recipients and senders, which include an impression of security, privacy, affordability, speed, and convenience. The research suggests that implementing direct deposit for wages has proven highly beneficial for factory workers, increasing savings and enhancing financial security (Breza et al., 2020). Entrepreneurs can leverage digital payment methods to broaden their network of buyers, suppliers, and service providers, enabling a smooth transition into the digital economy. By embracing digital payments, farmers can enhance their financial inclusion and gain access to a broader range of formal financial services such as credit and insurance.

The global communities have widely acknowledged the recognition of digital payments in transitioning to a digital economy. Considering the pressing need for the diffusion of digital payments, the estimates depict that 42 per cent of individuals in the OIC use digital payment (see Figure 7). On the other hand,

Figure 7. Use of digital payment across the OIC and non-OIC

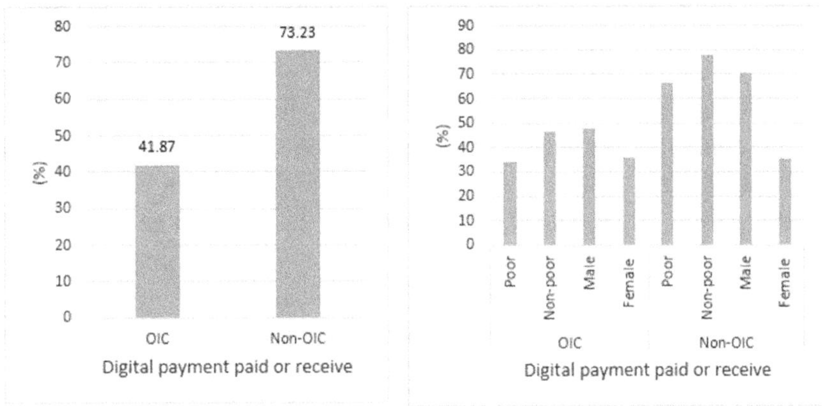

the count of individuals using digital payments has soared to 73 per cent in non-OIC. The lack of digital payment adoption in Islamic countries is primarily influenced by socio-cultural factors, religious considerations, limited trust in financial institutions, and cultural preferences for cash. In addition, a lack of awareness and education regarding the advantages of digital payments, a lack of competition, and high transaction fees can also impede the adoption of such payment methods.

The presence of gender and income disparities in the use of digital payment methods is apparent in both OIC and non-OIC nations. For example, 48 per cent of the non-poor population in the OIC made digital payments, whilst just 33 per cent of the poor population did the same. An analogous disparity is also observed between the males and females of OIC. The gender and income gaps are also present in the non-OIC countries, although the magnitude of these gaps is smaller when comparing them to those within the OIC countries. Notably, the non-poor population in non-OIC countries has a 30 per cent greater digital payment usage rate than in the OIC countries. The 22 per cent disparity is evident when comparing the use of digital payment by males in OIC and non-OIC regions. The lower usage rates of digital payments among marginalised groups – poor or female – can be attributed to various factors. These include their disproportionate participation in informal economies, limited income, digital divide in access and usage, and safety concerns.

6.2. Savings

Financial inclusion aims to create opportunities for saving within the formal sector. On a global scale, nearly 49 per cent of adults have managed to save or put aside money in the past year (Demirgüç-Kunt et al., 2021). A significant portion of individuals (around 31 per cent) globally reported saving money through formal means such as financial institutions or mobile money accounts. People have different motivations for saving, such as preparing for future expenses, making investments, planning for retirement, and being prepared for unexpected emergencies. Regular savings habits foster better budgeting and management skills while reducing reliance on debt and predatory lending practices. Formal saving accounts provide numerous benefits to individuals and communities, including financial security, increased income, improved financial planning, reduced risk, enhanced financial literacy, access to credit, and empowerment. They also contribute to capital formation, financial stability, economic growth, financial inclusion, resource allocation, increased tax revenue, and improved financial market efficiency. They also play a vital role in advocating for greater financial access, increased tax earnings, and enhanced market effectiveness.

The importance of savings at formal financial accounts in generating economic activities has been widely recognized. The savings count in the formal sector is higher in non-OIC than the OIC. In the OIC unit, 11 per cent of individuals have saved formally using financial institutions, while 33 per cent in the non-OIC unit (see Figure 8). The savings in mobile money accounts are higher in OIC than in non-OIC, with a difference of 4 per cent. The lower formal savings can be attributed to various religious and cultural factors, among others. For instance, traditional saving practices, like gold, land, and family networks, are more familiar and trusted. Religious considerations surrounding interest-based financial products and the limited availability of Islamic-compliant financial products may also play a role. Although the Islamic finance sector has expanded, finding a wide range of Sharia-compliant saving products may be challenging.

The gender and income gap in saving at formal institutions is evident within OIC and non-OIC countries. For instance, 13 per cent of the non-poor in OIC reported saving at formal institutions, while this count is only 6 per cent for the poor. A similar difference is also observed for the males and females. The gender and income gap is also evident in the non-OIC; it is higher in magnitude when compared to the gap within the non-OIC. Noteworthy is the extent of saving at formal institutions across non-poor non-OICs, which is 25 per cent higher than the non-poor OIC. The 23 per cent gap is evident when comparing the outcome of formal savings by males across the OIC and non-OIC. Individuals of OIC are more inclined to mobile money accounts than non-OIC individuals across the income group and gender categories.

Lower rates of formal saving account ownership among women and the poor are attributed to three main factors: economic and financial, social and cultural, and institutional and market barriers. Women often have lower incomes due to gender pay gaps and limited employment opportunities, making it difficult for them to accumulate savings consistently. They also often work in informal sectors, lack access to financial services, and face high transaction costs. On the other hand, the poor have limited disposable income, high financial burdens, and limited financial literacy, leading to informal saving methods, lack of social support, and inadequate financial education.

Figure 8. Savings across the OIC and non-OIC

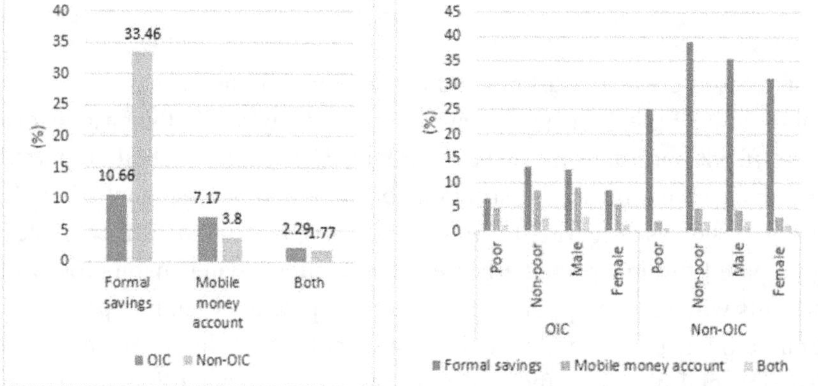

6.3. Borrowing

Financial inclusion aims to enable formal sector borrowing. Formal sector borrowing includes financial institution loans, credit cards, and mobile money accounts, a widely used source of credit. On the other hand, informal borrowing involves seeking credit from family and friends and participating in rotation savings and credit associations. In 2021, a significant portion of the global population, 53 per cent, indicated that they had taken out loans within the previous year, encompassing both formal and informal sources (Demirgüç-Kunt et al., 2021). Borrowing formally is desirable because it provides numerous benefits to individuals. It offers access to larger sums, lower interest rates, flexible repayment terms, legal protection, credit history building, financial discipline, and emergency funds. Formal lenders typically offer lower interest rates, reducing the overall cost of borrowing and making repayments more manageable. They also provide structured repayment plans with predictable instalments, allowing borrowers to budget effectively and avoid financial strain. Legal protection ensures fairness and protects both parties from misunderstandings or disputes. Formal borrowing plays a vital role in social cohesion, expansion of entrepreneurial activities, and support of economic activities.

The distribution of borrowing in OIC and non-OIC is presented in Figure 9. In the OIC unit, 49 per cent of individuals borrowed last year, while it is 52 per cent in the non-OIC unit. The rate of formal borrowing in the OIC is 17 per cent from formal financial institutions and 15 per cent from mobile money accounts. The distribution of borrowing in non-OIC is 26 from formal financial institutions and 18 per cent from the mobile money account. The phenomenon of borrowing informally is higher in OIC than in non-OIC, with a difference of 7 per cent. The lower formal borrowing rates in Islamic countries are attributed to religious and cultural factors, among others. Islamic financial principles, such as avoiding usury and interest payments, discourage borrowing. The limited availability of Sharia-compliant borrowing products and the reliance on informal borrowing mechanisms, such as family loans, also contribute to hesitancy among potential borrowers.

The gender and income gaps in the borrowing formal institutions are evident within OIC and non-OIC countries. For instance, 18 per cent of the non-poor in OIC reported borrowing from formal institutions, while this count is only 16 per cent for the poor. A difference of 2 per cent is also observed for the male and female borrowing from formal institutions. The gender gap and income gap are also evident in the

Figure 9. Borrowing across the OIC and non-OIC

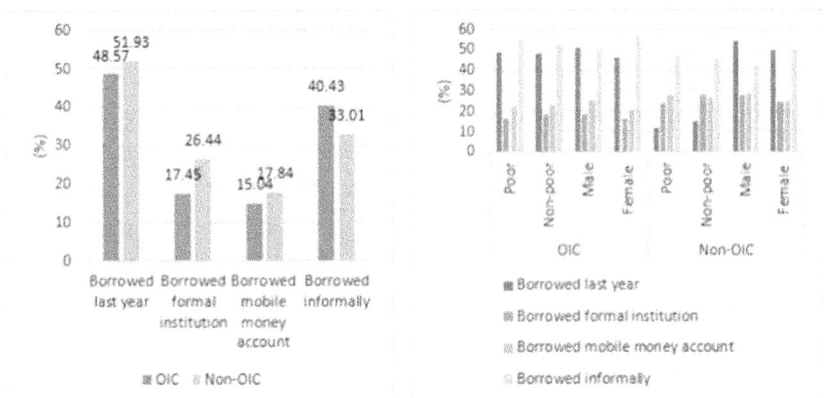

non-OIC. Noteworthy, borrowing from formal institutions across non-poor non-OIC is 10 per cent higher than the OIC. The 11 per cent gap is apparent when comparing the outcome of formal institution borrowing by males across the OIC and non-OIC. The lower inclusiveness in access to borrowing (either for the poor or females) in the traditional society is characterised by similar deprivations in observed metrics. These include economic disparity, informal economy participation, limited access to financial services, limited disposable income, high financial burdens, and limited financial literacy. In addition, other factors like cultural norms, social exclusion, and limited access to education and technology further hinder financial inclusion in formal borrowing.

7. FINANCIAL WELLBEING

Financial well-being is a state of financial stability and security that enables individuals and families to meet their current and future financial needs. Financial inclusion is also subject to enhanced well-being by enhancing financial resilience, stress management, and confidence in financial resources. Financial well-being is characterised by advocating for people to feel secure in their financial future. It involves a steady income, responsible debt management, adequate savings, access to financial services, financial literacy and knowledge, financial resilience, and financial confidence. The subject matter of the study covers financial resilience and financial worrying.

7.1. Financial Resilience

Financial resilience is the ability of adults to cope with sudden income drops or unavoidable expenses. Financial resilience is the extent of ease of access to emergency funds. The common approaches to cope with emergency funds include relying on family and friends, working extra hours, drawing down savings, taking out a loan, or selling an asset. However, these strategies may be challenging due to slow labour markets, systemic shocks like the COVID-19 pandemic, or inaccessible savings in community groups. Building financial resilience is crucial for avoiding short-term harm and long-lasting consequences.

The sources of emergency funds are savings, borrowing, family or friends, sale of assets, and earnings from work. In developing economies, 87 per cent of adults said they could access one of several emergency money sources within a month (Demirgüç-Kunt et al., 2021). The extent of financial resilience on a global scale shows that only 55 per cent of individuals could access emergency money within a month without much difficulty. In this study, we measure financial resilience on the ease of accessing the equivalent amount of 5 per cent of the Gross National Income (GNI) per capita within 7 days. The estimates of financial resilience for the OIC and non-OIC are presented in Figure 10. In the OIC unit, 39 per cent of individuals responded they had no or relatively less difficulty getting emergency funds in 7 days, while 61 per cent were in the non-OIC unit. The phenomena of financial resilience are higher in non-OIC than in the OIC. The lower level of financial resilience in OIC is due to lower per capita incomes, reliance on informal employment, limited access to financial services, gender disparities, cultural norms, and limited financial literacy. These factors make it difficult for individuals and communities to build financial resilience and manage financial risks, particularly in deprived areas.

The gender and income gaps in financial resilience are evident within OIC and non-OIC countries. For instance, 54 per cent of the non-poor in OIC reported difficulty in getting emergency funds, while this count is 70 per cent for the poor. A similar difference is also observed for the males and females.

Figure 10. Financial resilience across the OIC and non-OIC

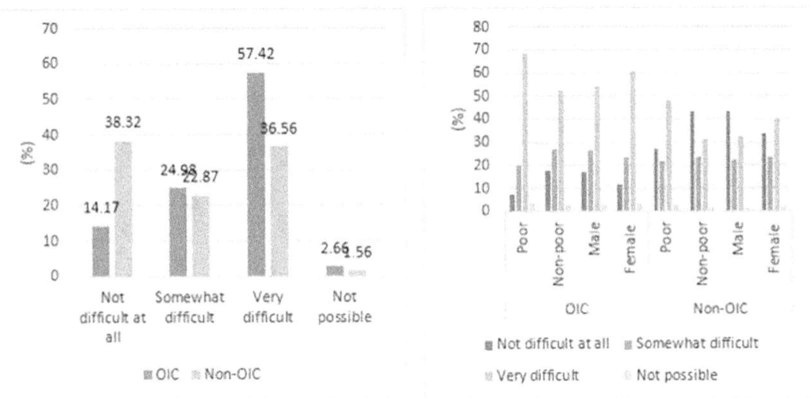

The gender gap and income gap are also evident in the non-OIC. It is lower in magnitude when compared to the gap within the non-OIC. Noteworthy, financial resilience across non-poor non-OIC is 23 per cent higher than the OIC. The 22 per cent gap is evident when comparing the outcome of financial resilience by males across the OIC and non-OIC. The marginalized segment of society faces challenges in building financial resilience, making them more vulnerable to financial shocks. Factors contributing to this disparity include limited income, informal employment, limited access to financial services, social and cultural factors, limited financial literacy and awareness, institutional and market barriers, and unconscious bias and discrimination.

7.2. Financial Worrying

Financial worrying, or financial anxiety, is a persistent concern about finances that can cause stress, anxiety, and uncertainty. Factors contributing to financial worrying include financial strain, relying on a single income source, lack of financial planning, limited financial literacy, and difficulty paying for basic needs. These factors can exacerbate financial worry, impacting mental well-being, relationships with others, and overall quality of life. Poor people, especially those with limited savings and credit, are more likely to worry about money. Addressing these issues can help individuals manage their finances and maintain a healthy financial life.

The financial worrying is quantified by asking respondents about the extent of worry on the specific issues of living expenses for old age, medical costs arising from a serious illness or accident, monthly bills and expenses, and school or education fees. On a global scale, 25 per cent of individuals in developing economies responded very worried about the four issues (Demirgüç-Kunt et al., 2021). This counts for 4 per cent for high-income economies. In the OIC unit, 59 per cent of individuals responded that they are very worried about their financial lives, while 41 per cent in the non-OIC unit (Figure 11). The phenomenon of financial worrying is higher in OICs than the non-OICs. Financial worry is influenced by lower per capita incomes, reliance on informal employment, limited access to financial services, educational disparities, employment opportunities, financial literacy, lack of risk management practices, underdeveloped financial infrastructure, and inadequate financial safety nets. These factors can amplify financial worries and increase financial insecurity, especially during difficult economic periods.

Figure 11. Financial worrying across the OIC and non-OIC

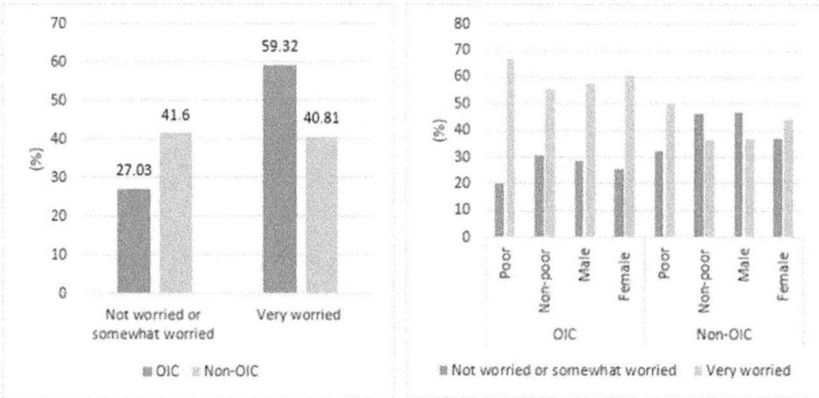

The gender and income gaps in financial worries are evident within OIC and non-OIC countries. For instance, 55 per cent of the non-poor in OIC reported being very worried about their financial lives, while this count is 67 per cent of the poor. A similar difference is observed for males and females with relatively less magnitude. The gender gap and income gap are also evident in the non-OIC. It is lower in magnitude when compared to the gap within the non-OIC. Noteworthy, financial worry across non-poor OICs is 18 per cent higher than the non-OICs. The 23 per cent gap is evident when comparing the outcome of financial worrying by males across the OIC and non-OIC. Due to limited income, resources, and low financial literacy, financial worrying is a common issue among the poor and females. These individuals may face economic shocks, difficulties accessing financial services, and a lack of representation in financial institutions. Additionally, they may have different financial needs and preferences, which the existing financial system may need to adequately address. These factors contribute to higher financial worries, negatively impacting mental and physical health and social and economic participation.

8. CONCLUSION

This study compares financial inclusion, its various dimensions, sustainability, and financial well-being within the OIC and non-OIC groups. The access rate to financial institution accounts is lower in OIC countries than in non-OIC countries. Similarly, the level of financial services such as digital payment, savings, and borrowing is also lower in the OIC. The level of financial resilience and financial worry in the OIC could be better when compared to the non-OIC. Financial inclusion is also less prevalent among marginalised groups in society, particularly those who are poor and female.

Financial inclusion in the OIC countries is crucial for economic growth, poverty reduction, and empowering individuals and businesses. For smooth penetration of financial inclusion, some strategic measures are required to develop Sharia-compliant financial products, promote Islamic finance awareness, and enhance financial literacy and education. In addition, expanding access to formal financial services, promoting digital financial solutions, expanding branch networks, and simplifying account opening procedures can further fuel the momentum of financial inclusion.

Long-term policy measures are required to bridge the income gap and achieve gender parity in access and use of financial services. Financial inclusion is a complex and dynamic process that requires continuous learning, adaptation, and collaboration among various actors and stakeholders, including governments, development agencies, financial institutions, and civil society organizations. The specific challenges and contexts of each country and population will determine the most effective approach.

REFERENCES

Abdelghaffar, R. A., Emam, H. A., & Samak, N. A. (2023). Financial inclusion and human development: Is there a nexus? *Journal of Humanities and Applied Social Sciences*, *5*(3), 163–177. doi:10.1108/JHASS-11-2021-0178

Agner, M. G., & Desello, J. M. U. (2023). Financial inclusion and the role of financial literacy in the Philippines. *International Journal of Economics and Finance*, *15*(6), 12–31.

Allen, F., Demirguc-Kunt, A., Klapper, L., & Peria, M. S. M. (2016). The foundations of financial inclusion: Understanding ownership and use of formal accounts. *Journal of Financial Intermediation*, *27*, 1–30. doi:10.1016/j.jfi.2015.12.003

Anarfo, E. B., Abor, J. Y., & osei, K. A. (2020, January). Africa: Does financial stability play a moderating role? *Research in International Business and Finance*, *51*, 101070. doi:10.1016/j.ribaf.2019.101070

Ashraf, N., Karlan, D., & Yin, W. (2010). Female empowerment: Impact of a commitment savings product in the Philippines. *World Development*, *38*(3), 333–344. doi:10.1016/j.worlddev.2009.05.010

Bhandari, A. (2009) Access to banking services and poverty reduction: a state-wise assessment in India. *IZA Discussion Paper, 4132*.

Breza, E., Kanz, M., & Klapper, L. F. (2020). Learning to navigate a new financial technology: Evidence from payroll accounts. *Policy Research Working Paper 9495*, World Bank, Washington, DC.

Bruhn, M., & Love, Y. (2017). Financial inclusion and economic development: A review of the literature and new evidence. *The Review of Economics and Statistics*, *99*(4), 667–687.

CFPB. (2015). *Measuring financial well-being: A guide to using the CFPB financial well-being scale.* Retrieved October 13, 2023 from https://fles.consumerfnance.gov/f/201512_cfpb_fnancial-wellbeing-user-guide-scale.pdf

Demirgüç-Kunt, A., Klapper, L. F., & Singer, D. (2013). Financial inclusion and legal discrimination against women: evidence from developing countries. *World Bank Policy Research Working Paper*, (6416).

Duvendack, M., Palmer-Jones, R., Copestake, J. G., Hooper, L., Loke, Y., & Rao, N. (2011). *What is the evidence of the impact of microfinance on the well-being of poor people? EPPI-Centre, Social Science Research Unit, Institute of Education*. University of London.

Fitzpatrick, K. (2015). The effect of bank account ownership on credit and consumption: Evidence from the UK. *Southern Economic Journal*, *82*(1), 55–80. doi:10.4284/0038-4038-2013.027

Fungáčová, Z., & Weill, L. (2015). Understanding financial inclusion in China. *China Economic Review*, *34*, 196–206. doi:10.1016/j.chieco.2014.12.004

Ghosh, S., & Vinod, D. (2017). What constrains financial inclusion for women? Evidence from Indian micro data. *World Development*, *92*, 60–81. doi:10.1016/j.worlddev.2016.11.011

Grohmann, A., Kluhs, T., & Menkhoff, L. (2018). Does financial literacy improve financial inclusion? Cross country evidence. *World Development*, *111*, 84–96. doi:10.1016/j.worlddev.2018.06.020

Gupte, R., Venkataramani, B. & Gupata, D. (2012). Computation of financial inclusion index for India. *International Journal of Procedia - Social and Behavioural Sciences, 37*, 133-149.

Gutter, M., & Copur, Z. (2011). Financial behaviours and financial wellbeing of college students: Evidence from a national survey. *Journal of Family and Economic Issues*, *32*(4), 699–714. doi:10.1007/s10834-011-9255-2

Kim, D. W., Yu, J. S., & Hassan, M. K. (2018). Financial inclusion and economic growth in OIC countries. *Research in International Business and Finance*, *43*, 1–14. doi:10.1016/j.ribaf.2017.07.178

Malone, K., Stewart, S. D., Wilson, J., & Korsching, P. F. (2010). Perceptions of financial well-being among American women in diverse families. *Journal of Family and Economic Issues*, *31*(1), 63–81. doi:10.1007/s10834-009-9176-5

Nandru, P., Byram, A., & Rentala, S. (2016). Determinants of financial inclusion: Evidence from account ownership and use of banking services. *International Journal of Entrepreneurship and Development Studies*, *4*(2), 141–155.

Neaime, S., & Gaysset, I. (2018). Financial inclusion and stability in MENA: Evidence from poverty and inequality. *Finance Research Letters*, *24*, 230–237. doi:10.1016/j.frl.2017.09.007

Ozili, P. K. (2020). Theories of financial inclusion. In *Uncertainty and challenges in contemporary economic behaviour* (pp. 89–115). Emerald Publishing Limited. doi:10.1108/978-1-80043-095-220201008

Ozili, P. K. (2023). Can social inclusion policies promote financial inclusion? *The International Journal of Sociology and Social Policy*, *43*(11), 1138–1155. doi:10.1108/IJSSP-03-2023-0054

Park, C. Y., & Mercado, R. (2021). Understanding financial inclusion: What matters and how it matters. *ADBI Working Paper no. 1287.*

Prina, S. (2015). Banking the poor via savings accounts: Evidence from a field experiment. *Journal of Development Economics*, *115*, 16–31. doi:10.1016/j.jdeveco.2015.01.004

Sarkar, S., Nair, S., & Rao, M. V. V. (2023). Exploring the gender dimension in financial inclusion in India: Insights from the Global Findex Database. *Journal of Development Policy and Practice*, *8*(2), 141–161. doi:10.1177/24551333221141570

Sen, A. (2000). *Social exclusion: Concept, application, and scrutiny.* Social Development Papers No. 1. Office of Environment and Social Development Asian Development Bank.

Sethi, D., & Acharya, D. (2018). Financial inclusion and economic growth linkage: Some cross country evidence. *Journal of Financial Economic Policy*, *10*(3), 369–385. doi:10.1108/JFEP-11-2016-0073

Shim, S., Xiao, J. J., Barber, B. L., & Lyons, A. C. (2009). Pathways to life success: A conceptual model of financial well-being for young adults. *Journal of Applied Developmental Psychology*, *30*(6), 708–723. doi:10.1016/j.appdev.2009.02.003

United Nations. (2016). *Digital Financial Inclusion*. Retrieved from https://www.un.org/esa/ffd/ wpcontent/uploads/2016/01/Digital-Financial-Inclusion_ITU_IATF-Issue-Brief.pdf

Xiao, J. J., & O'Neill, B. (2018). Propensity to plan, financial capability, and financial satisfaction. *International Journal of Consumer Studies*, *42*(5), 501–512. doi:10.1111/ijcs.12461

Zins, A., & Weill, L. (2016). The determinants of financial inclusion in Africa. *Review of Development Finance, 6*(1), 46-57.

APPENDIX 1

Discussion Questions

1. Global account ownership has increased by 50 per cent over the past decade. What are the primary factors driving this surge in context of OIC and non-OIC economies?
2. Financial inclusion pertains to equal access to financial services. However, multiple types of disparities hinder individuals from engaging in the financial sector. Discuss these disparities.
3. What factors contribute to the lower utilization of financial services by individuals of OIC?
4. In both OIC and non-OIC countries, how can financial inclusion be elevated amongst marginalized groups?
5. Why financial resilience is lower in OIC and financial worrying is higher in OIC than the non-OIC economies?

Short Questions

What are dimensions of sustainable development?
What is developmental impact of financial inclusion?
What are dimensions of financial inclusion?
Write a note on public good theory of financial inclusion.
What is financial wellbeing?

Assignments

1. The social and economic dimension of sustainable development is closely linked to the financial inclusion. Do you think any causality or reverse causality between environmental dimension and financial inclusion. Is there any relationship between the environmental dimension of sustainable development and financial inclusion?
2. Based on recent Global Findex report, only 10 per cent unbanked adults globally identified religion as a hindrance. How can Sharia-compliant financial products help alleviate this obstacle to financial inclusion?
3. Is financial resilience and financial worrying a more accurate indicator of financial wellbeing? Are there alternative indicators of financial wellbeing in the existing literature? Examine and analyze these measures of financial wellbeing in depth.
4. It has been identified that 20 per cent of OIC and 88 per cent non-OIC economies have an account ownership rate of 50 per cent or above. What are the primary factors at macro level that predict these variations in account ownership?
5. Why are non-poor individuals in OIC countries less financially included than poor individuals in non-OIC countries? Why is the financial inclusion rate lower for females in OIC countries compared to females in non-OIC countries?

Multiple choice questions

<table>
<tr><td colspan="4">1. Digital payment is a following dimension of the financial inclusion:</td></tr>
<tr><td>(a) access</td><td>(b) usage</td><td>(c) quality</td><td>(d) quantity</td></tr>
<tr><td colspan="4">2. Which of the following Islamic country has higher proportion of individuals responded religion as a hinder in bank account:</td></tr>
<tr><td>(a) Pakistan</td><td>(b) Iran</td><td>(c) Iraq</td><td>(d) Morocco</td></tr>
<tr><td colspan="4">3. Which of the following is marginalized group of the society:</td></tr>
<tr><td>(a) illiterate</td><td>(b) part-time worker</td><td>(c) male</td><td>(d) poor</td></tr>
<tr><td colspan="4">4. Sustainable development goal pertains to enhancing access to financial services for poor individuals is target:</td></tr>
<tr><td>(a) 1.2</td><td>(b) 1.4</td><td>(c) 2.2</td><td>(d) 2.4</td></tr>
<tr><td colspan="4">5. Which of the following is not dimension of financial inclusion:</td></tr>
<tr><td>(a) access</td><td>(b) usage</td><td>(c) stability</td><td>(d) quality</td></tr>
<tr><td colspan="4">6. Which of the following target of sustainable development goal is related to the attainment of gender parity in financial services.</td></tr>
<tr><td>(a) 5.a</td><td>(b) 5.b</td><td>(c) 5.c</td><td>(d) 5.d</td></tr>
<tr><td colspan="4">7. There is no gender gap in account ownership in:</td></tr>
<tr><td>(a) OIC</td><td>(b) non-OIC</td><td>(c) both OIC and non-OIC</td><td>(d) South Asian countries</td></tr>
<tr><td colspan="4">8. The lack of digital payment adoption in Islamic countries is primarily influenced by:</td></tr>
<tr><td>(a) gender-disparity</td><td>(b) unemployment</td><td>(c) poverty</td><td>(d) cultural preferences for cash</td></tr>
<tr><td colspan="4">9. The lower formal borrowing rates in Islamic countries are attributed to:</td></tr>
<tr><td>(a) higher income</td><td>(b) lower education</td><td>(c) avoiding usury</td><td>(d) role of gender</td></tr>
<tr><td colspan="4">10. Financial resilience is the extent of ease of access to:</td></tr>
<tr><td>(a) emergency funds</td><td>(b) formal savings</td><td>(c) digital payments</td><td>(d) formal borrowing</td></tr>
</table>

Chapter 9
Impact of Financial Inclusion on SME Growth:
A Bibliometric Analysis of OIC and Non-OIC Countries

Humera Tariq Mahmood
Birmingham City University, UK

Deniz E. Yoruk
Birmingham City University, UK

Mark Gilman
University of Derby, UK

ABSTRACT

Financial inclusion (FI) is perceived as an imperative tool for reducing poverty and stimulating economic growth. In particular, FI provides access to capital and financial services to small and medium-sized enterprises (SMEs) and enables them to manage their finances, mitigate risks, expand operations, facilitate innovation, and drive job creation. SMEs are considered the backbone of an economy regardless of the level of development of that economy. However, their potential is not fully tapped yet and is hindered due to several constraints. Among its constraints, the unavailability of financial resources is considered a major barrier to SME growth. The International Finance Corporation (IFC) evidenced that 40% of formal SMEs in emerging economies suffer from unmet yearly financial needs of USD 5.2 trillion. Despite all the advantages of FI, it is argued that FI is contingent upon various factors such as structural and policy-related factors and cannot be achieved in isolation. The effectiveness of FI requires collective effort. On the other hand, information and communication technology (ICT) is considered a key enabler of FI. The existing literature has been debated the relationship between FI and SME growth; nonetheless, a lack of consensus exists for the role of FI in SMEs' performance and/or growth. It is also evidenced that the level of FI varies among countries as well as within a country. Therefore, this chapter reviews the academic literature on FI in SMEs by employing bibliometric analysis methods. A total of 62 publications related to FI in SMEs between 2206 and 2024 were identified from a widely recognised Scopus online database. Using VOSviewer software, the analysis established how research has evolved in this area. The authors identified main current themes, emerging trends, and gaps for future research

DOI: 10.4018/979-8-3693-1475-3.ch009

directions.

1. INTRODUCTION

The promotion of financial inclusion has emerged as a crucial element in the advancement of worldwide economic growth, with SMEs being the main agents of innovation, employer of choice, and major contributors to GDP. SMEs' access to financial services becomes critical as they become major forces behind economic growth. Nevertheless, small businesses face particular challenges that could impede their development and long-term sustainability. Among those challenges, access to finance is considered a major barrier to their development. However, there is a lack of consensus regarding the influence of FI on SMEs growth. Some studies advocate that FI has a positive impact on SMEs (Okello, 2017). On the contrary, another argument supports the view that FI alone cannot bring improvement in SMEs, rather it requires collective efforts (Matama, 2016; Mwangi & Cheluget, 2018). In a similar vein, it is emphasized that to leverage financial resources wisely, financial literacy is important particularly in the case of SMEs which are already resources constrained (Junoh, et al., 2019). In addition, in the era of rapid evolution of technology fintech has received attention. It is argued that Fintech can increase financial inclusion of SMEs in developing economies where SMEs suffer lack of finances and lack of financial knowledge (Nugraha et al.,2022). Despite all the factors influencing FI-SME nexus, the level of FI varies in each country. The dynamics of each country is different. For instance, Islamic countries provide Islamic finance options which can increase financial inclusion of Muslims who are interested in ethical and shariah compliant financing options.

Therefore, this book chapter intends to provide a deep insight into current trends on FI-SME nexus by considering OIC and non-OIC countries dynamics. To do this, bibliometric analysis will be employed to evaluate current trends, emerging patterns, and gaps in existing literature in Organization of Islamic Cooperation (OIC) and non-OIC nations on FI-SME literature. Given the unique economic, cultural, and legal contexts of OIC member countries—where Sharia-compliant FI concepts are common—FI in SMEs is an important component. A comparative viewpoint is also provided by non-OIC countries because of their different economic and regulatory frameworks, Islamic faith-based SMEs may have limitations in accessing interest free finance.

A systematic approach to mapping and analyzing the scholarly landscape that offers insights into the works that have shaped the discourse on the financial inclusion in SMEs is provided by bibliometric analysis, a quantitative tool. This method makes it possible to identify key publications, prominent research themes, well-known authors, and important journals surrounding the main topic of FI in SMEs. This chapter intends to undertake a thorough bibliometric analysis of the body of literature in order to identify gaps in the literature, highlight emerging patterns, and establish a foundation for future research endeavors.

Through the analysis of bibliometric methods such as co-authorship networks, co-citation patterns, and co-word clusters, the study seeks to determine the intellectual structure of the academic field. Prominent authors and highly cited papers can serve as indicators of knowledge leaders who can direct future research and policymaking endeavors. Analyzing academics' and institutions' patterns of collaboration may highlight chances to support interdisciplinary and global partnerships, boosting the field's research and policymaking. In addition, this book chapter intends to add value to the book by providing updated information on the influence of various factors that can lead to sustainability of SMEs by enabling them to access finances.

Policymakers, scholars, and practitioners all benefit from understanding the trends and shifts in concentration across the academic community to address the difficulties SMEs have in accessing financial services and to develop targeted programs to improve SMEs' access to funding both of which contribute to promoting sustainable economic growth in both OIC and non-OIC nations. In addition, by offering insights into how Islamic finance principles affect FI, the research aims to shed light on the evolution of research on Sharia-compliant financial inclusion for SMEs in OIC member nations. It also seeks to make clear how various legal frameworks and financial systems affect SMEs' access to financial services in non-OIC nations.

This book chapter addresses the following research questions:

Q1. What are the publication trends in FI and SMEs literature?

Q2. Which are the top contributing authors, journals, and countries for financial inclusion and SMEs research area?

Q3. How do the bibliometric performances of OIC and non-OIC countries compare in the FI and SMEs nexus?

2. RELATIONSHIP BETWEEN FINANCIAL INCLUSION AND SME GROWTH

Financial inclusion (FI) has become a prominent topic in the academic literature (Nurohman et al., 2021). It is perceived as an imperative tool for reducing poverty and stimulating economic growth (Nurohman et al., 2021). Earlier studies by Beck et al. (2007) and Claessens and Perotti (2007) laid the foundation for our current knowledge of the significance of FI globally. Beck et al. (2007) noted that broader access to financial services is necessary, while Claessens and Perotti (2007) highlighted the relationship between finance and inequality. Demirguc-Kunt and Klapper (2013) analysed cross-national data on enterprises' access to finance in developing nations and found that half of adults around the world remain unbanked because of cost, distance, and documentation requirements. It is also evidenced that the level of FI varies among countries as well as within a country. Contributing to these debates methodologically, Demirguc-Kunt and Leora (2012) offered a method for gauging FI.

In particular, FI provides access to capital and financial services to Small and Medium-sized Enterprises (SMEs) and enables them to manage their finances, mitigate risks, expand operations, facilitate innovation, and drive job creation. Claessens and Perotti (2007) and Demirguc-Kunt and Klapper (2012) investigated how regulatory frameworks affect SMEs' access to financial services.

SMEs are considered the backbone of an economy regardless of the level of development of that economy. They play a crucial role in job creation and economic activity. However, their potential remains untapped due to various constraints. Access to finance is considered a major barrier to SME growth. In particular, SMEs in developing countries struggle to access finance due to the unavailability of financial resources, such as collateral options and the difficulty in recovering in case of default. 40% of formal SMEs in emerging economies suffer from unmet yearly financial needs of USD 5.2 trillion (International Finance Corporation, 2017).

Due to the critical role that SMEs play in promoting economic growth, FI in SMEs has drawn more and more scholarly attention. Examining the body of research on the subject reveals a complex environment that encompasses many aspects of FI, especially when considering both OIC and non-OIC nations. Due to different dynamics such as cultural, legal, and religious differences, the magnitude of this barrier may vary among SMEs in OIC and non-OIC countries. At the same time, despite all the advantages of FI, Naceur et al. (2015) argue that FI is contingent upon various factors such as structural and policy-related factors, and cannot be achieved in isolation (Nagpal et al., 2020). The effectiveness of FI requires collective efforts and the design of policies that support in eradicating barriers and promoting financial inclusion (Demirguc-Kunt and Klapper, 2013). For instance, evidence from an OIC country in Africa revealed that access to loan financing can positively impact permanent employment growth, especially in labour-intensive sectors such as manufacturing (Brixiova et al, 2020). Authors therefore suggest that the sectoral targeting of finance could be an effective policy tool to promote industrialization. Therefore, removing structural barriers to credit supply by establishing accurate asset valuation, strengthening property rights, and implementing partial credit guarantees are suggested. In the same vein, other evidence supports the view that access to finance is strongly linked to the performance of firms (Ayyagari, Demirguc-Kunt, and Maksimovic, 2008).

On the contrary, it is also argued that small firms are more growth-constrained than their large firms' counterparts and have more limited access to finance both in developing and advanced countries (Beck et al., 2005). Evidence from Croatia also advocates that firm size plays a crucial role in determining borrowing costs, alongside factors like collateral and internal credit rating (Kundid, A., & Ercegovac, R., 2011). Nevertheless, Ethiopian SMEs' FI is positively impacted by supply, demand, market opportunity, and collateral factors. Negative impacts come from the institutional framework and borrowing costs. Ethiopia's financial system needs strengthening to provide affordable and sustainable services to SMEs (Fekete-Farkas et al., 2021). Furthermore, bank concentration and financial inclusion both positively affect SME credit availability. In China, excessive financial inclusion reduces the beneficial effect of bank concentration, suggesting that financial inclusion substitutes for bank concentration in improving SME credit availability (Lu, Z., et al., 2020).

To reduce the financial exclusion of SMEs, various countries are making endeavours suitable to their dynamics. For instance, SMEs in the United Kingdom (West Midlands) are struggling for credit access due to the financing gap created after the 2008 global financial crisis. Community Development Financial Institutions (CDFIs) are introduced to bridge the gap between traditional and alternative finance to address financial exclusion. However, to create a more inclusive financial landscape, a national fund could be established to increase its scale and geographical coverage. Greater cooperation between banks and CDFIs is also required to continue the positive impact (Appleyard, L., 2013). Nonetheless, SMEs in Uganda are struggling with FI issues mainly due to high costs, limited access to certain financial products and poor treatment of users. SMEs are suggested to focus on innovation to stay competitive and adopt cost-effective solutions such as digital financial services (Eton et al., 2021).

Moreover, information and communication technology (ICT) is considered a key enabler of FI (Chatterjee & Anand, 2017). More precisely, digital innovation is witnessed to outperform inclusive banking. It eases borrowing constraints and enhances productivity for SMEs, leading to better financial access across the Currency Union (Babilla, T. U. K., 2023). Moreover, evidence from China supports that digital financial services like payments, funds, credit, insurance, and investment reduce information asymmetry and facilitate SMEs' access to finance (Zhang, X. et al., 2023). Likewise, Fintech adoption in Indonesia's SMEs is driven by practicality, user-friendliness, reliability, and user-driven advancements.

Collaborative efforts between the government, financial institutions, and fintech entities are crucial for navigating regulatory obstacles and fostering trust (Nugraha, D. P. et al., 2022). Adoption of these technologies requires management support and external pressures influence firms in Canada for e-business technology acceptance (Ifinedo, P., 2011). Reforms in banks and digital financial inclusion can empower SMEs to overcome financial constraints and contribute to the economy (Lu Z. et al., 2022). It is endorsed that financial inclusion, digital financing, and the Technology Acceptance Model (TAM) positively impact SME performance in Sri Lanka. Digital finance and TAM mediate the relationship between financial inclusion and SME performance. In addition, promoting affordable and secure digital financing services and financial literacy can highly benefit SMEs (Thathsarani, U. S., & Jianguo, W., 2022).

Despite technological revolutions to promote FI and boost SME growth, these technologies such as fintech depend on some factors for their effectiveness. For instance, financial literacy is considered crucial in this regard. SMEs are advised to prioritize improving financial literacy, while governments are informed to refine regulations to support financial literacy, fintech, and financial inclusion, with emphasis on SMEs in Indonesia (Mutamimah, M., & Indriastuti, M., 2023). However, it is argued that financial inclusion is positively linked with SME performance in East Java. Whereas financial knowledge, behaviour, and digital capability are its significant drivers, however, SME performance is not influenced by them individually (Sari, Y., et al., 2023). In addition, having knowledge about insurance, managing risks effectively, and willingness to take risks can have a positive impact on economic sustainability, as revealed by (Garba et al., 2022) while examining the moderating effect of FI on the relationship between insurance literacy, risk knowledge management, risk-taking propensity and economic sustainability of Nigerian SMEs. Notwithstanding the effect of FI on SME performance and financial stability, it is argued that improving financial inclusion for SMEs can have both positive and negative impacts on financial stability. It can diversify bank assets but compromise credit standards. However, measures like credit databases and broadening collateral options can lead to favourable effects on financial stability (Morgan, P. J., & Pontines, V., 2018).

The integration of various advanced models and technologies brings opportunities and challenges as well for SMEs. To overcome these challenges, regulations and revisiting of existing policies are crucial. To help SMEs access finance, policies should focus on narrowing the financial inclusion gap, strengthening infrastructure, reducing barriers, leveraging technology, and implementing adequate regulation (Lam, W. R., & Liu, Y., 2020). In addition, technological infrastructure can help mitigate information asymmetry and transaction costs (Agyekum, F. K. et al., 2022). Despite the significant revolutionary developments in the financial technology (Fintech) industry in China, there remains a pressing need for improved coordination of regulatory policies and innovative policy tools such as Regtech and Fintech development 2.0. Achieving a balance between innovation and stability is crucial to ensure the sustainable growth of the industry (Hua, X., & Huang, Y., (2021). Moreover, regulatory sandboxes and a risk-based approach balance supporting FinTech start-ups and managing systemic risk. Light-touch regulation promotes financial stability, allowing innovative FinTech markets to develop (Tsai, C. H., & Kuan-Jung, P., 2017). However, to prevent opportunistic lenders from causing financial distress to SMEs, policymakers should reshape lender practices to ensure responsible and sustainable financing (Arvind, T. T., 2021). Moreover, the policymakers in countries (such as the EU) with high financial inclusion where SMEs are still struggling to access financial services due to unemployment and cuts in social assistance need to adopt flexible monetary policies and differential fiscal consolidation. In addition, moving towards a banking and fiscal union can help promote a more inclusive financial market in those countries (Gomez Urquijo, L., 2015).

Therefore, while the extant literature has greatly advanced our understanding of FI, most research on FI tends to ignore the difficulties that SMEs experience. Moreover, our knowledge of the various economic and regulatory contexts is limited by the paucity of studies that compare financial inclusion in SMEs across OIC and non-OIC nations. This literature review highlights the importance of FI for SMEs, identifies barriers in OIC and non-OIC nations and provides suggestions to improve the access to finance for SMEs. This analysis intends to add value to current knowledge in the area of FI in SMEs and to provide a mapping of the literature for policymakers and practitioners to found their strategies and policies on informed decisions.

3. METHODOLOGY AND DATA

Bibliometric analysis is a scientific mapping of academic literature that analyzes and quantifies patterns of publications, citation, and scientific collobaration within a given area or topic (Zupic and Cater, 2015). In the framework of this study, bibliometric analysis was used to offer a thorough overview of the academic research regarding the FI of SMEs. This strategy enables us to identify major patterns and trends in the literature for a better understanding of the changing discourse on the subject.

To conduct a comprehensive review of knowledge base in FI of SMEs, we collected bibliometric data from Scopus, an extensive database of scholarly papers that is widely recognized and regarded as a reputable scientific database. The Scopus database was preferred because there are a greater number of articles available for review, e.g. than the Web of Science (WoS) (Paul et al., 2021). In addition, the software we chose for analysis, VOSviewer (version 1.6.20, Centre for Science and Technology Studies, Leiden University, Leiden, The Netherlands), better supports databases obtained from Scopus.

VOSviewer is a powerful tool for bibliometric analysis that enables researchers to conduct in-depth analysis, visualize and interpret scholarly literature. With features such as network visualization, citation analysis, clustering analysis, and keyword co-occurrence analysis, it helps uncover hidden patterns and trends within bibliographic datasets (van Eck and Waltman, 2010). The network visualization feature enables visual exploration of interconnections between various elements in bibliographic data such as publications, authors, references, countries and keywords. The citation analysis helps assessing citation counts, networks, and impact metrics to evaluate the influence and visibility of publications, authors, and journals. The clustering analysis in bibliographic networks allows identification of thematic clusters, research communities, and emerging trends within the literature. The keyword co-occurrence detects common themes, predominant topics, concepts and research domains through analysis of keyword patterns that frequently appear together in documents. The co-author analysis reveals collaboration networks uncovering the social ties and scientific relationships between authors and their institutions (co-affiliation), helping to gain insight into influential authors, research teams, and valuable collaborative partnerships within the scholarly community.

Figure 1. Collection of data on Scopus by applying syntax and filter

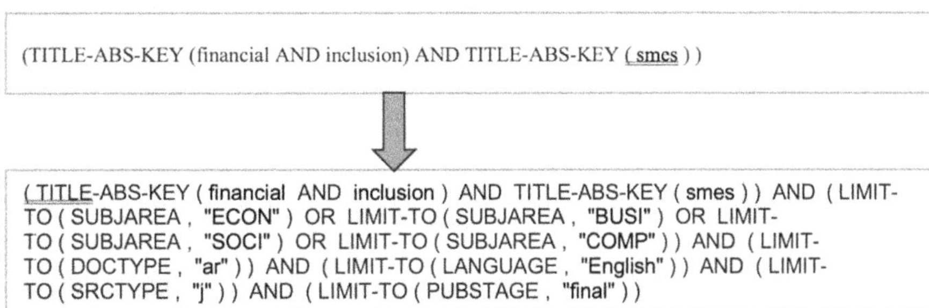

We started our search query in broader terms by using the syntaxes "Financial inclusion" AND "SMEs", which yielded 136 documents ranging from 2006 to 2024. Then we applied several filters to refine our database (Figure 1). First, we limit the subject area to Business Management and Accounting, Economics, Econometrics and Finance, Computer Science and Social Sciences. Then we excluded any form of publication other than articles that were only published in 'journals. We included only published articles, and not the ones 'in press'. Any articles published in languages other than English were also eliminated. This filtering process refined the data to 85 documents. Finally, we reviewed the abstracts of each document and any article outside our scope was excluded from the list. After assembling and arranging data, 62 articles ranging from 2011 to 2023 were finalized as our sample to assess in VOS-viewer. A full list of publications used in this dataset can be found in Appendix A in full reference form with their citation count and affiliated country.

4. RESULTS OF BIBLIOMETRIC ANALYSIS

This section provides quantitative insight into FI in SMEs through identifying current research trends and contributions of authors. Table 1 below exhibits a summary of the characteristics of the publications in our dataset. Around one fifth (21%) of our dataset is comprised of publications in the context of OIC countries. Half of the publications in our dataset are on non-OIC countries. Almost one third is without a specific country context. While the international and single country collaboration are on a par (42% vs 58%), co-authorship (82%) is presented significantly more than single authorship (18%). Similarly, the number of publications with quantitative research methods (63%) are double that of with qualitative research methods (32%). Mixed research methods represent 6% of the data.

Figure 2 presents development of research on FI in SMEs from 2011 to 2023. Data collected from Scopus on FI in SMEs present a significant increase in the number of publications since 2019 in this field.

Table 1. Summary table for the characteristics of data

	Frequency	Percentage
OIC	13	21%
Non-OIC	31	50%
General context	18	29%
Study approaches		
Quantitative	39	63%
Qualitative	19	31%
Mixed methods	4	6%
Authorship		
Single authored	11	18%
Co-auothored	51	82%
Collaboration		
International collaboration	26	42%
Single country collaboration	36	58.%

Figure 2. Number of publications per year
Source: Scopus

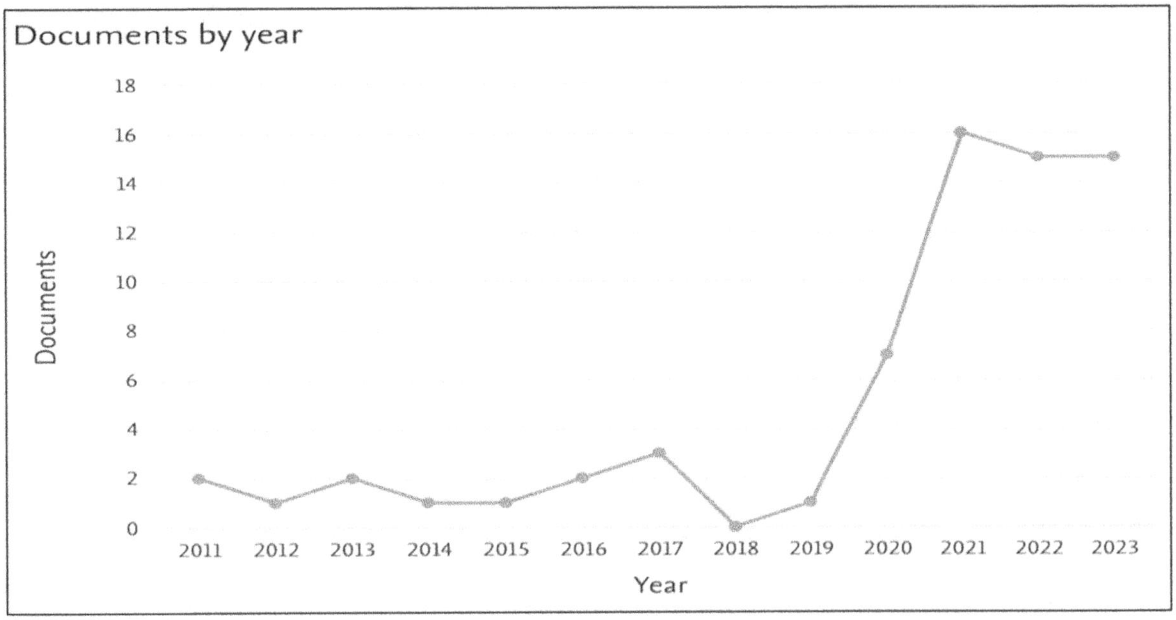

4.1 Citation Analysis

The aim of citation analysis is to identify the most influential studies, authors and journals that contribute to the literature on FI in SMEs. This measure of influence is based on being most cited in top-N lists and reinforced by the assumption that publications that are considered to be most important are cited most. Because getting cited requires time, most cited articles tend to be older publications.

Princely Ifinedo's (2011) article receives the highest number of citations (163), making the journal his article was published, "Internet Research", one of the most influential journals in the FI in SMEs field (Tables 2 and 3). The study titled 'Internet/e-business technologies acceptance in Canada's SMEs: An exploratory investigation' examines the hindering factors of the acceptance of Canadian SMEs in adopting internet and e-business technologies in their operations and finds that, among other factors, the availability of financial support did not influence technology acceptance, in particular, such support was hard to be obtained from local financial institutions.

Despite being a recent publication, Junjie Wu, Zhiqiang Lu, Hongyu Li and Duc Khuong Nguyen (2022) share the second ranking in most influential authors with 70 citations on their article called 'Local Bank, Digital Financial Inclusion and SME Financing Constraints: Empirical Evidence from China'. The study covers a ten-year period between 2007 and 2017 and finds that local bank branches and digital finance technologies could alleviate SME financial constraints through enhancing digital financial inclusion and traditional SME-banking relations.

Kuan-Jung Peng and Chang-Hsien Tsai (2017) ranked third with 52 citations on their article titled "The FinTech Revolution and Financial Regulation: The Case of Online Supply-Chain Financing". The study highlights how Fintech regulations should be adaptive to promote innovation in improving digital

Table 2. Most cited authors

Author	Articles	Total Citations	Average Citations
ifinedo, princely	1	163	163
lu, zhiqiang	2	86	43
wu, junjie	2	86	43
li, hongyu	1	70	70
nguyen, duc khuong	1	70	70
peng, kuan-jung	1	52	52
tsai, chang-hsien	1	52	52
huang, yiping	2	49	24.5
hua, xiuping	1	48	48
fahma, farah	1	43	43
najib, mukhamad	1	43	43
hudaefi, fahmi ali	1	42	42
morgan, peter j.	1	38	38
pontines, victor	1	38	38
coffie, cephas paa kwasi	1	35	35
hongjiang, zhao	1	35	35
kiconco, rebecca	1	35	35
mensah, isaac adjei	1	35	35
simon, abraham emuron otim	1	35	35
fekete-farkas, maria	3	35	11
ercegovac, roberto	1	32	32
kundid, ana	1	32	32

Source: VOSviewer based on Scopus data

financial inclusion through fintech-enabled financial services such as online supply-chain financing, which is a relatively novel funding channel for small and medium-sized suppliers.

Authors with two publications in the field are abovementioned second most cited authors Junjie Wu, Zhiqiang Lu (whose second publication received 16 citations), Yiping Huang and Maria Fekete-Farkas. The first article by Huang is co-authored with Xiuping Hua, published in 2021 and received 48 citations. It touches upon the role of Chinese fintech sector in promoting financial inclusion of SMEs and low-income households through digital technology and more tolerant regulatory environment. His second article, published in 2023, received only 1 citation, probably due to being very recent.

Fekete-Farkas co-authored three recent publications, one in 2021 and two in 2022 with 14, 17 and 4 citations respectively. Two of her publications are on financial inclusion in Ethiopia; the first article focuses on the determinants of FI in SMEs while the second is about increasing women economic empowerment through FI. The third one is on Indonesian SMEs to understand what drives these SMEs for Fintech adoption to promote firm innovation.

The top cited journals directly match with the above discussion on the most cited authors. "Internet Research", which is a relatively highly ranked 3* journal in Chartered Association of Business School

Table 3. Most cited journals

Journal Name	Total Citations	Publication Number
Internet research (CABS 3*)	163	1
Emerging markets finance and trade (CABS 2*)	70	1
Asian journal of law and society	52	1
European journal of finance (CABS 3*)	48	1
International journal on advanced science, engineering and information technology	43	1
Qualitative research in financial markets (CABS 1*)	42	1
Singapore economic review	38	1
Information technology for development (CABS 2*)	35	1
International journal of law and management	32	1
Regional studies (CABS 4*)	21	1
Structural change and economic dynamics (CABS 2*)	20	1
Journal of risk and financial management	18	2
Gender in management (CABS 1*)	17	1
Global finance journal (CABS 2*)	17	1
Journal of open innovation: technology, market, and complexity	17	1
Economic modelling (CABS 2*)	16	2
International journal of bank marketing (CABS 1*)	16	1
Journal of entrepreneurship, management and innovation	14	1
Journal of innovation and entrepreneurship	14	2
Forecasting	13	1
Journal of small business and enterprise development (CABS 2*)	13	1
International journal of business and management science	12	1
Sustainability (switzerland)	11	3
Annals of economics and finance (CABS 2*)	10	1
Economy of regions	10	1
Information (switzerland)	10	1

Source: VOSviewer based on Scopus data

(CABS) is the top cited journal and it is followed by other CABS 3* and 2* journals,namely "Emerging markets finance and trade", "Asian Journal of law and Society", European Journal of finance" that rank second, third and fourth with one document in each receiving number of citations 70, 52, 48 respectively.

Some journals become the most influential journals in terms of number of documents published in this field such as "Sustainability" with 3 articles, and "Journal of risk and financial management", "Journal of innovation and entrepreneurship", "Economic modelling", with 2 articles each.

Figure 3 indicates that there is no particular clustering among journals where publications FI in SMEs are focused. Authors publish whichever journal they can find as an outlet for their research.

Figure 3. Journals vs. citations
Source: VOSviewer

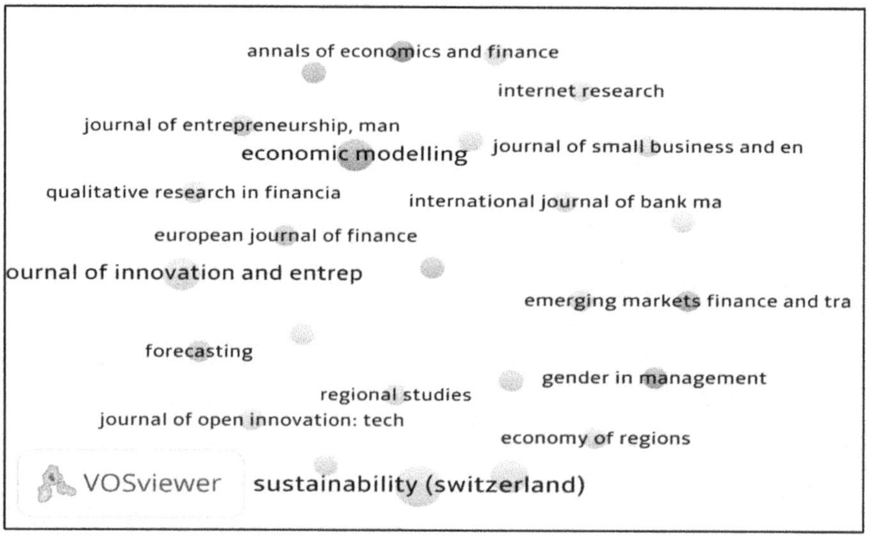

4.2 Co-Authorship Analysis

Co-author analysis measures the degree of scientific collaboration on publications. In other words, it produces social interactions and networks among authors based on their scientific collaborations. By analysing the patterns in co-authorship, researchers can complement their insights from citation analysis and estimate the effect of collaborations on the development of the research field (Zupic and Cater, 2015, Donthu et al. 2017).

4.2.1 Collaboration Among Authors

Our co-authorship analysis identified 3 clustered research among scholars based on their collaboration in research on FI in SMEs (Figure 4). The clusters present collaboration among more than four authors and shed light on the social structure of the field. Their main characteristics can be summarized as:

(i) A high 'degree centrality' around one author, namely, Maria Fekete-Farkas, who is at the centre of three clusters in the academic community of FI in SMEs, indicating that she is a bridge between different regions in the world and different research streams (Fischbach et al., 2011). Fekete-Farkas also presents a high 'betweenness centrality' due to her distinguished capacity to connect other authors within the network compared to other authors, creating links among authors and developing social network which would have not happened if it was not for her (Acedo et al, 2006).
(ii) A geographical focus on Ethiopia (Africa) and Indonesia (an OIC country),
(iii) The fact that the collaborations are fairly recent.

Cluster 1 is a collaboration between six authors (Nguse T, Desalegn D, Oshora B, Tangl A.; Nathan R.J.; Fekete-Farkas M) on article titled "Enhancing women economic empowerment through financial

Figure 4. Social networks of authors

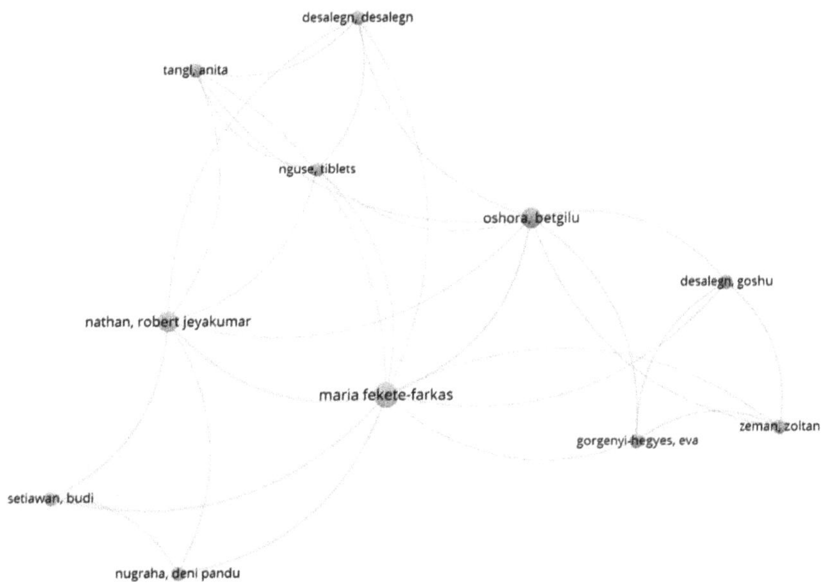

inclusion: Evidence from SMEs in Ethiopia", published in Polish Journal of Management Studies. The article received only 4 citations probably because it is a new publication in 2022 that had not sufficient time to accumulate citations. Co-authors' affiliation are from Hungarian and Malaysian universities.

Cluster 2 is another prominent collaboration by five authors (Oshora B., Desalegn G., Gorgenyi-Hegyes E, Fekete-Farkas M., Zeman Z.) for the article titled "Determinants of Financial Inclusion in Small and Medium Enterprises: Evidence from Ethiopia" and published in Journal of Risk and Financial Management in 2021. The study received 14 citations. Collaborating authors are affiliated with universities in Hungary and Ethiopia.

Cluster 3 is a collaboration of four authors (Nugraha D.P.; Setiawan B.; Nathan R.J.; Fekete-Farkas M) for the article titled with title of "Fintech Adoption Drivers for Innovation for SMEs in Indonesia". Their article was published in "Journal of Open Innovation: Technology, Market, and Complexity" in 2022. The paper was cited by 17. This collaborative research by universities from Hungary, Malaysia, Indonesia, Czech Republic is a good example of international collaboration in this field.

This analysis also reveals current trends in FI in SMEs. As well as focus geographical studies on FI in SMEs, studies that integrate financial technology and women economic empowerment into FI in SMEs have been emerging.

4.2.2 Collaboration Among Countries

Figures 5, 6 and 7 explain scholarly networks at international level. VOSviewer provides visualization of collaboration among countries based on co-authorship in two main groups. Each group have a predominant country, China and Indonesia, as seen in Figure 5. The group under China's leadership for collaboration has five clusters and the group under Indonesia has three clusters, in total eight clusters (Table 4). Figures 6 and 7 are zoom-ins of the Figure 5 for better depiction of the two groups. While

Figure 5. International collaborations

Table 4. Clusters of country collaboration analysis

Clusters under **China's** leadership for collaboration through co-authorship	1	China, Pakistan (OIC), Sri Lanka, Tanzania
	2	France, United Kingdom, Viet nam
	3	Australia, New Zealand
	4	Ghana, Uganda (OIC)
	5	Switzerland, United States
Clusters under **Indonesia's** leadership for collaboration through co-authorship	1	Indonesia (OIC), Japan, Malaysia (OIC), Nigeria (OIC), Saudi Arabia (OIC)
	2	Africa Development Bank, Czech Republic, World Bank
	3	Ethiopia, Hungary

Figure 6. International collaborations – China

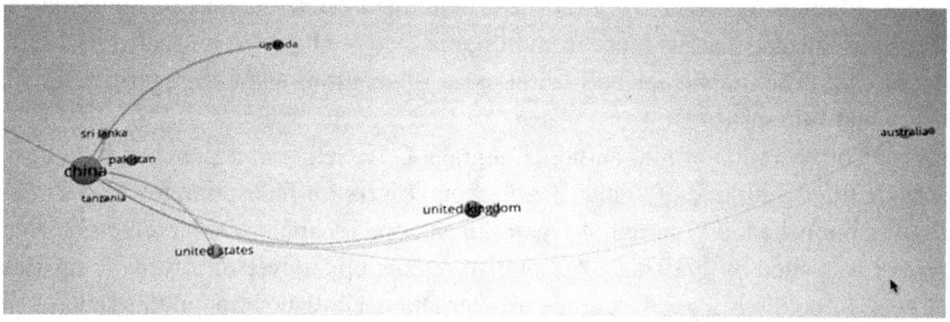

China has a sizable significance in co-authorship collaborations all over the world (Figure 5), Indonesia presents more and focused co-authorship with other OIC countries (Figure 6).

4.3 Co-Citation Analysis

Co-citation analysis is the most commonly used and validated bibliometric method due to its connecting two publications that co-occur in the list of references in another publication (Donthu et al. 2021; Leung et al., 2017). Co-citation is measured by the frequency with which two articles are cited together (Small, 1973), indicating a relatedness of their content (Zupic and Cater, 2015). The analysis helps shaping the

Figure 7. International collaborations – Indonesia

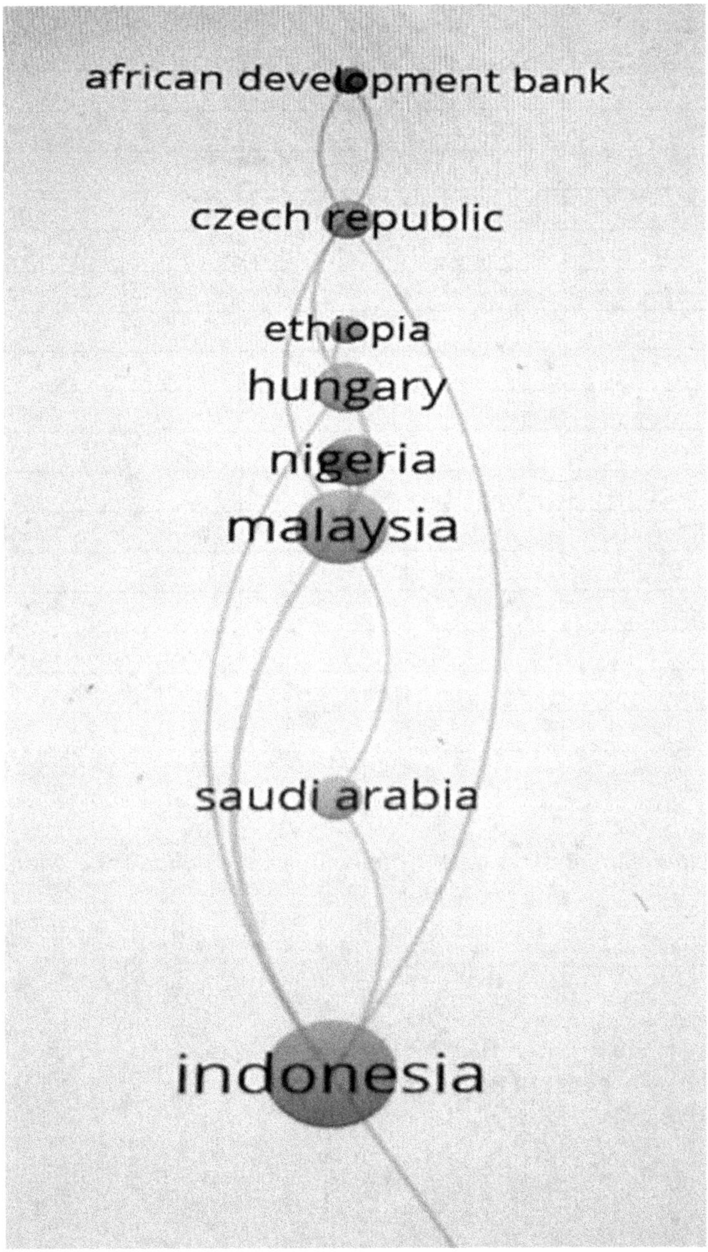

intellectual structure of a research field, uncovering seminal publications, major themes, and developing thematic clusters based on highly co-cited articles (Leung et al., 2017; Donthu et al. 2021).

4.3.1 Author Co-Citation Analysis

Author co-citation analysis identifies most important authors through their citation records and connects them (Zupic and Cater, 2015). The authors who are frequently co-cited with each other are considered

Table 5. Author Co-citation analysis results

Author	Frequency of Co-Citations	Total Link Strength
demirguc-kunt a.	89	85.72
beck t.	60	58.59
klapper l.	30	29.86
maksimovic v.	23	22.56
levine r.	20	19.86
huang y.	17	16.13
ayyagari m.	15	14.69
singer d.	15	14.98
berger a.n.	14	13.87
caputo f.	13	12.26
sarstedt m.	13	12.93
ansar s.	12	11.98
sarma m.	12	11.99
saviano m.	12	11.11
barile s.	11	10.26
hess j.	11	10.95
udell g.f.	11	10.92

Source: VOSviewer

Figure 8. Author co-citation analysis results (with minimum 5 co-citations of authors)

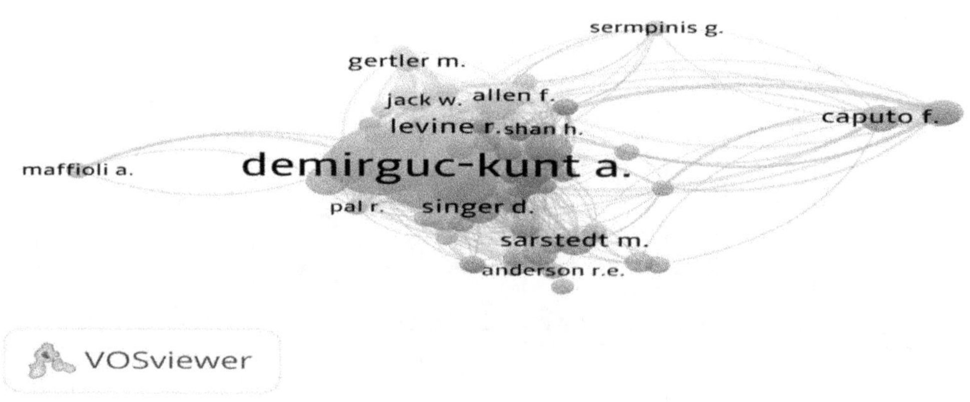

influential figures in their fields, as their work is widely acknowledged and referenced by other researchers. In Table 4, a high number of co-citations indicates that A. Demirguc-Kunt, T. Beck, L. Klapper and V. Maksimovic are prominent figures who have left a lasting impact on the research field of FI in SMEs and their work is highly regarded. Their work on financial constraints and SME growth, financial inclusion, technology, and new methodological approaches were highly co-cited.

Table 6. Clusters of author co-citation analysis

Cluster	Co-Cited Authors	Their Research Focus
1	Ansar; Ayyagari; Beck; Berger; Cull; Demirguc-Kunt; Hess; Klapper; Levine; Love; Maksimovic; Pais; Perian; Rajan; Singer; Udell	financial & legal constraints, SMEs, growth, SME finance, fintech, financial inclusion and Islamic finance, Africa
2	Hair; Ringle; Sarstedt;	methodological contribution
	Sarma; Taghizadeh-Hesari; Yoshino	Asian SMEs and their challenges, financial inclusion
3	Frost; Gamacorta; Huang; Li; Wang; Wu J	digital financial inclusion, fintech, bigtech credit and its risk, SME finance, SME financing constraints, Asia, China
4	Leyshon	financial geography, financial exclusion
	Zhang X; Zhang Y	digital financial inclusion, SMEs, China
	Khan S	SMEs, financial inclusion, digital financial services, Saudi Arabia, Islamic finance
5	Allen; Gertler; Sari	financial intermediation, fintech, financial inclusion
6	Barile; Caputo F.; Saviano	fintech, financial gap, MENA region, systems (market, decision making, information sharing, stakeholders, digital ecosystems, etc.)

Figure 8 exhibits six clusters of author co-citation analysis. Demirguc-Kunt is at the centre of the co-citation analysis. Her work is exceptionally cited. She and her co-authors consist of a cluster.

VOSviewer provided us with the clusters and we identified the co-cited authors' research focus from the reference lists of our dataset. While main themes FI in SMEs and technology simultaneously run in most of the clusters, the clustered authors distinguish with regard to geographic focus, theoretical vs empirical work, and/or their methodological contribution (Table 6).

4.3.2 Journal Co-Citation Analysis

Journal co-citation analysis indicates intellectual influence and impact within a particular field or discipline by mapping the association between scientific journals. By analyzing the frequency of the citations received by the publications together in other works, researchers can gain insights into influence of journals in a particular academic field, i.e. which ones are the important and impactful journals in that field. In addition, it helps researchers understand the interconnectedness of ideas within a specific field of study.

Table 7 and Figure 9 provide information on influential journals which are co-cited by scholars investigating FI in SMEs. Sustainability journal in the dataset is highly influential source for intellectual work with co-citation frequency of 51. Likewise, Small Business Economics journal is second influential source for scholarly publications on FI in SMEs research area with co-citation frequency of 46. The most influential journals listed in Table 7 are by no surprise are the highest ranked journals in CABS.

Figure 9 exhibits the visualization of 12 influential journals into 2 big clusters. Each cluster has a prominent journal that are the first two top journals in our Journal Co-citation Analysis. The first cluster consists of 8 journals where Sustainability journal is prominent and associates with journals in finance, small business and information management disciplines. The formation of this cluster indicates that, in the field of FI in SMEs, co-citations in publications take a multi-disciplinary approach and incorporate

Table 7. Journal co-citation analysis results

Journal	CABS Ranking	Citations	Total Link Strength
Sustainability	-	51	46.85
Small Business Economics	3	46	42.51
Journal of Financial Economics	4*	28	27.01
Journal of Banking & Finance	3	23	21.64
The Journal of Finance	4*	19	18.02
American Economic Review	4*	18	14.88
World Development	3	18	17.74
American Economic Journal: Macroeconomics	4	16	13.55
Journal of Business Research	3	14	13.82
MIS Quarterly (Management Information Systems)	4*	14	13.49
International Small Business Journal	3	12	11.91
Journal of Small Business and Enterprise Development	2	11	10.79
Review of Development Finance	2	11	10.82
Information and Management	3	9	8.33
Internet Research	3	9	8.61

Figure 9. Journal Co-citation analysis results (minimum co-citations 10 per journal)

sustainability and technology into FI and SME literatures. The second cluster however consists of 4 journals where Small Business Economics journal leads the association with journals in Finance discipline, presenting a more focused approach on the FI in SME research.

4.4 Co-Word Analysis

The co-word analysis is based on the co-occurrence of author keywords. It creates clusters of words that meaningfully link to each other to reveal a thematic relationship. Co-word analysis supplements co-citation analysis and uncovers common themes, trends, interdisciplinary connections, and under-represented areas that necessitate further investigation.

Figures 10, 11, 12 clearly demonstrate the strong link between financial inclusion and SMEs. Figure 10, based on minimum three co-occurrences of keywords, provide the main themes in the FI and SME literature in two clusters. The green cluster consists of financial inclusion, financial literacy and fintech, while red cluster consists of SMEs, access to finance, digital financial inclusion, and China. Figure 11, based on minimum two co-occurrences of keywords, indicates additions to the financial inclusion main theme (i.e. financial behavior, financing gap, financial stability), to SMEs main theme (i.e.entrepreneurship), to technology main theme (i.e.Technology Acceptance Model (TAM)), and additional sub-theme of sustainability (i.e. SDGs). These themes appear in six clusters, in which empirical studies in specific geographies are also highlighted, such as China with financial stability (blue cluster), Indonesia with SDGs (purple cluster), and Sri Lanka with TAM (turquoise cluster). Red cluster consists of financial inclusion, financial literacy, fintech, and financial behavior, green cluster consists of SMEs, financing gap and digital financial inclusion, yellow cluster consists of access to finance and entrepreneurship.

Figure 12, based on minimum one co-occurrences of keywords, is a nice depiction of the bigger picture. It produced 29 clusters, which we will not go into detail. The most novel finding in this analysis is the coupling of specific countries with specific concepts. While linking to SMEs and financial inclusion main themes, China being coupled with financial stability is instructive for other emerging economies and Sri Lanka with TAM indicates the influence of technology adoption in developing countries. Indonesia, on the other hand, is coupled with SDGs when linked only with financial inclusion indicates a strong emphasis on achieving sustainability in relation to FI. In Chinese context, financially fit SMEs can survive in evolving environment and upgrade with latest trends. For Sri Lankan context, among the FI-SME trends, technological advancement is crucial. It is considered a critical driver for development

Figure 10. Main themes (keywords minimum three co-occurrences)

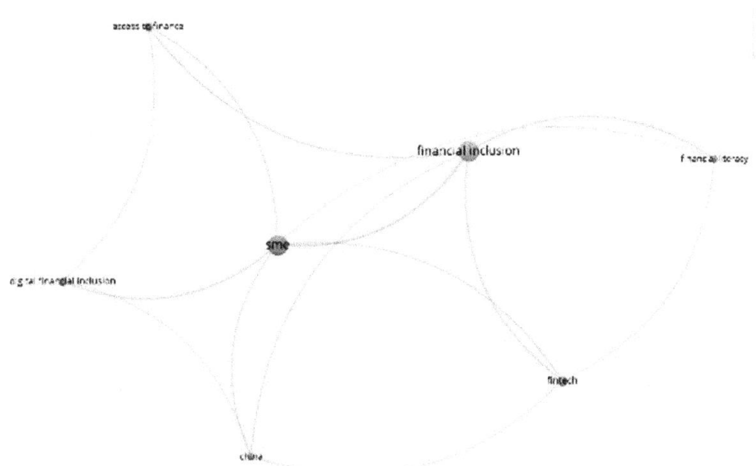

Figure 11. Keywords minimum two co-occurrences

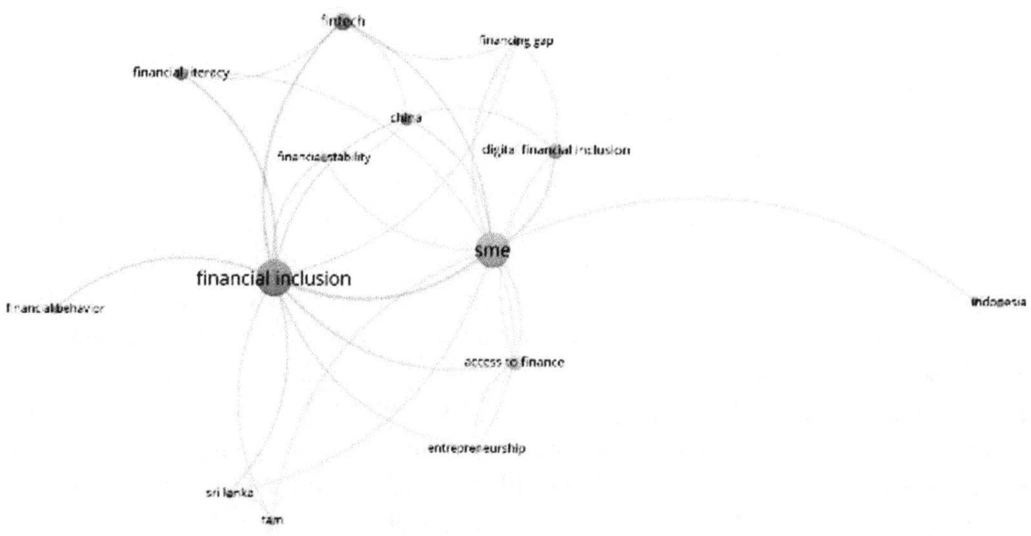

Figure 12. Keywords minimum one co-occurrence

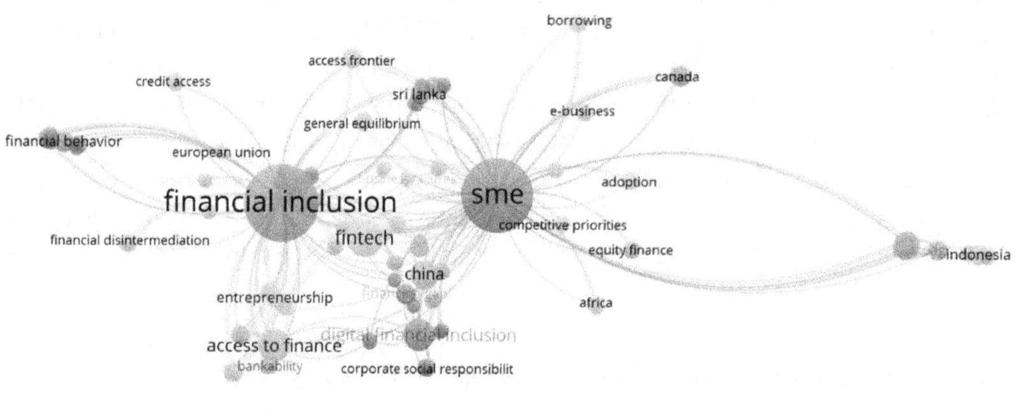

as it leads to efficiency and productivity. However, fintech, which through various technological applications are enabling entrepreneurs to deal with finances and business transactions without getting support from accounting and finance experts, is linked to China and financial stability rather than Sri Lanka.

4.5 Thematic Analysis

The co-citation analyses of authors and journals and co-word analyses above highlight three main themes in the scholarly area of FI in SMEs (Table 8).

The first is financial inclusion in SMEs, which are pivotal to the economic growth of countries. However, because they face challenges in accessing finance, the extant literature discusses determinants of their financial inclusion in the form of enablers and hindrances, such as firm size, high costs, collateral, internal credit rating, bank concentration, supply-side factors, demand-side factors, institutional framework factors and information asymmetry between lenders and SMEs. They argue that community development financial institutions, community banking, credit and repayment schemes for SMEs and cost-effective technological solutions can reduce the financing gap.

A concept that has both direct and indirect relationship with FI-SME nexus, financial literacy is crucial for individuals and SMEs to make informed financial decisions. It improves access to financial services and decision-making, however, research on financial literacy receives least citations. Findings, however, reveal that financial knowledge, financial behavior, and digital financial capability significantly influence financial inclusion. They do not significantly affect SME performance individually, but financial inclusion and financial concerns positively influence SME performance. Financial literacy also moderates fintech's impact on FI; FI enhances financial performance, thereby fostering SMEs' business growth. SMEs are advised to enhance financial literacy, while governments work towards refining regulations regarding financial literacy, fintech, and financial inclusion, especially for SMEs.

In addition, greater financial inclusion for SMEs can lead to both positive and negative impacts on financial stability. While it can diversify bank assets and reduce riskiness, it can also erode credit standards and increase the loan-to-GDP ratio. However, implementing policies like credit databases and expanded collateral options can generate positive spillover effects on financial stability.

The transformative power of digital technologies in financial inclusion is a second dominant concept in the literature, in particular, through e-business, fintech and other digital apps for finance increase ef-

Table 8. Thematic analysis results based on co-citation analysis, key publications and their citations

Themes	Key Articles
Financial inclusion in SMEs Financial literacy Financial stability	(Kundid A.; Ercegovac R., 2011) Cited by 32 (Appleyard L., 2013) Cited by 21 (Brixiová Z.; Kangoye T.; Yogo T.U., 2020) Cited by 20 (Lu Z.; Wu J.; Liu J., 2020) Cited by 16 (Oshora B, Fekete-Farkas M., et al., 2021) Cited by 14 (Eton et al., 2022) Cited by 10 (Ali M.et al., 2017) Cited by 10 (Shinozaki S., 2014) Cited by 7 (Sari Y.W.; Nugroho M.; Rahmiyati N., 2023) cited by 0 (Mutamimah M.; Indriastuti M., 2023) Cited by 1 (Garba M.; Salleh F.; Hafiz U.A.; Bakar N.M.A., 2022) Cited by 2 (Irman M.; Budiyanto; Suwitho., 2021) Cited by 0 (Morgan P.J.; Pontines V., 2018) Cited by 38
Technology adoption in FI	(Ifinedo P., 2011) Cited by 163 (Lu Z.; Wu J.; Li H.; Nguyen D.K., 2022) Cited by 70 (Najib M.; Fahma F., 2020) Cited by 43 (Coffie et al., 2021) Cited by 35 (Nugraha D.P.; Setiawan B.; Nathan R.J.; Fekete-Farkas M., 2022) Cited by 17 (Thathsarani U.S.; Jianguo W., 2022) Cited by 10 (Kame Babilla T.U., 2023) Cited by 10 (Bui T.Q.; Do A.V.P., 2022) Cited by 8 (Zhang X.; Li J.; Xiang D.; Worthington A.C., 2023) Cited by 6 (Mamaro L.P.; Sibindi A.B., 2022) Cited by 4
Islamic Finance	(Hudaefi F.A., 2020) Cited by 42 (Okfalisa et al., 2022) Cited by 5 (Sabiu T.T.; Abduh M., 2021) Cited by 3 (Ibrahim A.-J.; Kahf M., 2020) Cited by 1

ficiency and productivity of SMEs while reducing the barriers in accessing finance. These technologies have been shown to boost access to financial goods, raise awareness, and facilitate transactions. The importance of financial technology gradually increases in developing countries where FI is one of major constraints for SMEs. However, these technological advancements are also accompanied by issues such as behavioral resistance in acceptance of these advancements, management support and commitment, government support, user innovativeness, trust, and regulatory challenges. Moreover, fintech, Technology Acceptance Model (TAM), digital payment system, digital funding, and crowdfunding are suggested to increase efficiency by providing easy and affordable access to finance. The evidence for effectiveness of financial technology in FI-SME relationship are found in OIC and non-OIC countries, yet leveraging technology and fostering an innovative ecosystem can empower SMEs and promote FI. Digital innovation complements inclusive banking in addressing credit discrepancies among firms, easing collateral and borrowing constraints for SMEs, and enhancing productivity growth. Digitalization is becoming more effective than traditional methods in alleviating SMEs' financing constraints and enhancing financial inclusion and play a pivotal role in mitigating information asymmetry.

Third main theme that arose from the co-citation analyses is Islamic finance. A subset of studies by S. Khan focuses on the relationship between SMEs and Islamic finance, especially in countries that are members of the OIC. Islamic finance plays a vital role in financial inclusion of SMEs as a Shariah-compliant alternative financing solution for faith-based and others who do not want interest-based financing. It offers potential for financial inclusion in OIC countries and caters to unbanked communities and promotes SME growth with instruments like as Ijarah and trade finance. However, knowledge and proper utilization of shariah complaint tools is crucial to get benefit from it. In addition, proper knowledge of Islamic principles becomes more important in revolution of financial technology. Furthermore, Shariah-compliant instruments can be used to protect investments and incentivize potential investors to promote investments in SMEs. Evidence from Nigeria indicates positive effect of Islamic financing on MSMEs' employment growth and recommends enhancing the Islamic banking system by emphasizing Profit and Loss Sharing (PLS) financing, particularly Musharakah for FI and job creation of MSMEs. Another evidence from Indonesia reveals the FI of SME sector through Islamic social funds which subsequently promotes SDGs as well. Quadruple Helix (government, investors, academics, and communities) ensures SMEs' financial stability through Shariah Fintech presents new post-Covid-19 challenges and opportunities. There's a recommendation to develop a new Shariah Fintech quadruple helix model that assesses SMEs' digital readiness to enhance proper Shariah Fintech product utilization.

5. COMPARISON OF OIC AND NON OIC COUNTRIES

Table 9 exhibits the frequency of the articles published by authors or institutions in OIC and non-OIC countries. It also shows the impact of research generated in OIC and non-OIC countries through citation rate.

These publications are recognized in other countries. High citations from a country not only reflect the strength of its research output, but also highlight the country's ability to foster collaboration and establish meaningful partnerships with researchers and institutions worldwide.

Table 9 depicts that Indonesia is first major contributor with 11 publications, followed by Malaysia with 6 and Nigeria with 3 articles. With regard to average citations, Uganda ranks first with 23.5 citations per article (47/2) while Indonesia and Malaysia share second position with 11 citations per publication.

Table 9. Frequency of publications and citation on FI and SMEs in OIC and non-OIC countries

OIC Countries	Citation	Pub	Avg cit.	Non-OIC Countries	Citation	Pub	Avg cit.	Non-OIC Countries	Citation	Pub	Avg cit.
Saudi Arabia	6	2	3	China	201	13	15	Greece	2	1	2
Indonesia	121	11	11	South Africa	7	2	4	India	0	1	0
Uganda	47	2	24	Spain	7	2	4	Japan	38	1	38
Malaysia	66	6	11	Sri Lanka	10	2	5	Philippines	17	3	6
Bangladesh	10	1	10	Italy	73	3	24	Kenya	3	1	3
Cameroon	10	1	10	Viet Nam	78	2	39	Mexico	3	1	3
Nigeria	6	3	2	United Kingdom	121	5	24	New Zealand	17	1	17
Pakistan	2	2	1	Australia	23	3	8	Poland	33	3	11
Brunei Darussalam	3	1	3	Hungary	35	3	12	United States	13	3	4
Jordan	0	1	0	Canada	163	1	163	Switzerland	1	1	1
Qatar	1	1	1	Croatia	32	1	32	Thailand	10	1	10
Sudan	1	1	1	Ethiopia	14	1	14	Taiwan	52	1	52
Turkey	1	1	1	France	70	1	70	Czeck Republic	37	2	19
				Ghana	35	1	35	Tanzania	0	1	0
				Germany	52	2	26	Ukraine	6	1	6
				Netherlands	52	2	26				

Note: Decimals are rounded due to lack of space.

Bangladesh and Cameroon bot have one article published on FI in SMEs and received 10 citations each, so they come third in the ranking of OIC countries. When compared with the non-OIC countries, it is clear that OIC countries do not perform as good as non-OIC countries.

Among non-OIC countries, China has the highest contribution to FI in SMEs literature with 13 publications and 201 citations, corresponding to an average of 15 citations per publication. However, it needs to be noted that Canada with one publication on technology perspective to FI in SMEs receives 163 citations. Similarly, France and Taiwan with one publication receive 70 and 52 citations respectively. While these mean high impact publications, the United Kingdom follows them with 5 publications receiving 121 citations, which comes to an average or 24 citations per publication. Italy shares the same average citation with the UK.

Despite two publications produced on FI in SMEs by Vietnamese authors, Vietnam has an average of 39 citations, which ranks the country above West European countries, such as Germany and the Netherlands which also have two publications each but received 26 citations on average.

As a result, the data analysis reveals that the contribution of OIC countries to this research field is low as compared to non-OIC countries. More production of scholarly work from OIC countries can have positive implications for policymakers, and industrialists due to the provision of better insight into developing strategies and policies. Moreover, future research can add value by adopting qualitative or mixed-method approaches to the literature of FI-SME in OIC and non-OIC countries.

Table 10. Major gap in the FI in SMEs literature

Major Gap	Key Articles
Policies, Rules & Regulations (Sandbox, Regtech, Fintech development 2.0)	(Tsai C.-H.; Peng K.J., 2017) Cited by 52 (Hua X.; Huang Y., 2021) Cited by 48 (Agyekum F.K.; Reddy K.; Wallace D.; Wellalage N.H., 2022) Cited by 17 (Tasak P. 2022) Cited by 14 (Lam W.R.; Liu Y., 2020) Cited by 10 (Gómez Urquijo L., 2015) Cited by 4 (Arvind T.T., 2021) cited by 1

6. DISCUSSION AND CONCLUSION

Financial inclusion is a vital factor in the success and sustainability of SMEs. This chapter reviews the literature on FI in SMEs employing bibliometric analysis methods. A sample of 62 publications from various journals is used to understand the main themes, new emerging trends and the gaps that needs addressing through future research. The main themes are identified as (i) FI in SMEs with financial literacy and financial stability as sub-themes, (ii) technology adoption in FI (fintech, digital FI) and its impact on SMEs, and (iii) Islamic finance and explained in detail in Section 4.5.

A major gap in the literature is in policies, rules and regulations that align with the fast penetration of technology into FI (Table 10). Despite the pivotal role of financial technology in promoting FI, and supporting business, and bridging the financing gap, some regulatory issues are risen. Policymakers need to pay attention towards revisiting their policies and make regulatory reforms in various dimension. For instance, regulatory sandboxes and a risk-based approaches are proposed to strike a balance between supporting FinTech start-ups and managing potential systemic risk.

Furthermore, improved coordination of regulatory policies, innovative policy tools and a balance between innovation and stability are required. Enhancing technological infrastructure can help reduce information asymmetry and transaction costs, while donor agencies can play a crucial role in supporting these efforts. There is need for communication between policymakers and the private sector and implementation of other ways of financing such as microfinance and crowdfunding. Advancing towards a banking union and, crucially, a fiscal union can promote a more uniform and inclusive financial market, addressing challenges faced by vulnerable European citizens and enterprises amid the current crisis. To avoid financial distress to SMEs caused by opportunistic lenders, policymakers should focus on reshaping lender practices to ensure and foster responsible and sustainable financing for SMEs.

6.1 Future Directions for Main Themes

In the main field of FI in SMEs, there are still many research areas are waiting to be explored, such as understanding the determinants of FI among developing country SMEs other than African countries. Investigating the role of banks and formal and informal institutions, exploring credit access dynamics, assessing transmission mechanism from access to finance to job creation, the effects of formal and informal firms, and the role of gender in FI and SME nexus could enhance our knowledge of differences between OIC and non-OIC and developed and developing countries. Conducting sector specific analysis could bring a different perspective to FI in SMEs than country level studies, and lead to targeted sectoral policy development. In addition, relationship between SMEs and networking for FI can be investigated.

Future research can explore primary data sources to implement community banking for converting micro-savings into micro-investments to promote social justice.

As one of the main determinants of FI, financial literacy is another theme that needs further studies, such as evaluating financial literacy and FI relationship from both demand and supply sides by incorporating other variables in developing and developed countries or OIC and non-OIC countries context. We also suggest exploring effective methods for financial literacy education for SMEs and evaluating the impact of financial literacy programs on SME outcomes.

Technology has significant bearing on the FI research through e-business, fintech, digital financial inclusion and so on. The adoption of internet and e-business technologies (IEBT) could be examined in other regions of developed countries and government support could be factored in into the analysis. Banks, SMEs and digital financial inclusion relationship can be investigated in regions where technology adoption is widely observed. Exploring different digital business models across emerging markets would provide valuable insights. A possible extension of the study could look at an open economy model to experience whether the adoption of a flexible exchange rate regime may affect the dynamics of digital innovation in SMEs relative to the fixed exchange rate. We suggest examining the effect of digital finance on business financing at different stages of business cycle and the long-term impact of FinTech on SME development and sustainability. Finally, identifying best practices for integrating FinTech into SME financial services would serve as exemplars to the SMEs in OIC countries.

While technology is widely integrating into finance, public sector delays in devising policies, rules & regulations in fintech area that facilitate digital financial inclusion. There is urgent need for studies that investigate the effect of regulation apps (Sandbox, Regtech, Fintech development 2.0) in OIC and non-OIC countries and assess the impact of policy recommendations from extant literature in terms of fintech, FI and SMEs development.

In the area of Islamic finance, there is lack of research on evaluating Quadruple Helix Engagement for Shariah Fintech-Based SMEs' Digitalization Readiness. More research needed to generate in this area. Further studies are needed, especially to understand some of the instruments used for Islamic Venture Capital to protect investors in practice and attract investments that can finance SMEs. We suggest conducting empirical studies on the effectiveness of Islamic finance for SME inclusion, exploring Islamic finance's role in promoting sustainable finance and ethical business practices, and investigating the regulatory landscape for Islamic finance in different countries.

6.2 Directions for Future Research: Emerging Trends

A major emerging trend in this field is economic empowerment of women entrepreneurs. Women entrepreneurs in the MENA region face challenges due to scarcity of collateral & credit history. Customized financial products & access to savings services can help them overcome these barriers & flourish as entrepreneurs (Saviano, et al., 2017). Likewise, evidence revealed that female entrepreneurs in Ethiopia encounter several obstacles, such as collateral requirements, limited start-up capital, illiteracy, high-interest rates, bureaucratic procedures, and a lack of technical expertise. To address these barriers and to improve financial inclusion for women entrepreneurs, it is crucial to provide women with customized financial products and services, to streamline credit processes, offer training programs on financial literacy, integrate financial technology, and reduce interest rates. Improving access to savings services can be just as critical as access to credit for women business owners. However, the role of government and policymakers can play a crucial role in the economic empowerment of women by promoting their financial inclusion (Nguse, T., et al., 2022).

Government policies and regulations positively impact women's economic empowerment, both directly and indirectly through financial inclusion. However, various constraints like collateral requirements, start-up capital, illiteracy levels, high-interest rates, bureaucratic procedures, and lack of technical skills hinder women's economic empowerment, evidenced particularly in Ethiopia. simplifying credit processes and training programs of financial literacy, incorporating financial technology and reducing interest rates can enhance financial inclusion in women entrepreneurs.

Future studies can extend theoretical work by conducting empirical research on women entrepreneurs' challenges in accessing finance in regions other than MENA region and compare developing countries with developed countries in this research area. Exploring the role of government support and available financial access opportunities for women-led SMEs in OIC and non-OIC countries can add value to the literature.

Another emerging trend in FI-SME literature is the importance of ethical and socially responsible finance options for the sustainable growth of SMEs and their financial stability. For instance, Islamic finance can help boost the financial stability of SMEs through multiple channels. It prioritizes ethical and fair financial dealings and offers benefits like Risk-Sharing Mechanisms, Asset-Backed and interest-free Financing, Islamic Socially Responsible Investments, and Flexible Repayment Structures. By collaborating with SME-Islamic finance institutions, businesses can achieve stability and promote responsible economic development. In addition, Shariah-compliant instruments also protect investments and promote SME investments (Ibrahim, A. J., & Kahf, M. (2020).

Encouragingly, SMEs' employment growth in Nigeria experiences a positive impact from Islamic financing. To further financial inclusion and job creation, the Islamic banking system should prioritize Profit and loss sharing (PLS) financing, particularly the beneficial Musharakah option (Sabiu, T. T., & Abduh, M., 2021). However, for long-term sustainability, SMEs are stressed to embrace digitalization. Faith-based SME owners are inclined toward Shariah-compliant financial technology solutions. Shariah-compliant Fintech firms promote financial inclusion and collect/distribute Islamic social funds. They also initiate charity programs for underprivileged communities to achieve the SDGs of ending poverty, and hunger, and reducing inequalities (Hudaefi, F. A., 2020). Nevertheless, the Quadruple Helix approach is considered vital in sustaining and strengthening industry creativity, capability, and competitiveness. Islam recognizes this approach as pivotal in SMEs' sustainability and compliance strategies during disasters in developing countries. The rise of Shariah Fintech presents both challenges and opportunities for the quadruple helix to support SMEs. Therefore, to fully leverage the benefits of Shariah Fintech products, it's recommended that a new quadruple helix model be developed, specifically tailored to assess SMEs' digital readiness (Okfalisa, O. et al., 2022).

To conclude, our bibliometric analysis gave useful insights into the literature on FI in SMEs. This thorough analysis explored a number of influential publications to pinpoint themes, major contributors, and emerging trends. Our bibliometric study in this chapter paved the way for future research and policy interventions. The identified study directions highlight the importance of targeted financial education programs for financial literacy, regulatory issues in FinTech adoption, a better knowledge of the role of Islamic finance in FI and SME development, and creative policies to increase SME financial inclusion. Ultimately, resolving these issues will help to create a more equitable and sustainable financial situation for SMEs worldwide.

REFERENCES

Acedo, F. J., Barroso, C., Casanueva, C., & Galan, J. L. (2006). Co-authorship in management and organizational studies: An empirical and network analysis. *Journal of Management Studies*, *43*(5), 957–983. doi:10.1111/j.1467-6486.2006.00625.x

Adesola, W. A., Ewa, U. E., & Arikpo, O. F. (2020). Microfinance Banks Dynamics Effect on Small-Scale Enterprise Development in Nigeria. International Journal of Applied Economics. *Finance and Accounting*, *6*(2), 64–75.

Agyekum, F. K., Reddy, K., Wallace, D., & Wellalage, N. H. (2022). Does technological inclusion promote financial inclusion among SMEs? Evidence from South-East Asian (SEA) countries. *Global Finance Journal*, *53*, 100618. Advance online publication. doi:10.1016/j.gfj.2021.100618

Al-Hakim, M. S., Al-Hamad, R. A. A. S., & Ghaith, M. A. (2021). The Role Of Financial Inclusion In Bridging SMEs Financing Gap-The Viewpoint Of Credit Employees At Jordanian Islamic Banks. *Turkish Journal of Computer and Mathematics Education*, *12*(14), 2763–2776.

Alrababah, Z. (2023). Barriers to Cloud Computing Adoption Among SMEs in The Middle East: A Systematic Review. *Journal of Theoretical and Applied Information Technology*, *101*(17).

Appleyard, L. (2013). The geographies of access to enterprise finance: The case of the West Midlands, UK. *Regional Studies*, *47*(6), 868–879. doi:10.1080/00343404.2012.748979

Arcuri, M. C., & Pisani, R. (2021). Is trade credit a sustainable resource for medium-sized Italian Green companies? *Sustainability (Basel)*, *13*(5), 2872. doi:10.3390/su13052872

Arvind, T. T. (2021). Too Big to Care?: Financial Contracts and the Problem of Transactional Asymmetry. *Law and Contemporary Problems*, *84*, 35.

Ayyagari, M., Demirgüç-Kunt, A., & Maksimovic, V. (2008). How important are financing constraints? The role of finance in the business environment. *The World Bank Economic Review*, *22*(3), 483–516. doi:10.1093/wber/lhn018

Babilla, T. U. K. (2023). Digital innovation and financial access for small and medium-sized enterprises in a currency union. *Economic Modelling*, *120*, 106182. Advance online publication. doi:10.1016/j.econmod.2022.106182

Beck, T., Demirgüç-Kunt, A. S. L. I., & Maksimovic, V. (2005). Financial and legal constraints to growth: Does firm size matter? *The Journal of Finance*, *60*(1), 137–177. doi:10.1111/j.1540-6261.2005.00727.x

Bhattacharyya, A., Rahman, M. L., & Wright, S. (2023). Improving small and medium-size enterprise performance: Does working capital management enhance the effectiveness of financial inclusion? *Accounting and Finance*, *63*(4), 3943–3969. doi:10.1111/acfi.13081

Brixiová, Z., Kangoye, T., & Yogo, T. U. (2020). Access to finance among small and medium-sized enterprises and job creation in Africa. *Structural Change and Economic Dynamics*, *55*, 177–189. doi:10.1016/j.strueco.2020.08.008

Bui, T. Q., & Do, A. V. P. (2022). Does technological inclusion reduce financial constraints on small and medium sized enterprises? The case of Vietnam. *Finance Research Letters*, *47*, 102534. Advance online publication. doi:10.1016/j.frl.2021.102534

Chatterjee, A. (2020). Financial inclusion, information and communication technology diffusion, and economic growth: A panel data analysis. *Information Technology for Development*, *26*(3), 607–635. do i:10.1080/02681102.2020.1734770

Claessens, S., & Perotti, E. (2007). Finance and inequality: Channels and evidence. *Journal of Comparative Economics*, *35*(4), 748–773. doi:10.1016/j.jce.2007.07.002

Coffie, C. P. K., Hongjiang, Z., Mensah, I. A., Kiconco, R., & Simon, A. E. O. (2021). Determinants of FinTech payment services diffusion by SMEs in Sub-Saharan Africa: Evidence from Ghana. *Information Technology for Development*, *27*(3), 539–560. doi:10.1080/02681102.2020.1840324

Czerwonka, L., & Jaworski, J. (2021). Capital structure determinants of small and medium-sized enterprises: Evidence from Central and Eastern Europe. *Journal of Small Business and Enterprise Development*, *28*(2), 277–297. doi:10.1108/JSBED-09-2020-0326

Dela Cruz, N. A., Villanueva, A. C. B., Tolin, L. A., Disse, S., Lensink, R., & White, H. (2023). PROTOCOL: Effects of interventions to improve access to financial services for micro-, small-and medium-sized enterprises in low-and middle-income countries: An evidence and gap map. *Campbell Systematic Reviews*, *19*(3), e1341. Advance online publication. doi:10.1002/cl2.1341 PMID:37415851

Dluhopolskyi, O., Pakhnenko, O., Lyeonov, S., Semenog, A., Artyukhova, N., Cholewa-Wiktor, M., & Jastrzębski, W. (2023). Digital financial inclusion: COVID-19 impacts and opportunities. *Sustainability (Basel)*, *15*(3), 2383. doi:10.3390/su15032383

Donthu, N., Kumar, S., Mukherjee, D., Pandey, N., & Lim, W. M. (2021). How to conduct a bibliometric analysis: An overview and guidelines. *Journal of Business Research*, *133*, 285–296. doi:10.1016/j.jbusres.2021.04.070

Eton, M., Mwosi, F., Okello-Obura, C., Turyehebwa, A., & Uwonda, G. (2021). Financial inclusion and the growth of small medium enterprises in Uganda: Empirical evidence from selected districts in Lango sub-region. *Journal of Innovation and Entrepreneurship*, *10*(1), 1–23. doi:10.1186/s13731-021-00168-2

Fazal, H., Muhammad, J., & Zahoor, U. H. (2020). Operational perspective of SMEs performance and competitive priorities practices: Path analytic approach. *Studies in Business and Economics*, *15*(1), 55–67. doi:10.2478/sbe-2020-0006

Fischbach, K., Putzke, J., & Schoder, D. (2011). Co-authorship networks in electronic markets research. *Electronic Markets*, *21*(1), 19–40. doi:10.1007/s12525-011-0051-5

Garang, J. A. (2015). How to leverage oil resources to enhance SME financing in South Sudan. *International Journal of Economic Policy in Emerging Economies*, *8*(2), 119–137. doi:10.1504/IJEPEE.2015.069604

Garba, M., Salleh, F., Hafiz, U. A., & Bakar, N. M. A. (2022). Insurance Literacy, Risk Knowledge Management, Risk-Taking Propensity and Economic Sustainability among SMEs: The Moderating Effect of Financial Inclusion. *Journal of Social Economics Research*, *9*(2), 92–110. doi:10.18488/35.v9i2.3120

Gomez Urquijo, L. (2015). Financial exclusion in the European Union: Addressing difficulties in accessing finance within the current integration framework. *Journal of Contemporary European Studies, 23*(1), 100–117. doi:10.1080/14782804.2014.961059

Hu, D., Fang, X., & DiGiovanni, Y. M. (2023). Technological progress, financial constraints, and digital financial inclusion. *Small Business Economics*, 1–29.

Hua, X., & Huang, Y. (2021). Understanding China's fintech sector: Development, impacts and risks. *European Journal of Finance*, *27*(4-5), 321–333. doi:10.1080/1351847X.2020.1811131

Huang, Y., Li, Z., Qiu, H., Tao, S., Wang, X., & Zhang, L. (2023). BigTech credit risk assessment for SMEs. *China Economic Review*, *81*, 102016. Advance online publication. doi:10.1016/j.chieco.2023.102016

Hudaefi, F. A. (2020). How does Islamic fintech promote the SDGs? Qualitative evidence from Indonesia. *Qualitative Research in Financial Markets*, *12*(4), 353–366. doi:10.1108/QRFM-05-2019-0058

Ibrahim, A. J., & Kahf, M. (2020). Instruments for investment protection when structuring Islamic venture capital. *Journal of Islamic Accounting and Business Research*, *11*(9), 1907–1920. doi:10.1108/JIABR-01-2019-0025

Ifinedo, P. (2011). Internet/e-business technologies acceptance in Canada's SMEs: An exploratory investigation. *Internet Research*, *21*(3), 255–281. doi:10.1108/10662241111139309

International Finance Corporation. (2017). *SME Finance.* Retrieved February 22, 2021, from IFC:https://www.ifc.org/wps/wcm/connect/Industry_EXT_Content/IFC_External_Corporate_Sit e/Financial+Institutions/Priorities/SME+Finance/

Irman, M. (2021). Financial inclusion as mediator in the relationship of social capital and financial literacy towards business performance of the trade sector SMEs in Pekanbaru, Indonesia. *Economic Annals-XXI*, 194.

Junoh, M. Z. B. H., Hidthiir, M. M. H. B., & Basheer, M. F. (2019). Entrepreneurial financial practices in Pakistan: The role of access to finance and financial literacy. International Journal of Innovation. *Creativity and Change*, *7*(9), 210–231.

Khan, S., & Alhadi, F. A. F. (n.d.). Fintech and Financial Inclusion in Saudi Arabia. *Review of Economics and Finance, 20*(1), 857-866.

Kotsios, P. (2023). Business resilience skills for SMEs. *Journal of Innovation and Entrepreneurship, 12*(1), 37. doi:10.1186/s13731-023-00304-0 PMID:37274429

Kundid, A., & Ercegovac, R. (2011). Credit rationing in financial distress: Croatia SMEs' finance approach. *International Journal of Law and Management*, *53*(1), 62–84. doi:10.1108/17542431111111890

Lam, W. R., & Liu, Y. (2020). Tackling Small and Medium-Sized Enterprises (SMEs) Financing in China. *Annals of Economics and Finance*, *21*(1).

Łasak, P. (2022). The role of financial technology and entrepreneurial finance practices in funding small and medium-sized enterprises. *Journal of Entrepreneurship. Management and Innovation*, *18*(1), 7–34.

Leung, X. Y., Sun, J., & Bai, B. (2017). Bibliometrics of social media research: A co-citation and co-word analysis. *International Journal of Hospitality Management*, *66*, 35–45. doi:10.1016/j.ijhm.2017.06.012

Li, Y., Stasinakis, C., & Yeo, W. M. (2022). A hybrid XGBoost-MLP model for credit risk assessment on digital supply chain finance. *Forecasting*, *4*(1), 184–207. doi:10.3390/forecast4010011

Lu, Z., Wu, J., Li, H., & Nguyen, D. K. (2022). Local bank, digital financial inclusion and SME financing constraints: Empirical evidence from China. *Emerging Markets Finance & Trade*, *58*(6), 1712–1725. doi:10.1080/1540496X.2021.1923477

Lu, Z., Wu, J., & Liu, J. (2020). Bank concentration and SME financing availability: The impact of promotion of financial inclusion in China. *International Journal of Bank Marketing*, *38*(6), 1329–1349. doi:10.1108/IJBM-01-2020-0007

Mabula, J. B., Dong Ping, H., & James, M. (2023). The Impact of African Firms' Utilization of Financial and Technology Resource on Innovation: A Simple Mediation. *SAGE Open*, *13*(1). Advance online publication. doi:10.1177/21582440231153037

Mahboob, A. M., Vichayanan, R., & Abusayed, K. A. (2017). Comparative positioning of Small and Medium enterprises in Bangladesh, Thailand and the Philippines. *Экономика региона, 13*(2), 381-395.

Mahmood, S., Shuhui, W., Aslam, S., & Ahmed, T. (2023). Financial Inclusion: Does it matter in Alleviating Poverty in Pakistan. *Social Indicators Research*, *169*(3), 1125–1146. doi:10.1007/s11205-023-03200-y

Mamaro, L. P., & Sibindi, A. B. (2022). Entrepreneurial Financing in Africa during the COVID-19 Pandemic. *Journal of Risk and Financial Management*, *15*(11), 511. doi:10.3390/jrfm15110511

Matama, R. (2016). Analysis of education levels and small business financial worth in Uganda. In*Analysis of education levels and small business financial worth in Uganda*. Matama, Rogers.

Morgan, P. J., & Pontines, V. (2018). Financial stability and financial inclusion: The case of SME lending. *The Singapore Economic Review*, *63*(01), 111–124. doi:10.1142/S0217590818410035

Mutamimah, M., & Indriastuti, M. (2023). Fintech, financial literacy, and financial inclusion in Indonesian SMEs. *International Journal of Entrepreneurship and Innovation Management*, *27*(1-2), 137–150. doi:10.1504/IJEIM.2023.129331

Mutamimah, M., & Indriastuti, M. (2023). Fintech, financial literacy, and financial inclusion in Indonesian SMEs. *International Journal of Entrepreneurship and Innovation Management*, *27*(1-2), 137–150. doi:10.1504/IJEIM.2023.129331

Naceur, S. B., Barajas, A., & Massara, A. (2017). Can Islamic banking increase financial inclusion? In *Handbook of empirical research on Islam and economic life* (pp. 213–252). Edward Elgar Publishing. doi:10.4337/9781784710736.00017

Nagpal, A., Jain, M., & Jain, A. (2020). Determining the role of digital technology, governance and institutions in advancing financial inclusion in BRICS nations using probit regression analysis. *Journal of Social and Economic Development*, *22*(2), 443–459. doi:10.1007/s40847-020-00112-2

Najib, M., & Fahma, F. (2020). Investigating the adoption of digital payment system through an extended technology acceptance model: An insight from the Indonesian small and medium enterprises. *International Journal on Advanced Science, Engineering and Information Technology*, *10*(4), 1702–1708. doi:10.18517/ijaseit.10.4.11616

Nanziri, L. E., & Wamalwa, P. S. (2021). Finance for SMEs and its effect on growth and inequality: Evidence from South Africa. *Transnational Corporations Review*, *13*(4), 450–466. doi:10.1080/19186444.2021.1925044

Nguse, T., Desalegn, G., Oshora, B., Tangl, A., Nathan, R. J., & Fekete-Farkasne, M. (2022). Enhancing Women Economic Empowerment Through Financial Inclusion: Evidence from SMEs in Ethiopia. *Polish Journal of Management Studies*, *25*(1), 270–291. doi:10.17512/pjms.2022.25.1.17

Nugraha, D. P., Setiawan, B., Nathan, R. J., & Fekete-Farkas, M. (2022). FinTech adoption drivers for innovation for SMEs in Indonesia. *Journal of Open Innovation*, *8*(4), 208. doi:10.3390/joitmc8040208

Okello Candiya Bongomin, G., Mpeera Ntayi, J., Munene, J. C., & Akol Malinga, C. (2017). The relationship between access to finance and growth of SMEs in developing economies: Financial literacy as a moderator. *Review of International Business and Strategy, 27*(4), 520-538.

Okfalisa, O., Mahyarni, M., Anggraini, W., Saeed, F., Moshood, T. D., & Saktioto, S. (2022). Quadruple helix engagement: Reviews on shariah fintech based SMEs digitalization readiness. *Indonesian Journal of Electrical Engineering and Informatics*, *10*(1), 112–122. doi:10.52549/ijeei.v10i1.3455

Onodugo, C., Ogbo, A., & Ogbaekirigwe, C. (2021). Moderating role of social capital on the effect of financial behavior on financial inclusion. *Problems and Perspectives in Management*, *19*(3), 502–512. doi:10.21511/ppm.19(3).2021.41

Oshora, B., Desalegn, G., Gorgenyi-Hegyes, E., Fekete-Farkas, M., & Zeman, Z. (2021). Determinants of financial inclusion in small and medium enterprises: Evidence from Ethiopia. *Journal of Risk and Financial Management*, *14*(7), 286. doi:10.3390/jrfm14070286

Roa, M. J., Villegas, A., & Garrón, I. (2022). Interest rate caps on microcredit: Evidence from a natural experiment in Bolivia. *Journal of Development Effectiveness*, *14*(2), 125–142. doi:10.1080/19439342.2021.1968934

Sabiu, T. T., & Abduh, M. (2021). Impact of Islamic banking inclusion on SME employment growth in Nigeria. *Journal of Islamic Monetary Economics and Finance*, *7*(1), 77–106. doi:10.21098/jimf.v7i1.1354

Sari, Y., Nugroho, M., & Rahmiyati, N. (2023). The effect of financial knowledge, financial behavior and digital financial capabilities on financial inclusion, financial concern and performance in MSMEs in East Java. *Uncertain Supply Chain Management*, *11*(4), 1745–1758. doi:10.5267/j.uscm.2023.6.016

Saviano, M., Nenci, L., & Caputo, F. (2017). The financial gap for women in the MENA region: A systemic perspective. *Gender in Management*, *32*(3), 203–217. doi:10.1108/GM-07-2016-0138

Shinozaki, S. (2014). A new regime of SME finance in emerging Asia: Enhancing access to growth capital and policy implications. Journal of International Commerce. *Economic Policy*, *5*(03), 1440010. Advance online publication. doi:10.1142/S1793993314400109

Small, H. (1973). Co-citation in the scientific literature: A new measure of the relationship between two documents. *Journal of the American Society for Information Science, 24*(4), 265–269. doi:10.1002/asi.4630240406

Thathsarani, S., Jianguo, W., & Alariqi, M. (2023). How Do Demand, Supply, and Institutional Factors Influence SME Financial Inclusion: A Developing Country Perspective. *SAGE Open, 13*(3). Advance online publication. doi:10.1177/21582440231187603

Thathsarani, U. S., & Jianguo, W. (2022). Do Digital Finance and the Technology Acceptance Model Strengthen Financial Inclusion and SME Performance? *Information (Basel), 13*(8), 390. doi:10.3390/info13080390

Toni, N., Theng, B., & Calen, C. (2024). Investigating the effect of financial literacy and financial inclusion on operational and sustainable supply chain performance of SMEs. *Uncertain Supply Chain Management, 12*(1), 573–582. doi:10.5267/j.uscm.2023.8.014

Tsai, C. H., & Kuan-Jung, P. (2017). The FinTech revolution and financial regulation: The case of online supply-chain financing. *Asian Journal of Law and Society, 4*(1), 109–132. doi:10.1017/als.2016.65

Utamaa, A. G. S., & Hariantob, S. (2020). Information System of" Laku Pandai": Achieving Financial Inclusion-Financial Technology SMEs Sector in Banyuwangi. *Transactions, 13*(10).

van Eck, N. J., & Waltman, L. (2010). Software survey: VOSviewer, a computer program for bibliometric mapping. *Scientometrics, 84*(2), 523–538. doi:10.1007/s11192-009-0146-3 PMID:20585380

Wambugu Mwangi. (2018). *Role of financial literacy, financial innovation, financial inclusion on SME access to credit in Kenya: A case of Kumisa Sacco* (Doctoral dissertation). MUA.

Yakubi, Y., Basuki, B., & Purwono, R. (2019). Financial Inclusion and Digital Finance in the Arab World: Current Status and Future Priorities. International Journal of Innovation. *Creativity and Change, 6*(3), 132–143.

Yang, Y., Shi, S., & Wu, J. (2022). Digital Financial Inclusion to Corporation Value: The Mediating Effect of Ambidextrous Innovation. *Sustainability (Basel), 14*(24), 16621. Advance online publication. doi:10.3390/su142416621

Yanto, H., Handayani, B. D., Solikhah, B., & Mula, J. M. (2016). The behavior of Indonesian SMEs in accepting financial accounting standards without public accountability. *International Journal of Business & Management Science, 6*(1).

Zhang, X., Li, J., Xiang, D., & Worthington, A. C. (2023). Digitalization, financial inclusion, and small and medium-sized enterprise financing: Evidence from China. *Economic Modelling, 126*, 106410. Advance online publication. doi:10.1016/j.econmod.2023.106410

Zupic, I., & Cater, T. (2015). Bibliometric Methods in Management and Organization. *Organizational Research Methods, 18*(3), 429–472. doi:10.1177/1094428114562629

APPENDIX A.

Table 11. Publications dataset used in the bibliometric analysis

	Authors	Title	Year	Source Title	Cited by	Country
1	Ifinedo P.	Internet/e-business technologies acceptance in Canada's SMEs: An exploratory investigation	2011	Internet Research	163	Canada
2	Lu Z.; Wu J.; Li H.; Nguyen D.K.	Local Bank, Digital Financial Inclusion and SME Financing Constraints: Empirical Evidence from China	2022	Emerging Markets Finance and Trade	70	UK/ France/ China/ Viet Nam
3	Tsai C.-H.; Peng K.-J.	The FinTech Revolution and Financial Regulation: The Case of Online Supply-Chain Financing	2017	Asian Journal of Law and Society	52	Taiwan/ Netherlands
4	Hua X.; Huang Y.	Understanding China's fintech sector: development, impacts and risks	2021	European Journal of Finance	48	China
5	Najib M.; Fahma F.	Investigating the adoption of digital payment system through an extended technology acceptance model: An insight from the Indonesian small and medium enterprises	2020	International Journal on Advanced Science, Engineering and Information Technology	43	India/ USA
6	Hudaefi F.A.	How does Islamic fintech promote the SDGs? Qualitative evidence from Indonesia	2020	Qualitative Research in Financial Markets	42	Indonesia
7	Morgan P.J.; Pontines V.	FINANCIAL STABILITY AND FINANCIAL INCLUSION: THE CASE OF SME LENDING	2018	Singapore Economic Review	38	Malaysia/ Japan
8	Coffie C.P.K.; Hongjiang Z.; Mensah I.A.; Kiconco R.; Simon A.E.O.	Determinants of FinTech payment services diffusion by SMEs in Sub-Saharan Africa: evidence from Ghana	2021	Information Technology for Development	35	China/ Ghana/ Uganda
9	Kundid A.; Ercegovac R.	Credit rationing in financial distress: Croatia SMEs' finance approach	2011	International Journal of Law and Management	32	Croatia
10	Appleyard L.	The Geographies of Access to Enterprise Finance: The Case of the West Midlands, UK; [Les géographies de l'accès au financement des entreprises: Étude de cas de la région des West Midlands, au Royaume-Uni]	2013	Regional Studies	21	UK
11	Brixiová Z.; Kangoye T.; Yogo T.U.	Access to finance among small and medium-sized enterprises and job creation in Africa	2020	Structural Change and Economic Dynamics	20	Czech Republic
12	Saviano M.; Nenci L.; Caputo F.	The financial gap for women in the MENA region: a systemic perspective	2017	Gender in Management	17	Italy
13	Agyekum F.K.; Reddy K.; Wallace D.; Wellalage N.H.	Does technological inclusion promote financial inclusion among SMEs? Evidence from South-East Asian (SEA) countries	2022	Global Finance Journal	17	Australia/ New Zealand
14	Nugraha D.P.; Setiawan B.; Nathan R.J.; Fekete-Farkas M.	Fintech Adoption Drivers for Innovation for SMEs in Indonesia	2022	Journal of Open Innovation: Technology, Market, and Complexity	17	Hungary/ Indonesia/ Malaysia/ Czech Republic
15	Lu Z.; Wu J.; Liu J.	Bank concentration and SME financing availability: the impact of promotion of financial inclusion in China	2020	International Journal of Bank Marketing	16	UK/ China
16	Oshora B.; Desalegn G.; Gorgenyi-Hegyes E.; Fekete-Farkas M.; Zeman Z.	Determinants of Financial Inclusion in Small and Medium Enterprises: Evidence from Ethiopia	2021	Journal of Risk and Financial Management	14	Hungary/ Ethiopia
17	Łasak P.	The role of financial technology and entrepreneurial finance practices in funding small and medium-sized enterprises	2022	Journal of Entrepreneurship, Management and Innovation	14	Poland
18	Li Y.; Stasinakis C.; Yeo W.M.	A Hybrid XGBoost-MLP Model for Credit Risk Assessment on Digital Supply Chain Finance	2022	Forecasting	13	UK
19	Czerwonka L.; Jaworski J.	Capital structure determinants of small and medium-sized enterprises: evidence from Central and Eastern Europe	2021	Journal of Small Business and Enterprise Development	13	Poland

	Authors	Title	Year	Source Title	Cited by	Country
20	Yanto H.; Handayani B.D.; Solikhah B.; Mula J.M.	The behavior of Indonesian SMEs in accepting Financial Accounting Standards without Public Accountability	2016	International Journal of Business and Management Science	12	Indonesia/ China
21	Eton M.; Mwosi F.; Okello-Obura C.; Turyehebwa A.; Uwonda G.	Financial inclusion and the growth of small medium enterprises in Uganda: empirical evidence from selected districts in Lango sub-region	2021	Journal of Innovation and Entrepreneurship	12	Uganda
22	Lam W.R.; Liu Y.	Tackling small and medium-sized enterprises (SMEs) financing in China	2020	Annals of Economics and Finance	10	World Bank
23	Ali M.M.; Rattanawiboonsom V.; Perez C.M.; Khan A.A.	Comparative positioning of Small and Medium Enterprises in Bangladesh, Thailand and the Philippines	2017	Economy of Regions	10	Bangladesh/ Philippines/ Thailand
24	Thathsarani U.S.; Jianguo W.	Do Digital Finance and the Technology Acceptance Model Strengthen Financial Inclusion and SME Performance?	2022	Information (Switzerland)	10	Sri Lanka/ China
25	Kame Babilla T.U.	Digital innovation and financial access for small and medium-sized enterprises in a currency union	2023	Economic Modelling	10	Cameroon
26	Bui T.Q.; Do A.V.P.	Does technological inclusion reduce financial constraints on small and medium sized enterprises? The case of Vietnam	2022	Finance Research Letters	8	Viet Nam
27	Shinozaki S.	A New Regime of SME Finance in Emerging Asia: Enhancing Access to Growth Capital and Policy Implications	2014	Journal of International Commerce, Economics and Policy	7	Asian development Bank
28	Zhang X.; Li J.; Xiang D.; Worthington A.C.	Digitalization, financial inclusion, and small and medium-sized enterprise financing: Evidence from China	2023	Economic Modelling	6	China/ Australia
29	Dluhopolskyi O.; Pakhnenko O.; Lyeonov S.; Semenog A.; Artyukhova N.; Cholewa-Wiktor M.; Jastrzębski W.	Digital Financial Inclusion: COVID-19 Impacts and Opportunities	2023	Sustainability (Switzerland)	6	Poland/ Ukrain
30	Okfalisa; Mahyarni; Anggraini W.; Saeed F.; Moshood T.D.; Saktioto	Quadruple Helix Engagement: Reviews on Syariah Fintech Based SMEs Digitalization Readiness	2022	Indonesian Journal of Electrical Engineering and Informatics	5	Indonesia/ Saudi Arabia/ Malaysia
31	Gómez Urquijo L.	Financial Exclusion in the European Union: Addressing Difficulties in Accessing Finance within the Current Integration Framework	2015	Journal of Contemporary European Studies	4	Spain
32	Onodugo C.; Onodugo I.; Ogbo A.; Okwo H.; Ogbaekirigwe C.	Moderating role of social capital on the effect of financial behavior on financial inclusion	2021	Problems and Perspectives in Management	4	Nigeria
33	Nguse T.; Desalegn D.; Oshora B.; Tangl A.; Nathan R.J.; Fekete-Farkasne M.	ENHANCING WOMEN ECONOMIC EMPOWERMENT THROUGH FINANCIAL INCLUSION:EVIDENCE FROM SMEs IN ETHIOPIA; [ZWIĘKSZANIE WŁASNOŚCI GOSPODARCZEJ KOBIET POPRZEZ WŁĄCZENIE FINANSOWE: DOWODY Z MŚP W ETIOPII]	2022	Polish Journal of Management Studies	4	Hungary/ Malaysia
34	Mamaro L.P.; Sibindi A.B.	Entrepreneurial Financing in Africa during the COVID-19 Pandemic	2022	Journal of Risk and Financial Management	4	Africa
35	Arcuri M.C.; Pisani R.	Is trade credit a sustainable resource for medium-sized italian green companies?	2021	Sustainability (Switzerland)	4	Italy
36	Nanziri L.E.; Wamalwa P.S.	Finance for SMEs and its effect on growth and inequality: evidence from South Africa	2021	Transnational Corporations Review	3	South Africa/ Kenya
37	Roa M.J.; Villegas A.; Garrón I.	Interest rate caps on microcredit: evidence from a natural experiment in Bolivia	2022	Journal of Development Effectiveness	3	Mexico/ Spain
38	Sabiu T.T.; Abduh M.	IMPACT OF ISLAMIC BANKING INCLUSION ON SME EMPLOYMENT GROWTH IN NIGERIA	2021	Journal of Islamic Monetary Economics and Finance	3	Brunei Darussalam
39	Kotsios P.	Business resilience skills for SMEs	2023	Journal of Innovation and Entrepreneurship	2	Greece
40	Garba M.; Salleh F.; Hafiz U.A.; Bakar N.M.A.	INSURANCE LITERACY, RISK KNOWLEDGE MANAGEMENT, RISK-TAKING PROPENSITY AND ECONOMIC SUSTAINABILITY AMONG SMEs: THE MODERATING EFFECT OF FINANCIAL INCLUSION	2022	Journal of Social Economics Research	2	Malaysia/ Nigeria

	Authors	Title	Year	Source Title	Cited by	Country
41	Fazal H.; Muhammad J.; Zahoor U.H.	Operational Perspective of SMEs Performance and Competitive Priorities Practices: Path Analytic Approach	2020	Studies in Business and Economics	2	Pakistan
42	Hu D.; Fang X.; DiGiovanni Y.M.	Technological progress, financial constrains, and digital financial inclusion	2023	Small Business Economics	2	China/ USA
43	Khan S.; Alhadi F.A.F.	Fintech and Financial Inclusion in Saudi Arabia	2022	Review of Economics and Finance	1	Saudi Arabia
44	Huang Y.; Li Z.; Qiu H.; Tao S.; Wang X.; Zhang L.	BigTech credit risk assessment for SMEs	2023	China Economic Review	1	China/ Switzerland/ United States
45	Ibrahim A.-J.; Kahf M.	Instruments for investment protection when structuring Islamic venture capital	2020	Journal of Islamic Accounting and Business Research	1	Qatar/ Turkey
46	Arvind T.T.	Too Big To Care?:Financial Contracts And The Problem Of Transactional Asymmetry	2021	Law and Contemporary Problems	1	UK
47	Yang Y.; Shi S.; Wu J.	Digital Financial Inclusion to Corporation Value: The Mediating Effect of Ambidextrous Innovation	2022	Sustainability (Switzerland)	1	China
48	Mutamimah M.; Indriastuti M.	Fintech, financial literacy, and financial inclusion in Indonesian SMEs	2023	International Journal of Entrepreneurship and Innovation Management	1	Indonesia
49	Garang J.A.	How to leverage oil resources to enhance SME financing in South Sudan	2015	International Journal of Economic Policy in Emerging Economies	1	Sudan
50	Yakubi Y.A.Y.; Basuki B.; Purwono R.	Financial inclusion and digital finance in the Arab world: Current status and future priorities	2019	International Journal of Innovation, Creativity and Change	1	Indonesia
51	Sari Y.W.; Nugroho M.; Rahmiyati N.	The effect of financial knowledge, financial behavior and digital financial capabilities on financial inclusion, financial concern and performance in MSMEs in East Java	2023	Uncertain Supply Chain Management	0	Indonesia
52	Alrababah Z.	BARRIERS TO CLOUD COMPUTING ADOPTION AMONG SMEs IN THE MIDDLE EAST: A SYSTEMATIC REVIEW	2023	Journal of Theoretical and Applied Information Technology	0	Malaysia
53	Mahmood S.; Shuhui W.; Aslam S.; Ahmed T.	Financial Inclusion: Does it matter in Alleviating Poverty in Pakistan	2023	Social Indicators Research	0	Pakistan
54	Toni N.; Theng B.P.; Calen	Investigating the effect of financial literacy and financial inclusion on operational and sustainable supply chain performance of SMEs	2024	Uncertain Supply Chain Management	0	Indonesia
55	Al-Hakim M.S.; Al-Hamad A.A.-S.; Ghaith M.A.	The Role of Financial Inclusion in Bridging SMEs Financing Gap The Viewpoint of Credit Employees at Jordanian Islamic Banks	2021	Islamic Quarterly	0	Jordan
56	Mabula J.B.; Dong Ping H.; James M.	The Impact of African Firms' Utilization of Financial and Technology Resource on Innovation: A Simple Mediation	2023	SAGE Open	0	China/ Tanzania
57	Bhattacharyya A.; Rahman M.L.; Wright S.	Improving small and medium-size enterprise performance: Does working capital management enhance the effectiveness of financial inclusion?	2023	Accounting and Finance	0	Australia
58	Irman M.; Budiyanto; Suwitho	Financial inclusion as mediator in the relationship of social capital and financial literacy towards business performance of the trade sector SMEs in Pekanbaru, Indonesia	2021	Economic Annals-XXI	0	Indonesia
59	Dela Cruz N.A.; Villanueva A.C.B.; Tolin L.A.; Disse S.; Lensink R.; White H.	Effects of interventions to improve access to financial services for micro-, small- and medium-sized enterprises in low- and middle-income countries: An evidence and gap map	2023	Campbell Systematic Reviews	0	Philippines/ Netherlands/ India
60	Utama A.A.G.S.; Harianto S.	Information System of "Laku Pandai": Achieving Financial Inclusion-Financial Technology SMEs Sector in Banyuwangi	2021	Review of International Geographical Education Online	0	Indonesia
61	Thathsarani S.; Jianguo W.; Alariqi M.	How Do Demand, Supply, and Institutional Factors Influence SME Financial Inclusion: A Developing Country Perspective	2023	SAGE Open	0	China
62	Wasiu Adebisi A.; Uket Eko E.; Oka Felix A.	Microfinance Banks Dynamics Effect on Small-Scale Enterprise Development in Nigeria	2020	International Journal of Applied Economics, Finance and Accounting	0	Nigeria

APPENDIX B: CLASS ACTIVITIES FOR STUDENTS

Class Assignment 1

Analysing the Regional Differences in Financial Inclusion of SMEs

Instructions: Based on the provided information in this chapter, conduct further research and answer the following questions:

- Identify cultural, legal, and religious differences in OIC and non-OIC countries.
- Evaluate the impact of these differences on varying magnitudes of access to finance barriers for SMEs in OIC and non-OIC countries.
- Identify influential publications in this research area and explain their contribution and collaboration of OIC and non-OIC countries to develop this FI-SME research area.

Class Assignment 2

Role of Regulatory Policies in Fostering or Hindering FinTech Development for SMEs

Instructions: Based on the provided information in this chapter, conduct further research and answer the following questions:

- Discuss the challenges and opportunities presented by the integration of advanced models and technologies.
- Provide insights into how policy-makers can strike a balance between innovation and stability to ensure sustainable growth of SMEs.
- Analyze the regulatory issues in OIC and non-OIC countries.

Class Assignment 3

Women-Led SMEs and Islamic Finance

- **Discuss the specific challenges faced by women entrepreneurs in accessing finance in OIC and non-OIC countries.**
- **Compare and contrast the potential of Islamic finance products and services in addressing these challenges in both regions.**
- **What policy recommendations could be made to enhance the effectiveness of Islamic finance for women-led SMEs?**

Class Assignment 4

Digitalization and Sustainability in SMEs

- **Analyze the key features and benefits of Shariah-compliant Fintech solutions for SMEs.**
- **Discuss the potential challenges and limitations of adopting these solutions, particularly in developing countries.**
- **Propose a revised Quadruple Helix model tailored to assess the digital readiness of SMEs and leverage Shariah Fintech for sustainable growth, especially in disaster-prone areas.**

Assessment Questions

Question 1: What is a major barrier hindering SME potential?

Question 2: How can access to loan financing impact employment growth in labor-intensive sectors in OIC country Africa?

Question 3: How does digital innovation benefit SMEs, and what's the impact of digital financial services on SMEs in the Currency Union?

Question 1: How can Islamic finance contribute to SME financial stability, and what are the mentioned benefits?

Question 2: What challenges do SMEs in the United Kingdom (West Midlands) face for credit access, and what solution is proposed to address the financing gap created after the 2007 crisis?

Question 3: How is the economic empowerment of women entrepreneurs discussed in the text, and what barriers do female entrepreneurs in the MENA region and Ethiopia face?

Assessment MCQs

1. **The main driver behind financial inclusion (FI) research is:** (a) Understanding the specific challenges faced by SMEs. (b) Comparing FI across OIC and non-OIC nations. (c) Reducing poverty and stimulating economic growth. (d) Analyzing the effectiveness of existing FI policies.
2. **A major barrier to FI for SMEs in developing countries is:** (a) Lack of government support. (b) Complex regulatory frameworks. (c) Limited access to collateral options. (d) All of the above.
3. **Which factor does NOT positively impact FI for Ethiopian SMEs?** (a) Market opportunities. (b) Institutional framework. (c) Supply-side factors. (d) Borrowing costs.
4. **According to the study, excessive financial inclusion in China can:** (a) Reduce the benefits of bank concentration. (b) Increase access to finance for large firms. (c) Encourage innovation in the financial sector. (d) Lead to higher borrowing costs for SMEs.
5. **A key challenge for Community Development Financial Institutions (CDFIs) in the UK is:** (a) Lack of regulatory support. (b) Limited geographical reach. (c) Insufficient funding. (d) All of the above.
6. **How do digital financial services benefit SMEs in China?** (a) Reduce information asymmetry. (b) Facilitate access to various financial products. (c) Increase borrowing limits. (d) Both (a) and (b).
7. **What factor is considered MOST crucial for successful Fintech adoption by SMEs?** (a) Regulatory support. (b) User-friendliness of technology. (c) Management understanding. (d) All of the above.
8. **According to the paper, financial literacy has a:** (a) Negative impact on SME performance. (b) Positive impact on financial stability. (c) No significant impact on financial inclusion. (d) Positive impact on SME performance and financial stability.

9. **Regtech and Fintech development 2.0 are examples of:** (a) Risk management tools for SMEs. (b) Innovative policy tools for the Fintech industry. (c) Regulatory sandboxes for new financial products. (d) Both (b) and (c).
10. **The paper recommends flexible monetary policies and differential fiscal consolidation for:** (a) OIC countries with high financial inclusion. (b) Non-OIC countries with limited access to finance. (c) Countries aiming to promote a more inclusive financial market. (d) All of the above

Answers to MCQs

1. (c) Reducing poverty and stimulating economic growth
2. (d) All of the above
3. (b) Institutional framework
4. (a) Reduce the benefits of bank concentration
5. (d) All of the above
6. (d) Both (a) and (b)
7. (d) All of the above
8. (d) Positive impact on SME performance and financial stability
9. (b) Innovative policy tools for the Fintech industry
10. (a) OIC countries with high financial inclusion

Section 3
Challenges and Opportunities

Chapter 10

Inflation-targeting monetary policy framework in Nigeria: The Success Factors

Peterson K. Ozili
https://orcid.org/0000-0001-6292-1161
Central Bank of Nigeria, Nigeria

ABSTRACT

Many developing countries are facing high inflation, and the central banks in these countries have adopted several solutions to tame rising inflation. Nigeria transitioned to an inflation targeting monetary policy framework in late 2023 from a monetary targeting monetary policy framework. There is high prospect that the inflation targeting monetary policy framework will tame high inflation in Nigeria. This study identifies the important success factors for an effective inflation targeting monetary policy framework in Nigeria. The identified success factors include the size of economic agents monitoring the inflation target, the credibility of the central bank, the degree of central bank independence, reduction in budget deficit, limited dollarization of the Nigerian economy, effective central bank communication, avoidance of fiscal dominance, financial development, greater financial inclusion, financial stability, and insecurity caused by farmer-herder clashes and terrorism.

1. INTRODUCTION

This study identifies the success factors for an effective inflation targeting monetary policy framework in Nigeria.

The goal of most central banks is to achieve price stability which is generally interpreted as low inflation. Inflation is a general and persistent increase in the price of goods and services in an economy (Barro, 1996). Many central banks have adopted an inflation targeting monetary policy framework and have made the inflation rate the most superior objective of monetary policy.

The literature document some motivations for adopting an inflation targeting monetary policy framework (Bernanke and Mishkin, 1997; Svensson, 1997). For instance, a central bank may adopt an inflation

DOI: 10.4018/979-8-3693-1475-3.ch010

targeting monetary policy framework when it wants to refocus on price stability as the primary goal of monetary policy (Svensson, 1999), or when it wants to avoid potential loss of credibility from frequent changes to monetary aggregates (Neuenkirch and Tillmann, 2014), or when it wants to provide an anchor for inflation expectations (Bundick and Smith, 2018). Other advantages of an inflation targeting monetary policy framework include a low and less variable inflation rate and interest rate, stable economic growth, and greater ability to respond to shocks without losing credibility (Mishkin, 2000; Bernanke, 2003). Adopting an inflation targeting monetary policy framework may yield significant economic benefits in developing countries that are facing high inflation, large external shocks and are facing difficulties in designing sound domestic macroeconomic policies (Lin and Ye, 2009; Thornton, 2016).

Nigeria recently adopted an inflation targeting monetary policy framework. In late 2023, the central bank transitioned to a floating exchange rate system and adopted an explicit inflation targeting monetary policy framework which allows the Nigerian central bank to set an inflation target for the coming quarters or year and use its monetary policy instruments to meet the inflation target while taking into account the lags between policy decisions and their effect on output and prices. It is important to understand how inflation targeting monetary policy framework might work in Nigeria and the factors that determine its success.

This study contributes to the monetary policy literature in several ways. It contributes to the economic literature that examine the efforts of developing countries to combat high persistent inflation (Vega and Winkelried, 2005; Taylor, 2019). This study contributes to the literature by analyzing the case of Nigeria which recently adopted an inflation targeting monetary policy framework to combat high inflation. The study also contributes to the literature that explore several monetary policy frameworks for controlling inflation (e.g., Dua, 2023; Bianchi et al, 2021). This study focuses on a specific type of monetary policy framework which is the inflation targeting monetary policy framework.

The remainder of this study is structured as follows. Section 2 presents an overview of the monetary policy framework in Nigeria. Section 3 presents the literature review. Section 4 presents the success factors affecting the inflation targeting regime. Section 5 concludes.

2. LITERATURE REVIEW

Several studies have investigated inflation targeting as an approach of central banks in controlling inflation. Svensson (2010) suggests that inflation targeting is a monetary policy strategy that involves announcing an inflation target. It was first introduced in New Zealand in 1990 and it was successful in stabilizing both inflation and the real economy in New Zealand. As of 2010, about 25 industrialized and emerging-market economies had adopted inflation targeting (Svensson, 2010). Ball and Sheridan (2004) showed that inflation-targeting regimes have worked well as it led to significant reduction in both the rate of inflation and inflation expectations. They also observed that shocks to inflation die away more quickly under inflation targeting than in other monetary policy regimes. Mishkin and Schmidt-Hebbel (2001) undertook a review of the inflation targeting regimes adopted in 18 countries and compared it with the non-inflation targeting regime used in other countries. They found that inflation targeting is successful in controlling inflation. However, they showed that there is still much to learn about inflation targeting as an approach to conduct monetary policy. In a related study, Mishkin and Schmidt-Hebbel (2007) empirically examined the efficacy of inflation targeting in countries that adopt inflation targeting, and found that inflation targeting helps countries to achieve low inflation in the longrun, and it helps to obtain inflation outcomes that are closer to the inflation target. However, they emphasise that their result does not suggest that countries adopting inflation targeting have better monetary policy performance than countries that adopt a non-inflation targeting regime. De Mendonça and Souza (2012) examined the adoption of inflation targeting in 180 countries from 1990 to 2007. They used the propensity score matching methodology and found that the adoption of inflation targeting yield good results by reducing inflation volatility in developing economies. However, inflation targeting adoption does not offer much benefits in advanced economies. They conclude that the adoption of inflation targeting is useful for countries that want to increase the credibility of the management of monetary policy. Kumar et al (2015) study whether inflation targeting can assist in the anchoring of inflation expectations in New Zealand. They survey a large number of firms and found that managers of these firms display little anchoring of inflation expectations, they are poorly informed about recent inflation dynamics, and their forecasts of future inflation reflect high levels of uncertainty in the economy. Mishkin and Posen (1998) examine the operation of inflation targeting in some countries. They found that all of the inflation targeting countries have low inflation rates and greater monetary policy transparency without harming the real economy. Fratzscher et al (2020) examine whether inflation targeting acts as a shock absorber during crises or disasters. They use quarterly data of many countries and found that inflation targeting leads to better macroeconomic performance after crises or disasters. Inflation targeting decreases inflation, increases output growth, and lowers inflation and growth variability compared to other monetary regimes. They also show that only hard inflation targets, but not soft targets, will reap fruits in an inflation targeting regime. While these studies have examined inflation targeting in several contexts, these studies have not examined inflation targeting in Nigeria. This study examines the case of Nigeria.

3. MONETARY POLICY IN NIGERIA

3.1. Exchange Rate and Monetary Targeting Regime

The objective of monetary policy in Nigeria is to achieve and maintain price, monetary and financial stability. Over the years, one of the major characteristics of the Nigerian economy is the persistent double-digit inflation (see figure 1). Between 2014 and mid-2023, the central bank adopted a monetary targeting framework and maintained a managed float exchange rate system. The 'monetary targeting' monetary policy framework yielded positive results in managing inflation during the time. It led to low double-digit inflation and significant growth in non-oil export between 2014 and mid-2023 (see figure 2). However, the gains of the central bank's 'monetary targeting' monetary policy framework was marred by the occurrence of two economic recessions in 2016 and 2020, insecurity arising from farmer-herder clashes, and low revenue generation by the fiscal authorities. The central bank's monetary policy also led to negative economic consequences which include high budget deficit financing (see figure 3), a wide gap in the exchange rate in the official and parallel foreign exchange rate markets, preferential access to cheap foreign exchange, and restricted access to foreign exchange for dealers of 43 items which led to significant market distortion.

Figure 1. Inflation, consumer prices (annual %)
Source: World Bank

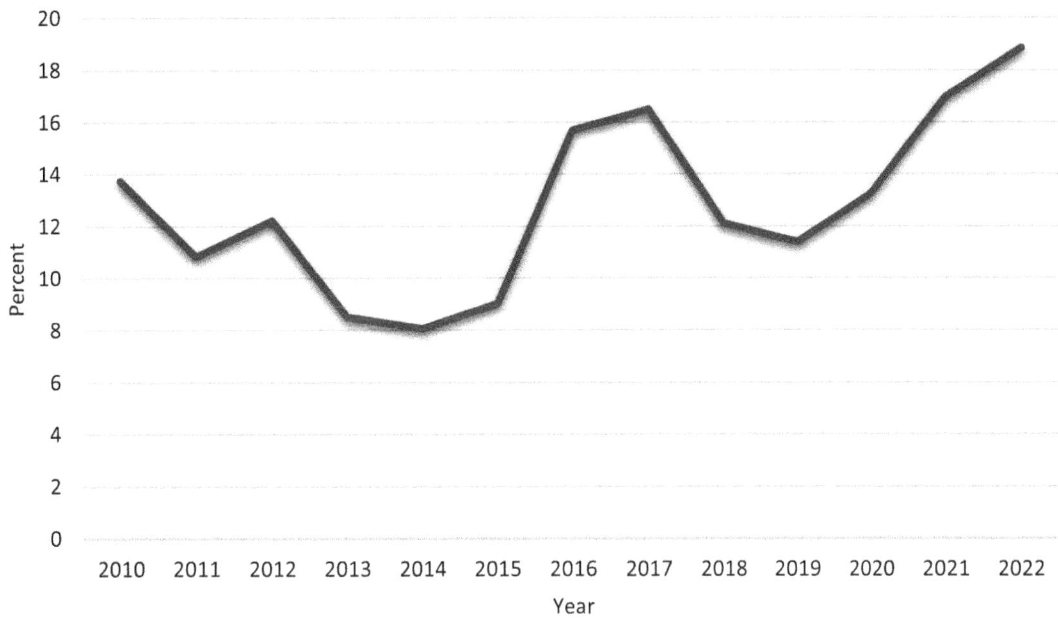

Figure 2. Non-oil export to GDP ratio
Source: World Bank

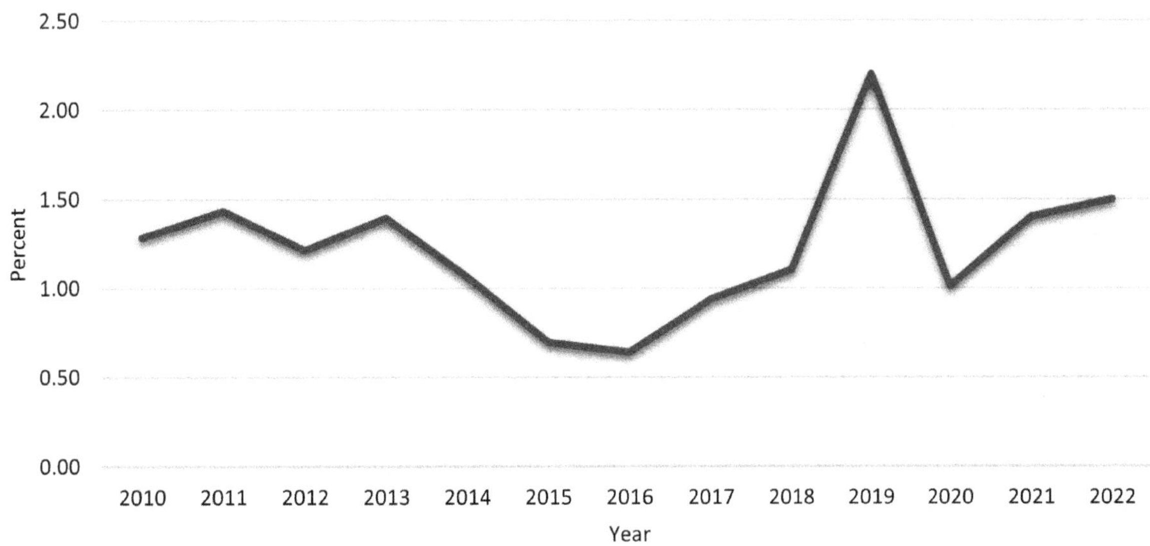

Figure 3. Nigeria budget defit financing (general government borrowing as percent of GDP)
Source: World Bank

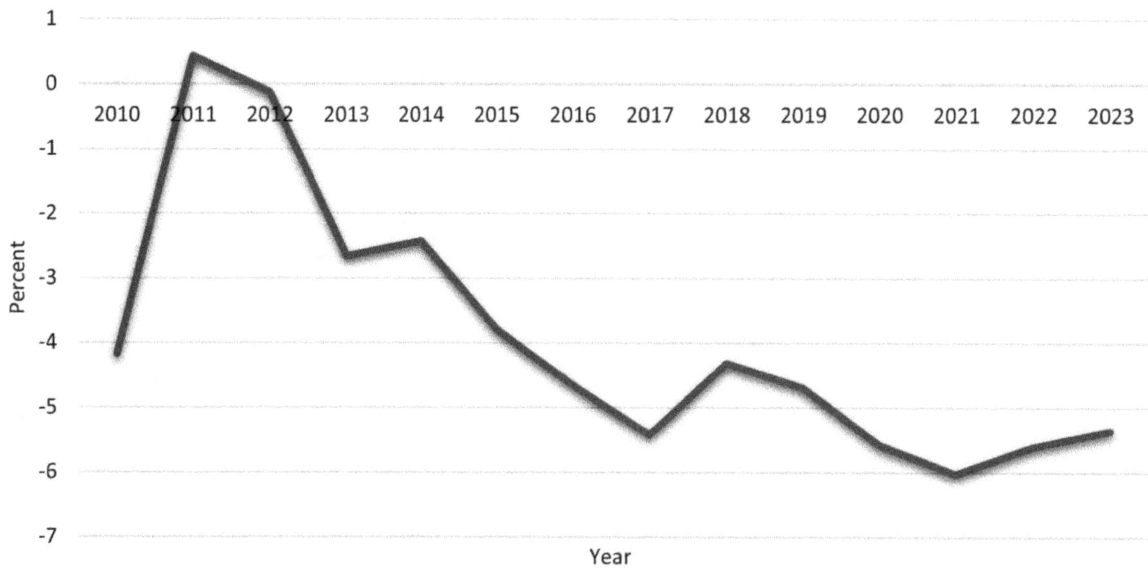

3.2. Inflation Targeting Monetary Policy Regime

The central bank in November 2023 abandoned the managed-float exchange rate system and the 'monetary targeting' monetary policy framework. It adopted an inflation targeting monetary policy framework designed to allow the central bank to set an inflation target for the medium-term, announce the inflation target to the public to manage inflation expectations, and use its monetary policy instruments to meet the inflation target. The inflation targeting monetary policy framework was introduced alongside the unification of exchange rates, the lifting of the ban on the forty-three items, increasing the capital requirement of banks and the introduction of new foreign exchange guidelines. The central bank adopted the inflation targeting monetary policy framework towards the end of 2023 at a time when there was high public debt stock, low government revenue, low foreign direct investment, rapid currency depreciation and rising energy prices due to fuel subsidy removal. Due to these factors, I argue that the success of the inflation targeting regime will depend on several factors some of which I will discuss in the next section.

4. FACTORS DETERMINING THE SUCCESS OF AN INFLATION-TARGETING REGIME IN NIGERIA

4.1. Size of Economic Agents Monitoring the Inflation Target

The expectation is that once the central bank announces an inflation target, economic agents in Nigeria will monitor the movements in the monetary base and they should be aware of its influence on prices. In simple terms, the central bank expects economic agents to monitor the movements in the inflation target and factor-in the movement in the inflation target in their consumption behavior and pricing decisions. This is the expectation in theory (D'Acunto et al, 2019). However, a problem that arises is that many economic agents in Nigeria pay little attention to a central bank inflation target, and those that pay attention to the inflation target announcement are usually less than 1 percent of the population. As a result, the announcement of an inflation target may have little impact on the inflation expectations of economic agents in Nigeria if the segment of the population that respond to the inflation target announcement is small.

4.2. Credibility of the Central Bank

Inflation targeting would be effective if the reputation of the central bank is credible. Ideally, when the central bank announces the inflation target, the general public will [or should] become aware of the inflation target. If the central bank misses the inflation target for any reason, even when it missed the target through no fault of its own, the central bank will immediately lose credibility. As a result, the general public or economic agents will disregard the importance of the inflation target. This will make inflation targeting ineffective to rein in the inflation expectations of economic agents. To avoid this effect, the central bank will be under pressure to do all it can to meet the inflation target it has set in order to preserve its existing credibility or to regain its lost credibility. Often, a central bank that has a weak reputation and is unable to control inflation may choose to adopt an inflation targeting monetary policy framework with the hope that setting and meeting the inflation target will help the central bank regain its credibility. The central bank may set an inflation target that is too easy to achieve even without the central bank doing anything. This will help the central bank to meet the inflation target and preserve or regain its credibility.

4.3. The Degree of Central Bank Independence

Central bank independence refers to the ability and the right of the central bank to set its own monetary policy goals with or without coordination with the fiscal authorities and without undue political interference. In Nigeria, central bank independence does not mean that there should be no coordination between the central bank and the fiscal authority. Rather, it means that the central bank of Nigeria should determine by itself the specific areas where it will coordinate with the fiscal authority and the areas where it will not coordinate with the fiscal authority. The degree of independence of the Nigerian central bank will be pivotal for the success of the newly adopted inflation targeting monetary policy framework. However, too much central bank independence has several disadvantages for inflation targeting. First, it could reduce the transparency of inflation forecast because nobody outside the central bank will be able to question or challenge the assumptions made by an independent central bank in determining the inflation target. As a result, the transparency of the inflation target will be diminished. Second, central bank independence could diminish the credibility of the central bank's inflation target because an independent central bank can undertake frequent changes in interest rate within a short time to achieve the inflation target. But the market may interpret the frequent changes in interest rate within a short time as an attempt to cover up the failure of the central bank to meet its inflation target using fewer changes in interest rate. To mitigate these consequences, there is a need for a degree of central bank independence that encourage monetary and fiscal policy coordination so that the fiscal authority can help to curtail excessive monetary policy activism by an independent central bank.

4.4. Reduction in Budget Deficits

The central bank's financing of budget deficit will lead to money creation which will hinder the central bank's effort to achieve the inflation target under an inflation targeting monetary policy regime. If the central bank has low independence, one channel through which inflation targeting would reduce inflation is through the reduction of budget deficits. In the case of Nigeria, the central bank can achieve its inflation target if it fully resists the pressure by politicians to fund large fiscal deficits. Adopting an inflation targeting monetary policy framework, in collaboration and consultation with politicians, can make politicians support the central bank's commitment to reduce inflation and would make politicians to stop pressuring the central bank to fund the budget deficit. This will not only increase the central bank's independence, but it will also bring an end to budget deficit financing by the central bank, thereby curbing inflation that is induced by rising budget deficit.

4.5. Limited Dollarization of the Nigerian Economy

Financial dollarization of the Nigerian economy frustrates the central bank's effort to reduce inflation because dollarization reduces the efficiency of monetary policy instruments, increases Nigeria's sensitivity to external shocks, increases money supply and exchange rate, and increases exchange rate pass-through to price, thereby increasing inflation and inflation expectations. The recent adoption of an inflation targeting monetary policy framework in Nigeria should be supported by the de-dollarization of the economy to obtain maximum results. To de-dollarize the Nigerian economy, the central bank must achieve a sustained reduction in inflation. The reduction in inflation must be substantial and visible to the general public through a significant increase in their purchasing power. This will encourage the general public to stop saving their wealth in dollars or in any other foreign currencies, thereby leading to a gradual de-dollarization of the Nigerian economy.

4.6. Effective Central Bank Communication

Another factor that is crucial for the success of inflation targeting in Nigeria is effective central bank communication. The central bank should constantly communicate to the public its own assessment, evidence, and policy strategy. The central bank should also make clear its limitations too. The central bank can use three communication tools, namely, inflation targets, inflation forecasts, and quarterly reports that present the assessments of inflation factors (Baranowski et al, 2021). Furthermore, announcing the entire policy process upon which the inflation target is based will amount to full communication and it will give households, firms, and government a more accurate forecast of future macroeconomic conditions, and lead to greater stability in firm output, inflation, and nominal interest rates. But if the central bank only announces the variables upon which interest rate decisions are made, it will amount to partial communication and may produce less stability in firm output, inflation, and nominal interest rates.

4.7. Avoidance of Fiscal Dominance

Fiscal dominance exists when Nigeria's public debt, budget deficit and external debt levels are too high that monetary policy ceases to be an effective tool for controlling inflation. When there is fiscal dominance, the government through the central bank will either service domestic debt by printing more money which will lead to inflation, or the central bank will reduce interest rate to reduce the cost of debt servicing, but this will also lead to rising inflation and cause the central bank to miss the inflation target. Either way, the central bank will miss the inflation target. Furthermore, when debt is sufficiently high, it will lead to concerns about debt overhang, debt sustainability and the possibility of fiscal dominance which will induce the central bank to pay more attention to decreasing the cost of debt servicing instead of focusing on achieving its inflation target (Blanchard, 2004). Fiscal dominance will pressure the central bank to deviate from the inflation target in ways designed to ease the debt burden of the government (Ahmed et al, 2021). When this happens, the central bank will miss its inflation target. Therefore, the central bank must oppose fiscal dominance if the inflation targeting framework is to succeed and the central bank should advise the federal government against increasing public debt.

4.8. Financial Development

The inflation targeting monetary policy framework in Nigeria will lead to a shift towards a more market-oriented and developed financial system. High level of financial development is essential to meeting the inflation target of Nigeria's central bank because greater levels of financial development are associated with greater access to finance (and credit) and greater financial intermediation (see figure 4), which makes the interest rate channel of monetary policy transmission more effective and enables greater consumption-smoothing which leads to a decrease in the inflation rate.

Figure 4. Inflation and financial development (proxy by private credit to GDP ratio
Source: World Bank

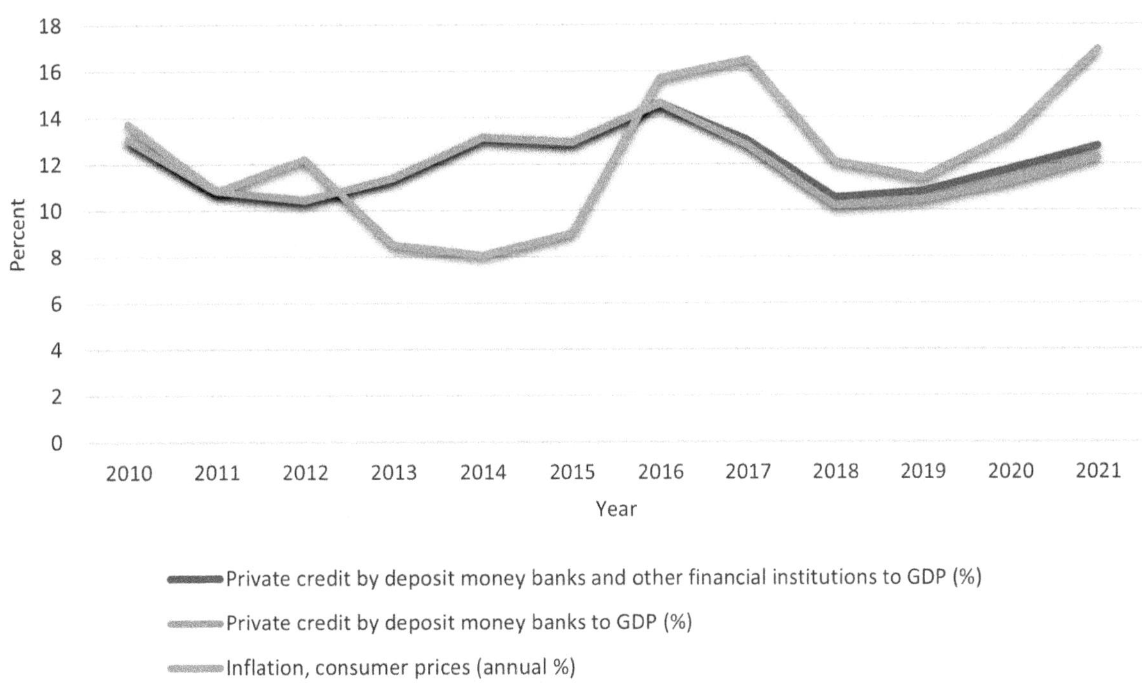

4.9. Greater Financial Inclusion

Greater financial inclusion enhances inflation targeting by bringing people into the formal financial system and bringing their monies as deposits into the financial system. This will decrease the amount of money outside banks. Greater financial inclusion brings money into the formal banking sector so that central bank interest rate can affect all financial system deposits. Greater financial inclusion also allows households and firms to smooth consumption thereby decreasing the inflation rate.

4.10. Financial Stability

Under inflation targeting, the central bank should aim to achieve a low inflation target and should meet the inflation target. Meeting the inflation target will lead to correct inferences about future real returns of investments. This, in turn, will lead to accurate and well-informed lending/borrowing decisions, decrease in loan defaults, and lower bankruptcies which will improve financial stability. However, the central bank faces the risk of setting an easy-to-achieve inflation target in order to increase its credibility but may fail to detect early the build-up of financial imbalances that increase financial instability risks. These imbalances can show up in the form of credit market imperfections or financial frictions that hinder the transmission mechanism between monetary policy and inflation by reducing welfare through mechanisms that are not fully reflected in the inflation target. The central bank can strive to meet its inflation target by increasing interest rate to mitigate risks to financial stability. Increasing interest rate to meet the inflation target can decrease financial instability risk because increasing interest rate will make borrowing become expensive and will decrease economic activity. High interest rate will induce financial sector agents to decrease leverage in the financial system. The decrease in leverage, with equity levels remaining unchanged, will decrease the debt-to-equity ratio, decrease insolvency risk and bankruptcy risks in the financial system and improve financial stability (Woodford, 2012).

4.11. Insecurity Farmer-Herder Clashes and Terrorism

Farmers/herders clash could make the central bank miss its inflation target. The farmers/herders clashes over the years have restricted farmers from accessing their farmlands, leading to food price inflation. If the central bank sets a low inflation target, there is the risk that the central bank may miss the inflation target if unexpected escalation in farmers/herders clashes occur, leading to farmers avoiding their farmlands. This will increase the farmgate price of food and lead to food price inflation. Terrorism in Northern Nigeria also contributes to the increase in food price inflation because terrorists impose levies on farmers who want to access their farmlands in terrorized areas. As a result, farmers will increase the price of farm produce, leading to food price inflation and a higher risk of the central bank missing the inflation target.

5. CONCLUSION

The purpose of this paper was to identify the success factors that will be crucial for an effective inflation targeting monetary policy framework in Nigeria. Several success factors were considered. These include the size of economic agents monitoring the inflation target, the credibility of the central bank, the degree of central bank independence, reduction in budget deficit, limited dollarization of the Nigerian economy, effective central bank communication, avoidance of fiscal dominance, financial development, greater financial inclusion, financial stability, and insecurity caused by farmer-herder clashes and terrorism. Many countries such as New Zealand, Canada, the U.S., the U.K., and many others have adopted inflation targeting. Nigeria's central bank adopted the inflation targeting monetary policy framework as its monetary policy framework for achieving price stability or low inflation. Nigeria is not the first country to adopt an inflation targeting monetary policy framework. Having adopted inflation targeting in Nigeria, the central bank of Nigeria should view inflation targeting as a policy framework rather than as a system of rules to increase its acceptance. There is a need to customise the inflation targeting approach to fit Nigeria's peculiarities provided that its core features remain which is the announcement by the central bank that in the future it intends to hold inflation at a specified level. Furthermore, special consideration must be given to the risks associated with an inflation targeting monetary policy framework. The significant risks are that inflation targeting may not be operational because of the time that it takes for monetary policy actions to affect inflation. Another risk relates to the difficulty in forecasting inflation. There is also the potential for exchange rate volatility because adopting inflation targeting in open economies, such as Nigeria, can lead to changes in interest rates, and the changes in interest rates can affect capital flows and exchange rates. Notwithstanding the challenges, the implication of adopting an inflation targeting monetary policy framework in Nigeria is that the central bank has a full understanding of the benefits and risks of an inflation targeting monetary policy framework. Finally, it is too early to determine whether the inflation targeting monetary policy framework will succeed or fail. The best we can do is to give it a chance to work. But I think it will work because the advantages outweigh the risks. Future studies can examine whether an explicit inflation targeting framework might be more appropriate in Nigeria. Future studies can also examine whether an implicit inflation targeting regime or an average inflation targeting regime would be more appropriate to adopt in Nigeria.

REFERENCES

Ahmed, R., Aizenman, J., & Jinjarak, Y. (2021). Inflation and exchange rate targeting challenges under fiscal dominance. *Journal of Macroeconomics*, *67*, 103281. doi:10.1016/j.jmacro.2020.103281

Ball, L. M., & Sheridan, N. (2004). Does inflation targeting matter? In *The inflation-targeting debate* (pp. 249–282). University of Chicago Press. doi:10.7208/chicago/9780226044736.003.0007

Baranowski, P., Doryń, W., Łyziak, T., & Stanisławska, E. (2021). Words and deeds in managing expectations: Empirical evidence from an inflation targeting economy. *Economic Modelling*, *95*, 49–67. doi:10.1016/j.econmod.2020.12.003

Barro, R. J. (1996). Inflation and growth. *Review - Federal Reserve Bank of St. Louis*, *78*(3), 153–169. doi:10.20955/r.78.153-169

Bernanke, B. (2003). A perspective on inflation targeting: Why it seems to work. *Business Economics (Cleveland, Ohio)*, *38*(3), 7–16.

Bernanke, B. S., & Mishkin, F. S. (1997). Inflation targeting: A new framework for monetary policy? *The Journal of Economic Perspectives*, *11*(2), 97–116. doi:10.1257/jep.11.2.97

Bianchi, F., Melosi, L., & Rottner, M. (2021). Hitting the elusive inflation target. *Journal of Monetary Economics, 124*, 107–122. doi:10.1016/j.jmoneco.2021.10.003

Blanchard, O. J. (2004). *Fiscal dominance and inflation targeting: lessons from Brazil.* Academic Press.

Bundick, B., & Smith, A. L. (2018). Does communicating a numerical inflation target anchor inflation expectations? Evidence & bond market implications. *Federal Reserve Bank of Kansas City, Research Working Paper*, (18-01).

D'Acunto, F., Hoang, D., & Weber, M. (2022). Managing households' expectations with unconventional policies. *Review of Financial Studies, 35*(4), 1597–1642. doi:10.1093/rfs/hhab083

De Mendonça, H. F., & Souza, G. J. D. G. (2012). Is inflation targeting a good remedy to control inflation? *Journal of Development Economics, 98*(2), 178–191. doi:10.1016/j.jdeveco.2011.06.011

Dua, P. (2023). Monetary policy framework in India. In *Macroeconometric Methods: Applications to the Indian Economy* (pp. 39–72). Springer Nature Singapore. doi:10.1007/978-981-19-7592-9_3

Fratzscher, M., Grosse-Steffen, C., & Rieth, M. (2020). Inflation targeting as a shock absorber. *Journal of International Economics, 123*, 103308. doi:10.1016/j.jinteco.2020.103308

Kumar, S., Afrouzi, H., Coibion, O., & Gorodnichenko, Y. (2015). *Inflation targeting does not anchor inflation expectations: Evidence from firms in New Zealand (No. w21814)*. National Bureau of Economic Research.

Lin, S., & Ye, H. (2009). Does inflation targeting make a difference in developing countries? *Journal of Development Economics, 89*(1), 118–123. doi:10.1016/j.jdeveco.2008.04.006

Mishkin, F. S. (2000). Inflation targeting for emerging-market countries. *The American Economic Review, 90*(2), 105–109. doi:10.1257/aer.90.2.105

Mishkin, F. S., & Posen, A. (1998). *Inflation targeting: lessons from four countries.* Academic Press.

Mishkin, F. S., & Schmidt-Hebbel, K. (2001). *One decade of inflation targeting in the world: what do we know and what do we need to know?* Academic Press.

Mishkin, F. S., & Schmidt-Hebbel, K. (2007). *Does inflation targeting make a difference?* Academic Press.

Neuenkirch, M., & Tillmann, P. (2014). Inflation targeting, credibility, and non-linear Taylor rules. *Journal of International Money and Finance, 41*, 30–45. doi:10.1016/j.jimonfin.2013.10.006

Svensson, L. (1997). Monetary policy and inflation targeting. *Research summary, NBER Reporter*, 5-8.

Svensson, L. E. (1999). Inflation targeting as a monetary policy rule. *Journal of Monetary Economics, 43*(3), 607–654. doi:10.1016/S0304-3932(99)00007-0

Svensson, L. E. (2010). Inflation targeting. In *Handbook of monetary economics* (Vol. 3, pp. 1237–1302). Elsevier.

Taylor, J. B. (2019). Inflation targeting in high inflation emerging economies: Lessons about rules and instruments. *Journal of Applied Econometrics, 22*(1), 103–116.

Thornton, J. (2016). Inflation targeting in developing countries revisited. *Finance Research Letters*, *16*, 145–153. doi:10.1016/j.frl.2015.10.024

Vega, M., & Winkelried, D. (2005). Inflation targeting and inflation behavior: A successful story? *International Journal of Central Banking*, *1*(3), 153–175.

Woodford, M. (2012). Inflation targeting and financial stability (No. w17967). National Bureau of Economic Research.

APPENDIX

Discussion Questions

1. Identify three types of inflation targeting frameworks.
2. Identify the three success factors for inflation targeting in Nigeria

Assessment Questions

1. Which of the following is NOT a type of inflation targeting.
   (a) Explicit inflation targeting
   (b) Average implicit inflation targeting
   (c) Implicit inflation targeting
   (d) Reverse inflation targeting
2. What type of communication is useful for inflation targeting.
   (a) Commercial banking communication
   (b) Central bank communication
   (c) Fiscal policy communication
   (d) Presidential communication
3. Which of the following countries adopted inflation targeting in 2023.
   (a) Canada
   (b) Germany
   (c) United States
   (d) Nigeria
4. Which country in the world was the first to adopt inflation targeting
   (a) New Zealand
   (b) Finland
   (c) India
   (d) France

Answers to Discussion Questions

1. Explicit inflation targeting, implicit inflation targeting, average implicit inflation targeting
2. Credibility of the central bank; The degree of central bank independence; Reduction in budget deficits; Limited dollarization of the Nigerian economy; Effective central bank communication; Financial development; Avoidance of fiscal dominance

Assessment Questions

1. D.
2. B.
3. D.
4. A.

Chapter 11
The Interplay Among Financial Inclusion, Corruption, and Phishing

Bilal Ahmed Chishty
Institute of Business Management, Karachi, Pakistan

Rafia Ayub
Institute of Business Management, Karachi, Pakistan

Syed Sarmad Hasan
Institute of Business Management, Karachi, Pakistan

ABSTRACT

The intersection of financial inclusion, corruption, and phishing poses issues in our digital age. This chapter explores their complex relationship, with a focus on technology and sustainability. Financial inclusion, which is essential for fair access, suffers from playing the dual roles of corrupting agent and enabler, undermining goals and destroying confidence. Fintech solutions, which leverage technology as a disruptor and enabler, improve accessibility while also posing cybersecurity and phishing dangers. In order to create resilient financial ecosystems, the chapter emphasizes the need for holistic approaches that strike a balance between the requirement for inclusivity and protections against corruption and cyberthreats. Scholars, policymakers, and practitioners must collaborate and consider a range of view-points in order to effectively handle difficulties and capitalize on possibilities in our globalized society.

INTRODUCTION

The advent of digital finance era opened up new opportunities for the financial service providers to include people who earlier had no access to such services. In the year 2000 just 276 people per 1000 adults had a bank account which rose to 692 people in 2023 (The World Bank, 2024). However, the blessing came

DOI: 10.4018/979-8-3693-1475-3.ch011

with new challenges such as inadequate regulatory mechanisms, poor technical and financial literacy among users and technical glitches resulting in vulnerability to corruption and fraud.

The chapter describes in detail the significance of financial inclusion and explores the intricate web it makes with corruption and phishing. Inevitable advancement in technology in enabling and disrupting the financial inclusion is also discussed along with different theories which current literature has used to explain the relationships in this web are presented. In the end, the chapter identifies gaps observed and potential areas of research.

Financial Inclusion

There are numerous ways to define "Financial Inclusion", most commonly it is understood as the extent to which underprivileged and impoverished individuals have access to financial services. Nevertheless, there exists substantial difference in the usage and subtleties of the term. Asian Development Bank has defined it as "easy access for households and enterprises to fairly priced financial services" (ADB, 2015). According to the World Bank, financial inclusion is the ratio of persons and firms that use financial services (The World Bank, 2014). Financial inclusion is also defined in the context of promoting financial well-being along with economic and social inclusion. According to this concept, financial inclusion is the process of encouraging and promoting access to an extensive range of regulated financial products and services that is affordable, timely, and sufficient to all segments of society. It can be accomplished by implementing innovative and existing approaches of financial awareness and education specifically tailored to meet the needs of society (Atkinson & Messy, 2012). Lastly, the idea of "unbanking," or financial exclusion, is also implied by the term "financial inclusion." Financial exclusion means not using any financial product or service, such as microfinancing facilities or saving or deposit products, offered by the financial institutions. However, it is also critical to clearly distinguish between individuals who are unable to or do not wish to use financial services from those who want to but due to various reasons such as, lack of resources, are unable to do so because of limited resources, difficult access, expensiveness, complex, doubtful, obliviousness, or identity requirements.

Why Is Financial Inclusion Important?

There are several justifications for increased financial inclusion. Innovations that improve the effectiveness of impoverished households' cash management and enable them to smooth consumption can have a substantial influence on welfare because these households are frequently extremely cash-constrained. Using cash for transactions comes with its hazards. For instance, most transactions require carrying substantial sums of cash, sometimes over great distances, which raises security concerns.

By increasing the earnings of the lowest income quintile, more financial inclusion can also aid in the reduction of income inequality (Beck et al., 2007). Additionally, diversifying bank assets and thereby lowering their risk as well as strengthening the steady funding base of bank deposits, may promote financial stability (Morgan & Pontines, 2014). It has also been identified that a larger number of bank branches lowers poverty and increases income and employment (Bruhn & Love, 2013). Governments may decide to switch from inefficient subsidies to cash transfer programmes in response to increased financial accessibility, and the increased openness of electronic funds transfers may also aid in the fight against corruption.

Figure 1. High income economies

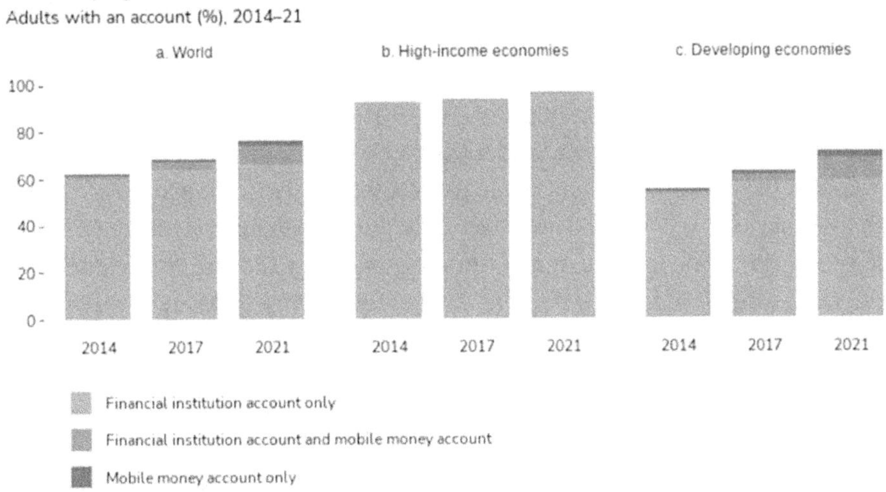

Source: Global Findex Database 2021

Financial Inclusion and Corruption

The extent of financial inclusion has increased dramatically in both industrialized and developing nations in recent years (Duvendack & Mader, 2020). It has been noted that as time goes on, the impoverished and disadvantaged groups in society have more access to and use official financial services and goods (Hussain et al., 2021). Adults from middle-class and low-class nations routinely use various forms of formal financial services in their daily lives, just like those from high-income nations. The current widespread use of digital payment systems by all demographic groups has significantly increased the volume of financial transactions. 76% of adults now have a bank or mobile account, up from just 51% in 2011, according to the report. Yet, until recently, a large proportion of adults in developing nations remained without an account. But inclusion is now increasing rapidly, says the World Bank. Account ownership in developing economies grew from 63% to 71% between 2017 and 2021, driven by services like mobile money. The mobile money service M-Pesa, for example, has lifted 2% of the Kenyan population out of poverty, according to research from Georgetown University and MIT (World Economic Forum).

In particular, the COVID-19 pandemic's quick adoption of digital technologies has drawn attention from throughout the world (Barik & Lenka, 2023; Sornaganesh et al., 2020). Over 80 million adults in India and more than 100 million in China made a digital merchant payment for the first time after the onset of the pandemic. In developing economies, 40% of adults made transactions using a card, phone, or the internet for the first time, Findex found. Fintech adoption was 50% higher in countries with strict lockdown measures than those without such restrictions, according to the World Economic Forum. Therefore, given the increasing prevalence of digital technology and the easy access to financial services for large segments of the population, it is important to analyse how the broad availability of basic finance has affected national corruption patterns.

Broadly, corruption is the abuse of governmental authority for personal gain. Therefore, the other socioeconomic results are significantly impacted by the dishonest actions of public authority. For as long as there has been economic development, reducing poverty, inequality (Gupta et al., 2002), and unemployment (Adjor & Kebalo, 2018), controlling corruption has been essential. Given the importance of preventing corruption and the widespread availability of financial services for all demographic groups, a global discussion among academics and decision-makers has arisen regarding the need to present convincing evidence of the connection between financial inclusion and corruption.

It has been argued that with the evolution of digital finance and financial inclusion – for example internet, mobile banking, linking biometric identity to bank account etc. the corrupt practices can be stopped. Conversely, the counterargument made for this is that the combination of high level financial inclusion with low financial literacy and awareness rate, improper supervison and in absence of proper regulations can result in exponential increment in corruption by allowing individuals to be able to receive large debts and using it in various illicit and unlawful activities like money laundering, gambling or insider trading (Ajide, 2020).

Evidence and Theories on Financial Inclusion and Corruption

The "sand the wheels" hypothesis does a good job of describing the theoretical underpinnings of corruption and money. This theory states that corruption can have a negative impact on the growth of the financial sector (Cooray & Schneider, 2018). The hypothesis also stresses how insufficient supervisory rules, extensive regulation, insider trading, and a lack of transparency can result in increased corruption practices are caused by, that ultimately hinders the growth of the financial sector (Barik & Lenka, 2023; Park, 2012; Song et al., 2021). That is to say, in the context of financial inclusion, it can be claimed that financial resources are diverted, which results in an inefficient allocation of money, due to the issues of moral hazard and adverse selection (Barth et al., 2004; Cooray and Schneider, 2018). Misallocation of financial resources increases the amount of non-performing assets, which further undermines the nation's financial stability because of the system's lack of transparency and oversight.

According to "Rationale Choice Theory" corruption arises due to asymmetric information that exists in between principal and agent. The government or the public authority is the agent who has monopolistic power that enables it to hide the information and use for the individuals' benefits only (Dupuy & Neset, 2018; Windhoff-Héritier, 2019). In the concept of financial inclusion all banking information is held by agents or bank employees who deceive customers. Most commonly in emerging and underdeveloped nations, due to lack of financial literacy, people have unequal knowledge about banking services (Hussain et al., 2021). It provides the bank agent with an opportunity to conceal important information by deceiving clients and accepting payment in exchange for supplying financial services.

A substantial number of past studies on corruption have concentrated on the relationship between corruption and economic expansion. Research on the connection between corruption and growth has produced contradictory findings. According to some researchers, corruption hinders growth in the economy (Graeff & Mehlkop, 2003; Mauro & Driscoll, 1997; Thach et al., 2017). While others argued that corruption promotes economic growth (Chakravorty, 2019; Méon & Weill, 2010). Many researches focused on identifying the relationship between financial crisis and financial corruption; for instance, Kane, (1993) in his study has asserted that various forms of financial corruption were prevalent in Japanese banking system which contributed to the financial crisis of 1990s. Similarly, McFarlane, (2001) has stated that Japanese banking crisis can be linked with fraud, syatmeic corruption as well as the loan sharking by certain bankers. Cooray and Schneider, (2018) and Song et al., (2021) also supported the view that corruption hinders the economic growth and has a negative impact on development of financial industry. Ahlin and Pang, (2008) in their study found that on one hand underdevelopment of financial system fosters corruption in the system, while on the other hand, financial system strengthens due to corruption. Because corruption increased the need for liquidity in the system.

The research by Barik and Lenka, (2023) and Thornton, (2010) also presented contrasting results. According to there findings, the progression in financial sector has resulted in reduced corruption. Sharma and Paramati, (2021) conducted an empirical analysis of 140 countries to study the impact of growth of financial industry on level of corruption. Their results showed that, not only in low- and lower-middle-income nations but also in upper-middle- and high-income countries, the growth of the financial sector significantly inhibits the spread of corruption in all sample countries. These results were supported by Setor et al., (2021) as well. In their study of 111 developing countries, it was found that corruption was reduced with the increase in digital financial transactions in the country.

Two distinct areas of research look at the connection between money and corruption. The first collection of studies provides empirical evidence that corruption stifles financial development (Cooray & Schneider, 2018; Yaroson, 2013). This indicates a negative correlation between higher levels of financial sector development and corruption. Due to adverse selection and moral hazard, affects the financial system's efficient allocation of resources, creating disincentives among financial players and undermining the process of financial decision-making (Cooray & Schneider, 2018).

Three important aspects have been identified in the literature related to financial inclusion: financial service utilisation, availability, and penetration (Ajide, 2020). The penetration dimension indicators are the number of adults with deposit, loan, and mobile money accounts per adult; the availability dimension indications are the number of branches of financial institutions, the accessibility of ATMs, and the availability of mobile money outlets. The payment system, remittances and transfers, deposits and credits from financial institutions are among the utilisation dimension indicators. Each of these aspects is helpful in the battle against corruption. For example, Sidibe, (2015) claims that access to official financial facilities has been facilitated by mobile banking. Additionally, he stated that the access rate is roughly 49.5%. Because this innovation is transparent and traceable, the African government has been able to reduce corruption in the agriculture sector. Because of its degree of payment system accountability, the mobile banking system M-Paisa plays a vital and important role in Afghanistan's efforts to reduce corruption (Lianju & Luyan, 2011). According to a study by Krolikowski et al., (2013), mobile payments reduce corrupt practices in Tanzania.

In banking industry, financial inclusion provides a tool for reporting suspicious banking activities, therefore has an impact on controlling corruption (Ajide, 2020). This financial development can help in monitoring and identifying potential criminal activities such as money laundering that is a component of economic corruption. One of the most key function of banking industry is the financial intermediation. It is closely governed and safeguarded by using the program "Know your Customers (KYC)" that is to maintain the depositors records. This suggests that there is a heavy responsibility on banks to document and disclose unlawful and other criminal activities. To do this, though, banks require a large number of experienced employees as well as robust technology assistance.

Citizens are urged to create bank accounts since financial inclusion involves the construction of biometric IDs. These accounts can be linked to support technologies that can follow individual citizens' records for any illicit deals in the economy. The direct distribution of funds in the form of salaries and unemployment benefits rather than through dishonest middlemen is another way that financial inclusion minimizes corruption. Jungo et al. (2021) found that financial literacy and financial inclusion reduce credit risk, increase bank profits, and help underpin financial stability. Similarly, Klapper and Lusardi (2020) confirm that financial literacy increases bank resilience and improves stability. Through an increase in economic formality, financial inclusion also lowers corruption. Increased financial inclusion has reduced the prevalence of tax avoidance and evasion, and tax collection is now relatively simple (Ozili, 2018, 2021). Digital technology makes tracking and traceability easier. One example is the infrastructure for e-government. This indicates that inclusive finance can be used to a greater extent in countries to combat terrorism and corruption.

Phishing Hazards

Advances in financial inclusion are not only beneficial; they also have drawbacks. Even highly advanced technology is not without flaws. Many intelligent but flawed individuals wish to take advantage of the system. . Since the creation of the ATM, there have been reports of skimming occurrences, which predate the emergence of phishing, which was more often known as "ATM duplication." Phishing—the theft of a victim's data—rose as a result of the large number of transactions made without the use of an ATM (Andriani & Hermantoro, 2023).

The name "phishing" comes from the comparison of "fishing" for victims' login credentials and passwords over the internet. The term "phone phreaking," which was a popular method of attacking phone systems in the 1970s, is where the word "ph" originates. When a group of hackers utilized the Internet to steal America Online (AOL) accounts in 1996 by pulling unsuspecting AOL users into divulging their passwords, they coined the term "phishing."

Phishing, sometimes known as automated identity theft, is a scam that deceives millions of people and steals substantial sums of money by taking advantage of human nature and the Internet.(Gupta, Agrawal, Tewari, & Jain, 2017). Social engineering is the foundation for the crime of phishing (Chen & Chen, 2019). A phishing assault is described by Sameen et al. (2020) as a deceptive attempt to pose as a reliable source in order to gain private information. It is noteworthy to mention that, according to IBM (2022), phishing emerged as the most expensive attack avenue in 2022, with an average cost of $4.91 million USD per data breach.

Phishing can be carried out utilizing a variety of platforms and routes; the three most popular platforms are voice, short messaging services, and the Internet (Chiew, Yong, & Tan, 2018). Different routes of attack are used in each of these media to carry out the attack. Using the Internet as an example, common phishing routes include websites, social networks, email, eFax, instant messaging, and Wi-Fi. Smishing and Vishing are the pertinent routes of attack for phone and short messaging systems, respectively. Phishing attempts have been recorded in many industries, including financial institutions like banks, educational institutions, political organizations, and the healthcare industry, according to recent trends (IBM, 2022).

In 2018, the World Economic Forum noted that fraud and financial crime was a trillion-dollar industry, reporting that private companies spent approximately $8.2 billion on anti–money laundering (AML) controls alone in 2017. The crimes themselves, detected and undetected, have become more numerous and costly than ever. In a widely cited estimate, for every dollar of fraud institutions lose nearly three dollars, once associated costs are added to the fraud loss itself. Risks for banks arise from diverse factors, including vulnerabilities to fraud and financial crime inherent in automation and digitization, massive growth in transaction volumes, and the greater integration of financial systems within countries and internationally. Cybercrime and malicious hacking have also intensified. In the domain of financial crime, meanwhile, regulators continually revise rules, increasingly to account for illegal trafficking and money laundering, and governments have ratcheted up the use of economic sanctions, targeting countries,

Figure 2. Total observed phishing attacks by year

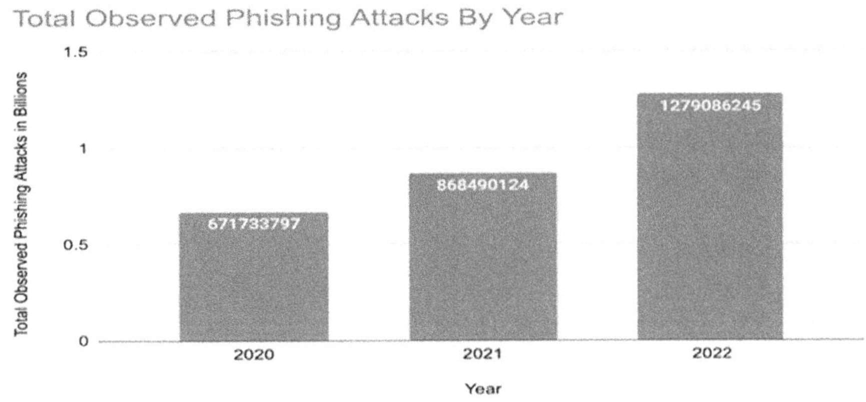

public and private entities, and even individuals. Institutions are finding that their existing approaches to fighting such crimes cannot satisfactorily handle the many threats and burdens.

Phishing attacks continue to be one of the most significant threats facing organizations today. As businesses increasingly rely on digital communication channels, cybercriminals exploit vulnerabilities in email, SMS, and voice communications to launch sophisticated phishing attacks. With the COVID-19 pandemic leading to a surge in remote work over the past several years, the risk of phishing attacks has only increased.

The latest phishing report from Zscaler ThreatLabz reveals that phishing attacks are still on the rise, detailing a 47.2% increase in phishing attacks in 2022 compared to the previous year.

Motivation Behind the Phishing

The reason for the phishing attack is that its perpetrators always capitalize on people's tendency to overlook important warning signs. The primary reason phishing assaults have been so successful is that people in society are largely unaware of them. Phishers attempt to identify related loopholes to launch effective attacks whenever an expert discovers a way to stop these assaults. Though money gain is the primary motivation for phishing, there are additional motives that drive individuals who engage in this criminal activity. The following are the reasons underlying these activities:

Theft of login credentials: Phishers employ spoof emails that look like emails warning users to change their passwords and include a hyperlink to steal login credentials from users of online services like eBay, Amazon, and Gmail.

Theft of banking credentials: Passwords for online accounts, credit card information (number, expiration and issue dates, cardholder name, CCV number), and information from a number of other well-known financial institutions, including PayPal, as well as other personally identifiable bank data.

Acquisition of Personal Data: Direct marketing organizations are always looking for personal data, such as phone numbers and addresses, because it is very marketable.

Theft of trade secrets and private papers: Phishers utilize spear phishing tactics to target certain companies in an effort to obtain proprietary information that may either be used directly or sold to interested parties.

Fame and notoriety: This is a very intriguing psychological side of phishing, where information is phished primarily for peer recognition and renown rather than financial gain.

Take advantage of security flaws: Individuals who are inquisitive about a system's resilience may attempt to create programs that hack systems in order to conduct phishing attacks against others or to resell the compromised systems to other phishers.

Attack Propagation: Phishers can exploit a single compromised host as an internal "jump point" within the system by combining spear phishing with the installation of bot agents.

Challenges and Risks

The literature has provided a number of ways to prevent phishing assaults. On the other hand, we can state that there is no "bulletproof" method to stop phishing. Phishing attacks are growing more frequent and a prevalent way for cybercriminals to conduct fraud. Every time researchers discover a way to manage this issue, phishers modify their attack plan by taking advantage of flaws in the available fix. Therefore, we might conclude that there is aggressive competition between researchers and phishers. Malicious coding or social engineering could be used to perpetrate phishing scams (Gupta et al., 2017). To trick consumers and steal money phishers employ spoof emails or phony websites in social engineering schemes. Those with low digital literacy have the potential to compromise the financial assets and sensitive information of those. Even with strong security measures in place, financial institutions are nevertheless vulnerable to data breaches that reveal user information to phishing scams.

Strategies for Mitigating Phishing Risks

- **Cybersecurity Measures:** with the use of encryption and multi-factor authentication, financial institutions should continuously invest in cybersecurity infrastructure to detect and prevent phishing attempts.
- **Education and Awareness:** Users can become more resilient against cyberthreats by learning to identify and steer clear of phishing attempts. Therefore, enhancing awareness initiatives and encouraging digital literacy can mitigate the risk.
- **Regulatory Frameworks:** Regulatory support is always crucial to control such risks. In order to foster a safe digital financial environment, governments and regulatory organizations are essential in setting and enforcing cybersecurity requirements for financial institutions.

FUTURE RESEARCH AND CONTRIBUTION

As the financial industry is rapidly evolving research needs should also be constantly reviewed. One area where the gap is glaring and also expanding instantly is public policy and regulation (Zanardi, Castellani & Zarazua, 2022). Bank for International Settlements, (2021) identifies barriers to reaching excluded populations as the one prickly constant in this industry. Although Artificial Intelligence is not a new phenomenon recent geometric progression in AI is certainly going to have a big impact on financial industry necessitating a need to keep in at the top of future research agenda (Boeddu, Chien & Istuk, 2021). Future researchers should also look into identifying financial services need of the millennials by including the youth in surveys. Furthermore, exploring the emerging phenomena of social impact investing, gender Bonds, green Bonds, vis-à-vis financial inclusion have immense potential in creating value for different stakeholders.

The chapter contributes to the understanding of the importance of financial inclusion whilst identifying the challenges of increased corruption and potential frauds. The identification of vulnerabilities created in the financial ecosystem due to difference in the pace of progress in technology and regulations can help the policy makers to plan and formulate rues accordingly which would help in reducing corruption and fraud. Similarly, the financial institutions and even the consumers can benefit by developing an understanding provided by this chapter to guard against potential phishing. Finally, the future researchers can benefit from this chapter in determining their priorities.

CONCLUSION

Financial inclusion has shown a huge potential in promoting the economic growth and empowering individuals, but its impact on corruption is still a debatable issue. It is unanimously agreed that growth financial inclusion results in transparency and reduced reliance of conventional system that is more prone to corruption. Also, it gives individual financial tools that can help in reporting suspicious activities. However, it is accompanied with phishing and other financial scams. It is therefore important to maintain a balance between both opportunities and threats offered by financial inclusion. It is of utmost importance that cybersecurity measures are strengthen, financial literacy is promoted and robust financial regulatory framework is formed to create a more inclusive and equitable society.

REFERENCES

ADB. (2015). *Asian development outlook: financing asia's future growth.* Asian Development Bank. https://www.adb.org/sites/default/files/pu blication/154508/ado-2015.pdf

Adjor, D. M., & Kebalo, L. (2018). Does corruption matter for unemployment in SADC countries? *Review of Economic and Business Studies, 11*(2), 65–92. doi:10.1515/rebs-2018-0074

Ahlin, C., & Pang, J. (2008). Are financial development and corruption control substitutes in promoting growth? *Journal of Development Economics, 86*(2), 414–433. doi:10.1016/j.jdeveco.2007.07.002

Ajide, F. M. (2020). Can financial inclusion reduce the presence of corruption? Evidence from selected countries in Africa. *International Journal of Social Economics, 47*(11), 1345–1362. doi:10.1108/IJSE-03-2020-0145

Andriani, & Hermantoro, B. (2023). Optimizing Financial Technology Literacy in Minimizing Phishing Threats (Case Study of Indonesian Sharia Bank Customers). *Proceeding of International Conference on Islamic Philantrophy, 1*, 38–52.

Atkinson, A., & Messy, F.-A. (2012). *Measuring Financial Literacy: Results of the OECD/International Network on Financial Education (INFE) pilot study (15).* doi:10.1787/20797117

Bank for International Settlements. (2021). *The fintech gender gap.* Author.

Barik, R., & Lenka, S. K. (2023). Does financial inclusion control corruption in upper-middle and lower-middle income countries? *Asia-Pacific Journal of Regional Science*, *7*(1), 69–92. doi:10.1007/s41685-022-00269-0

Beck, T., Demirgüç-Kunt, A., & Levine, R. (2007). Finance, inequality and the poor. *Journal of Economic Growth*, *12*(1), 27–49. doi:10.1007/s10887-007-9010-6

Boeddu, G., Chien, J., & Istuk, I. (2021). *Consumer Risks of Fintech.* https://figi.itu.int/wp-content/uploads/2021/06/Consumer-Risks-of-Fintech.pdf

Bruhn, M., & Love, I. (2013). The economic impact of expanding access to finance in Mexico. *Banking the World: Empirical Foundations of Financial Inclusion*, 137–156.

Chakravorty, N. N. (2019). How Does Corruption Affect Economic Growth? An Econometric Analysis. *Journal of Leadership, Accountability and Ethics*, *16*(4).

Chen, Y. H., & Chen, J. L. (2019). AI@NTIPHISH — Machine learning mechanisms for cyber-phishing attack. *IEICE Transactions on Information and Systems, E102D*(5), 878–887.

Chiew, K. L., Yong, K. S. C., & Tan, C. L. (2018). A survey of phishing attacks: Their types, vectors and technical approaches. *Expert Systems with Applications*, *106*, 1–20. doi:10.1016/j.eswa.2018.03.050

Cooray, A., & Schneider, F. (2018). Does corruption throw sand into or grease the wheels of financial sector development? *Public Choice*, *177*(1-2), 111–133. doi:10.1007/s11127-018-0592-7

Dupuy, K., & Neset, S. (2018). The cognitive psychology of corruption. *Micro-Level Explanations for Unethical Behavior*, *U4*, 2.

Duvendack, M., & Mader, P. (2020). Impact of financial inclusion in low-and middle-income countries: A systematic review of reviews. *Journal of Economic Surveys*, *34*(3), 594–629. doi:10.1111/joes.12367

Graeff, P., & Mehlkop, G. (2003). The impact of economic freedom on corruption: Different patterns for rich and poor countries. *European Journal of Political Economy*, *19*(3), 605–620. doi:10.1016/S0176-2680(03)00015-6

Gupta, B. B., Tewari, A., Jain, A. K., & Agrawal, D. P. (2017). Fighting against phishing attacks: State of the art and future challenges. *Neural Computing & Applications*, *28*(12), 3629–3654. doi:10.1007/s00521-016-2275-y

Gupta, S., Davoodi, H., & Alonso-Terme, R. (2002). Does corruption affect income inequality and poverty? *Economics of Governance*, *3*(1), 23–45. doi:10.1007/s101010100039

Hussain, M., Yahya, F., & Waqas, M. (2021). Does strong governance stimulate the effect of economic freedom and financial literacy on financial inclusion? a cross-country evidence. *Future Business Journal*, *7*(1), 1–10. doi:10.1186/s43093-021-00090-9

IBM. (2022). *Cost of a Data Breach Report 2022.* Available at: https://www.ibm.com/sg-en/security/data- breach

Jungo, J., Madaleno, M., & Botelho, A. (2021). Financial literacy and financial inclusion effects on sta bility and competitiveness indicators in the banking sector: Cross country evidence for Africa and the world. *Global Economy Journal, 21*(2), 1–30. doi:10.1142/S2194565921500093

Kane, E. J. (1993). What lessons should Japan learn from the US deposit-insurance mess? *Journal of the Japanese and International Economies*, *7*(4), 329–355. doi:10.1006/jjie.1993.1021

Khan, A., Mubarik, M. S., & Naghavi, N. (2023). What matters for financial inclusions? Evidence from emerging economy. *International Journal of Finance & Economics*, *28*(1), 821–838. doi:10.1002/ijfe.2451

Klapper, L., & Lusardi, A. (2020). *Financial literacy and financial resilience: evidence from around the world.* https://www.weforum.org/agenda/2022/07/global-digital-financial-inclusion-findex/ doi:10.1111/fima.12283

Krolikowski, A., Fu, X., & Hope, R. (2013). *Wireless Water: Improving Urban Water Provision Through Mobile Finance Innovations Opens in a new t. Smith School of Enterprise and the Environment.* https://www.oxfordtmcd.org/publication/improving-urban-water-governance-through-mobile-finance-innovations

Mauro, P., & Driscoll, D. D. (1997). *Why worry about corruption?* (Vol. 6). International Monetary Fund Washington.

McFarlane, J. (2001). Corruption and the financial sector: The strategic impact. *Journal of Financial Crime*, *9*(1), 8–21. doi:10.1108/eb026002

Méon, P.-G., & Weill, L. (2010). Is corruption an efficient grease? *World Development*, *38*(3), 244–259. doi:10.1016/j.worlddev.2009.06.004

MorganP.PontinesV. (2014). *Financial stability and financial inclusion* (Working Paper 488). ADBI Working Paper 488. https://doi.org/http://dx.doi.org/10.2139/ssrn.2464018

Ozili, P. K. (2018). Impact of digital finance on financial inclusion and stability. *Borsa Istanbul Review*, *18*(4), 329–340. doi:10.1016/j.bir.2017.12.003

Ozili, P. K. (2021). Financial inclusion research around the world: A review. *The Forum for Social Economics*, *50*(4), 457–479. doi:10.1080/07360932.2020.1715238

Park, J. (2012). Corruption, soundness of the banking sector, and economic growth: A cross- country study. *Journal of International Money and Finance*, *31*(5), 907–929. doi:10.1016/j.jimonfin.2011.07.007

Setor, T. K., Senyo, P. K., & Addo, A. (2021). Do digital payment transactions reduce corruption? Evidence from developing countries. *Telematics and Informatics*, *60*, 101577. doi:10.1016/j.tele.2021.101577

Sharma, C., & Paramati, S. R. (2021). Does financial development reduce the level of corruption? Evidence from a global sample of 140 countries. *International Journal of Finance & Economics*, *26*(4), 5093–5109. doi:10.1002/ijfe.2056

Sidibe, T. (2015). *Mobile banking and mobile money: a highly instrument against corruption*. Academic Press.

Song, C.-Q., Chang, C.-P., & Gong, Q. (2021). Economic growth, corruption, and financial development: Global evidence. *Economic Modelling, 94*, 822–830. doi:10.1016/j.econmod.2020.02.022

Sornaganesh, V., Ganesh, S., Sathish, M. T., & Chellamma, A. V. (2020). Impact of COVID-19 outbreak in digital payments. *Int J Innov Res Multidiscip Field, 6*(8), 159–164.

Thach, N. N., Duong, M. B., & Oanh, T. T. K. (2017). Effects of corruption on economic growth-empirical study of Asia countries. *Imperial Journal of Interdisciplinary Research, 7*, 791–804.

The World Bank. (2014). *Global Financial Development Report 2014: Financial inclusion* (Vol. 2). World Bank Publications. doi:10.1596/978-0-8213-9985-9

The World Bank. (2024), *Global Financial Development Report*. https://databank.worldbank.org/source/global-financial- development/Series/GFDD.AI.01#

Thornton, J. (2010). *Does Financial Development Reduce Corruption?* Bangor Business School Research Paper, 09/003.

Yaroson, E. (2013). Corruption and financial sector performance: Empirical evidence from Nigeria. *Int. J. Multidiscip. Thought, 3*(2), 507–519.

Zanardi, Castellani, & Niño-Zarazua. (2022). *European Microfinance Platform (e-MFP) 'From Research to Practice and Back Again' Action Group*. Academic Press.

APPENDIX

Assessment Material

MCQs

1. How is financial inclusion most commonly defined?
   a) access to luxury goods
   b) access to educational services
   c) access to financial services for underprivileged individuals
   d) access to healthcare services
2. Which organization defined financial inclusion as "easy access for households and enterprises to fairly priced financial services"?
   a) world bank
   b) imf
   c) asian development bank
   d) federal reserve
3. What is the primary motivation behind phishing attacks?
   a) to gain fame and notoriety
   b) to improve cybersecurity measures
   c) to protect personal data
   d) to steal sensitive information for financial gain
4. What is the primary reason for the success of phishing attacks?
   a) lack of internet connectivity
   b) advanced cybersecurity measures
   c) people's tendency to overlook warning signs
   d) lack of phishing attempts
5. Which theory describes corruption as arising due to asymmetric information between principal and agent?
   a) rational choice theory
   b) behavioral economics
   c) game theory
   d) chaos theory
6. What is the impact of financial inclusion on corruption, according to setor et al. (2021)?
   a) financial inclusion increases corruption
   b) financial inclusion has no effect on corruption
   c) financial inclusion reduces corruption
   d) financial inclusion exacerbates corruption
7. How do phishing attacks typically exploit vulnerabilities?
   a) through physical break-ins
   b) through advanced encryption methods
   c) through social engineering and deception
   d) through legal means

8. What is the primary reason behind the rise in phishing attacks during the covid-19 pandemic?
   a) increased cybersecurity awareness
   b) decreased reliance on digital communication
   c) surge in remote work and digital communication channels
   d) decreased internet usage
9. What is the primary tool used by banks to monitor and identify potential criminal activities such as money laundering?
   a) cash transactions
   b) financial inclusion programs
   c) know your customer (kyc) procedures
   d) internal audits
10. How does financial inclusion contribute to reducing corruption in the banking industry?
   a) by increasing cash transactions
   b) by reducing the need for cybersecurity measures
   c) by promoting transparency and accountability
   d) by limiting access to financial services

Answers to MCQs

1. c) Access to financial services for underprivileged individuals
2. c) Asian Development Bank
3. d) To steal sensitive information for financial gain
4. c) People's tendency to overlook warning signs
5. a) Rational choice theory
6. c) Financial inclusion reduces corruption
7. c) Through social engineering and deception
8. c) Surge in remote work and digital communication channels
9. c) Know Your Customer (KYC) procedures
10. c) By promoting transparency and accountability

Assignment Topics

1. **The Impact of Financial Inclusion on Economic Development**: Explore how increased access to financial services for underprivileged individuals affects overall economic development, including factors such as GDP growth, income inequality, and poverty alleviation. Future research could delve into specific case studies or conduct longitudinal analyses to assess long-term impacts.
2. **Cybersecurity Challenges in Financial Inclusion**: Investigate the cybersecurity risks associated with expanding financial inclusion, focusing on phishing attacks, identity theft, and data breaches. Future research could explore emerging threats, develop strategies for mitigating risks, or evaluate the effectiveness of cybersecurity measures in the context of financial inclusion initiatives.
3. **Innovations in Digital Financial Services**: Analyze the role of digital technologies in advancing financial inclusion, such as mobile banking, digital payments, and biometric authentication. Future research could assess the adoption and impact of these innovations among different demographic

groups, explore barriers to access, or investigate best practices for implementing digital financial services.

4. **Policy Implications of Financial Inclusion**: Examine the policy frameworks and regulatory environments that facilitate or hinder efforts to promote financial inclusion. Future research could evaluate the effectiveness of government interventions, analyze the role of public-private partnerships, or propose policy recommendations for enhancing financial inclusion outcomes.
5. **Financial Inclusion and Social Impact**: Explore the broader social implications of financial inclusion beyond economic outcomes, including its effects on education, healthcare, gender equality, and empowerment. Future research could investigate the intersectionality of financial inclusion with other social determinants, identify marginalized groups who may be left behind, or assess the potential for financial inclusion to address social inequalities

Short-Answer Questions

1. Define financial inclusion and provide two key elements that contribute to its definition.
2. What are the primary motivations behind phishing attacks, and how do cybercriminals exploit vulnerabilities to carry out these attacks?
3. Explain the concept of "unbanking" and its implications for financial inclusion. Provide examples of barriers that contribute to financial exclusion.
4. Identify two theories discussed in the text that explain the relationship between financial inclusion and corruption. Briefly explain each theory and its implications.
5. Describe one innovation in digital financial services that has contributed to advancing financial inclusion. Discuss its impact on access to financial services for underprivileged individuals.

Long-Answer Questions

1. Discuss the importance of financial inclusion in promoting economic development. Explain how increased access to financial services can contribute to poverty alleviation, income equality, and overall economic growth. Provide examples from both developed and developing countries to support your arguments.
2. Analyze the cybersecurity challenges associated with expanding financial inclusion, focusing on phishing attacks and data breaches. Discuss the potential risks for individuals and financial institutions, as well as strategies for mitigating these risks. Provide recommendations for enhancing cybersecurity measures in the context of financial inclusion initiatives.
3. Evaluate the effectiveness of government policies and regulatory frameworks in promoting financial inclusion. Discuss key policy interventions, such as financial literacy programs, microfinance initiatives, and mobile banking regulations. Assess their impact on increasing access to financial services for marginalized populations and address any limitations or challenges they may face.
4. Explore the social impact of financial inclusion beyond economic outcomes. Discuss how increased access to financial services can empower individuals, improve healthcare and education outcomes, and promote gender equality. Provide examples of successful interventions or programs that have addressed social inequalities through financial inclusion initiatives.

5. Critically assess the role of digital technologies in advancing financial inclusion. Discuss the benefits and challenges associated with digital financial services, such as mobile banking, digital payments, and biometric authentication. Analyze how these technologies have expanded access to financial services for underprivileged individuals and identify areas for future innovation and improvement.

Chapter 12
Unleashing the Potential of Industry 4.0 for Financial Inclusion

Saeed Mousa
Rennes School of Business, France

ABSTRACT

In an era marked by rapid technological advancement, the dynamic interplay between financial inclusion and Industry 4.0 holds immense potential to reshape economies and empower marginalized communities. This chapter explores how Industry 4.0 technologies, such as mobile devices, the internet, blockchain, and AI, can bridge the gap in financial inclusion. Industry 4.0, with its digital integration and automation across industries, goes beyond efficiency gains to address financial exclusion. Case studies, including M-Pesa's mobile money platform and Singapore's Project Ubin, illustrate how these technologies empower individuals, transform cross-border payments, and redefine currency in an increasingly digital world. This chapter provides an in-depth examination of the benefits, challenges, and ethical considerations associated with Industry 4.0's role in promoting financial inclusion. It argues that Industry 4.0 is not just a technological evolution but a catalyst for societal transformation, fostering a more inclusive and equitable global economy.

I. INTRODUCTION

The intersection of Financial Inclusion and Industry 4.0 has enormous potential to transform economies and give voice to underserved groups in an era of fast technological innovation[1]. The purpose of this chapter is to delve into the complex interplay between Industry 4.0 technology and financial inclusion initiatives, highlighting their potential to propel revolutionary shifts and promote economic parity on a global scale.

The term "Industry 4.0" has been used to describe the widespread use of digital technologies, data-driven insights, and automated processes across multiple industries. Mpofu and Mhlanga (2022) argued that Industry 4.0 has the potential to impact every aspect of human daily lives including how people

DOI: 10.4018/979-8-3693-1475-3.ch012

work and interact. Its significance goes beyond efficiency improvements; it presents a rare chance to tackle the pervasive problem of financial exclusion.

Access to formal financial services is a fundamental human right, and financial inclusion has been a priority for governments, international organisations, and enterprises for quite some time. The prevalence of unbanked and underbanked communities, however, highlights the need for creative solutions outside of conventional banking. There's a great chance for economic progress and growth due to Industry 4.0[2].

Mobile devices, the internet, the blockchain, and artificial intelligence are the backbone of Industry 4.0 and can help break down financial boundaries[3]. In this chapter, we look at how the mobile money platform M-Pesa has revolutionised financial services in Kenya and throughout Sub-Saharan Africa, illuminating how new technologies contribute to financial inclusion. It delves into how mobile financial solutions alter the course of economies and give people more control over their money.

The chapter also delves into Singapore's groundbreaking Project Ubin to investigate Central Bank Digital Currency (CBDCs) via blockchain technology. It offers a thorough evaluation of CBDCs' potential to transform international transactions, broaden access to financial services, and redefine money in our increasingly digital society. This chapter provides a balanced look at the benefits and drawbacks of Industry 4.0's efforts to expand access to banking services. It addresses ethical concerns, data protection issues, and disruptions to established banking structures, while highlighting efficiency improvements, increased financial service accessibility, and democratised economic potential.

In conclusion, this chapter argues that we should look at Industry 4.0 not just in terms of technology advancement, but as a driver of fundamental societal transformation. It foresees a future where financial inclusion and Industry 4.0 merge to change capitalism in a way that benefits a wider range of people. The purpose of this chapter is to encourage thought, provide insight for policy development, and highlight the importance of capitalising on Industry 4.0's disruptive potential to expand access to financial services for all. To that end, we employ in-depth case studies, analyses, and observations. The following section is a literature review that will highlight gaps in literature and major contribution of this chapter to the research.

II. LITERATURE REVIEW

It is important to define the key concepts that are Industry 4.0 and financial inclusion. The advent of Industry 4.0 signifies a period characterised by remarkable progress in technology, where the physical and digital domains converge to establish a novel framework for industrial development Ustundag &Cervikcan, 2018). Fundamentally, Industry 4.0 embodies the confluence of advanced technologies that are positioned to fundamentally transform various sectors, economies, and communities. Rosin et al (2020) further posit that Industry 4.0 refers to the trends in data exchange and automation between manufacturing technologies. The key enabling technologies for Industry 4.0 such as big data analytics, the Internet of Things (IoT), Artificial Intelligence (AI), augmented and virtual reality, and blockchain technology amongst others (Gialanza, Aiello, & Marannano, 2021). Industry 4.0 has greatly contributed to the digitisation of financial services as well as how people interact with technology.

Mhlanga (2020) refers to financial inclusion as the total number of adults having access to financial services and or banking. The research further revealed that 3.5 billion people in the world have no access to financial services that is they are unbanked or underbanked[4]. Industry 4.0 has triggered an increase in digital payments resulting in an increase in access to financial services especially among the underserved populations (Alameda, 2020; Xiong, Jenny &Wang, 2023). This has resulted in digital financial inclusion which enables the financially excluded persons to access formal financial services in ways that meet their needs. The reliance on digital technologies has stirred economic growth, especially in African countries with more than 40% of the population in the sub-Saharan having mobile money accounts (Munoz et al., 2022; Kijikasiwat &Chancharat, 2022). To benefit from the digitization processes, governments introduce a tax on Digital Financial Services (DFS) through charges on transactions and transfers (Mpofu and Mhlanga, 2022).

The continued increase in taxation on these financial services has contributed to negative externalities including considerable market distortions. Research shows that high taxation on the DFS has had noticeable impacts on financial inclusion as many low-income earners resort to cash transactions or end up being unbanked (Demirguc-Kun et al., 2018; Santoro et al., 2022). It implies that financial exclusion is one of the fundamental negative externalities that can emerge as a result of the implementation of DFS taxes. Therefore, as Industry 4.0 continues to influence economic growth across the different sectors, its effects on financial inclusion are largely contested (Mpofu &Mhlanga, 2022).

Several studies on Industry 4.0 and financial inclusion agree that digitisation has greatly contributed to improved access to financial services resulting in financial inclusion (Killeen &Chan, 2018; Ozili, 2020; Ahmed et al., 2021; Rauniyar, Rauniyar &Sah, 2021; Santoro et al., 2022). In the study conducted by Siwela and Njaya (2021), industry 4.0 has made considerable inroads in Africa leading to increased uptake of DFS. However, the researchers acknowledge the marginalisation leading to financial inclusion among the African population, especially women and girls. It means that despite the positive role of Industry 4.0 in enhancing economic growth and access to financial services, the negative externalities can have a counterproductive impact on financial inclusion. In an attempt to address these gaps, this chapter contributes by outlining the role of Industry 4.0 on financial inclusion and how negative externalities create challenges. To provide an insight into Industry 4.0 as a technological advancement that transforms society in terms of access to financial services, this chapter focuses on Industry 4.0 especially its key enabling technologies which are Artificial Intelligence (AI), Blockchain technology, Internet of Things (IoT), Robotics, and Data Analytics as explained in the subsequent sectors.

II. Industry 4.0: A Primer

This part functions as a complete introduction, providing readers with a thorough understanding of Industry 4.0 and explaining how its major technologies have the potential to significantly reshape the finance industry with a focus on financial exclusion.

A. Artificial Intelligence (AI): Pioneering Intelligence Amplification

AI, a dynamic field that combines human inventiveness with machine skills, is at the heart of Industry 4.0's disruptive power. The value of AI stems from its potential to improve upon and replace human intelligence, hence opening up new avenues of opportunity in the financial sector and beyond[5].

The success of AI depends on a comprehensive framework that includes cutting-edge algorithms, Machine Learning (ML), and Deep Learning (DL). With these components, AI systems may mimic human cognition by learning to automatically extract insights from data, recognise patterns, and make educated decisions[6]. Predictive analytics, a vital resource for developing Industry 4.0 financial inclusion plans, is supported by this fusion.

AI has the potential to dramatically improve the efficiency and reach of financial inclusion initiatives. Institutions can take advantage of AI's analytical capabilities to perform credit risk assessments at a previously unattainable level of precision. AI creates complex risk profiles by analysing data like repayment behaviour and socioeconomic characteristics, allowing access to credit for people who wouldn't have otherwise qualified[7]. This foresightful evaluation improves the lives of traditionally disenfranchised groups while easing the financial strain on service providers.

In addition, AI makes it easier for businesses in the financial sector to implement individualised strategies. By poring over mountains of data, AI systems can identify subtle monetary trends that inform product and service personalization. Financial inclusion programmes can reach more people by using AI to recommend personalised savings plans, investment portfolios, and insurance policies.

Chatbots and virtual assistants driven by AI are prime examples of the interaction between AI and accessibility. These electronic companions eliminate communication barriers by providing intuitive interfaces that may be controlled via speech or text. The growing use of AI in interactions reduces barriers to participation for people with low literacy or technical proficiency, closing a major accessibility gap.

However, there are some obstacles to overcome when introducing AI into the financial sector. Problems with algorithmic bias and data privacy also need serious thought. Impartial decision-making processes and strong data protection within AI technology are essential for financial inclusion projects to maintain confidence and ethical norms[8],[9].

One cannot overstate the importance of AI's effects on financial inclusion in Industry 4.0. Predictive capacities, individualised solutions, and increased accessibility are just a few ways in which these technological breakthroughs have the potential to increase economic autonomy. Ethical and legal considerations must be taken into account if AI is to realise its full potential. According to Paul (2019) when used carefully, AI has the potential to expand access to resources for underserved populations and help build a more equitable global economy for all through financial inclusion.

B. Blockchain: Redefining Trust and Transparency

Blockchain technology has emerged as a powerful force in the ever-changing world of Industry 4.0, altering trust and transparency in the realm of financial inclusion[10]. Notably, the potential of blockchain to transform and revolutionize the financial industry cannot be overlooked. Research shows that blockchain technology has enabled a secure and cost-effective extension of financial services to the underbanked population given its decentralized nature (Lawal, Ahmed, &Abdulkadir, 2023). Blockchain is often associated with digital currency, but it has far-reaching implications for the financial sector beyond that.

Blockchain is essentially a distributed ledger that records transactions across a network of computers in a permanent and unalterable format[11]. There is an immutable chain of data that results from the cryptographic linking of each transaction, or "block," to the one before it. By removing the need for centralised entities like banks or government agencies, this architecture greatly lowers transactional friction and costs.

The effect that blockchain technology has on broadening access to financial services is significant. Its immutability makes transactions reliable and less prone to fraud, which is especially helpful for those who lack access to conventional financial institutions. Peer-to-peer lending is made possible by blockchain technology since it eliminates the need for intermediary banks in the loan transaction.

In addition, blockchain's ability to improve the efficiency of international transactions can promote financial inclusion on a worldwide scale[12]. Transferring money internationally through the traditional banking system can be a costly and time-consuming operation. Individuals' ability to send and receive international payments quickly and efficiently can be revolutionised by blockchain technology due to its borderless and speedy transaction capabilities.

Blockchain's ability to provide digital identities is extremely consequential in the field of financial inclusion (Grosse, Guerpinar, &Henke, 2021). People from underprivileged backgrounds often face obstacles when trying to access financial services due to a lack of required paperwork. The distributed ledger technology known as blockchain provides a safe way to keep and share sensitive data like names, addresses, and financial histories, opening up opportunities for people to gain access to banking services like loans, insurance, and savings accounts.

However, there are still problems that need to be worked out before blockchain can fully live up to its potential. To guarantee consumer safety, data privacy, and security, regulatory frameworks and standards must be developed. De Filippi and Hassan (2018) argued that blockchain is one of the technologies that opens new avenues for regulation among private actors to ensure values are integrated into the technological artefacts.

Therefore, blockchain is a foundational component of Industry 4.0 with far-reaching potential for promoting financial inclusion[13]. It promotes honesty and eliminates middlemen, making it easier for underprivileged people to use banking services. Successfully harnessing blockchain while resolving its inherent obstacles is necessary to successfully reshape financial ecosystems, which will ultimately pave the way for a more inclusive and fair global economy[14].

C. Internet of Things (IoT): Connecting the Unconnected

The Internet of Things (IoT) is a key enabler within the context of Industry 4.0, facilitating connections between previously unrelated things and people, places, and things. The IoT transcends the constraints of traditional communication to include a wide variety of smart devices, from simple household items to sophisticated industrial systems[15]. In this analysis, we focus on the revolutionary potential of IoT in the context of financial inclusion, showing how its seamless connectivity may fill in the gaps in financial services and make them available in the most inaccessible parts of the world.

Connecting inanimate objects to a network so that they may share information and gain insight is the foundation of the Internet of Things[16]. A complicated ecology powered by sensors, actuators, and communication protocols is responsible for the revolutionary effect on the availability of financial services. By facilitating instantaneous data transmission, IoT paves the way for individuals, especially those living in rural or underserved areas, to enter the formal financial system.

IoT's potential impact on financial inclusion is substantial. IoT liberates hitherto unrealized economic potential in underdeveloped regions. Devices with Internet of Things functionality can act as digital bank branches, remotely keeping tabs on all monetary dealings and exchanges. IoT-enabled point-of-sale terminals and mobile devices, for instance, can quickly process transactions and update account balances, providing easy access to monetary data notwithstanding the user's physical location.

One of the most promising aspects of IoT for expanding access to financial services is its ability to simplify the process of making and processing financial transactions. IoT-enabled devices provide for safe and convenient financial transactions in areas with a dearth of traditional banking infrastructure[17]. People can send money to one another, make bill payments, and conduct other financial transactions without visiting a bank branch, all thanks to mobile money networks. This helps more people gain access to financial services and gives voice to those who have been silenced by traditional financial structures.

One way in which the Internet of Things can promote inclusion is by helping to improve risk assessment and increase access to financing. Financial institutions may now collect real-time data from IoT devices, allowing them to gain a more in-depth understanding of customers' financial behaviours (Mishra & Sant, 2021; Harsheela, Happonen &Julius, 2023). These data-driven inferences allow for accurate credit profiling, which in turn enables banks to give credit to people who might not have qualified for it before. To facilitate economic mobility and provide people more agency in their pursuit of financial independence, accurate risk assessment methodologies must be developed.

However, the Internet of Things' potential as a driver of financial inclusion needs serious thought. Privacy and data security are of the utmost importance, especially when dealing with money. Trust in financial services offered by the Internet of Things relies on strict adherence to security protocols and data protection rules. In addition, closing the digital divide and eliminating disparities in access to the Internet of Things technology are critical steps towards realising the sector's potential for universal financial inclusion (Anam &Nisar, 2023).

Finally, the Internet of Things is a powerful resource inside Industry 4.0, with the potential to significantly alter the landscape of financial inclusion. Its importance in ensuring that everyone has access to financial services is highlighted by the fact that technology can bring together previously isolated people, make transactions safer, and lead to more accurate risk assessments[18]. A more equitable global economic system can be fostered by addressing the issues posed by the Internet of Things and maximising its potential to uplift underserved groups.

D. Robotics: Automating Efficiency and Accessibility

Robotics plays a crucial role in improving operational efficiency and accessibility in the context of Industry 4.0's integration into financial services. Automating routine processes using robots can speed up operations and cut down on human error. In the long run, this boosts customer satisfaction for the underserved groups served by microfinance organisations. Additionally, automated advisory services enabled by robotics provide customised financial advice, enabling people to make educated decisions and interact with conventional financial institutions[19].

Robotics is a foundational component of Industry 4.0 that will drastically alter the financial services industry (Dirican, 2015). Automation, and Robotic Processing Automation (RPA) in particular, makes short work of mundane jobs, which leads to streamlined operations, faster processing, and fewer mistakes. These efficiencies allow us to save money while providing better service to our customers.

As a key component of the robotics revolution ushering in Industry 4.0, RPA ensures the timely and accurate execution of rule-based processes[20]. There are many upsides to using it in financial institutions, such as lower costs and happier customers. These savings are very important for microfinance firms since they help people who otherwise wouldn't have access to credit or banking services. Loan processing, account management, and transaction reconciliation are just a few examples of how automation can improve service delivery for customers who place a premium on timeliness and accuracy.

Automated advice services are another game-changing application of robots in the realm of financial inclusion. With the use of robot-driven technologies, banks can provide customers with tailored financial advice. Machine learning algorithms analyse a person's financial habits and goals to provide specific recommendations for budgeting and saving. Financially savvy individuals from underserved communities who lack access to traditional financial advisors can benefit greatly from automated advising services (Vermeulen, Pyka, &, Omerovic, 2017).

In addition, by filling in information gaps, people are better able to make decisions about their finances, including their investments, savings, and risk management (Hasheela, Haopponen, & Julius, 2023). Financial literacy is strengthened, and more people are encouraged to participate in mainstream financial institutions, as a result of this democratisation of financial information. By increasing people's familiarity with financial concepts and possibilities, robotics can help promote financial inclusion and help eliminate inequities.

Addressing ethical and regulatory frameworks is becoming increasingly important as the financial uses of robotics grow[21]. Transparency, fairness, and the absence of algorithmic bias in automated processes are essential for maintaining confidence and defending consumers' interests. Recognising the possibility of job loss to automation also highlights the significance of reskilling and upskilling programmes to prepare the workforce with digital-era skills.

In conclusion, robotics plays a crucial role in Industry 4.0, creating transformative impacts through increased efficiency and accessibility, and so aiding the development of initiatives to broaden access to financial services. When used in the microfinance industry, RPA speeds up operational procedures and improves customer experiences. At the same time, automated advising services make it easier for people to get the individualised financial advice they need, which has positive effects on both financial literacy and interest. To ensure that all segments of society benefit from automation, financial institutions must strike a balance between rapid technological advancement and ethical concerns as they continue to employ robotics.

E. Data Analytics: Insights for Inclusion

To get useful insights from large datasets, data analytics play a pivotal role in Industry 4.0. Organisations can gain insight into the financial habits and requirements of the underserved, which paves the way for more tailored financial services. Risk assessment and fraud detection are two further areas where data-driven insights improve the stability and longevity of financial organisations.

The advent of Industry 4.0 has pushed data analytics to the forefront as a game-changing tool for all sectors. When data analytics and technology are combined, it becomes possible to provide financial services in a way that is targeted, inclusive, and individual.

The goal of data analytics is to get actionable insights from large datasets. The data collecting and analysis features of Industry 4.0 shed light on the spending habits and requirements of the economically excluded. Based on these findings, banks can better serve customers by creating products that are tailored to their needs[22].

When data analytics and technology are combined, insights into the preferences, spending habits, and transaction dynamics of traditionally underserved groups can be gained, all to the benefit of financial inclusion[23]. This in-depth knowledge allows for the development of financially viable solutions that remove conventional obstacles to participation.

Financial institutions can provide individualised loan products, repayment plans, and savings strategies thanks to data analytics. As a result, access to data-driven financial opportunities is expanded. Ravi and Kamarudin (2017) posit that the impacts of Industry 4.0 especially data analytics have triggered digital evolution among customers as well as financial providers

By highlighting suspicious behaviour patterns, data analytics also improves the safety and reliability of financial institutions[24]. Assessing risks ahead of time strengthens the financial system and protects institutions and their clients[25]. Yet, cautious thought is required when merging data analytics and financial inclusion. Keeping sensitive financial information private and secure is of the utmost importance. Maintaining public confidence requires stringent security measures and compliance with data privacy legislation. To combat the possibility of algorithmic bias and the perpetuation of current imbalances, it is essential to continuously evaluate and alter algorithms used in data analytics.

Industry 4.0's use of data analytics has far-reaching consequences for broadening access to financial services. Institutions can follow its lead in providing personalised financial services for underserved communities, which benefits such communities by enhancing risk analysis and security. This has a profound impact on economies and communities, fostering equality and fostering a sense of agency (Holanders, 2020).

As seen, unprecedented financial inclusion can be achieved through the confluence of Industry 4.0 with AI, blockchain, the IoT, robots, and data analytics. In what follows, we'll examine how these industry 4.0 technological innovations may be put into practice to help marginalised populations thrive and expand access to financial services.

III. ADVANCING FINANCIAL INCLUSION THROUGH INDUSTRY 4.0

In an epoch characterised by swift technological progress and significant changes in multiple industries, the notion of financial inclusion has assumed a novel perspective, propelled by the advent of Industry 4.0[26]. The current era is distinguished by the amalgamation of digital technology, data analytics, automation, and connectivity, which has significantly transformed our way of life, professional endeavours, and engagement with financial institutions (Mpofu &Mhlanga, 2022). With the imminent transformation in the field of finance, there is an increasingly urgent need to advocate for the advancement of financial inclusion within the context of Industry 4.0.

Financial inclusion, as a fundamental concept, promotes the idea of ensuring that individuals and businesses have equal and inexpensive opportunities to receive financial services, irrespective of their socioeconomic background or geographical position[27]. Throughout human history, a considerable segment of the populace has experienced exclusion from the established financial sector, so constraining their capacity to engage in saving, investing, and attaining economic well-being. Nevertheless, the emergence of Industry 4.0 can challenge the existing state of affairs by presenting novel approaches to tackle persistent inadequacies in financial accessibility and services.

This section provides an analysis of the confluence between Industry 4.0 and financial inclusion, focusing on the transformative technologies and policies that are redefining the landscape of the financial sector. This report examines how artificial intelligence, blockchain technology, fintech firms, and the IoT are reshaping the financial industry. Moreover, this study explores the ramifications of these alterations on individuals, enterprises, governmental bodies, and the worldwide economy.

The endeavour to achieve improved financial inclusion within the framework of Industry 4.0 poses a multitude of obstacles and intricacies. Although these technical advancements provide significant potential, they also give rise to problems about privacy, security, and the fair distribution of access. This analysis delves into the complexities involved and investigates the requisite strategies to effectively leverage the advantages of Industry 4.0 inclusively, so assuring equitable participation for all individuals and groups.

In the course of this inquiry, we aim to demonstrate that Industry 4.0 transcends being solely a technological paradigm change, instead functioning as a catalyst for economic empowerment, poverty reduction, and societal advancement. The advent of Industry 4.0 presents a promising avenue for attaining financial inclusion, as it redefines our understanding of currency and utilises it as a constructive force for empowering individuals and communities worldwide. In this section, we highlight the impacts of four industry 4.0 technologies including blockchain, smart banking and IoT, AI-powered Credit Scoring, and digital identity to discuss their contribution to financial inclusion.

A. Digital Identity and Biometrics: Empowering Financial Inclusion Through Secure and Tamper-Proof Identities

Identity verification is of utmost importance in the contemporary period dominated by digital advancements, as it facilitates the provision of various services, with a special emphasis on the financial industry. Nevertheless, conventional approaches to identity verification are plagued by inefficiencies, vulnerabilities in terms of security, and practices that lead to exclusion. As the complexities of attaining financial inclusion are confronted, the amalgamation of biometric authentication and blockchain technology emerges as a potentially auspicious avenue to surmount these barriers and augment the accessibility of financial services for marginalised populations.

Biometrics comprises a range of modalities, including fingerprint scanning, iris identification, and facial recognition, which collectively offer a unique and exceptionally dependable method for authenticating an individual's identity. The integration of blockchain technology with digital identity identification results in a formidable architecture characterised by enhanced security and transparency. In contrast to centralised databases that are susceptible to security breaches and unauthorised modifications, blockchain technology employs a decentralised and immutable ledger for the storage of identity data[28]. The use of this measure guarantees the safeguarding of personal data, by restricting access solely to authorised entities and effectively deterring any unauthorised alterations.

An intriguing facet of this groundbreaking approach lies in its capacity to facilitate the democratisation of financial services. Individuals who are marginalised and do not possess conventional means of identity, such as birth certificates or government-issued documents, can face substantial obstacles when attempting to obtain banking and credit services. Biometric-based digital identification systems provide the capability to mitigate this disparity. The establishment of personal identity can be facilitated by the utilisation of biometric scans, which are then cryptographically connected to a blockchain. This procedure generates dependable and immutable documentation of individuals' identities, which financial institutions may rely upon.

This technological innovation provides an avenue for persons who lack access to conventional banking services to participate in the financial domain. This technology empowers individuals to commence the procedure of establishing bank accounts, obtaining credit, and participating in financial transactions with an unparalleled degree of security and convenience, surpassing prior anticipations. The notion of inclusion carries substantial ramifications for the mitigation of poverty, as it enables the empowerment of individuals and communities to engage in saving, investing, and attaining economic stability.

Nevertheless, it is imperative to recognise and confront the obstacles linked to the implementation of this innovative methodology. The effective management of privacy problems necessitates a methodical strategy, wherein individuals maintain authority over their biometric data and possess a complete comprehension of its utilisation. Furthermore, it is imperative to guarantee the accessibility of biometric technologies in geographically remote or socioeconomically deprived areas.

In essence, the integration of biometric authentication and blockchain technology signifies the advent of a novel era characterised by robust and unalterable digital identities. The integration of technology provides a significant opportunity for persons who are marginalised inside the financial system, as it enables them to gain access to banking and credit services[29]. In the pursuit of this transformational strategy, it is imperative to adopt a diligent approach towards privacy and equity to effectively harness the complete potential of financial inclusion.

B. AI-Powered Credit Scoring: Expanding Financial Inclusion Through Innovative Data Analysis

Within the conventional domain of credit evaluation, the fundamental metrics for ascertaining an individual's eligibility for credit have historically revolved around their financial backgrounds and credit ratings. Nevertheless, the traditional method frequently disregards significant portions of society, particularly individuals who do not own an extensive credit record. Welcome to the era of credit scoring powered by AI, where sophisticated algorithms leverage unconventional data sources, such as mobile phone usage and social media behaviour, to transform the assessment of creditworthiness. This innovative solution possesses the capacity to facilitate access to financial services for individuals who were previously excluded from traditional credit systems, thereby reducing the existing disparity[30].

The rapid advancement of data and computer capacity has enabled AI algorithms to efficiently analyse extensive datasets with exceptional speed and accuracy. This capacity empowers individuals to analyse non-traditional sources of information, such as the utilisation of mobile phones and participation in social media platforms by individuals. These behaviours offer distinctive perspectives into an individual's financial tendencies, accountability, and steadfastness.

Financial organisations can develop more comprehensive and complex credit profiles by utilising AI[31]. For instance, the examination of mobile phone usage patterns can provide insights into the regularity of bill payments and the prudent utilisation of communication services. Likewise, the use of social media can expose an individual's social connections, associations, and even their inclination towards fiscal accountability, as inferred from the information they interact with or disseminate.

The adoption of non-traditional data-driven credit evaluation has the potential to significantly impact financial inclusion[32]. The assessment of creditworthiness for individuals who have been marginalised by traditional credit systems, either owing to an absence of credit history or other socioeconomic circumstances, has improved in terms of accuracy. This provides access to crucial financial services like as loans and credit cards that were previously unattainable.

Nevertheless, this novel methodology is not without its obstacles. It is imperative to thoroughly address issues about privacy concerns, ethical considerations, and any biases inherent in AI systems. It is of utmost importance to prioritise the establishment of mechanisms that empower individuals to exercise control over the data utilised in their credit evaluations, while simultaneously promoting transparency and fairness in the algorithms employed.

In summary, the utilisation of artificial intelligence in credit scoring signifies a fundamental transformation inside the realm of finance. Through the utilisation of non-traditional data sources, these sophisticated algorithms have the potential to promote enhanced financial inclusiveness, thereby granting possibilities to individuals who were previously marginalised by the conventional lending system. In the process of traversing this revolutionary landscape, it is imperative to establish a harmonious equilibrium between innovation and ethical considerations. This entails guaranteeing that the advantages derived from credit scoring facilitated by artificial intelligence are utilised fairly and conscientiously.

C. Smart Banking and IoT: Bridging Geographical Gaps for Financial Inclusion

In the contemporary era of digitalization, the availability of financial services has been closely associated with the accessibility to various chances, enhanced security, and overall economic advancement. Nevertheless, in numerous rural and underserved regions, the presence of conventional banking infrastructure remains limited, resulting in financial isolation within these communities. The convergence of Smart Banking and IoT is a significant development with the potential to revolutionise how financial transactions are carried out[33]. This partnership can transcend geographical limitations and promote enhanced financial inclusion.

IoT encompasses a wide-ranging network of networked devices, including smart appliances and sensors, which can gather and exchange data via the internet[34]. When incorporated into the domain of banking and finance, IoT devices emerge as potent instruments for the augmentation of financial services.

The introduction of smart automated teller machines (ATMs) stands as a very influential implementation of IoT inside the banking sector. Modern machines are fitted with a variety of sensors, cameras, and connection technologies that serve to enhance both security and accessibility. For example, organisations can verify the identity of users by employing biometric authentication methods, thereby mitigating the potential for fraudulent transactions[35]. In addition, the implementation of intelligent ATMs offers a viable solution in geographically isolated regions where the establishment of conventional banking facilities is not economically viable. This enables individuals to avail themselves of crucial financial services around the clock.

Mobile banking vans provide a creative solution driven by IoT. The mobile units are outfitted with financial infrastructure, which encompasses ATM capabilities and mobile point-of-sale systems. These vehicles possess the capability to traverse difficult terrains and access isolated villages that are devoid of conventional banking infrastructure. By engaging in this process, they enable immediate availability of financial services, granting individuals the ability to engage in transactions, save money, and obtain credit without the requirement of a physical banking institution.

Point-of-sale (POS) gadgets represent an additional aspect of this transformation. The deployment of IoT-enabled POS systems presents a convenient solution for small companies and shops, effectively expanding the reach of banking services to previously underserved regions. These gadgets let consumers engage in digital transactions, access banking services, and even apply for loans or insurance policies inside the confines of their local communities.

IoT has been instrumental in facilitating the expansion of financial services accessibility and improving the overall banking experience. Digital payment systems can facilitate instantaneous transactions, diminish the reliance on tangible currency, and improve the safety and ease of banking operations. These factors all contribute to the promotion of financial inclusion.

However, the effective use of IoT technology in the context of smart banking necessitates a meticulous examination of security and infrastructure obstacles, with the guarantee of affordability and accessibility for all individuals within the community. Ensuring the utmost importance is placed on privacy concerns and data security is vital.

In summary, the integration of Smart Banking and IoT devices is effectively dismantling geographical obstacles to foster financial inclusivity. Smart ATMs, mobile banking vans, and IoT-enabled POS systems are facilitating instantaneous access to financial services, hence revolutionising the livelihoods of those residing in geographically isolated and underprivileged regions. As society embraces the ongoing revolution of Smart Banking and the IoT, it becomes imperative to approach the associated problems with caution and prudence. This approach is necessary to ensure that the advantages of these technologies are utilised in a manner that is inclusive and responsible.

D. Blockchain for Financial Inclusion: Revolutionizing Cross-Border Finance and Empowering the Unbanked

Blockchain technology, sometimes linked with digital currencies such as Bitcoin, is not alone in disrupting the financial sector, but it also serves as a potent catalyst for promoting financial inclusion[36]. This innovative technology possesses the capacity to enhance the cost-effectiveness, transparency, and accessibility of cross-border transactions, remittances, and microfinance, particularly for individuals who lack access to traditional banking services or have limited access to them.

Fundamentally, blockchain is a distributed and unalterable ledger that documents transactions over a network of computational devices[37]. This architectural framework possesses numerous significant benefits in the context of promoting financial inclusion.

One of the advantages of utilising blockchain technology for cross-border transactions and remittances is the potential for cost reduction. Conventional methods sometimes involve substantial fees, which can have a disproportionate impact on persons with lower incomes. In contrast, blockchain-based systems have the potential to substantially decrease these expenses through the removal of intermediaries and the optimisation of the process.

Transparency and security are inherent features of blockchain technology, as each transaction is meticulously documented in a manner that is both transparent and resistant to tampering[38]. The implementation of transparency measures not only mitigates the potential for fraudulent activities but also fosters a sense of trust among individuals who have been marginalised from conventional financial institutions as a result of inadequate transparency.

A third advantage is the accessibility, where the Blockchain networks exhibit a high degree of accessibility, as they can be accessed through any internet-enabled device[39]. This characteristic enables the provision of financial services to anybody possessing a smartphone or computer, hence extending the reach of such services to even those residing in geographically isolated regions where conventional banking infrastructure is absent.

There are ongoing implementations of blockchain technology in real-world scenarios to promote financial inclusion. As an illustration,

- The utilisation of blockchain technology by companies such as Ripple is facilitating expedited and cost-effective cross-border payment transactions. Through establishing collaborations with financial institutions, they enable the prompt settlement of transactions in real time, leading to a substantial reduction in the duration and expenses connected with international money transfers.
- Remittances are being facilitated through the utilisation of blockchain-based platforms such as Stellar, catering to individuals who lack access to conventional banking systems. These platforms facilitate the transfer of funds between users at a relatively low cost, which is particularly significant for the substantial number of individuals who depend on financial support from their relatives employed in foreign countries.
- Microfinance: The utilisation of blockchain technology has the potential to facilitate peer-to-peer microfinance platforms, establishing direct connections between lenders and borrowers, hence obviating the necessity for conventional banking institutions. This enables small-scale entrepre-

neurs and people to avail themselves of finance and investment opportunities that were previously unattainable.

Nevertheless, despite its vast potential, the utilisation of blockchain technology for financial inclusion is not devoid of obstacles (Chinaka, 2016). To achieve widespread adoption and promote responsible usage, it is imperative to address various challenges, including scalability, energy consumption (particularly in the context of proof-of-work blockchains), and regulatory considerations.

In summary, blockchain technology is revolutionising the financial sector, offering individuals and communities a means to attain crucial financial services. Blockchain technology is facilitating greater financial inclusion and economic empowerment by enhancing the affordability, transparency, and security of cross-border transactions, thereby benefiting unbanked and underserved groups. The ongoing evolution of blockchain technology is expected to have a profound disruptive effect on financial inclusion. In as much as the major industry 4.0 have considerable disruptive impacts on financial inclusion, they are also associated with challenges. In the following section, we look at the challenges and risks of these technologies on financial inclusion and solutions through socioeconomic and regulatory approaches.

IV. OVERCOMING CHALLENGES AND RISKS

As we commence the endeavour of augmenting financial inclusion through advanced technologies such as blockchain, credit scoring powered by artificial intelligence, identification through biometrics, and smart banking driven by the IoT, it is imperative to recognise that advancements are accompanied by obstacles and potential hazards (Adegoke, 2018). Although disruptive technologies have the potential to address longstanding obstacles to financial access, they also offer novel intricacies that necessitate cautious manoeuvring.

This section explores the primary concerns that various players, such as governments, financial institutions, technology developers, and society, need to solve to guarantee the fair and just distribution of the advantages associated with financial inclusion. The aforementioned concerns span a range of topics including privacy, ethics, legislation, and the digital divide. By comprehending and actively resolving these concerns, we may pave the way towards a future in which financial inclusion transcends mere ambition and becomes an attainable actuality for every individual. By doing so, we may effectively harness the potential of Industry 4.0 to establish a society that is more equitable and affluent. This entails ensuring that financial services are readily available, affordable, and secure for everybody, irrespective of their socioeconomic background or geographical position.

A. Addressing the Digital Divide for Widespread Adoption of Industry 4.0 in Financial Inclusion

The concept of the digital divide refers to the disparity between individuals who possess access to digital technologies and those who lack such access. This discrepancy presents a notable obstacle to the widespread implementation of Industry 4.0 technologies in the context of financial inclusion. It is imperative to establish a connection between different groups to guarantee that the revolutionary capabilities of these technologies may be accessed by marginalised populations and underserved communities. This discourse will examine the issues of the digital divide and examine approaches and endeavours aimed at reducing this disparity.

Understanding the Digital Divide

The digital divide spans multiple dimensions, which include:

- Access: This concerns the physical availability of the internet and tech devices. Many remote and underserved areas lack reliable internet access and face limitations in obtaining essential tech tools like smartphones or computers.
- Affordability: Even if access is available, the cost of internet services and devices can be a significant barrier for individuals and households, especially in economically disadvantaged regions.
- Digital Literacy: It's not just about having access; individuals also need the skills and knowledge to navigate the digital world effectively, including safely using online financial services.
- Relevance: Providing services and content that meet users' needs is crucial for digital technologies. The digital divide persists because there's often a mismatch between what's offered and what a particular community requires.

Strategies to Bridge the Digital Divide

- The imperative of infrastructure development necessitates the allocation of resources by both governmental and commercial entities towards the expansion of broadband infrastructure in places that currently lack adequate coverage. Initiatives such as the implementation of public Wi-Fi hotspots, establishment of community internet centres, and deployment of satellite internet projects have the potential to enhance connection in geographically isolated areas.
- Enhancing Accessibility to Internet Services: To promote affordability, governmental entities may consider implementing subsidy initiatives, providing tax incentives for Internet Service Providers (ISPs), and enacting regulatory measures that foster competitive pricing. Zero-rating programmes have the potential to decrease the expenses associated with accessing vital information and services by exempting specific internet services from data costs.
- Device accessibility can be improved through the implementation of programmes that offer subsidised or low-cost gadgets to individuals and families with low income, thereby serving as a means to address the device gap. Recycled or refurbished electronics can be procured at a significantly reduced price compared to their brand-new counterparts.
- Digital literacy initiatives should be implemented to augment individuals' proficiency in using digital technologies. These initiatives might take the shape of educational programmes, both official and informal, aimed at improving individuals' digital literacy skills. These projects have the potential to educate users on the effective and secure utilisation of technology, encompassing the acquisition and administration of digital financial services.
- Community Engagement: Collaborative efforts among local community organisations, non-governmental organisations (NGOs), and governmental entities can be employed to evaluate the distinct requirements of particular communities and develop tailored responses. Community-driven approaches have demonstrated a higher level of effectiveness in tackling local obstacles to digital inclusion.

- Content localization is a crucial aspect of enhancing the accessibility and relevance of online content and services to various populations. By ensuring that digital material is available in local languages and culturally appropriate, the digital world may become more inclusive and meaningful for a wider range of individuals.
- Public-private partnerships (PPPs) involve the collaboration of governmental entities, private sector enterprises, and non-profit organisations. This collaborative approach enables the pooling of resources and knowledge, hence facilitating the expeditious advancement in efforts to bridge the digital divide.
- Regulatory Support: Governments can enact laws and regulations that facilitate digital inclusion, including the establishment of minimum broadband coverage requirements, the promotion of net neutrality principles, and the assurance of consumer protection in online financial transactions.

The digital divide poses a significant barrier to the complete utilisation of Industry 4.0 technology in achieving financial inclusion[40]. Nevertheless, by coordinated endeavours, inventive resolutions, and cooperative alliances, it is feasible to overcome this disparity and expand the advantages of modern technologies to every area of the world. By placing digital inclusion as a top priority, it is possible to establish a financial landscape that is characterised by fairness, ensuring that individuals from all geographical areas and socioeconomic backgrounds have equal access to the necessary tools and services required for the development of a more prosperous financial future.

B. Balancing Data Privacy and Security in the Era of Financial Inclusion

One of the primary considerations in the utilisation of Industry 4.0 technologies to enhance financial inclusion is the safeguarding of confidential financial data. Ensuring data privacy and security is of utmost importance, requiring careful attention to cultivate confidence among users, organisations, and governments[41]. This discourse aims to delve into the intricacies associated with data privacy and security within the context of financial inclusion. It will scrutinise regulatory frameworks and technical interventions designed to protect user data and uphold confidence.

The Importance of Data Privacy and Security

- Financial data sensitivity refers to the inherent sensitivity of financial information, which includes personal and frequently confidential aspects. The potential consequences of the loss or improper handling of this data encompass financial fraud, identity theft, and significant violations of privacy.
- Trust has a pivotal role in the establishment and acceptance of a financial system. To fully adopt digital financial services, individuals, organisations, and governments alike must possess a sense of assurance regarding the security and privacy of their financial transactions and data.
- Regulatory compliance has become a significant concern as governments and regulatory bodies across the globe are implementing rigorous data protection legislation, exemplified by the General Data Protection Regulation (GDPR) in Europe and the California Consumer Privacy Act (CCPA) in the United States. Failure to comply with regulations can lead to significant monetary fines and detrimental harm to the reputation of an entity.

Methods for Ensuring Data Privacy and Security

- The topic of discussion pertains to regulatory frameworks. Governments assume a crucial role in the preservation of data privacy and security. It is recommended that complete legislation and regulations be implemented to ensure data protection, encompassing measures such as data encryption, mandatory breach disclosure, and rigorous security protocols. Adherence to these legislations guarantees that organisations exercise responsible handling of sensitive data.
- Data encryption is a crucial measure that should be implemented to safeguard financial data against unauthorised access. It is imperative to utilise strong encryption techniques for data protection both during transmission and while stored. The implementation of encryption should encompass various aspects, including communication methods, databases, and storage systems.
- The implementation of Multi-Factor Authentication (MFA) enhances the security of financial transactions by incorporating an additional layer of protection. Access to user accounts often necessitates the provision of several forms of identification, including a password and a biometric scan.
- The decentralised and tamper-proof characteristics of blockchain technology can potentially boost the security of data. The use of this measure guarantees the maintenance of transparency in financial data, while simultaneously mitigating the risk of unauthorised modifications.
- It is recommended that organisations engage in routine security audits and penetration testing as a means of identifying potential vulnerabilities and flaws inside their systems. The prompt resolution of these concerns is crucial to protect the integrity of data security.
- User Education: Financial institutions and service providers must provide knowledge to consumers regarding optimal data privacy practices. This encompasses the establishment of robust passwords, identification of phishing endeavours, and comprehension of individuals' entitlements about data confidentiality.
- The use of a "privacy by design" strategy ensures that the integration of data protection is a fundamental aspect of the creation of financial services and technologies, rather than being considered as an afterthought.
- The principle of data minimization emphasises the need to collect and retain only the essential data that is required for the specific reason for which it was originally obtained. The act of minimising data mitigates the potential risks that arise from the storage of an excessive amount of personal information.

The preservation of data privacy and security is an essential and indisputable aspect of the endeavour to achieve financial inclusion through the utilisation of Industry 4.0 technology[42]. The protection of sensitive financial information is primarily achieved by the implementation of regulatory frameworks, encryption techniques, multi-factor authentication protocols, and user education initiatives. By taking proactive measures to address these concerns, stakeholders may lay the groundwork for establishing trust and confidence, so assuring the efficacy and security of financial inclusion initiatives, while safeguarding the privacy and security of both individuals and organisations.

C. Regulatory Considerations in the Era of Industry 4.0 and Financial Inclusion

Regulations have a significant impact on the financial services business within the dynamic context of Business 4.0. In addition to establishing guidelines for participation, these regulations serve to protect the welfare of consumers, uphold the integrity of the market, and foster equitable competition. In light of the evolving nature of the sector, regulators are confronted with the formidable undertaking of formulating flexible frameworks that effectively reconcile the promotion of innovation with the safeguarding of consumer interests[43]. One of the key imperatives in this digital revolution is ensuring financial inclusion, which refers to providing access to essential financial services to all individuals, especially those historically underserved or excluded from the formal financial system. However, as financial services increasingly digitize and evolve, regulatory frameworks play a crucial role in safeguarding consumer rights, promoting market stability, and fostering innovation while ensuring that the benefits of Industry 4.0 are accessible to all. Arner et al (2022) highlighted four main regulatory approaches including financial, telecommunication and internet, data protection, as well as antitrust and competition regulations that remain to be important in realizing financial inclusion.

Notably, various regulator approaches are applied to ensure regulations in the provision of financial services. In Industry 4.0, digital identities serve as the gateway to financial services, enabling individuals to access banking, payments, and other financial products remotely. Regulatory bodies establish robust frameworks to safeguard the privacy and security of personal data, ensuring that individuals have control over their information (Li, Maiti & Fei, 2023). Compliance with data protection laws such as GDPR (General Data Protection Regulation) or equivalent standards is imperative to build trust in digital financial services. Additionally, regulatory efforts should focus on promoting financial literacy programs and consumer protection measures to empower individuals to make informed financial decisions and safeguard against digital fraud and exploitation.

On the other hand, regulatory sandboxes provide a controlled environment for fintech startups and incumbents to test innovative products and services under the supervision of regulatory authorities. These sandboxes enable regulators to gain insights into emerging technologies and business models while ensuring that consumer protection and regulatory compliance remain paramount. Additionally, establishing innovation hubs fosters collaboration between regulators, industry stakeholders, and academia to promote responsible innovation and address regulatory challenges in real-time. In the context of financial inclusion, regulatory bodies should promote interoperable payment systems and standards to facilitate cross-border transactions and enhance financial access for underserved populations. Standardization of APIs (Application Programming Interfaces) and data formats enables interoperability between financial institutions and fintech firms, driving innovation and reducing barriers to entry in the digital financial ecosystem. Joia and Cordeiro (2021) further pointed out that by incorporating inclusive regulatory impact assessments into the policymaking process, regulators can identify potential barriers to access and design targeted interventions to promote inclusive growth and economic empowerment.

This discourse aims to explore the complex realm of regulatory considerations about financial services provided by Industry 4.0, encompassing perspectives at both national and international levels.

The Evolving Regulatory Landscape

- National Regulations: At the national level, various countries are currently confronting the challenge of developing regulatory frameworks to govern the integration of nascent technologies such as blockchain, AI, biometrics, and the IoT inside the financial domain. The aforementioned legislation encompasses a range of domains, including but not limited to data privacy, cybersecurity, digital identity, and electronic transactions. The shaping of these factors is frequently influenced by the distinct economic, political, and cultural conditions that exist inside each respective country.

- International Coordination: The role of international regulatory agencies and coalitions is increasingly significant as financial services continue to transcend national borders. The Financial Stability Board (FSB), the Basel Committee on Banking Supervision, and the International Organisation of Securities Commissions (IOSCO) are dedicated to the task of promoting regulatory harmonisation across nations to safeguard worldwide financial stability.

The Need for Adaptive Regulatory Frameworks

- Facilitating Innovation: To promote innovation within the financial services sector driven by Industry 4.0, regulators must establish conducive settings that facilitate the growth and development of novel technologies. This entails the provision of explicit directives that promote the conduct of experiments while upholding a dedication to safeguarding the interests and well-being of consumers.
- Consumer protection remains of utmost importance as new and innovative financial services continue to develop. Regulatory bodies must guarantee that the introduction of novel technology does not undermine the security and privacy of individuals' financial data. The presence of sufficient safeguards and effective enforcement mechanisms is of utmost importance.
- Adaptability: To effectively respond to the quickly changing technology landscape, regulatory frameworks must possess the ability to be flexible and adjustable. Excessive rigidity in regulations might impede the progress of innovation, whilst insufficient stringency may potentially subject customers to unwarranted hazards. The attribute of flexibility enables regulators to achieve a harmonious equilibrium between these two polarities.
- Interoperability is a crucial aspect of Industry 4.0 technologies, as it pertains to the capacity of disparate systems to effectively collaborate and function in unison. Regulatory bodies ought to actively advocate for the establishment of standards that guarantee the smooth interoperability of systems, all the while upholding the principles of security and data integrity.
- Data Governance: Data plays a crucial role in the context of Industry 4.0. Regulatory frameworks must set comprehensive norms about data governance, encompassing aspects such as data ownership, permission, and utilisation. Achieving an optimal equilibrium between innovation and privacy poses a nuanced challenge.
- Cross-Border Collaboration: In light of the international scope of financial services, regulators must engage in cross-border collaboration to effectively tackle regulatory arbitrage, which refers to the practice of corporations exploiting regulatory discrepancies across different jurisdictions. International collaboration plays a pivotal role in the harmonisation of standards and the promotion of uniformity.

Challenges and Considerations

- The rapid evolution of Industry 4.0 technology frequently surpasses the pace at which rules can be formulated and implemented. The existence of this gap can potentially give rise to ambiguity and expose both enterprises and customers to various dangers.
- Achieving a Harmonious Equilibrium between Innovation and Risk: The perpetual task of finding the optimal equilibrium between fostering innovation and managing potential hazards poses an ongoing challenge. Regulatory sandboxes and pilot programmes exemplify methodologies that facilitate regulated testing.
- Compliance costs can pose a significant financial burden for firms, as they are required to adhere to intricate and ever-changing regulatory frameworks. Regulators are obligated to take into account these expenses and strive for optimal efficiency in the execution of compliance procedures.

The regulatory considerations about financial services in the era of Industry 4.0 are characterised by a multitude of facets[44]. Developing adaptable and innovation-supportive frameworks that effectively protect the interests of consumers is a multifaceted undertaking. The promotion of responsible technology usage, the cultivation of competition, and the preservation of financial system integrity should be key objectives of effective regulatory measures. Achieving this equilibrium is of utmost importance in leveraging the complete capabilities of Industry 4.0 to advance financial inclusion, while simultaneously safeguarding the security and trust that serve as the foundation of the financial sector. To effectively address these difficulties, regulatory agencies, industry players, and governments must engage in collaborative efforts. To deepen the analysis, the following section will cover two main case studies at the global level that are Mpesa, as well as, Project Ubin which have demonstrated success in using industry 4.0 technologies in financial inclusion.

V. CASE STUDIES: TRANSFORMATIVE INITIATIVES

The emergence of Industry 4.0, which is distinguished by the integration of digital technology and automation, has a significant potential for addressing a crucial global issue: financial inclusion. The objective of this part is to investigate the use of Industry 4.0 technologies to advance financial inclusion. This will be accomplished through an examination of case studies that demonstrate the various outcomes, both advantageous and disadvantageous, resulting from these endeavours. Through an exploration of transformational endeavours like as M-Pesa and Project Ubin, this analysis aims to elucidate the capacity of technology-driven financial solutions to reconfigure economies, enhance the agency of marginalised populations, and mitigate the disparity between individuals lacking access to formal financial systems and those who possess it.

A. M-Pesa and Mobile Money

The case study of M-Pesa serves as a prime example of the profound impact that Industry 4.0-driven financial inclusion can have. This study examines the influence of mobile money platforms, such as M-Pesa, in Sub-Saharan Africa, with a specific emphasis on how these platforms empower individuals and small firms through accessible mobile solutions. These solutions provide crucial financial services, including payments, transfers, and savings options. M-Pesa, a mobile money transfer service launched in Kenya in 2007, has revolutionized the landscape of financial inclusion not only in Kenya but also across various emerging economies. Developed by Safaricom, Kenya's leading mobile network operator, M-Pesa enables users to deposit, withdraw, transfer money, pay bills, and access a range of financial services using their mobile phones. Further, M-Pesa has had a transformative impact on financial inclusion, serving as a catalyst for socio-economic empowerment and inclusive growth. By democratizing access to financial services, M-Pesa has enabled millions of individuals to participate more actively in the formal economy, improve their livelihoods, and build a better future for themselves and their communities.

Analysis of M-pesa focuses on its adoption and use within the households. In terms of the socio-economic variables that determine M-pesa such as uptake education, age, and location have been investigated in extant literature (Hove & Dubus, 2019). Notably, M-pesa adoption has contradicted the initial findings on socio-demographic characteristics and revealed that accessibility, financial services demand, and perceived usefulness are key factors in determining its adoption among the households[45]. In terms of use, remittances and saving are the two major aspects that have been revealed in research (Hove & Dubus, 2019). Analysis of the trends of use shows a significant flow of money from urban to rural areas in what is seen as supporting relatives in rural areas. The economic implications such as cost-effectiveness as well as the service immediateness have contributed to its role in financial inclusion.

This case study highlights the significant benefits of M-Pesa, namely community empowerment, economic growth, and enhanced accessibility to financial services[46]. Through a critical analysis of this phenomenon, valuable insights can be obtained regarding the positive transformations that Industry 4.0 brings to the realm of financial inclusion. In this context, mobile phones play a crucial role as facilitators of financial empowerment, providing economic opportunities for a vast number of individuals.

Positive Aspects of M-Pesa and Mobile Money

- Accessibility: M-Pesa has emerged as a shining example of how Industry 4.0-driven financial inclusion can overcome traditional barriers[47]. In Sub-Saharan Africa, where banking infrastructure is often limited, M-Pesa offers a lifeline. With just a basic mobile phone, even in remote villages lacking banks, individuals can send and receive money, pay bills, and access financial services. This accessibility has significantly reduced the geographical constraints that once hindered financial inclusion.
- Empowerment of Women: One of the remarkable outcomes of M-Pesa's success is its role in empowering women entrepreneurs. In many Sub-Saharan African countries, women are the backbone of small businesses. M-Pesa enables them to take control of their finances, manage cash flow, and engage in economic activities that were previously hampered by distance and lack of access to formal banking services. This newfound financial independence has not only improved the lives of individual women but has also had a positive impact on entire communities.
- Economic Growth: M-Pesa has catalysed economic growth in Sub-Saharan Africa. By providing a means for individuals and small businesses to save, invest, and access credit, it has unlocked entrepreneurial potential. Savings and investments lead to capital accumulation, which, in turn, fosters economic development. This culture of savings and investment has contributed to the overall economic growth of the region, creating opportunities for wealth creation and poverty reduction.

Negative Aspects of M-Pesa and Mobile Money

- Security Considerations: Notwithstanding the indisputable advantages, the security of mobile money systems continues to be a significant area of concern. Cybersecurity dangers, such as phishing attacks, fraudulent schemes, and data breaches, provide potential hazards to individuals' financial stability and personal data. Users of M-Pesa, similar to anyone utilising any financial service, need to maintain a state of constant vigilance and stay well-informed to safeguard themselves against potential risks. Furthermore, it is imperative for financial service providers to consistently allocate resources towards the implementation of resilient security measures to effectively mitigate the ever-changing cyber threats.
- The persistence of the digital divide is evident despite the notable advancements made in promoting financial inclusion through mobile-based financial services such as M-Pesa. Certain marginalised communities face a lack of accessibility to smartphones or dependable network coverage, resulting in their exclusion from the advantages offered by mobile money systems. The disparity in access underscores the necessity for more extensive infrastructure development and initiatives aimed at narrowing the digital divide.
- Regulatory issues: The exponential expansion of mobile money platforms has presented governments and regulatory bodies with a set of issues about regulation. Achieving a harmonious equilibrium between promoting innovation and safeguarding consumer interests is a nuanced endeavour. Regulators must maintain alignment with the dynamic financial technology landscape, by modifying legislation to ensure the protection of users' interests, while simultaneously fostering an environment conducive to innovation. To uphold trust in mobile money systems, regulatory frameworks must effectively tackle concerns about fraud prevention, safeguarding client data, and facilitating dispute resolution.

The M-Pesa case study exemplifies the profound impact of Industry 4.0-driven financial inclusion, showcasing a range of good and negative observations. Mobile money platforms such as M-Pesa have made notable advancements in enhancing the availability of financial services, empowering individuals, and stimulating economic development[48]. However, these platforms also raise security concerns, contribute to the persistence of the digital divide, and pose a challenge for regulators in finding an optimal equilibrium between innovation and safeguarding consumer interests[49]. The aforementioned intricacies highlight the significance of ongoing adjustment and cooperation among relevant parties to optimise the advantages of mobile money and comparable advancements, while also minimising potential threats.

B. Project Ubin: Central Bank Digital Currencies (CBDCs)

The combination of blockchain technology with Central Bank Digital Currencies (CBDCs) represents a significant turning point in the realm of financial inclusion. The effort known as Project Ubin serves as an exemplary case study that sheds light on the various ramifications of CBDCs in the pursuit of improving financial inclusion[50].

This section explores the subject of Project Ubin, delving into the various aspects of integrating CBDCs into the financial ecosystem. It examines both the potential benefits and the obstacles associated with this integration. Through an examination of the knowledge and results derived from Project Ubin, significant perspectives can be obtained regarding the transformative potential of CBDCs supported by blockchain technology in redefining the landscape of financial inclusivity.

Positive Aspects of Project Ubin and CBDCs

- One notable benefit highlighted by Project Ubin is the capacity of CBDCs to significantly transform international payment systems in terms of efficiency. By harnessing the efficiency of blockchain technology, transactions involving CBDCs can be executed smoothly, thereby mitigating the typically burdensome administrative processes, reducing transaction durations, and eventually decreasing expenses. Efficiency plays a vital role in the context of international remittances, as it addresses the persistent challenges of exorbitant fees and protracted processing times that have historically imposed significant burdens on both individuals and organisations.
- The primary objective of CBDCs is to enhance financial inclusivity by expanding access to financial services for marginalised communities. Project Ubin serves as a prime illustration of how CBDCs can effectively empower those who lack access to traditional banking services or have limited access to such services, by providing them with the means to engage with digital financial assets. By use of easily navigable digital wallets, those lacking access to conventional banking services can engage in the official financial system, thereby promoting economic stability and facilitating growth.
- Enhanced Transparency: The utilisation of blockchain technology as the underlying framework for CBDCs enhances the levels of transparency and traceability associated with financial transactions. The Project Ubin initiative demonstrates the effectiveness of transparency in mitigating the potential risks associated with corruption, fraud, and illicit financial activities. All financial activities are meticulously documented on an unalterable ledger, facilitating the ability of auditors, regulators, and users to see and authenticate transactions with unparalleled transparency.

Negative Aspects of Project Ubin and CBDCs

- The increasing integration of CBDCs into the financial landscape has led to heightened apprehensions regarding user privacy and the safeguarding of personal data. The Project Ubin initiative highlights the necessity of implementing strong protective measures to mitigate the risk of unauthorised intrusion into individuals' financial data. Achieving an optimal equilibrium between the principles of transparency and privacy is a complex and multifaceted dilemma that necessitates the attention and resolution of both regulatory bodies and software developers.
- Disruption of the Banking System: The extensive implementation of CBDCs presents a possible source of disruption to conventional banking systems. The success of Project Ubin in showcasing the efficacy of CBDCs prompts inquiries on the prospective involvement of financial intermediaries in the future. The growing adoption of CBDCs necessitates a thorough examination of the implications for financial institutions and other intermediaries, with a focus on minimising any unforeseen negative effects.
- The use of CBDCs brings about a heightened level of regulatory intricacy. The importance of establishing a comprehensive regulatory framework to mitigate potential dangers, enforce adherence to regulations, and safeguard the interests of users is highlighted by Project Ubin. Regulatory agencies are confronted with the challenge of formulating flexible regulations that promote innovation while ensuring the preservation of financial stability and the protection of consumers.

The examination of Project Ubin, which involves the integration of CBDCs with blockchain technology, provides significant insights into the possible advantages and obstacles associated with this financial innovation. To promote financial inclusion using CBDCs, it is imperative to establish a nuanced equilibrium that encompasses effectiveness, openness, privacy, and adherence to regulatory frameworks. The examination of Project Ubin's discoveries has the potential to provide valuable insights for the development of CBDCs, enabling them to function as efficient instruments for advancing financial inclusivity while upholding the principles of security and privacy.

This chapter delves into the potentially transformative impact of Industry 4.0 on financial inclusion, with a particular focus on notable case studies such as M-Pesa and Project Ubin. These studies provide insights into the benefits and drawbacks associated with the utilisation of technology in facilitating access to financial services for disadvantaged populations, as well as bridging the gap between these individuals and conventional financial institutions. As the global initiatives aimed at enhancing financial inclusion continue to expand, these case studies offer valuable perspectives for politicians, regulators, and industry participants who are interested in leveraging the opportunities presented by Industry 4.0 to further societal advancement.

VI. CHAPTER CONCLUSION

The concluding section of this chapter underscores the capacity of Industry 4.0 to facilitate significant and enduring financial inclusion. This highlights the necessity for cooperative endeavours between governments, financial institutions, technological pioneers, and international organisations to proficiently utilise new technologies and establish a financial ecosystem that is more comprehensive and fairer. This chapter aims to inspire readers to explore the limitless possibilities that arise from the convergence of financial inclusion and technical innovation by emphasising success stories, addressing obstacles, and picturing a future where Industry 4.0 catalyzes positive transformation.

REFERENCES

Abdulghani Taha, M. (2020). Block Chain Technology and Financial Inclusion-A Systematic Review of Literature. *International Journal of Advanced Science and Technology*, *29*(7), 14479–14486.

Adegoke, Y. (2018). Ugandans are Furious with a New Tax for Using social media and Mobile Money. *Quartz Africa*, *1*, 1–3.

Agarwal, S., Alok, S., Ghosh, P., & Gupta, S. (2020). Financial inclusion and alternate credit scoring for the millennials: role of big data and machine learning in fintech. *Business School, National University of Singapore Working Paper, SSRN, 3507827*.

Ahmed, S., Chinembiri, T., & Govan-Vassen, N. (2021). *Exposes the Contradictions of Social Media Taxes in Africa*. Academic Press.

Alameda, T. (2020). *Data, AI and Financial Inclusion: The Future of Global Banking—Responsible Finance Forum*. Responsible Finance ForumBBVA 2020.

Allioui, H., & Mourdi, Y. (2023). Exploring the full potentials of IoT for better financial growth and stability: A comprehensive survey. *Sensors (Basel), 23*(19), 8015. doi:10.3390/s23198015 PMID:37836845

Anam, A., & Nisar, S. (2023). Artificial Intelligence and Financial Inclusion: A Systematic. *Journal of Asian Development Studies, 12*(3).

Andrian, R., & Kurniawan, B. (2018, October). Blockchain technology and implementation: A systematic literature review. In 2018 international conference on information technology systems and innovation (ICITSI) (pp. 370-374). IEEE. doi:10.1109/ICITSI.2018.8695939

Barajas, A., Beck, T., Belhaj, M., & Naceur, S. B. (2020). Financial inclusion: What have we learned so far? What do we have to learn? *IMF Working Paper, 2020*(157).

Bisht, D., Singh, R., Gehlot, A., Akram, S. V., Singh, A., Montero, E. C., Priyadarshi, N., & Twala, B. (2022). Imperative role of integrating digitalization in the firm's finance: A technological perspective. *Electronics (Basel), 11*(19), 3252. doi:10.3390/electronics11193252

Brambilla, I., César, A., Falcone, G., & Gasparini, L. (2023). The impact of robots in Latin America: Evidence from local labor markets. *World Development, 170*, 106271. doi:10.1016/j.worlddev.2023.106271

Chinaka, M. (2016). *Blockchain technology--applications in improving financial inclusion in developing economies: case study for small scale agriculture in Africa* (Doctoral dissertation). Massachusetts Institute of Technology.

Criado, J. I., & Gil-Garcia, J. R. (2019). Creating public value through smart technologies and strategies: From digital services to artificial intelligence and beyond. *International Journal of Public Sector Management, 32*(5), 438–450. doi:10.1108/IJPSM-07-2019-0178

De Filippi, P., & Hassan, S. (2018). Blockchain technology as a regulatory technology: From code is law to law is code. *arXiv preprint arXiv:1801.02507.*

Demirgüç-Kunt, A., & Klapper, L. F. (2012). Financial inclusion in Africa: An overview. *World Bank Policy Research Working Paper*, 6088.

Demirgüç-Kunt, A., Klapper, L. F., Ansar, S., & Jagati, A. (2017). Making it easier to apply for a bank account: a study of the Indian market. *World Bank Policy Research Working Paper*, (8205).

Dirican, C. (2015). The impacts of robotics, artificial intelligence on business and economics. *Procedia: Social and Behavioral Sciences, 195*, 564–573. doi:10.1016/j.sbspro.2015.06.134

Giallanza, A., Aiello, G., & Marannano, G. (2021). Industry 4.0: Advanced digital solutions implemented on a close power loop test bench. *Procedia Computer Science, 180*, 93–101. doi:10.1016/j.procs.2021.01.133

Gillpatrick, T., Boğa, S., & Aldanmaz, O. (2022). How can blockchain contribute to developing country economies? A literature review on application areas. *Economics, 10*(1), 105–128. doi:10.2478/eoik-2022-0009

Gortsos, C. (2015). *Financial inclusion: An overview of its various dimensions and the initiatives to enhance its current level.* Academic Press.

Grosse, N., Guerpinar, T., & Henke, M. (2021, July). Blockchain-enabled trust in intercompany networks applying the agency theory. In *Proceedings of the 2021 3rd Blockchain and Internet of Things Conference* (pp. 8-14). 10.1145/3475992.3475994

Hasheela, V., Happonen, A., & Julius, L. (2023). Assessing The Status Quo Of Fintech In Africa. The Role of African Fintech & Financial Inclusion Promotion: A Systematic Literature Review. *Journal of Namibian Studies: History Politics Culture, 37*, 321–348.

Hendrix, N., Veenstra, D. L., Cheng, M., Anderson, N. C., & Verguet, S. (2022). Assessing the economic value of clinical artificial intelligence: Challenges and opportunities. *Value in Health, 25*(3), 331–339. doi:10.1016/j.jval.2021.08.015 PMID:35227443

Hollanders, M. (2020). FinTech and financial inclusion: Opportunities and challenges. *Journal of Payments Strategy & Systems, 14*(4), 315-325.

Iphofen, R., & Kritikos, M. (2021). Regulating artificial intelligence and robotics: Ethics by design in a digital society. *Contemporary Social Science, 16*(2), 170–184. doi:10.1080/21582041.2018.1563803

Kaur, P., & Parashar, A. (2021). A systematic literature review of blockchain technology for smart villages. *Archives of Computational Methods in Engineering*, 1–52. PMID:34720578

Kijkasiwat, P., & Chancharat, N. (2022). Financial inclusion in the industry 4.0: The effects of financial inclusion on electronic payments in Thailand. *International Journal of Trade and Global Markets, 15*(1), 70–78. doi:10.1504/IJTGM.2022.120884

Kshetri, N. (2016). Big data's role in expanding access to financial services in China. *International Journal of Information Management, 36*(3), 297–308. doi:10.1016/j.ijinfomgt.2015.11.014

Lawal, A. B., Ahmed, F., & Abdulkadir, J. (2023). Blockchain Technology and Financial Inclusion In Nigeria: An Analysis Of The Missing Link. *Gusau Journal of Business Administration, 2*(1), 97–106.

Mhlanga, D. (2020). Industry 4.0 in finance: The impact of artificial intelligence (ai) on digital financial inclusion. *International Journal of Financial Studies, 8*(3), 45. doi:10.3390/ijfs8030045

Mishra, P., & Sant, T. G. (2021, October). Role of artificial intelligence and Internet of Things in promoting banking and financial services during COVID-19: Pre and post effect. In *2021 5th International Conference on Information Systems and Computer Networks (ISCON)* (pp. 1-7). IEEE.

Mpofu, F. Y., & Mhlanga, D. (2022). Digital financial inclusion, digital financial services tax and financial inclusion in the fourth industrial revolution era in africa. *Economies, 10*(8), 184. doi:10.3390/economies10080184

Munoz, L., Mascagni, G., Prichard, W., & Santoro, F. (2022). Should governments tax digital financial services? A research agenda to understand sector-specific taxes on DFS. *Economies, 10*(8), 184. doi:10.3390/economies10080184

Ozili, P. K. (2020). Social inclusion and financial inclusion: International evidence. *International Journal of Development Issues, 19*(2), 169–186. doi:10.1108/IJDI-07-2019-0122

Paul, S. (2019). *Use of Blockchain and Aritificial Intelligence to Promote Financial Inclusion in India Smita Miglani Indian Council for Research on International Economic Relations*. Available online: https://economictimes

Preuveneers, D., & Ilie-Zudor, E. (2017). The intelligent industry of the future: A survey on emerging trends, research challenges and opportunities in Industry 4.0. *Journal of Ambient Intelligence and Smart Environments*, *9*(3), 287–298. doi:10.3233/AIS-170432

Rauniyar, K., Rauniyar, K., & Sah, D. K. (2021). Role of FinTech and innovations for improvising digital financial inclusion. *Int. J. Innov. Sci. Res. Technol*, *6*(5), 1419–1424.

Ravi, V., & Kamaruddin, S. (2017). Big data analytics enabled smart financial services: opportunities and challenges. *Big Data Analytics: 5th International Conference, BDA 2017, Hyderabad, India, December 12-15, 2017 Proceedings*, *5*, 15–39.

Rosin, F., Forget, P., Lamouri, S., & Pellerin, R. (2020). Impacts of Industry 4.0 technologies on Lean principles. *International Journal of Production Research*, *58*(6), 1644–1661. doi:10.1080/00207543.2019.1672902

Santoro, F., Munoz, L., Prichard, W., & Mascagni, G. (2022). *Digital financial services and digital IDs: What potential do they have for better taxation in Africa?* Institute of Development Studies.

Verma, D., Valentina, B., Sindhwani, N., & Anand, R. (2022). *IoT Based Smart Applications*. Springer International Publishing.

Vermeulen, B., Pyka, A., & Omerovic, M. (2017). The economic impact of robotics and artificial intelligence. *REELER Working Paper Series*.

Xiong, M., Li, W., Jenny, C., & Wang, P. (2023). Financial Inclusion through Digitalization: Improving Emerging Drivers of Industrial Pollution—Evidence from China. *Sustainability (Basel)*, *15*(13), 10203. doi:10.3390/su151310203

ENDNOTES

1. Refer to Xiong et al (2023) on the potential of digitalization to enhance financial inclusion- Evidence from China
2. Jamwal et al (2021) Industry 4.0 technologies for manufacturing sustainability: a systematic review and future research directions. Applied Sciences 11.12 (2021): 5725.
3. See The United Nations Industrial Development Organizations (2017) Background Paper on Industry 4.0: Opportunities Behind the Challenge. Available at https://www.unido.org/sites/default/files/files/2017-11/UNIDO%20Background%20Paper%20on%20Industry%204.0_27112017.pdf
4. See Mhlanga (2020) on Industry 4.0 on Finance. The Impact of artificial Intelligence on Digital Financial Inclusion.
5. See Hendrix, N., Veenstra, D. L., Cheng, M., Anderson, N. C., & Verguet, S. (2022). Assessing the economic value of clinical artificial intelligence: challenges and opportunities. *Value in Health*, *25*(3), 331-339.

6 Criado, J. I., & Gil-Garcia, J. R. (2019). Creating public value through smart technologies and strategies: From digital services to artificial intelligence and beyond. *International Journal of Public Sector Management*, *32*(5), 438-450.

7 Ibid

8 Read Barajas, A., Beck, T., Belhaj, M., & Naceur, S. B. (2020). Financial inclusion: what have we learned so far? What do we have to learn?. *IMF Working Papers*, *2020*(157).

9 See also Lopes, J., & Pereira, J. L. (2019). Blockchain technologies: Opportunities in healthcare. In *Digital Science* (pp. 435-442). Springer International Publishing.

10 See Lawal, B., Ahmed, F., & Abdulkadir, J. (2023). Blockchain Technology and Financial Inclusion in Nigeria: An Analysis of The Missing Link. *Gusau Journal of Business Administration*, *2*(1), 97-106.

11 See also Abdulghani Taha, M. (2020). Block Chain Technology and Financial Inclusion-A Systematic Review of Literature. *International Journal of Advanced Science and Technology*, *29*(7), 14479-14486.

12 Read & Kurniawan (2018) on Blockchain technology and implementation and its contribution to financial inclusion.

13 See also Gillpatrick, T., Boğa, S., & Aldanmaz, O. (2022). How can blockchain contribute to developing country economies? A literature review on application areas. *Economics*, *10*(1), 105-128.

14 Read Kaur, P., & Parashar, A. (2021). A systematic literature review of blockchain technology for smart villages. *Archives of Computational Methods in Engineering*, 1-52.

15 Allioui and Mourdi (2023) Explores the full potential of IoT for better financial growth and sustainability. The review of literature revealed that IoT application has a great potential to meet the evolving needs among the population.

16 See also Bisht, D., Singh, R., Gehlot, A., Akram, V., Singh, A., Montero, C., ... & Twala, B. (2022). Imperative role of integrating digitalization in the firms finance: A technological perspective. *Electronics*, *11*(19), 3252.

17 Read also IoT Based Smart Applications. (2022). Switzerland: Springer International Publishing.

18 See Gortos (2015) in Exploring the Financial inclusion: an overview of its various dimensions and the initiatives to enhance its current level.

19 Read also Dhanabalan, T., & Sathish, A. (2018). Transforming Indian industries through artificial intelligence and robotics in industry 4.0. *International Journal of Mechanical Engineering and Technology*, *9*(10), 835-845.

20 Brambilla, I., César, A., Falcone, G., & Gasparini, L. (2023). The impact of robots in Latin America: Evidence from local labor markets. *World Development*, *170*, 106271.

21 See Iphofen, R., & Kritikos, M. (2021). Regulating artificial intelligence and robotics: ethics by design in a digital society. *Contemporary Social Science*, *16*(2), 170-184.

22 Read Ravi, V., & Kamaruddin, S. (2017). Big data analytics enabled smart financial services: opportunities and challenges. In *Big Data Analytics: 5th International Conference, BDA 2017, Hyderabad, India, December 12-15, 2017, Proceedings 5* (pp. 15-39). Springer International Publishing.

23 Ibid

24 See Kshetri, N. (2016). Big data's role in expanding access to financial services in China. *International journal of information management*, *36*(3), 297-308.

[25] Read Agarwal et al (2020) In Exploring financial inclusion among Millennials, revealed discriminatory tendencies in the use of mobile money using Data Analytics.

[26] See Demirgüç-Kunt, A., & Klapper, L. F. (2012). Financial inclusion in Africa: an overview. *World Bank policy research working paper*, (6088).

[27] Read Demirgüç-Kunt, A., & Klapper, L. F. (2012). Financial inclusion in Africa: an overview. *World Bank policy research working paper*, (6088). The working covers critical insights into the African financial landscape.

[28] See also Schuetz, S., & Venkatesh, V. (2020). Blockchain, adoption, and financial inclusion in India: Research opportunities. *International journal of information management*, *52*, 101936.

[29] Ibid

[30] See Kumar, A., Sharma, S., & Mahdavi, M. (2021). Machine learning (Ml) technologies for digital credit scoring in rural finance: a literature review. *Risks*, *9*(11), 192.

[31] Read also Sadok, H., Sakka, F., & El Maknouzi, M. E. H. (2022). Artificial intelligence and bank credit analysis: A review. *Cogent Economics & Finance*, *10*(1), 2023262.

[32] Marques, A. I., García, V., & Sánchez, J. S. (2013). A literature review on the application of evolutionary computing to credit scoring. *Journal of the Operational Research Society*, *64*(9), 1384-1399.

[33] Indriasari, E., Prabowo, H., Gaol, F. L., & Purwandari, B. (2022). Intelligent Digital Banking Technology and Architecture: A Systematic Literature Review. *International Journal of Interactive Mobile Technologies*, *16*(19).

[34] Ibid

[35] Paul, S. (2019). Use of Blockchain and Aritificial Intelligence to Promote Financial Inclusion in India Smita Miglani Indian Council for Research on International Economic Relations. *Availableonline: https://economictimes*.

[36] Lawal, A. B., Ahmed, F., & Abdulkadir, J. (2023). Blockchain Technology and Financial Inclusion In Nigeria: An Analysis Of The Missing Link. *Gusau Journal of Business Administration*, *2*(1), 97-106.

[37] Abdulghani Taha, M. (2020). Block Chain Technology and Financial Inclusion-A Systematic Review of Literature. *International Journal of Advanced Science and Technology*, *29*(7), 14479-14486.

[38] Mishra, L., & Kaushik, V. (2023). Application of blockchain in dealing with sustainability issues and challenges of financial sector. *Journal of Sustainable Finance & Investment*, *13*(3), 1318-1333.

[39] Ibid

[40] See also Ali, A. J., Arora, A., & Rathi, J. (2023). Navigating the Digital Divide: Integrating Industry 4.0 Technologies in Modern Management Practices. *European Economic Letters (EEL)*, *13*(4), 53-60.

[41] Malladi, C. M., Soni, R. K., & Srinivasan, S. (2021). Digital financial inclusion: Next frontiers—Challenges and opportunities. *CSI Transactions on ICT*, *9*(2), 127-134.

[42] Ibid

[43] Parvin, S. R., & Panakaje, N. (2022). A Study on the Prospects and Challenges of Digital Financial Inclusion. *Education (IJCSBE)*, *6*(2), 469-480.

[44] See Preuveneers, D., & Ilie-Zudor, E. (2017). The intelligent industry of the future: A survey on emerging trends, research challenges and opportunities in Industry 4.0. *Journal of Ambient Intelligence and Smart Environments*, *9*(3), 287-298.

45 See Morawczynski, O. (2008, September). Surviving in the‗ dual system ': How M-PESA is fostering urban-to-rural remittances in a Kenyan Slum,|| in. In *Proceedings of the IFIP WG* (Vol. 9, pp. 110-127).

46 Read Ahmad, A. H., Green, C., & Jiang, F. (2020). Mobile money, financial inclusion and development: A review with reference to African experience. *Journal of economic surveys*, *34*(4), 753-792.

47 See Ahmad, A. H., Green, C., & Jiang, F. (2020). Mobile money, financial inclusion and development: A review with reference to African experience. *Journal of economic surveys*, *34*(4), 753-792.

48 Ibid

49 Read Nan, W., Zhu, X., & Lynne Markus, M. (2021). What we know and don't know about the socioeconomic impacts of mobile money in Sub-Saharan Africa: A systematic literature review. *The Electronic Journal of Information Systems in Developing Countries*, *87*(2), e12155.

50 See Athanassiou, P. (2020). Wholesale central bank digital currencies: an overview of recent central bank initiatives and lessons learned. In *European Central Bank. European System of Central Banks Legal Conference* (pp. 191-216).

APPENDIX

Discussion Questions

1. How can regulatory bodies strike a balance between fostering innovation in financial services through Industry 4.0 technologies and ensuring consumer protection and financial stability?
2. In what ways can digital literacy initiatives and community engagement strategies be leveraged to bridge the digital divide and promote financial inclusion on a global scale?
3. What are the potential risks and benefits associated with the widespread adoption of Central Bank Digital Currencies (CBDCs) in transforming traditional banking systems, and how can regulatory frameworks adapt to this evolving landscape?
4. How can public-private partnerships play a pivotal role in advancing digital inclusion and ensuring equal access to financial services for individuals from diverse geographical and socioeconomic backgrounds?
5. Considering the challenges of compliance costs and regulatory arbitrage in the financial services sector, how can collaborative efforts between regulatory agencies, industry players, and governments lead to more effective and efficient regulatory frameworks that support innovation while safeguarding consumer interests?

Assessment Tools

Multiple-Choice Questions (MCQs)

1. Which of the following best describes regulatory arbitrage in the context of financial services?
   A) Exploiting regulatory discrepancies across different jurisdictions
   B) Promoting regulatory harmonization across nations
   C) Enhancing consumer protection measures
   D) Facilitating compliance with rigid regulations
2. What role do regulatory sandboxes play in fostering innovation in the financial services sector?
   A) Restricting experimentation with new technologies
   B) Allowing fintech startups to test innovative products under supervision
   C) Eliminating compliance costs for firms
   D) Promoting regulatory arbitrage practices
3. Why is data governance crucial in the context of Industry 4.0 technologies?
   A) To limit access to financial services
   B) To ensure compliance with data protection laws
   C) To hinder interoperability between systems
   D) To discourage innovation in the financial sector
4. How can public-private partnerships contribute to advancing digital inclusion in financial services?
   A) By increasing compliance costs for firms
   B) By promoting financial literacy programs
   C) By limiting access to innovative technologies
   D) By discouraging collaboration between stakeholders

5. What is the primary objective of regulatory frameworks in the era of Industry 4.0?
   A) To hinder innovation in the financial sector
   B) To promote regulatory arbitrage practices
   C) To safeguard consumer interests and financial stability
   D) To eliminate compliance costs for firms
6. Which positive aspect of M-Pesa is NOT mentioned in the text?
   (a) Increased access to financial services for remote populations
   (b) Reduced transaction costs compared to traditional banking
   (c) Enhanced opportunities for women entrepreneurs
   (d) Elimination of the digital divide
7. What is a major SECURITY concern regarding M-Pesa and mobile money platforms?
   (a) Lack of government regulation
   (b) High fees associated with transactions
   (c) Phishing attacks and fraudulent schemes
   (d) Limited availability of smartphones
8. Which is a TRUE statement about Project Ubin and CBDCs?
   (a) They aim to replace traditional banking systems entirely.
   (b) They can potentially improve efficiency of international payments.
   (c) They guarantee complete privacy for user data.
   (d) They have no impact on financial inclusion.
9. A potential NEGATIVE impact of Project Ubin is:
   (a) Increased access to credit for small businesses
   (b) Reduced risk of corruption and fraud
   (c) Disruption of the existing banking system
   (d) Improved transparency in financial transactions
10. What is the main takeaway from the chapter regarding Industry 4.0 and financial inclusion?
    (a) Technology can solve all financial inclusion issues without challenges.
    (b) Case studies like M-Pesa and Project Ubin offer valuable insights and considerations.
    (c) Financial inclusion is solely dependent on government initiatives.
    (d) Traditional banking methods are more effective than technology.

Answers to MCQs

1. Exploiting regulatory discrepancies across different jurisdictions is the most accurate description of regulatory arbitrage in the context of financial services. This practice involves companies taking advantage of different regulatory environments to their benefit, typically by moving operations to jurisdictions with less stringent regulations.
2. Allowing fintech startups to test innovative products under supervision best describes the role of regulatory sandboxes. These sandboxes provide a safe space for startups to experiment with new technologies and business models without being subject to all the usual regulatory requirements. This helps foster innovation while protecting consumers and preventing systemic risks.
3. To ensure compliance with data protection laws is the crucial role of data governance in the context of Industry 4.0 technologies. As vast amounts of data are generated and used in financial services,

it's critical to have frameworks in place to manage, protect, and ethically utilize this data while adhering to data privacy regulations.

4. B) By promoting financial literacy programs is a key way public-private partnerships can contribute to advancing digital inclusion. Partnerships between governments, technology companies, and NGOs can create programs that educate individuals on how to use digital financial services safely and effectively, bridging the digital divide.
5. To safeguard consumer interests and financial stability is the primary objective of regulatory frameworks in the era of Industry 4.0. While adapting to rapid technological advancements, these frameworks need to ensure consumer protection, data security, and prevent systemic risks arising from new financial technologies
6. (d) Elimination of the digital divide - the text acknowledges the persistence of the digital divide even with advancements like M-Pesa.
7. (c) Phishing attacks and fraudulent schemes - the text specifically mentions these as security risks for users.
8. (b) They can potentially improve efficiency of international payments - this is highlighted as a benefit of CBDCs in Project Ubin.
9. (c) Disruption of the existing banking system - the text discusses this as a potential challenge to consider.
10. (b) Case studies like M-Pesa and Project Ubin offer valuable insights and considerations - the chapter emphasizes learning from real-world examples.

Short Answer Questions

1. Explain the concept of regulatory arbitrage and discuss its implications for the financial services sector.
2. How can regulatory sandboxes facilitate innovation while ensuring consumer protection in the financial industry?
3. Discuss the importance of data governance in the context of Industry 4.0 technologies and its impact on financial services.
4. Analyze the role of public-private partnerships in promoting digital inclusion and expanding access to financial services.
5. Evaluate the challenges and benefits of achieving a harmonious equilibrium between fostering innovation and managing risks in the financial sector.

Assignment Topics

1. Conduct a case study analysis of a successful regulatory sandbox initiative in the financial services sector and evaluate its impact on innovation and consumer protection.
2. Develop a proposal for a public-private partnership project aimed at promoting financial inclusion through the adoption of Industry 4.0 technologies.
3. Compare and contrast the data governance regulations in two different countries and assess their effectiveness in ensuring data security and privacy in financial services.

4. Create a regulatory framework outline that addresses the challenges of compliance costs and regulatory arbitrage in the era of Industry 4.0, emphasizing consumer protection and innovation.
5. Explore the potential implications of Central Bank Digital Currencies (CBDCs) on traditional banking systems and propose regulatory measures to mitigate risks and ensure financial stability.

Compilation of References

Abdelghaffar, R. A., Emam, H. A., & Samak, N. A. (2023). Financial inclusion and human development: Is there a nexus? *Journal of Humanities and Applied Social Sciences*, *5*(3), 163–177. doi:10.1108/JHASS-11-2021-0178

Abdu, E., & Adem, M. (2021). Determinants of financial inclusion in Afar Region: Evidence from selected woredas. *Cogent Economics & Finance*, *9*(1), 1920149. doi:10.1080/23322039.2021.1920149

Abdulghani Taha, M. (2020). Block Chain Technology and Financial Inclusion-A Systematic Review of Literature. *International Journal of Advanced Science and Technology*, *29*(7), 14479–14486.

AbdulKareem, I. A., Mahmud, M. S., & Elbishr Ali Hassan, E. M. (2023). The Application of Legal and Beneficial Ownership in Sukuk Structure in Malaysia and Nigeria. *Turkish Journal of Islamic Economics*, *10*(1).

Abdullah, A. (2016). Examining U.S. approvals of Islamic financing products and the Islamic theory of lawful profit. *International Journal of Islamic and Middle Eastern Finance and Management*, *9*(4), 532–550. doi:10.1108/IMEFM-09-2015-0107

Abdullah, N., & Tan, Y. (2017). Profitability of commercial banks revisited: New evidence from oil and non-oil exporting countries in the MENA region. *Investment Management and Financial Innovations*, *14*(3), 62–73. doi:10.21511/imfi.14(3).2017.06

Abdul-Rahman, A., & Mohd nor, S. (2016). Challenges of profit-and-loss sharing financing in Malaysian Islamic banking. *Geografia : Malaysian Journal of Society and Space*, *12*, 39–46.

Abel, S., & Le Roux, P. (2016). Determinants of banking sector profitability in Zimbabwe. *International Journal of Economics and Financial Issues*, *6*(3).

Abubakar, Y. S., Nafees, S. M., Dorloh, S., & Aji, R. H. (2023). *The Concept of Sukuk and Its Applications in Contemporary Islamic Financial System*. Academic Press.

Acedo, F. J., Barroso, C., Casanueva, C., & Galan, J. L. (2006). Co-authorship in management and organizational studies: An empirical and network analysis. *Journal of Management Studies*, *43*(5), 957–983. doi:10.1111/j.1467-6486.2006.00625.x

ADB. (2015). *Asian development outlook: financing asia's future growth.* Asian Development Bank. https://www.adb.org/sites/default/files/pu blication/154508/ado-2015.pdf

Adegoke, Y. (2018). Ugandans are Furious with a New Tax for Using social media and Mobile Money. *Quartz Africa*, *1*, 1–3.

Adelopo, I., Lloydking, R., & Tauringana, V. (2018). Determinants of bank profitability before, during, and after the financial crisis. *International Journal of Managerial Finance*, *14*(4), 378–398. doi:10.1108/IJMF-07-2017-0148

Adesola, W. A., Ewa, U. E., & Arikpo, O. F. (2020). Microfinance Banks Dynamics Effect on Small-Scale Enterprise Development in Nigeria. International Journal of Applied Economics. *Finance and Accounting*, *6*(2), 64–75.

Adjor, D. M., & Kebalo, L. (2018). Does corruption matter for unemployment in SADC countries? *Review of Economic and Business Studies*, *11*(2), 65–92. doi:10.1515/rebs-2018-0074

Adzimatinur, F., & Manalu, V. G. (2021). The Effect of Islamic Financial Inclusion on Economic Growth: A Case Study of Islamic Banking in Indonesia. Budapest International Research and Critics Institute (BIRCI-Journal): Humanities and Social Sciences, 4(1), 976–985. doi:10.33258/birci.v4i1.1699

Aebi, V., Sabato, G., & Schmid, M. (2012). Risk management, corporate governance, and bank performance in the financial crisis. *Journal of Banking & Finance*, *36*(12), 3213–3226. doi:10.1016/j.jbankfin.2011.10.020

Agarwal, S., Alok, S., Ghosh, P., & Gupta, S. (2020). Financial inclusion and alternate credit scoring for the millennials: role of big data and machine learning in fintech. *Business School, National University of Singapore Working Paper, SSRN, 3507827.*

Agner, M. G., & Desello, J. M. U. (2023). Financial inclusion and the role of financial literacy in the Philippines. *International Journal of Economics and Finance*, *15*(6), 12–31.

Agyekum, F. K., Reddy, K., Wallace, D., & Wellalage, N. H. (2022). Does technological inclusion promote financial inclusion among SMEs? Evidence from South-East Asian (SEA) countries. *Global Finance Journal*, *53*, 100618. Advance online publication. doi:10.1016/j.gfj.2021.100618

Ahamed, M. M., & Mallick, S. K. (2019). *Is financial inclusion good for bank stability? International Evidence, 157*, 403–427.

Ahlin, C., & Pang, J. (2008). Are financial development and corruption control substitutes in promoting growth? *Journal of Development Economics*, *86*(2), 414–433. doi:10.1016/j.jdeveco.2007.07.002

Ahmad, F., Hussain, R. T., & Shahzad, S. M. (2020). Measuring Financial Permanency of Firms in Emergent Economy: A Comparative Study on Financial Institutions of Pakistan. *Int. J. of Multidisciplinary and Current Research, 8*(2), 534-544.

Ahmad, M., Majeed, A., Khan, M. A., Sohaib, M., & Shehzad, K. (2021). Digital financial inclusion and economic growth: Provincial data analysis of China. *China Economic Journal*, *14*(3), 291–310. doi:10.1080/17538963.2021.1882064

Ahmad, S. (2019). The Role of Musharakah in the Economic Development of Tehsil Dargai, District Malakand, Khyber Pakhtunkhwa, Pakistan. *Islamic Banking and Finance Review*, *6*(1), 80–97. doi:10.32350/ibfr.2019.06.05

Ahmad, S., Lensink, R., & Mueller, A. (2023). Religion, social desirability bias and financial inclusion: Evidence from a list experiment on Islamic (micro-) finance. *Journal of Behavioral and Experimental Finance*, *38*, 100795. doi:10.1016/j.jbef.2023.100795

Ahmed, E. R., Islam, M. A., Alabdullah, T. T. Y., & Amran, A. B. (2019). A qualitative analysis on the determinants of legitimacy of sukuk. *Journal of Islamic Accounting and Business Research*, *10*(3), 342–368. doi:10.1108/JIABR-01-2016-0005

Ahmed, R., Aizenman, J., & Jinjarak, Y. (2021). Inflation and exchange rate targeting challenges under fiscal dominance. *Journal of Macroeconomics*, *67*, 103281. doi:10.1016/j.jmacro.2020.103281

Ahmed, S., Chinembiri, T., & Govan-Vassen, N. (2021). *Exposes the Contradictions of Social Media Taxes in Africa.* Academic Press.

Ajide, F. M. (2020). Can financial inclusion reduce the presence of corruption? Evidence from selected countries in Africa. *International Journal of Social Economics*, *47*(11), 1345–1362. doi:10.1108/IJSE-03-2020-0145

Alam, A., Ratnasari, R. T., Jannah, I. L., & Ashfahany, A. E. (2023). Development and evaluation of Islamic green financing: A systematic review of green sukuk. *Environment and Ecology, 14*(1), 61–72.

Alameda, T. (2020). *Data, AI and Financial Inclusion: The Future of Global Banking—Responsible Finance Forum.* Responsible Finance ForumBBVA 2020.

Alam, M. M., Hassan, S., & Said, J. (2015). Performance of Islamic microcredit in perspective of Maqasid Al-Shariah: A case study on Amanah Ikhtiar Malaysia. *Humanomics, 31*(4), 374–384. doi:10.1108/H-12-2014-0072

Alam, N., Duygun, M., & Ariss, R. T. (2016). Green sukuk: An innovation in Islamic capital markets. In *Energy and finance: Sustainability in the energy industry* (pp. 167–185). Springer. doi:10.1007/978-3-319-32268-1_10

Albert, A. (2016a). Le genre du prêt sur gage: rapports de pouvoir au Mont-de-Piété de Paris (années 1850 – années 1920). *Genre & Histoire*. Printemps. doi:10.4000/genrehistoire.2462

Albert, A. (2016b). Une incomprehension de la pauvreté? La crise du Mont-de-Piété de Paris à la Belle Époque. *Les Études Sociales, 2*(164), 63-86. https://www.cairn.info/revue-les-etudes-sociales-2016-2-page-63.htm doi:10.3917/etsoc.164.0063

Albertazzi, U., & Gambacorta, L. (2009). Bank profitability and the business cycle. *Journal of Financial Stability, 5*(4), 393–409. doi:10.1016/j.jfs.2008.10.002

Al-Hakim, M. S., Al-Hamad, R. A. A. S., & Ghaith, M. A. (2021). The Role Of Financial Inclusion In Bridging SMEs Financing Gap-The Viewpoint Of Credit Employees At Jordanian Islamic Banks. *Turkish Journal of Computer and Mathematics Education, 12*(14), 2763–2776.

Alhassan, A. L., Tetteh, M. L., & Brobbey, F. O. (2016). Market power, efficiency and bank profitability: Evidence from Ghana. *Economic Change and Restructuring, 49*(1), 71–93. doi:10.1007/s10644-015-9174-6

Alighieri, D. (1996). The Divine Comedy. Volume 1, Inferno. Oxford University Press.

Ali, M. M., Devi, A., & Bustomi, H. (2020). Determinants of Islamic financial exclusion in Indonesia. *Journal of Islamic Monetary Economics and Finance, 6*(2), 373–402. doi:10.21098/jimf.v6i2.1093

Ali, M. M., Devi, A., Furqani, H., & Hamzah, H. (2020). Islamic financial inclusion determinants in Indonesia: An ANP approach. *International Journal of Islamic and Middle Eastern Finance and Management, 13*(4), 727–747. doi:10.1108/IMEFM-01-2019-0007

Ali, M., & Puah, C. H. (2019). The internal determinants of bank profitability and stability. *Management Research Review, 42*(1), 49–67. doi:10.1108/MRR-04-2017-0103

Aliyu, S., Yusof, R. M., & Naiimi, N. (2017). The role of moral transaction mode for sustainability of banking business: A proposed conceptual model for Islamic microfinance banks in Nigeria. *International Journal of Social Economics, 44*(12), 2238–2256. doi:10.1108/IJSE-07-2016-0205

Allam, A. (2020). *Doctor of philosophy Three Essays on Financial Inclusion Allam.* Academic Press.

Allen, F., Demirguc-Kunt, A., Klapper, L., & Peria, M. S. M. (2016). The foundations of financial inclusion: Understanding ownership and use of formal accounts. *Journal of Financial Intermediation, 27*, 1–30. doi:10.1016/j.jfi.2015.12.003

Allioui, H., & Mourdi, Y. (2023). Exploring the full potentials of IoT for better financial growth and stability: A comprehensive survey. *Sensors (Basel), 23*(19), 8015. doi:10.3390/s23198015 PMID:37836845

Alrababah, Z. (2023). Barriers to Cloud Computing Adoption Among SMEs in The Middle East: A Systematic Review. *Journal of Theoretical and Applied Information Technology, 101*(17).

Al-Sayed, O. (2013). Sukuk risk: Analysis and management. *European Journal of Applied Social Sciences Research, 1*(3), 67–76.

Althalathini, D., Al-Dajani, H., & Apostolopou, N. (2020). Muslim women's entrepreneurship in conflict zones: Religiosity, culture, and gender egalitarianism. *Proceedings - Academy of Management, 2020*(1), 13878. doi:10.5465/AMBPP.2020.13878abstract

Alvi, I. (2009, May). *Standardization of Documentation in Islamic Finance & Role of the International, Islamic Financial Market (IIFM).* Paper presented at Islamic Financial Sector Development (IFSD), Forum 2009, Ashgabat, Turkmenistan.

Amaroh, S., & Masykuroh, E. (2023). Financial Attitude, Trust, and ROSCAs' Member Commitment: Social Relations as Mediating Factor. *Global Business & Finance Review, 28*(3), 35–49. doi:10.17549/gbfr.2023.28.3.35

Amin, M. A. M., Sanusi, N. A., Kusairi, S., & Abdallah, Z. M. (2019). Inverse relationship of financial risk and performance in commercial banks in Tanzania. *Innovations, 11*, 4–1.

Ammar, N., & Boughrara, A. (2019). The impact of revenue diversification on bank profitability and risk: Evidence from MENA banking industry. *Macroeconomics and Finance in Emerging Market Economies, 12*(1), 36–70. doi:10.1080/17520843.2018.1535513

Ammerman, N. T. (2020). Rethinking religion: Toward a practice approach. *American Journal of Sociology, 126*(1), 6–51. doi:10.1086/709779

Anam, A., & Nisar, S. (2023). Artificial Intelligence and Financial Inclusion: A Systematic. *Journal of Asian Development Studies, 12*(3).

Anarfo, E. B., Abor, J. Y., & osei, K. A. (2020, January). Africa: Does financial stability play a moderating role? *Research in International Business and Finance, 51*, 101070. doi:10.1016/j.ribaf.2019.101070

Andrian, R., & Kurniawan, B. (2018, October). Blockchain technology and implementation: A systematic literature review. In 2018 international conference on information technology systems and innovation (ICITSI) (pp. 370-374). IEEE. doi:10.1109/ICITSI.2018.8695939

Andriani, & Hermantoro, B. (2023). Optimizing Financial Technology Literacy in Minimizing Phishing Threats (Case Study of Indonesian Sharia Bank Customers). *Proceeding of International Conference on Islamic Philantrophy, 1*, 38–52.

Appleyard, L. (2013). The geographies of access to enterprise finance: The case of the West Midlands, UK. *Regional Studies, 47*(6), 868–879. doi:10.1080/00343404.2012.748979

Arcuri, M. C., & Pisani, R. (2021). Is trade credit a sustainable resource for medium-sized Italian Green companies? *Sustainability (Basel), 13*(5), 2872. doi:10.3390/su13052872

Aria, M., & Cuccurullo, C. (2017). Bibliometrix: An R-tool for comprehensive science mapping analysis. *Journal of Informetrics, 11*(4), 959–975. doi:10.1016/j.joi.2017.08.007

Aristotle. (1996). Politics, Book. In *Aristotle. The politics and The Constitution of Athens*. Cambridge University Press.

Arvind, T. T. (2021). Too Big to Care?: Financial Contracts and the Problem of Transactional Asymmetry. *Law and Contemporary Problems, 84*, 35.

Ashraf, N., Karlan, D., & Yin, W. (2010). Female empowerment: Impact of a commitment savings product in the Philippines. *World Development, 38*(3), 333–344. doi:10.1016/j.worlddev.2009.05.010

Ashta A., Assadi D., & Durand N. (2021). Capture d'innovation: étude de cas d'une néo-banque à mission sociale et défis pour les pays en développement. *ISTE OpenScience*, 1–21 doi:.OP.2021.0673 doi:10.21494/ISTE

Aslam, E., Ashraf, M. S., & Iqbal, A. (2022). Impact of corporate image on customer loyalty of Islamic banks: The role of religiosity, collectivism, sight cues and CSR. *Journal of Islamic Marketing, 14*(5), 1310–1324. doi:10.1108/JIMA-09-2021-0314

Aslam, E., Ur-Rehman, A., & Iqbal, A. (2021). Does Corporate Governance Matter for Asset Quality of Islamic Banks? *Bulletin of Monetary Economics and Banking, 24*(2), 221–236. doi:10.21098/bemp.v24i2.1344

Aslan, I. (2017). Interest- free banking: reasons for choosing Islamic banking in bingol city. *Press academia, 3*(1), 257-268. doi:10.17261/Pressacademia.2017.411

Asnaini, F., Isnaini, D., & Fryanti, Y. E. (2023). Exploring the potential of Islamic financial instruments in addressing economic challenges: the role of financial inclusion and institutional quality. *International Journal of Economics and Finance Studies, 15*(1), 204–224.

Atkinson, A., & Messy, F.-A. (2012). *Measuring Financial Literacy: Results of the OECD/International Network on Financial Education (INFE) pilot study (15).* doi:10.1787/20797117

Ayaz, M., Shah, H. S., Shaheen, S., & Yusuf, J. B. (2019). *Islamic microfinancing by the banking sector of Pakistan: Problems and solutions*. Academic Press.

Ayyagari, M., Demirgüç-Kunt, A., & Maksimovic, V. (2008). How important are financing constraints? The role of finance in the business environment. *The World Bank Economic Review, 22*(3), 483–516. doi:10.1093/wber/lhn018

Azhgaliyeva, D., Kapoor, A., & Liu, Y. (2020). Green bonds for financing renewable energy and energy efficiency in South-East Asia: A review of policies. *Journal of Sustainable Finance & Investment, 10*(2), 113–140. doi:10.1080/20430795.2019.1704160

Aziz, A., & Naima, U. (2021). Rethinking digital financial inclusion: Evidence from Bangladesh. *Technology in Society, 64*, 101509. doi:10.1016/j.techsoc.2020.101509

Babajide, A. A., Adegboye, F. B., & Omankhanlen, A. E. (2015). Financial inclusion and economic growth in Nigeria. *International Journal of Economics and Financial Issues, 5*(3), 629–637. doi:10.38157/business-perspective-review.v2i2.149

Babilla, T. U. K. (2023). Digital innovation and financial access for small and medium-sized enterprises in a currency union. *Economic Modelling, 120*, 106182. Advance online publication. doi:10.1016/j.econmod.2022.106182

Bach, L., Ghio, N., Guillouzouic, A., & Malgouyres, C. (2021). *Rapport d'évaluation de la contrainte pour les entreprises du remboursement des prêts garantis par l'État (PGE)* [Rapport de recherche]. Rapport IPP n°32, Institut des politiques publiques (IPP). https://shs.hal.science/halshs-03693262

Bader-Saye, S. (2013). Disinterested Money. Islamic Banking Monti di Pietà, and the Possibility of Moral Finance. *Journal of the Society of Christian Ethics, 33*(1), 119-138. doi:10.1353/sce.2013.0015

Baita, A. J., Malami, H. U., & Al-Faryan, M. A. S. (2023). Fiscal policy and sukuk market development in OIC countries. *Journal of Islamic Accounting and Business Research, 14*(8), 1216–1231. doi:10.1108/JIABR-06-2022-0159

Baker, H. K., Pandey, N., Kumar, S., & Haldar, A. (2020). A bibliometric analysis of board diversity: Current status, development, and future research directions. *Journal of Business Research, 108*, 232–246. doi:10.1016/j.jbusres.2019.11.025

Ball, L. M., & Sheridan, N. (2004). Does inflation targeting matter? In *The inflation-targeting debate* (pp. 249–282). University of Chicago Press. doi:10.7208/chicago/9780226044736.003.0007

Bank for International Settlements. (2021). *The fintech gender gap*. Author.

Banna, H., & Alam, M. R. (2020). Islamic banking efficiency and inclusive sustainable growth: The role of financial inclusion. *Journal of Islamic Monetary Economics and Finance*, *6*(1), 213–242. doi:10.21098/jimf.v6i1.1089

Banna, H., Alam, M. R., Ahmad, R., & Sari, N. M. (2022). Does financial inclusion drive the Islamic banking efficiency? A post-financial crisis analysis. *The Singapore Economic Review*, *67*(01), 135–160. doi:10.1142/S0217590819420050

Banna, H., Hassan, M. K., & Alam, M. R. (2020). Digital financial inclusion, Islamic banking stability and sustainable economic growth. *Islamic Perspective for Sustainable Financial System*, *20*(1), 131–152.

Barajas, A., Beck, T., Belhaj, M., & Naceur, S. B. (2020). Financial inclusion: What have we learned so far? What do we have to learn? *IMF Working Paper*, *2020*(157).

Baranowski, P., Doryń, W., Łyziak, T., & Stanisławska, E. (2021). Words and deeds in managing expectations: Empirical evidence from an inflation targeting economy. *Economic Modelling*, *95*, 49–67. doi:10.1016/j.econmod.2020.12.003

Barik, R., & Lenka, S. K. (2023). Does financial inclusion control corruption in upper-middle and lower-middle income countries? *Asia-Pacific Journal of Regional Science*, *7*(1), 69–92. doi:10.1007/s41685-022-00269-0

Barro, R. J. (1996). Inflation and growth. *Review - Federal Reserve Bank of St. Louis*, *78*(3), 153–169. doi:10.20955/r.78.153-169

Bateman, M., Blankenburg, S., & Kozul-Wright, R. (2019). The rise and fall of microfinance. *The Journal of Development Studies*, *55*(7), 1205–1221.

Beck, T., Demirgüç-Kunt, A. S. L. I., & Maksimovic, V. (2005). Financial and legal constraints to growth: Does firm size matter? *The Journal of Finance*, *60*(1), 137–177. doi:10.1111/j.1540-6261.2005.00727.x

Beck, T., Demirgüç-Kunt, A., & Levine, R. (2007). Finance, inequality and the poor. *Journal of Economic Growth*, *12*(1), 27–49. doi:10.1007/s10887-007-9010-6

Benavent C. (2017). Disruption à l'âge des plateformes. *Économie & Management, 165*, 11-17.

Bentham, J. (2014). *A Defense of Usury. Shewing the Impolicy of the Present Legal restraints on the Terms of Pecuniary Bargains, in a Series of Letters to a Friend.* Cambridge University Press.

Bernanke, B. (2003). A perspective on inflation targeting: Why it seems to work. *Business Economics (Cleveland, Ohio)*, *38*(3), 7–16.

Bernanke, B. S., & Mishkin, F. S. (1997). Inflation targeting: A new framework for monetary policy? *The Journal of Economic Perspectives*, *11*(2), 97–116. doi:10.1257/jep.11.2.97

Bhandari, A. (2009) Access to banking services and poverty reduction: a state-wise assessment in India. *IZA Discussion Paper, 4132.*

Bhardwaj, M., Hedrick-Wong, Y., & Howard, T. (2018). *Financial inclusion for Asia's unbanked.* World Bank Blogs.

Bhattacharyya, A., Rahman, M. L., & Wright, S. (2023). Improving small and medium-size enterprise performance: Does working capital management enhance the effectiveness of financial inclusion? *Accounting and Finance*, *63*(4), 3943–3969. doi:10.1111/acfi.13081

Bhatti, F. A., & Aslam, E., ur Rehman, A., Ashraf, S., Aslam, M., & Shabbir, M. S. (2023). Does intellectual capital efficiency spur the financial performance of banks? A comparative analysis of Islamic and conventional banks in Pakistan. *Al-Qantara*, *9*(3), 55–67.

Bhuiyan, A. B., Siwar, C., Ismail, A. G., & Omar, N. (2017). The Islamic microfinancing contributions on sustainable livelihood of the borrowers in Bangladesh. *International Journal of Business and Society, 18*(S1), 79–96.

Bianchi, F., Melosi, L., & Rottner, M. (2021). Hitting the elusive inflation target. *Journal of Monetary Economics, 124*, 107–122. doi:10.1016/j.jmoneco.2021.10.003

Billah, M., Elsayed, A. H., & Hadhri, S. (2023). Asymmetric relationship between green bonds and Sukuk markets: The role of global risk factors. *Journal of International Financial Markets, Institutions and Money, 83*, 101728. doi:10.1016/j.intfin.2022.101728

Bisht, D., Singh, R., Gehlot, A., Akram, S. V., Singh, A., Montero, E. C., Priyadarshi, N., & Twala, B. (2022). Imperative role of integrating digitalization in the firm's finance: A technological perspective. *Electronics (Basel), 11*(19), 3252. doi:10.3390/electronics11193252

Bitar, M., Saad, W., & Benlemlih, M. (2016). Bank risk and performance in the MENA region: The importance of capital requirements. *Economic Systems, 40*(3), 398–421. doi:10.1016/j.ecosys.2015.12.001

Blanchard, O. J. (2004). *Fiscal dominance and inflation targeting: lessons from Brazil*. Academic Press.

Boadi, I., Dana, L. P., Mertens, G., & Mensah, L. (2017). SMEs' financing and banks' profitability: A "good date" for banks in Ghana? *Journal of African Business, 18*(2), 257–277. doi:10.1080/15228916.2017.1285847

Boeddu, G., Chien, J., & Istuk, I. (2021). *Consumer Risks of Fintech*. https://figi.itu.int/wp-content/uploads/2021/06/Consumer-Risks-of-Fintech.pdf

Bonin, H. (1992). *La banque et les banquiers en France, du Moyen-Âge à nos jours*. Larousse.

Boujlil, R., Hassan, M. K., & Grassa, R. (2020). Sovereign debt issuance choice: Sukuk vs conventional bonds. *Journal of Islamic Monetary Economics and Finance, 6*(2), 275–294. doi:10.21098/jimf.v6i2.1104

Brahmana, R. K., & You, H. W. (2022). Do Muslim CEOs and Muslim stakeholders prefer Islamic debt financing? *Global Finance Journal, 54*, 100625. doi:10.1016/j.gfj.2021.100625

Brambilla, I., César, A., Falcone, G., & Gasparini, L. (2023). The impact of robots in Latin America: Evidence from local labor markets. *World Development, 170*, 106271. doi:10.1016/j.worlddev.2023.106271

Breza, E., Kanz, M., & Klapper, L. F. (2020). Learning to navigate a new financial technology: Evidence from payroll accounts. *Policy Research Working Paper 9495*, World Bank, Washington, DC.

Brixiová, Z., Kangoye, T., & Yogo, T. U. (2020). Access to finance among small and medium-sized enterprises and job creation in Africa. *Structural Change and Economic Dynamics, 55*, 177–189. doi:10.1016/j.strueco.2020.08.008

Broadus, R. N. (1987). Toward a definition of "bibliometrics.". *Scientometrics, 12*(5–6), 373–379. doi:10.1007/BF02016680

Bruhn, M., & Love, I. (2013). The economic impact of expanding access to finance in Mexico. *Banking the World: Empirical Foundations of Financial Inclusion*, 137–156.

Bruhn, M., & Love, Y. (2017). Financial inclusion and economic development: A review of the literature and new evidence. *The Review of Economics and Statistics, 99*(4), 667–687.

Brundtland, G. H. (1987). *Our Common Future: The World Commission on Environment and Development*. Oxford University Press. Available at https://shorturl.at/hnOT6

Bui, T. Q., & Do, A. V. P. (2022). Does technological inclusion reduce financial constraints on small and medium sized enterprises? The case of Vietnam. *Finance Research Letters*, *47*, 102534. Advance online publication. doi:10.1016/j.frl.2021.102534

Bundick, B., & Smith, A. L. (2018). Does communicating a numerical inflation target anchor inflation expectations? Evidence & bond market implications. *Federal Reserve Bank of Kansas City, Research Working Paper*, (18-01).

Burton, B., Kumar, S., & Pandey, N. (2020). Twenty-five years of The European Journal of Finance (EJF): A retrospective analysis. *European Journal of Finance*, *26*(18), 1817–1841. doi:10.1080/1351847X.2020.1754873

Cabeza-García, L., Del Brio, E. B., & Oscanoa-Victorio, M. L. (2019). *Female financial inclusion and its impacts on inclusive economic development.* Paper presented at the Women's Studies International Forum. 10.1016/j.wsif.2019.102300

Cao, Y. (2022). Bank earnings management and performance reporting of comprehensive income. *Journal of Accounting and Public Policy*, *41*(5), 106996. doi:10.1016/j.jaccpubpol.2022.106996

Castriotta, M., Loi, M., Marku, E., & Naitana, L. (2019). What's in a Name? An exploration of the emerging organisations conceptual structure. *Scientometrics*, *118*(2), 407–437. doi:10.1007/s11192-018-2977-2

CFPB. (2015). *Measuring financial well-being: A guide to using the CFPB financial well-being scale.* Retrieved October 13, 2023 from https://fles.consumerfnance.gov/f/201512_cfpb_fnancial-wellbeing-user-guide-scale.pdf

Chaibi, O. (2014). Le crédit des travailleurs »: un aperçu du crédit populaire en France de 1848 à 1914. *Vie sociale*, *3*(7), 13-29.

Chaibi, O. (2010). *Proudhon et la banque du peuple (1648-1849).* Éditions Connaissances et Savoirs.

Chakravorty, N. N. (2019). How Does Corruption Affect Economic Growth? An Econometric Analysis. *Journal of Leadership, Accountability and Ethics*, *16*(4).

Chatterjee, A. (2020). Financial inclusion, information and communication technology diffusion, and economic growth: A panel data analysis. *Information Technology for Development*, *26*(3), 607–635. doi:10.1080/02681102.2020.1734770

Chen, Y. H., & Chen, J. L. (2019). AI@NTIPHISH — Machine learning mechanisms for cyber-phishing attack. *IEICE Transactions on Information and Systems, E102D*(5), 878–887.

Chesneau, D. I. (2019). Fintechs et banques coopération et coopétition, *Réalités industrielles. Annales des Mines*, 45–50.

Chidozie, U. E., & Ayadi, F. S. (2017). Macroeconomy and banks' profitability in Nigeria. *African Research Review*, *11*(2), 121–137. doi:10.4314/afrrev.v11i2.10

Chiew, K. L., Yong, K. S. C., & Tan, C. L. (2018). A survey of phishing attacks: Their types, vectors and technical approaches. *Expert Systems with Applications*, *106*, 1–20. doi:10.1016/j.eswa.2018.03.050

Chinaka, M. (2016). *Blockchain technology--applications in improving financial inclusion in developing economies: case study for small scale agriculture in Africa* (Doctoral dissertation). Massachusetts Institute of Technology.

Chong, F. H. L. (2021). Enhancing trust through digital Islamic finance and blockchain technology. *Qualitative Research in Financial Markets*, *13*(3), 328–341. doi:10.1108/QRFM-05-2020-0076

Christen-Lécuyer. (2004). *Histoire sociale et culturelle des Caisses d'Epargne en France: 1818–1881.* Economica.

Claessens, S., & Perotti, E. (2007). Finance and inequality: Channels and evidence. *Journal of Comparative Economics*, *35*(4), 748–773. doi:10.1016/j.jce.2007.07.002

Coffie, C. P. K., Hongjiang, Z., Mensah, I. A., Kiconco, R., & Simon, A. E. O. (2021). Determinants of FinTech payment services diffusion by SMEs in Sub-Saharan Africa: Evidence from Ghana. *Information Technology for Development, 27*(3), 539–560. doi:10.1080/02681102.2020.1840324

Cohen, L. J., Cornett, M. M., Marcus, A. J., & Tehranian, H. (2014). Bank earnings management and tail risk during the financial crisis. *Journal of Money, Credit and Banking, 46*(1), 171–197. doi:10.1111/jmcb.12101

Comerio, N., & Strozzi, F. (2019). Tourism and its economic impact: A literature review using bibliometric tools. *Tourism Economics, 25*(1), 109–131. doi:10.1177/1354816618793762

Coninck, S. de. (2012). *Le livret de Caisse d'épargne (1818-2008): une "passion" française*. Economica.

Cooray, A., & Schneider, F. (2018). Does corruption throw sand into or grease the wheels of financial sector development? *Public Choice, 177*(1-2), 111–133. doi:10.1007/s11127-018-0592-7

Cornut-Gentille, P. (2010). *Un scandale d'État: l'affaire Prince*. Perrin.

Criado, J. I., & Gil-Garcia, J. R. (2019). Creating public value through smart technologies and strategies: From digital services to artificial intelligence and beyond. *International Journal of Public Sector Management, 32*(5), 438–450. doi:10.1108/IJPSM-07-2019-0178

Croutsche, J.-C., & Roux, M. (2015). La fixation du prix des produits et services bancaires. *La Revue des Sciences de Gestion, 271*, 89-95. doi:10.3917/rsg.271.0089

Cull, R., Demirgüç-Kunt, A., & Lyman, T. (2012). *Financial inclusion and stability: what does research show?* openknowledge.worldbank.org

Czerwonka, L., & Jaworski, J. (2021). Capital structure determinants of small and medium-sized enterprises: Evidence from Central and Eastern Europe. *Journal of Small Business and Enterprise Development, 28*(2), 277–297. doi:10.1108/JSBED-09-2020-0326

D'Acunto, F., Hoang, D., & Weber, M. (2022). Managing households' expectations with unconventional policies. *Review of Financial Studies, 35*(4), 1597–1642. doi:10.1093/rfs/hhab083

Daly, S., & Frikha, M. (2016). Banks and economic growth in developing countries: What about Islamic banks? *Cogent Economics & Finance, 4*(1), 1168728. doi:10.1080/23322039.2016.1168728

Danisman, G. O., Demir, E., & Ozili, P. (2021). Loan loss provisioning of US banks: Economic policy uncertainty and discretionary behavior. *International Review of Economics & Finance, 71*, 923–935. doi:10.1016/j.iref.2020.10.016

Daumy, J.-C. (2023). Des salons à l'Assemblée constituante: le du de Liancourt ou la formation d'un aristocate libéral et réformateur (1768-1827). *Parlements(s), Revue d'histoire politique, 2*(38), 159-175.

De Filippi, P., & Hassan, S. (2018). Blockchain technology as a regulatory technology: From code is law to law is code. *arXiv preprint arXiv:1801.02507.*

de Lutzel, E. (2008). Prêter aux pauvres avec intérêt? Une révolution du XVème Siècle. *Finance & Bien Commun, 1*(30), 115-119. https://www.cairn.info/revue-finance-et-bien-commun-2008-1-page-115.htm doi:10.3917/fbc.030.0115

De Mendonça, H. F., & Souza, G. J. D. G. (2012). Is inflation targeting a good remedy to control inflation? *Journal of Development Economics, 98*(2), 178–191. doi:10.1016/j.jdeveco.2011.06.011

Dela Cruz, N. A., Villanueva, A. C. B., Tolin, L. A., Disse, S., Lensink, R., & White, H. (2023). PROTOCOL: Effects of interventions to improve access to financial services for micro-, small-and medium-sized enterprises in low-and middle-income countries: An evidence and gap map. *Campbell Systematic Reviews*, *19*(3), e1341. Advance online publication. doi:10.1002/cl2.1341 PMID:37415851

Demirgüç-Kunt, A., Klapper, L. F., & Singer, D. (2013). Financial inclusion and legal discrimination against women: evidence from developing countries. *World Bank Policy Research Working Paper*, (6416).

Demirgüç-Kunt, A., Klapper, L. F., Ansar, S., & Jagati, A. (2017). Making it easier to apply for a bank account: a study of the Indian market. *World Bank Policy Research Working Paper*, (8205).

Demirgüç-Kunt, A., Klapper, L., & Singer, D. (2017a). *Financial Inclusion and Inclusive Growth: A Review of Recent Empirical Evidence.* World Bank Policy Research Working Paper, (8040). Available at: https://shorturl.at/JORS4

Demirguc-Kunt, A., Klapper, L., Singer, D., Inclusion, F., & Inclusive, G. A. (2017). *Review of Recent Empirical Evidence.* World Bank Group, Policy Research working paper 8040.

Demirgüç-Kunt, A., & Klapper, L. F. (2012). Financial inclusion in Africa: An overview. *World Bank Policy Research Working Paper*, 6088.

Demirgüç-Kunt, A., Klapper, L., & Singer, D. (2017b). Financial inclusion and legal discrimination against women: Evidence from developing countries. *The World Bank Economic Review*, *31*(3), 1–22.

Dempsey, N., Bramley, G., Power, S., & Brown, C. (2011). The social dimension of sustainable development: Defining urban social sustainability. *Sustainable Development (Bradford)*, *19*(5), 289–300. doi:10.1002/sd.417

Deschodt, E. (1993). *Histoire du Mont-de-Piété, Collection « Documents.* Le Cherche Midi Editeur.

Dhaoui, E. (2015). *The role of Islamic Microfinance in Poverty Alleviation: Lessons from Bangladesh Experience.* Tunisian Institute for Competitiveness and Quantitative Studies, Munich Personal RePEc Archive, Paper No. 63665.

Dienillah, A. A., & Anggraeni, L. (2016). Impact of Financial Inclusion on Financial System Stability in Asia. *Inclusion on Financial System Stability in Asia. Bulletin of Monetary Economics and Banking.*

Dietrich, A., & Wanzenried, G. (2011). Determinants of bank profitability before and during the crisis: Evidence from Switzerland. *Journal of International Financial Markets, Institutions and Money*, *21*(3), 307–327. doi:10.1016/j.intfin.2010.11.002

Dirican, C. (2015). The impacts of robotics, artificial intelligence on business and economics. *Procedia: Social and Behavioral Sciences*, *195*, 564–573. doi:10.1016/j.sbspro.2015.06.134

Dluhopolskyi, O., Pakhnenko, O., Lyeonov, S., Semenog, A., Artyukhova, N., Cholewa-Wiktor, M., & Jastrzębski, W. (2023). Digital financial inclusion: COVID-19 impacts and opportunities. *Sustainability (Basel)*, *15*(3), 2383. doi:10.3390/su15032383

Donthu, N., Kumar, S., Mukherjee, D., Pandey, N., & Lim, W. M. (2021). How to conduct a bibliometric analysis: An overview and guidelines. *Journal of Business Research*, *133*, 285–296. doi:10.1016/j.jbusres.2021.04.070

Donthu, N., Kumar, S., Pandey, N., & Lim, W. M. (2021c). Research constituents, intellectual structure, and collaboration patterns in Journal of International Marketing: An analytical retrospective. *Journal of International Marketing*, *29*(2), 1–25. doi:10.1177/1069031X211004234

Donthu, N., Kumar, S., Pattnaik, D., & Lim, W. M. (2021d). Abibliometric retrospection ofmarketing from the lens of psychology: Insights from Psychology & Marketing. *Psychology and Marketing*, *38*(5), 834–865. doi:10.1002/mar.21472

Du Toit, E., & Cuba, Y. Z. (2018). Cost and profit efficiency of listed South African banks pre and post the financial crisis. *Research in International Business and Finance*, *45*, 435–445. doi:10.1016/j.ribaf.2017.07.175

Dua, P. (2023). Monetary policy framework in India. In *Macroeconometric Methods: Applications to the Indian Economy* (pp. 39–72). Springer Nature Singapore. doi:10.1007/978-981-19-7592-9_3

Duet, D. (1991). *Les Caisses d'Epargne*. PUF.

Dulac, S. (1993). *Histoire du Mont-de-Piété en France*. Rondeau. https://www.historia.fr/les-mauvaises-affaires-dalexandre-stavisky

Dupuy, K., & Neset, S. (2018). The cognitive psychology of corruption. *Micro-Level Explanations for Unethical Behavior*, *U4*, 2.

Durisin, B., & Puzone, F. (2009). Maturation of corporate governance research, 1993–2007: An assessment. *Corporate Governance*, *17*(3), 266–291. doi:10.1111/j.1467-8683.2009.00739.x

Duvendack, M., & Mader, P. (2020). Impact of financial inclusion in low-and middle-income countries: A systematic review of reviews. *Journal of Economic Surveys*, *34*(3), 594–629. doi:10.1111/joes.12367

Duvendack, M., Palmer-Jones, R., Copestake, J. G., Hooper, L., Loke, Y., & Rao, N. (2011). *What is the evidence of the impact of microfinance on the well-being of poor people? EPPI-Centre, Social Science Research Unit, Institute of Education*. University of London.

Dziopa, F., & Ahern, K. (2011). A systematic literature review of the applications of Q-technique and its methodology. *Methodology: European Journal of Research Methods for the Behavioral and Social Sciences*, *7*(2), 39–55. doi:10.1027/1614-2241/a000021

Eid, Q. M. A., Al Houl, M. A. A., Alqudah, M. T. S., & Almomani, M. A.-A. (2023). The Role of Financial Inclusion in the Stability of Islamic Banks. *International Journal of Professional Business Review: Int. J. Prof. Bus. Rev.*, *8*(4), 7–19.

Elasrag, H. (2011). *Principals of the Islamic finance: A focus on project finance*. Munich Personal RePEc Archive, MPRA Paper No. 30197.

Elhaj, M. A. A., Muhamed, N. A., & Ramli, N. M. (2015). The influence of corporate governance, financial ratios, and Sukuk structure on Sukuk rating. *Procedia Economics and Finance*, *31*, 62–74. doi:10.1016/S2212-5671(15)01132-6

Elkhayat, N., & ElBannan, M. A. (2018). State Divestitures and Bank Performance: Empirical Evidence from the Middle East and North Africa Region. *Asian Economic and Financial Review*, *8*(2), 145–171. doi:10.18488/journal.aefr.2018.82.145.171

Ellegaard, O., & Wallin, J. A. (2015). The bibliometric analysis of scholarly production: How great is the impact? *Scientometrics*, *105*(3), 1809–1831. doi:10.1007/s11192-015-1645-z PMID:26594073

Elouaourti, Z., & Ezzahid, E. (2022a). Factors of regional financial inclusion in Morocco. *Regional Science Policy & Practice*, rsp3.12516. Advance online publication. doi:10.1111/rsp3.12516

Elouaourti, Z., & Ezzahid, E. (2022b). Financial services and firm performance, are there any differences by size? Worldwide evidence using firm-level data. *Journal of Economic Studies (Glasgow, Scotland)*, *50*(4), 858–880. Advance online publication. doi:10.1108/JES-10-2021-0526

Elouardighi, I., & Oubejja, K. (2023). Can Digital Financial Inclusion Promote Women's Labor Force Participation? Microlevel Evidence from Africa. *International Journal of Financial Studies*, *11*(3), 87–87. doi:10.3390/ijfs11030087

Elouardighi, I., & Oubejja, K. (2023). COVID-19 and the fate of Moroccan female-led firms: Regional level evidence. *Regional Science Policy & Practice*, *15*(8), 1740–1767. doi:10.1111/rsp3.12703

Ernawati, E., Rosnawintang, R., & Nusantara, A. (2022). The Effect of Public Awareness on the Islamic Financial Industry's Development. *Significant: Journal Ilma Ekonomi.*, *11*(2), 399–414. doi:10.15408/sjie.v11i2.25816

Ertan, A. (2022). Real earnings management through syndicated lending. *Review of Accounting Studies*, *27*(4), 1157–1198. doi:10.1007/s11142-021-09607-7

Esquiros, A. (1844, September). Les Caisses d'Epargne. *Revue des Deux Mondes (Paris, France)*, *7*(5), 751–782. https://www.jstor.org/stable/44690223

Eton, M., Mwosi, F., Okello-Obura, C., Turyehebwa, A., & Uwonda, G. (2021). Financial inclusion and the growth of small medium enterprises in Uganda: Empirical evidence from selected districts in Lango sub-region. *Journal of Innovation and Entrepreneurship*, *10*(1), 1–23. doi:10.1186/s13731-021-00168-2

Ezzahid, E., & Elouaourti, Z. (2019). Financial development and total factors productivity channel: Evidence from Africa. *Indonesian Capital Market Review*, *10*(2). Advance online publication. doi:10.21002/icmr.v10i2.10827

Ezzahid, E., & Elouaourti, Z. (2021). Financial inclusion, mobile banking, informal finance and financial exclusion: Micro-level evidence from Morocco. *International Journal of Social Economics*, *48*(7), 1060–1086. doi:10.1108/IJSE-11-2020-0747

Ezzahid, E., & Elouaourti, Z. (2022). Financial inclusion, financial frictions, and economic growth: Evidence from Africa. *Journal of African Business*, *23*(3), 731–756. doi:10.1080/15228916.2021.1926856

Faisal, Y. A., Gunawan, I., Cupian, Hayati, A., Apriliadi, A., & Fajri, M. (2023). Examining the Purchase Intentions of Indonesian Investors for Green Sukuk. *Sustainability (Basel)*, *15*(9), 7430. doi:10.3390/su15097430

Farooqi, A. H., Qamar, M. U. R., & Chachi, A. (2017). Role of Islamic microfinance scheme in poverty alleviation and well-being of women implemented by Islami Bank Bangladesh Limited. *İslam Ekonomisi ve Finansı Dergisi, 3*(1), 1-32.

Fathallah, R., Sidani, Y., & Khalil, S. (2020). How religion shapes family business ethical behaviors: An institutional logics perspective. *Journal of Business Ethics*, *163*(4), 647–659. doi:10.1007/s10551-019-04383-6

Fazal, H., Muhammad, J., & Zahoor, U. H. (2020). Operational perspective of SMEs performance and competitive priorities practices: Path analytic approach. *Studies in Business and Economics*, *15*(1), 55–67. doi:10.2478/sbe-2020-0006

Fernández-Olit, B., Martín Martín, J. M., & Porras González, E. (2020). Systematized literature review on financial inclusion and exclusion in developed countries. *International Journal of Bank Marketing*, *38*(3), 600–626. doi:10.1108/IJBM-06-2019-0203

Fichtenau, H. (1966). *Carolingian Empire. The Age of Charlemagne*. Harper Torchbooks.

Fischbach, K., Putzke, J., & Schoder, D. (2011). Co-authorship networks in electronic markets research. *Electronic Markets*, *21*(1), 19–40. doi:10.1007/s12525-011-0051-5

Fitzpatrick, K. (2015). The effect of bank account ownership on credit and consumption: Evidence from the UK. *Southern Economic Journal*, *82*(1), 55–80. doi:10.4284/0038-4038-2013.027

Fortescue, W. (2000). *The Third Republic in France: 1870 - 1940*. Routledge.

Francis, M. E. (2013). Determinants of commercial bank profitability in Sub-Saharan Africa. *International Journal of Economics and Finance*, *5*(9), 134–147.

Franzoni, S., & Allali, A. (2018). Principles of Islamic Finance and Principles of Corporate Social Responsibility: What Convergence. *Sustainability (Basel)*, *10*(3), 637. Advance online publication. doi:10.3390/su10030637

Fratzscher, M., Grosse-Steffen, C., & Rieth, M. (2020). Inflation targeting as a shock absorber. *Journal of International Economics*, *123*, 103308. doi:10.1016/j.jinteco.2020.103308

Fried, J. (2016). Charlemagne (P. Lewis, Trans.). Harvard University Press.

Fungáčová, Z., & Weill, L. (2015). Understanding financial inclusion in China. *China Economic Review*, *34*, 196–206. doi:10.1016/j.chieco.2014.12.004

Garang, J. A. (2015). How to leverage oil resources to enhance SME financing in South Sudan. *International Journal of Economic Policy in Emerging Economies*, *8*(2), 119–137. doi:10.1504/IJEPEE.2015.069604

Garba, M., Salleh, F., Hafiz, U. A., & Bakar, N. M. A. (2022). Insurance Literacy, Risk Knowledge Management, Risk-Taking Propensity and Economic Sustainability among SMEs: The Moderating Effect of Financial Inclusion. *Journal of Social Economics Research*, *9*(2), 92–110. doi:10.18488/35.v9i2.3120

Garcia, M. T. M., & Trindade, M. J. (2019). Determinants of banks' profitability in Angola. *African Journal of Economic and Management Studies*, *10*(1), 116–128. doi:10.1108/AJEMS-06-2018-0161

Gaudez, P., & Schacchi, P.-H. (1989). *Les Caisses d'Epargne en Europe*. ESKA.

Ghosh, S. (2016). Political transition and bank performance: How important was the Arab Spring? *Journal of Comparative Economics*, *44*(2), 372–382. doi:10.1016/j.jce.2015.02.001

Ghosh, S., & Vinod, D. (2017). What constrains financial inclusion for women? Evidence from Indian micro data. *World Development*, *92*, 60–81. doi:10.1016/j.worlddev.2016.11.011

Giallanza, A., Aiello, G., & Marannano, G. (2021). Industry 4.0: Advanced digital solutions implemented on a close power loop test bench. *Procedia Computer Science*, *180*, 93–101. doi:10.1016/j.procs.2021.01.133

Gillpatrick, T., Boğa, S., & Aldanmaz, O. (2022). How can blockchain contribute to developing country economies? A literature review on application areas. *Economics*, *10*(1), 105–128. doi:10.2478/eoik-2022-0009

Gilormini, P. (2013). *Aux origines du groupe Banque Populaire Caisse d'Epargne: Philantropie libérale et solidarisme républicain.* Electronic Working Paper Series, ESDES Recherche.

Goetzmann, W. N., & Rouwenhorst, K. G. (2005). *The Origins of Value. The Financials Innovations that Created Modern Capital Markets.* Oxford University Press. doi:10.1093/oso/9780195175714.001.0001

Gomez Urquijo, L. (2015). Financial exclusion in the European Union: Addressing difficulties in accessing finance within the current integration framework. *Journal of Contemporary European Studies*, *23*(1), 100–117. doi:10.1080/14782804.2014.961059

Gortsos, C. (2015). *Financial inclusion: An overview of its various dimensions and the initiatives to enhance its current level.* Academic Press.

Goyal, K., Kumar, S., & Xiao, J. J. (2021). Antecedents and consequences of personal financial management behavior: A systematic literature review and future research agenda. *International Journal of Bank Marketing*, *39*(7), 1166–1207. Advance online publication. doi:10.1108/IJBM-12-2020-0612

GPFI. (2012). The G20 Basic Set of Financial Inclusion Indicators. Global Partnership for Financial Inclusion.

Graeff, P., & Mehlkop, G. (2003). The impact of economic freedom on corruption: Different patterns for rich and poor countries. *European Journal of Political Economy, 19*(3), 605–620. doi:10.1016/S0176-2680(03)00015-6

Grais, W., & Pellegrini, M. (2006). *Corporate governance and Shariah compliance in institutions offering Islamic financial services* (Vol. 4054). World Bank Publications. doi:10.1596/1813-9450-4054

Greene, W. H. (2003). *Econometric analysis*. Pearson Education India.

Grohmann, A., Kluhs, T., & Menkhoff, L. (2018). Does financial literacy improve financial inclusion? Cross country evidence. *World Development, 111*, 84–96. doi:10.1016/j.worlddev.2018.06.020

Grosse, N., Guerpinar, T., & Henke, M. (2021, July). Blockchain-enabled trust in intercompany networks applying the agency theory. In *Proceedings of the 2021 3rd Blockchain and Internet of Things Conference* (pp. 8-14). 10.1145/3475992.3475994

GSMA. (2019). *State of the industry report on mobile money*. GSMA. https://www.gsma.com/sotir/#download

Gueslin, A. (1987). *L'invention de l'économie sociale. Le XIXème siècle français*. Economica.

Gueslin, A. (2007). *Mythologies de l'argent: essai sur l'histoire des representations de la richesse et de la pauvreté dans la France contemporaine (XXe-XXe siècles)*. Economica.

Gueslin, A. (1989). *L'invention des Caisses d'épargne en France: une grande utopie libérale. Revue Historique, 282*. https://www.jstor.org/stable/40955304

Gueslin, A. (1991). *Aux origines de l'État-providence: la mise en place du modèle français des Caisses d'épargne. Revue d'histoire moderne et contemporaine, 38*[e]. https://www.jstor.org/stable/20529732

Gu, F., Gao, J., Zhu, X., & Ye, J. (2023). The impact of digital inclusive finance on SMEs' technological innovation activities—Empirical analysis based on the data of new third board enterprises. *PLoS One, 18*(11), e0293500. doi:10.1371/journal.pone.0293500 PMID:37917741

Guillen-Royo, M. (2018). *Sustainability and wellbeing: Human-scale development in practice*. Routledge. doi:10.4324/9781315762135

Gupta, B. B., Tewari, A., Jain, A. K., & Agrawal, D. P. (2017). Fighting against phishing attacks: State of the art and future challenges. *Neural Computing & Applications, 28*(12), 3629–3654. doi:10.1007/s00521-016-2275-y

Gupta, S., Davoodi, H., & Alonso-Terme, R. (2002). Does corruption affect income inequality and poverty? *Economics of Governance, 3*(1), 23–45. doi:10.1007/s101010100039

Gupte, R., Venkataramani, B. & Gupata, D. (2012). Computation of financial inclusion index for India. *International Journal of Procedia - Social and Behavioural Sciences, 37*, 133-149.

Gutter, M., & Copur, Z. (2011). Financial behaviours and financial wellbeing of college students: Evidence from a national survey. *Journal of Family and Economic Issues, 32*(4), 699–714. doi:10.1007/s10834-011-9255-2

Gyapong, E., Gyimah, D., & Ahmed, A. (2021). Religiosity, borrower gender and loan losses in microfinance institutions: A global evidence. *Review of Quantitative Finance and Accounting, 57*(2), 657–692. doi:10.1007/s11156-021-00958-5

Hafssa, Y., & Oumaima, B. (2020). *Blockchain and smart sukuk: new determinant of development of the sukuk market.* Paper presented at the 2020 IEEE International Conference on Technology Management, Operations and Decisions (ICTMOD). 10.1109/ICTMOD49425.2020.9380613

Halay, T. (1994). *Le Mont-de-Piété des origines à nos jours*. L'Harmattan.

Haneef, M., Manu, L. P., Adjasi, C. K. D., Abor, J., Harvey, S. K., Dienillah, A. A., ... Doan, T. P. L. (2020). The impact of financial inclusion on financial stability in Asian countries. *Journal of Asian Finance. Economics and Business*, *7*(6), 47–59. doi:10.13106/jafeb.2020.vol7.no6.047

Hania, B. T., Endri, E., & Indra, I. (2022). Identify the Issuance Problem of Corporate Green Sukuk in Indonesia. *Islamic Economics Journal*, *8*(2), 187–204. doi:10.21111/iej.v8i2.8404

Hasan, A., Gupta, S., Irfan, M., & Dias, R. M. (2024). Assessing Public Awareness of Islamic Finance and Interest-Free Banking in India. In Fintech Applications in Islamic Finance: AI, Machine Learning, and Blockchain Techniques (pp. 80-92): IGI Global.

Hasan, Z. (2015). *Risk sharing versus risk transfer in Islamic Finance: A critical appraisal.* . doi:10.12816/0021394

HasanM. (2023)The Impact of Financial Technology (Fintech) on the Financial and Banking Services Sector and Its Applications in the Islamic Financial Industry. doi:10.2139/ssrn.4369683

Hasan, R., Ahmad, A. U. F., & Parveen, T. (2019). Sukuk risks–a structured review of theoretical research. *Journal of Islamic Accounting and Business Research*, *10*(1), 35–49. doi:10.1108/JIABR-06-2015-0026

Hasheela, V., Happonen, A., & Julius, L. (2023). Assessing The Status Quo Of Fintech In Africa. The Role of African Fintech & Financial Inclusion Promotion: A Systematic Literature Review. *Journal of Namibian Studies: History Politics Culture*, *37*, 321–348.

Hassan, M. K. (2020). Introduction: Islamic Finance and Contemporary Challenges. *Arab Law Quarterly, 35*(1-2), 1-5. https://www.isdb.org/sites/default/files/media/documents/2021-02/ISLAMIC%20MICROFINANCE%20FOR%20WOMEN%20FINAL.pdf doi:10.1163/15730255-BJA10067

Hassan, A., & Saleem, S. (2017). An Islamic microfinance business model in Bangladesh: Its role in alleviation of poverty and socio-economic well-being of women. *Humanomics*, *33*(1), 15–37. doi:10.1108/H-08-2016-0066

Hassan, M. K., Alshater, M. M., Hasan, R., & Bhuiyan, A. B. (2021). Islamic microfinance: A bibliometric review. *Global Finance Journal*, *49*, 100651. doi:10.1016/j.gfj.2021.100651

Hendrix, N., Veenstra, D. L., Cheng, M., Anderson, N. C., & Verguet, S. (2022). Assessing the economic value of clinical artificial intelligence: Challenges and opportunities. *Value in Health*, *25*(3), 331–339. doi:10.1016/j.jval.2021.08.015 PMID:35227443

Henley, A. (2017). Does religion influence entrepreneurial behaviour? *International Small Business Journal*, *35*(5), 597–617. doi:10.1177/0266242616656748

Hoffman, P., Postel-Vinay, G., & Rosenthal, J.-L. (2001). *Des marchés sans prix, une économie politique du crédit à Paris.* EHESS.

Hollanders, M. (2020). FinTech and financial inclusion: Opportunities and challenges. *Journal of Payments Strategy & Systems, 14*(4), 315-325.

Homer, S., & Sylla, R. (2005). *A History of Interest Rates* (4th ed.). Wiley.

Homsi, M. A., Muhamad Sori, Z., & Mohamad, S. (2023). Determinants of Sukuk credit rating: Evidence from issuing firms in Malaysia. *Journal of Islamic Accounting and Business Research*, *14*(8), 1324–1343. doi:10.1108/JIABR-05-2022-0127

Huang, Y., Li, Z., Qiu, H., Tao, S., Wang, X., & Zhang, L. (2023). BigTech credit risk assessment for SMEs. *China Economic Review*, *81*, 102016. Advance online publication. doi:10.1016/j.chieco.2023.102016

Hua, X., & Huang, Y. (2021). Understanding China's fintech sector: Development, impacts and risks. *European Journal of Finance, 27*(4-5), 321–333. doi:10.1080/1351847X.2020.1811131

Hu, D., Fang, X., & DiGiovanni, Y. M. (2023). Technological progress, financial constraints, and digital financial inclusion. *Small Business Economics*, 1–29.

Hudaefi, F. A. (2020). How does Islamic fintech promote the SDGs? Qualitative evidence from Indonesia. *Qualitative Research in Financial Markets, 12*(4), 353–366. doi:10.1108/QRFM-05-2019-0058

Hussain, M., Shahmoradi, A., & Turk, R. (2015). *An Overview of Islamic Finance.* IMF Working Paper, International Monetary Fund, WP/15/120.

Hussain, R. T., & Ahmad, F. (2021). Measuring Financial Longevity of Firm in Emerging Economy: A Study on Islamic Financial Institutions of Pakistan. *Minhaj Journal of Economics and Organization Science, 1*(2), 9-27.

Hussain, M., Nawaz, M. A., Aqdas, R., & Riaz, M. (2020). The Influence of Islamic Finance. *Financial Inclusion and Governance on the Economic Growth of Islamic Countries., 25*, 216–226.

Hussain, M., Shahmoradi, A., & Turk, R. (2016). An overview of Islamic finance. *Journal of International Commerce. Economic Policy, 7*(01), 1650003.

Hussain, M., Yahya, F., & Waqas, M. (2021). Does strong governance stimulate the effect of economic freedom and financial literacy on financial inclusion? a cross-country evidence. *Future Business Journal, 7*(1), 1–10. doi:10.1186/s43093-021-00090-9

Huston, S. J. (2010). Measuring financial literacy. *The Journal of Consumer Affairs, 44*(2), 296–316. doi:10.1111/j.1745-6606.2010.01170.x

IBM. (2022). *Cost of a Data Breach Report 2022.* Available at: https://www.ibm.com/sg-en/security/data- breach

Ibrahim, A. J., & Kahf, M. (2020). Instruments for investment protection when structuring Islamic venture capital. *Journal of Islamic Accounting and Business Research, 11*(9), 1907–1920. doi:10.1108/JIABR-01-2019-0025

Ifinedo, P. (2011). Internet/e-business technologies acceptance in Canada's SMEs: An exploratory investigation. *Internet Research, 21*(3), 255–281. doi:10.1108/10662241111139309

IFSB, I. F. S. B. (2020). Retrieved from Karim, S., & Naeem, M. A. (2022). Do global factors drive the interconnectedness among green, Islamic and conventional financial markets? *International Journal of Managerial Finance, 18*(4), 639–660.

International Finance Corporation. (2017). *SME Finance.* Retrieved February 22, 2021, from IFC:https://www.ifc.org/wps/wcm/connect/Industry_EXT_Content/IFC_External_Corporate_Sit e/Financial+Institutions/Priorities/SME+Finance/

Iphofen, R., & Kritikos, M. (2021). Regulating artificial intelligence and robotics: Ethics by design in a digital society. *Contemporary Social Science, 16*(2), 170–184. doi:10.1080/21582041.2018.1563803

Irman, M. (2021). Financial inclusion as mediator in the relationship of social capital and financial literacy towards business performance of the trade sector SMEs in Pekanbaru, Indonesia. *Economic Annals-XXI*, 194.

Islamic Development Bank. (2018). An overview of Islamic banking and finance in Asia. Routledge Handbook of Banking and Finance in Asia. doi:10.4324/9781315543222-28

Islam, M. (2020). Role of Islamic microfinance in women's empowerment: Evidence from rural development scheme of Islami bank Bangladesh limited. *Isra International Journal of Islamic Finance, 13*(1), 26–45. doi:10.1108/IJIF-11-2019-0174

Jain, V., Ramos-Meza, C. S., Aslam, E., Chawla, C., Nawab, T., Shabbir, M. S., & Bansal, A. (2023). Do energy resources matter for growth level? The dynamic effects of different strategies of renewable energy, carbon emissions on sustainable economic growth. *Clean Technologies and Environmental Policy*, *25*(3), 771–777. doi:10.1007/s10098-022-02432-9

Jankowki, P. (2002). *A Confidence Man in the Republic of Virtue*. Cornell University Press.

Jeanblanc, H. (2002). Karl Marx à la découverte des mystères de Paris. *Cahiers d'Études Germaniques*, *42*, 135-153. https://www.persee.fr/doc/cetge_0751-4239_2002_num_42_1_1590 doi:10.3406/cetge.2002.1590

Jungo, J., Madaleno, M., & Botelho, A. (2021). Financial literacy and financial inclusion effects on sta bility and competitiveness indicators in the banking sector: Cross country evidence for Africa and the world. *Global Economy Journal*, *21*(2), 1–30. doi:10.1142/S2194565921500093

Jungo, J., Madaleno, M., & Botelho, A. (2022). The Effect of Financial Inclusion and Competitiveness on Financial Stability: Why Financial Regulation Matters in Developing Countries? *Journal of Risk and Financial Management*, *15*(3), 122. Advance online publication. doi:10.3390/jrfm15030122

Junoh, M. Z. B. H., Hidthiir, M. M. H. B., & Basheer, M. F. (2019). Entrepreneurial financial practices in Pakistan: The role of access to finance and financial literacy. International Journal of Innovation. *Creativity and Change*, *7*(9), 210–231.

Kamal, A., Khan, M. M. S., Kazmi, U. E. R., Anis, W., Hussain, T., & Sualeh, M. (2021). Impact of Financial Inclusion and Corporate Social Responsibility on Islamic Banks Financial stability with the Moderating Role of Corporate Governance. *Indian Journal of Economics and Business*, *20*(1), 1–13.

Kane, E. J. (1993). What lessons should Japan learn from the US deposit-insurance mess? *Journal of the Japanese and International Economies*, *7*(4), 329–355. doi:10.1006/jjie.1993.1021

Kania, R. (2022). *Why and how financial inclusion policy develop? A case study from Indonesia*. University of Birmingham.

Kapur, D., & Gualu, A. K. (2012). Financial performance and ownership structure of Ethiopian commercial banks. *Journal of Economics and International Finance*, *4*(1), 1–8.

Kaur, P., & Parashar, A. (2021). A systematic literature review of blockchain technology for smart villages. *Archives of Computational Methods in Engineering*, 1–52. PMID:34720578

Kazim, S. (2008). Islamic Finance for Micro and Medium Enterprises. Islamic Research Training Institute and University Brunei Darussalam.

Keshminder, J., Singh, G., Wahid, Z., & Abdullah, M. (2019). Green sukuk: Malaysia taking the lead. *Malaysian Journal of Consumer and Family Economics*, *22*(2), 1–22.

Khan, S., & Alhadi, F. A. F. (n.d.). Fintech and Financial Inclusion in Saudi Arabia. *Review of Economics and Finance*, *20*(1), 857-866.

Khan, A., Mubarik, M. S., & Naghavi, N. (2023). What matters for financial inclusions? Evidence from emerging economy. *International Journal of Finance & Economics*, *28*(1), 821–838. doi:10.1002/ijfe.2451

Khan, H. R. (2011). Financial Inclusion and Financial Stability; Are They Two sides of the Same Coin? In *Address at BANCON 2011*. Reserve Bank of India.

Khan, M. A., Pattnaik, D., Ashraf, R., Ali, I., Kumar, S., & Donthu, N. (2021). Value of special issues in the Journal of Business Research: A bibliometric analysis. *Journal of Business Research*, *125*, 295–313. doi:10.1016/j.jbusres.2020.12.015

Khan, S. (2023). The impacts of Sukuk on financial inclusion in selected Sukuk markets: An empirical investigation based on generalized method of moments (GMM) analysis. *International Journal of Social Economics*, *50*(8), 1153–1168. doi:10.1108/IJSE-06-2022-0424

Khan, S. A., & Aslam, E. (2018). Partnership Based Microfinance in Islamic Banks: Need, Application and Commandments in Modern Age. *Journal of Islamic Thought and Civilization*, *8*(1), 192–208. doi:10.32350/jitc.81.13

Khmous, D. F., & Besim, M. (2020). Impact of Islamic banking share on financial inclusion: Evidence from MENA. *International Journal of Islamic and Middle Eastern Finance and Management*, *13*(4), 655–673. doi:10.1108/IMEFM-07-2019-0279

Kijkasiwat, P., & Chancharat, N. (2022). Financial inclusion in the industry 4.0: The effects of financial inclusion on electronic payments in Thailand. *International Journal of Trade and Global Markets*, *15*(1), 70–78. doi:10.1504/IJTGM.2022.120884

Kim, W.C., Mauborgne, R., & Pipino, M. (2020). *Fintech: Compte-Nickel Creating New Demand in the Retail Banking Sector*. INSEAD.

Kim, D. W., Yu, J. S., & Hassan, M. K. (2018). Financial inclusion and economic growth in OIC countries. *Research in International Business and Finance*, *43*, 1–14. doi:10.1016/j.ribaf.2017.07.178

Kim, D.-W., Yu, J.-S., & Hassan, M. K. (2020). The influence of religion and social inequality on financial inclusion. *The Singapore Economic Review*, *65*(01), 193–216. doi:10.1142/S0217590817460031

Kitchenham, B., Brereton, O. P., Budgen, D., Turner, M., Bailey, J., & Linkman, S. (2009). Systematic literature reviews in software engineering–a systematic literature review. *Information and Software Technology*, *51*(1), 7–15. doi:10.1016/j.infsof.2008.09.009

Klapper, L., & Lusardi, A. (2020). *Financial literacy and financial resilience: evidence from around the world.* https://www.weforum.org/agenda/2022/07/global-digital-financial-inclusion-findex/ doi:10.1111/fima.12283

Kodongo, O., Mokoaleli-Mokoteli, T., & Maina, L. N. (2015). Capital structure, profitability and firm value: Panel evidence of listed firms in Kenya. *African Finance Journal*, *17*(1), 1–20.

Konyak, O., Das, S., & Patra, N. (2022). Impact of Nagaland state rural livelihood mission (nsrlm) on livelihood status of women in Nagaland. *Agricultural Reviews.* , doi:10.18805/ag.R-2358

Koseoglu, M. A., Rahimi, R., Okumus, F., & Liu, J. (2016). Bibliometric studies in tourism. *Annals of Tourism Research*, *61*, 180–198. doi:10.1016/j.annals.2016.10.006

Kotsios, P. (2023). Business resilience skills for SMEs. *Journal of Innovation and Entrepreneurship*, *12*(1), 37. doi:10.1186/s13731-023-00304-0 PMID:37274429

Krolikowski, A., Fu, X., & Hope, R. (2013). *Wireless Water: Improving Urban Water Provision Through Mobile Finance Innovations Opens in a new t. Smith School of Enterprise and the Environment.* https://www.oxfordtmcd.org/publication/improving-urban-water-governance-through-mobile-finance-innovations

Kshetri, N. (2016). Big data's role in expanding access to financial services in China. *International Journal of Information Management*, *36*(3), 297–308. doi:10.1016/j.ijinfomgt.2015.11.014

Kumar, R., & Pathak, D. (2022). Financial awareness: A bridge to financial inclusion. *Development in Practice*, *32*(7), 968–980. doi:10.1080/09614524.2022.2028731

Kumar, S., Afrouzi, H., Coibion, O., & Gorodnichenko, Y. (2015). *Inflation targeting does not anchor inflation expectations: Evidence from firms in New Zealand (No. w21814)*. National Bureau of Economic Research.

Kumar, S., Sahoo, S., Lim, W. M., & Dana, L.-P. (2022). Religion as a social shaping force in entrepreneurship and business: Insights from a technology-empowered systematic literature review. *Technological Forecasting and Social Change*, *175*, 121393. doi:10.1016/j.techfore.2021.121393

Kumbirai, M., & Webb, R. (2010). A financial ratio analysis of commercial bank performance in South Africa. *African Review of Economics and Finance*, *2*(1), 30–53.

Kundid, A., & Ercegovac, R. (2011). Credit rationing in financial distress: Croatia SMEs' finance approach. *International Journal of Law and Management*, *53*(1), 62–84. doi:10.1108/17542431111111890

Kuyateh, M. A. (2022). Shariah Compliance Prohibitions in Islamic Banking and Finance: The Case of Riba, Gharar and Maysir. *Journal of Islamic Banking & Finance*, *39*(1).

Lam, W. R., & Liu, Y. (2020). Tackling Small and Medium-Sized Enterprises (SMEs) Financing in China. *Annals of Economics and Finance*, *21*(1).

Lanzara, F. (2021). Islamic finance and Sustainable Development Goals. A bibliometric analysis from 2000 to 2021. *European Journal of Islamic Finance*. https://ssrn.com/abstract=3857617

Lapidus, A. (1991). Information and Risk in the Medieval Doctrine of Usury during the Thirteenth Century. In *Perspectives on the History of Economic Thought*. Edward Elgar. https://paris1.hal.science/hal-00721678

Laroche-Signorile. (2019), Affaire Stavisky: la mort de l'escroc a fait vaciller la République en 1934. *Le Figaro Histoire*. https://www.lefigaro.fr/histoire/archives/2019/01/07/26010-20190107ARTFIG00261-affaire-stavisky-la-mort-de-l-escroc-fit-vaciller-la-republique-en-1934.php

Łasak, P. (2022). The role of financial technology and entrepreneurial finance practices in funding small and medium-sized enterprises. *Journal of Entrepreneurship. Management and Innovation*, *18*(1), 7–34.

Latridis, G. E., & Persakis, A. D. (2012). Bank profitability determinants under IFRSs. *International Journal of Economics and Accounting*, *3*(1), 77–99. doi:10.1504/IJEA.2012.045523

Lawal, A. B., Ahmed, F., & Abdulkadir, J. (2023). Blockchain Technology and Financial Inclusion In Nigeria: An Analysis Of The Missing Link. *Gusau Journal of Business Administration*, *2*(1), 97–106.

Le Bret, H. (2016). Le Compte-Nickel: un compte pour tous, sans banque. *Le Journal de l'école de Paris du Management*, *6*, 24–30.

Le Bret, H. (2017). Vers un monde sans banques? [Towards a world without banks?]. In Annales des Mine- Réalités industrielles (n° 4, pp. 56–59). FFE.

Le Bret, H. (2013). *No Bank. L'incroyable histoire d'un entrepreneur de banlieue qui veut révolutionner la banque*. Les Arènes.

Le Goff, J. (2019). *Le Moyen Âge et l'argent. Essai d'anthropologie historique*. Perrin.

Lee, T. H., & Chih, S. H. (2013). Does financial regulation affect the profit efficiency and risk of banks? Evidence from China's commercial banks. *The North American Journal of Economics and Finance*, *26*, 705–724. doi:10.1016/j.najef.2013.05.005

Lelissa, T. B. (2014). The determinants of Ethiopian commercial banks performance. *European Journal of Business and Management*, *6*(14), 52–62.

Le, T. D. (2020). The interrelationship among bank profitability, bank stability, and loan growth: Evidence from Vietnam. *Cogent Business & Management*, *7*(1), 1840488. doi:10.1080/23311975.2020.1840488

Leung, X. Y., Sun, J., & Bai, B. (2017). Bibliometrics of social media research: A co-citation and co-word analysis. *International Journal of Hospitality Management*, *66*, 35–45. doi:10.1016/j.ijhm.2017.06.012

Leyshon, A., & Thrift, N. (1995). Geographies of financial exclusion: Financial abandonment in Britain and the United States. *Transactions of the Institute of British Geographers*, *20*(3), 312–341. doi:10.2307/622654

Liaqat, W., Altaf, M. T., Barutçular, C., Zayed, E. M., & Hussain, T. (2023). Drought and sorghum: A bibliometric analysis using VOS viewer. *Journal of Biomolecular Structure & Dynamics*, •••, 1–13. doi:10.1080/07391102.2023.2269279 PMID:37837436

Lim, W. M., Yap, S. F., & Makkar, M. (2021). Home sharing in marketing and tourism at a tipping point: What do we know, how do we know, and where should we be heading? *Journal of Business Research*, *122*, 534–566. doi:10.1016/j.jbusres.2020.08.051 PMID:33012896

Lin, S., & Ye, H. (2009). Does inflation targeting make a difference in developing countries? *Journal of Development Economics*, *89*(1), 118–123. doi:10.1016/j.jdeveco.2008.04.006

Liu, F. H., & Lai, K. P. (2021). Ecologies of green finance: Green sukuk and development of green Islamic finance in Malaysia. *Environment and Planning A. Economy and Space*, *53*(8), 1896–1914.

Li, Y., Stasinakis, C., & Yeo, W. M. (2022). A hybrid XGBoost-MLP model for credit risk assessment on digital supply chain finance. *Forecasting*, *4*(1), 184–207. doi:10.3390/forecast4010011

Llorca, M. (2017). Les banques aux prises avec les fintech. *L'économie politique*, *3*(75).

Lusardi, A., & Mitchell, O. S. (2014). The economic importance of financial literacy: Theory and evidence. *Journal of Economic Literature*, *52*(1), 5–44. doi:10.1257/jel.52.1.5 PMID:28579637

Lu, Z., Wu, J., Li, H., & Nguyen, D. K. (2022). Local bank, digital financial inclusion and SME financing constraints: Empirical evidence from China. *Emerging Markets Finance & Trade*, *58*(6), 1712–1725. doi:10.1080/1540496X.2021.1923477

Lu, Z., Wu, J., & Liu, J. (2020). Bank concentration and SME financing availability: The impact of promotion of financial inclusion in China. *International Journal of Bank Marketing*, *38*(6), 1329–1349. doi:10.1108/IJBM-01-2020-0007

Mabula, J. B., Dong Ping, H., & James, M. (2023). The Impact of African Firms' Utilization of Financial and Technology Resource on Innovation: A Simple Mediation. *SAGE Open*, *13*(1). Advance online publication. doi:10.1177/21582440231153037

Machkour, B., & Abriane, A. (2020). Industry 4.0. and its Implications for the Financial Sector. *Procedia Computer Science*, *177*, 495–502. doi:10.1016/j.procs.2020.10.068

Mahboob, A. M., Vichayanan, R., & Abusayed, K. A. (2017). Comparative positioning of Small and Medium enterprises in Bangladesh, Thailand and the Philippines. *Экономика региона*, *13*(2), 381-395.

Mahmood, S., Shuhui, W., Aslam, S., & Ahmed, T. (2023). Financial Inclusion: Does it matter in Alleviating Poverty in Pakistan. *Social Indicators Research*, *169*(3), 1125–1146. doi:10.1007/s11205-023-03200-y

Malik, A. H., Md Isa, A. H., Jais, M., Ur Rehman, A., & Ali Khan, M. (2022). Financial stability of Asian Nations: Governance quality and financial inclusion. *Borsa Istanbul Review*, *22*(2), 377–387. doi:10.1016/j.bir.2021.05.005

Malone, K., Stewart, S. D., Wilson, J., & Korsching, P. F. (2010). Perceptions of financial well-being among American women in diverse families. *Journal of Family and Economic Issues*, *31*(1), 63–81. doi:10.1007/s10834-009-9176-5

Mamaro, L. P., & Sibindi, A. B. (2022). Entrepreneurial Financing in Africa during the COVID-19 Pandemic. *Journal of Risk and Financial Management, 15*(11), 511. doi:10.3390/jrfm15110511

Manu, L. P., Adjasi, C. K. D., Abor, J., & Harvey, S. K. (2011). Financial stability and economic growth: A cross-country study. *International Journal of Financial Services Management, 5*(2), 121. doi:10.1504/IJFSM.2011.041920

Matama, R. (2016). Analysis of education levels and small business financial worth in Uganda. In *Analysis of education levels and small business financial worth in Uganda*. Matama, Rogers.

Maulayati, R. R., & Iswati, S. (n.d.). *Sukuk Trend Analysis: Bibliometric and Systematic Literature Review from 2011-2021*. Academic Press.

Mauro, P., & Driscoll, D. D. (1997). *Why worry about corruption?* (Vol. 6). International Monetary Fund Washington.

McFarlane, J. (2001). Corruption and the financial sector: The strategic impact. *Journal of Financial Crime, 9*(1), 8–21. doi:10.1108/eb026002

McIntyre, N., Quaye, E. S., Anning-Dorson, T., Lanivich, S., & Adomako, S. (2023). Investigating the impact of religiosity on entrepreneurial intentions. *Journal of Business Research, 156*, 113528. doi:10.1016/j.jbusres.2022.113528

McKitterick, R. (2008). Charlemagne. The Formation of a European Identity. Cambridge University Press.

Mdoe, I. J., Omolo, J. O., & Wawire, N. H. (2018). Bank Competition in Kenya. *Journal of Industry, Competition and Trade*, 1–20.

Mehry, E.-B., Ashraf, S., & Marwa, E. (2021). The Impact of Financial Inclusion on Unemployment Rate in Developing Countries. *International Journal of Economics and Financial Issues, 11*(1), 79–93. doi:10.32479/ijefi.10871

Méon, P.-G., & Weill, L. (2010). Is corruption an efficient grease? *World Development, 38*(3), 244–259. doi:10.1016/j.worlddev.2009.06.004

Mhlanga, D. (2020). Industry 4.0 in finance: The impact of artificial intelligence (ai) on digital financial inclusion. *International Journal of Financial Studies, 8*(3), 45. doi:10.3390/ijfs8030045

Mirakhor, A., & Iqbal, Z. (2012). *Financial Inclusion: Islamic Finance Perspective*. . doi:10.12816/0004974

Mireku, K., Sakyi, E. A., & Agana, J. A. (2018). Does Commercial Banks Presence Enhance Profitability in Ghana? *Global Business Review, 19*(6), 1449–1461. doi:10.1177/0972150918794969

Mishkin, F. S., & Posen, A. (1998). *Inflation targeting: lessons from four countries*. Academic Press.

Mishkin, F. S., & Schmidt-Hebbel, K. (2001). *One decade of inflation targeting in the world: what do we know and what do we need to know?* Academic Press.

Mishkin, F. S., & Schmidt-Hebbel, K. (2007). *Does inflation targeting make a difference?* Academic Press.

Mishkin, F. S. (2000). Inflation targeting for emerging-market countries. *The American Economic Review, 90*(2), 105–109. doi:10.1257/aer.90.2.105

Mishra, P., & Sant, T. G. (2021, October). Role of artificial intelligence and Internet of Things in promoting banking and financial services during COVID-19: Pre and post effect. In *2021 5th International Conference on Information Systems and Computer Networks (ISCON)* (pp. 1-7). IEEE.

Mohieldin, M. (2012). Realizing the potential of Islamic finance. World Bank Publications.

MohieldinM.IqbalZ.RostomA.FuX. (2015)The Role of Islamic Finance in Enhancing Financial Inclusion in Organization of Islamic Cooperation (OIC) Countries. *Islamic Economic Studies, 20*(2). https://ssrn.com/abstract=3158639

Morea, D., & Poggi, L. A. (2016). *Islamic finance and renewable energy: An innovative model for the sustainability of investments.* Paper presented at the 2016 AEIT International Annual Conference (AEIT). 10.23919/AEIT.2016.7892766

Morea, D., & Poggi, L. A. (2017). An innovative model for the sustainability of investments in the wind energy sector: The use of green sukuk in an Italian case study. *International Journal of Energy Economics and Policy*, *7*(2), 53–60.

Morgan, P. J., & Pontines, V. (2018). Financial stability and financial inclusion: The case of SME lending. *The Singapore Economic Review*, *63*(01), 111–124. doi:10.1142/S0217590818410035

MorganP.PontinesV. (2014). *Financial stability and financial inclusion* (Working Paper 488). ADBI Working Paper 488. https://doi.org/http://dx.doi.org/10.2139/ssrn.2464018

Mpofu, F. Y., & Mhlanga, D. (2022). Digital financial inclusion, digital financial services tax and financial inclusion in the fourth industrial revolution era in africa. *Economies*, *10*(8), 184. doi:10.3390/economies10080184

Muhammad, S., Ximei, K., Saqib, S. E., & Beutell, N. J. (2021). Entrepreneurial income and wellbeing: Women's informal entrepreneurship in a developing context. *Sustainability (Basel)*, *13*(18), 10262. doi:10.3390/su131810262

Mukit, M. M. H., Muneeza, A., & Paltrinieri, A. (2021). Contributions of Professor M. Kabir Hassan to the Islamic finance literature: A bibliometric study. *Jurnal Ekonomi Malaysia*, *55*(3), 49–76. doi:10.17576/JEM-2021-5503-04

Muneer, M. (2022, September). Fintech in Islamic finance literature: A review. *Heliyon*, *8*(9), e10385. doi:10.1016/j.heliyon.2022.e10385 PMID:36060472

Musari, K. (2022). Integrating green sukuk and cash waqf linked sukuk, the blended Islamic finance of fiscal instrument in Indonesia: A proposed model for fighting climate change. *International Journal of Islamic Khazanah*, *12*(2), 133–144. doi:10.15575/ijik.v12i2.17750

Musari, K., & Hidayat, S. E. (2023). The role of green sukuk in maqasid al-shariah and SDGs: Evidence from Indonesia. In *Islamic finance, fintech, and the road to sustainability: Reframing the approach in the post-pandemic era* (pp. 181–203). Springer. doi:10.1007/978-3-031-13302-2_9

Musau, S., Muathe, S., & Mwangi, L. (2018). Financial inclusion, bank competitiveness and credit risk of commercial banks in Kenya. *International Journal of Financial Research*, *9*(1), 203–218. doi:10.5430/ijfr.v9n1p203

Mutamimah, M., & Indriastuti, M. (2023). Fintech, financial literacy, and financial inclusion in Indonesian SMEs. *International Journal of Entrepreneurship and Innovation Management*, *27*(1-2), 137–150. doi:10.1504/IJEIM.2023.129331

Naceur, B. S., Goaied, M. (2010). The determinants of commercial bank interest margin and profitability: evidence from Tunisia. *Frontiers in Finance and Economics*, *5*(1), 106-130.

Naceur, S. B., Barajas, A., & Massara, A. (2017). Can Islamic banking increase financial inclusion? In *Handbook of empirical research on Islam and economic life* (pp. 213–252). Edward Elgar Publishing. doi:10.4337/9781784710736.00017

Naeem, M. A., Raza Rabbani, M., Karim, S., & Billah, S. M. (2023). Religion vs ethics: Hedge and safe haven properties of Sukuk and green bonds for stock markets pre-and during COVID-19. *International Journal of Islamic and Middle Eastern Finance and Management*, *16*(2), 234–252. doi:10.1108/IMEFM-06-2021-0252

Nagpal, A., Jain, M., & Jain, A. (2020). Determining the role of digital technology, governance and institutions in advancing financial inclusion in BRICS nations using probit regression analysis. *Journal of Social and Economic Development*, *22*(2), 443–459. doi:10.1007/s40847-020-00112-2

Najeeb, S. F., Bacha, O., & Masih, M. (2017). Does a held-to-maturity strategy impede effective portfolio diversification for Islamic bond (sukuk) portfolios? A multi-scale continuous wavelet correlation analysis. *Emerging Markets Finance & Trade, 53*(10), 2377–2393. doi:10.1080/1540496X.2016.1205977

Najib, M., & Fahma, F. (2020). Investigating the adoption of digital payment system through an extended technology acceptance model: An insight from the Indonesian small and medium enterprises. *International Journal on Advanced Science, Engineering and Information Technology, 10*(4), 1702–1708. doi:10.18517/ijaseit.10.4.11616

Nandru, P., Byram, A., & Rentala, S. (2016). Determinants of financial inclusion: Evidence from account ownership and use of banking services. *International Journal of Entrepreneurship and Development Studies, 4*(2), 141–155.

Nanziri, L. E., & Wamalwa, P. S. (2021). Finance for SMEs and its effect on growth and inequality: Evidence from South Africa. *Transnational Corporations Review, 13*(4), 450–466. doi:10.1080/19186444.2021.1925044

Neaime, S., & Gaysset, I. (2018). Financial inclusion and stability in MENA: Evidence from poverty and inequality. *Finance Research Letters, 24*, 199–220. doi:10.1016/j.frl.2017.09.007

Nehal, S. (2023). Green Sukuk–A Viable Global Financing option for Climatic and Environmental Revolution (A Practical Instrument for the Development of Sustainable Energy Projects in Pakistan). *Karachi Islamicus, 3*(1).

Neuenkirch, M., & Tillmann, P. (2014). Inflation targeting, credibility, and non-linear Taylor rules. *Journal of International Money and Finance, 41*, 30–45. doi:10.1016/j.jimonfin.2013.10.006

Ngoc, N. M., & Tien, N. H. (2023). Quality of Scientific Research and World Ranking of Public and Private Universities in Vietnam. *International Journal of Public Sector Performance Management.*

Nguse, T., Desalegn, G., Oshora, B., Tangl, A., Nathan, R. J., & Fekete-Farkasne, M. (2022). Enhancing Women Economic Empowerment Through Financial Inclusion: Evidence from SMEs in Ethiopia. *Polish Journal of Management Studies, 25*(1), 270–291. doi:10.17512/pjms.2022.25.1.17

Nikunj Kumar Gor. (2013). Microtakaful-islamic insurance for deprived: innovation, sustainability and inclusive growth. *International Journal of Business, Economics and Law, 3*(2).

Nugraha, D. P., Setiawan, B., Nathan, R. J., & Fekete-Farkas, M. (2022). FinTech adoption drivers for innovation for SMEs in Indonesia. *Journal of Open Innovation, 8*(4), 208. doi:10.3390/joitmc8040208

Nurhanifah, A., & Khomsatun, S. (2023). Literature analysis of sukuk ratings in Indonesia bibliometric approach. *Journal of Science, 12*(03), 4191–4201.

Obaidullah, M., & Khan, T. U. (2008). *Islamic Microfinance Development: Challenges and Initiatives.* Islamic Research & Training institute Policy Dialogue Paper No. 2. doi:10.2139/ssrn.1506073

Okello Candiya Bongomin, G., Mpeera Ntayi, J., Munene, J. C., & Akol Malinga, C. (2017). The relationship between access to finance and growth of SMEs in developing economies: Financial literacy as a moderator. *Review of International Business and Strategy, 27*(4), 520-538.

Okfalisa, O., Mahyarni, M., Anggraini, W., Saeed, F., Moshood, T. D., & Saktioto, S. (2022). Quadruple helix engagement: Reviews on shariah fintech based SMEs digitalization readiness. *Indonesian Journal of Electrical Engineering and Informatics, 10*(1), 112–122. doi:10.52549/ijeei.v10i1.3455

Okonkwo, J., & Nwanna, I. (2021). Financial Inclusion and Economic Growth in Nigeria: An Empirical Study. *International Journal of Research and Innovation in Social Science, 05*(01), 323–330. doi:10.47772/IJRISS.2021.5113

Onodugo, C., Ogbo, A., & Ogbaekirigwe, C. (2021). Moderating role of social capital on the effect of financial behavior on financial inclusion. *Problems and Perspectives in Management, 19*(3), 502–512. doi:10.21511/ppm.19(3).2021.41

Oseni, A., U. (. (2014). Dispute management in Islamic financial institutions: A case study of near sukuk defaults. *Journal of International Trade Law & Policy, 13*(3), 198–214. doi:10.1108/JITLP-12-2013-0034

Oshora, B., Desalegn, G., Gorgenyi-Hegyes, E., Fekete-Farkas, M., & Zeman, Z. (2021). Determinants of financial inclusion in small and medium enterprises: Evidence from Ethiopia. *Journal of Risk and Financial Management, 14*(7), 286. doi:10.3390/jrfm14070286

Ozili & Opene. (2021). The role of banks in the circular economy. *World Journal of Science, Technology and Sustainable Development.*

Ozili, P. K. (2021). *Financial inclusion research around the world: A review.* Paper presented at the Forum for social economics. 10.1080/07360932.2020.1715238

Ozili, P. K. (2021a). Banking sector earnings management using loan loss provisions in the Fintech era. *International Journal of Managerial Finance.*

OziliP. (2020). Financial Inclusion Research Around the World: A Review. Socially Responsible Investment journal. doi:10.2139/ssrn.3515515

Ozili, P. K. (2017). Bank profitability and capital regulation: Evidence from listed and non-listed banks in Africa. *Journal of African Business, 18*(2), 143–168. doi:10.1080/15228916.2017.1247329

Ozili, P. K. (2018). Impact of digital finance on financial inclusion and stability. *Borsa Istanbul Review, 18*(4), 329–340. doi:10.1016/j.bir.2017.12.003

Ozili, P. K. (2019). Bank income smoothing, institutions and corruption. *Research in International Business and Finance, 49*, 82–99. doi:10.1016/j.ribaf.2019.02.009

Ozili, P. K. (2020). Social inclusion and financial inclusion: International evidence. *International Journal of Development Issues, 19*(2), 169–186. doi:10.1108/IJDI-07-2019-0122

Ozili, P. K. (2020). Theories of financial inclusion. In *Uncertainty and challenges in contemporary economic behaviour* (pp. 89–115). Emerald Publishing Limited. doi:10.1108/978-1-80043-095-220201008

Ozili, P. K. (2021). Measuring financial inclusion and financial exclusion. In *New Challenges for Future Sustainability and Wellbeing* (pp. 411–427). Emerald Publishing Limited. doi:10.1108/978-1-80043-968-920211022

Ozili, P. K. (2021b). Bank profitability determinants: Comparing the United States, Nigeria and South Africa. *International Journal of Banking and Finance, 16*(1), 55–78.

Ozili, P. K. (2022). Big 4 auditors, bank earnings management and financial crisis in Africa. *Journal of Financial Reporting and Accounting, 20*(2), 215–232. doi:10.1108/JFRA-10-2020-0306

Ozili, P. K. (2023). Can social inclusion policies promote financial inclusion? *The International Journal of Sociology and Social Policy, 43*(11), 1138–1155. doi:10.1108/IJSSP-03-2023-0054

Ozili, P. K., & Inclusion, F. (2022)Sustainability and Sustainable Development. Advance online publication. doi:10.2139/ssrn.4185735

Ozili, P. K., & Outa, E. (2017). Bank loan loss provisions research: A review. *Borsa Istanbul Review, 17*(3), 144–163. doi:10.1016/j.bir.2017.05.001

Ozili, P. K., & Uadiale, O. (2017). Ownership concentration and bank profitability. *Future Business Journal, 3*(2), 159–171. doi:10.1016/j.fbj.2017.07.001

Paltrinieri, A., Hassan, M. K., Bahoo, S., & Khan, A. (2019). A bibliometric review of sukuk literature. *International Review of Economics & Finance.*

Park, C. Y., & Mercado, R. (2021). Understanding financial inclusion: What matters and how it matters. *ADBI Working Paper no. 1287.*

Park, J. (2012). Corruption, soundness of the banking sector, and economic growth: A cross- country study. *Journal of International Money and Finance, 31*(5), 907–929. doi:10.1016/j.jimonfin.2011.07.007

Pasiouras, F., & Kosmidou, K. (2007). Factors influencing the profitability of domestic and foreign commercial banks in the European Union. *Research in International Business and Finance, 21*(2), 222–237. doi:10.1016/j.ribaf.2006.03.007

Passmore, K. (2013). The Right in France from the Third Republic to Vichy. Oxford University Press.

Pastureau, G. (2011). Le Mont-de-piété en France: une réponse économique aux problèmes sociaux de son époque (1462-1919). *Revue d'histoire de la protection sociale, 1*(4), 25-40. doi:10.3917/rhps.004.0025

Pastureau, G. (2013). Le microcrédit social: un "argent secours" en perspective historique - Le cas du prêt sur gages au Crédit municipal de Bordeaux. In *Economies et finances*. Université Montesquieu - Bordeaux IV.

Paul, S. (2019). *Use of Blockchain and Aritificial Intelligence to Promote Financial Inclusion in India Smita Miglani Indian Council for Research on International Economic Relations.* Available online: https://economictimes

Paul, J., Lim, W. M., O'Cass, A., Hao, A. W., & Bresciani, S. (2021). Scientific procedures and rationales for systematic literature reviews (SPAR-4-SLR). *International Journal of Consumer Studies, 45*(4), O1–O16. doi:10.1111/ijcs.12695

Peni, E., & Vähämaa, S. (2012). Did good corporate governance improve bank performance during the financial crisis? *Journal of Financial Services Research, 41*(1-2), 19–35. doi:10.1007/s10693-011-0108-9

Pinos, F. (2015). *Inclusion financière et populations précarisées: effets des business models des services financiers en France. Economies et finances* [Thèse]. Université de Bordeaux.

Pirgaip, B., Arslan-Ayaydin, Ö., & Karan, M. B. (2021). Do Sukuk provide diversification benefits to conventional bond investors? Evidence from Turkey. *Global Finance Journal, 50*, 100533. doi:10.1016/j.gfj.2020.100533

Pontet, J. (1991). *Histoire de Bayonne, ebook.* Privat.

Praszkier, R. (2023). Three-dimensional delineation of Changers-for-Good: From practice to conceptualization. *Possibility Studies & Society, 1*(3), 361–379. doi:10.1177/27538699231177149

Preuveneers, D., & Ilie-Zudor, E. (2017). The intelligent industry of the future: A survey on emerging trends, research challenges and opportunities in Industry 4.0. *Journal of Ambient Intelligence and Smart Environments, 9*(3), 287–298. doi:10.3233/AIS-170432

Prina, S. (2015). Banking the poor via savings accounts: Evidence from a field experiment. *Journal of Development Economics, 115*, 16–31. doi:10.1016/j.jdeveco.2015.01.004

Pritchard, A. (1969). Statistical bibliography or bibliometrics. *The Journal of Documentation, 25*, 348.

Puglisi, C. R., & Barcham, W. L. (2008). Bernardino da Feltre, the Monte di Pieta and the man of sorrows: Activist, microcredit and logo. *Artibus et Historiae, 29*(58), 35–63. https://www.jstor.org/stable/40343649

Qosim, N., Ratnasari, R. T., Wardhana, A. K., Fauziana, H., & Barkah, T. T. (2023). Eight Years of Research Related to the Green Sukuk in the Global Stock Exchange Market to Support the Implementation of SDG: A Bibliometric Review. *Journal of Islamic Economic and Business Research*, *3*(2), 161–180. doi:10.18196/jiebr.v3i2.204

Rabbani, M. R., Bashar, A., Nawaz, N., Karim, S., Ali, M., Rahiman, H. U., & Alam, M. S. (2021). Exploring the role of Islamic fintech in combating the aftershocks of covid-19: The open social innovation of the Islamic financial system. *Journal of Open Innovation*, *7*(2), 136. doi:10.3390/joitmc7020136

Rabbani, M. R., Billah, S. M., Shaik, M., Rahman, M., & Boujlil, R. (2023). Dynamic connectedness, spillover, and optimal hedging strategy among FinTech, Sukuk, and Islamic equity markets. *Global Finance Journal*, *58*, 100901. doi:10.1016/j.gfj.2023.100901

Rahman, A., Ahmad, A. U. F., Bin-Nashwan, S. A., Muneeza, A., Abdul Halim, A. H., & Markom, R. (2023). Policy approach adopted for issuance of Green Sukuk: Is priority given to priority needed areas? *Journal of Islamic Accounting and Business Research*. Advance online publication. doi:10.1108/JIABR-10-2022-0279

Rahman, M., Isa, C. R., Tu, T.-T., Sarker, M., & Masud, M. A. K. (2020). A bibliometric analysis of socially responsible investment sukuk literature. *Asian Journal of Sustainability and Social Responsibility*, *5*(1), 1–19. doi:10.1186/s41180-020-00035-2

Rahman, R. A., & Dean, F. (2013). Challenges and solutions in Islamic microfinance. *Humanomics*, *29*(4), 293–306. doi:10.1108/H-06-2012-0013

Ramadhan, I. A. (2020). *Green Sukuk issuance as an investment instrument for sustainable development*. Paper presented at the International Conference on Law, Governance and Islamic Society (ICOLGIS 2019). 10.2991/assehr.k.200306.189

Ramady, M. A. (2012). *The GCC economies: Stepping up to future challenges*. Springer Science & Business Media. doi:10.1007/978-1-4614-1611-1

Ratnawati, K. (2020). The Impact of Financial Inclusion on Economic Growth, Poverty, Income Inequality, and Financial Stability in Asia. *The Journal of Asian Finance. Economics and Business*, *7*(10), 73–85. doi:10.13106/jafeb.2020.vol7.no10.073

Rauniyar, K., Rauniyar, K., & Sah, D. K. (2021). Role of FinTech and innovations for improvising digital financial inclusion. *Int. J. Innov. Sci. Res. Technol*, *6*(5), 1419–1424.

Ravi, V., & Kamaruddin, S. (2017). Big data analytics enabled smart financial services: opportunities and challenges. *Big Data Analytics: 5th International Conference, BDA 2017, Hyderabad, India, December 12-15, 2017 Proceedings*, *5*, 15–39.

Rayhan, A. (2023). *Interest-Free Finance for A More Equitable Future*. doi:10.13140/RG.2.2.33212.21129/1

Rehman, A., Aslam, E., & Iqbal, A. (2022). Intellectual capital efficiency and bank performance: Evidence from islamic banks. *Borsa Istanbul Review*, *22*(1), 113–121. doi:10.1016/j.bir.2021.02.004

Rezkyarta, A., & Irfany, M. I. (2023). Bibliometric Analysis of Sukuk Literatures. *Journal of Islamic Economics Literatures*, *4*(2). Advance online publication. doi:10.58968/jiel.v4i2.314

Riaz, U., Burton, B., & Fearfull, A. (2023). Emotional propensities and the contemporary Islamic banking industry. *Critical Perspectives on Accounting*, *94*, 102449. doi:10.1016/j.cpa.2022.102449

Rizvi, S. K. A., Naqvi, B., Mirza, N., & Umar, M. (2022). Safe haven properties of green, Islamic, and crypto assets and investor's proclivity towards treasury and gold. *Energy Economics*, *115*, 106396. doi:10.1016/j.eneco.2022.106396

Roa, M. J., Villegas, A., & Garrón, I. (2022). Interest rate caps on microcredit: Evidence from a natural experiment in Bolivia. *Journal of Development Effectiveness*, *14*(2), 125–142. doi:10.1080/19439342.2021.1968934

Rocchi, J. M. (2020). *Des banques en ligne aux néobanques*. Franel Editions. doi:10.14375/NP.9782384910243

Rocchi, J. M. (2021). Competition Between Neobanks and Online Banks in the French Retail Banking Market and Reactions from Universal Banks. In A. Sghari & K. Mezghani (Eds.), *Influence of FinTech on Management Transformation* (pp. 191–216). IGI Global. doi:10.4018/978-1-7998-7110-1.ch009

Rocchi, J. M. (2022). How to Build a Leading So-Called Neobank and Pursue its Growth? The Case of the FinTech Nickel in Europe. In J. D. Santos (Ed.), *Cases on Digital and Management Issues in Modern Organizations* (pp. 177–199). IGI Global.

Rosin, F., Forget, P., Lamouri, S., & Pellerin, R. (2020). Impacts of Industry 4.0 technologies on Lean principles. *International Journal of Production Research*, *58*(6), 1644–1661. doi:10.1080/00207543.2019.1672902

Rzegocki, M. (2021). *The mounts of piety: A case study in Christian innovation*. Acton Institute. https://www.acton.org/publications/transatlantic/2021/06/23/mounts-piety-case-study-christian-innovation

Sa'ad, A. A., & Ali, E. R. A. E. (2023). Developing Smart Green Sukuk Structure Using Blockchain Technology. *Journal of Islamic entrepreneurship (Majallatu Riyadati Al-aamali Al-islamiati), 8.*

Sabiu, T. T., & Abduh, M. (2021). Impact of Islamic banking inclusion on SME employment growth in Nigeria. *Journal of Islamic Monetary Economics and Finance*, *7*(1), 77–106. doi:10.21098/jimf.v7i1.1354

Sachs, J., Thye, W. W., & Yoshino, N. (2019). *Handbook of Green Finance: Energy Security and Sustainable Development*. Springer. doi:10.1007/978-981-13-0227-5

Salman, A., & Nowacka, K. (2020). *Innovative financial products and services for women in Asia and the pacific*. Academic Press.

Santoro, F., Munoz, L., Prichard, W., & Mascagni, G. (2022). *Digital financial services and digital IDs: What potential do they have for better taxation in Africa?* Institute of Development Studies.

Sari, Y., Nugroho, M., & Rahmiyati, N. (2023). The effect of financial knowledge, financial behavior and digital financial capabilities on financial inclusion, financial concern and performance in MSMEs in East Java. *Uncertain Supply Chain Management*, *11*(4), 1745–1758. doi:10.5267/j.uscm.2023.6.016

Sarkar, S., Nair, S., & Rao, M. V. V. (2023). Exploring the gender dimension in financial inclusion in India: Insights from the Global Findex Database. *Journal of Development Policy and Practice*, *8*(2), 141–161. doi:10.1177/24551333221141570

Sarma, M., & Pais, J. (2011). Financial inclusion and development. *Journal of International Development*, *23*(5), 613–628. doi:10.1002/jid.1698

Sarofim, S., Minton, E., Hunting, A., Bartholomew, D. E., Zehra, S., Montford, W., Cabano, F., & Paul, P. (2020). Religion's influence on the financial well-being of consumers: A conceptual framework and research agenda. *The Journal of Consumer Affairs*, *54*(3), 1028–1061. doi:10.1111/joca.12315

Sarpong-Kumankoma, E., Abor, J., Aboagye, A. Q., & Amidu, M. (2018). Differences in bank profit persistence in Sub-Saharan Africa. *African Journal of Economic and Management Studies*, *9*(4), 512–522. doi:10.1108/AJEMS-03-2017-0037

Saviano, M., Nenci, L., & Caputo, F. (2017). The financial gap for women in the MENA region: A systemic perspective. *Gender in Management*, *32*(3), 203–217. doi:10.1108/GM-07-2016-0138

Seemule, M., Sinha, N., & Ndlovu, T. (2017). Determinants of Commercial Banks' Profitability in Botswana: An Empirical Analysis. *IUP Journal of Bank Management, 16*(2).

Seghezzo, L. (2009). The five dimensions of sustainability. *Environmental Politics, 18*(4), 539–556. doi:10.1080/09644010903063669

Seglen, P. (1989). Use of citation analysis and other bibliometric methods in evaluation of the quality of research. *Tidsskrift for den Norske Laegeforening: Tidsskrift for Praktisk Medicin, ny Raekke, 109*(31), 3229-3224.

Sen, A. (2000). *Social exclusion: Concept, application, and scrutiny.* Social Development Papers No. 1. Office of Environment and Social Development Asian Development Bank.

Sethi, D., & Acharya, D. (2018). Financial inclusion and economic growth linkage: Some cross country evidence. *Journal of Financial Economic Policy, 10*(3), 369–385. doi:10.1108/JFEP-11-2016-0073

Setor, T. K., Senyo, P. K., & Addo, A. (2021). Do digital payment transactions reduce corruption? Evidence from developing countries. *Telematics and Informatics, 60,* 101577. doi:10.1016/j.tele.2021.101577

Shahid, M. R., Khin, A. A., Seong, L. C., Shahbaz, M., & Ahmad, F. (2024). Mapping the Relationship of Research and Development Expenditures and Economic Growth through Bibliometric Analysis: A Theoretical Perspective. *Journal of the Knowledge Economy.* Advance online publication. doi:10.1007/s13132-024-01781-8

Sharma, C., & Paramati, S. R. (2021). Does financial development reduce the level of corruption? Evidence from a global sample of 140 countries. *International Journal of Finance & Economics, 26*(4), 5093–5109. doi:10.1002/ijfe.2056

Sharma, H., & Díaz Andrade, A. (2023). Digital financial services and human development: Current landscape and research prospects. *Information Technology for Development, 29*(4), 1–25. doi:10.1080/02681102.2023.2199189

Shihadeh, F. H., Hannon, A. M. T., Guan, J., Ul Haq, I., Wang, X., & Haq, I. ul, & Wang, X. (2018). Does Financial Inclusion Improve the Banks' Performance? Evidence from Jordan. In J. W. Kensinger (Ed.), Global Tensions in Financial Markets (pp. 117–138). Emerald Publishing Limited. doi:10.1108/S0196-382120170000034005

Shim, S., Xiao, J. J., Barber, B. L., & Lyons, A. C. (2009). Pathways to life success: A conceptual model of financial well-being for young adults. *Journal of Applied Developmental Psychology, 30*(6), 708–723. doi:10.1016/j.appdev.2009.02.003

Shinozaki, S. (2014). A new regime of SME finance in emerging Asia: Enhancing access to growth capital and policy implications. Journal of International Commerce. *Economic Policy, 5*(03), 1440010. Advance online publication. doi:10.1142/S1793993314400109

Siddik, M. N. A., & Kabiraj, S. (2018). Does financial inclusion induce financial stability? Evidence from cross-country analysis. *Australasian Accounting. Business and Finance Journal, 12*(1), 33–46. doi:10.14453/aabfj.v12i1.3

Sidibe, T. (2015). *Mobile banking and mobile money: a highly instrument against corruption.* Academic Press.

Sinclair, S. P. (2001). Financial exclusion: An introductory survey. CRSIS, Edinburgh College of Art/Heriot Watt University.

Small, H. (1973). Co-citation in the scientific literature: A new measure of the relationship between two documents. *Journal of the American Society for Information Science, 24*(4), 265–269. doi:10.1002/asi.4630240406

Smith, A. (1999). *The Wealth of Nations, Books IV-V.* ePenguin.

Smith, A. (2003). *The Wealth of Nations.* Books I-III. Penguin Classics.

Smolo, E., & Ismail, A. G. (2011). A theory and contractual framework of Islamic micro-financial institutions' operations. *Journal of Financial Services Marketing, 15*(4), 287–295. doi:10.1057/fsm.2010.24

Song, C.-Q., Chang, C.-P., & Gong, Q. (2021). Economic growth, corruption, and financial development: Global evidence. *Economic Modelling*, *94*, 822–830. doi:10.1016/j.econmod.2020.02.022

Sornaganesh, V., Ganesh, S., Sathish, M. T., & Chellamma, A. V. (2020). Impact of COVID-19 outbreak in digital payments. *Int J Innov Res Multidiscip Field*, *6*(8), 159–164.

Sufian, F. (2009). Determinants of bank profitability in a developing economy: Empirical evidence from the China banking sector. *Journal of Asia-Pacific Business*, *10*(4), 281–307. doi:10.1080/10599230903340205

Sufian, F. (2011). Profitability of the Korean banking sector: Panel evidence on bank- specific and macroeconomic determinants. *Journal of Economics and Management*, *7*(1), 43–72.

Surachman, E. N., Hermawan, R. P., Handayani, D., & Astuti, E. (2023). Evaluation of Sovereign Sukuk as a government financing instrument with stakeholder theory: A moving forward policy from Indonesia's experience. *Journal of Islamic Accounting and Business Research*, *14*(2), 315–338. doi:10.1108/JIABR-03-2022-0066

Svensson, L. (1997). Monetary policy and inflation targeting. *Research summary, NBER Reporter*, 5-8.

Svensson, L. E. (1999). Inflation targeting as a monetary policy rule. *Journal of Monetary Economics*, *43*(3), 607–654. doi:10.1016/S0304-3932(99)00007-0

Svensson, L. E. (2010). Inflation targeting. In *Handbook of monetary economics* (Vol. 3, pp. 1237–1302). Elsevier.

Svoboda, A. (2024). Investing in the Islamic world: Opportunities, challenges, and implications. *Economics and Finance*, *12*(1), 13–21. doi:10.51586/2754-6209.2024.12.1.13.21

Tahir, H., Hussain, S., Iqbal, A., Aslam, E., & Masri, R. (2020). Determinants of Return on Assets of Non-Financial Firm of Malaysia. *International Transaction Journal of Engineering, Management, &. Applied Sciences & Technologly*, *11*(11), 1–11.

Tarus, D. K., & Manyala, P. O. (2018). What determines bank interest rate spread? Evidence from Sub-Saharan Africa. *African Journal of Economic and Management Studies*, *9*(3), 335–348. doi:10.1108/AJEMS-05-2017-0094

Taylor, J. B. (2019). Inflation targeting in high inflation emerging economies: Lessons about rules and instruments. *Journal of Applied Econometrics*, *22*(1), 103–116.

Thach, N. N., Duong, M. B., & Oanh, T. T. K. (2017). Effects of corruption on economic growth-empirical study of Asia countries. *Imperial Journal of Interdisciplinary Research*, *7*, 791–804.

Thathsarani, S., Jianguo, W., & Alariqi, M. (2023). How Do Demand, Supply, and Institutional Factors Influence SME Financial Inclusion: A Developing Country Perspective. *SAGE Open*, *13*(3). Advance online publication. doi:10.1177/21582440231187603

Thathsarani, U. S., & Jianguo, W. (2022). Do Digital Finance and the Technology Acceptance Model Strengthen Financial Inclusion and SME Performance? *Information (Basel)*, *13*(8), 390. doi:10.3390/info13080390

The World Bank. (2014). *Global Financial Development Report 2014: Financial inclusion* (Vol. 2). World Bank Publications. doi:10.1596/978-0-8213-9985-9

The World Bank. (2024), *Global Financial Development Report*. https://databank.worldbank.org/source/global-financial-development/Series/GFDD.AI.01#

Thivaud, J.-M., & Kang, Z. (1991). Épargne, retraite, prévoyance idéale: Les caisses d'épargne, la Caisse des retraites et la Caisse des dépôts et consignations (1816-1850). *Revue d'Economie Financiere*, *1*(1), 65–92. doi:10.3406/ecofi.1991.1779

Thomson Reuters. (2018). *Islamic Finance Development Report 2018.* Thomson Reuters. Retrieved from: https://ceif.iba.edu.pk/pdf/Reuters-Islamic-finance-development-report2018.pdf

Thornton, J. (2010). *Does Financial Development Reduce Corruption?* Bangor Business School Research Paper, 09/003.

Thornton, J. (2016). Inflation targeting in developing countries revisited. *Finance Research Letters, 16*, 145–153. doi:10.1016/j.frl.2015.10.024

Tinta, A. A., Ouédraogo, I. M., & Al-Hassan, R. M. (2022). The micro determinants of financial inclusion and financial resilience in Africa. *African Development Review, 34*(2), 293–306. doi:10.1111/1467-8268.12636

Toaff, A. (2004). Jews, Franciscans, and the First monti di Pieta in Italy (1462–1500). In *Friars and Jews in the Middle Ages and Renaissance*. Leiden: Koninklijke Brill.

Toni, N., Theng, B., & Calen, C. (2024). Investigating the effect of financial literacy and financial inclusion on operational and sustainable supply chain performance of SMEs. *Uncertain Supply Chain Management, 12*(1), 573–582. doi:10.5267/j.uscm.2023.8.014

Trabelsi, N., Umar, Z., Dogah, K. E., & Vo, X. V. (2024). Are investment grade Sukuks decoupled from the conventional yield curve? *International Review of Financial Analysis, 91*, 102981. doi:10.1016/j.irfa.2023.102981

Trianto, B., & Masrizal, M. (2021). Sukuk and Islamic banking financing: Their impacts on the real sector. *Journal of Islamic Monetary Economics and Finance, 7*(4), 671–686. doi:10.21098/jimf.v7i4.1407

Truby, J., Dahdal, A., & Ismailov, O. (2022). The Role and Potential of Blockchain Technology in Islamic Finance. *European Business Law Review, 33*(2), 175–192. Advance online publication. doi:10.54648/EULR2022005

Tsai, C. H., & Kuan-Jung, P. (2017). The FinTech revolution and financial regulation: The case of online supply-chain financing. *Asian Journal of Law and Society, 4*(1), 109–132. doi:10.1017/als.2016.65

Ulfah, I. F., Sukmana, R., Laila, N., & Sulaeman, S. (2023). A structured literature review on green sukuk (Islamic bonds): Implications for government policy and future studies. *Journal of Islamic Accounting and Business Research.* Advance online publication. doi:10.1108/JIABR-10-2022-0255

Ullah, Dey, Shahriar, & Shahriar. (2023). *A Review of Literature on Takaful and Conventional Insurance. Evidence from Bangladesh.* Munich Personal RePEc Archive, MPRA Paper No. 117463.

Uluyol, B. (2023). A comprehensive empirical and theoretical literature survey of Islamic bonds (sukuk). *Journal of Sustainable Finance & Investment, 13*(3), 1277–1299. doi:10.1080/20430795.2021.1917224

Umar, U. H., Ado, M. B., & Ayuba, H. (2019). Is religion (interest) an impediment to Nigeria's financial inclusion targets by the year 2020? A qualitative inquiry. *Qualitative Research in Financial Markets, 12*(3), 283-300.

UNDP. (2020). *Sustainable Development Goals.* Retrieved from United Nations Development Programme website. Available at: https://www.undp.org/sustainable-development-goals

United Nations. (2016). *Digital Financial Inclusion.* Retrieved from https://www.un.org/esa/ffd/ wpcontent/uploads/2016/01/Digital-Financial-Inclusion_ITU_IATF-Issue-Brief.pdf

Ur Rehman, A., Aslam, E., & Iqbal, A. (2021). Factors influencing the intention to give Zakat on employment income: Evidence from the Kingdom of Saudi Arabia. *Islamic Economic Studies, 29*(1), 33–49. doi:10.1108/IES-05-2020-0017

Utamaa, A. G. S., & Hariantob, S. (2020). Information System of" Laku Pandai": Achieving Financial Inclusion-Financial Technology SMEs Sector in Banyuwangi. *Transactions, 13*(10).

Van de Mieroop, M. (1997). *The Ancient Mesopotamian City*. Oxford University Press. doi:10.1093/oso/9780198150626.001.0001

van Eck, N. J., & Waltman, L. (2010). Software survey: VOSviewer, a computer program for bibliometric mapping. *Scientometrics*, *84*(2), 523–538. doi:10.1007/s11192-009-0146-3 PMID:20585380

Van Eck, N. J., & Waltman, L. (2017). Citation-based clustering of publications using CitNetExplorer and VOSviewer. *Scientometrics*, *111*(2), 1053–1070. doi:10.1007/s11192-017-2300-7 PMID:28490825

Van, L. T.-H. H., Vo, A. T., Nguyen, N. T., & Vo, D. H. (2021). Financial Inclusion and Economic Growth: An International Evidence. *Emerging Markets Finance & Trade*, *57*(1), 239–263. doi:10.1080/1540496X.2019.1697672

Vega, M., & Winkelried, D. (2005). Inflation targeting and inflation behavior: A successful story? *International Journal of Central Banking*, *1*(3), 153–175.

Verma, D., Valentina, B., Sindhwani, N., & Anand, R. (2022). *IoT Based Smart Applications*. Springer International Publishing.

Vermeulen, B., Pyka, A., & Omerovic, M. (2017). The economic impact of robotics and artificial intelligence. *REELER Working Paper Series*.

Vo, D. H., Nguyen, N. T., & Thi-Hong Van, L. (2021). Financial inclusion and stability in the Asian region using bank-level data. *Borsa Istanbul Review*, *21*(1), 36–43. doi:10.1016/j.bir.2020.06.003

Wajdi Dusuki, A. (2008). Banking for the poor: The role of Islamic banking in microfinance initiatives. *Humanomics*, *24*(1), 49–66. doi:10.1108/08288660810851469

Wallin, J. A. (2005). Bibliometric methods: Pitfalls and possibilities. *Basic & Clinical Pharmacology & Toxicology*, *97*(5), 261–275. doi:10.1111/j.1742-7843.2005.pto_139.x PMID:16236137

Wambugu Mwangi. (2018). *Role of financial literacy, financial innovation, financial inclusion on SME access to credit in Kenya: A case of Kumisa Sacco* (Doctoral dissertation). MUA.

Wani, Tali, Ashraf, & Sikandar. (2022). An Over view of Islamic micro finance. *Journal of Emerging Technologies and Innovative Research, 9*(9), 422-429.

Weber, M. (2002). *The protestant ethic and the "spirit" of capitalism and other writings*. Penguin.

Weeks, M. (2002). *Introductory econometrics: a modern approach*. JSTOR.

Wei, W., Sarker, T., Żukiewicz-Sobczak, W., Roy, R., Alam, G., Rabbany, G., Hossain, M. S., & Aziz, N. (2021). The influence of women's empowerment on poverty reduction in the rural areas of bangladesh: Focus on health, education and living standard. *International Journal of Environmental Research and Public Health*, *18*(13), 6909. doi:10.3390/ijerph18136909 PMID:34199117

Widarjono, A., & Mardhiyah, Z. (2022). Profit-loss sharing financing and stability of Indonesian Islamic banking. *International Journal of Islamic Business and Economics (Ijibec)*, *6*(1), 1–16. doi:10.28918/ijibec.v6i1.4196

Widiyanto, W., Mutamimah, S., & Hendar, H. (2011). *Effectiveness of Qard Al-Hasan financing as a poverty alleviation model. Economic Journal of Emerging Markets, 3, 27-42.* doi:10.20885/EJEM.V3I1.2318

Woodford, M. (2012). Inflation targeting and financial stability (No. w17967). National Bureau of Economic Research.

World Bank. (2018). *Global Financial Development Report 2017/2018: Bankers without Borders*. Available at: https://shorturl.at/pr028

World Bank. (2018). *The Global Findex Database 2017: Measuring Financial Inclusion and the Fintech Revolution.* World Bank Group. https://documents.worldbank.org/curated/en/332881525873182837/The-Global-Findex-Database-2017-Measuring-Financial-Inclusion-and-the-Fintech-Revolution

World Bank. (2022). *Financial Inclusion.* Available at: https://shorturl.at/bgqsv

Xiao, J. J., & O'Neill, B. (2016). Consumer financial education and financial capability. *International Journal of Consumer Studies, 40*(6), 712–721. doi:10.1111/ijcs.12285

Xiao, J. J., & O'Neill, B. (2018). Propensity to plan, financial capability, and financial satisfaction. *International Journal of Consumer Studies, 42*(5), 501–512. doi:10.1111/ijcs.12461

Xiong, M., Li, W., Jenny, C., & Wang, P. (2023). Financial Inclusion through Digitalization: Improving Emerging Drivers of Industrial Pollution—Evidence from China. *Sustainability (Basel), 15*(13), 10203. doi:10.3390/su151310203

Xu, M. T., Hu, K., & Das, M. U. S. (2019). *Bank profitability and financial stability.* International Monetary Fund. doi:10.5089/9781484390078.001

Yaacob, H., & Abdullah, A. (2012). Standards Issuance for Islamic Finance in International Trade: Current Issues and Challenges Ahead. *International Congress on Interdisciplinary Business and Social Science 2012, Social and Behavioral Sciences, 65*, 492 – 497.

Yakubi, Y., Basuki, B., & Purwono, R. (2019). Financial Inclusion and Digital Finance in the Arab World: Current Status and Future Priorities. International Journal of Innovation. *Creativity and Change, 6*(3), 132–143.

Yangdol, R., & Sarma, M. (2019). Demand-side factors for financial inclusion: A cross-country empirical analysis. *International Studies, 56*(2–3), 163–185. doi:10.1177/0020881719849246

Yang, Y., Shi, S., & Wu, J. (2022). Digital Financial Inclusion to Corporation Value: The Mediating Effect of Ambidextrous Innovation. *Sustainability (Basel), 14*(24), 16621. Advance online publication. doi:10.3390/su142416621

Yanto, H., Handayani, B. D., Solikhah, B., & Mula, J. M. (2016). The behavior of Indonesian SMEs in accepting financial accounting standards without public accountability. *International Journal of Business & Management Science, 6*(1).

Yaroson, E. (2013). Corruption and financial sector performance: Empirical evidence from Nigeria. *Int. J. Multidiscip. Thought, 3*(2), 507–519.

Yıldırım, S., Yıldırım, D. C., & Diboglu, P. (2020). Does Sukuk market development promote economic growth? *PSU Research Review, 4*(3), 209–218. doi:10.1108/PRR-03-2020-0011

Yilmaz, E. (2023). Analyzing investor types and marketing strategies for sukuk: Insights from preference similarity theory and protection motivation theory. *Journal of Islamic Accounting and Business Research.* Advance online publication. doi:10.1108/JIABR-03-2023-0097

Yuanita, N. (2019). Competition and bank profitability. *Journal of Economic Structures, 8*(1), 31. doi:10.1186/s40008-019-0164-0

Zaccheaus, O. D., & Ajuwon, O. S. (2019). Oil Price Dynamics and The Nigerian Banks Profitability. *Journal of Developing Areas, 53*(2), 91–107. doi:10.1353/jda.2019.0023

Zain, N. S., & Muhamad Sori, Z. (2020). An exploratory study on Musharakah SRI Sukuk for the development of Waqf properties/assets in Malaysia. *Qualitative Research in Financial Markets, 12*(3), 301–314. doi:10.1108/QRFM-09-2018-0099

Zanardi, Castellani, & Niño-Zarazua. (2022). *European Microfinance Platform (e-MFP) 'From Research to Practice and Back Again' Action Group*. Academic Press.

Zhang, X., Li, J., Xiang, D., & Worthington, A. C. (2023). Digitalization, financial inclusion, and small and medium-sized enterprise financing: Evidence from China. *Economic Modelling*, *126*, 106410. Advance online publication. doi:10.1016/j.econmod.2023.106410

Zhang, Y., Posso, A., & Swanepoel, J. (2021). Financial inclusion and poverty reduction in Sub-Saharan Africa. *Economic Modelling*, *94*, 387–396.

Zhao, M., Yang, R., & Li, Y. (2020). Financial leverage, economic growth and environmental degradation: Evidence from 30 provinces in China. *International Journal of Environmental Research and Public Health*, *17*(3), 831. Advance online publication. doi:10.3390/ijerph17030831 PMID:32013117

Zins, A., & Weill, L. (2016). The determinants of financial inclusion in Africa. *Review of Development Finance*, *6*(1), 46-57.

Zupic, I., & Čater, T. (2015). Bibliometric methods in management and organisation. *Organizational Research Methods*, *18*(3), 429–472. doi:10.1177/1094428114562629

About the Contributors

Awais Ur Rehman is a Finance, Law, and Islamic Finance expert, holding a PhD in Finance, MS Finance, LLB, and MSc in Economics. With over 5 years of experience, he has excelled as an Assistant Professor, and Lecturer and also in the applied corporate world as Factory Manager. Driven by a passion for research, he has published in esteemed journals, focusing on Financial inclusion, Islamic finance, and behavioral finance.

Arsalan Haneef Malik is an academician and experienced professional in accounting and finance. He is affiliated with the Institute of Business Management (IoBM) Karachi, Pakistan. With a PhD from the University of Malaysia Sarawak, he has published extensively in the social sciences in highly reputed journals. Among his research areas are financial inclusion, financial stability, institutional quality, and environmental and social sustainability. He inspires and mentors students to think critically and apply their knowledge to real-world situations. Arsalan Haneef Malik is committed to academic excellence and shaping the next generation of financial professionals. Research work can be followed on the links below.

* * *

Mr. Fiaz Ahmad is a PhD scholar at Sunway Business School, Sunway University Malaysia. He has diversified experience in industry and academia, serving as an Internal Shari'ah Auditor in the Banking sector and as a Research Officer at the Vice Chancellor's Office Minhaj University Lahore. He holds a bachelor's in accounting and finance with Glod Medal. His areas of expertise include Corporate Finance, Corporate Finance, and Islamic Finance. He is a member of the review board of many international publishers, including Springer Nature and IGI Global publisher. He is currently working as President of the Pakistani community of Sunway University Malaysia and a member of Pentland Centre for Sustainability in Business, Lancaster University United Kingdom (UK). He has published in top research journals, including Environmental Science and Pollution Research, Journal of the Knowledge Economy, and The International Journal of Management Education. He has also edited one book with Vice Chancellor Minhaj University Lahore titled "Impact of Pakistan Maritime Affairs on Blue Economy in the backdrop of CPEC.

Sara Akram is a research scholar with a strong academic background in the field of environmental and health sociology, Sun yat sen University, China. Sara, motivated by an unyielding passion to understand the complex relationship between society, health, and the environment, has embarked on an academic pursuit to elucidate these subtleties. She aims to contribute significantly to the collective knowledge that informs our understanding of how social institutions impact the well-being of persons and the environment, using her acute mind and commitment to thorough study. Sara's academic pursuits demonstrate her steadfast dedication to advancing a sustainable and healthier global environment via thorough research and innovative problem-solving methods.

Ejaz Aslam is a highly accomplished academic and researcher, specializing in the field of Islamic Banking and Finance. With a PhD in Islamic Banking and Finance from the International Islamic University Malaysia, Dr. Aslam brings a wealth of knowledge and expertise to his work. Throughout his career, Dr. Aslam has taught a diverse range of courses in Islamic finance to undergraduate, graduate, and executive students. His dedication to education is reflected in his extensive publication record, which includes over 30 research papers in renowned international refereed journals such as Borsa Istanbul Review, Environmental Science and Pollution Research, and Corporate Governance: The International Journal of Business in Society, Clean Technologies and Environmental Policy, Global Business Review, Asian Journal of Accounting Research, International Journal of Business Excellence, Journal of King Abdulaziz University, Islamic Economics, Journal of Islamic Marketing, Islamic Economic Studies, Business & Economic Review, Journal of Islamic Thought and Civilization, International Transaction Journal of Engineering, Management, & Applied Sciences & Technology, Buletin Ekonomi Moneter Dan Perbankan, Islamic Banking and Finance Review. In addition to his academic contributions, He has authored two book chapters on corporate finance and corporate governance, published by IGI Global. He is an active participant in national and international conferences, workshops, and webinars, where he has served as a speaker, session chair, and presenter. Dr. Ejaz Aslam's impressive academic achievements and vast research experience make him a valuable asset in the field of Islamic Banking and Finance. His commitment to advancing knowledge and his contributions to the academic community is truly commendable.

Calvin Cheong is an Associate Professor, the Deputy Dean and Associate Dean (Education) at Sunway Business School. He is also Associate Editor of the Asia Pacific Journal of Business Administration, and an Editorial Board Member of the International Journal of Emerging Markets. He also currently serves as Senior Policy Advisor for various ministerial committees across the globe. He was formerly a senior partner of an international management consulting firm that specializes in providing strategic advisory and leadership advice to corporations in over 20 countries.

Mark Gilman is a Professor of Economics with lead responsibilities within the University of Derby Regional Economic Observatory whose purpose is to build a robust evidence base to inform economic and social policy deliberations, engage with people and businesses, and produce analysis to support engagement with national government policy. He continues to research and publish extensively on SME Growth and Human Resource Management issues faced by business owners and their organisations.

Sarmad Hasan is a finance professional with 30 years of experience of which he spent 25 years in the corporate and development sectors, and for the past 5 years he is working full time in the academia. His current research interest is in the qualitative aspects of finance. Furthermore, he volunteers his time in helping the local NGOs for setting up financial monitoring and donor reporting systems.

Mr. Saem Hussain is pursuing PhD economics at Technological University Dublin, Ireland. He has completed his MPhil. Economics from the reputed university of Pakistan. He holds a Post Graduate Diploma (PGD) in management from the BPP University London. He has published research papers and book chapters in well-reputed national and international journals. Moreover, he has presented research papers at different conferences on the socio-economic and political challenges faced by Pakistan. Mr. Saem Hussain is a highly analytical and researched-focused professional. He possesses more than 9 years of experience in delivering proactive assistance to seniors in planning, organizing, and conducting research; whilst synthesizing and summarising findings and results.

Anam Iqbal is an assistant professor of Islamic Banking and Finance. She holds a PhD in Islamic Banking and Finance from International Islamic University Malaysia, Kuala Lumpur, Malaysia and an M.Phil degree from the University of Management and Technology Lahore. She has taught various Islamic finance courses for undergraduates, graduates, and executives in several institutions. She has also published several academic papers in international refereed journals, including; Borsa Istanbul Review, Corporate Governance, Asian Journal of Accounting Research, International Journal of Business Excellence, Journal of King Abdulaziz University, Islamic Economics, Journal of Islamic Marketing, Islamic Economic Studies, Business & Economic Review, Journal of Islamic Thought and Civilization. Furthermore, she has also participated in several national and international conferences, workshops, and Webinars as well.

Muhammad Ishfaq is an Assistant Professor at the School of Commerce and Accountancy at Minhaj University Lahore. He holds PhD in Finance from China. He has taught various Islamic finance courses at undergraduate, graduate, and executive level in several institutions. He has also published several academic papers in international refereed journals.

Saeed Mousa is an adjunct professor at Rennes school of business. He has received his PhD degree from Lille university in the domain of economics of innovation and technology. His main research interests are in the applications of new technology and how those applications impact the market and society through building new business models, in addition to market resilience and shocks absorption strategies. Dr. Mousa is currently a reviewer at some international peer reviewed journals like "international journal of innovation science".

Farah Naz is an Assistant Professor in the Accounting and Finance department at Kinnaird College for Women, Lahore, Pakistan. She holds a PhD in finance from the School of Accounting and Finance, University of Central Punjab. Her research interests include Microfinance, Fintech, Financial Inclusion and Diversity, Financial Markets and Risk Management.

Muhammad Roman is Assistant Professor and Head of Sociology Department in University of Jhang. He did his PhD in Rural Sociology from University of Agriculture Faisalabad. His area of research is transforming dynamics of family with the invasion of technology and modernization. During his doctoral studies, he presented his work in various public and private sector universities and national forums. He also served as faculty member in renowned universities (UAF, GCUF and MUL) and HEIs. He has number of research publications in various national and international journals on vibrant social issues. He has also evaluated a number of M.Phil and Doctoral research projects as an external evaluator from the forum of

University of Jhang. His Master of Philosophy is in Sociology with particular focus on social safety nets and their implications for the people. During his MPhil studies, he got some professional diplomas as well in the fields of Journalism, advertising, and public relationing. He also worked in different projects of development sector i.e. BISP-NSER and Rural Development Organization in Faisalabad.

Ahmad Salman is a seasoned academician and researcher with a focus on sustainability and community engagement. He is dedicated to utilizing his interdisciplinary expertise and robust organizational skills to enhance academic excellence and promote the progress of sustainable practices.

Muhammad Khalid Shahid stands at the forefront of cutting-edge research in the realm of quantitative data and business economics. As an early career researcher, he exhibited early academic prowess, paving the way for a remarkable journey that melds mathematical acumen with a profound understanding of economic forces. Armed with a Certified Management Accountant (CMA) from ICMAP and Becker's Friedman Institute, he is actively pursuing his PhD from Universiti Tunku Abdul Rahman (UTAR) currently embarked on a career marked by groundbreaking contributions to the intersection of data and economics. Joining numerous research projects at the University of the Punjab, Lahore Pakistan and Universiti Tunku Abdul Rahman, Malaysia he quickly distinguished himself through his innovative approach to unravelling complex economic and business phenomena. Beyond research, Mr. Shahid shares his wealth of knowledge as a visiting lecturer for Cambridge University's Education System, the University of the Punjab and the College of Financial Excellence (CFE). The impact of Mr. Shahid's work extends beyond academia, influencing business leaders and policymakers alike.

Waqas Shair is a research associate at the Center of Economic Planning and Development (CEPD), Minhaj University Lahore, Pakistan. He also holds the position of Lecturer at Minhaj University Lahore, Pakistan. He is pursuing his Doctor of Philosophy degree at the esteemed University of the Punjab, Pakistan. The primary focus of his research lies in the fields of Labour Economics, Household Economics, Applied Microeconomics, and Development Economics. He has authored research papers and contributed book chapters in esteemed international journals. He has also written various newspaper columns on contemporary economic issues that have been published in reputable newspapers such as "Dawn," "The Nation," "Pakistan Today," "Daily Times," and "Global Village Space."

Humera Tariq Mahmood is a PhD Student at Birmingham City University, Graduate School of Management, UK. Her PhD research looks into what drives SME growth in the Pakistani context. Humera also teaches "SMEs-Microfinancing from an Islamic Perspective" as a visiting faculty to undergraduate students at the International Islamic University in Islamabad, Pakistan. She also holds MSc in Islamic Finance from Hamad Bin Khalifah University in Qatar, and an MA in Business Administration from Punjab University in Pakistan.

Deniz E. Yoruk is a Research Fellow in SME Development and Growth in the Centre for Enterprise, Innovation and Growth (CEIG) at Birmingham City University, Graduate School of Management, UK. She holds a PhD from the University of Sussex, Science Policy Research Unit (SPRU), UK. Her research focuses on sustainable business growth in SMEs. Her research interests include organizational learning and innovation, networks and GVCs, international business and strategy, industrial and regional development. Her publications in these areas cover a diverse range of industries in advanced and emerging market economies.

Index

G

I

M

N

O

P

R

S

T

U

V

W

www.ingramcontent.com/pod-product-compliance
Lightning Source LLC
LaVergne TN
LVHW062140300926
849161LV00010B/2586